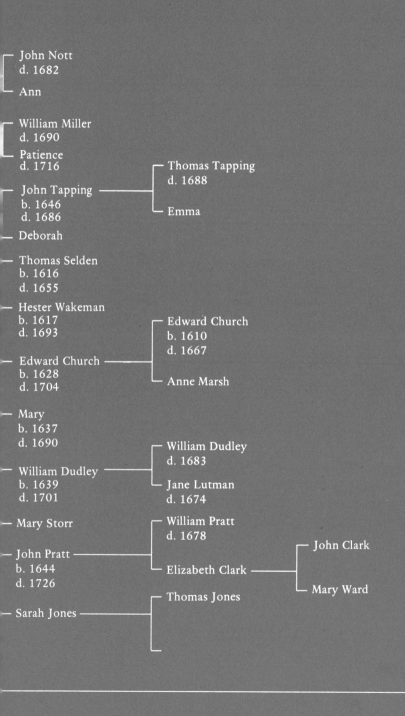

John Nott
d. 1682

Ann

William Miller
d. 1690

Patience
d. 1716

John Tapping
b. 1646
d. 1686

Deborah

Thomas Selden
b. 1616
d. 1655

Hester Wakeman
b. 1617
d. 1693

Edward Church
b. 1628
d. 1704

Mary
b. 1637
d. 1690

William Dudley
b. 1639
d. 1701

Mary Storr

John Pratt
b. 1644
d. 1726

Sarah Jones

Thomas Tapping
d. 1688

Emma

Edward Church
b. 1610
d. 1667

Anne Marsh

William Dudley
d. 1683

Jane Lutman
d. 1674

William Pratt
d. 1678

Elizabeth Clark

Thomas Jones

John Clark

Mary Ward

ELIPHALET NOTT

ELIPHALET NOTT: 1773-1866. Portrait by Henry Inman, 1839. Owned by Union College; photograph, Schaffer Library, Union College.

Eliphalet Nott

By CODMAN HISLOP

WESLEYAN UNIVERSITY PRESS

Middletown, Connecticut

ISBN: 0–8195–4037–4

Library of Congress Catalog Card Number: 71–161696

Manufactured in the United States of America

First edition

For my beloved
and wonderfully patient wife
GERTRUDE H. HISLOP

Albert Camus, on the function of biography:

> "It teaches that a man defines himself by his make-believe, as well as by his sincere impulses."
>
> — from "The Myth of Sisyphus"

Henry Thoreau, on the words of ministers:

> ". . . though you trade in messages from heaven, the whole curse of trade attaches to the business."
>
> — from *Walden*

Captain Frederick Marryat, on Eliphalet Nott:

> ". . . seriously speaking, Professor Nott is a very clever man, and I suspect [Union College] will turn out more clever men than any other in the Union."
>
> — from *A Diary in America*, New York, 1839

Contents

Illustrations

Foreword

TO relive the life of another and to put what is learned justly into words is an undertaking both formidable and perilous. When executed successfully, as it is here, it is among the major human achievements. President Eliphalet Nott of Union College lived for nearly a century, spanning American history from colonial days until after the Civil War as one of the educational "movers and shakers" of his times. Few leaders did as much as Eliphalet Nott to determine the shape that higher education was to take in this country. During his fantastic sixty-two-year reign as the President of Union he pioneered in many fields, such as the development of the elective system, of scientific and engineering education, to mention only a few. In addition, as the versatile inventor and promoter of improved stoves and steamboats, he was almost a da Vinci among college heads. This intense and broad-gauge practicality he imparted to many of his four thousand students, an extraordinary number of whom have taken their place in the pages of the *Dictionary of American Biography*.

It might be said that Professor Codman Hislop's preparation for the writing of this book began almost forty years ago with his arrival as a student at Union. He had only to look about him to become acquainted with Dr. Nott. There was that awesome Inman portrait of him in the Nott-Potter Memorial building, and all around was the beautifully planned campus which the Doctor had induced the gifted French architect Joseph Jacques Ramée to design in 1813, payment for the construction of which was to embroil President and College in the nightmare of the "Literature Lottery." Few scholars would have had the patience and ingenuity to master the intricacies of Nott's financial buccaneering and its moral ambiguities as Dr. Hislop has done. The documentation required, and provided, has been immense, and its interpretation scrupulously fair.

Eliphalet Nott was a dreamer of spacious dreams for his country, his college, and perhaps his own pocketbook. Revered by the multitude and by generations of his students, he has been virtually canonized by those who have previously written about him. It has remained for his present biographer to tackle the needed but unwelcome task of showing that his subject's flaws were proportionate to his virtues, and that the absolute "power to do assumed good" can be just as corrupting as any other kind of power. "Intense avarice in a good cause," as Nott's close observer and critic Jonathan Pearson put it, remains a vice.

Dr. Nott's good cause was "university" higher education for the many. But to promote it he stooped to the questionable means of the lottery and devious real-estate speculations. The philosopher Jacques Maritain has warned us that in our choice of means "our ends are already realized." But President Nott was blinded by the rectitude of his intentions, and his religion somehow failed to alert him to the moral implications of his deeds. In his day he had a towering reputation as an analyst of human passions and as an adroit manipulator of legislators and businessmen. Unfortunately he seems to have imbibed from some of the latter a few of the shoddier standards of business and political ethics which prevailed in the first half of the nineteenth century. Before we judge him too harshly by twentieth-century rules of behavior, we should recall that, after more than a century of moral and legal condemnation, New York State has recently re-entered the slippery field of lotteries for education.

No reader can fail to find in these pages the dramatic playing out of a true Greek tragedy: the story of a gifted man who rose to the heights of power and esteem, only to be undone by defects in his own character. That they were bared to the world by the machinations of less worthy personages cannot obscure the fact that Dr. Nott's deviousness and lack of caution in speculation were his own worst enemies. In sum, his intensely American life-story as vividly related by Codman Hislop gives us a memorable example of what Premier Clemenceau called "the grandeur and the misery of the human condition."

Harold A. Larrabee

Acknowledgments

A book which was begun thirty years ago has, as a project, outlived many of those who have made it possible. The very listing of the names of colleagues and friends who gave of their time and experience would take pages, and, I am afraid, would reduce a debt I cannot repay to a statistic.

Four Presidents of Union College, however, I must thank here: Frank Parker Day (1928–1933), Dixon Ryan Fox (1934–1945), Carter Davidson (1946–1965), and Harold C. Martin who, believing wholeheartedly in the value of a biography of Eliphalet Nott, never withheld their support when I needed it. President Martin read the manuscript, and his suggestions and encouragement during the final year of work on it have meant much to me.

As its library is one measure of the worth of a college, so its librarians are the test of the usefulness of its library; without their special dedication few of us would have books to publish. For helping to make this biography possible I also want to record my debt to three chief librarians of Union: James Brewster, Helmer Webb, and Edwin Tolan, and, because my memory is so fallible as I look back over the years I have been writing, I dare add only my thanks to the many members of their staffs who so often did more for me than I knew how to do for myself. Within the last five years five members of the staff of the new Schaffer Library at Union College have aided me beyond measuring: Miss Ruth Ann Evans, Mrs. Francis Miller, and the Messrs. Charles Wilde, Edward Elliott, and Wayne Somers.

Harold A. Larrabee, emeritus Professor of Philosophy at Union, has been the sort of critic few authors are fortunate enough to find. His work on the manuscript has retaught me much of what I once taught others and then, seemingly, forgot. I also wish to thank Professor Michael Schinagel, Chairman of the Union College English Department, for establishing the contact which led to this book's publication under its present auspices.

The staffs of so many libraries and organizations have been helpful I can name only those to which I have had to return again and again: The New-York Historical Society, the New York State Library, the Widener and Houghton Libraries at Harvard, Brown University, Columbia University, Hamilton College, the Albany Institute of History and Art, and the Schenectady Historical Society. This biography itself must be the witness to my gratitude to several hundred correspondents, among whom are many descendents of Eliphalet Nott, who have troubled themselves to answer my many inquiries. Particular debts I have tried to acknowledge in the appropriate footnotes.

To those writers without whose biographies and studies of the American scene I could not have worked I owe the debt of all authors; for what I have taken from them I hope I have accounted, but if I have borrowed far more than I realize, at least what I have taken now becomes once more available.

I also owe a great debt to Professor Jonathan Pearson— "Pinky" Pearson to Eliphalet Nott's young gentlemen—whose monumental diary covering the vital Nott years was an open window on the Union College he knew so intimately. I want also to thank his great-grandson Jonathan Pearson III, Alumni Secretary of Union College, who so generously shared his knowledge of the "Thinking Books" with me.

There is one man, beyond all others, to whom this book owes its origin: Charles Newman Waldron, emeritus Professor of American History, and the retired Alumni Secretary of Union College. He taught me to seek out the life and the drama which is also the history of this college, and, in doing so, he introduced me to a source of knowledge in the field of American studies which would enrich the curriculum of any college or university which would make use of its own institutional and regional records.

The last is seldom least: Indexing is imaginative drudgery and the results seldom please the specialist. Gloria Berry, to whom all thanks, has labored with me to produce the best general guide we could.

Introduction

Eliphalet Nott became a giant in his time. In an age that conferred certain, if temporary, dignity upon anyone elevated to a college presidency, Nott quickly assumed heroic stature. From the outset he was a very public man, not apparently ambitious of notice but irresistibly drawn to actions and utterances that effectively marked him off not only from the crowd but even from his colleague presidents. A child of the eighteenth century, theist and rationalist at once — and, like other eighteenth-century worthies, in some measure sentimentalist to boot — Nott provoked and welcomed controversy. The best measure of his size, indeed, may be that he seems to have wasted no time in victory celebrations, though he had occasion for many. Probably not more than a half-dozen other college presidents in the history of this country can be said to have done so much so quickly with so little initial advantage.

Lest his achievement or that of others equally remarkable be diminished by the easy reflection that times were easier a hundred or a hundred and fifty years ago, the record reminds us that they were in many ways very like our own. Students were rebellious and frequently savage; faculty members contended unscrupulously with presidents and among themselves; money was scarce; the public carped and condemned, and legislative bodies enacted punitive measures even as both paid tribute (literally and figuratively) to the institutions they reproved. The presidents who today remain visible from past generations all bear scars of battle. What distinguishes them, and gives hope to their successors, is that they survived their wounds. On that score, none outdid Eliphalet Nott: sixty-two years president of Union College, he outlasted the critics whom he could not convert and died blessedly unaware that the institution he had created, almost single-handed, in the wilderness was on the verge of a forty-year exile in the spiritual and academic desert of post–Civil War America.

Professor Hislop's book — more than a biography, less than a social history — restores to Nott a reputation earned in times of great difficulty and strangely eclipsed in the near eclipse of the college he served. Nott was a prophet honored in his own country and his own time; he does not appear to have asked for anything more, but it is decidedly to our advantage that his career and character, both flawed in ways we shall have no trouble recognizing, should now be so richly recalled for us.

Harold C. Martin
President, Union College
Chancellor, Union University

September, 1970

BOOK ONE

Boyhood and Priesthood, 1773-1804

CHAPTER I

New Ashford to "Pisgah's Top"

"September, 1805:
   President Nott preached in the Brattle Street Church. The fullest audience ever known there, except ordination day. The Epigram made on him by Josiah Quincy:
   'Delight and instruction have people, I wot,
      who in seeing NOT see, and in hearing, hear NOT.' "[1]

THE brevity of this diary entry, made by the Reverend Joseph Stevens Buckminster, the new Unitarian pastor of the Brattle Street Church, may indicate that he was a little irked by this outpouring of Bostonians in honor of an outsider. Who was this Connecticut man turned Yorker who had left the Congregational Way to embrace the Presbyterian discipline and who, within the year, had resigned his pulpit to become the President of a new college on the frontier of New York?

Josiah Quincy could not resist punning. If this future President of Harvard, however, had "a strong distaste for nonsense" as Van Wyck Brooks writes, he forgot it on this occasion, and beat out an epigram which, puns and paradoxes to the contrary, speaks enthusiastically of the new President of Union College.[2] Ezekiel Webster seems to have been there, too, for he reported to his brother Daniel in this same month from Boston that he had just heard a sermon preached by Eliphalet Nott, "a man of abilities and a scholar."[3]

The Reverend Joseph Buckminster's church had heard that September Sunday the Lord's Word preached strong, with fermentation well begun in the grapes of wrath. There was honest heat in the hellfire Dr. Nott kindled for his audience. Here was no

"Boston Religion," no "mild and tolerant Unitarianism, rational-
istic, torpid, utilitarian."[4] Here, rather, was the Bible whole, with
grace and redemption, and its fear of the Lord. Boston heard Nott
preach a simpler Christianity than the Orthodox Calvinism he had
taken out of New England into New York ten years before and
had preached among the Scotch-Presbyterians of that Cherry
Valley enclave of New Englanders whose knowledge of God's
wrath had been made doubly vivid in the horrors of the Cherry
Valley massacre and the miseries of the border warfare of the late
Revolution.[5]

By September, 1805, Dr. Eliphalet Nott was a famous man.
Bostonians were reading a local edition of his electrifying sermon
on the death of Alexander Hamilton.[6] The New York State
Legislature had acknowledged his eloquence on behalf of education by granting in March of that year the first of the Literature
Lotteries to be given to the young and debt-ridden college to
which he had been called as President.[7] The "Doctor" on the lips
of his students was new, for the College of New Jersey, in
Princeton, had just awarded him its divinity degree.[8] The road he
had travelled in acquiring his reputation, however, was a sinuous
one; it stretched back from the door of the Brattle Street Church
into Dutch Schenectady and Albany, New York, further west to
the Oneida Indian country, and then east into his native
Connecticut, where it began as a farmer's lane, rocky and steep as
the pastures of the town of Ashford to which the defeated
Stephen Nott, his father, had brought his family in 1772.

The bare record of Eliphalet Nott's inheritance would bring
comfort to those who measure a man in terms of his blood lines.
The genealogists of the family, of course, have given especial
attention to those forebears who bore the name of NOTT.[9] "John
Nott, Sergeant," of Nottingham, England, appears in Wethersfield,
Connecticut, in the not unusual role of "considerable landholder"
about 1640; for several years after 1665 he is mentioned as the
Wethersfield representative in the General Assembly. Somewhat
unusually for a colonial father, and particularly for a Nott, he
sired only three children, two of whom were among the
progenitors of two notable Americans. Elizabeth, his firstborn,
married Robert Reeve from whom was descended Judge Tapping

Reeve, founder of the Litchfield Law School. Hannah, second daughter of the "Sergeant," married John Hale, and so anticipated fame by becoming the grandmother of the patriot Nathan Hale.

John, the third child, upon whom devolved the duty of passing on the Nott name, faced his responsibility to a sparsely settled colony and fathered seven sons and two daughters. The genealogists fail to say what else he did. John Nott, of this second generation, and his father, John, the "Sergeant," thus appear in these brief but necessary roles of progenitors, theirs the undelineated parts of Prologue.

The mighty Abraham Nott, in the minds of Eliphalet and Samuel, his grandsons, begins the meaningful record. The Notts who lived and died within their memory are recorded in the family Bible,[10] and in the voluminous manuscript *Autobiography* written by the older of them, the Reverend Samuel Nott, D.D., of Franklin, Connecticut.[11]

Abraham appears to have been the first of the "educated" Notts. Yale College had been in New Haven three years when he was graduated from it in 1720. Although he died in 1756, seventeen years before Eliphalet was born and three years before the birth of Samuel, he left not only a useful estate and a reputation as an efficient minister of the Second Congregational Church of Saybrook, Connecticut, but also a legacy of tall stories about his feats of strength, which was cherished by his grandsons.[12] In the dark days which descended on the household of Stephen Nott, the second of Abraham's four sons and Eliphalet's father, it must have been good, at times, to make much of the family hero. He was one of that mighty band who could raise the cider barrel above his head, hold it at arm's length, and drink from the bunghole. It was reported that more than one Connecticut strong man came to Abraham Nott's parsonage door and demanded that the pastor of the Second Congregational Church prove himself the better man. There was none of them, according to Abraham's report, he could not pin to the ground. In addition to "his uncommon muscle and force—he was an excellent preacher, a sound theologian . . . gifted with a keen and vigorous intellect . . . a warm heart and unaffected piety."[13] It was the hand of Abraham Nott of Saybrook which was laid on the grandsons. He gave direction to the career of Eliphalet's brother Samuel, and through Samuel he helped to add Eliphalet's name to the roll of American educators.

If Samuel and Eliphalet Nott probably knew less about their ancestry than does the modern genealogist, they knew intimately and grimly how their father, Stephen, had been forced to bring his family to the rude house and the poor acres of Ashford. As Samuel tells the story in his *Autobiography* the feeling grows that Connecticut, too, may have bred its Furies, for certainly Stephen Nott, through no apparent fault of his own, suffered one shattering reverse after the other.[14] The *Autobiography*, it must be said, reports the tragic events which beset Stephen and Deborah without rancor. What happened to this hard-pressed family, their son believed, was one with God's plan to shape the tough Nott clay into images to His own liking. Samuel, Eliphalet's older brother, saw the process beginning with himself when he wrote:

> Self-gratification was my lot. I thought myself born to good fortune and to be in the high road to pleasure and honor. Pride goeth before destruction and a haughty spirit before a fall. God saw a check was necessary for me. The pleasant scene before me suddenly changed for one solemn and alarming.[15]

First, God's wrath was vented, not only on Samuel, but on the whole family because the boy was full of vanity over his learning. "My instructor and friends," he writes, "always caressed me. That pleased my vanity. I increased, therefore, much faster in self-importance than in real knowledge. . . . I thought nothing of God. . . ."[16] Then the blow fell. Fire swept the Saybrook house where the then five-year-old sinner had been born on January 23, 1754. "My mother," Samuel remembered, "caught me and an apprentice by the hair of our heads and dragged us into the street."

Not fire the next time, but a highwayman was the agent of chastisement. About a year following the first disaster Stephen was in New Jersey, selling horses he had taken in trade for his store goods. The *Autobiography* puts the event succinctly: "About the time he was looked for at home, news arrived that, after he had sold his horses and received his money, he was robbed and, that by reason of a wound received in his head, though not dangerous, he was unable immediately to return to his family."[17]

At this point in the *Autobiography* Deborah Nott, mother of Samuel and later of Eliphalet, emerges as a woman of considerable character. As Deborah Selden, second daughter of Samuel Selden of Lyme, Connecticut, "a large and respectable farmer," she "possezzed (*sic*)" according to her son Samuel, "a very sprightly mind, and was favoured with the best early education," and he adds, of his parents she was "the most extraordinary person."[18]

At this juncture in the Nott family affairs she needed to be a most extraordinary person. More and more the management of their lives was becoming her problem. As soon as Stephen Nott arrived back in Saybrook, carrying a scar and toting his empty saddlebags, his creditors began to seize what property he still owned. Samuel, now six, reported that his chief fears were only that they would be poor, and that he would be bound out to learn a trade.

The first of these fears was realized almost at once. Stephen Nott's chief creditor, a Mr. Webb of Wethersfield, had recently died and his widow, a first cousin of Stephen's, had just married Silas Deane, "the same mercenary S.D. who was during the Revolutionary War appointed an ambassador from the United States to France."[19]

> The settlement of Mr. W.'s estate fell into Mr. D.'s hands. . . . He had no bowels of compassion. He soon began to seize my father's property. An alarm was instantly given. A host of small creditors soon appeared. Everything was directly seized by the officers. One attachment was put upon the back of another. Many who had been friends became enemies. The selfishness of the human heart was strikingly manifested.[20]

For Deborah Nott there was the overpowering sense of family disgrace. "The idea that my father could not pay his debts. . . . wounded family pride and touched all the tender feelings of her soul."[21] The loyalty of Saybrook friends and relatives and the care of three small daughters helped Deborah Nott through the weeks of Stephen's understandable absence on a long fishing voyage. He returned, finally, to Saybrook, hoping to win leniency from his creditors. Their answer was to clap him in the Hartford jail, from which, Samuel writes, "having some money in his pockets, and friends without, he very soon made his escape."[22] Not long after this second flight the Connecticut lawmakers passed an Insolvency Act and Stephen "took the benefit of it." *Benefit* was a cruel word to give to the freedom the act provided, for its beneficiaries were left with nothing but their wearing apparel and their necessary household furniture.[23]

Deborah Nott had to call more and more on her deep reservoirs of strength in order to hold her growing family together. Temperance, her firstborn, had died in Saybrook, in 1757,[24] but Phebe and a second Temperance and Charlotte had gone with the parents to the new home in East Haddam, where a fifth daughter, Lovice, was born in February, 1764. Samuel, still burdened with pride and a wickedness to which he constantly returned, he wrote, "like a dog to its vomit"—was released from his apprenticeship to a blacksmith and returned to his parents. All of them leaned on Deborah Nott.

> The great poverty of the family and the ill health of my father at this time, called for great exertions from my mother. She often besides doing the common work of the family used to spin three runs of linning yearn [sic] in a day. At length she took up the business of mantua-making and drawing. She was of consequence very full of business. She often had a young child to nurse and the other children to instruct and to attend to, as well as myself.[25]

Education, in the family of Stephen Nott, was concerned, not with spiritual milk, but with the hard realities of the everyday Yankee world of a shoemaker-farmer. The practical education for which the names of Eliphalet Nott and Union College became synonymous in the early nineteenth century had roots, in part, in the concern of Deborah Nott for the welfare of her ragged children. Samuel, busy in the fields, busy with his several brands of wickedness, hoodwinking the neighbors with fortune-telling tricks, gossiping about the activities of the local witches, would be pulled up short with Deborah's, "I fear you will never know how to keep a book or to do common business." "Often," he wrote in the *Autobiography*, "she set me copies and taught me how to write and spell."[26]

In 1772 the Nott family ended a long apprenticeship to poverty. Saybrook and Lyme relatives and friends had never been more than a day's journey away. In that year, however, Stephen Nott, now long inured to the fruits of barter and credit, traded off his house and small lot to a local character known as "King Fox" for a run-down house and some sixty acres of land in Westford, a society in the town of Ashford, about thirty miles northeast of Hartford, Connecticut.[27]

II

Here, in "Westford meeting," Eliphalet ["God is deliverance"] Nott was born on the 25th of June, 1773. He was the ninth and the last child Deborah Nott was to bear.[28] During his first eight years his world was bounded by Lawry Brook on the west and Squaw Bottom Brook on the east. The greatest natural wonder of his world was "Frog Rock," a huge glacial boulder precariously balanced on a granite ledge, still to be seen some ten miles east of the Stephen Nott farm and shoe-shop. Wild grapes, elms, oaks, maples, sumac, wild cherry trees, crowded up to the stone fences which marked the clearings. The ash trees were useful to Stephen in tanning leather for country clothes and boots.

No time was lost in acquainting young Eliphalet with the Puritan's guide to God's Plan.[29] During his fourth year he read the Bible through, or so it is reported.[30] A boyhood companion, Vine Utley, in 1830 wrote a reminiscing letter to his then famous friend in which he recalled the young Eliphalet's astounding feats in scripture recitation, "performed at the instance of (your) mother". Vine Utley was particularly impressed with Eliphalet's behavior in Brother Lampson's meeting house, where, "during the service, I observed that you frequently took pen, ink, and paper, and wrote, or appeared to write the sermon down as delivered by the clergyman."[31]

The nearest schoolhouse to Stephen Nott's farm was a lonely five miles away. Whatever the reason—too little money to meet the small common school tax, the distance from home, or the fact that Deborah Nott knew herself to be the better instructor—Eliphalet knew no other teacher than his mother until he was eight years old. He had only the family's stories of more opulent days to make him long for greener fields than Ashford's. The violent upheavals in the family fortunes, as he heard about them from his parents and from Samuel, the older brother reportedly newly touched by Grace, must have appeared as salutary warnings of God's concern for them all. The "humble cottage" and the "adjacent rough country" Vine Utley recalled in his letter were themselves quiet, secure check points, however, in the exploding British-American world of Eliphalet Nott's boyhood.

Deborah Nott, in spite of her waning strength, communicated much of herself to her younger son. "She was acquainted with character. She was the only person who, in my early years, fully understood me, and knew just what was the proper treatment to pursue."[32] Eliphalet Nott's grandchildren remembered being told the grim tale of a certain breakfast in Ashford, and

> how, when he was a small boy, he refused to eat his Indian meal mush . . . one morning. When dinner came the same mush was served to him, but nothing else, and when again he refused to eat it it was again served to him at supper. He was still resolute, but when it turned up again at breakfast the next day he gave in, ate the mush and in addition the red ants which had been attracted to it by the sugar on it.[33]

Not only discipline but justice was meted out by Deborah Nott in terms the small boy, grown to manhood, never forgot. On one occasion not only was justice done, but with the punishment was delivered, by implication, a clear rebuke to those who read God's Word too narrowly. The young Eliphalet heard the Baptist preacher inveigh against some sort of cushion headdress the girls of the parish had taken a fancy to. The hat was denounced as a device of the devil, a proper object for prompt destruction. The boy knew exactly where one of his sisters had hidden her version of this abomination. The pulpit charge was all he needed. On arriving home, he went directly to the place where the offensive article had been hidden, rooted it out, tore it up, and scattered the evidence of God's Wrath over the floor of his sister's bedroom. Deborah Nott and the outraged girl read the evidence differently. "The culprit was duly arraigned, confessed, but pleaded in justification the preacher's lessons and his own conviction of duty. Spite of the plea, the offense brought a sound maternal chastisement upon him; the justice of which, however, under the circumstances, he ever afterward denies."[34]

These incidents have little importance in themselves, but they reveal something of the resolute woman who began the education of one of the country's most notable teachers. Eliphalet's father, Stephen, seems to have made little or no impression on the mind of the younger son, nor are the Notts who preceded him, the "Sergeant" of Saybrook, or even the well-muscled and scholarly grandfather, the Reverend Abraham Nott of barrel-hoisting fame, referred to in the considerable correspondence of Eliphalet Nott's which has survived. But Deborah, mantua-making, child-tending, spinning the "linning yearn," holding together a family in spite of the many disasters which they all seemed to have accepted as chastening experience, she is the one he remembered. His tall, spare frame and the giant's head, grey eyes set deep under a wall of forehead, nose and mouth and jaw to suit, these he got from unnamed progenitors, but the first set of his mind, this came from Deborah.[35] "I not only owe my early education," he said, "but under God, all that I have been and am to the tutelage and council of the best of mothers."[36]

Samuel Nott, the older brother, who once blamed his pride and his love of the world for the chastising meted out to his family by their New England God, must have wondered at the relentlessness with which Deborah was pursued and punished. When Eliphalet was fifteen she died; "being worn down," Samuel wrote, "with trouble and hard labor [she] fell into a kind of religious melancholy which continued two years. The sun finally set in a cloud. She died at Ashford, October 24, 1788, in the 56th year of her age."[37] For Eliphalet, her death was the end of one way of life and the beginning of another. "The light of my life went out," he said in later years, "when my mother died."[38] From the time of Deborah's death until he left Connecticut for the wilderness of western New York Eliphalet was to live now, with, or within the reach of Samuel Nott.

III

Patriotism had burned bright in many an idealist's heart in 1776, but for Samuel, it had illuminated only the inside of his empty purse. If the local recruiting sergeant had been at home when he called, he would have joined "the northern army," so he wrote, in order to fill his purse.[39] His mind at this time was set on going to Yale College, however, not to war. The next year, as a Yale freshman, he joined his classmates in a brief interruption of their education by helping to defend New Haven against a British landing. From that time on, however, the Revolution was hardly more than sound and fury for the now busy theological student.

Samuel Nott, by 1780, had become a dedicated "New Light" Congregationalist, "saved" by his emotional conviction rather than by any rational argument. Behind him was a childhood steeped in what he had come to think of as sheer wickedness. Because he now thought of himself as a "hopeful" Christian he felt himself charged with the awful responsibility of attempting to impose upon young and old alike any discipline which might lead to their own Christian rebirth.

During the winter of 1780 the young Yale graduate devoted himself not only to school teaching, but "to the regular study of divinity under Dr. Edwards."[40] The brother under whom Eliphalet Nott was soon to receive most of his secular education and a part of his training for the ministry thus committed himself to the world of the Calvinist theologians, even though the force of its gravitational pull was lessening with every decade as the new attractions of politics, economic exploitation, and the rational philosophies of the Age of Enlightenment drew men into new orbits. For the dedicated "New Light" Calvinists, however, for men like Samuel Nott and his instructor in divinity, the Reverend Jonathan Edwards the Younger, the new forces were manifestations only of man's perversity, of his godlessness, and of the fearful imminence of the final judgment.

Samuel Nott, the Yale divinity student of 1780, was thus exposed to an embattled Calvinism; neither for him nor for most of his contemporaries was there the vitality and the quickening sense of mystery with which the elder Jonathan Edwards had infused it. The year after Samuel was graduated by Yale College, the thunder of the Revolution echoing comfortably in distant valleys, he became a licentiate of the New Haven East Association, and so a member of one of the oldest Congregational Associations in Connecticut, "a battlefield for the discussion of some of the most important questions relating to ecclesiastical order, theological doctrine, ministerial duty and covenant obligations that have ever agitated the churches of the state."[41] During March, 1782, he was settled as the third minister of the Congregational Church of Norwich, West Farms, Connecticut, a community which four years later became the town of Franklin.[42]

"As it was in my heart," the new minister wrote in the *Autobiography* he prepared for his children, "to relieve as far as I was able, my parents, I very soon after my settlement took my brother and my younger sister to educate and provide for as my own. This added greatly to my cares and my expense."[43] The young pastor, who had just married Lucretia Taylor of nearby Mansfield, had other cares, for he had also "bought a small house and garden."[44]

"Pisgah's Top," as the Nott family came to call Samuel's parsonage, was in many ways like the ark of Noah, a self-contained community afloat on the troubled waters of Franklin Society. "Franklin Parish," the new minister noted on his arrival, "was cold and independent. God's people appeared to be fed."[45] His chief concern was that his church had degenerated with the times and that "it was permitting merely moral persons to own the covenant, to bring their children to baptism, and to live, if they pleased, all their days in the neglect of the Lord's Supper themselves."[46] All this to the Reverend Samuel Nott, student of Edwardsian Calvinism, was unscriptural.

Life for the members of the Reverend Samuel Nott's family (three sons and four daughters) was circumscribed indeed. Carefully enumerated in the *Autobiography* are rules of conduct which have all the shrewd practicality of "Poor Richard" for whom the town was renamed. Added to these rules, however, are a dozen directions for religious conduct which might have seemed arduous to that Yankee eclectic. One may be sure, however, that young Eliphalet and his nieces and nephews hewed to the line drawn by the master of Pisgah's Top, who wrote solemnly on another occasion that "It has always been my notion of government that when I commanded, I executed."[47]

If there was any gaiety in this Calvinist household it must have expressed itself secretly, behind closed doors, for there was little place for it where each day's events were weighed in terms of their significance as Christian acts. The family of the Reverend Samuel Nott was taught "subjection . . . and kept from wicked and gay company." Early rising and retiring were ordered in the spirit of Yankee thrift: "The sun," wrote this Reverend task-master, "gives cheaper and better light than a candle. No time need be lost in snuffing it."[48]

Other Yankee precepts were "commanded" into young Eliphalet and his brother's children:

> Be industrious whilst up, and have a place for everything and everything in its place.
>
> Live within your income. If you cannot eat white bread eat brown bread. 'Dip and deal, and take a little at every meal.'
>
> . . . . pay mechanics and common laborers promptly . . . most of their debts are on interest.
>
> Keep the best company, the *most moral and religious.* It will be the most pleasing and the most improving if your hearts are right and ordinarily will be the least expensive.[49]

The practical Yankee note sounded through much of the noise and bustle of this busy family. "Good Works" as epitomized in those who carefully husbanded their resources and who increased them at the legal rate of interest were among the approved evidences of a "holiness of heart and faith in the Great Redeemer."[50]

The Reverend Samuel Nott stimulated his younger brother Eliphalet by rod and by example not only to attend to the elements of Yankee thrift, classical learning, and Edwardsian Calvinism, but he also exposed him to definite social and political attitudes. In the "intolerable little business of the pew," as the irate pastor referred to a protracted quarrel with a group of his parishioners over the right of the minister to a free family pew, the whole pattern of New England's political loyalties came to the surface. Those "dissident" members of the Franklin congregation who, in 1795, demanded that he buy his pew as did the other members of his church were "all upon the Republican side," from whence one always heard, Samuel noted, "a general cry against the clergy."[51] Not only did these Republicans (those Jeffersonian radicals of the day) make an issue of his right to a pew in his own church, but they complained bitterly that he "had bought a good farm, built the best house in Franklin, had horses and carriages, all this supported by many who are abjectly poor." "Of the 16 dissidents," he later wrote, "three eventually came back to the Federalist side and made good parishioners."[52]

I V

Here, at "Pisgah's Top" Eliphalet Nott, aged nine, first encountered Yale learning, presented by his brother with the help of the rod and the enthusiasm of the reformed sinner. "In addition to warnings and admonitions daily," he wrote to Henry Barnard years later, "if I was not whipped more than three times a week, I considered myself for the time peculiarly fortunate."[53] The victim of this iron discipline took to his heels on one occasion and returned to Ashford, "pretending," wrote Samuel, "that my government was too severe."[54]

The paying scholars could, if their parents chose, leave Franklin and pursue their education under more congenial conditions. Eliphalet Nott, however, had no choice. Until he was eighteen he lived under his brother's roof and by his rules, hating much of this life, apparently, but earning Samuel Nott's praise for studiousness. Here, in Franklin, he made an important resolution: "If I lived to be a man, I would not be like other men in regard to their treatment of children." The resolution became the rock on which he built the whole structure of his educational philosophy. Deborah Nott, the mother who knew character, who knew precisely what course to take with a boy, helped to shape that resolution; the Reverend Samuel Nott, intent on heaven, denying his own boyhood, gave his younger brother new reasons to ponder on the needs of children and men within the framework of this world.

How much of Eliphalet Nott's success as a schoolmaster at the Pautapaug Road School, not far from "Pisgah's Top," was owing to his use of "moral motives" as he called them, and how much of it was the result of the sympathetic personality of the tall, earnest boy who had already had too much of the rod would be hard to say. Eliphalet and his pupils, however, pooled their enthusiasms. They "played and gamboled together during play hours," procedures somewhat different from those implied in the Reverend Samuel Nott's "Regulations for my Pupils . . ." in which permission "to walk for an hour if they choose" was the limit of frivolity.[55] Saturday afternoons at the Pautapaug schoolhouse were devoted to play, a custom in considerable contrast to the one outlined in Regulation Number Five for the boys at "Pisgah's Top," where "Saturday afternoon [was] study time till 3 P.M. in the winter and 2 P.M. in the summer. The rest of the time they may have to get ready for the Sabbath."

The ordinary district school and the parsonage-school, however, were no longer adequate to the new times. The ministers were no longer looked upon as competent to explain the world; heaven yes, but laymen were finding more satisfactory answers to their practical questions in secular history and in the papers read before the multiplying philosophical societies. New England Congregationalists now had to share the land with increasing numbers of Episcopalians and Baptists and Quakers and Free Thinkers. Merchants and lawyers had taken over public life. Their innovations, however, did not often include spending public money to educate every man's son. Free public schools had, generally, to wait on the humanitarians of the Nineteenth Century, among the first of whom would be the young teacher of Pautapaug Road.

The Reverend Samuel Nott had other reasons than a consideration for Yankee thrift to be glad that his younger brother in the fall of 1793 gave up his local school to become the "Principal Instructor" of the Plainfield Academy, and so put some fifteen miles between him and Franklin Society.[56] Exactly what Eliphalet Nott and his brother's student, David Mason, had done while at "Pisgah's Top" to justify the charge lodged against them that year by irate members of the Franklin congregation is only briefly noted on the 23rd of August, 1793, in the official prose of the church record and the somewhat misleading comments in the Reverend Samuel Nott's *Autobiography*. The complaint of "brethren Phineas Peck, Elisha Edgerton, and William Ellis" is unequivocal: Eliphalet Nott and David Mason were guilty of "injurious tattling, falsehood, a manifest disposition to disturb the peace of the church, and to set the young people at variance."[57]

The storm the two young men raised in the church-bound community was violent enough to cause its frightened minister to write that it appeared to him, "as though universal desolation was about to take place."[58] He went on to state that his brother and David Mason had busied themselves with publicly censuring "a practice of some of the young men of the town, with respect to the virtue of some of the young women of the town." A satirical poem, presumably composed by Eliphalet, had been circulated, as well as "sundry letters much to the discredit of the young people. . . ." The victims belonged to the first families of Franklin, and the parents, once the censures had become generally known, laid their charges before the church membership for action. "Party spirit arose," the frightened minister wrote, "and my brother was marked for destruction, being, if not the most criminal of the two, a public professor of religion."

The tensions which this parish upheaval developed must have helped to shape Eliphalet Nott's decision to leave Franklin, and finally, to quit Connecticut altogether. Plainfield Academy, in the fall of 1793, was certainly a more comfortable vantage point from which to view the "universal desolation" which he and David Mason had released on the Reverend Samuel Nott's parish, for the embittered Franklin families, wrote their frightened minister, "permitted no chance of any accommodation through my mediation" and proceeded to keep the town in a state of turmoil for the two years young Eliphalet was head of the Academy.

The storm which the young schoolmaster and his friend David Mason had stirred up with their satiric poem and their "sundry letters very injurious" in the summer of 1793 came to a climax in November, 1795. The frustrated Samuel Nott now took the last recourse open to him: he called a church council made up of Congregational clergymen from five neighboring societies, two of them from Norwich, the others from Bozrah, Preston, and Lisbon.[59] The council met on the 13th of November, 1795, and proceeded to review the record of the earlier trial. Most of the witnesses of the earlier hearings were recalled, as was a harried Eliphalet Nott, who by this time had resigned the principalship of the Plainfield Academy and had returned to "Pisgah's Top" to become a student of divinity. The best the ecclesiastical jurists could do was to recommend that both sides give ground, and that a reasonable basis for settlement of the two-year-old dispute was to be found in the admonition already given to the erring brother by the congregation of the Franklin Church itself.

It took another month to put an official end to a controversy which the Reverend Samuel Nott had seen as "universal desolation" and as a time of real danger to himself and his family. By the middle of December, 1795, the church minutes recorded that Eliphalet Nott and the dissident members could be reconciled to each other "on condition that a certain *paper* should be publicly read on the 20th inst . . . said paper to be read in church meeting."

And so five days before Christmas, 1795, Eliphalet Nott stood up in public meeting in the Reverend Samuel Nott's church and read "a certain *paper*," probably a more satisfactory version, so far as Brother Edgerton and his backers were concerned, of the compliance the then Proctor of Plainfield Academy had sent back to Franklin the preceding May.[60]

The two years' storm must have left wide and lasting scars in the community, although Eliphalet Nott never alluded to the charges or the ecclesiastical trials. The Reverend Samuel Nott's comments are somewhat misleading, inasmuch as he writes in his *Autobiography* as though his brother had first endured the two years of attack, and had then left Franklin in 1793 for Plainfield and the principalship of its academy.

Eliphalet Nott's refusal to accept the offer of New Salem, Connecticut, to settle him in 1796, following his licensing to preach, and his decision to "go into the state of New York," as his brother wrote, may have been made, in part, because of the ill feeling which the two years' disturbance in Franklin had undoubtedly left.[61] A great many people had been involved in charges which in a less conventional and disciplined community would have been sufficient to precipitate shot-gun justice.

Perhaps the most important aspect of "Franklin Society's" ecclesiastical storm was that young Eliphalet Nott, overzealous in policing his neighbors' morals, was deemed not only capable of creating a satiric poem virulent enough to throw his brother's parish into violent upheaval, but that he could also tack well enough to ride out the storm and then steer himself back to the safe harbor of official approval.

In any event Eliphalet Nott was now almost the educated man his grandfather, the Reverend Abraham Nott, that mighty keeler of casks and bester of local toughs, had hoped his grandsons would be. Unlike the Reverend Abraham, however, "ambitious 'Liph," as Samuel Nott was to call his younger brother, was soon to accept challenges on a scale beyond the imagining of all the Puritan Notts who had proceded him.

CHAPTER 2

The "Principal Instructor" of Plainfield Academy

ALONG the Moosup and Quinebaug Rivers were the "fine water privileges" where such Plainfield citizens as Dr. Elisha Perkins had built their mills. Wool growing, potash works, a hat factory, and an establishment for making "pocketbooks and portmanteaus" gave the town a place of importance in the eastern Connecticut economy.[1] Town meetings between 1790 and 1800 were taken up largely with the problems which the new commercial enterprises were forcing on many strategically located New England communities. New roads and bridges were built to move the products of the new mills and to make the town more accessible to the neighboring villages. By 1795 the main county roads out of Plainfield had been turned over to the turnpike companies whose toll gates were soon looming up as undemocratic barriers, according to some of the countrymen.[2]

The new "Principal Instructor" of the Plainfield Academy, as the Trustees called Eliphalet Nott in their Norwich *Packet* advertisement, or "Principal" as the Reverend Samuel Nott referred to him, or the "Rector" if the Plainfield historians are followed, was, for the first time, his own man.[3] Life at "Pisgah's Top" had matured him. "His development," according to Robert Benedict, son of the Plainfield Congregationalist minister, and soon to be Eliphalet Nott's brother-in-law, "both mental and physical, at the age of twenty was so extraordinary that more than one person warned him that his early maturity presaged an early death."[4]

The new "Principal Instructor," mature far beyond his twenty years, had become responsible for the continued success of one of the most important academies in the State. "The Brick

School House," "The White Hall," and "The New Hall," the three buildings which comprised the academy as early as 1784, represented Plainfield's response to the growing demands for educated laymen.[5] The Academy to which young Nott came in 1793 had its beginnings twenty-three years earlier when a number of local citizens, including Dr. Perkins, developer of the "Metallic Tractors," a magnetic cure-all device, became dissatisfied with the uncertain achievements of their district schools and banded together into an association to provide facilities "for the more complete education of the youth."[6] There, in the brick schoolhouse which they built in the year of the Boston Massacre, boys and girls assembled to study "the common English branches," a curriculum probably much like that taught by Eliphalet Nott to his awed students at Franklin.

Young Nott apparently pleased his Trustees from the outset, for their Norwich *Packet* notice of March, 1794, published some months after he had begun his service, noted that, "the School under their direction again appears in a very respectable and flourishing situation." It seems likely that the end of the war had reduced the demands on Plainfield Academy, for the new principal referred to it as "an institution in which several hundred children of both sexes were in the same building successfully taught and governed for years without the use of the rod. . . ."[7] Possibly again a one-building school in 1793, but still drawing on a wide territory for its students, the academy must have dominated the town.

On Tuesday, the 30th of September, 1794, Plainfield Academy held its Public Exhibition at the Meeting House. Principal Nott, all of twenty-one years old, his assistant instructors and "the Procession" walked from Captain Eaton's to the place of the exhibition.[8] The Trustees of the Academy must have been delighted with the results and with Principal Nott's whole record for the year; two weeks after the exhibition they ran another advertisement in the *Packet* which would have challenged the modesty of a teacher far older than young Eliphalet. "The unexpected revival of the Schools since Mr. Nott has had the care of them, evince the public confidence in him. . . ." The Trustees went on to state that Mr. Nott would continue that winter as the principal instructor and added that the curriculum would consist of "the learned languages, arts and sciences . . . and Children (will be) instructed in Reading, Writing, English Grammar, Arithmetic, etc."[9]

What of this young "Principal Instructor" himself? At Franklin, in spite of the beatings received and the unrelenting Calvinism of his brother, he had enlarged his world to include the Greece and Rome of the classics. At "Pisgah's Top" he had also added the subjects dear to Yankee Connecticut: mathematics, geography, composition, and speaking, and had synthesized his knowledge in order to share it with his pupils in the Franklin district school. Eliphalet Nott, at twenty-one, had extended his paternal control over several hundred boys and girls, and had done it so successfully that Plainfield Academy enjoyed what its Trustees called "an unexpected revival."

At Plainfield he took an active part in the undramatic revolution which was quietly aligning American education with the day-to-day aspirations of his pupils and their families. Although he would soon begin his ministerial career as an Edwardsian Calvinist he never left the world in which schoolboys live, as had the Reverend Samuel Nott, nor ignored the concerns of their parents, who were more and more rephrasing the older Calvinists' question, "How am I to be saved?" into one befitting the times, "How am I to succeed?"

The younger brother of the Reverend Samuel Nott, born into Federalist-Republican America, was to spend his talents in trying to comprehend the problems posed by these two questions. The salvation his brother and his forebears prayed for by the mill streams of a new land, and the success which many of his contemporaries and their offspring measured in terms of their conquest over the land itself, he was eventually to synthesize in his own mind. "Salvation" and "success" were thus to become common terms for God's grace, and the church and the school to him were to become agents or means in soliciting that grace.

II

The Reverend Joel Benedict of Plainfield rather than the stern Puritan of Franklin was to be the teacher who planted the seeds of a new optimism in Eliphalet Nott. The Reverend Mr.

Benedict (the Doctorate of Divinity was not conferred on him until 1808, the gift of his son-in-law, by then President Nott of Union College) was as much the product of the revolutionary forces at work in America as were the new Plainfield mills and the network of turnpikes which were changing the ancient ways of Windham County.

Where the Reverend Samuel Nott's world was largely a seventeenth-century enclave, a world in which his long pastorate was spent in preserving the social and religious sanctions of an earlier Connecticut, the world in which the Reverend Joel Benedict had been reared and in which he spent his years as a Congregational pastor was very much one with the revolutionary Eighteenth Century. He was a New Englander only by adoption. His father, Deacon Peter Benedict, had moved his family from Norwalk, Connecticut, to Salem, Westchester County, New York, sometime before 1745, where he and his Connecticut neighbors had settled on the manorial lands of Stephen VanCortland.[10]

Joel Benedict's young manhood was spent in one of the most active breeding grounds of social discontent in mid-eighteenth-century America. Westchester and the other Hudson River Valley counties were practically medieval fiefs. The pattern of land tenure and legal procedure and the economic and political dependence in which the Dutch patroons and the English landlords kept their tenants contributed to produce the "riotous farmers" of the area, men who were, in the main, reduced to a state of peasantry, bitterly protesting a social and economic system which was an affront to their New England tradition.[11] Deacon Benedict's Calvinism taught him that all men were brothers in ruin; within the framework of this leveling doctrine there was little room for the kind of aristocracy he and his Norwalk neighbors found in the Crown Colony of New York.

It was at the College of New Jersey that young Joel Benedict got his enthusiasm for the classics, and particularly for Hebrew, "the language of the angels," as he called it, a subject taught to the seniors by President Finley. Where Samuel Nott had spent his college years in bolstering his pocketbook and following the Calvinist doctrine as laid down by Yale and Jonathan Edwards the Younger (Joel Benedict's classmate at the College of New Jersey), Joel Benedict had developed into an outstanding mathematician, a student of languages, and a Vergilian scholar whose talents were "so remarkable that the Professors sometimes set him to reading Vergil merely for their own gratification."[12]

As a theology student, Joel Benedict stood one generation closer to the source of the "New Light" theology than did Samuel Nott. Both Joel Benedict and Jonathan Edwards the Younger had been students of the Reverend Joseph Bellamy, the elder Edwards's close friend and enthusiastic disciple. By 1769 that big-voiced, powerful preacher had made Bethlehem, Connecticut, famous as a center of "New Light" Calvinism. From his pulpit he had defended the ancient doctrine of the Trinity against the Arianism of the Reverend Jonathan Mayhew.[13] Joel Benedict and his fellow students took their instructions from one of the most militant revivalists of the Great Awakening itself, an itinerant "New Light" pastor to whom Jonathan Edwards' preaching on "distinterested benevolence," the self-forgetful love of God, was the very essence of religion.

The vital element in his thinking, however, a departure from the teaching of Edwards himself, the Reverend Joseph Bellamy reiterated time and again to his pupils. Joel Benedict seems to have been especially sensitive to Bellamy's clear assertion of a general atonement, the conclusion that Christ died, not for the elect alone, but for all men.[14] This optimist's conception which the later Edwardsians, especially Jonathan Edwards the Younger and the Reverend Samuel Hopkins, conditioned by elaborate theological systems, was accepted without conditions or system by Joel Benedict.

If the Reverend Joel Benedict never went beyond the New Testament's mystical presentation of Christ's death into the wide realms of philosophical speculation as did both Edwardses, neither was he led into the spiritually desiccating theological controversies which were of constant concern to many later Edwardsians, including Eliphalet Nott's brother, the Reverend Samuel Nott. It seems likely that Joel Benedict's chief contribution to the religious development of their young student was the awakening within him of his own poetic response to the central mystery of Christianity. Ten years after Eliphalet Nott had left Plainfield, he would write out his once famous series of sermons on "The Resurrection," a series in which he dramatically restated Joel Benedict's humble acceptance of the offer of salvation to all men on the basis of a simple faith in the atonement and resurrection of Christ. The Reverend Samuel Nott's doctrine of salvation of the "saints" alone, those arbitrarily elected to everlasting life, had by then lost its conviction for his "too ambitious" younger brother, as "Liph" then seemed to be to the authoritarian master of "Pisgah's Top."

If the Reverend Joel Benedict left a deep impression on Eliphalet Nott, so, too, did the religious revivals, the "Second Awakening" which began to leaven the life of Plainfield and of many other New England towns during the young teacher's principalship of the Academy. This "downpouring of the spirit," as he was later to call it, began as early as 1791 in southern Maine and became, by the end of the decade, a vast and unpredictable flood moving west and south along the channels of emigration.[15]

It was undoubtedly a sorrow to the Reverend Joel Benedict that his own flock was so little stirred by the enthusiasm which began in Plainfield in 1792. From then until 1803 only twenty-two "were moved by the spirit" to join his church, and of these only three were men.[16] The success of the Baptists of the town, however, with their eighty-seven converts, and of the Methodists, does not seem to have affected the generosity of Eliphalet Nott's first instructor in theology. "Plainfield," one writer has said, "was a school for prophets, and Dr. Benedict was the master of the school."[17]

That the young head of the Plainfield Academy was undergoing instruction in theology from the Reverend Joel Benedict during these first years of the new revival, however, is significant. It was Joel Benedict, he remembered, who had found "greatness and goodness . . . in other denominations . . . [who could] take an interest in their prosperity . . . which made an impression on my mind which has never been effaced." Unitarians and Universalists, Baptists and Methodists, all of these were subject to God's grace, he was discovering, as, too, were even those Republicans who had looked askance at the Reverend Samuel Nott's fine house and coach and horses, and dubiously at a Federalism which many of them concluded would hardly provide a suitable government for either a "New Jerusalem" or a democratic America.

III

By May of 1795 the young Preceptor believed he was ready for advanced standing at Rhode Island College in Providence. Having terminated his agreement with the Trustees of the Plainfield Academy, he went up to the college in order to be examined by President Jonathan Maxcy and the Fellows, planning, apparently, to stay on as a student until he was ready to take his first degree. Instead of being enrolled, however, he was told he might spend the following summer studying for the senior class examination, which he could take in the fall.[18] His studies with his older brother and with Dr. Benedict apparently had carried him a longer way than he had realized.

Eliphalet Nott was no student novice. Plainfield Academy, during his principalship, had offered "the learned languages, Arts and Sciences." He must have known his mathematics and his astronomy, for he later told Henry Barnard that "though inferior in attainments to some of my classmates, I published successfully myself an almanac when about twenty-one years old."[19] The fact that Rhode Island College, at the end of that summer's review, awarded Eliphalet Nott its honorary degree of Master of Arts for work done out of course is testimony enough that his attainments did not seem inferior to the Board of Fellows which granted the honor. An entry in the Reverend Samuel Nott's *Autobiography* indicates that the degree was not a casual gesture made to please a friend of the institution, but an earnest of real achievement: at Providence, the older brother wrote, "he pursued his studies with attention. He became acquainted with the President and Officers of the College and though he never became a member of it himself, his reputation as a scholar was so good that he was at the Commencement honored with a degree of Master of Arts."[20]

The long summer of 1795 was important to Eliphalet Nott also for the impressions he received of undergraduate life and of college administration. What little first-hand knowledge he had of colleges he got in Providence, and what he learned there he later took to Schenectady. The "Eliphalet Nott, of Plainfield," however, named in the Minutes of the Rhode Island College Board of Fellows on September 2, 1795, then knew only that he believed his goal was to preach the Gospel of Edwards.

He had now to prepare himself for the examination given to prospective ministers by the Congregational Association of New London, an examination in "experimental, doctrinal, polemic, and practical divinity." From September, 1795, until the following June, according to the Reverend Samuel Nott, there was "the study of divinity under my direction." For the kinds of divinity which seemed important to the Association of New London one could hardly have gone to a better, more orthodox teacher. Eliphalet Nott himself has left no record of his own feelings about returning to "Pisgah's Top," but at least there could have been no rod this time.

Precisely what combination of events moved the newly licensed preacher of the New London Association in 1795 "to go into New York" that summer is beyond knowing, but the urge to enter "the vacant ground" had never been stronger than in this last decade of the century, during those years when the Reverend Samuel Nott's younger brother was preparing himself to serve the church of the Puritans. He may have been influenced by the fact that his brother and his father-in-law were planning to go on missions themselves into the new settlements along both sides of the upper Connecticut River.

Franklin Society, and much of eastern Connecticut, certainly, must have still echoed with the noise and gossip aroused by young " 'Liph's" recent church trial. Young Eliphalet, with a career to make, might justifiably have decided that he would find his life on "vacant ground" in New York State less handicapped. Whatever the reasons, they must have been urgent, for not only did he turn down a parish at New Salem, Connecticut, but he left behind him Sarah Maria Benedict, the fey and frail daughter of the Reverend Joel Benedict, who had become his wife on Independence Day that year.[21] His bride was not even to have her honeymoon until her husband had been "settled" as pastor to the Scotch Presbyterians of Cherry Valley, New York, that November.

It does not seem possible to say who exactly, sponsored what Eliphalet Nott many years after the event called his "mission" to the Otsego Lake Country. The "Domestic Missionary Society" of Connecticut, according to one source, "on learning of Mr. Nott's wish to undertake a mission to the State of New York, accepted his services, giving him a commission to go forth and labor in such parts of the proposed field as Providence might open before him."[22]

> The vacant settlements on the tract south of those on the Mohawk River, between that and the Great Bend and Wyoming in Pennsylvania, and between Hudson's and Genesee River, are very numerous; for that in all these extensive regions, north and west, we suppose, there are between 200 and 300 vacant towns and settlements. Such is their state that they have as yet little advantage for schooling, and there is a great searcity [*sic*] of books, especially of the religious kind.[23]

Letters such as this one from Otsego County, New York, written in 1794 to the General Association of the Connecticut Congregational Churches, were read by these churches as earnest pleas to send out missionaries to the so-called "vacant ground" of Vermont, New Hampshire, and those vast frontier areas of western New York which, since the days of the Revolution, had been drawing off thousands of Connecticut families.

In these "Narratives of Missions to the New Settlements" one finds the record of one phase of the Second Awakening which revitalized many of the Connecticut churches during Eliphalet Nott's years as the "Principal Instructor" of the Plainfield Academy. These "Narratives" forcefully illustrated the great demand for dedicated men, young men who could cope with the rugged life of the frontier. The need in New York State was obviously great. Ministers were wanted who could organize churches among the "vacant towns," who could bring schooling to those places suffering from a "searcity" of books and who could collect the frontier statistics the General Association was amassing. Tours of four months were available at five dollars a week for those who could supply a horse and pay their expenses out of the stipend.[24]

The name of Eliphalet Nott, however, does not appear anywhere in the records of the General Association as undertaking a New York State Mission in its behalf. According to a ruling of the Association adopted on the 21st of June, 1796, he would actually have been ineligible for its missionary service, for it was agreed at that time that only "settled" ministers should be engaged.[25] Nor had the area young Nott visited been neglected by the General Association: a "Mr. Starr . . . with Mr. Robbins went on a mission to Lattonia, Cherry Valley, and the settlements about Lake Otsago [*sic*] and on the Mohawk River in the autumn of 1796."[26]

Sixty-four years later, however, President Nott, out of his octogenarian's memory, gave an explanation for his leaving Connecticut to one of his faculty members at Union College, an explanation completely at variance with the record. "Pinky" Pearson, Professor Jonathan Pearson, a student and then a long-time associate of President Nott, recorded the old man's reminiscence:

> Dr. Nott told me the other day that he studied medicine with "Metallic Tractors" Perkins in Connecticut and practised it until he was frightened out of it by the Scarlet Fever which about '95 committed awful ravages in some Connecticut towns. At first he had good success with a few cases but saw so many die around him, that he became alarmed and started for New York State to get clear of any farther concern for the healing art.[27]

For lack of any final evidence that Eliphalet Nott went into the "vacant ground" as a representative of any of the developing missionary enterprises of the period, one is thrown back on the Reverend Samuel Nott's simple and perhaps revealing statement on the subject of his brother's departure: "He decided to go into New York."[28] The Calvinism which he then embraced, the population movement westward, the stimulation of the Second Awakening, and the recent unsettling events in his personal history were more then enough to justify the decision.

CHAPTER 3

"Is This the Way to Zion?"

THE newly licensed Congregationalist preacher broke his journey long enough, apparently, to make his first public address in New York State to a Union College audience. There in Schenectady, on the edge of the frontier, he met the man who was now to become a major influence in his life, who was to change not only his immediate plans, but his very allegiance to the church he had declared it was his intention to extend among the new settlements.

> In passing through Schenectady [the young missionary recalled], I stopped overnight at a public house opposite the academy building, then occupied by the college, and learned that there was to be a prayer meeting or lecture there that evening. I felt it my duty to attend, and was solicited to preach by Dr. Smith, then President of Union College, who, after the service invited me to his house to spend the night.[1]

From the Schenectady Coffee House, across the street from Union College, to the frontier was a matter of a day's horseback ride in 1796, if one went north or southwest. If one rode or took the stagecoach or went by batteau up the Mohawk River, there was civilization of a sort for about ninety miles, until one came to the cabins and lean-tos and the rotting timbers of Fort Stanwix, at Rome, New York. Beyond Rome was the thinly settled wilderness, its millions of acres west of the Appalachian Divide to the Great Lakes still subject to the ownership quarrels of Massachusetts, Connecticut, and New York, of the huge land companies and the cowed tribes of the Iroquois.[2]

The young Connecticut preacher was in a new world. The village of Schenectady had fewer than a thousand inhabitants, Dutchmen, most of them, to whom the town was known as "the Dorp." Strung west along the river were the remains of the forts of the French and Indian Wars and of the Revolution. Dutchmen and Germans, but mostly Germans, descendants of the great Palatine immigration into the valley in the second and third decades of the Eighteenth Century, farmed the flats. The stage road up the north side of the river was the one followed by westbound settlers heading for the Genesee Road and the land speculators' paradise through which it passed. The best road south, out of the little Palatinate of the Mohawk Valley, began at the village of Canajoharie and inched southwest up the broad flanks of the Susquehanna highlands until it came to the village of Cherry Valley. Beyond Cherry Valley, some fifteen miles west, lay Otsego Lake, Fenimore Cooper's "Glimmerglass," and the object of Eliphalet Nott's journey.[3]

A half century later the events of 1796 had arranged themselves within the pattern of a romantic landscape in the mind of the still active President of Union College, events which he described for an audience assembled at Cherry Valley fifty-five years after he had left Connecticut. He remembered his youth and his inexperience. He remembered his hardihood at taking what he called "The New State Road," known later as the Great Western Turnpike. He recalled that he was the first man to travel west on it. He painted a Thomas Cole landscape for his hearers:

> On the forenoon of the second day, as I emerged from the dense forest which covered the summit of yon eastern hills, this beautiful valley, with its rich pasture grounds and golden harvest fields, ripe for the sickle, broke unexpectedly upon my view. . . . I checked my horse, and in amazement looked down upon it. It seemed like the vision of enchantment. . . . I descended yon hillside, and entered the then thriving village. What an exchange it was for the gloom of the forest, where, at intervals the howl of the wolf fell upon my ear, and where, a short time thereafter, a traveller was devoured by these ferocious animals.[4]

He remembered his greatest joy was that the men and women of Cherry Valley "spoke the same language and professed the same religion as myself." The *mannen and vrouwen* of Dutch Albany and Schenectady and the German teamsters (whose manners had affronted him) had little to do with the world he had left and with the New England settlements he had come to find. The old president remembered the affection with which the fathers and mothers of his hearers had received him a half century earlier and that he had then promised them to come back to Cherry Valley as soon as his mission was fulfilled.

If Eliphalet Nott went on to Otsego Lake, however, as he had declared it was his intention to do, he left no record of the journey. He would have found more civilization than he had expected. The valleys that ran south into the greater valley of the Susquehanna River were already filled with clearings and tote-road communities which bore familiar names. South of Otsego Lake were Franklin and Plainfield. And there was a Norwich, and Guilford and Windsor, New Berlin and Exeter, and Lisbon, names of towns he had known all his life. These were the upper Susquehanna settlements that were "more indebted to Connecticut than to any other part of the country."[5]

It is fair to assume that Nott probably visited a number of these transplanted Connecticut communities, and that after considerable wrestling with the problem, he then decided to go back to Cherry Valley. By September 5, 1796, the Trustees of the Cherry Valley Presbyterian Church were circulating a subscription "respecting the having of the Reverend Mr. Eliphalet Nott."[6] But what had happened to his Congregationalist missionary ardor? Cherry Valley, in contrast to the many churchless communities west of it, was for Nott truly a "Solitary Zion," a ready-made congregation of Calvinists living a New England village life. There was already standing the chief building of the Connecticut scene: "a new, but old-fashioned, square, wooden meeting-house, with its square high-backed pews," the "Lord's barn," according to one traveller.[7]

The Cherry Valley massacre of 1778 had swept the physical evidences of the then frontier settlement into a ruin of cellar holes and broken families. Five years later, however, the survivors had gathered in the rubble of their meeting-house yard and incorporated the Presbyterian Church whose "new, square, wooden meeting house" and "affectionate" parishioners had seemed so inviting to Eliphalet Nott, fresh from the organized life of Connecticut.

If there was invitation to settlement in the warmth of the parish's call late that summer of 1796, there was also the attractive prospect for the young ex-schoolmaster of running the Cherry

Valley Academy. That second important prop of the New England scene was also standing, "a large and commodious building for an academy."

Here then, in this growing town, inside the eastern edge of the New York frontier, straddling the cleared path of what was soon to become the vital Great Western Turnpike, Eliphalet Nott gave up the purpose which he had declared was responsible for his leaving his native state. Not for him the missionary life of a Father Nash, who in 1797 took for his Episcopal parish the whole county of Otsego, and who, with his wife, "lived in rude cabins of unhewed logs," preaching the doctrine of the Church of England to Connecticut Congregationalists until his death in 1836.[8] Eliphalet Nott made an important decision when he eschewed the life of the frontier for that of a settled community cast in the mold of the New England towns he had left. The cities, President Smith had told him, were the centers of influence; they were the places to which the Apostles had gone to preach the Word.[9] Cherry Valley was no city, but by definition it was a more important center of influence than the crossroad communities of the Susquehanna wilderness.

As pastor of the Cherry Valley Church young Nott apparently wrote nothing which he or others thought significant enough to commit to print. It was rather as Principal Nott of the Academy that he was remembered. It was as the educator once more that he published in April, 1797, *Federal Money*, a seven-page pamphlet describing the "money of account of United America," an ironic little book, considering the title of "Money King" a Union College poet would one day award him.[10] Here in convenient form "for the use of schools" was the arithmetic of dollars, dimes, cents, and mills. Schoolmaster Nott and his pupils had grown up with the clipped and mutilated hard money of foreigners. By 1797, however, the United States mint, established five years earlier, was distributing its silver dollars, dimes, half-dimes, and cent pieces, and until the new money obtained the ascendancy, adding confusion among people brought up with Spanish dollars and English pounds and pence.

Federal Money, by Eliphalet Nott of the Cherry Valley Academy, offered no comments on the new coinage but got down at once to the business of multiplication, division, subtraction, and simple interest, with examples. If the author's example under "Division" can be trusted, it offers a startling comment on commodity prices, to say nothing of a somewhat painful regard for decimal points:

If 122 Oranges cost 109D. 8d. 0c. 0m. what were they apiece?

```
      D.  d.  c.  m.       D.  c.  m.
122)  109.  8  0  0  ( .9  0  0
      109.  8
      ───────
       0    0  0  0
```

Eliphalet Nott's rule for changing cents into pence was probably the most useful one from the point of view of his Cherry Valley pupils, who were now faced with the problem of Lawful money as opposed to York money:

"Multiply the given pence by 100, and divide them by 96, if the pence be York currency—if Lawful, then multiply by 100 and divide by 72."

Sarah Maria, waiting in Plainfield, had her wedding journey soon after her new husband completed his arrangements with his Cherry Valley parishioners. The tall, handsome old-young minister and "Mrs. Nott . . . small of stature, complexion fair, countenance expressive . . . enlivened by an eye uncommonly brilliant. . . ." were undoubtedly welcome tenants of the Cherry Valley parsonage. Her vivacity and "her talent for satire" were leavening qualities in a household whose head must epitomize the virtues of the community. A minister with his way to make, he was apparently bothered a little by her candor, although he was generous in his appraisal; he "thought it sometimes made enemies, [though] it always endeared her to her friends."[11] Their first child, Joel Benedict Nott, was born in Cherry Valley on the 14th of December, 1797. The young mother failed to regain her strength and the following summer she was driven to Ballston Spa, a dozen miles north of Schenectady, where it was hoped she would improve by drinking the mineral waters.

II

It was during this summer that President Smith of Union College completed his reorientation of Eliphalet Nott's thinking about a proper "field of usefulness." Apparently the older man took every occasion possible to urge the younger one to give up not only his missionary zeal to spread Congregational churches along the New York frontier, but also to leave his Cherry Valley parish. In addition to heeding Dr. Smith's arguments for accepting a call to the "Court Church" of Albany, the new capital of New York State, he must have considered the economic opportunities offered by the proposed change; there would be $1000 a year from the trustees of the Albany church, plus the New Year's perquisites and the usual "extras" to be derived from weddings, christenings, and funerals. Such things were important in view of Sarah Maria's illness and the advent of a son. The fact that he was wanted by the most influential church in the Albany Presbytery was itself flattering. Albany, not New York City, was now the State capital and the minister who spoke from the First Church pulpit would face some of the nation's first citizens during the legislative sessions: Alexander Hamilton, Chancellor Kent, Gouverneur Morris, Aaron Burr, Brockholst Livingston, and a good many other state officers and legislators.

Events moved fast during Sarah Maria's absence at Ballston Spa. At President Smith's urging, her husband preached in Albany on the second Sunday in July. He must have been eloquent, for five days later, on the 13th of July, 1798, the "electors" of the First Church invited him to become their pastor.[12] He remained in the city a week, discussing parish problems, preached on the 16th, and then, his mind made up to accept the Albany call, returned to Cherry Valley to end his first ministry and his work as principal of the academy. When he left the valley toward the end of that summer for the city, he left behind him the earnest boy from Connecticut who had come into New York State two years earlier with two fixed purposes: to make his home in the country, and to carry the church of the Puritans to the New England men on the New York frontier.

President Smith of Union College was sure his handsome young disciple from Connecticut would serve God best by establishing his ministry in the city; it was, he had insisted, what the apostles had done. What these men of God could not calculate, however, was the effect of the city on their ministries and on their own purposes. Beginning in Albany and throughout his extra-ordinarily long life, Eliphalet Nott, as had President John Blair

Smith, was to force his talents as a peacemaker, a harmonizer, harnessing when he could the conflicting and competing ambitions of urban men to the common work of building the American Zion. Though the city seemed to be the place for such work, it is difficult now to recapture that enthralling vision which animated these vigorous ministers of Nott's generation, men whose lives were intimately associated with a social and political revolution which had spread before them an almost vacant continent. West of Albany and the barrier of the Appalachians stretching south to Georgia was that "vacant ground" where "the downpouring of the spirit," many believed, would surely germinate the seeds of a new civilization.

This dream of a new Zion, the redeemed land, which Protestant Christian Americans were to build beyond the shadow of infidel Europe, was chiefly responsible for bringing the young Cherry Valley pastor to his new pulpit in the capital city of New York State. To make a reality of such a dream was worth any sacrifice, and especially any "accommodation." One has only to read that sermon Nott was to preach to an audience gathered in his Albany church on the fourth of July, 1801, to realize what a hold this dream had on the imagination and the will of the ambitious young pastor. Because of that dream he had already committed himself to the first of those "accommodations," as he was to call them, in 1796, in response to the special pleading of the man who was soon to wean him from his country parish.

If the dream of an American Zion was to be realized, President Smith had argued—and the hope was never stronger than during these first decades of the Second Awakening—the church of Calvin must truly consolidate its strength. "The arguments employed by Dr. Smith were deemed conclusive by me," Eliphalet Nott recalled. He had agreed with the older man's observation that "the orthodox churches of New England had substantially the same faith as the Presbyterians, of which the Shorter Catechism is the common symbol". He had agreed that "those two divisions should make mutual concessions, and thus effect a common organization" so that the "full means to grace" might be sooner enjoyed by the swelling population of "this vast new territory." [13]

What, however, had seemed to be a simple "accommodation plan" in the mind of President Smith, and later a "Plan of Union" in the mind of his successor, President Jonathan Edwards the

Younger of Union College, soon became, in Eliphalet Nott's thinking, a call "to a new direction in my efforts, and led, through the influence of other Congregationalists whom I induced to cooperate, to the formation, on this plan, of those large Presbyterian Churches of which, though the plan has been abandoned, the fruits remain to the present day." [14]

The "accommodation" which President Smith of Union had urged on Nott in 1796 became, in fact, not "accommodation," but assimilation. Smith's "Plan of Union," as it was to operate in fact was slowly to close the West to the successful extension of that milder, democratic Congregational discipline of associations and consociations which Nott had known as a theology student in Connecticut. In order to promote the interests, however, of that "modern and western Israel" which would be the subject of his Independence Day address in 1801, Nott and his Presbyterian colleagues deliberately made the original "Plan of Union" a device for absorbing a friendly rival for recruits in the war against infidelity.

Eliphalet Nott was twenty-five years old in 1798 when he allowed President Smith to persuade him to turn his back on his "solitary Zion" of Cherry Valley and on country living. The "inexperience and want of ability" which had deterred him from a too hasty acceptance of the call to Cherry Valley in 1796 were, apparently, no longer stumbling blocks two years later to accepting the call to Albany. Either enormous self-confidence or a sense of destiny must have fortified him, for Albany was an old and sophisticated community and many of his new parishioners were among its most worldly citizens. [15]

It was a city of Dutch houses, high gable ends facing the crowded streets with here and there an architectural intruder, a Georgian house or a public building such as Philip Hooker's new Dutch Reformed Church, with its pediment and Doric columns and twin baroque towers.

New York City, 150 miles down the Hudson River, had six times as many people, but Albany was the new Capital of the State and the distribution center for much of the western country. Its 5000 citizens, the majority of Dutch descent, supported four churches. Many in the Dutch Reformed congregation, the oldest and the largest in 1798, still resented the substitution of English for Dutch in the service. There was an Episcopalian Church and a small Roman Catholic society which completed its building the year Nott arrived to occupy the pulpit of the First Presbyterian Church, the "Court Church," so-called because of the notable names on its roster.

Albanians, during the last years of the Eighteenth Century, were largely manufacturers and middlemen, suppliers and carriers for the Yankee hordes thronging through the capital to western counties. During Eliphalet Nott's six-year stay in the city as many as one hundred sloops a season were engaged in carrying goods to and from the port of New York. In order to supply the frontier, New Englanders, settled in Albany, set up mills to manufacture nails, glass, plows, tobacco and "segars," chocolate, and wagons. New Englanders printed the four Albany newspapers, which were established with varying degrees of success during these years. The conservative Dutch majority resented the Yankees, but were glad to invest their money in the banks the Yankees established in Albany and in the turnpike companies they organized.[16]

This city economy, expanding in every direction, was creating its own revolution. The young minister of the First Presbyterian Church was to meet it among his parishioners: the city's factory workers with their new and puzzling social problems, the rising tide of materialism and corruption, these were now to become daily challenges to his traditional Christian formulas for saving men.

The First Presbyterian Church of Albany, in its role as the "Court Church," designated another aspect of that new world which was beginning to absorb the Reverend Eliphalet Nott.[17] The uncomplex relationships of his brother's Congregational Parish in Franklin, Connecticut, and the working democracy of the New England town itself were no guides to conduct in the capital city of New York State. From his Albany pulpit Eliphalet Nott would face such political opponents as Alexander Hamilton and Aaron Burr; their bitter political and personal quarrels need not be rehearsed here, but the aristocratic-democratic issues which divided them divided Albany and the nation, and those issues were forced upon the young minister. It required no small talent to preach God's Word to the satisfaction of both Federalists and Republicans, to the traditionally conservative merchants and professional men of his parish, and to the followers of the Livingstons and the Clintons, those purveyors of states' rights doctrines, backers of Jefferson and his "mad French philosophy." [18] Albany presented a cultural medium in which Nott learned rapidly to force his talents for "accommodation" and for the management of men.

Within less than a month the new minister's "handling the word of God" was rudely challenged by a committee representing part of the First Church's membership which claimed he was "settled contrary to our desire." [19] "His mode and his manner of preaching is such that we cannot profit from his labours; he being in our judgment the least qualified of any we could possibly have got." The committee must have represented a sizable portion of the congregation, for they proceeded to petition the Trustees for the use of "the old church" as a compensation for their property in the new building opened in 1796. They then added insult to injury by pointing out that they wanted a minister "who will compose with accuracy, speak correctly, and preach without reading; one qualified to inform the minds and improve the morals of those committed to his charge."

What percentage of these charges were based on a real dislike of Eliphalet Nott and what on local disagreements which antedated his coming to Albany is largely conjectural. Possibly the dissidents had heard of his trial by his brother's church in Franklin, Connecticut. The Scotch Presbyterians were traditionally opposed to a clergy which read its sermons, whereas in Connecticut, as President Nott wrote to the Reverend W. B. Sprague a half-century after he had left his Albany charge, "the discourses were for the most part argumentative, carefully written, and calmly and deliberately read from the pulpit." [20]

The First Church had been without a settled pastor for three years, a fact which in itself is testimony to discord among the members. President Smith, who had preached to them on many occasions during these years, had a pulpit manner and an address which pleased them and which had filled Nott "with admiration and amazement." His "impassioned and extemporaneous efforts," as he wrote years later to Dr. Sprague, "his addresses to the hopes of Christians were most cheering; his appeals to the consciences of sinners, terrific." Here, then, at the beginning of his career in Albany was a challenging example of the effective minister in action.

The effect of this schism in the "Court Church" and all that it implied as to his effectiveness as a minister account, in part, for the extreme measures Eliphalet Nott now took to please his Trustees and his audiences. For the first time in his brief professional career, he had met really violent opposition, enough, certainly, to become a *cause célèbre* within the confines of the Albany community. A part of the remedy was to model himself after President Smith of Union College or at least to do whatever was necessary to "command that rapt attention of audiences" which had already excited admiration and amazement in the young disciple.

He was still too young a man and too inexperienced to achieve the effects the older man did, whose "preparations for the pulpit were meditation and prayer." "Dr. Smith," he noted, "seldom wrote his sermons; at most he wrote only a few brief hints on a slip of paper. . . ."; but the hints were enough and the effect was magnificent and it was the effect the younger man set about to produce. He established a regimen which almost ruined his health. "From 1798 to 1814," he wrote many years later, "I studied hard, often from twelve to fourteen hours a day. I slept little, and took but little exercise." He "visited on Monday, studied on Tuesday and Wednesday, commenced [his] sermons on Thursday, and gave to them the residue of the week."[21]

The success of the young minister as a pulpit orator, however, now grew rapidly. It was a success based on the hardest kind of work, for in order to approach Dr. Smith's effects he had to write out his two Sunday sermons and commit them to memory. But the Scotch-Irish Albanians who remained in his parish soon had little cause to complain. "So true was his memory to the trust he was wont to impose in it," wrote his one time student, Professor Tayler Lewis of Union College, "that there was no sign of constraint in his utterance, or of effort to recall a word, or of misgiving as to what he was about to put forth; but his speech flowed easily and naturally, as if premeditated. He had the art to make what was really an artistic work seem like nature herself. . . ."[22]

Being the State capital, Albany was not unfamiliar with eloquent men, yet within five years Eliphalet Nott made himself one of a notable company of impressive speakers. "Dr. Nott," wrote Gorham A. Worth in 1803, "drew together the largest congregation—made the deepest impression, and commanded the profoundest respect. His church was filled to overflowing. His elocution was admirable, and his manner altogether better, because more impressive than that of any other preacher of the day; yet he could not, I think, have been over twenty-eight years of age when I first heard him. . . ."[23]

In an era when the theatre was anathema to many Christians, Nott seems to have made his pulpit a stage, and to have given his hearers that catharsis which Aristotle argued was the theatre's *raîson d'étre*. Francis Wayland testified to this effect on Nott's audiences in a comment on a series of sermons on the Resurrection which Nott delivered first in Albany and later to his students at Union College:

> I remember at the present time the effect of them. Each sermon seemed to the audience about twenty minutes long, though in reality three-quarters of an hour in delivery. I sat all this time perfectly entranced, chills running over me from nearly the commencement to the close. When he uttered the Amen, the whole audience experienced a sensible relief. The strain of attention was so great, that men hardly breathed, and as soon as it was over, everyone took a long inspiration, and felt that he could hardly have endured the effect of concentration much longer.[24]

III

Nott and his contemporaries in the first decade of the Nineteenth Century shared a world view which must be kept constantly in mind. Archbishop Ussher's chronology according to the Bible had not yet been challenged. Sir James Lyell's studies of the geological evidences of the antiquity of man had not yet set the clergy to reconciling religion and science. God's special act of creation on behalf of man was still to be repealed by Charles Darwin. And in western New York a school-teacher could still upset his community by declaring that the earth was round.[25] If the deists were then "exposing" revelation, it was solely on the basis of that so-called "common sense" among men which the orthodox Christian knew could easily be betrayed by the devil.

The American republic, for Eliphalet Nott, was now that wonder, "which God hath wrought for our fathers and for us."

This was the young pastor's theme which he developed for his Albany parish on Declaration Day, 1801.[26] His tact before a mixed audience of Federalists and Republicans was exemplary: he would "not act the partisan, and thus lead into the uncertain fields of political discussion. . . ." Instead, he struck out at once on a parallel which illustrated his theme: America, before her triumph, was as Israel had been, groaning in bondage to a Britain as vile as Egypt. Extending this parallel, he matched every Israelite trial with an American one. Petitions from the colonists, "like the groanings of Israel in Egypt, only provoked new grievances and drew down heavier burdens upon them." Finally war, "to defend our liberties," and the years of unequal contest "when America, like Israel upon the brink of the sea, stood trembling, unable to withstand, having no refuge from her enemies; then the Almighty appeared for the deliverance of his suffering people. "The arm of Omnipotence," he declared, "then stretched down from heaven, smote the wave that was overwhelming us: it divided; and we passed through into a new world, from which our feet were to return no more into the land of oppression."

Eliphalet Nott left no useful or dramatic metaphor unexploited. In the spirit of the Connecticut Wits, he raised the history of the American Revolution to the level of a holy war and cast Washington in the role of a Moses sent "to rescue this western and modern Israel."

God's wonder-working, however, did not stop with the release of the colonies from bondage to England. In the midst of the darkest days of the Confederacy which followed appeared "the pillar of divine glory . . . the finger of Providence," which again pointed the way: wise Americans produced their Constitution, "the *magnum opus*, which hath proved a rock of safety." Eliphalet Nott was now on secure ground from which he could point the lessons he felt the occasion and the times justified. He knew his hearers were glad to accept the thesis that America was the special object of heavenly solicitude. He addressed them now as though they were all New Englanders, all descendants of those Calvinist fathers who, "when they landed on these shores . . . made a covenant with God."

What, then, must be done twenty-five years after the Revolution to keep that contract with God which He, on His part, had so signally honored? "Choose this day," charged the young pastor, "whom you will serve . . . your all is at stake." The contract must be kept, and the blandishments of an infidel Europe must not be heeded. Partisan Americans, he declared, must elect to become patriots, and cease their party quarreling. "Why," he asked, "will you weaken each other's influence by division?" United, all Americans must withstand "foreign influence," and that "Infidelity" which, he warned, "has already converted Europe into one vast Golgotha."

Such injunctions to unity and patriotism, and to politics according to God's oracles, to respect even for leaders contaminated with "democracy," was fine Sunday talk, but young Nott's Federalist hearers gladly continued in sin when speaking of such as Jefferson. As the Federalist-Republican quarrels sharpened and the break between the Livingstons and the Clintonians split the New York Republican ranks into noisy factions, Eliphalet Nott of the "Court Church" had more and more cause to question his choice of a city pulpit as his final "field of usefulness." If he was sincere in believing that the Americans of 1801 would heed his Sunday injunctions, that they could live in a modern Israel, abiding by covenants with God made explicit by Mathers, and Edwardses, by the Samuel Notts, and John Blair Smiths, he must have been soon disillusioned.

By the end of that year the Reverend Eliphalet Nott and "Mrs. Sally Nott," as Sarah Maria was known in Albany, were living on North Pearl Street, probably a little north of the "Vanderheyden Palace," a twin-gabled, Dutch mansion about which Washington Irving was to write in *Bracebridge Hall*.[27] Their household now included three children, Joel, born in Cherry Valley, Sarah Maria, born during a visit her mother made to her family in Plainfield, Connecticut, in the spring of 1799, and John, born in the North Pearl Street house on December 14, 1801.[28]

More and more the young minister of the "Court Church" found himself taxed by those additional duties imposed upon him. President Smith of Union College resigned his office in January, 1799, and, "sunk into extreme debility", returned to his congregation in Philadelphia; "the business of presiding over a college," he had written two years earlier to a former parishoner, "was an object of disgust to me."[29] John Blair Smith's departure left the administrative work of the Northern Missionary Society in his ambitious young disciple's hands. As Secretary of the society Nott now found himself busy promoting religious education among the Indian tribes, particularly the Oneidas of western New York who in 1798 had given the society 400 acres of land for the support of a mission among them.

During January, 1800, Nott was also made a co-chaplain of the New York State Legislature, sharing that office with the Reverend J. B. Johnson, the pastor of the Dutch Reformed Church in Albany, and a Trustee of Union College, that debt ridden, frontier institution to which Eliphalet Nott himself would soon be going as a fellow trustee.

The roads leading to the New Zion were beginning to seem as numerous as were those roads which, proverbially, led into and out of Rome.

CHAPTER 4

The Pastor of the "Court Church"

ELIPHALET NOTT had charged himself with a task which, with the advent of the Nineteenth Century, suddenly seemed possible to fulfill, the work of mapping for mankind the return route to a lost Eden. He charged himself with traveling as much of the route as time, events, and men would permit, a journey of "accommodations." His was an arrogant undertaking, perhaps, for he assumed the route, an often frightening one as he searched it out, would lead, indeed, to Zion or Eden. Ahead lay that perfected world he had come to believe would evolve, not from the cloister and the church, but from the market place, from the workshop, and especially from the schools of a science-oriented America.

"Accommodation," for Eliphalet Nott, was also to mean bending to those demands of "Capt. Edgerton and others . . ." during his boyhood trial before the congregation of his brother's church in Franklin, Connecticut; it was to mean his acceptance of the younger Jonathan Edwards's ironically named "Plan of Union" with which, in effect, he was to disrupt the spread of Congregational parishes on the New York frontier; "accommodation" was to be reflected in that change of mind which, following President John Blair Smith's arguments on the virtues of a city ministry, took him from Cherry Valley to Albany; and "accommodation" was again responsible for that first major relocation of his personal route to Zion which was to take him from the pulpit of the "Court Church" into the presidency of Union College. By 1804 he was sure at last that Zion lay that way, beyond the sin-drenched cities, through the portals of the nation's schools, and for him, by way of a college he might shape to greatness.

Evidence that the Reverend Eliphalet Nott was still at heart the schoolteacher of "Pautapaug Road" is seen in two developments which were to lead to that "accommodation" which so suddenly closed his ministry to the "Court Church." The first involved what he called his "Utopian institution," an academy designed especially for the city of Albany, which he outlined in March, 1803.[1] It is significant that he addressed this "reverie," as he also called it, to his friend John V. Henry, a trustee of his church who was also a member of the Union College Board of Trustees, and to Professor Benjamin Allen, his wife's brother-in-law, who had recently come to Union College by way of the two educational institutions Nott knew so well: The Academy at Plainfield and Rhode Island College, from which both men held degrees.

Eliphalet Nott's "reverie" was utopian only when considered in relation to the schools then available in Albany. There were no free public schools, although the new capital city was making a small contribution to the support of common schools as early as 1799.[2] The author of the "reverie" contemplated a complete school system designed to educate the children of the entire city, rich and poor alike, "from the first rudiments of English reading to the last finish of classic culture." To accomplish his purpose he wanted, first, a building designed especially to make teaching an efficient operation, a true schoolhouse in which there would be one room devoted exclusively to one of each of the four grand divisions into which he divided his curriculum.

At the base of his system Nott wished to establish in the various wards of the city, "smaller houses where little children might be taught the alphabet, and to spell," before being admitted to the first year of his four-year academy. His "Utopian" plan was logical, and based on a realistic appraisal of Albany's special needs. "I am more inclined," the author wrote, "to aim at this because I suppose Utopia to be, like Albany, peopled with emigrants from various nations, among whom there is the Dutch dialect, the Irish dialect, the Scotch dialect, along with our peculiar Yankee dialect." He hoped his primary schools "where the poor will be furnished at their doors with the means of attaining [an education]," and his academy's department of elocution would go a long way to end the confusion of tongues in this American Babel.

The young pastor of the "Court Church" held no brief for those schools which attempted "to blend . . . the lower branches and the higher together." His plan of specialized instruction, graded to suit the needs of his students, would save, he believed, "at least six months to the pupil," at the primary level, and uncounted time during the following years of instruction. A regulated system, attention to one subject at a time, and carefully selected teachers who themselves had been instructed in the art of teaching, these provisions for an academy at Albany indicate the author's educational reach and his willingness to challenge the class-conscious, *laissez-faire* educational doctrines of his fellow citizens. He undoubtedly introduced much of the program of the Plainfield Academy into his ironically labeled "Utopian institution," for the course arrangement he proposed in 1803 resembles to some extent the advertised curriculum of his successful Connecticut school.

He closed his "reverie" with two paragraphs which seem touched with the spirit of Jonathan Swift and certainly with the spirit of the practical Yankee:

> I am aware that to carry the above plan into execution, considerable funds will be necessary; but as I can command these much easier in Utopia than in Albany, I shall, notwithstanding, adopt it, and, when laying the foundation for the chief school of a wealthy and growing city, endeavor to make it so broad that a suitable superstructure may be raised upon it.
>
> Should I succeed in my proposed plan, two advantages not yet mentioned will result from it. The expense of education will be diminished; and the poor will be furnished at their doors with the means of attaining it.[3]

Three years before he developed his "Utopian institute" Eliphalet Nott on May 14, 1800, was made a Trustee of the then five-year-old Union College in Schenectady. He appears to have been on intimate terms with the college's second President, the Reverend Jonathan Edwards the Younger, who, twenty years earlier, had been the Reverend Samuel Nott's strict guide through the maze of a scholar's Calvinism.[4] Among the college's Trustees was John V. Henry, a member of the Board of the young minister's Albany church; and there were also on the Board three of his fellow members of the Northern Missionary Society.

To be a Trustee of Union College in 1800 was to be associated with some of the most able men of the period, many of them veterans of the Revolution, and most of them active partisans in the violent struggle then going on between Federalists and Republicans. Here was an association to challenge one's tact and to sharpen one's talent for dealing with men. Among these Trustees was General Abraham Ten Broeck, an active Federalist, recently mayor of Albany for two terms, and husband of the daughter of the Patroon, Stephen VanRensselaer, who, himself, had been a Trustee until 1800. The family of the Patroon was also represented by Philip S. VanRensselaer, Stephen's younger brother, and mayor of Albany at the time of Eliphalet Nott's election to the board.

Here at the Union College Trustees' meetings, the young minister of the Court Church would come to know Goldsbrow Banyar, the son-in-law of John Jay, and one of the most noted land speculators in New York State, a Federalist who, during the ascendancy of DeWitt Clinton, finding "accommodation" expedient, became a Republican.

On this strongly Federalist Board there were at least two radical Republicans, Joseph C. Yates, the first mayor of Schenectady (1798), who became, in 1808, Judge of the New York State Supreme Court, and, in 1822, Governor of the state, and John Frey, an earnest Whig lawyer of Palatine, a hero to his western New York neighbors because of his participation in the decisive battle of Oriskany during the Revolution. Here, too, Nott had an opportunity to meet with seven of his ministerial colleagues, the most important of whom, in the history of Union College, was the Reverend Theodoric, or "Dirck" Romeyn, pastor of the Dutch Reformed Church in Schenectady, a member of George Washington's intelligence service during the Revolution, and the chief promoter of the program which resulted, in 1795, in the chartering of Union College.[5]

It would be hard to exaggerate the importance of this new office to Eliphalet Nott. On Independence Day the year following his appointment to the Board he pictured to an Albany audience the forces which must conquer the wilderness of the New Jerusalem and of the America God had destined for a race reborn. Here, in Schenectady, was a new training ground for Christian leaders. Union College had emerged in 1795 as a nonsectarian institution from a welter of conflicting interests, a "union" in fact of Presbyterians, Congregationalists, the Dutch Reformed, Episcopalians, of Federalists and Republicans, of the Hudson River aristocracy, and the vigorous democracy of the western reaches of the Mohawk country. The composition of its Board of Trustees itself foreshadowed the democratic pattern which, in the minds of the chiliasts, the new America was to take, where union would lead to understanding, where the growth of knowledge would have its reward in grace.

What, in 1800, was the state of this college to which this newest and youngest member of the Board was to give the remaining sixty-six years of his life?

President Edwards, by the time Nott joined the Board, was not well. He must have been dismayed at this May meeting of the Trustees when they proceeded to cut the salaries of his small staff: "considering the present state of the funds [the Board] do not conceive themselves able to pay the professors at the rate of three hundred and fifty pounds per annum." Following this resolution, the Trustees cut Professor Colonel John Taylor's salary to three hundred pounds a year, a figure that matched what the Board had just agreed to pay their new Professor of Mathematics, Benjamin Allen, husband of Maria Nott's sister and so closely related to the young pastor of the "Court Church."

If the prospects looked dark that May, the Board seems to have felt they would brighten. The project for a new and handsome "College Hall" was one which had enlivened almost every Trustees' meeting since the granting of the charter in 1795. It had taken until the spring of 1800 to erect the first three stories of their new building and until that time to persuade the legislature to grant the funds necessary to cover the building's cost, a grant which was proving to be an embarrassment, for none of the Trustees had yet found a way to convert the State's promises into usable credit.

The last piece of business which the Board of Trustees discharged that May day in 1800 was far more significant for the future of their college than any other action they had ever taken, though none of the members present could have realized it. "Wherefore," the clerk of the Board wrote in his minutes, "it was resolved the Rev'd Eliphalet Nott be and is hereby elected a member of the Board."

For Eliphalet Nott it was an action which was to raise again that question which had led him from Connecticut into the "vacant ground" of frontier New York, then to Albany and his city church: "is *this* the way to Zion?"

II

The new Trustee faithfully attended seventeen of the eighteen meetings held between the date of his appointment to the Board and his election, in 1804, to the presidency, a record hardly equalled by any of the other Trustees. He undertook the responsibilities of membership on fourteen Trustee committees, a labor which embraced every possible collegiate activity from the consideration of a proper steward for the new college building occupied the year of his election to the presidency through the study of a student petition "to speak a comedy and a tragedy" in the College Hall, to an examination of the treasurer's report for 1800 and the preparation of "a plan for the conducting of the business of the college."

It was not, however, in the new Trustee's ability to deal with such situations that his service to Union College during these years is to be remembered. The real weight of his personality, of his training as an educator, and of his growing conviction that the college should be a marshalling ground for citizens of the New Zion were shown in two major instances: the first, his year and a half consideration of the proper "laws" to govern the college, and the second, in his behind-the-scenes maneuvering or "accommodating," which resulted in the election of his friend, President Jonathan Maxcy of Rhode Island College to succeed President Edwards, who died suddenly on the first of August, 1801.

There seems to be little doubt that Nott was the prime mover in bringing about the election of the young President from Rhode Island, then only thirty-three years old. The brief announcement in the Trustees' Minutes for the 29th of September, 1801, that Jonathan Maxcy "is hereby elected President of this College . . . and that he be allowed a salary of one thousand five hundred dollars per annum to be paid in quarterly payments together with the usual fees attached to the office and a house," gives little of the drama behind the election, and suggests nothing of Nott's involvement in it.

Ten days before this meeting the Reverend John B. Johnson, Trustee of Union College and minister of the Albany Dutch Reformed Church, wrote to a fellow trustee, the Reverend Alexander Proudfit, of Salem, New York, that it was fortunate for the college that Dr. Proudfit had been unable to attend the last meeting of the Board of Trustees since if he had, there would have been a quorum present and the Board, owing to Nott's enthusiastic endorsement, would undoubtedly have proceeded to elect Jonathan Maxcy, and so have inflicted a serious injury on the college.[6]

Dr. Johnson's letter indicated that his young Presbyterian colleague in Albany had precipitated a crisis. Behind Dr. Johnson's concern for the Reverend Jonathan Maxcy's orthodoxy, or lack of it, lay the fact that in this pending election the influence of the Dutch Reformed ministers on the Board of Trustees was being challenged. The Reverend Theodoric Romeyn could remember his hope that the president of the college which finally grew out of that Schenectady Academy his parish had sponsored, would "forever be a member of the Dutch Reformed Church."[7] It had been suggested sixteen years earlier that should the faltering Dutch Reformed Church's Queen's College in New Brunswick, New Jersey, fail, the proposed college in Schenectady might well become the new "Door of Hope for our Zion."[8]

The Trustees' meeting on the 29th of September, 1801, marks the last of any serious attempt by the Dutch Reformed Church to influence the affairs of the new institution, for the Board on that day did, indeed, elect Jonathan Maxcy, Baptist President of Rhode Island College, to be the third President of Union College, a signal triumph for the young pastor of the "Court Church."

The chief supporters of Jonathan Maxcy, two vigorous Federalist Trustees, John V. Henry and James Emott, as well as

"Mr. Not" himself, were satisfied with their new President's views on Christianity. To the opposition, however, the rationalizations of "Mr. Not" on his behalf were nothing but the "language of a Gibbon." Maxcy's Christianity was not theirs. "Gentlemen," it had been argued by Maxcy's proponents, "did not send Youth to College to learn Religion, but Languages and the Arts."[9] For those who were turning from orthodoxy, however, the way was now opening for the establishment of a new religious equation: knowledge of the "Languages and the Arts" could lead to virtue, and such a course, according to Jonathan Maxcy, might be enough to win regeneration and "eternal felicity."

The Maxcy affair indicates "Mr. Not's" growing ability to maneuver men and events to suit his own purpose. His "determination to support Maxcy," according to the frustrated Reverend J. B. Johnson, was known to "a Mr. Bassett" sometime before the September 29th meeting of the Board, although Nott seems to have purposefully concealed his determination from two members of the opposition until the meeting itself. His ability to "explain away" Maxcy's unorthodoxies seemed the height of unreason to the Dutch Reformed pastor, but it was effective with those whose support Eliphalet Nott needed. Whether his opposition was aware of it or not, this successful ex-Connecticut schoolteacher was preparing the way at Union College for a new kind of education which he believed would be more useful to the church and so to God's purposes than the sectarianisms which Jonathan Maxcy and he had come to deplore.

Jonathan Maxcy, too, had his dream of the New Zion. In this poem, "On the Prospects of America," written in 1787, he had pictured the college of the future, where

> shall bright learning fix her last retreat,
> Her joyous sons, a num'rous concourse meet;
> Each art shall there to full perfection grow,
> And all be known that man shall ever know;
> There shall religion pure from heav'n descend,
> Her influence mild thro' all degrees extend;
> Each different sect shall then consenting join,
> Walk in her domes, and bend before her shrine;
> Virtue shall reign, each heart expand with praise,
> And hail the prospect of celestial days.[10]

Promulgation of the Union College "Laws of 1802" waited until the new "Edifice" was occupied, the new tutors were engaged, and President Maxcy in residence. The latter had begged Nott's leave "to advise a little in this business" of revision and it was the part of a new Trustee to listen, not only to the voice of experience, but also to a friend from whom he had received his Master's Degree at Rhode Island College and in support of whose election to the presidency of Union he had "preconcerted the trustees" vote. But the result was an unhappy one, both for the college and for Eliphalet Nott. The young Trustee set aside all he had learned about the nature of his fellow men and joined with Jonathan Maxcy in fixing on Union "a new system" which borrowed too generously from Rhode Island College. Maxcy assumed there was only one avenue to the heart, that it was controlled by force made manifest through tutorial spying, a bewildering array of fines, trials before a Faculty Court, and appeals to the final authority of the Board of Trustees. Years later, an aged President Nott, looking back on this unfortunate period, wrote that "the faculty met and sat as a court, arraigned offenders, examined witnesses and passed judgment, with all the solemnity of a civil tribunal,.... [the "new system"] was found practically to array the students against the faculty, to prevent mutual confidence, and to provoke, rather than deter from transgression."[11]

The "Laws of 1802" reshaped Union College into the likeness of Rhode Island College. Of its 139 sections, 69 of them are either borrowed word for word from or are paraphrases of the 113 sections which make up the "Laws of 1793" of the college in Providence.[12] The Union College student who lived under these "Laws" walked in the shadow of the "Old Brick," the huge dormitory at Providence where, in the March preceding Jonathan Maxcy's resignation, there was "No study! No Prayers! Nothing but riot and confusion! No regard paid to Superiors."[13]

The Rhode Island College "Laws of 1793" represented an eager searching on the part of the Rhode Island Trustees and faculty for a discipline to re-establish, following the Revolution, what Professor Bronson, in his history of Brown University, calls a "due deference to superior station." The lack of "regard paid to Superiors" within the college walls at Providence, however, was but one more reflection of the unsettled times: a revolution had just been won by those who had lost respect for orthodoxy and a variety of conventional obligations.

Eliphalet Nott, in 1802, accommodating himself to the wishes of Jonathan Maxcy, had yet to discover that the "New Zion" he was envisaging had need of newer "Laws," and a different discipline from that which Maxcy now imposed on Union College.

III

The following year was a year of climax and decision for the new Trustee and pastor of the "Court Church." New Year's Day, 1803, began as it traditionally did in Albany, "with the firing of guns," wrote Nott, "the beating of drums, the sound of musical instruments . . . and a group of boys on your stoop, vociferating 'Happy New Year', for which they expect cookies in return."[14]

His New Year's letter, written to the Reverend Samuel Nott, is also important in reflecting the young minister's distress that his people had not yet felt the "down pouring of the Spirit" which appeared to be flooding many congregations with new hope, especially in New England: "we have had more seriousness than usual among our youth. Some have been added to the church, some are now seeking after God, as is also the case with some heads of families. Our praying societies have for some time been crowded, and we have hoped that God was about to pour his Spirit among us. As yet, alas! our hopes have not been realized."

In a year when almost every Protestant pulpit had become a watch tower from which its occupant scanned the heavens for signs of grace, it was a matter of concern to Nott that his city parish was largely untouched by the religious excitement of the period. Three years earlier the Reverend John Blair Smith, recently retired from the presidency of Union College, wrote to his admiring young follower just returned from visiting Connecticut, "If you can bring back with you a portion of the fervour which usually attends revivals of religion . . . your journey may be blest. Albany and the adjacent churches very much need some such refreshing time as is said to have taken place in Massachusetts and Connecticut. These are recruiting seasons which preserve a succession of Christians in the Churches. . . . we have reason to look for such things as are now taking place on earth previous to the universal prevalence of the Gospel. . . ."[15]

The signs seemed to be everywhere. The Reverend Edward D. Griffin, who accepted the call of the Park Street Church in Boston in 1811, the year after Nott refused it, thought that 1847 might mark the end of the papal regime; he was sure the Napoleonic rise proved to everyone "how far we are advanced under the seven vials."[16] Jedediah Morse was certain the Eastern and Western anti-Christs had risen in 606 A.D. and would therefore disappear in 1866, after which the Jews would return to Palestine, both Gentiles and Jews would become Christians, and the Millennium would follow.[17] He was sure also that the Napoleonic Wars, the rise of Bible societies, and the spread of missionary activities were clear signs of God's purpose toward men. The Reverend John B. Romeyn, holder of an honorary M.A. from Union College, speaking from the pulpit of the First Presbyterian Church in Albany in 1808, had calculated the opening of the new age exactly: Napoleon's Concordat with the Pope, he said, would last fifty years, after which there would be 1000 years of peace.[18]

Eliphalet Nott's distress over "the general dissoluteness of manners and awful insensibility to eternal concerns" is clearly stated in a letter he wrote in the spring of 1800, reviewing the effects of the revival in Berne, New York. "No place," he then informed the editor of the *New York Missionary Magazine*," [existed] perhaps in all this country, where there was less religion." And,

> notwithstanding these things, God has singled out that people as the objects of his sovereign grace, and visited them with salvation; while many of our churches, in circumstances apparently more hopeful, still mourn the absence of his Spirit. So great has been the change that has been effected in Berne, so very striking the incidents that have led to it, that he must be blind who does not see the Divine Agency through the whole. He must be more than infidel, who is not concerned that the finger of God is in this.[19]

Between 1798 and 1804, the year he left Albany, Nott delivered a notable series of sermons, ten of which were gathered together fifty years later under the general title, "The Resurrection."[20] Professor Tayler Lewis, editor of the collection, had himself heard most of the sermons, recast in part to meet the special requirements of the campus and delivered during his own undergraduate years which ended in 1820. The body of these sermons represent the answer of the pastor of the Court Church to that question he had heard so often asked during the Berne revival: "What must I do to be saved?" These "Resurrection Sermons" were his response to the challenge of the Second Awakening, his apostle's plea to the people of the market place that they, too, step forward and ask the same question.

Here, as Tayler Lewis writes, is the "impassioned preacher . . . a true preacher in distinction from the logical casuist or the methodical, didactic lecturer, a preacher in the old sense of the term—of the herald, the proclaimer—calling aloud to men, demanding their attention to some great fact, and setting it forth in language exuberant and superlative. . . ."[21] Nott, indeed, had traveled far from "Pisgah's Top," the Connecticut household of his brother whose concern was solely with the reasoned theology of the later Edwardsians.

The resurrection of Jesus Christ had now become for Nott the final assurance that God had accepted the Savior's death as a vicarious sacrifice, as a total erasure of the Adam-Sin, and that man's salvation depended solely on the recognition of that fact, on his wholehearted acceptance of it, and on his repentance for sin. This was not the Covenant religion he had known at "Pisgah's Top."

"Dr. Nott, I would say," wrote Gorham A. Worth in 1803, "was neither a Calvinist nor a Lutheran. In other words, he was no bigoted sectarian; and in this respect he bore . . . but little resemblance to many of his clerical brethren. In mind as well as in manner, he stood alone. The narrow dogmas and the commonplace oratory of the churches were beneath him."[22]

The Calvinist conviction that salvation is predetermined and the idea that man cannot influence God's judgment by the practice of works were now behind him; "since repentance will insure forgiveness," the author of the Resurrection Sermons wrote, "why will you die?" The repenting sinner, he told Albanians, must and will be punished, but his voluntary act of repentance will insure eternal life.[23]

The force of this affirmative thinking in the 19th Century is incalculable. "Faith," the Pelagians claimed, "is not the effect, but the cause of election to salvation." Nott, in accepting this mystical conclusion, now denied what his brother affirmed, that man's will was wholly subject to that divine necessity which, in the Edwardsian system, ultimately denied man everything but hope. Nott had found certainty in the resurrection of Christ, for it was to him "a proof of the certainty of our own resurrection at the last day."[24] The nature of God for him was now no longer what it had been for his Calvinist forebears. He now knew the answer, he proclaimed, to the question, "How am I to be saved?"

> Has [Christ's] sacrifice been accepted? Will it be availing? On this point the Church hesitated; faith wavered; hope wavered. The first and the second day elapsed, and no tiding was received from the sepulchre. Still, the great question that involved the destiny of so many millions was not decided. Neither heaven nor earth, however, remained long in suspense. Suddenly an unknown glory lit up the moral firmament; the night of death and of nature fled together; and the third day dawned on the world, the ascertained, the *accredited* Messiah came forth from the sepulchre, 'the resurrection and the life.'[25]

Men, in the 1800s, had only to look about them, he said, to see the same regenerating spirit at work. New England and western New York had known its wonder-working and it was his greatest hope that Albany, too, would be moved by it.

From his "Court Church" pulpit Nott reinforced this message in every way possible. The "Resurrection Sermons" became essays in Christian evidence. His hearers were led through the story of the apostles, and of the defeat by the church of enemy after enemy. Proof that God intended to Christianize the world during the lives of many then living could be seen in the rapid spread of the gospels from continent to continent: "Century after century rolls away; still the work progresses. As the world grows older, the vast design opens, and act following act, the grand drama still continues advancing to its ultimate result." Here was the source of much of that optimism which energized so many in pre-Civil War America.

The Second Awakening, though it had scarcely touched Albany, was offering signs to those who would heed them that the Millennium itself was approaching.

> Whence even *now* that shaking so perceptible among the nations? [Nott asked] It comes from heaven. It is the moving of the Holy Ghost. . . . Whether kingdoms rise or fall, every change accelerates His

progress; all events bend unto His purpose . . . the way is opening for His triumphant entry. The glad tidings have already reached many, and they will soon have reached every nation. Then will the purpose of grace be consummated, and the millenial jubilee begin.[26]

"His church," wrote Gorham A. Worth of this period, "was filled to overflowing. His appearance in the pulpit, his style of eloquence, his very look 'Drew audience and attention still as night, or summer's noontide air. . . .' "[27]

The excitement of the Second Awakening is long gone, and the excitement of the personality of the man who preached the "Resurrection Sermons" is gone. It is hard to remember the temper of many Americans in this first decade of the 19th Century, men fearful of a Napoleon who quite possibly was Satan incarnate, fearful of the communism which had been preached by French deists, fearful of those forces of Republicanism then the essence of democracy in an America symbolized by the presence of Thomas Jefferson in the White House. Were these things, too, Nott was asking, part of the "vast design"?

Certain now of the key to salvation, animated by the chiliast's vision of the Millennium, Eliphalet Nott was discovering that life was charged with purpose. By abandoning that which was inhuman in Calvinism, by accepting Jonathan Maxcy's injunction "to form your faith immediately from the Sacred Scriptures," Nott was now prepared to be a leader among the humanitarians of the 19th Century. Their work was clear; the world must be readied for the millennial jubilee, the way prepared "for His triumphant entry."

The happiness he must have felt at the birth of his fourth child and third son, Benjamin, on the 20th of November, would have been tempered on New Year's Day, 1804, by the fact that "Sally Nott," the small and sprightly wife he had married in Plainfield, Connecticut, failed to rally following the birth of the boy. She had never regained her strength after her serious illness in Cherry Valley in 1797, though she never gave in to being an invalid. For Sally Nott the Albany years had meant the end of a vivacious girlhood. They were the years when her "talent for satire," wrote her husband, was "concealed beneath the veil of discretion. . . ."[28] It must have been difficult at times for the daughter of the democratic Reverend Joel Benedict of Plainfield, Connecticut, a girl who "seldom ever disguised her feelings or her sentiments," to adjust herself to the class-conscious, sophisticated capital of New York State. It was not until 1800 that she felt herself sufficiently "under conviction" to join her husband's congregation.

For some months before the birth of Benjamin, Sally Nott had been assuring her friends that she had only a short time to live. Unlike her sister ("who thought herself possessed of the sin of vanity, particularly on account of her eyes . . . so, mindful of the scriptural injunction, 'If thine eye offend thee, pluck it out,' . . . took a teaspoon and plucked it out,") Sally Nott suffered none of the religious melancholia which so often seized the oversensitive and the impressionable.[29] Although for more than a year before her death "she became less social and more contemplative," she "beguiled almost everyone with her cheerfulness which accompanied her to the end."[30]

Sarah Maria Nott died in Ballston Springs, New York, on the 9th of March, 1804. Four days earlier she had asked to be taken there in the hope that the spring waters might bring her some of the relief they had apparently brought her seven years before, but soon, "nature being exhausted, she expired without a struggle and without a groan."[31]

For the young husband, now left with four small children, the death of this attractive wife was the severest kind of blow: "In that care and responsibility and severe pressure upon the brain (such as led himself to say that he could hardly have lived through it long) he relied exceedingly upon his gifted and devoted wife. He had never thought, he said, that *she* would die. . . ."[32]

Four years after Sally Nott's burial, John Howard Payne, remembered as the author of "Home, Sweet Home," then a precocious student at Union College, printed three stanzas in *The Pastime*, the college paper which he edited, taken, he said, from Mrs. Nott's gravestone, discovered "in a ramble amongst the tombs." The lines were quite possibly composed by her husband, but whether they were or not, they are a capsule statement of his faith:

> Rest, precious Dust, beneath this mound,
> Which the lorn mourner raises here;
> Whilst lisping orphanage around,
> Pours forth the filial tear.

Can this Dust live? blind Nature cries!
  The Gospel answers, Yes; it can—
When Christ descends, the saints shall rise,
  And hail Thy Advent, Son of Man.

Why then indulge the flowing tear—
  We check our grief, and kiss the rod,
No more thy triumphs, Death, we fear,
  The grave conducts us home to God.[33]

The sense of failure in his mission to the city which he had read in the spiritual drought among Albanians, and now in this personal loss, was soon to be dramatically reinforced by the death at the hands of Aaron Burr of the young pastor's friend and his most famous parishioner, Alexander Hamilton. Zion, Nott now had reason to conclude, was not to be entered by him through the doors of the "Court Church."

CHAPTER 5

Schenectady via Weehawken

Last Saturday were interred, with all possible respect, the remains of General Alexander Hamilton, the enlightened statesman, the skillful lawyer, the eloquent orator, the distinguished patriot, and the honest man. Never was the sensibility of the citizens awakened to such a degree, and never did they witness so mournful a scene.[1]

IN New York City "immediately after his decease, the Bells announced that he was no more." They tolled from six until seven the morning of Hamilton's funeral, and again from ten until the funeral procession reached the church, and again that evening. Minute guns were fired from the forts around Manhattan Island, and the ships in the harbor broke out their funeral pennants.

Suddenly, above these tear-choked voices which had been calling the nation to an orgy of self-pity a new voice rang out, charging the mourners themselves with being accessories to the murder of Hamilton. Eighteen days after the fatal duel on the heights of Weehawken, a spare, black-gowned Presbyterian minister stood in the pulpit of the North Dutch Church in Albany, the capital of New York State, and prosecuted his charge of the nation's complicity in the murder.[2] Many who had known Hamilton agreed that the great Federalist himself had never been more eloquent or more successful in bringing a criminal to justice than was his friend, the Reverend Eliphalet Nott, in this memorable indictment. Never before had they witnessed such a scene: the church a courtroom, the minister turned prosecutor, and the audience brought to the bar before a judge from whom there was no appeal.

For Eliphalet Nott, standing in the pulpit of the North Dutch Church of Albany, the death of Hamilton at the hands of Aaron Burr, that "Prince of Plausibilities," so Nott called him, was no "customary providence" as had been the death of Washington. First the son, Philip Hamilton, and now the father, each of them had gone down on the same shores at the hands of the duelist; these dreadful events, too, were signs of the time. Atheism, anarchy, and communism had already made of Europe a Golgotha and now the infection was threatening America, "this western and modern Israel of the Lord." The task before the orator was clear: not eulogy again, but the club of Hercules. His, too, must be a triumph of eloquence over the passions of men. Hamilton himself might well have hesitated to put the nation on trial, but Nott believed he had no choice. God had moved him to speak as He, in His wisdom, had also directed the bullet which killed Hamilton.

First, there was the crime:

> Before such an audience, and on such an occasion, I enter on the duty assigned me with trembling. . . .
>
> You will ask, then, why I tremble? I tremble to think that I am called to attack from this place a crime, the very idea of which almost freezes one with horror—a crime, too, which exists among the polite and polished orders of society, and which is accompanied with every aggravation; committed with cool deliberation—and openly in the face of day!

Hamilton's death, Nott continued, was the result of "mad deliberation . . . marked by violence." Pathos, to which his Albany hearers were ready to respond, must have knelled in Nott's voice as he evoked the scene of the duel:

> The time, the place, the circumstances are arranged with barbarous coolness. The instrument of death is leveled in daylight, and with well directed skill pointed at his heart. Alas! the event has proven that it was too well directed. Wounded, mortally wounded, on the very spot which still smoked with the blood of a favorite son, into the arms of his indiscreet and cruel friend, the father fell.

Hamilton, in exposing his own life, presumptuously set aside God's law, that law of Nature which forbids the taking of life, except under those conditions which the Gospels make explicit.

Although Hamilton was willful in assuming the obligations of a barbarous code of honor, "think not," the speaker thundered, "that the issue of the late inhuman interview was fortuitous." God directed Aaron Burr's bullet "as a loud and awful warning to a community where justice has slumbered—and slumbered—and slumbered. . . ."

Nott's faith in the miraculous aspects of Christianity had resolved for him the Calvinist problem of Free Will and Permission; the problem, for him, simply did not exist: Hamilton had freely elected to meet Aaron Burr in the fatal duel, and God, in the interest of social and divine justice had then brought about his death. The speaker had seen the evidence of the intervention of God in the affairs of men in the town of Berne, outside of Albany, and in other places marked by the still active revivals of the "Second Awakening." Here, in this tragedy and with awful force, so he believed, God was intervening again, and in such a way that "the polite and polished orders of society" must now be aware of the divine anger.

Hamilton was guilty of complicity in murder, and the "auditory," as Nott called his audience, an accessory to the fact. The dramatic reversal of roles which Hamilton and the audience had played all their lives was a masterly piece of casting on the part of the speaker. In the age of sensibility the courtroom and the church were, in many ways, theaters to those who attended them, and the lawyer and the minister who could evoke the theater's excitement and catharsis were the popular leaders. It took courage on the part of the speaker to put Alexander Hamilton and his mourners on trial, but in such a courtroom and before such a judge the prosecutor had rather special advantages, and the Reverend Eliphalet Nott capitalized them to the fullest.

> I cannot forgive you my brethren, who till this late hour have been silent, whilst successive murders were committed.

Ministers, public prosecutors, judges, governors, the public, then each received separate and dramatic indictments. In their tacit support of dueling they were all as barbarians, he charged, to the more cultivated citizen of ancient Greece and Rome. Nott's hearers must be reasoned with as inferiors; they must be told what was obvious, he argued, to the Greek and the Roman: Dueling is absurd to men of reason.

Irony, which Hamilton had used so effectively in his appeal of the case of Harry Croswell, Nott now turned against the duelists themselves:

> One man of honor by some inadvertence, or perhaps with design, injures the sensibilities of another man of honor. In perfect character the injured gentleman resents it. He challenges the offender. The offender accepts the challenge. The time is fixed. The place is agreed upon. The circumstances, with an air of solemn mania are arranged; and the principals, with their seconds and surgeons, retire under the covert of some solitary hill, or upon the margin of some unfrequented beach, to settle this important question of honor by stabbing or shooting at each other.
>
> One or the other, or both the parties fall in this polite and gentlemanlike contest. And what does this prove? It proves that one or the other or both of them, as the case may be, are marksmen. But it affords no evidence that either of them possess honor, probity, or talents.
>
> It is true that he who falls in single combat, has the honor of being murdered; and he who takes his life, the honor of a murderer.

Although the vitality of this speech is gone, for Nott's power lay in "the tones of the voice," as Francis Wayland remembered, there is ample evidence to judge the speaker's skill in playing upon the sensibilities of his audience. So far he had assumed the roles of prosecutor and instructor exclusively; pathetic at times, ironic, speaking with the authority of one who prosecutes in the name of immutable law, patiently reasonable, he brought in the awful indictment and explained the nature of the crime. Now, however, as though he, too, were caught up in the emotion of the hour, he became in a moment the stricken friend, searching for words of praise.

> O that I possessed the talent of eulogy, and that I might be permitted to indulge the tenderness of friendship in paying the last tribute to his memory. O that I were capable of placing this great man before you. . . . I can only hint at the variety and exuberance of his excellence.

This sudden merging of his mood with that of his hearers was an effective and calculated shift of position, a skillful prelude to the terrifying final scene which he was to open before them.

Eliphalet Nott's "hint" at the variety and exuberance of Hamilton's character now became a paean to his virtues as fulsome as the newspapers of the country and the Albany Common Council and his audience could have wished. In his eulogy of Hamilton, THE STATESMAN, he indicated his own acceptance of Hamilton's political tenets, and his disapproval of his partisan activities.

> Hamilton, the correctness of whose principles and the strength of whose mind, are inscribed on the records of congress and on the annals of the council chamber. Whose genius inscribed itself upon the CONSTITU-TION of his country; and whose memory, the government, ILLUS-TRIOUS FABRIC, resting on this basis, will perpetuate while it lasts; and shaken by the violence of party, should it fall, which may heaven avert, his prophetic declarations will be found inscribed on its ruins.

As if this evocation of a hardly mortal man were not enough, the speaker again pictured the scene of death, this time in terms which lie outside the range of modern criticism; they represent, however, an orator's triumph to an Albanian of 1804, crepe about his arm, one of tens of thousands of citizens making a public display of their grief at the unnatural death of a national hero. Granted the climate of opinion at the turn of the century there can be no question of the speaker's skill in preparing his audience for what was now to follow, the terrible lesson which he, as a Christian minister, must draw from what he had said was a murderer's meeting on the "tragic shores of Hoboken."

> Approach, and behold—while I lift from his sepulchre its covering. Ye admirers of his greatness, ye emulous of his talents and his fame, approach and behold him now. How pale! How silent! No martial bands admire the adroitness of his movements. No fascinated throngs weep—and melt—and tremble at his eloquence!—Amazing change. A shrowd! a coffin! a narrow, subterranean cabin! This is all that now remains of *Hamilton*! . .

The murdered statesman at least had risen above the times "when skepticism, shallow and superficial, but depraved and malignant, is breathing forth its pestilential vapours, and polluting by its unhallowed touch, everything divine and sacred."

Eliphalet Nott had spoken with passion and eloquence. He ended, not with praises for his dead friend, but with a chiliast's prophecy of the terror to precede the Millennium. The speaker had carefully enlarged his subject until his audience found itself no longer by the bier of Hamilton, accessories to his murder, but "standing on the borders of an AWFUL GULF." Behind them, he said, were "the ruins of the tomb . . . an emblem of the ruins of the world."

> Anticipate the concluding scene, the final catastrophe of nature. When the sign of the Son of Man shall be seen in heaven . . . the fiery desolation envelops towns, palaces and fortresses. The heavens pass away! The earth melts! and all those magnificent productions of art which ages heaped on ages have reared up, are in one awful day reduced to ashes.

This must have been that moment when, as one Nott parishioner remembered, "his eloquence, his very look, drew audience and attention still as night."

> Against the ruins of that day, as well as the ruins of the tomb which precede it, the gospel in the CROSS of its great HIGH PRIEST, offers you all a sanctuary . . . thither fly, ye prisoners of hope! . . . that . . . you may perpetuate the song which lingered on the faltering tongue of HAMILTON, 'Grace, Rich Grace.'

I I

The "Amen" which closed Eliphalet Nott's charge against a heedless nation ended also one phase of the speaker's life. He left the North Dutch Church that day in 1804 a famous man. William Coleman, editor of the New York *Evening Post*, the chief Federalist journal of the time, wrote that Nott's "sermon has deservedly engaged a universal share of public attention . . . in the passage beginning with the apostrophe, 'APPROACH AND BEHOLD' how elegant, how deeply affecting, how sublime he is! Perhaps a passage of equal length is not to be anywhere found in our language superior to this." [2]

"In the state of New York, at least," one writer commented, "dueling was extirpated by a single sermon; for every duelist knew that should he be brought to trial, probably half the jury, and certainly the court, would have read Dr. Nott's sermon on the death of Hamilton." [3]

The duel on the heights of Weehawken which ended the life of Alexander Hamilton elevated his friend Eliphalet Nott to national prominence and contributed to a reputation which resulted in the offer to him of the presidency of Union College within days after his dramatic indictment of the nation for its part in the tragedy. "He had so improved the occasion of a conspicuous violation of the law of God and man," wrote one commentator, "that his discourse and elegy . . . placed him in the front rank of orators, in the very place where Hamilton himself had stood."[4]

For the pastor of the "Court Church" there was now a brief interim, a time for spiritual inventory. In a letter that August addressed to the minister and associate pastors of the First Presbyterian Church of New York City he reviewed his own purposes and some of the advantages and disadvantages which his acceptance of the call to the presidency of Union College involved.

> Albany, August [3?] 1804
>
> Dear Sir: The object of this letter is to request your advice in a matter of no inconsiderable importance. At the last meeting of the Board of Trustees of Union College, it appeared to be the prevailing wish of the members present to commit the care of the institution, after the removal of Dr. Maxcy, to myself.
>
> As no one of the board had conferred with me on this subject previous to the day of the meeting, and as a refusal in case of appointment might tend to injure the institution, my friends obtained a postponement of the election for three weeks, that I might have an opportunity to reflect on the subject, to take advice, and to declare that I would not accept the appointment if such should be my determination previous to the election.
>
> Should I declare myself, it is not unlikely that the Rev. Mr.——will be elected. . . .[5]

This letter, written probably no more than five days following the delivery of the memorable "Discourse on the death of Hamilton" marked the approaching end of Eliphalet Nott's apostle's mission to the capital of New York State. At the Board meeting on July 31, 1804, the Trustees of Union College had accepted the resignation of the Reverend Jonathan Maxcy, their third President in the nine years the college had existed. Although Dr. Maxcy gave ill health as his reason for accepting the presidency of South Carolina College, there were undoubtedly other consider-ations. The Albany *Gazette* had noted on the 28th of May that his new appointment carried "a salary of $5000 and a house free"; at Union he had had to be content with $1500 and his house.

John Kirby, a Union College sophomore, in a letter addressed to a former classmate the 15th of August had inserted into his gossipy young man's report about college life some revealing information about the students' dissatisfaction with Jonathan Maxcy and about the division in the Board of Trustees over his successor:

> To leave us, [Maxcy] is determined, and that the coming vacation; and what then? Why probably we shall have another and if he shall attend to his business and discharge his duties with propriety Union College will receive no hurt by the exchange; for you know that students may as well be at home as to pretend to attend his recitations, seing [sic] they happen so seldom. But he is going, and I need make no further comment on it. The trustees had a meeting the last of July at which time Doct Green, of Philadelphia; Mr. Mason and Professor Wilson, of New York, and Rev. Mr. Not [sic] of Albany, were nominated as candidatus for the Presidency the Board of Trustees then adjourned untill [sic] somewhere about the 20th of the present month without electing anyone; It is thought the election rests between Mason and Not; however we shall soon know.[6]

And there the matter rested for three weeks. For John Kirby, the Union College sophomore, the trustees' problem was a simple one: find a man who will "attend to his business and discharge his duties with propriety." Union College, for him, in August 1804, was attractive for the very reason Eliphalet Nott found Albany and "the polite and polished orders of society" unattractive. The two student organizations of the college, so Kirby informed his friend "Carus Amicus," were busy with their heated bidding for the sixteen "perty [sic] smart fellows" and "yong [sic] men of good appearance" who had just entered. The "Adelphicks" and the "Philomatheons" were carrying on electioneering campaigns with all the enthusiasm of Federalists and Republicans hungry for office.

The young pastor's letter to his ministerial friends that August suggests that Eliphalet Nott, if he accepted the presidency of this nine year old frontier college, would give its Trustees something far more than simple propriety as he attended to his and their business:

If I know my own heart, to be useful is my great object. I think I am willing to go and to be whatever my Master directs. The questions to be decided are, whether it is prudent, at my time of life (thirty-one years), and with my inexperience, to accept a trust so important, and engage in duties so arduous; whether the prospect of usefulness is greater than in my present situation, and so much greater as to justify a removal from a people with whom I have lived for several years in harmony, among whom my labors appear in some measure to have been blessed, with whom rests the dust of a beloved partner, and to whom I am united by the strongest and tenderest ties. Into this account must be taken the state of my health, which has often, and for some time past, been such as to induce a serious apprehension that I should be obliged to resign my present charge and seek a situation favorable to exercise, which might furnish at least a partial respite from public speaking. Thus situated, I have thought it my duty to pause and consider.

There were important aspects to this problem of leaving Albany which the young pastor did not mention in his circular letter on the matter. He knew, of course, that if he accepted the new post he would have to commit himself wholly to being the President of Union College; in this respect, the College's charter of 1795 was unique in that it specifically stated that the incumbent of the office could not hold any other position in conjunction with it. During a period when so many college presidents were also settled and active pastors this would mean for Nott the official conclusion of a ministerial career in which he had been officially successful.

There were also economic considerations which, for a young widower with four small children, must have weighed heavily in favor of moving to Schenectady. His salary as pastor of the First Presbyterian Church was $1250 and perquisites which, in 1802, had amounted to $380, $130 of which had been in wine. As the President of Union College his salary would be $1500 a year, with perquisites, and a house rent free; and not only would his income be considerably higher in Schenectady, but he would find the cost of living in the then frontier town of less than 4000 inhabitants a good deal below that of fashionable Albany.

He knew the college intimately. As a Trustee since 1800 he was quite aware of the problems which had so far defeated three Presidents. Although the college budget was about $4000 a year the cash income was still less than half that sum. He was also aware the college had large though still frozen assets in the form of land gifts from the state legislature, that it had almost completed its handsome new building, and that, in spite of all its difficulties, it was attracting students.

Undoubtedly Nott was under considerable pressure to accept the appointment from those Trustees who, for lack of a better term, might be called "practical men." General Ten Broeck, president of the Board, Goldsbrow Banyar, Philip S. VanRensselaer, James Gordon, and John V. Henry, all noted and wealthy Albanians, were present at the July meeting which accepted Dr. Maxcy's resignation. These men knew how much better prepared their fellow Trustee was for the hard task ahead than had been the three preceding minister-scholars who had remained in office so short a time. As pastor of the "Court Church" Nott already knew many of those legislators who controlled the State's purse strings; as a Trustee he had negotiated successfully with the Albany and New York bankers. His reputation as an educator was well established, for he had not only developed the Cherry Valley Academy, served on an Albany citizens' committee charged with drawing up an educational plan for the city, but he had joined with President Maxcy in revising the "Laws" of Union College. He was no radical, for he had publicly decried the "poisonous French doctrines" of the time. And he was safe from the tar brush of party and factional disputes, as his so recent and notable sermon on the death of Hamilton demonstrated. As the pastor of the First Presbyterian Church of Albany he had preached a nonsectarian Christianity which, except to the most orthodox, should be welcome in a college chartered to educate men of all faiths.

Eliphalet Nott's letter asking for advice brought one answer which was of help to him in two respects; it laid to rest any doubts he had about his youth and his inexperience. The ministers of the First Presbyterian Church of New York City agreed that his age was actually "a favorable circumstance"; "Had you lived ten or fifteen years longer out of the habit of teaching, we should regard this as a much more serious difficulty than your want of years."[7] More important was their conclusion that a President of Union College was a man who would have an "extensive and commanding influence in respect to religion as well as literature. . . ."

If this last conclusion was true, why should he hesitate? The educator and the minister, he believed, both served the same Master, both worked toward the same end, their duty "in an ever reviving and dying universe" to clear the way to the New Zion, to prepare men for the millennial jubilee, for the triumphant entry of a returning Christ. He could quit the city with a clear conscience.

On the 24th of August, 1804, Eliphalet Nott was elected the fourth President of Union College.

BOOK TWO

President of Union College:
Two Decades, 1804-1824

CHAPTER I

President Nott and the White Moth of Hope

THERE was nothing unsteady about the men who welcomed the new President to his seat in "College Hall" that August afternoon following his election. Nott had known them for four years as a fellow Trustee. John V. Henry and William P. H. Beers had been members of his church in Albany, men who must have known of their pastor's success in leading several "in high place" away from the poisoned, green pastures of French thought. A number of them must have heard Nott declaim over Hamilton a month earlier with the fervor of an Antony over slain Caesar, a Hamilton "whose GENIUS," Nott had exclaimed, "inscribed itself upon the CONSTITUTION!" Nott, unlike some of his Trustees, held no reservations about the firmness of the rock on which the new United States was being reared. His only fear for his country was that the "frenzy of party" would destroy it before men of his own millennialist's vision could show the nation its destiny.

The majority of the Union College Trustees and their new President were one in their patriotism, though the ultimate use to which they would put it separated them by the width of the gulf which separates heaven and earth. Nott was a radical but seemingly, a safe one, a Christian who had lately preached of the Second Coming of Christ as though the calendar might soon be marked with the year, the month, and the day. He preached that the United States was a nation set apart for the next to the last act in the Christian drama, the Millenium itself. Land values, political ambitions, warehouse stocks, the relations between esquire and tenant, these staples of American culture were seemingly in no danger from the radicalism of the Reverend Eliphalet Nott. Little did the Union College Trustees know, however, of the ends to which their new President was to go to implement his vision of the new heaven and the new earth. They had all accepted the recently acquired college seal with its classic head of Minerva and its French motto: "Nous devenons tous frères sous les lois de Minèrve." These Trustees, however, were mostly eighteenth-century gentlemen for whom Minerva, Goddess of Wisdom, was a tasteful symbol to adorn their corporate documents. The French motto took them as far as they cared to go with the drift of the times: "We all become brothers under the laws of Minerva" was quite rational and quite safe, even though it was written, not in the language of the classics, but in that of *les philosophes*.[1] What would happen, though, if one translated the French, not only into English, but into the language of Christian theology? If one read, not "We all become brothers under the laws of Minerva," but, "We all become brothers under the laws of God"? The brotherhood of man was an idea which Nott now accepted unconditionally, a brotherhood to be achieved, not in heaven, but in this world. Because he talked about brotherhood, however, in the traditional language of the pulpit his Trustees felt no cause for alarm.

These New Yorkers who shook Nott's hand in congratulation that afternoon transmitted to him a different legacy from the spiritual inheritance he had received at his ordination in Albany as a young minister. They laid upon him a portion of Adam's world; they gave him unfinished buildings, and faculty rivalries, and debts. They laid on him the burden of building a college among men caught up in the bitterest partisan conflicts the country had yet known.

Goldsbrow Banyar, the President of the Board, had no reason to like the shape of things in August, 1804. With Hamilton in his grave barely a month and Governor Jay retired from politics, the oligarchy of Federalism in New York was falling apart for lack of leadership. Banyar, eighty years old, remembering his privileged niche in the colonial government of New York, could only shudder at the rage for democracy which had put the deist Jefferson in the White House and Morgan Lewis, a Republican, a brother-in-law to a Livingston, one of the tribe that had betrayed their class, in the governor's chair in Albany. Goldsbrow Banyar, in 1804, still owned vast tracts of land in western New York.[2] Since the Revolution he had faced west, doing those things which, as a land speculator, he knew would increase the value of his acres.

Canals and new banks, which he was then encouraging, would help to populate the wilderness of western New York, and, less directly, so would a college, one as close to the frontier as was the new college in Schenectady he had helped to sponsor when he became a charter Trustee nine years earlier.[3]

If Union College was, in some respects, a useful instrument in forwarding the frontier settlement plans of the New York land speculators, it was wholly a dream fulfilled for another of the Trustees who welcomed Eliphalet Nott that August afternoon. Abraham Oothout, "The General", was a strong-minded Dutchman, a resident since 1759 of the Dorp Schenectady; he had been a captain in the Revolution and, in 1804, was a general in the New York State militia. He, better than the other Board members, knew where lay the roots of this new college.

The General could remember being made a Trustee of Clinton College, that paper institution of 1772 which had been invented by Alexander Miller, an ambitious Presbyterian minister of Schenectady who had persuaded Governor George Clinton and his own fellow townsmen that this growing river port was "in every respect the most suitable and commodious seat for a seminary of learning in this state, or perhaps in America."[4] Disappointed, but not defeated when this paper college was consumed in the spreading fight for American Independence, the General and Schenectadians settled for a second best when they supported the local Dutch Reformed Church in its two-stage plan, following the Revolution, to found a college in the Dorp Schenectady. Abraham Oothout in 1785 became a Trustee of the revived Schenectady Academy which his church had appropriated from the Presbyterians. The pastor of the Dutch Church, Dirck Romeyn, although he had earlier declared Schenectady was no fit place for a college, had had his mind changed for him by the leaders of the Dutch Reformed Church in America. They were concerned that their center of higher education, Queen's College in New Brunswick, New Jersey, was a failing enterprise, and they had urged Dominie Romeyn to build a new college in Schenectady, a place to educate their ministers and laymen, "a new door of hope for our Zion," as one of their letters to Romeyn had phrased their vision.[5] First, the plan called for the Academy, and then, by careful maneuvering, a transformation of their Academy into a church college.

Perhaps the memory of these events would have annoyed such Trustees as old President Banyar of the Board, and Mayor Philip Schuyler of Albany, both of whom could recall the time when Albanians had expected to see a new college built on their own city common.[6] The General had shared in the ten years struggle the Dutch Church and Schenectady waged before they got their charter. The Columbia College men who then dominated the New York State Board of Regents had wanted no challenge to their pretensions to be the custodians of higher education in the state. The Trustees of the Schenectady Academy had had to contend not only against the delaying tactics of such Columbia supporters as Alexander Hamilton and General Philip Schuyler,[7] but also against a fiercely democratic majority of the state legislature which wanted no church domination of state chartered schools and colleges.[8]

General Oothout could remember it all: Alexander Miller's dream of a non-denominational "seminary of learning," then the scheme for a church college, much out of joint with the times. The General could remember too, when Dominie Romeyn and the Dutch Church had generously sacrificed their plan to control the new college in order that it might receive a $25,000 endowment from the Trustees of the huge Schenectady Patent, men who spoke for the town, and who refused their grant until it was certain the projected college would not be "the private body of the Dutch Church."[9]

The General and the whole town had turned out that cold February evening in 1795 when the doubts and conflicting ambitions of men and towns and the outmoded ideas of church controlled education and the fears of frontier democrats were resolved in the blaze of candlelight flooding from the windows of the transformed Schenectady Academy; the candles burned, that evening, in the windows of the newly chartered Union College.[10] Remembering these things, General Oothout's welcome to Eliphalet Nott that August afternoon in 1804 was probably an especially warm one; perhaps this young man from Albany could make Alexander Miller's dream of educational democracy come true.

A nineteenth-century Aeschuylus or Sophocles, dramatizing the fate of men against the gods of this new world, would have called for a thunderclap at least to mark the pleasantries which probably psssed between Eliphalet Nott and the Honorable Joseph Christopher Yates, also a charter Trustee, and Mayor of Schenectady. The Yateses, brothers and cousins, were destined to move in and out of the new President's career with the persistence and the effect of Furies.

The Yateses, two of whom were in College Hall that afternoon, were a family of radical Republicans whose English ancestor had lost all but the identity of his name among the Dutch families of Schenectady into which he and his descendants had married. Four generations earlier primitive America added the blood line of the Mohawk Indians to Mayor Yates's genealogy when his colonial grandfather, Cornelius VanSluyck, "Broer Cornelis" to the Indians of the Canajoharie Castle, married a chief's daughter and received as a dowry one-half of the big island in the Mohawk which still bears his name.[11] Cornelius and his son Jacques were among the fifteen original proprietors of the Schenectady Patent out of which Union College received that portion of its endowment which had made its chartering possible. Ryckmans, Bradts, Vroomans, one a tapster of Schenectady, another a translator of Iroquois for the colonial governors, fur traders, land speculators, militiamen, these Dutch ancestors of Mayor Yates had played important roles in the violent history of the Mohawk Valley.

Republican sympathies came naturally to the Yateses; their progenitors, unlike those of the aristocratic VanRensselaers and the Banyars, were a part of Schenectady's history; theirs was a frontier story of protests against established order and privilege, of Dutchmen who built plain, solid houses, cornered the Indian trade, intermarried with the Iroquois when it suited them, who fought and talked and pamphleteered against the sort of Athenian government Tories and Federalist politicians like Alexander Hamilton wished to impose upon America.[12]

The congratulations in "College Hall" were over at last, and the hands of welcome folded again, or fingered a snuffbox, a silver buckle, or a flowered waistcoat, or the plain cloth of the church. There was the smell of clothes hung in hot country bedrooms, or worn in the warehouses along the Binnekill, or in the cool parlors of the Albany town houses. Sounds and odors mingled with what the eye saw, the slack, old man's face of Isaac Vrooman, ninety-four, surveyor and farmer of Schenectady, of the scholar's face of President Maxcy, for whom Schenectady and its new college had proved too much, and who would soon leave for the easier life of the President of the College of South Carolina. There were the faces of main-chance men, and of ministers who believed America was God's choice for His New Jerusalem, of lawyers who had practiced with Hamilton and Burr, of men who looked back to George the Third's America as heaven enough, and of men whose thoughts were up-river with the Durham boats, or running lines for new townships, or wondering whether to back a Clintonian or a Livingston man at the next election.

Eliphalet Nott, looking at his Trustees, and at the raw, new room in which they met, aware, too, of the loyalties and antagonisms that moved them, their family ties and traditions, their acres and their goods, knew he had gone irrevocably from the certain, quiet Sunday world of his pulpit into a world of "partizan frenzy" and economic license which would sorely test his belief that Americans of his generation had a common destiny: to prepare themselves and their land for a certain and approaching Millenium. Men of different traditions and sympathies could be yoked in a Sunday effort in the name of religion or of education (the new college was proof of that), but could they work together in the service of a Minerva who was the symbol of Wisdom as well as a face on an official seal? And would they work together to build a college whose purpose would be to make brothers of men, *all* men, within the framework of a divine plan he believed he had read and understood? No leader of the French Revolution had been inspired with a more radical purpose than was the new President of Union College.

These, then, were the Trustees of the new college in Schenectady in August, 1804. To compound the doubts which already beset him, Eliphalet Nott received a letter later that year of restrained congratulations from his elder brother in Franklin, Connecticut. It was a blunt letter, written the day before Christmas. "Friends" were saying that nothing Eliphalet could do "can make the college flourish for any length of time . . . [they] say it does not stand in the right place." The Reverend Samuel Nott looked across the intervening miles straight at his brother:

"Knowing your ambition, I fear for your health . . . if that should remain good, you are at an age when you may make *great improvement.*"

"I have been glad to see by your publications, that you improve in your composition. Your sermon on the death of General Hamilton was the best of anything I have seen, though that, I think, was not without fault. . . ."[13] It was a salutary letter.

II

In nine years the three preceding Presidents of Union College had each found his own way to safe harbor. John Blair Smith, after two years of struggle, had given up and returned to his Philadelphia parish, "a shameful desertion," John Brodhead Romeyn had written to his father, Domine Dirck Romeyn, still pastor of the Schenectady Dutch Reformed Church. Jonathan Edwards the Younger, the dour, scholarly son of the Great Awakener of Northampton and uncle of Aaron Burr, had successfully lobbied for the contributions received from the legislature during the two years he spent in Schenectady before death ended a career so much like that of his father. Jonathan Maxcy had been chiefly concerned with organizing his rigid system for monitoring every moment of college life; financing the day-to-day operation of the college and of the mounting costs of the new stone building which was to house his students had proved too much for him. On the afternoon Eliphalet Nott, his one-time protégé at Rhode Island College, was welcomed to a dubious office, Jonathan Maxcy was saying his goodbyes, and excusing his retreat to the College of South Carolina on the grounds of poor health. He had no reason to thank Nott for the part the latter had played three years earlier in making him the third President of this poverty stricken place.

Three years earlier Eliphalet Nott, then a Trustee and a member of the auditing committee himself, had observed that the annual expenses were 1500 pounds, about $3750, and were being met by an income of 676 pounds. In the three years following, the college had solved its financial problems by sailing away from them out into a sea of debt.

Nothing was said officially of debts and income during his first meeting with the Board as President. Stephen Bayard, the owner of the Binnekill warehouses, was appointed a committee to procure a bell for the new building, and John V. Henry, the Albany lawyer and disgusted Federalist ex-comptroller of New York State, with Mayor Yates was made one of a committee to confer on the matter of Richard Allanson, then in the Albany jail for breach of his contract with the Trustees, a man whose failures as a builder were visible everywhere one looked about Stone College.[14]

Neither the faculty, nor the courses taught by Mrs. Nott's brother-in-law, Professor Benjamin Allen, and tutors Dunlap, Westbrook, and Younglove are mentioned in the Minutes of the Trustees' meeting for that August afternoon. Troubles are faced in the order of their urgency, and though stiff-necked Benjamin Allen, late of the Plainfield Academy and Rhode Island College, had already had trouble with his students and would soon have more of it, he and they could wait. Nott knew the faculty and their problems intimately; two years earlier he had helped to frame the curriculum they taught. If the "parental system," and Union College itself, were to survive, however, the balance in his treasurer's books must be changed soon and radically.

His treasurer, and soon, *his* trustees, and then *his* college. Neither Nott nor the Board could have realized, in August, 1804, the transforming power the presidency of Union College was to generate in this young Millennialist.

His first move had seemed obvious: go back along that well-travelled road to the legislative halls in Albany over which Presidents Smith and Edwards had gone. Where else could one find the money Union College must have to feed and house the new students he was expecting the following year, to pay his own salary and that of his four-man faculty, to pay carpenters and painters, and the contractor who was fitting up the new kitchen on the "Rumford Plan"?[15] The Trustees' "no" to this reasonable proposal to seek money from Albany must have seemed almost a betrayal to their new President; it was tantamount to a no-confidence vote in the future of the college, for certainly creditors were not going to wait for a rise in value of the earlier state gift of lots in the Military Grants in western New York and of the garrison lands at Ticonderoga and Lake George before presenting their bills!

Why this "no"? There is no record of the argument, which must have gone on for several months. The Board was never convened to air the difficulty, but Nott would prefer it that way; he liked the private talk, a time for persuasion and compromise, for men as individuals, he believed, had a pliability they lost when they became committeemen and board members. Nothing he could say moved enough of them, however, to give him the Board's sanction. Although the Trustees had paid President Edwards "to attend on the legislature," Nott was told further application for state funds would be useless.[16]

Unlike the health of his church, the health of this college, he was discovering, waxed and waned with the political health of the State. The leaders among his Trustees were, for the most part, Federalists, and some of them were still smarting from fresh, political wounds. A few of the members had been supporters of Aaron Burr in his recent fight for the governorship, and they were finding silence golden. Democracy was anathema to many of the Federalist members of his Board and they may well have reasoned that the college for which they were Trustees could expect little from the overwhelmingly Republican legislature of 1804.[17] A college, to these conservatives, was an undemocratic institution, for collegiate education was not yet designed for the sons of tradesmen and farmers. Nothing new, they may have observed, had been granted to Union since early in 1801. The conservative and respected voices which had once been raised in Albany on behalf of higher education were gone now with those Federalist majorities which had recently melted away in the heat of the Hamilton-Burr battles over the cause of national union, and in the political struggle for the control of New York State.

The Trustees' disapproval of Nott's plan was probably not unanimous, but its effect might well have been to set them looking for a new President if the man to whom they said "no" had not come to Schenectady braced with an indestructible faith. Two things were clear in Eliphalet Nott's mind: the first was that Union College was not the projection of a class of men, nor of the economic planning of land speculators and Schenectady traders, nor was it in any way to be an adjunct to the Dutch Reformed

Church or any other church, though such ideas may well have colored the thinking of the practical men and the ministers, who, as Trustees, had now apparently lost the power of action as they contemplated their empty treasury. God had purposes for America, Nott had told his audiences, and there were corollaries to that proposition: if his major premise was true, then it followed that God had purposes for Union College and for the men ordained to serve it. Although the inhuman theology of John Calvin, as it filtered down to Eliphalet Nott, had undergone the transmutations forced on it by such humanists as his "Father Benedict" and Joseph Bellamy, Joel Benedict's teacher, Nott still saw men acting involuntarily to serve ends not their own. If it was given to him to see the role of his college in terms his Trustees failed to grasp, so be it.

With one stride he now became the leader, not only of his divided Board, but of those who believed that America's future was one with the spread and growth of its schools. With the skill of an able general, Nott, on his own responsibility, moved through the legislative chambers in Albany during the winter session of 1804-1805, organizing its members in support of his two bills for education. Unlike Presidents Smith, Edwards, and Maxcy, Nott could now pass his snuff box to Federalist and Republican legislators alike as a man of consequence, an already famous New Yorker. His epic speech on the death of Alexander Hamilton delivered in Albany only a few months earlier was still echoing far beyond the State. The power of his preaching, the drama of his sermons on the Resurrection, and the promise of the new day they contained were well known to the men he now turned to for help. He had already served as a chaplain to the legislature in 1800. He had never publicly supported the partisan cause of any of these politicians so that he could go from Republican to Federalist, from Hollander to Yankee, confident that he was everywhere welcome.

If his Trustees had failed him, his legislative friends did not. Even the death of his wife made access easier to those Republicans who counted most in these dangerous, dry-leaf days of the nation. His daughter was now living at "Linden," in Rhinebeck on the Hudson, the home of Dr. Robert Tillotson, the new Republican Secretary of New York State.[18]   To little Sarah Maria, Mrs.

Tillotson, the "dear friend" of Mrs. Nott, was now "Mother Tillotson," and Mrs. Tillotson was a daughter of Chancellor Robert R. Livingston who was then engaged in promoting Robert Fulton's "folly," a boat the promotors said would be propelled by steam. "Clermont," the heart of the Livingston barony, was not far from "Linden." There Nott, whose wide-ranging interests had already made him the author of an almanac and a treatise on the new Federal coinage, may well have discussed the puzzle of pistons and gears and boiler pressures in this headquarters of New York democracy.[19] More important, however, were the political leaders who also shared the hospitality of the Livingstons and the Tillotsons: the nephew, Brockholst Livingston and Smith Thompson, who had married a Livingston, both of whom were judges of the New York State Supreme Court, Maturin Livingston, recently given the influential post of Recorder of New York City, and, vital in Nott's muster of forces, the governor himself, Morgan Lewis, whose wife was "Mother Tillotson's" aunt. Governor Lewis and Eliphalet Nott were already old friends; Nott had been a guest of the bench when Lewis, as Chief Justice of New York, had sat in judgment on Harry Croswell, the Hudson, New York editor who, as the "libeler" of Jefferson, had been so ably defended by Hamilton. Fortuitously, too, a Livingston had just taken his bachelor's degree from Union College that May, another was coming up for his degree the following year, as was Robert Tillotson, the son of the new Secretary of State.[20]

Nott's campaign consisted of two parts. Where Presidents Smith's and Edwards's pleas to earlier legislatures had been simply for funds for their new college, Nott's approach must be different, for there was a new breed of politician in Albany, and the old arguments had worn thin. Then too, Columbia College, the only other institution of higher education in New York State, wanted funds, and he knew that the old antagonism of Columbia men for Union College, again competing for endowments, was not dead.[21]

So Eliphalet Nott, on behalf of his unwilling Trustees, petitioned the legislature to finance "the plan for education and government . . . lately adopted in the college different from that which was lately intended and which in its consequences affords the most flattering prospects of extensive and permanent usefulness." He had outlined the new plan in December to his brother

Samuel: his students were "to be separated from the great world"; the President and faculty, with their families were "to lodge in college and board in commons . . ."; each class was to belong "to the family of the officer who instructs them"; the emphasis was to be placed "on the decorum, ceremony, and politeness of refined, domestic life"; and the ultimate object of the plan was "to furnish . . . complete security to the manners and morals of youth . . . to fill the week with collegiate, the Sabbath with religious exercises."

If any of the legislators had, by chance, met any of those "strangers" who Samuel Nott had been told "visit us with interest, and leave astonished at the order, punctuality, and diligence which prevails," they must have been impressed with the reports of the wonder-working of the new President of Union College. Two aspects of Nott's plan of collegiate education may have been even more influential with the democratic majority of the legislature than those to which he had given first place; board, they noted, had been reduced from $2.50 a week to $1.45, and, they were told, a further reduction was expected. Nor, they noted, was Nott concerned chiefly with enlisting students from among the gentry, for his proposal called for a state endowment "toward defraying the expenses of such indigent students as may be from time to time pursuing their education in said seminary."[22]

In 1804, with a tide of seemingly dangerous political and philosophical ideas flooding America, such an educational program had the widest possible appeal. Federalist conservatives who hated the leveling democrats pushing in from the new western settlements, and upriver from Tammany-tainted New York City could find in this country college, and in its President, a guarantee of safety for their sons from the dangerous "isms" of the day. For the responsible citizens of the new settlements, largely New Englanders, politically Republican, but conservatives in matters of religion and economics, Union College offered their sons the discipline and refinement of homes they had left east of the Hudson and were then rebuilding in the vast, new western counties. A gentleman's son and a worthy poor man's son, no matter what his religious beliefs, would be equally welcome at Union College so long as he subscribed to security measures designed to safeguard his manners and morals. Neither Federalist nor Republican could seriously object to the academic democracy Nott proposed, for he made it abundantly clear that it carried the sanction of both pagan Minerva and the God of his fellow Christians.

The second part of Nott's proposal to the legislature proved him the equal of any of its members in enlisting support for what he wanted. In offering them a twofold program he offered something the mid-Twentieth Century would recognize as a "package deal." Would it not be reasonable, he argued, to extend at this time the state's aid to common schools? "Provision," he said, "for collegiate instruction must be in vain, unless the masses were educated from which the College must receive its pupils to educate." [23] Connecticut men would recognize the logic of this statement; most of them had been educated in the "parish" schools of their old homes, schools which had been long supported by contributions from a state school fund. [24]

Nott, in 1804, recognizing the pressure which had already developed behind the common school movement and sensing its value in forwarding his own measure, linked it at once to his new plan for education at Union College. [25] What he now proposed was actually the then radical idea of a state supported plan of education which would, in part, at least, carry a young New Yorker from his three "Rs" to his bachelor's degree. [26] It was Nott's recent "Utopian Plan" for a school system for the city of Albany, scaled to the realities of the moment. [27] And like a good general, Nott developed the logistics without which his bills would never have gone beyond their first reading.

Governor Morgan Lewis, Nott liked to recall years later, "was induced to send to the legislature a special message in favor of these objects." [28] Actually there was a hurly-burly, give-and-take struggle to pass the two bills which the dignified measures of early nineteenth-century prose reduces to an exercise in the amenities of snuff-box passing. "I trust the effort which is now making," Nott wrote to the Patroon, Stephen VanRensselaer, the epitome of Federalist conservatism, "to refund and renovate a seminary in which so many youths are educated is one in which every great and good man in this community will unite. . . ." [29] Nine years, Nott hoped, had softened the patroon's disappointment that Schenectady, not Albany, had captured Union College.

Nott soon recognized his own role in the violent contests which developed over the two bills; it was a role he had found himself playing on other occasions: the peacemaker, the pacifier, the compromiser, in a word better suited to our twentieth-century vocabularies, the psychologist. As the debates of the winter season began to degenerate into Republican-Federalist bickering, Nott undertook to focus the strength of the men he needed. [30]

That Nott was optimistic, even visionary about the effects he expected would follow the state's generosity stands out in a revealing story W. W. VanNess, the young Assemblyman and floor leader for Nott's two bills, told about the help Nott gave him. [31] That Nott repeated the story himself reveals that he as well as VanNess had a saving sense of humor.

> On one occasion [VanNess], having made a somewhat less elaborate and impressive speech than he was accustomed to make, when discussing the merits of the College appropriation, . . . said . . . that the President of the College had been at his room, and undertook to show him that if this bill passed, it never would thereafter cost anybody anything to educate their sons at College, and that he so presented the facts and arguments that went to establish this position, that he himself thought he saw the connection between the proposition and the proof of its truth, and that he could make the House see it. But when he arose in his place to do so, those facts and arguments had entirely escaped him, and he could not, for his life, recollect one of them . . . which was the reason for the brevity . . . and the apparent want of connection between his premises and his conclusion.[32]

It was a mean building, this legislative meeting house of 1805, stone and brick, three stories high, five windows wide and two deep, on South Market Street, Albany, close to the fever breeding Hudson River. Assemblymen and Senators, Federal and State Courthouse officers, rubbed shoulders here and shared its cramped rooms with officials of Albany County. In the cupola above their heads was the alarm bell which had called Albanians to their ancient Stadt Huys to hear the Declaration of Independence read. The new capital, to stand well up State Street hill, was still on Philip Hooker's drawing board. [33]

Early in the winter session Nott recognized that in its Senate room the success or failure of his bills for education lay with two men.[34] The contrast between the dour, sarcastic Federalist Hollander, Abraham VanVechten, and Jedidiah Peck, full of bustle, in appearance "diminutive and almost disgusting," fanatical in his Christianity, "a man who would survey your farm in the daytime, exhort and pray in your family at night, and talk on politics the rest of the time,"[35] was, basically, the contrast between the old world of the Hudson River aristocracy and the new world of frontier democracy, of stump farms and clapboard towns. Education at public expense seemed to Judge Peck, Republican Senator from Otsego County, a natural right; to Senator VanVechten of Albany it was a wretched, leveling device to reshape his Federalist world; it was an invasion of property rights and a challenge to social order.

VanVechten had no intention of talking the bill to death as his fellow Albanian in the Assembly, Stephen Lush, was prepared to do. Instead, he approached Nott with a Machiavellian measure about which he made no secret:

> You and your friends have got up such an excitement in favor of Common Schools that it is perhaps necessary to do something for them. Now if you will consent to have that bill so amended that no money shall be distributed till the annual income of the lands sold shall amount to $50,000, we will pass the Bill through the Senate . . . long before that period arrives, however, we shall repeal the law. [36]

Nott agreed. If the Senator from Albany thought the democratic excitement was only a passing storm through his ordered, Federalist world, the President of Union College would compromise, and so keep the peace, and the half-loaf received now would be a baker's dozen in due time. Men and events in these days were shaping toward ends hidden from a Senator Van-Vechten, and Eliphalet Nott, who believed he knew their direction, would accept any man's contribution, made knowingly or not.

If, as seems likely, this settling for half-loaves between Nott and the Federalist senatorial leader was reported to the quick tempered Senator Peck then the latter's sudden hostility to Nott becomes understandable. Although Jedidiah Peck was himself an uneducated Connecticut emigrant to the New York frontier, he had been among the first legislators to fight for state aid to common schools. He had helped to establish the short-lived Common School Fund of 1795, and now with a great victory for the fund almost in sight the President of Union College, who had proposed the method for winning it at the beginning of the session, was seemingly willing to sell it out on Senator Van-Vechten's disgraceful terms in order, apparently, to guarantee the success of his College Bill.

> The session was far advanced, [Nott recalled], before (Judge Peck's) doubts were so far overcome as to admit of bringing the friends of these two interests to act in concert. This, however, was finally effected, and the influence in favor of education became, in the Assembly, the controlling interest of the session.[37]

Nott remembered that that was the way things were, though the newspapers of the day, and the older historians of New York State political history reflect events of a more dramatic nature: the corruption which surrounded the Merchants' Bank bill that session, and the promise of even worse to come as the ghost of Hamilton continued to walk the political byways.

On the 27th of March, 1805, Nott, without waiting to carry the news to Schenectady, wrote to his father-in-law in Plainfield, Connecticut: "My two bills this day passed the Senate." The Reverend Joel Benedict, as he read his son-in-law's letter telling of his great success may have remembered the intense, tall boy, too old for his years, who had gone before Samuel Nott's riven church in Franklin during the winter of 1795 and there had played the peacemaker and the compromiser so well that a divided church had been made whole again.

How wrong his Trustees had been! Individuals among them may have helped during his three months of lobbying, but there is no evidence they did. In any event here was a result they could understand: on his own responsibility their new President had won an endowment for Union College far in excess of even his own unrestrained hopes.

But at what cost? That the question must have been asked, and repeated, and asked again seems evident in the fact that there was no comment, no official action recorded in the Trustees' Minutes on this most important event since the charter itself had been granted until the fourth meeting following the passage of the

college bill. [38] Not even a quorum could be got together for the
April 30th meeting. On the first of May there was a quorum, but
there was no record that the great endowment had ever been heard
of. There was nothing noted but the faculty report: 55 students:
13 seniors, 14 juniors, 15 sophomores, 13 freshmen, and 34 boys
in the grammar school. Ten weeks later, a special meeting was
called, and again no quorum. By the next Wednesday, the 17th of
July, however, the question had been settled, though with what
misgiving will never be known.

The cost to some of the Trustees must have seemed
outrageous: as a Board they were now to lose their autonomy. For
those who were superstitious there may have been confirmation
for their doubts in the numbering of the paragraphs of the
Legislature's Endowment Act, passed on March 30, 1805. Paragraph 13, had these Trustees realized it, was to be like a key to
Pandora's Box; in return for $80,000 to be raised for Union
College through a series of state-controlled lotteries:

> "*be it further enacted*: That the grant of the aforesaid lotteries is upon
> the express condition and stipulation, that the said trustees of Union
> College, shall make application, under their common seal, to the regents
> of the university of this state, for an amendment of the charter of said
> college, so as to reduce the number of trustees to twenty-one, and so as
> to constitute the chancellor, the justices of the supreme court, the
> secretary, the comptroller, the treasurer, the attorney-general, and
> surveyor-general of this state respectively, for the time being, ex-officio,
> trustees of said college; as also for the said regents, to fill all vacancies of
> the said trustees, from time to time, which shall take place. . . ." [39]

Legally, the Endowment Act of March 30, 1805 changed the
nature of the control of Union College as much as unfinished
Stone College would have been changed by blocking up its
windows. In return for a Republican legislature's eighty thousand
dollar lottery grant Eliphalet Nott joined the State to those then
governing Union; he had not only added eleven State officers to
his Board, but he had made them, if the test should come, the
ruling members.

The shift in control was eased only by the provision in the
Endowment Act which declared the Regents of the University
were directed to fill all vacancies on the Board of Trustees which
occurred after the then existing Board of twenty-four members

was reduced to ten through death, resignation, or removal from the State. As the passage of time reduced the Board the control of the State would become stronger and stronger. Eventually the Board would consist of eleven state officers: the Governor, the Chancellor of the University, the five justices of the Supreme Court, the Secretary of State, the Comptroller, the Attorney-General, and the Surveyor-General; and those chosen by the state-appointed Board of Regents.

In these first months of success Nott may have believed he could deal with whatever Board of Trustees a benevolent State might contrive. There would be no difficulty, certainly, with these new state officers and good friends, with Governor Lewis, who was also chancellor of the University, with Dr. Tillotson, Secretary of State, and with Supreme Court Judge Brockholst Livingston. These Republicans, in 1805, however, had taken away the corporate freedom Federalists had granted Union College in 1795 and Columbia College in 1787. In appropriating control of the Board of Trustees they had, whether intentionally or not, established a Republican collegiate counterbalance to Federalist-dominated Columbia College. Eliphalet Nott had talked persuasively of educational democracy, a language not often heard among the older alumni of the late King's College. And the President of Union College, whether intentionally or not, had established himself as the particular friend of Republicans, of a party distributing generous gifts to its supporters.

There seems little doubt that Nott presented this legislative endowment to his Trustees as a *fait accompli*; take it, and the college lives, "the new plan of education" will have its chance; refuse it. . . . but such a course must have been unthinkable to Eliphalet Nott, and, by the 17th of July, 1805, he had made it seem so to the majority of the Trustees who had offered no alternative for filling an empty treasury.

Goldsbrow Banyar, however, the old Tory land speculator, was no longer seen at Trustees' meetings in College Hall. James Emott, the Federalist lawyer and legislator, resigned his seat, as did Isaac Vrooman and Dirck Ten Broeck, two "Hollanders" who may have thought Nott had struck a devil's bargain.[40]

The acquiescent majority of the Board, on July 17th quickly elected two new members, one of whom was James C. Duane, grandson of Robert R. Livingston; the other was the Reverend Samuel Blatchford of Lansingburgh, a Greek scholar whose new grammar would soon be in use at the college. These two men were the last an independent Board of Trustees could hope to elect before Paragraph 13 of the Endowment Act went into effect. The final business of that fateful Wednesday morning was to accept the Legislative Endowment Act and all its provisions, a vote which sealed Nott's fate, and which was to cast a deepening shadow on the college for the rest of the century.

In March, 1805, doubt as to the consequences or the morality of the State's lottery grant to Union College would not have occurred to its young President, vindicated now before his Board of Trustees. Eighty thousand dollars to be collected from willing adventurers in chances was far better than the substitute endowment it was rumored some legislators had had in mind for Union College, the out-of-repair "Government House" in New York City which stood until 1815 near the lower end of Broadway.[41]

The State's gift seemed, indeed, munificent. The "New plan of education lately adopted" could go forward. "Stone College" would be finished, a bulwark in the chain of fortifications America must rear against the atheists and communists then arms-rattling in Europe. Nott, in April, 1805, returned to a Schenectady warming in a spring sun, to his pupils for whom spring had other messages, to certain Trustees winter-cold to the conditions attached to the gift of their state legislature. The new President had opened a Pandora's Box from which emerged, many were later to agree, the moths of evil, as well as the one white moth of hope.

CHAPTER 2

"Novelties Worse than Paine!"

FOR the Dorp Schenectady the spring of 1805 was a season of beginnings. Drifting across the half Dutch, half Yankee town warming in a May sun were the pig odors and river smells released by the south wind. The new bell in "Stone College" could be heard along the Binnekill wharves when the wind shifted to the east.

For Eliphalet Nott the spring of this year was also a season of beginnings. This village of elms and lilacs and streets going down to willow brakes and river views was home to him now, although he had known it as a frequent visitor for nine years. The changes in Schenectady since the summer of 1796 were in their way as marked as were the changes in the then inexperienced, young Congregationalist preacher who had gone in search of a parish and a home for his bride among the Connecticut settlers of western New York.

John Hudson's "stage-wagons" had then brought him across the pine plains from Albany on the old Normanskill Road, a four shilling ride of twenty miles, and deposited him at the Schenectady Coffee House, the center of the town's social life, the meeting place of "the high rollers of the day."[1] The year old Union College in 1796 stood about opposite the Coffee House on Niskayuna Street, a name soon to be changed to Union Street. Nine years later the college had retreated a full block west of its birthplace, to safer ground, for even that much distance was a gain in protecting the morals of young students for whom the midget Golden Horn of the Binnekill was both bazaar and port of great adventure.

The Reverend Timothy Dwight, that peripatetic President of Yale College, put his finger on both the source of the corruption and the source of the change coming over Schenectady when, in 1798, a violent three-day rain forced him to stay long enough to survey the town. "Few collections of men," he wrote in his *Travels*, "are more dissolute, than the boatmen on the Mohawk."[2] "The corruption," he said, "which they contribute to spread among the ordinary inhabitants, is a greater evil than a stranger can easily imagine." The growing crowds of rivermen, however, and the new wharves along the Binnekill were visible evidence of new vitality. "The merchandise which passes into the western country," President Dwight continued in his bleached prose, "is usually embarked here on the Mohawk." The traders of Schenectady were no longer waiting for redskins to bring in their bales of furs; that trade died with the Revolution, and moved now down the St. Lawrence. Freight handlers had taken their place, noisy, blasphemous German teamsters, carting over the new turnpike, it seemed, half of everything movable in New England. Furniture and families were crowded into the Durham boats and ferried west through the Mohawk rifts and the new locks at Little Falls and Rome. Schenectady's post-war boom was under way in the decade Eliphalet Nott and Timothy Dwight first visited it; by 1805, the ancient Dorp had become the center of the wonderful commotion of settling the west.

Teamsters and boatmen were almost more than the newly reorganized Night Watch could handle. Its members now traveled in pairs, armed with five foot pikes. The curfew they called at nine o'clock was scarcely heard along "Frog Alley River," the name by which the Binnekill was best known to those who sailed it and those who built the boats crowding its ways along "The Strand," between Washington Street and the Poor Pasture.[3]

If a spring evening during May, 1805, had prompted President Nott to put by the pressing problems of lotteries and Trustees, of the unfinished College Hall and his "new plan of education," he could have found within walking distance of the President's House a dozen yardsticks to measure this changing town. It was a "modern" house the Trustees had provided for the President of Union College, one of "the great number of new ones built in the English style," which Timothy Dwight of Connecticut compared to the disadvantage of the majority of "ancient structures of brick, in the Dutch style: the roofs sharp; the ends toward the street; and the architecture uncouth."[4] From Front Street, where the President's house stood near the site of the old Queen's Fort whose rotting timbers had recently been carted away, it was only a few blocks west to the shops, with their diamond paned windows and to the wharves close by, backing onto Washington Street. He would have crossed Ferry Street first, a narrow lane which now continued north as New Street to the ferry landing where scows had been operated until recently on lease from the town to General Abraham Oothoudt, devoted Trustee of the college. On the east side of Ferry Street, between the site of the Fort and Union Street stood the Episcopal Church where, it was rumored, Walter Butler was buried, that Tory raider whose Indians had perpetrated the terrible Cherry Valley Massacre during the Revolution. Timothy Dwight's comment on the architecture of Schenectady's three churches was succinct: "all of them ordinary buildings." The Dutch church still blocked coaches and wagons at the crossing of Union and Church Streets; it was a blue stone, gambrel-roofed house of worship as much a part of Holland as any church in a Ruysdael landscape. Here, too, was change, for just the year before Nott became a permanent resident of Schenectady the consistory had elected to hear the preaching done in English.[5]

A spring evening could be ruined by pondering the troubles of the Presbyterians, whose church stood close to Union Street, looking, in 1805, more like the Lord's barn, where pastors had come and gone, even their poor salaries too much for the members to meet.[6] The new President of Union College would bring their quarreling factions together in time, but that May he had as much trouble as he could handle.

A walk in the spring of 1805 would have circled Schenectady in little more than a half hour; a brisk walker in that time could have traveled the boundary of the once palisaded colonial village to which the name "Schenectady" had clung, a name which meant "the place beyond the pine plain," in the gutterals of the now scattered Mohawks.

Not only was the Dorp Schenectady changing, with its new English houses and English speech in place of gable ends and colonial Dutch, its city charter only seven years old, busy now with wagon building and ship building to serve an expanding frontier, but its inhabitants themselves were changing in response to a new democracy in manners as well as in politics. Dress and courtesies were "leveling," were becoming more and more sober. Many of the older citizens, especially those who remembered a colonial New York with regret, still wore their flowered vests, gold trimmed cocked hats and clocked stockings, and were as mannered in their coming and going as had been the Patroon and the British aristocracy they admired. Powdered wigs were passé, however, and a busy merchant now had his hair banged in the front, and tied behind in a queue.[7] The Dorp's citizens were now, most of them, Americans on the move as never before, bargaining, buying, building and selling, and none more so than the hordes moving west by way of Albany, through Schenectady to the democratic frontier. The customary ways of their fathers were often a burden where the eye was on the main chance, and talk was in dollars and cents.

Eliphalet Nott, too, was changing. His brother, the Reverend Samuel Nott, still preaching the inhuman Calvinism of the followers of Jonathan Edwards from a village pulpit in Connecticut, had recognized the change and warned his younger brother of the dangers he believed were threatened by his too-powerful ambition. The older Nott was concerned too, that his brother, anxious to please the taste for sensation in "his part of the country," was accepting without proper safeguards the currently popular Millennialism for which his own reading of the Bible offered little support.[8]

By 1804, that "Second Awakening" which swept rural America and which Nott had so dramatically underscored by charging the death of Hamilton to a nation which was deaf to the sounds of the approaching "chariot of the Lord," had convinced him a benevolent God was offering mankind its second chance. In many places, he had said, the perceiving eye could see the regenerating Spirit pour into the open heart.[9] There *was* now salvation for men who would seek it.

By 1804, God's purpose seemed very clear to Eliphalet Nott, and so, too, did his own part in bringing it to fulfillment. The new Zion was to be America, and his own role was to help educate its citizens, as Hamilton had hoped to see them educated, in their duties and opportunities in a Christian Commonwealth. [10] The second coming of Christ was imminent, and his own work was to help prepare men for the universal Christian brotherhood to follow.

These were in part the new convictions which had stimulated Nott's ambition, which were changing his world view, and which had given him the driving purpose in his first year as the President of Union College, to deal with a violently partisan legislature and a timid Board of Trustees. With a new optimism and with that talent for compromise which the Reverend Samuel Nott had good reason to remember, the young President of a new college on the main east-west highway of burgeoning America was ready for the men and events of his time.

II

The Frog Alley boys and the boatmen of the Mohawk probably had no representatives in the Dutch Church that May Day morning, 1805, when Eliphalet Nott delivered his first baccalaureate. There may have been palms itching for brickbats among those rivermen who watched the little parade of Trustees, the four-man faculty of Union College, the gowned student body, thirteen seniors, the underclassmen, and the corporation of the city of Schenectady as the column moved into the old blue stone building in sight of the Binnekill, the whole procession preceded by the sheriff with his staff of office. Although the ancient wars of "Town and Gown" were new to Schenectady, a few skirmishes had already been fought, and the uneasy truce would never be hard to break.

There had been no inaugural ceremonies to mark the new President's election, so the occasion was to be more than the customary goodbye to a senior class; it would also be a demonstration for Schenectadians of Eliphalet Nott's talents and a guide to his convictions.

Nott spoke directly to his "Young gentlemen"; he also called them "adventurers" and, in what must have been an unexpectedly brief address, armed them for their journey through a "fascinating but illusive world. . . ." [11] He was no attorney for heaven this time, as he stood in the high pulpit centered above his audience.

His words were for young men in a lilac season, when "happiness, smiling but deceitful . . . beckons to her embrace."

Those who had heard him speak on Hamilton may have been disappointed. He presented himself to his audience as a pater-familias, once an adventurer himself, returned home now with a wisdom imparted by his studies, and by those teachers he had met on his travels. He spoke as a man of reason, intent on sharing with his students the fruit of his experience. Here was none of the drama of his massive indictment of the nation for its part in the death of Hamilton, and few of the pathetic epithets and of those "blasphemies" which had worried the Reverend Samuel Nott. The new President of Union College had gauged the audience and the moment; on this occasion he would deal primarily with Man, not with the Spirit.

His theme was progress: "In the acquisition of knowledge, you are never to be stationary, but always progressive." [12] No boundary is to be set to the range of the mind. The duty of the true student is to expand his knowledge of Nature and, by doing this, of his own rational being until, "touching the earth, it can look above the clouds and reach beyond the stars. "Go (he exclaimed), with Newton, span the heavens, and number and measure the orbs which decorate them; with Locke, analyze the human mind; with Boyle, examine the regions of organic nature . . . in one word, go . . . and trace the Everlasting in His word and in His works." [13]

Here was Nott explaining the object of education; men who "spanned—and analyzed—and examined" would put by self-interest and "partisan frenzy" as they grew in knowledge; they would come to understand their common humanity. His seniors, however, must look beyond their finite world, must stretch their beings taut as they

> pondered the mysteries of Infinite Wisdom . . . (for then) a wide and unbounded prospect spreads itself before you in every point of which Divinity shines conspicuous; and on whichever side you turn your enraptured eyes, surrounded with uncreated majesty, and seen in the light of his own glory, God appears.

He had asked his students to embrace the world in order to know God. He would give them Newton, Locke, and Boyle to study for the same reason the novice priest was given the Lives of the Saints; "seen in the light of His own glory, God appears" he had assured them. Behind Nott were Jonathan Edwards, Joseph Bellamy, and Joel Benedict, who had had their own moments of insight and prescience.

The new President's thirteen seniors, however, had neither been asked to mortify the flesh nor to hold their gaze on heaven. He, too, he told them, had been an "adventurer" through the world. He, too, had allowed human reason to lure him into the embrace of "erring and blind philosophy." He, as had they, had watched the march of atheism through Europe. They had all heard the French "openly abjure their God . . . with one hand they seized the thunders of heavens, and with the other smote His throne who inhabits them. . . ." [14]

Nott, his voice vibrating that May morning with the emotion aroused by his vision of a France in ruins, where "Blasphemy waved its terrific sceptre," of a "great nation . . . delivered from the restraints of moral obligation, and enfranchised with all the liberties of infidelity," must have seemed a tall man indeed to the boys of the grammar school and the young gentlemen of Union College. One listened to him as one listened to men home from voyages to China and India; there was the excitement of wonders seen in the reports he brought of his own "adventuring."

If the death of Alexander Hamilton had been proof of God's anger at a heedless America, the end of the French Revolution and the rebuilding "of the altars they had demolished" was proof to Nott that "God formed man to be religious." A nation could be seduced into atheism, but it could not continue in it. He knew these young men. What sophistication there was in America belonged largely to its college families by inheritance and education. If their sons were to become Christians, prepared for a new America, the New Zion he envisaged, it would be because the mind was convinced. Not many of them would be moved by the revival spirit he had seen operating among the country people of the village of Berne near Albany. Reason, not the heart, would control them.

Nations, he continued, live through a time of passion, even as do young men. There had followed for France, as it would for his boys, "the calm of reason," a period when the enlightened man and nation read "Responsibility," when men from necessity turn to religion because, in doing so, they then respond to the dictates of their nature.

III

East of Schenectady three days horseback ride was Cambridge and Harvard College where, for 169 years, Calvin's "Institutes" and the Westminister Confession had framed the lives of its graduates. By 1805 the intellectual revolution of the Eighteenth Century had done no more than leaven Harvard with a mild Unitarianism. Connecticut and Yale College to the south were now safer havens for the sons of orthodox Calvinists, for there President Dwight, the "Pope of New England," a grandson of Jonathan Edwards, tolerated no ideas, native or foreign, which did not square with the gospel life as he understood it. South from Schenectady, down the Hudson River, in New York City was Columbia College, which reflected its cosmopolitan location in its law school and school of medicine. From the point of view of the Hudson River families who patronized it, conservatives, Federalists, many of them, Columbia was a "safe" college, even though it was unduly exposed, in a port city, to the influences of democracy and was without the safeguards of Eliphalet Nott's "New Plan" of education. The Columbia College curriculum, however, was made up of that solid classical fare so little changed from colonial days. In those dangerous areas of religion and the new philosophies there could be no cause for alarm, for under the presidency of Bishop Moore of the Episcopal Diocese of New York and the constant attention of representatives of the City's Protestant churches, Columbia, too, was maintaining the watch against the dreadful "isms": deism, idealism, and scepticism.

It was at the College of New Jersey, however, on the crossroads between town-meeting New England and the plantation south where the struggle for the minds of young Americans was being fought in terms the majority of the new generation of students could understand. It was at Princeton that that "erring and blind philosophy" which so concerned Nott in 1805 was being challenged by a counter-philosophy as palatable to expanding America as the arithmetic of dollars and cents.

At the College of New Jersey, and at other colonial colleges before the Revolution students and faculty had debated, often with misgivings, the implications of Newtonian physics. Newton's mathematical proofs of an orderly universe, earth, planets, and stars endlessly moving in the patterns of a heaven-directed quadrille had seemingly robbed Calvinism of one of its most fearful assumptions, that of an angry and arbitrary God using eclipses, comets and, astral chastisements against a sin-drenched earth: discipline by cosmic disorder. Newtonian physics implied a benevolent deity administering cosmic harmony.

By 1805 the Reverend Eliphalet Nott could say to his seniors, "Go, with Newton span the heavens and number and measure the orbs which, decorate them. . . ." In that directive one begins to measure the extent of the great compromise which Nott and most of the popular Christian apologists at the turn of the Nineteenth Century had made with the new physics. God had moved outward from the edge of Boston and the elbow of sinners, and had become also "Infinite Wisdom," and "The Everlasting," a God seen in the wonders of a Newtonian, orderly cosmos. God had permitted men to progress through reason to this ecstatic vision of the universe, but for the still unanswered questions of purpose and destiny, human reason, Nott argued, was useless: not reason, but revelation alone could give the answers.

If the new physics inadvertently gave the student arguments which led away from Christianity toward deism, and worse, the psychology of John Locke in the same hands could, so Nott and the watchers for the millennial dawn believed, lead the unsuspecting out of a real world down darkening corridors to lunacy.

"Go, with Locke," Nott directed his first seniors, "analyze the human mind . . ."; his young gentlemen, however, and the seniors at Harvard, Yale, Columbia, the College of New Jersey, and the other American colleges, knew at what point they were expected to conclude their analysis. As college men they had been permitted to study the new modes of thought, to develop a rational world-view as dangerous when out of control as is the unguarded atomic pile in an age less certain of the ultimate uses of physics and psychology.

We read today in a single-page Union College catalogue issued during the first decade of the new century what subjects Nott's seniors were studying, as well as evidence that he intended to limit their scope: "Select portions of ancient and modern history; such portions of Locke's Essay on the Human Understanding as the president shall direct, Stewart's Elements of the Philosophy of the Human Mind . . . Virgil, Cicero, and Horace. . . ." [15]

We may be inclined to sympathize with Nott's young men and with the senior classes in other American colleges in the first decades of the Republic because of the bland fare they were offered. Outrage and denunciation, however, were soon heaped on Nott for what he had given his students. To the orthodox he was teaching dangerously in a country whose revolution seemed to be over, where the weapons which had won it, and the radical ideas which had justified it could now become a threat to the authority of churchmen and the moulders of constitutions.

John Locke, friend of Newton and as devout a Christian, had unleashed ideas which erring philosophers were twisting into philosophical conclusions as dangerous to look on, it was argued, as had been the pillar of salt. Locke, in his *Essay on Human Understanding*, developed a psychology which presented the processes of human thought as orderly, harmonious functions as much a part of the Universal Harmony as was the new physics of Newton. What a man knows, Locke reasoned, his store of ideas, depends wholly on what his five senses convey to his mind of the physical world about him. What the mind receives through experience by way of the senses becomes transformed by the understanding, the "inner sense," into his view of the world, into the complex of ideas he will have about every phase of existence, including his perception of God.[16]

Nott, by 1805, believed Newton and Locke had cleared away, by the reasonableness of their deductions, the distorted world-view of the traditional theologians, that picture of God's wonder-working which was without order or harmony, in which events followed unknowable sequences imposed upon them by a capricious deity. There was, by contrast, an awful beauty in the vast design of the heavens Newton offered Christians in his *Principia*, and there was the same wonderful evidence of divine and benevolent planning in the mechanism of the senses which Locke had described whereby all men were progressively discovering the wonders of earth and of the universe.

Nott's seniors and the educated, older members of the audience in the Dutch Church in Schenectady that May Day thirty years after the battles of Lexington and Concord knew, however, what fatal consequences had followed the undisciplined and unchristian extension of the new physics and the new psychology. They knew what impetus Newton and Locke had given to the spreading idea of Natural Rights, the essentially Christian idea that all men have certain "inalienable rights," as the Declaration of Independence had called them, which are antecedent to man-made laws. If Nott's students in 1805 had no first-hand knowledge of the events, the speech making and the pamphlets which led up to the American Revolution only thirty years passed, their fathers had: the natural-rights arguments had been thrown in the face of King and Parliament, developed in lawyers' briefs and taproom oratory. Men and their governments, it had been argued, must conform to the laws of God, to His universal laws of Nature which natural and moral philosophy were at last revealing. Life, liberty, and the pursuit of happiness were Natural Rights: if kings and governments interfered with these rights, men, in order to guard their divine inheritance, must find new rulers and devise new governments dedicated to preserving them.

Nott and his baccalaureate audience in 1805 knew, however, that what had emerged in America was not the harmonious nation. Between the winning of the Revolution and the establishment of the Constitution the dreadful dangers inherent in the doctrine of Natural Rights had become frighteningly apparent. New York had seen the wild mobs fanning out from its Liberty Poles. Tom Paine's *Common Sense* had framed the apologies for revolution in non-religious terms even farmers and mechanics could understand. Shay had led his debtors' rebellion in Massachusetts. The voteless, the poor, the landless, the malcontents had also read the mellifluous phrase, "life, liberty, and the pursuit of happiness" as a message from heaven directed to them.

"Consequences are disregarded," Nott exclaimed to his graduating seniors, "and (Man) madly pressing forward to the object of desire, exclaims, 'My honour, my property, my pleasure'; but is never heard to say, 'My religion, my duty, my salvation....' "

His students knew why the flood tide of the Age of Enlightenment had receded, why the marsh-light phrases of the Declaration of Independence had had to be translated into the monitorial language of a Constitution based on a less exalted view of human nature. Erring philosophy, so they were told, had perverted right reason. Godless men, Nott declared, had used the heaven-inspired insights of Newton and Locke to formulate appeals to the baser passions. Government was no instrument to be wielded by Liberty Pole mobs, by an undisciplined democracy. The principles of a Hamilton, so he had said in 1804, were written on the Constitution; should the nation itself fall, he had then proclaimed, "shaken by the violence of party . . . [Hamilton's] prophetic declarations will be found inscribed on its ruins." [17] The order and harmony of the universe which informed Christians were seeing in the new astronomy were an imposed cosmic discipline, the visible expression of God's Law. So, too, was order and harmony among men a divine discipline. Civil government was its visible expression, so Nott then believed, to be discovered by Christians through the same avenues of the senses which had revealed the wonders of sidereal motion and of gravitation. God, Eliphalet Nott taught and preached in 1805, offered "the great, the wise, and the good of all nations . . ." a developing knowledge of the constitution of the universe, of the laws of Nature which the great, the wise, and the good, and they only, could translate into constitutions for the harmonious ordering of men. Not the theologians, the new President of Union College was saying in effect, but the godly scientists, the educated men of right reason were the proper interpreters of the Natural Law, a dangerous conclusion to offer young men, he was soon to be told.

His theme that first Commencement had been limitless "Progress". Education was presented as a planned march on heaven for the human race. Union College students were to be trained to join the new Christian leaders, men of right reason who, as they grew in knowledge of the laws of Nature, would come to see ever more clearly the wonders of the ordered universe which an attainable salvation would guarantee to them forever. Nott's thirteen seniors were given their degrees that May day as though they were commissions in the service of God.

I V

For a few weeks only the new President of Union College was allowed "to enjoy the many commendations which had been bestowed" upon his first baccalaureate. On July 9, 1805, in the Albany *Centinel* a writer who signed himself "C" read Nott a public lecture on composition which would have embarrassed a schoolboy: "ornaments and flowers of speech incongruous with the subject or the occasion . . . a fondness for a florid style . . . allowed to youth in their first essays . . . his faults are dangerous." Nott's comments on a France in ruins had been, for "C," "rather a revery of a very poetic imagination than a description, however exaggerated, of real events." After citing more than a dozen examples of Nott's "ornaments and flowers," "C" noted that the new President's regard for the classic writers "will have a tendency to restore an amiable simplicity and elegance of style. I antici-pate," he continued, "when that ardent ambition and those benevolent and unremitting exertions which have already procured Mr. Nott a well earned fame, will render him an ornament to American literature. In the pulpit his bold, simple, unaffected eloquence has left him almost without a rival."

Sarcasm with "C" had become irony. In the pulpit, certainly, Eliphalet Nott was bold, but as to being "simple, unaffected," no, for Nott aimed at the emotions of his hearers. He knew, as had Jonathan Edwards, how to move an American audience of his time, even though he did those things which "C" pointed out "the writers of the English Augustan Age . . . considered highly unwarrantable."

"C" judged the new President of Union College according to an Augustan model. "It seems to me," he wrote,

> that the manner and topic of this address are extremely unlike those that have been ordinarily adopted on similar occasions . . . Presidents of colleges, in their valedictory addresses to the graduated students, have, in humble prose, with exhortations to embrace Christianity, given them plain directions with regard to the conduct of life, the acquisitions of knowledge, the improvement of virtue, and the means of usefulness.

Nott, however, was neither an Augustan nor an ordinary man, and, for him, the means to usefulness had changed with the times. Three days later he found a champion among the contributors to the Hudson (New York) *Balance*, possibly Harry Croswell, that stormy editor who had been so recently defended against charges of libel by Alexander Hamilton. "C's" criticism was the fruit of "viperous envy and malice". The very oddity of Nott's sentences, according to his defender, his very "singularities," have "established his fame above that of any snarling critic." Not only did the writer in the Hudson *Balance* approve Nott's reading of French history, but he told his public that Nott "as a moral philosopher and metaphysician . . . stands almost without . . . rival. . . . He is one of the first characters in our country."

V

Dugald Stewart's *Elements of the Philosophy of the Human Mind*, introduced to the Union College Catalogue as early as 1802, revealed at once the nature of the campaign to be waged against infidelity. The writings of the tough minded Scottish judge and his fellow Scottish Realists had come to Princeton with President John Witherspoon before the Revolution, an effective prescription for Americans exposed to the infections of eighteenth-century radicalism.

If reason, without God, these Scotchmen argued, could do away with matter and mind, with God's help it could demonstrate their reality, and the reality of the God-head of which they were a part. These philosophers of Common Sense had answered the deists and sceptics for Nott, as they had for Jonathan Maxcy, and John Blair Smith who preceded him as Presidents of Union, and for many others educated at or influenced by the College of New Jersey.

The dark lunacy of scepticism, with all its inherent dangers to the order of nations, faded, it seemed to these Scottish Realists, before the fact of human intuition. The logic of cause and effect, they said, cannot be denied; it is "backed by certain first principles, or dictates of common sense . . . [which are] the foundations of all reasoning. . . . without them to reason is a word without meaning . . . they can be no more proved than you can prove an axiom in mathematical science." [18]

The Scottish and American Realists offered their students a new system of thought posited on a real world, on minds designed to comprehend it and themselves, on an inner sense, or intuition, or conscience capable of moral perceptions and of distinguishing between good and evil. Thomas Reid and Dugald Stewart,

Presidents Witherspoon and Samuel Smith of Princeton, and their followers, were not men who would have been welcome in Calvin's Geneva, but in the America of 1805, a new nation sensing power in machines and factories and banks, their philosophy of Common Sense bestowed sanctions on the world as it was and offered a logic to justify using power where the men of "right reason" found it.

The terrible threat, they believed, was that deism and scepticism could be used not only to destroy the orderly state obedient to Natural Law, but to destroy religion itself, and so the logic on which men submitted to the discipline of government and moral law. If the extremes to which deists and sceptics carried the analysis of the mind were accepted by those who control policy, then mechanical principles and custom, not Natural Rights, must be acknowledged to be the basis of government. If, as the radical philosophers believed, "Truth" is a concept as meaningless as the idea of Natural Rights, then there are only relative relationships, a universe without constants in which there is no guaranteed sequence of cause and effect, a world in which "divinity" is an archaic synonym for "change."

If Nott had had a friend from childhood in the audience on the Commencement Days from 1805 through 1809, a critical friend who had followed his career from their student days in Franklin, Connecticut, one concerned about matters of consistency, such a friend might well have asked himself if Nott, who had traveled into New York State nine years earlier as an avowed Calvinist, had become, indeed, a man for whom expediency was the rule of conduct. What kind of Christian had he become? Was he, as some had charged, experimenting privately with ideas "worse than Paine"? Was he skirting infidelity? What really was his world-view? What were its compass points, where was its horizon, and what lay beyond it?

Nott, one suspects, was at this time a little like Captain Lemuel Gulliver, whose adventuring Jonathan Swift designed to show the relativity of all compass points, geographical, moral, and intellectual. Nott, like Gulliver when the last half of that poor mariner's enlightenment was still ahead of him, was, in these first years of his presidency, on the threshold of a multiple vision of the world. He still saw the world chiefly with the eyes of the heaven-seeking Christian American of his day, just as Captain Gulliver viewed Lilliput and Brobdingnag with the eyes of the early eighteenth-century Englishman. But, even as Gulliver, who slowly and painfully came to see England through the eyes of those who were not English, to recognize that England and things English were not the absolutes of civilization, so too, Nott, an "adventurer" as he described himself to his first Commencement audience, was discovering that the world as seen through the eyes of a country boy from Connecticut and the eyes of his Calvinist brother were only two views of a world which might be surveyed from an infinite number of vantage points, that Connecticut and Geneva were not the only guides to conduct, or the measures of "truth." Like Gulliver after his humbling experience in Brobdingnag at the hands of the king of the giants, a Gulliver whose profounder discoveries about England and about his fellowmen were still to be made, Nott, in the first decade of the Nineteenth Century was still midway in his own travels, publicly proselytizing for a view of life which he was privately beginning to question, whose compass points he had been taught to describe exactly, but which, as he examined them, changed before his eyes. In trying to harmonize the new physics and the new psychology with a traditional Christianity, Nott, as had other Christian liberals, had opened up disquieting views of the world and the universe which required a new vocabulary to describe.

Up to 1809 the new concepts were being guardedly reflected in his baccalaureates. His seniors had gone with him into the new worlds charted by Newton, Locke, Boyle, and other writers of the Age of Reason. But to those audiences whose view of the world had not been affected by the intellectual adventuring he and his seniors had shared he spoke in the pulpit language of the day. Only a severe critic would have been concerned about the differences in the words and images, in the several ways he spoke of deity, of heaven, and of salvation on these different occasions, but there were differences: the clear and certain compass points of the Calvinist's view had blurred. He had ceased some years earlier to be a Congregationalist. He was a Presbyterian only by association. As the President of Union College and a clergyman he must talk from the pulpit in the language of the absolutes and axioms Christian Americans expected of him. Like Captain

Gulliver, however, he had become aware of certain things he would not and dared not discuss with those who had not "adventured" with him. "Truth" was becoming variable.

CHAPTER 3

"The Purposes of Minerva and of God"

IF Nott, seeking God, had trouble holding his course for Zion during these years, Nott, "the intellectual adventurer," discovered new assurances that his route was the right one in his observations as a natural philosopher.

The new President of Union College and James Fenimore Cooper each recorded the events of June 16, 1806, a day their generation never forgot. All across a wide belt on either side of the forty-second degree of latitude Americans had been arranging themselves and their affairs according to their understanding of the significance of the awful event they were told was to take place.

Cooper's "Leatherstocking Tales" were then far in the future, but their author, seventeen years old that year, was already an able reporter, capable of noting what he was to call God's "lesson of humility to man" as he and the Cooper family and their neighbors saw it written across the Otsego hills and on the face of Cooper's beloved Glimmerglas.[1]

Farther east, in Schenectady, Eliphalet Nott, too, had been making ready to record the Great Eclipse, an event he called "one of the most sublime and awful spectacles this age has witnessed." He had returned to the college the end of May in order to be ready for the event, "the most *charming* man in the world, he approaches the nearest perfection of any being I ever knew" according to a young lady passenger on the New York-Albany sloop which had brought him up the Hudson.[2] The Union College telescope had unfortunately been set up in the wrong place, so the observers missed the exact moment when the penumbra swept by them, the awful shadow rushing west across the land.

The day, however, was perfect for the event, windless and hot and not a cloud in the sky. The Coopers had had the forethought to provide themselves with pieces of smoked glass so they could watch the moon's inexorable slow curtaining of the sun. Many of the farm women and children, clustered in ever quieter groups along the road below Judge Cooper's big house were too frightened to use the sooty panes. Before the penumbra reached them there was talk that here, now, this next moment was the beginning of the Last Judgment, or of the Millennium, or world's end.

Young Fenimore Cooper remembered clearly what followed as the appalling eclipse swept in from the east and deepened into darkness at noon. Cheer and good will seemed to go out of the morning; the light on the hills and the lake became ever more lurid. As he watched and the shadows spread talk became whispers, and then stopped. Lark song and robin chatter stopped as the birds nested. One could sense fear rise as the unearthly light turned a familiar landscape into a strange country. Cows came in from their pastures.

At 11:12, at Otsego, the Eclipse was total. Stars filled a night sky. Dew fell. A bat flew among the unheeding women. A whippoorwill sang its night song.

And then the antistrophe: the awful event slowly reversed itself as the moon moved west. "Humiliation and awe," Cooper noted, "affected everyone." Remembering the day and recalling it in Paris many years later, he distilled the meaning the vast spectacle had for his generation when he said it had indeed been "designed by the Creator to reveal his Omnipotence to our race."[3]

Eliphalet Nott, who might well have been expected to make such a statement, spoke only of the "solemnities of the scene." His interest, as he precisely noted the stages of the eclipse, was of the order of a Newton's and his record of the event ended in no theologian's moral deductions. It was rather the vivid record of a man pledged to see and hear with all his being this cosmic witness of God-in-Nature. He saw the Great Eclipse far more exactly than did the excited young boy who watched the sun die above the Glimmerglas.

Nott, busy helping to find a better location for the college telescope, was disappointed when he could not set down the exact moment the leading edge of the penumbra reached Schenectady, but the hour, the minute, and the second of the beginning and the end of "the total obscuration" were noted minutely: At 11:7:30 A.M. the sun vanished. Four and a half minutes later its light broke out again along the near edge of the west moving moon. For the viewers in Cooperstown that was the mid-point, according to young Cooper, of total darkness.

At the instant the last direct ray was intercepted [Nott wrote] and the obscuration became total, a tremulous, undulating shadow, a kind of indescribable alternate prevalence and intermixture of light and shade struck the earth and played on its surface which gave to the most stable objects the semblance of agitation. It appeared as if the moon rode unsteadily in her orbit and the earth seemed to tremble on its axis. The deception was so complete that I felt instinctively, in spite of the dictates of my reason to the contrary, a tottering emotion. Some who were present I observed catching hold of whatever was near them for support whilst others suddenly leaned forward and insensibly flung themselves into an attitude which indicated that they found it difficult to stand. It was indeed an awful moment . . . every voice was hushed in silence and every mind was absorbed in the grandeur of the scene.

At the commencement of this singular phenomenon and while the surface of the earth appeared to be violently agitated the light and shade were irregularly intermixed and each seemed struggling for victory. In about five seconds the darkness prevailed. The light and shade suddenly separated into alternate and distinct arches. Instantly the arches of shade began to force the arches of light toward the horizon. The motion was at first very rapid . . . the alternate arches were narrow and followed each other in close succession: the motion gradually diminished, the streaks of light became less and less distinct for about fifteen seconds when, melting into each other, the appearance ceased, and a settled gloom ensued. The air became sensibly damp and cool, the swallows descended to the earth, the night birds began their flight and the pale stars looked forth thro' the yellow and sickly shades. It appeared as if the sun in the midst of his noontide splendors had been suddenly extinguished and was to be rekindled no more. Many of the inhabitants here were seized with horror, some broke forth in supplications, some fainted and some were flung into convulsions.[4]

Nott's record of the Great Eclipse, unlike young Cooper's, is primarily a scientist's record of physical phenomena carefully noted and timed, seen vividly; here were no oratorical tricks, few sonorities, or pulpit devices. Yet Nott's dramatist's imagination shown through; here also was the image maker at work who could stage the Christian cycle in terms so exciting his audience at times "scarcely breathed." Nott, no longer believing in a deity who capriciously altered the motions of planets and stars in order to frighten men into virtue and submission, saw the Great Eclipse as a triumphant assertion of his own growing conviction that Natural Law as men were coming to know it was one with universal law, that what he saw through the college telescope was neither "portentous" nor a spectacle to fill men with horror. "But what are all these phenomena," he concluded, as his mind swung through the great arc which spans reason and faith, "that now interest and astonish us compared with the closing scene, the final catastrophe of nature . . . when the sun shall be darkened and the moon turned to blood, and the stars of heaven fall as a fig tree casteth its untimely figs when it is shaken by a mighty wind?" Reason, and acceptance of the divine "reasonableness" of Revelation, seemingly so irreconcilable, here alternated in Nott's mind as easily and naturally as do the right and left positions of a swinging pendulum; it swings, and as it swings, the clock records that special time for which the pendulum is adjusted. What Nott had learned to read through the eyepiece of the Union College telescope and what he still read in Christian revelation seemed to him naturally encompassed within the arc of the divine pendulum, swinging between earth and heaven.

The new President of Union College, as a natural philosopher in 1806, had even less comfort to offer mankind than does the nuclear physicist of the mid-Twentieth Century.

"The sun," the President of Union College had told the General Assembly of the Presbyterian Church, meeting in Philadelphia a month before the Great Eclipse took place, "is burning out its splendours . . . subterranean fires are consuming the bowels of the earth . . . the planets are known by an examination of ancient eclipses, to be converging. . . . the present system," he informed his audience, "contains principles of decay."[5]

But then, neither the speaker nor his hearers had been confused, as are twentieth-century men, about their objective or their fate among these converging planets, on a world burning out in its own fires. For them, and for all Christians, as Nott then proclaimed, there "was certainty and perpetuity in the Kingdom of God." This had been his text. Christians had only to discover their roles in this awful drama to insure passport to a kingdom beyond the final catastrophe.

II

Much of what Nott saw from his Christian philosopher's mountain had to remain a private vision. To translate all that he could of what he continued to see from there of earth and heaven onto a comprehensible grid of latitudes and longitudes, however, was the work he now set for himself as a teacher. His skill in translating his widening vision for the following fifteen generations of college students was to make him, perhaps, the greatest single force in American higher education before the Civil War.

As an educator, however, the new President of Union College did not begin with a rush of classroom innovations. During his first two years in Schenectady he had had to fight for the very life of the college itself. He had first to deal as a general on maneuvers with an often hostile state legislature until he had persuaded compromising politicians to give him his "literature lottery" and with it the state's first practicable Common School program. His first year he had had to deal as a politician with his Board of Trustees until he had cajoled them into trading their corporate independence to the State in return for what at the time seemed adequate working funds. The result, however, was that "Stone College" was paid for; his professorships were endowed by the legislature's lottery grant; there were to be funds set aside for needy students, and for the appointment of new tutors to take care of a student body which strained the resources of the new building two years after it was opened.

Few of those autocrats of higher education who were the presidents of American colleges after 1800 and before the Civil War were classroom innovators. Education for doers, for citizens prepared to exploit the moment and the land, had been offered to but rejected by those New Yorkers who, in 1754, established King's College.[6] The pragmatic spirit with which that thorny Episcopal priest, the Reverend William Smith, had infused his idealized "Plan for a College in Mirania," had as yet little appeal for trustees, faculties, and students for whom Greek and Latin, and the classic authors still meant, in substance, "gentlemen." The College of Philadelphia, with Smith as its provost, at first borrowed much from his Miranian curriculum, but those practical subjects, useful to merchants, seamen, and builders of states were not yet looked upon as scholar's fare.

"Useful education," which was of so much concern to the framers of the state constitutions, was to remain largely the work of the common schools and academies until well into the new century. Eliphalet Nott, as the "principal tutor" of the Plainfield Academy in Connecticut, had, as early as 1794, offered parallel courses: one for young gentlemen going on to college, and a terminal course in the "Arts and Sciences," designed to prepare non-collegians "for the burden and the heat of the day."[7]

For a few decades only, following the Revolution, the guardians of the classic tradition listened to the enthusiasms of the philosophers of the Enlightenment, of those who believed education was a forge on which men were to be reshaped into the reasoning creatures a harmonious Nature intended them to be. Thomas Jefferson, while still a Virginia legislator, had proposed a scheme designed to educate young Virginians according to their natural abilities, raking, as he put it, "from the rubbish" the aristocrats of Nature and sending them through William and Mary College at state expense. "If humanity is susceptible of a certain degree of perfection, it is by means of education that it can reach it," La Chalotais had assured France in 1763, and the idea, once seeded, took many forms.[8] In America not only Jefferson but other idealists watered this democratic seed which had rooted and spread in Europe following the Eighteenth Century's two liberating revolutions. Many plans were proposed in America for publicly supported schools and colleges which should train citizens for that man-made Millennium, the New Age of Democracy.[9]

The flush of these dreams of men made wise and virtuous through education, however, rises into lurid contrast against the pale achievement. Human nature had not been changed by revolutions. Many conservative Americans, churchmen and men of property who had won their political and economic freedom from the threat of British control, still subscribed to the traditions which assured their status. The colleges of the new United States were run for the education of their sons. "Democrat" for these conservators became increasingly a lower case word, a label for the cheap money man, the debtor, the man without property. "Democrats" became, for them, the city rabble and the main-chance mob along the frontier.

Eliphalet Nott, during his first ten years as President of Union College, learned not only to recognize the new conservatism, but also the desirability of publicly damning those philosophers whose ideas threatened the status of the patrons of the colleges. He also acknowledged their status during this decade by giving his patrons ostensibly the sort of curriculum they still thought necessary to produce gentlemen and scholars.

John Seaman, for instance, might well have sent his ward, the stage-struck young John Howard Payne, to another college in 1806 if he had been shown the tainted, liberal curriculum offered in the Union College catalogue of 1796. Four years of French could then have been taken in place of Greek. The history of the French Revolution was taught. In the junior year students might elect Bossuet's *Universal History*, and in the senior year, Buffon's *Natural History*, both to be read in French. Other American colleges had dallied with French as a gentleman's accomplishment, but only Union had dared to carry the language of this unstable nation through four years of study. [10] Those "laws of Minerva" which the charter Trustees had advertised on their corporate seal, along with the classic head of the patroness of wisdom proclaimed a brotherhood of the enlightened, and an ideal of education which, by 1806, had gone out of favor with American conservatives. Seaman wrote to Nott in that year that he had selected Union College rather than Princeton because he believed it would be a safer haven for his giddy ward, far "from the devastating effects of democracy." [11]

Eliphalet Nott dropped all teaching of the language of his corporate seal in 1809, however, and accounted for the omission because "of a lack of patronage." The new times had indeed left those unidentified and adventurous curriculum makers of 1795-1796 back among the framers of the American Revolution. The propertied inheritors of that Revolution were looking for a safer, more conservative America and for an education which posed no serious challenge to their values.

The year following young Payne's admission to Union, Nott issued a new catalogue; French as a substitute for Greek was now eliminated and could be taken only after special arrangement with the President. Four courses in the classics were added to those listed in the catalogue for 1802, and then, in the tradition of curriculum makers, Nott assigned to the senior year those two new courses he found to his own liking: "Homer," and "Eminent Authors in the Learned Languages."

In the catalogue for the first time appeared "Kames," by name, or "Kaims," as it was listed, that senior course which Nott would slowly turn into a probe of the heart, the mind, and the universe. "Kames" through five decades, was to convince the thousands of seniors who were to take it and remember it, and live by it, that Eliphalet Nott was the supreme moralist, the most astute of political scientists, and a philosopher without equal. By the 1830s Kames' *Elements of Criticism* was to become only a shadow of a text book; the text would then be Nott himself.

If the conservative leaders of America at the beginning of the new century were garbling or turning away from the vocabulary of their own revolution and were allowing themselves to be frightened by the democratic idealism which had flamed out of hand in France, they were also finding exciting substitutes in a new language and in the startling and enthralling ideas it expressed. The physical sciences, not the philosophies of deists and atheists, were framed by a language Christian Americans could pronounce and pointed toward objects they could perceive. By 1800, they had a vocabulary of science which even gentlemen scholars in the colleges were anxious to study.

Nott's observations of the Great Eclipse and his new curriculum of 1807 reflect his own mounting enthusiasm for the sciences. One suspects that he was beginning to sense here a language through which he could reach the new generation far more effectively than he had been reaching them through the language of the theologians. His earlier "adventuring," his growing belief that Christians were charged with more to do than to wait prayerfully for their predestined careers to evolve, manifested itself in 1807 in the catalogue announcement that Union College was giving new emphasis to the subjects of mathematics and astronomy and that it had added a new study to the curriculum called "chymistry," a required course for all seniors.

The practical man might learn only so much of this new language as to become a better husbandman, or a useful physician, but beyond him were the men of Christian wisdom who, like Timothy Dwight, saw the retorts and the chemist's furnace as one sort of apparatus for the study of the Creation, or Nott himself, who was now convinced that one could read messages from heaven through his college telescope.

Algebra, trigonometry, and mensuration, which included navigation and surveying, sophomore subjects before 1807, were now made the chief fare of the junior year. Astronomy was moved up from the junior to the senior year, a time during which the seniors undoubtedly heard thrilling accounts of Nott's own observations.

Chemistry, however, for the seniors, was the important innovation. As a subject separate from Natural Philosophy and Natural History it had been taught for some years as an adjunct to the courses in medicine at Columbia and at least six other American colleges. [12] Columbia, in 1793, listed on its undergraduate faculty a "Professor of Chemistry and Agriculture," but it was the devout Timothy Dwight at Yale who, by 1802, set his seniors to studying the new course listed as "Chymistry," under his young disciple, Benjamin Silliman, for basically Christian reasons. Professor Meggs, who had long taught the course in Natural History at Yale was well qualified to expand the chemistry he had been teaching as a part of his course, but his strong sympathy for the French Revolution satisfied Timothy Dwight that he was not the man for the new assignment. [13]

Chemistry, according to Dwight and young Silliman, offered only associations that were "elevated and virtuous, pointing toward the infinite Creator." Science now offered the colleges under its new course headings a combination of motives for curriculum revision.

Nott made no pretense about copying President Dwight. In 1809, he, too, found a young and eager disciple to develop the new study in Thomas C. Brownell, who had graduated from Union in 1802, and who was to become the Episcopal Bishop of Connecticut. Young Brownell was made Union College's first professor of Chemistry and Mineralogy and was immediately sent to Europe to study his subject and to gather apparatus. "Professor Silliman," Brownell wrote in his journal, "had returned from

Europe with an imposing chemical apparatus. A fine cabinet of minerals had been procured . . . and these acquisitions had given to Yale College an imposing position which could not fail to stimulate the exertions of kindred institutions. . . ." [14]

Nott, at the time of the curriculum revision of 1807, was reacting to cross currents from many quarters; the competition of Yale College was exciting and worth meeting; his opportunities "for usefulness to the church" were multiplying in this new college, and in his role of natural philosopher he was reading what he believed were divine revelations in the language of those sciences which described the natural world around him.

It was to take two decades, however, for him to achieve a working synthesis of the new educational programs on which was to rest his great reputation as a college president. By 1830 he would find a rationale for uniting the ideal of education by way of the classics, of a pragmatic education for Americans who must be "made ready for the burden and the heat of the day," and of education for a Christian democracy through a knowledge of the Laws of Nature.

Until then he, too, learned to conform, though the evidence is strong that conformity was often a public exercise. Nott himself was being conditioned by events which were to shape not only gentlemen, or workaday citizens, or democrats, but that new American of the Nineteenth Century who might be all three of them.

If there seemed to be growing inconsistencies in what Nott said, or hypocrisy, these things lay, often, in the difficulty of finding the word and the image to move exploiting Americans at the turn of the Nineteenth Century. How does one describe or prepare men for a world which seems to change as one looks at it, a world in which an eclipse points out God's wrath to millions, and the order of God's universe to thousands, a world which was one thing to Christian scribes and another thing to the universe-embracing mind of a Newton, a world which was both reality and illusion? Nott, struggling to comprehend the many faces of nature, interpreted and misinterpreted; he used the language of theology and science according to his training and his awareness of his own limitations and the limitations of his hearers. If he was devious, if he compromised, if he was sometimes almost childishly literal, sometimes the philosopher, and at other times the orator, using a symbolism subject only to the range of the minds of his hearers and readers, these various ways of speaking seemed to him justified because he believed they all served to move lost men toward their lost brotherhood; they all served the purposes of Minerva and of the God he could call the Father, or the Unknowable, or the Everlasting.

CHAPTER 4

"The Illumination of the 13th of May."

IF a prospective second wife for the ambitious President of Union College had heard young John Howard Payne's report she might well have had doubts about committing herself to life in a place which Nott's new and arrogant student wrote was "railed at . . . for the excessive rigidity of its governors," a place "erected in one of the most unpleasant swamps in the United States."[1]

It was a softened and amenable John Howard Payne, however, the "chum" of Dr. Nott as he was soon calling himself, who first reported on those summer carriage jaunts to Troy which he shared with his new idol, and which resulted in Eliphalet Nott's second marriage, on the 3rd of August, 1807, to Gertrude Peebles Tibbits, the wealthy widow of Benjamin Tibbits, late Troy merchant in "grains, dry goods, and whale oil."[2]

In spite of young Payne's jaundiced report, the frail Mrs. Tibbits had good reason to look forward to becoming Mrs. Nott. She would have position; she would again have a home for her own son, Benjamin Tibbits Jr., who, ten years later would be graduated by the college, and she would be making a home for her new husband's children, Joel, John, Benjamin, and Maria. To what degree her considerable fortune was a factor in the marriage is beyond knowing; there is no doubt, however, that Union College has reason to remember the second Mrs. Nott with kindness, for it was undoubtedly her securities which now made it possible for her husband to acquire the great tract of land on which he was soon to raise the first buildings of a new, almost imperial campus. And there would be at least one occasion when her fortune would stand between her husband, Union College, and financial ruin for them all. Nott, years later, rummaging among his old man's memories, liked to say that he had married Gertrude Tibbits because he wanted someone to tell him "how to spell words." One hopes he laughed away his nonsense when he said it, for the widow from Troy freed him from the restraints of his modest salary, and made possible a free-wheeling career on a scale to please the "adventurer" in any man.

Sarah Maria Nott, who, at the time of her father's second marriage, was eight years old, became a problem for some months. She wanted nothing more than to go back to "Mamma Tillotson's care" and insisted that Mrs. Tillotson, Chancellor Livingston's daughter, couldn't do without her at Rhinebeck. During the summer of 1807 she had been with her father in Schenectady, attending Mr. Cuyler's grammar school, and listening, with growing apprehension, as her father wrote to Mrs. Tillotson, to "tales of another mamma, and another residence," until she was beside herself with fear.[3]

The little girl's summer of terrors may have been the beginning of that very special intimacy which was to grow through the years between father and daughter. Eliphalet Nott, unable to keep his promise to return Sarah Maria to Rhinebeck, seeing in her perhaps the fey Maria Benedict of the lost Connecticut days, made every effort to draw her into the new life in Schenectady, "to help her over her present pain," as he wrote to Mrs. Tillotson. The important thing was that father and sons and daughter were a family again. The threads that go into the pattern of a life are so cross-woven we can trace only the darkest and the brightest ones back to their skeins. Nott's love for Maria is one such bright thread. From the days of her frightened return from Rhinebeck to the new life her father and the new mother made for her and the three brothers and step-brother in the President's rooms of Stone College, on through the years of her married life to tutor Alonzo Potter of Union College, the man who was to become her father's counter-balance in the whirling years ahead, Sarah Maria seems more and more the brightest thread in the web of her father's life. For the man who wrote, "I love life, I sigh for immortality; I love my friends, my kindred, my species,"[4] this daughter, "plainly dressed, but always a belle," seems to have provided the effervescence and the gaiety he needed.

I I

Unhappily for both Nott and his new wife the order and peace of a reborn family life ended at the door to the President's apartment in Stone College. Beyond it was another kind of expanding family, 105 collegians at Commencement time in July, 1808, and the grammar school boys. Since the new building had been opened the juniors had roomed on the first floor, the seniors on the second floor, sophomores and freshmen on the third, and more freshmen on the fourth floor. North, about one hundred yards up College Street the overflow of boarders, collegians, and grammar school boys crowded the twenty rooms of the "Long College," a low, two-story brick building put up soon after Stone College was opened.[5]

At first privately, then publicly, trouble was acknowledged to be spreading through this academic family. Something had gone wrong with that model plan for college education of which the new President had boasted to his brother a few years earlier: "all our students, even as those in the Moravian schools . . . to be entirely separated from the great world: . . . the President to lodge in college: the President and the faculty and their families to take their meals in Commons . . . no disorders to be allowed; every minute of every day supervised. Strangers," the trusting younger brother had reported, "leave us astonished at the order, punctuality, and diligence which prevail."

Within months, however, after his arrival in Schenectady this Moravian pattern designed to achieve "complete security to the manner and morals of youth" began to fall apart. For the next three years, from that eventful drinking party in Freshman Hill's room to the nearly riotous student revolt over the "Illumination" of the 13th of May, 1809, Union College was increasingly a camp divided, its four-man faculty ranged in nervous postures of defense on one side, on the other a student body which picked champions, prepared petitions, and indulged in the heady joys of rebellion. Between both camps stood an increasingly embarrassed young President, too busy in these early years in refounding his own family, defending himself from charges of radicalism, and fighting for his college endowment and Common School Bills in the New

York State Legislature to see clearly the causes for the collapse of that "decorum, ceremony, and politeness" which he had been assuring the State's Assemblymen and Senators had made Union College unique.

John Howard Payne, that too-sophisticated child and "chum" of President Nott as he had styled himself soon after arriving in Schenectady, could have told him where the core of the trouble lay: "this college," Payne had written to his father in June, 1806, from Albany, "is universally railed at here for the excessive and unexampled rigidity of its governors."

Human nature, especially the nature of boys, does not lend itself naturally to decorum, or ceremony, or politeness. A senior over eighteen was then an oddity. Anthony VanBergen, age seven, by virtue of an "honorable dismissal from Williams College" had become a Union College sophomore in February, 1806. There were VanRensselaers and Livingstons and Tillotsons at the upper end of the social scale, and below them the sons of farmers from Washington County, the "hayseed" county at the turn of the century, and boys from the democratic towns of the Military Grants, and towns whose Indian names were good for the quick laugh over hot rum: Shawangunk, Caughnawaga, and Canandaigua. And there were the first contingents of the place-proud Southerners who later were to crowd the rolls, and New Englanders who could say things to put heat into Dutch tempers.

To this unstable brew of undergraduates, one must add the children of the grammar school who shared Stone College and its "subterranean portico" where faculty and students ate. The Union College "Laws of 1802" were never equal to the forces seething in this boy-man world, the horizons of which included the towering peaks of classical thought, candle-hour views of heaven and hell from the pulpit of the college chapel, the turmoil of class rivalries, and of the all absorbing Adelphic and Philomathean Literary Societies' elections, a world whose "governors," as Payne called them, must rule like armed priests to defend the pieties of their essentially theological scheme of education. Nott soon had good reason to regret embracing Jonathan Maxcy's fear-inspired plan for controlling undergraduates, one born of his predecessor's unhappy experiences at Rhode Island College.[6]

During the new President's long absences, the chief abbott of this overcrowded cloister was Benjamin Allen, Professor of Mathematics and Natural Philosophy, graduate of Rhode Island College, lately preceptor of the Plainfield Academy, husband of Mary Benedict, Nott's sister-in-law, and, if young Payne is to be believed, "the most learned man in college." A jealous man, jealous of his seniority and of his perogatives, he believed that order could only be the product of fines, public admonishments, and star chamber trials. He had come to Union in 1800 as the protégé of then Trustee Nott and President Maxcy, and had taken his stand quickly enough as a switch-and-rule harrier of the young; not for him were those "avenues to the heart" down which his predecessor, gentle Professor John Taylor, had traveled until his death the year after Allen arrived.

It was a mean little comedy, sometimes cruel, often ridiculous, which was played out behind Nott's back between 1806 and 1809. It was to end in the bitterness of a Trustees' investigation and trial, a faculty divided, student dismissals, and Professor Benjamin Allen's resignation.

The events which trigger revolutions are sometimes no more complex than was that forgotten toddy party held, probably on the top floor of Stone College in the early winter of 1806. The valley of the Mohawk is too often a great siphon, sucking polar days out of Canada. Heat to reach the marrow must have been impossible to generate in the iron chunk stoves of dormitory rooms. There are other sources for heat, however. Seth Baldwin, freshman, admitted bringing the toddy up to his classmate's room, but pointed out in the star chamber trial which Professor Allen set up to look into this challenge to authority that he did it only to bring warmth and comfort to his fellow students who "were unwell."[7]

Professors Allen, Macauley, and Brownell, and possibly several nonresident tutors, sat in their academic robes, took evidence, deliberated, and acted. The sketchy record of that trial indicates only that John Tillotson, a freshman probationer, was caught at Hill's medicinal toddy party, and whipped. If Allen thought he had extinguished the fires of student rebellion, he had picked the wrong boy. John Tillotson, grandson of Chancellor Robert R. Livingston and son of that "Mama Tillotson" with whom Eliphalet Nott's daughter, Sarah Maria, was then still living, was sent home to Rhinebeck. Poor Professor Macauley, who had been delegated to do the whipping, later reported he had had to face the boy's father, William R. Tillotson, the ex-Secretary of State of New York, himself still smarting from a political whipping received in that year at the hands of DeWitt Clinton.

The gossips were now well aware that all was not as it should be in this dangerously compounded community of boys and men. Embarrassed as the new President must have been, however, over the Tillotson case he seems to have taken no action to modify either the college laws or the proceedings of Professor Allen's high courts. Professor Henry Davis who was appointed in 1807 to teach the classics, recalled that in that year the President "apparently took great pains to consult Mr. Allen on every subject. . . ."[8]

Eliphalet Nott was then afloat on his own sea of troubles. Not only were such critics as Dr. John Mason of New York City, damning him for harboring ideas dangerous to the well-being of his students, but his success in getting money from the State by way of a state-run lottery had entailed joining eleven of the highest state officers and his no-longer self-perpetuating Trustees into a new Board which would work in harmony. His dream of a nonpareil Union College was beginning to take shape, though he had had little time to oversee the parochial affairs of the day-to-day Union College so dear to Professor Allen. If he had paid heed to the petition of his students in 1806, however, "against Benj. Allen, teacher," the disasters of the next two years which were to destroy Star Chamber Rule at Union might not have taken place.

Looking back over a century and a half of college history the "Sausage Plot" of 1807 seems all low comedy. If Professor Benjamin Allen had had good sense he would not have made villains of Ebenezer Bogue of the junior class, and freshman Phillip Livingston. It was again Professor Macauley who had the misfortune to look out of his study window just as the boys were attempting to lift a string of sausage up through the steward's window. Something happened; the pole slipped out of the fisherman's hands, and sausage, pole, and boys vanished. But the "Laws" had been challenged, and governors must govern, and the ponderous machinery which ground out dismissals and embarrassment began to turn once more. The investigation which followed makes one wonder if the steward, too, should not have been included, and charged with starving his boarders. The sausage fishing expedition Macauley witnessed had been one of many. The catch from earlier and more successful raids had been stored in dormitory trunks, and then, in response to some special Stone College economy, sausage had moved to customers "under the greatcoats" of the purveyors.[9]

Professor Allen's faculty court again sat and heard evidence, which included unnamed threats by Bogue against Professor Davis. Phillip Livingston, still a freshman probationer, was dismissed and Ebenezer Bogue expelled. It was a year and a day since the Tillotson trial and now a second grandson of Chancellor Livingston was discovering the unparental nature of the Union College system.

The Trustees the following July reviewed the case as the college charter required, and upheld the faculty's decision, but the Livingstons could not have been awed; sometime between that July and the following April Phillip returned to college to represent the Hudson River aristocracy again in an even more formidable assault on the "Parental System."

If Eliphalet Nott and his senior professor pondered the implications of toddy parties, sausage plots, and affronts to the dignity and authority of faculty members, their conclusions were capsuled in Eliphalet Nott's letter to President Samuel Smith of Princeton, written in March, 1807, on the occasion of the Princeton riots which almost closed the New Jersey college. Nott, in requesting a "catalogue" of those dismissed, congratulated harried President Smith for expelling the rioters and assured him that his firmness had saved other colleges from similar disorders. Smith's strong measures, Nott told him, "may check among your youth the leveling spirit of the times."[10]

Stiff-necked Professor Benjamin Allen seems never to have gone beyond that conclusion, to see through it to a less pat, deeper, and more sympathetic understanding of boys and of those "times" which no two generations ever see with the same eyes. That Nott could rediscover what he had known about boys as a Connecticut schoolmaster was one measure of the man, although it was to take another year and a half of sometimes almost riotous conditions at Union to clear his thinking.

These Union College boys protested, boy-fashion, against an outmoded system of government with petitions against their sheriffs which the Trustees refused to notice, with what Benjamin Allen stiffly called "desertions from the institution". They protested by illegally attending "parties of pleasure," "places of amusement," and what to a man of Professor Allen's stamp must have seemed evidence of leveling at its worst, by "mixing with the rabble on the fourth of July . . . and on parade days."[11]

Nott's awareness of the nature of the low comedy war being waged between his faculty and his students began with the Ebenezer Griffin affair in the spring of 1808. The "Laws" were clear on the matter of firearms. April, however, was in the blood and the guns were fired, and Griffin, of the junior class, caught in the act, was defiant. Professor Allen's court met again and rusticated Griffin to the Hamilton and Oneida Academy for five months, and a less defiant accomplice to the same limbo for three months. "No student to attend any ball, or to go to any place of amusement," read Benjamin Allen's notice to parents which was now attached to their term bills, "or even to go out of the College yard in the evening." He referred to students as "children," and to the Tom, Dick, and Harry of Schenectady as the "rabble."

On the 22nd of July Eliphalet Nott and Professor Allen constituted themselves a committee to draw up new, stricter by-laws to govern the college. Five days later the trustees met and passed a revision of the "Laws of 1802" which sanctioned the academic program introduced the preceding year and finally clarified, or so the Trustees, the now irritated President, and his faculty believed, the ways and means of discipline.

Instead of less of that rigidity about which John Howard Payne had complained, there was now more of it. In addition to those probations Allen had listed in his term bill notice, attendance at billiard rooms, horse races, "and the amusements of the fourth of July, parade days, and holy days" were specifically included among the new "don'ts"; there was to be no assembling of the classes at "public houses" following examinations. What to the students was to become more and more galling was the provision that an officer of the college was to visit each student's room "at least once each day and once in the evening." College officers, in 1802, were empowered to visit student rooms, but now they were commanded to do it. The fines officers might levy were raised from seventy-five cents to one dollar, and, in order to make the policing more palatable faculty members were promised that they would be given credit in the amount of the fines they levied "toward the education of their sons in the institution." Students now must not only know these new laws, but they must sign a book swearing to keep them.

If Allen's hand can be seen in these prison rules, particularly the last two, Nott's can be detected in one significant addition to them: college officers were now ordered "to report to the President daily in writing every transgression of the laws." He was fully aware at last that the "Parental System" as Jonathan Maxcy had envisioned it, was on trial, and that he could no longer stand aside leaving its operation to one who saw college life in terms of "children," and yet applied courtroom discipline to them, a man whose sense of superiority rolled the word "rabble" in his mouth.

On the night of the 13th of May, 1809, Edward Huntington of the junior class, responding either to spring or to his private demons, filled the windows of his room with lighted candles. Henry Bogart, his classmate, a New Orleans boy, perhaps remembering Mardi Gras, was delighted to copy him, and the "Great Illumination" was under way. Soon the windows across the face of Stone College blossomed with candle fire. Such a beautiful sight required viewers, who in a matter of minutes were crowding the yard in front of the building.

Professor Macauley, already out of student favor for his part in the Sausage Plot of 1807, perhaps the only faculty member in the building at the time and no doubt terrified that Stone College itself might soon become the chief illumination of these rites of spring, hurried from room to room, ordering the celebrants to put out their candles.

One by one the windows went blind. To the excited viewers milling on the "mound" in front of Stone College this must have seemed like the desecration of ritual fires. If Macauley's timing had been a little different, perhaps ten minutes one way or the other, there might have been no trouble; then viewers would have been boys and his the voice of authority. Instead, they became a mob, and stones were thrown at the windows of Macauley's study. Inside, in Huntington's room, the "Parental System" was falling into ruin. Huntington refused to extinguish his candles, and, in the manner of a barrack's room lawyer, argued that there was no "law" which required him to do so. One must imagine the exchange between the boy and his professor; the record only suggests that Macauley had to blow out the flames himself.

Spring, youth infected with the leveling spirit of the times, the rigidity of governors, these abstractions, caught up in the flame of dozens of candles, became a light strong enough at last to awaken Nott and a myopic Board of Trustees. By it Nott was forced at last to see the weaknesses of this "Parental System," that *reductio ad absurdum* of President Maxcy's eighteenth-century dream of decorum and civility.

In the past, trial by faculty had ended the matter: dismissal, suspension, rustication, public admonishment were routinely reported to the Trustees at their annual meeting where they were noted without comment. The Illumination of the 13th of May, however, and the train of events stretching back as far as that sad, cold weather toddy drinking party in probationer Hill's room three years earlier had produced penalties which so inflamed the students that a strong petition from them now confronted the Trustees at their July meeting.

There must be some measure of men in the assignment of their hours; a Board of Trustees which will meet at six in the morning is either excessively earnest, or seriously worried; in this instance one suspects both earnestness and concern hurried them to College Hall soon after sunup. Judge Palmer, surrogate of Saratoga County, was the only absentee. Archibald McIntyre, the State Comptroller, was there, to many of the older Board members a new and unwelcome symbol of the technical fact of the state's majority voice in all Union College decisions, and Eliphalet Nott was there, himself a symbol that morning of the world's troubles: his student body was in revolt, his faculty seething with resentments, his senior professor who was also his late wife's brother-in-law, openly questioning his authority, and, within hours, a Commencement address to deliver which had been designed to stop those who were criticizing him as a dangerous teacher, a radical "worse than Paine."

Sighs of relief, audible and inaudible, must have escaped Trustees, faculty and students at the end of Commencement week-end, 1809. The Illumination of the 13th of May had not turned into a Princeton riot, but it might have. The college, at least, had held together; face had been saved, and the Trustees' newly appointed Committee of Six had the summer to delve.

By the 19th of September the committee's report was ready: "after laborious investigation . . . it appears . . . the principal causes of the existing difficulties are want of unanimity and cooperation in the instruction and government of college in the members of the faculty, causes which have greatly impeded the progress of the institution and threaten it with incalculable injury . . . the subject is of such a delicate and important nature [your committee] deem the united exertions of the Board necessary for a full investigation, and would suggest the propriety of citing all members of the Faculty to appear before them. . . ."

A toddy party, the sausage plot, the Great Illumination, these were the crimes and misdemeanors of boys; adult evils lay behind the committee's officialese: "want of unanimity and cooperation . . . in the members of the Faculty." The full Board responded immediately, and the next day, Wednesday, the 20th of September, it sat as a star chamber. It was a memorable day at Union when civility, decorum, and politeness gave way before the charges and countercharges of frustrated and angry men, when Eliphalet Nott was forced at last to turn his back on a theory and practice of college administration he had inherited from colonial America.

"College Hall" that Wednesday morning became a courtroom. Not a young Tillotson, or Griffin, or Phillip Livingston this time, but the faculty itself was on trial. The life of the college depended on its outcome. Perhaps Beriah Palmer, the senior Trustee present, surrogate of Saratoga County in 1809, a New York militiaman in the Revolution, and a Massachusetts Yankee by birth, asked the questions. The reporter is nameless; his record is thin, terse, matter of fact.

Rumor, charge and countercharge, these things had been common property in Schenectady and Albany for several years. By the end of its three months of investigation the "Committee of Six" could have had little doubt left that it was Professor Benjamin Allen who "threatened the institution with incalculable injury." He seems to have been the second witness to be called. Nott's testimony was heard first, but it is not a part of the recorder's report. Then, apparently on a basis of their academic rank, Professors Brownell, Macauley and Davis were each heard in a proceeding which, under other circumstances, must have won Professor Allen's approval.

For one so used to passing judgment, this reversal of roles could only have been galling. By the time he entered "College Hall" to be questioned Allen seems to have decided the new Union College had no place for him; tact and compromise were not a part of his replies to his questioners. The recorder's notes only suggest the tension. "He had for some time," the recorder extracted from what must have been a long and defiant statement, "taken the lead in college and done more and now does not take the lead." Hurt pride, resentment, frustrated ambition, these things Allen could not rise above. "He will submit his resignation," the notes continue, "if a new opportunity present itself." Speaking with the freedom of a man who no longer needs to compromise, Professor Allen unburdened himself. The chief weakness, as he now saw things, lay in the failure of the Union College laws to give real power to the faculty. Faculty members should have final authority to lay fines; these should never be remitted. He denied advocating giving the fines collected to the Professor levying them, although Macauley testified later that Allen favored this, and that Allen had said he "could discover many improprieties among the students if it was made an object to him."

Trial by faculty and whippings he advocated. The punishments in the Tillotson and Griffin cases were quite proper, and he thought Professor Macauley had been unjustly blamed for administering the punishments. He declared he had never tried to undermine the Union College grammar school by encouraging a Mr. Thomas Clark to set up a competing one, although Professors Macauley and Davis later testified that he had.

Before the beleaguered Allen's hearing was over he had presented himself as the defender of a stern and virtuous code of academic conduct. The new President, he told his judges, "did not take the lead," and "none of the faculty wished to enter in"; yet he added that the President had too much power. He claimed he had never questioned the matter of equality among the professors, but he wanted more tutors. The difference between his own salary of $1000 and the $2000 the President received irked him.

The hearing finally ended and with it Professor Benjamin Allen's career at Union College, and with it ended also that system of discipline which Jonathan Maxcy and Benjamin Allen and Eliphalet Nott had shaped out of their Rhode Island College experience, a system which looked backward to pre-revolutionary America and to a medieval Europe for its authority. But Maxcy had resigned in 1804, and Eliphalet Nott, now viewing a world he knew was changing, seeing it through the eyes of a Boyle, a Newton, and a Locke, seeing the universe through the oculars of the college telescope, had lost his enthusiasm for a curriculum justified only by tradition and for a plan of discipline dear to the heart of such a man as Professor Allen.

This long forgotten academic tempest is important chiefly for the ground it cleared. With Benjamin Allen gone, Eliphalet Nott was free at last, free to be wholly his own President, his own man, to dominate Union College. [13] It was to be with relish that he would now set about to reorganize the faculty and the government of Union in order to bring about that "perfect and cordial cooperation" for which the Trustees now called and which he had already demonstrated he could impose when the situation demanded it.

CHAPTER 5

"We shall not be hereafter what heretofore we have been."

"With respect to the college," Eliphalet Nott wrote in April, 1810, to his elder brother Samuel who knew how full were the wellsprings of ambition in him, "it has never been in as good a state, or as agreeable to me, as at present. The mathematical professorship is filled by a learned Swiss—F. R. Hassler—confessedly the ablest mathematician and astronomer that was ever in America. He is the celebrated correspondent of De Le Sand, and goes through a course of lectures in the manner of the most approved European professors . . ."[1]

Nott had, indeed, pulled off an academic coup, or so it appeared in the spring of 1810. Hassler had been in America for almost five years, "encumbered with ninety-six trunks, boxes and bales, including a library of several thousand books, together with many art objects and scientific instruments." His friendship with the members of the American Philosophical Society had generated a plan to make him head of a trigonometric survey of the American coast, a plan which soon had President Jefferson's backing. During most of the long period it took this ambitious program to develop Hassler was employed at the United States Military Academy as Acting Professor of Mathematics until he was forced out of the post by a captious ruling of the War Department that only military personnel could be employed at West Point. Professor Benjamin Allen's recent resignation from Union College seemed well timed.

Nott's pleasure, however, at getting Hassler must have been tempered by that strange man's performance during his one year in Schenectady. The irascible Swiss certainly enlivened the scene. It was soon evident he had no ability to manage boys. One wonders what happened to those "most approved lectures and experiments," for it is said that bedlam reigned in his classroom where Hassler became so absorbed in his demonstrations he lost his students and talked to empty seats. Gossips reported the white dust which covered his coat when he came to Stone College in the morning was the residue of the bread he had been making, and others said they had seen him lay out his son on the floor at home in order to cut a bolt of cloth around the boy's figure for the suit of clothes he was making him.[2]

True or not, these stories characterize an extraordinary man whose scientific interests expanded Nott's horizons as an educator. Hassler, fortunately, was rescued early in 1811 from a position for which he was obviously unfitted. Albert Gallatin, a fellow countryman and Secretary of the Treasury, arranged for Hassler to begin his work that year for the government, and the harried professor departed from Schenectady to found the temperamentally run, but distinguished Coast Survey for his adopted country. Nott never forgot Benjamin Allen's successor, however; he remained Hassler's advisor in some of the latter's bitter arguments with those government leaders who could not get along with him, or without him; he encouraged Hassler's work as an author of mathematical texts, and, when learning of Hassler's death in 1843, wrote that "we have not such another man to die."[3]

Ferdinand Rudolph Hassler was only one of four new faculty members appointed at a special meeting of the Trustees on March 20, 1810, a far happier occasion for Nott than any that had preceded it for some time. Noah Wells, Henry Warner and Gideon Hawley, all recent graduates of the college, were made tutors, each to begin teaching at $400 a year. Besides Hassler there were three other professors, Davis, Macauley, and Brownell, the last of whom, Nott wrote in his April letter to his brother in Franklin, Connecticut, is "in Europe, [and] will return with a chemical apparatus and an addition to our library in September." The President of Union College was now presiding over an enterprise which was beginning to measure up to his ambitions for it. Although Timothy Dwight at Yale apparently thought Nott was in the wrong place, "most of my friends," he assured Samuel, "have thought with you that I ought not to leave the college. I have no idea that I shall."

He had been tempted to leave and there had been opportunities, but he was a stronger man moved by a greater vision than had been his predecessors. He was probably never aware of the fact, but three years earlier the Trustees of Bowdoin College, by a vote of eight to one had elected him to succeed President Joseph McKeen. The news never reached Schenectady, however, because the Overseers of Bowdoin were convinced Nott would refuse to leave a college he had served only two years.[4]

Nott himself had had ideas of returning to the ministry, and would have, he told his brother in 1810, "if I thought my health would stand it, and other circumstances would permit." It was those "other circumstances," however, intricately tied up with his conviction that he was serving God's purpose best by becoming an educator, which tied him irrevocably to Union College. He had said a firm "no" in 1810 to the commissioners representing the congregation of the then new Park Street Church of Boston. Although they pressed him again and again, he told Samuel they could "produce no change in my conviction of duty. I never did like the city," he continued in that long and revealing spring letter to the older brother, "I long for retirement and rest, and would sooner go into solitude than into a throng for the rest of my days, if I could, consistently with my duty, escape from responsibility."

The Boston offer had been tempting, and he seems to have considered it from every angle. "I am not fit for the place," he wrote. Ironically, for one viewing the panorama of Nott's career, he then went on to say Boston required "a man of manners and management, a man skilled in the subtleties of metaphysics, who loves, and is familiar with disputation. I apprehend," he told Samuel with a prescience which did him credit, "that the materials for a theological warfare are preparing at the East; and a warfare for which I have neither the talents nor the inclination to engage." There were other battlefields which suited Nott's temperament and ambition far better than would have those metaphysical cul-de-sacs into which Trinitarians, Socinians, and Unitarians, and their splinter groups were already journeying and in which many a New England theologian and metaphysician would be bloodied in the years to come.

Nott had chosen to serve in a day-to-day world. "Are you willing," he characteristically asked his graduating class in 1811, "to creep away from this seminary like unfledged reptiles from their cells, and, buried in obscurity, pass your years in inglorious sloth?" "Always," he counseled them, "be an enlightened adventurer, bent on glory, and setting out on a career of immortality . . . always be projecting and maturing new plans of public and glorious enterprise."

Public enterprises, not matters of closet doctrine, were now exciting Nott to pulpit sonorities. As early as 1811 he took his stand on slavery, praising, in his baccalaureate of that July, the work of those he called the "Negroes' advocates," the British anti-slavery leaders Howard, Sharp, and Clarkson, "whose fame," he declaimed, "I had rather inherit than that of Caesar."

Joseph Lancaster's scheme for mass learning then being urged by DeWitt Clinton won Nott's enthusiastic backing; the English visionary's monitorial system, designed, as Nott put it, to render "the houses of education, like the temples of grace, accessible to the poor . . . ," he hoped to see spread over the country. "Ah, had this man," he pondered for his audience in 1811, "but lived 2000 years ago. . . ."

Such orotund phrases, embarrassing to us, were a delight to Nott's hearers, a natural language to a man who saw the world as a theater, saw men as actors working from a script which permitted *ad-libbing*, but no deviation from the action of the overwhelming drama in which they were cast. There were the arras scenes within the walls of Stone College, courtyard scenes in Schenectady and Albany, and scenes enlarging until they embraced the nations, and Nott knew the appropriate language for all of them.

The President of Union College was certainly no man for the Boston of cerebral Christianity. By the time the Park Street Church delegations had given him up, he, in turn, had foresworn any idea of ever leaving Union. The world, he was to tell his audiences time and again, was God's beloved world, and their eyes must be fixed upon it. His intention as a man and a teacher, he said to his seniors in 1811, an intention which should be theirs, too, was to help "convert the very abodes of *ignorance and woe* into a theater of glory."

His nephew, Samuel Nott, Junior, who had graduated from Union the year before, taking such injunctions literally, had become a member of "The Brethren" at Andover Theological Seminary where orthodox Calvinism and such student activities as the making of coffins underscored the fact of man's mortality.

When young seminarian Nott and his wife and two other members of the Brethren sailed for India out of Philadelphia in the winter of 1812 as representatives of the newly organized American Board of Commissioners for Foreign Missions, they were the advance guard of an army of American missionaries who were to tap and hammer and thunder on the doors of the "abodes of ignorance and woe" around the world.[5]

Eliphalet Nott, although he optimistically became a member of the Board which the foreign mission dreams of the Brethren had brought into existence, had by now lost his enthusiasm for the theological austerities of Andover. There were wider, more encouraging entrances to his "theater of glory." He had watched the slow, hard birth of the Massachusetts seminary where young Calvinists were to be trained for the warfare against all theological heresies: of Papists, of Jews, Pelagians, Socinians, Antinomians, Universalists, and, in the minds of Andover's founders, those destroyers of Harvard, the Unitarians.

Let his brother in Franklin, Connecticut preach of "disinterested benevolence," and send young Samuel through Andover, he preferred the softer program of the new seminary at Princeton which the Presbyterian General Assembly at Philadelphia set up on the campus of the College of New Jersey in 1812. He had been moderator of the General Assembly the preceding year when the plans for the Seminary were settled, and he then became one of its directors, serving on the Board until 1828.[6] There *were* means a man might use to encourage the gift of grace, and the new seminary at Princeton did not deny them.

Ironically, the Princeton Seminary was to throw the College of New Jersey into a long eclipse, siphoning off church funds which had earlier gone to it, slowing down the development of a college from which Union had taken so much, including its first President, much of its original curriculum which had come to Schenectady from Princeton by way of the College of Rhode Island, and those rational arguments in defense of Christianity advanced by Presidents Witherspoon and Smith, those Scottish "Common Sense" doctrines which by now had rooted in Nott's mind.

As the eclipse deepened at the College of New Jersey, as Harvard was lapped by the mildly disturbing waves of Unitarianism, and Yale was bulwarked by a Timothy Dwight who stood belligerently by his Federalist and orthodox Calvinist principles, Union College, less inhibited, closest to the democratic frontier, grew rapidly along with an Eliphalet Nott who now exploited every opportunity he could to develop a college suitable for his student "adventurers."

"It is our lot," Nott told his expanding student body and his Commencement audience on July 22, 1812, a month after Congress had declared war on Great Britain, "To live at a time peculiarly disastrous . . . half the civilized world has been revolutionized . . . the current has at last reached us [and] we shall not hereafter be what heretofore we have been." If this Commencement audience expected him to fulminate against "Mr. Madison's War," it should have known him better by now. As he had done seven years earlier, when he saw destiny in the Hamilton-Burr duel, he did again, translating this second war with England into the only context which made sense to him. Instead of thundering as William Ellery Channing was doing in Boston against those Republican politicians who would not make a tradesman's peace with England, Nott, the Christian nonpartisan, meeting with Trustees who were then battling for their political lives, chose instead to see the War of 1812 as one more evidence of that "revolutionizing of the civilized world" which he now promised his hearers would eventually produce "great and beneficial changes."

A world in revolution: one has the feeling that the President of Union College more and more privately relished the idea, was invigorated by it, was glad "the current has at last reached us." The year before, at Commencement, he had told his graduating seniors that "that fatal explosion which shook the civilized world to its center" had begun with "Voltaire, Rousseau and their infidel coadjutors," and yet by that next year the lesson he drew from the careers of these rationalists was a new and curious one. These infidel Frenchmen, Nott said, were in fact, great men because they *achieved*; "theirs," he said, "was the success of individuals."

The teacher's responsibility ("my God, what a trust!" he declared), he had then told his hearers, is "to train and send abroad an annual corps of actors destined to corrupt or reform life's ever varying drama." The time might be "peculiarly disastrous," but one suspects in Nott's mind it was chiefly disastrous for those who resisted "the revolutionizing" which, in 1812, was turning Schenectady into a profitable armed camp.

And so the war itself, in 1812 beginning to make a military highway of the Mohawk Valley, was thus eliminated from Nott's immediate concern; he could concentrate his attention on a burgeoning Union College, on readying his students to play their part in the accelerating world revolution at that moment mustering the New York militia in the open fields west of the Mohawk Bridge. For both him and his students there was wonderful excitement in the promise that "we shall not hereafter be what heretofore we have been."

II

"Revolutionizing" appeared everywhere. The three great wooden arches of Theodore Burr's Mohawk Bridge, the first suspension bridge in American, now spanned the river a few blocks west and north of Stone College. The bridge, opened in 1809, and the Little Falls and Wood Creek locks of General Philip Schuyler's Inland Lock and Navigation Company had brought the speculator's west, and the new war theater of Lake Erie and the St. Lawrence Valley within reach of the town builders as well as the trappers and cabin builders of an earlier generation.

The Dorp Schenectady was booming, Dutchmen and Yankees taking their profit where they found it. The shipyards along "The Strand" were supplying the wide bottomed Durham boats which freighted the reluctant New York State militia to the less than successful campaigns of 1812. The common lands of Schenectady, including those acres which were part of the town's endowment of Union College, supplied the oak timbers that went into these hulking river carriers, sometimes one hundred of them on the stocks at a time.

Wheat was selling at two and sometimes three dollars a bushel. The price of butter, cheese, and river fish, local staples, had doubled since 1810, when eggs were quoted at a shilling a dozen, and twelve pounds of river fish sold for four shillings. New York City capital, seeking safe havens beyond the reach of the British fleet, was being converted into most of the available new Mohawk Bank stock.[7]

The *Western Budget*, the fifth of those ephemeral newspapers to try publication in Schenectady, died in June, 1810, but was reborn that same month as the Schenectady *Cabinet*, its very title an echo of the Dorp's growing self-consciousness. "Poverty, filth, and happiness," DeWitt Clinton reported that year were found everywhere along the much talked about Erie Canal route he was then surveying; Union College, he noted in his Journal on the fourth of July as he traveled west, had something of Oxford about it; its students, as did their English brothers, joined with the townsmen in making the most of a holiday.[8]

"Mr. Madison's War" dimmed, but did not extinguish the dream of New York State to link the Hudson with the Great Lakes. Astride the eastern end of the proposed Erie Canal route sprawled Schenectady, already the warehouse, the goods and traveler's depot for the freight wagons, the stage coaches and Durham boats bound for the Grants, the cabin clearings, and the pipe dream towns of the speculators.

It was the "West," the New York frontier, which sent back its vitality and excitement to Schenectady in these years, its "poverty, filth, and happiness" either a witch's brew to make irresponsible democrats, or, if your politics and sympathies were as were DeWitt Clinton's, an elixir to brew great schemes. Republicans and Federalists, agrarians and entrepreneurs for banks and factories, and the lines between them were not always clearly drawn, made the new State Capitol building in Albany a mirror of the times.

It was there among the legislators that the President of Union College, moved by that current which "has at last reached us," by the revolutionizing which was nowhere more evident than within sight and sound of his students, spent the winter of 1813.

Had David Parish, "the champion, the pearl of all the businessmen of Christendom on both sides of the Atlantic . . ." avoided Schenectady in January, 1813, Eliphalet Nott might well have had no reason to spend the following months in Albany, waging a campaign for an unprecedented state endowment to build a campus such as America had never seen.[9]

David Parish was a sophisticated European whose reach exceeded that of those speculators in America Nott already knew. The son of John Parish of Hamburg, one of the richest merchants and bankers on the Continent, he had been in America for seven years, making his headquarters in Philadelphia, managing the cloak and dagger affairs of Hope and Company of Amsterdam whose business it was to see that Talleyrand and Napoleon continued to receive Spanish gold from the mines of Mexico in spite of the tight British blockade. For the fifteen million dollars Parish smuggled past the British fleet, his fee had been one million dollars.

David Parish was a man, a friend wrote, "with great schemes in his head," schemes apparently easily brought to a focus by such Philadelphia friends as Gouverneur, Robert, and Lewis Morris, the Ogdens, and LeRay de Chaumont, men whose fever for land speculation was infectious. Gouverneur Morris's pamphlet on the limitless opportunities for the investor in northern New York State Lands, especially in lands held by the Morrises and their friends, was dedicated to Parish, and was persuasive enough to induce him to join their ranks. From the Morrises, Ogdens, and de Chaumont he bought land by the 100,000 acres, until, in 1814, his total investment in the Ogdensburg-St. Lawrence Valley region stood at "upward of six hundred thousand dollars."

By January, 1813, the outlines of the Parish barony were clearly drawn, a domain half feudal in its concept, an aristocrat's compromise with the American frontier, where the workmen were not peasants, and the owner's allegiance was to his ledger.

The month before his fateful stopover in Schenectady David Parish had written to his father as one eighteenth-century gentleman to another: "I have some of the most romantic situations you can possibly imagine [at Parishville, one of the several towns he was then building] and Ramée who made an excursion with me the other day to view them, declares he never saw anything as fine. . . ." Joseph Jacques Ramée, the sophisticated French architect whose work for the King of Denmark, the Duke of Mecklenburg-Schwerin and such commercial royalty as the father of David Parish, had viewed with delight his employer's site for his wilderness mansion.

These were the men who stepped out of their sleigh and into Nott's world at the precise moment when Ramée's reputation and romantic planning could so intrigue and move the President of Union College that he would once more commit himself and his Trustees to a calculated risk, one far greater, however, than that which had involved them in the Literature Lottery of 1805. What was left of the parochial Connecticut Yankee in Eliphalet Nott died during his January conversations with the banker from Hamburg and the French builder of ducal palaces and the Hamburg Bourse.

On March 17, 1813, Parish wrote directly to "Mr. Eliphalet Nott, Schenectady," thanking him for his recent letter sent to Philadelphia and for "its very friendly and polite comments—it gives me pleasure," Parish continued, "to hear that the acquaintance you made with my friend Mr. Ramée has fully justified the opinion I expressed and entertain of his tastes and talent. I have communicated your letter to him and beg leave to inform you that he is now occupied with making plans for the Central Building as also a sketch of the whole Plan including a disposition of all the buildings and of the grounds. . . ."

By the last of April, 1813, according to Parish, Jacques Ramée was in Schenectady, "to attend to the works of the Union College. . . ."

To understand the enormity of this calculated risk, this commitment to Ramée's vast design for a "new college," and "its 70 acres of pleasure grounds," one must survey the cellar hole Nott and his building committee had already dug in the fall of 1812, on their "large and airy site" on Nistiquona Hill. That cellar hole was the result of what was referred to in Professor Pearson's Diaries (those observations which were so often a wake on Nott's career) as "some horrible plan made by David Burt, perhaps!" A brick yard had already been built in the deep ravine to the north of their building site, in a cool glade through which ran Hans Groot's kill. Payments had already been made for "opening a quarry and making a road and bridges," for stone digging, for wagoning, for labor, and gallons of workmen's rum.

Six years before Ramée pictured for Nott the "pantheon," the "chapelle," and the dormitories, the arcades and the formal and romantic gardens of the vast academic forum he would erect on Nistiquona Hill, there were 115 undergraduates crowding Stone College just finished on the strength of the Literature Lottery of 1805. It was obvious Nott's predecessors as President had failed to read the significance of the rattling immigrant wagons which were rolling west down Union Street. When Parish and Ramée visited

Schenectady, instead of fifteen seniors, there were thirty-one. "The Long College" and "East College" had been hastily added in 1805 to take care of the swelling classes of collegians and grammar school boys, but these buildings, too, were soon overcrowded.

Nott had found it on the low green hill, "watered by a living stream" about a mile east of Stone College up which the Albany Turnpike climbed through pine groves to the wide, forested plain between Schenectady and Albany, the latter the new State Capital. On east of the new site there were only the distant white settlers along the banks of the Mohawk, the taverns of the Albany Road, and the clearings in the great plain where the Conestigione Indians scratched a thin living.

Lot by lot the new President bought the land himself, from owners whose Dutch names echo their lost New Amsterdam: John Groot, "Beekman Wessllse and mother," Barhydt, Veeder, Visscher, and there were others, whose 300 acres of glen and hillside cost Eliphalet Nott $13,692.96, a sum his Trustees refunded twelve years later. [10] The rich men on his new site committee, James C. Duane and Joseph C. Yates, had other plans for their own money; fortunately the young President's wife, the wealthy Troy widow who had recently become Mrs. Nott, solved many problems for her husband which, as a widower living on an annual salary of $2000 would have been beyond him.

By 1812 Nott had assembled a campus no college could expect to outgrow: the last lots were bought from Thomas C. Brownell, his Lecturer on Chemistry, and the mysterious David Burt, to whom he paid their cost and interest. One suspects them of having speculated a little, for it was David Burt who seems to have produced the "horrible plan" for the new building whose cellar hole had been covered with straw less than a month before Ramée raised in Nott's mind visions of a college scaled to match that coming America he repeatedly told his audiences God had prepared.

The Benjamin Allen episode and the turmoil which preceded it no doubt spurred Nott to speed up his plan for moving his students out of Stone College, away from the temptations of the city and the excitements of the nearby river docks. Although the President had bought almost all of the new land himself, his Trustees could hardly expect him to finance their new building.

From his first year in Schenectady Nott had accepted his role of fund raiser as an inevitable part of being the President of Union College. He had come to see the state government as his financial partner in education. The Literature Lottery of 1805 which he had pushed through the Legislature in the face of his Trustees' apathy proved to what extent he was willing to commit himself and them to great risks. Stone College and its dormitories had been built on expectations; they had been completed on $15,000 borrowed from the State on a credit of lottery hopes. New faculty members, new courses, new books, and apparatus had been added from what could be borrowed on earlier endowments made by the State or already held in bank stocks and land. It was not students who paid a tuition of $120 per year, or waiting donors who justified the purchase of the new site and the development of the "horrible plan" of 1812; rather it was those "Adventurers" in the Literature Lottery of 1805, the drawings for which were still being run off by the inefficient state managers. "Adventurers" in lottery tickets in spirit were ranked in thousands around the straw covered cellar hole which Nott was to abandon so soon on a "hazard" worthy of the biggest taker of risks among them all.

A man of smaller vision, less ambition, and less self-assurance could have murmured excuses involving the War of 1812, recommended a longer "Long College," stricter college laws, and put off building anything on the new campus until loans outstanding were repaid and the lottery grant of 1805 had become dollars, and was in the college treasury. Instead, on May 30, 1812, Nott and his Trustees sold their Stone College and "the East College," as buildings outgrown even before the initials of more than half a dozen classes scarred their woodwork. They had decided, apparently, that a new college could be paid for out of the lottery money still due, on the expected sales of the "military lots" in western New York, and of the Garrison tracts at Ticonderoga and Crown Point still held by Union and Columbia Colleges. The key to their hopes, however, was a new and ingenious real estate exchange with the city of Schenectady whereby, according to one old Dutch resident, Dr. Nott "yankee-doodled [them] out of their land."

This deal with the city fathers was a triumph of diplomacy, a carefully drawn plan to transfer to the college a speculation in land on which the college could not lose; "it has been represented by the citizens," the memorandum read, "that the purchase of Union College and its site would very much contribute to the wealth and prosperity of the city." Stone College was to become the Schenectady City Hall. The purchase price was 3000 acres of city owned land "to be selected by the Mayor, Aldermen, and Commonalty and the Union College Trustees." John I. Yates witnessed the memorandum for the city as Mayor, and also for the college as a Trustee.

All the citizens, however, were not convinced that Dr. Nott's first consideration in selling Stone College was the city's wealth and prosperity. John Sanders, member of a squirearchy of landowning Sanderses, recalled his father's comment that the county members of the Schenectady Common Council "were generally opposed to the grant," which Union College had so quickly elected to take in real estate, and which, Sanders recalled, consisted "of 3000 acres of the common lands under the designation of 'gores and gussets', about the most valuable tracts." The county members of the council, he told Professor Pearson almost seventy years after the transactions had taken place, "were greatly indignant with Dr. Nott's successful ingenuity." [11]

The Sanderses, and the other county citizens, many of them a little resentful of the hustling New Englanders settling among them or crowding on toward the frontier in the midst of the war, had no desire to be levered into the future by the Yankee President of Union College. Eliphalet Nott himself, years later, then less sure of God's planning for America, "spoke of the storm of wrath which was kindled against him . . . for the active part he took in getting the common lands of the city into the market and sold. One of the warmest contests," Nott remembered, "arose out of the question in which the two parties raised every influence possible to carry their point. The city was thoroughly canvassed and every voter brought out." Professor Pearson who delighted in looking backward over the then old President's shoulders, added to this the comment that "the lands were sold, and many have not forgiven the Dr. for his influence in this contest to this day." [12]

The profit to Union College from the sale of its "gores and gussets" eventually amounted to over $71,000. [13] In return the city received a ready-made City Hall, a building large enough to house the Schenectady County Court, the county offices, and the jail. From Nott's point of view a levy in gores and gussets was justified if it meant he could expand the education of the boys who were to build the America he believed he was intended to help bring to pass. Had he not told his seniors in his baccalaureate in 1812, the year before this land deal was completed, that they should always "be projecting and maturing great plans of public and glorious enterprise?" By the end of December, 1812, the brickyard, the new bridges and roads, and the then bleak cellar hole on the new college site testified he had taken his own counsel.

By January the County Members of the Common Council might well have won the vote and kept their gores and gussets, had the sequence of events been slightly different. Could they and their Dutch neighbors have heard the talk between David Parish, Joseph Jacques Ramée, and an Eliphalet Nott then much concerned with "public and glorious enterprise," heard talk of "Chappelles," and "Pantheons," and "pleasure grounds," they would have been dismayed. Their Dorp Schenectady was a cluttered river port of Holland houses, brick gable ends to the street, and Yankee clapboard interlopers. Their largest building was Stone College, soon to become their Court House, City Hall, and jail, a quarried oblong of Georgian solidity, suitable, dignified, and as useful as their Durham boats. Their churches had been likened to the Lord's barn. That early tourist, Timothy Dwight of Yale College, remembering his New England town commons, saw Schenectady only as an architectural cypher, and yet he might have been kinder, for there were graceful doorways; the Dutch houses had their charm, and there had been builders who could deal with the Five Orders, palladian windows, and wooden quoins.

Architecture, in the Mohawk Valley, had long been the province of local carpenters, their houses either copies or improvisations on those they saw in the imported style books. The County Members would have known the big houses designed by Massachusetts-born Samuel Fuller whose four-square buildings for Sir William Johnson and his heirs reflect Newburyport and Salem. Philip Hooker of Albany had built their "gussets-and-gores" City Hall as well as the new Capitol in Albany, work which would have given him a respectable following in Georgian England. What the

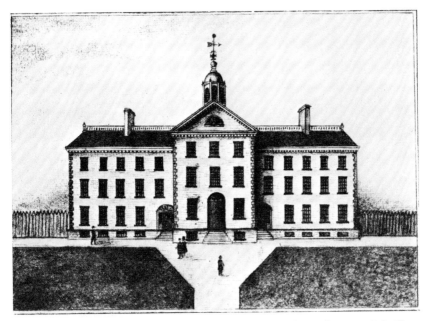

UNION COLLEGE ("Stone College") in 1805. Artist unknown. Schaffer Library, Union College.

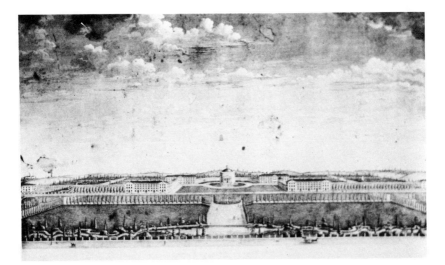

PROJECTED UNION COLLEGE CAMPUS, 1812-1813. Print after J. Klein drawing, after original design by Joseph Jacques Ramée. Print owned by Union College; photograph, Schaffer Library, Union College.

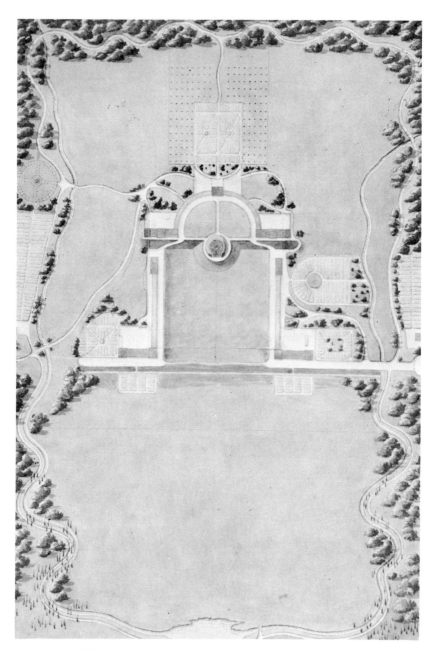

AERIAL VIEW OF THE PROJECTED UNION COLLEGE CAMPUS, 1812-1813. Design by Joseph Jacques Ramée. Drawing and photograph, Schaffer Library, Union College.

County Members would have thought of that romantic Frenchman, Joseph Jacques Ramée and his imperial plans for Nistiquona
Hill, however, his Union College which would dominate the Dorp,
his unity of buildings where Schenectadians had known only a
unity of roofs, is unknown, for the citizens seem never to have
been consulted. Schenectady was presented with Ramée's forum
campus as a *fait accompli.*

Nott and Ramée, standing on "the new and airy site" in
January, 1813, looked toward farther horizons; they shared the
geographical one only with the college's Dutch neighbors. Beyond
these two visionaries, toward the West, lay the almost empty
America for which Nott was then certain God had special plans.
The new college would face it, face Arendt VanCurler's "Most
beautiful land," built on a site John Jay had once hoped New
York would take for its new State Capitol. Such a site and such a
prospect and, for Nott, such a future, was justification enough to
take the calculated risk, to commit his Trustees and the
community to what one commentator later called the "great court
of honor, reminiscent of Versailles . . . a monument to learning for
royal occupancy."

Eliphalet Nott, too, was a Roman-American at heart, whose
dreams for his college came earlier and were as vast as were those
of that other educational innovator, Thomas Jefferson of Virginia.
Let the Anglophiles build their cautious Georgian buildings. For
Union College, however, the first college to be chartered under the
Constitution of the United States, a "union" in truth of men of
Dutch, English, and German stock, of many faiths, there would be
no turning again toward the meeting-house primness of the
Harvard Yard, or the closed monastic quadrangles of Oxford and
Cambridge. Nott seems to have needed little persuasion from the
Frenchman to accept his Roman scheme for the classic forum he
pictured flanking the empty hill above the town and the Mohawk
River, its domed Pantheon and "chappelles," and "pleasure
grounds," and framing dormitories connected with a great "U"
shaped colonnade. Unlike its European models, Union College
would be open to the west, the new America, flung wide, as the
architectural historian Christopher Tunnard has said, "as if to
express Dr. Nott's policy that education was not for the chosen
few. . . ."

III

The calculated risk accepted, Nott wasted no time. By April 1813, Ramée was back again in Schenectady with his "Plan for the Central Building, and a sketch of the whole Plan including a disposition of all the buildings and the grounds. . . ." Professor Thomas Macauley, who had survived student rebellions and Benjamin Allen's harsh regime in Stone College, was relieved of his Latin classes and made the superintendent of construction.

"Waste of time and stuff in working on the first plan" was charged off on the treasurer's books, and on May 13, 1813, "North and South Colleges," as Schenectady still knows them, were mentioned for the first time in a contract signed by superintendent Macauley and a George Cooper who agreed "to carry from Albany all the hewn stone which shall be required for the edifices. . . ." On May 20th the well diggers collected twenty-five dollars and eleven gallons of rum for work on the wells they were sinking in front of each of the "colleges." On the same day Asa Hewes, one of many laborers, carpenters, brick layers, and quarriers busy at the new site, collected nine dollars, his month's wages.

By June 24th the foundations were completed, and early in July "floor framing" began. A Mr. Crofoot supplied 15,000 shingles and 140,000 "warranted lath." In the heat of August there was more rum, a hogshead this time, brought over from Troy for $129.37 1/2.

What sanction had Nott's Trustees given to the activities on Nistiquona Hill? The only place Ramée's name is mentioned is in the record of the annual Board meeting held late in July, 1813, when they authorized the erection "of fencing designed by Mr. Ramée's plan. . . ." These Minutes acknowledged, at least, that there were "new Edifices" going up, for Henry Yates, the treasurer, was directed to buy suitable fire engines and buckets for their protection.[14]

If, however, the Trustees' Minutes speak only of Ramée's fences, their annual report to the Legislature, in February, 1813, does him more honor, and also foreshadows their President's scheme to pay for their "pantheon," "Chappelle," and their "pleasure grounds." It proved to be a scheme too complex, too finely balanced to suggest "yankeedoodling," and yet it had about it much that the irate Dutch citizen of Schenectady had capsuled in the term.

"During the year," the Trustees reported to the legislature, as though the war-frustrated and quarreling politicians in Albany had no other serious concerns, "the present College edifice and site have been disposed of, and new buildings are about to be erected on the high grounds that overlook the city of Schenectady. The plan of these buildings has been furnished by an architect of the highest reputation, and the Trustees confidently hope that when completed, they will be not only a convenience to the institution, but a Monument to the honour of the Legislature of this state, under whose fostering care, and by whose enlightened liberality they have been enabled to commence the erection of the same."

There was no request for more funds, but the seed words were there: "a Monument to the honour of the Legislature of this state . . . fostering care . . . enlightened liberality." And then the hint of things to come: It was the fruit of this legislative wisdom, this fostering care which had carried Union College through its infancy and which had now "enabled [the Trustees] to commence the erection" of the most sophisticated group of public buildings planned in America up to that time. To commence is not to complete, however, and so, Nott suggested, to whom but its foster mother should this child of the state turn for help?

On November 13th, 1813, there is a significant voucher for the payment of $11.19 "for digging at the chapel foundation . . ." and there the treasurer's building record ends. One begins to see, however, the dimensions of the calculated risk Eliphalet Nott had accepted after he had caught Ramée's vision "of the great court of honour . . . reminiscent of Versailles". By the end of 1813 Union College was more than $30,000 in debt for work done on the new site, and the two main buildings indicated on Ramée's monumental plan were barely roofed.

There is little doubt that Nott by now had designed a strategy to pay for his new campus as large in its conception and as artfully thought out as was Ramée's plan itself. "Yankeedoodled" gores and gussets might have provided most of the funds for the building which never rose over the first cellar dug in the fall of 1812. For the Union College, however, which Ramée projected, that "grand plan . . . which promises to rival in elegance any similar building in Europe," according to George Parish, the brother of David, a corollary grand plan to finance it was needed, and Eliphalet Nott had devised it.

BOOK THREE

The "Superintendent of the Literature Lottery," 1822-1828

CHAPTER I

The Lottery Act

PETER VAN SCHAIK'S letter to his son Peter, a senior in 1814, was a little fretful:

> The President of Union College is at Albany, and the Scholar is at Schenectady! Well—That the latter should receive the benefit from the instruction of the former is a problem which Euclid cannot solve. Whether Stewart is up to this, you will probably be ignorant of. Mr. Nott's address is pretty generally acknowledged, but while *he* is looking through a telescope for distant benefits *my* object in committing you to his charge is not answered. The Shepherd is mightily employed; but those Sheep, what have they, to be deprived of his care?[1]

At first glance it seems inconceivable that any promoter, no matter how foolhardy or how persuasive, could have elected to go before the New York State Legislature at the fateful time Eliphalet Nott chose in order to present such a Bill as he brought with him. Nott himself, remembering his extraordinary winter of lobbying, said "that so much should have been done at such a time by such a Legislature (one branch federal and the other democratic and both split into several violent parties) is a matter of astonishment to everybody."[2]

There had been only one bright moment to break the war gloom in New York during the year: as Asa Hewes and his fellow workmen were roofing and glazing the two "colleges" shown on Ramée's "Grand Plan," young Oliver Hazard Perry was destroying a British fleet on Lake Erie. November 8th, the day after the college treasurer had paid for digging at the chapel site, an excited Schenectady was entertaining Perry at Dow's Tavern on the Schenectady-Albany Turnpike. The rest of the war news had been bad and even disgraceful.

Two days after the Union College petition was read in the Assembly, February 4th, the anti-war party prepared a violent attack against Governor Tompkins; it omitted nothing: the failure of both the federal and state governments to prepare to fight the war, the devastation of the New York frontier, the destruction of Newark, the defeat at Queenstown, the shocking conduct of the New York militia in refusing to cross into Canada. England was pictured as the same vicious, massacring enemy of the days of the Revolution . . . and the democratic note: "the poor must serve, while the wealthy lordling riots in luxury and affluence at home."[3]

On February 2nd it had been the democratic note, too, which Nott had sounded:

> In attempting to re-found and reorganize Union College [the petition read], the Trustees have had respect to the encreasing population and future exigencies of this great and flourishing state. They have been desirous of exercising the trust reposed in them in such a manner as to furnish the youth in this vicinity with as great advantages as are furnished in any part of the United States.[4]

No invidious distinctions were made by the college petitioners, but even the Federalist-dominated Senate shortly recorded the fact that Columbia College was for the rich man, a place "too expensive for the accommodation of youth from the country."[5] Four Columbia College petitions to the New York Legislature for help were turned down between 1810 and 1814, a measure of the democratic opposition to what had been the "King's College" of the colonial aristocracy.[6]

The wording of the Union College petition was masterful, a compound of flattery, appeal to state pride, a challenge to Federalists and Republicans, and the factions within both parties.

> With a view to this [the Trustees' desire "to furnish the youth in this vicinity as great advantages as are furnished in any part of the United States"] they have selected an elevated and a beautiful site sufficiently large for all the purposes of exercise and gardening. They have also employed the first talents in the country in laying out the grounds and in projecting a plan of the buildings to be erected on the same which when completed will be of great utility to the public and remain a lasting monument to the honor of the state.

The Trustees, however, are under the necessity of representing to your honorable body, that they have already expended all the disposable funds in their possession, and that they have incurred a considerable debt in carrying forward the buildings to their present state. For the discharge of this debt as well as for the completion of the establishment, they have no further means in their power. All, therefore, that remains for them to do is to spread their wants before your honorable body, praying that you will grant such relief as may appear expedient. And the Trustees do this with a grateful rememberance [*sic*] of past favors, and confident that a liberal and enlightened legislature will not hesitate to cooperate with those who are struggling to improve the condition of a seminary in which so many of the youth of their own state are to be educated and with whose glory the glory of the republic is so intimately connected.

This "liberal and enlightened legislature," having forced itself on Union College as a major partner in order to protect the state's endowment resulting from the lottery grant of 1805, is now flatteringly shown the extent of its commitment. Eleven of the highest ranking state officers had been Trustees of the college for the preceding seven years; at least one of them, usually Archibald McIntyre, the state comptroller, had regularly attended the annual Board meetings, and these men, together with the elected Trustees, were responsible for this "rearranging and re-founding" of the college. Ironically, Columbia College four years earlier had fought off "the ignominy of having its charter changed . . . of being put on the same ground as Schenectady," and now Columbia, according to Provost Reverend John Mason, "was in ruin."[7]

Nott here gave the State, which, in 1805, had successfully demanded the right to share the college's future, such a bill as it had not anticipated, and in such a form it could hardly turn it down without destroying what it had created. This, in part, was the calculated risk Nott had accepted: would the Federalist Assembly and the Republican Senate accept the argument that they were already committed to honoring his bill, and that it was in the interest of the State to honor it generously? The gamble also accepted other imponderables: the reactions of politicians with supporters to please and the course of an unpopular war.

Young Peter VanSchaick and his fellow seniors had to get along as best they could that winter without their President. The new State House in Albany was now a more comfortable place to deal with members of select committees than had been the ancient and overcrowded Stadt Haus of Nott's first endowment campaign of 1805. Here again, however, was the charged atmosphere of the theater to which Eliphalet Nott reacted with the instincts of a stage manager; here bills died or were carried frequently on the strength of a politician's ability to skirt reason and take the heart. And it was here that Nott, the orator, found in Elisha Williams, young Federalist Assemblyman from Columbia County, the ideal protagonist-spokesman for the script the young President prepared and directed.

Williams, following directions, drew out the one emotional stop which had an especial appeal to the Republican members, the vibrato Nott had used so successfully in 1805. Here Williams spoke for a newer, more generous brand of Federalism; the State's children must not be told that the State will not prepare them for service to their country. One hears here an echo of the Union College petition, of the educated youth "with whose glory the glory of the Republic is so intimately connected." The heart of Williams's appeal was one which Nott undoubtedly counted on to win the wavering: the State, the select committee had agreed, must make further provision for its indigent students; it must do again for them "what Greece and Rome did for their youth." "The wealthy," Williams now proclaimed, "will not sacrifice to study for the professions; the rich can go to Europe; the state, in justice to itself must educate its poor."

Shame, patriotism, pride, the historical precedent of Greece and Rome, geographical advantage, promises given, and above all, the obligation of the State to educate its "talented, indigent students," these were the high cards Elisha Williams played for Eliphalet Nott in the opening round of the latter's bid to transfer to the State the financial responsibility for his "re-founded and reorganized" Union College and his vast Ramée campus already building. Elisha Williams's appeal suggests the idea that the legislature and the college in Schenectady, legally established partners in education, must now broaden the relationship so that Union, located near the seat of government, could become, under state patronage, what Columbia College partisans earlier thought Columbia was to be, the keystone of a state-supported university system.

The good news traveled fast that the Assembly was treating the Union College petition seriously. By the 23rd of February the Asbury African Church of New York City put its own petition before the House, asking for $4000 for a church school and the payment of part of the cost of its church building. The Assembly, after heated debate on the matter, split its vote, a division the chairman settled by supporting the church bill; it now became a rider to the Union College proposal following its third reading, and went to the Senate the next day.

Nott, "his eyes on distant benefits," was aware that others besides the African Church had caught the vision. Well before the final reading of the Union College petition in either house three other colleges filed their own requests for state bounty. Although Elisha Williams had already told his fellow Assemblymen that Hamilton, the new frontier college at Clinton, was handsomely provided for, Judge Platt of the New York State Supreme Court, a Hamilton Trustee and an old friend of the Nott family, wrote to Nott that Hamilton was "in great want, and that $30,000 would be of more aid then than at any future time"; it would be a special favor, he told Nott, if the latter would see to it that a clause proposing such a grant was added to the Union College Bill.[8]

The western vote, Republican, and even Federalist during these war years, was a large one. Nott remembered that he had replied at once to his old Federalist friend that "the cause in which he was engaged was a common cause," and that Hamilton's request should at once become one with Union's.

Neither Nott, his Trustees, nor any of these new petitioners, nor anyone in the legislature had any illusions as to where the money would be found, should it be granted. Tax receipts would not begin to pay war costs. The common schools now had the income derived from the sale of public lands. If the economy changed, however, human nature did not, and so legislators and petitioners comfortably accepted the idea that the State would again call on the "adventurers" among its citizens to subscribe to a new Literature Lottery which promised to be the biggest gambling venture in New York State history.

If Nott's scruples were not troubled by the prospect, their unnatural stirring among some he knew who were opposed to his bill must have amused him. The cry now went up that such financing was immoral, but politicians recognize their own kind, and one observer commented that "those whose consciences were most tender on the subject . . . would have voted against a grant . . . to Union College . . . if the money had been raised by any other means." [9]

All winter long Nott counseled, cajoled, mollified, adopted "that mode of address best suited to each"; he had personally "devised this grand scheme for the liberal and permanent endowment of the institution over which he presided," according to Jabez Hammond, the political historian, and he never for a moment relaxed his control of it, or trusted his political lieutenants to improvise their own strategy.

March was a dangerous period for the Union College Bill. News of the attention it and its accumulating riders were getting had moved the Trustees of the seven-year-old College of Physicians and Surgeons in New York City, now divorced from Columbia College, to ask Nott to assist them in getting a desperately needed $30,000 from the legislature. He replied to them at once and in the same spirit he had to Judge Platt, but there were now three institutional mendicants counting on his help.

The crisis came sometime between the 18th and the 29th of March when the Senate, sitting as a committee of the whole, began its final consideration of a Literature Lottery Bill bearing little resemblance to Nott's original petition. He recalled the events, but tactfully avoided naming those who almost destroyed his months of generalship.

> There were enemies to the measure, [he remembered], both in and out of the Legislature. Some of these individuals were known to have suggested to the friends of Columbia College, then at Albany, that, since grants were likely to be made to Union and Hamilton Colleges, it would be a good time for Columbia College to present its claims. Hence, when these claims were presented, many of the friends of Union College, believing that this move had been made with a view, not to aid Columbia College, but to defeat the whole bill in question, opposed the incorporating of the claims of the other colleges, and they tried to induce the President of Union College to cooperate with them in their opposition. [10]

Nott, however, was a far better strategist than were his friends. Even though he named no names, one suspects Senator

Erastus Root and his band of anti-Clintonians of most of the sappers' work. Nott, however, ear to ground, had heard enough to know that any opposition to the Columbia College petition was just what the enemies of his own Bill wanted. The legislature had far more men in it with Columbia College degrees than it had men with degrees from Union; General Root's long-time target, DeWitt Clinton, was also a loyal Columbia alumnus, as was Governor Tompkins.

To shut out Columbia from the lottery bounty would have been to lose the great gamble at once. Instead, the President of Union College welcomed this sister institution to the feast then preparing, and saw to it that his already well-amended bill made a modest provision for the New York City college.

If the Reverend Dr. John Mason, Provost of Columbia College, had not come up the Hudson to supervise Columbia's bid for lottery money, the New York City college might have gotten it, and so never have known the luxury of owning in perpetuity that land on which now stands Rockefeller Center; this small mid-Manhattan acreage was the compromise substitution for that lottery money grant requested by Columbia College which Nott feared would hopelessly bog down his own petition, already loaded with riders.

Provost Mason and President Nott had buried old and personal animosities a few years earlier in an emotional scene of reconciliation before a huge audience in Dr. Mason's church in New York City, but, though practicing Christians such as they were could find neutral ground on which to harmonize, practicing politicians seldom did. Nott, recalling the crowded events taking place in Albany that March, said that Dr. Mason "was personally offensive, on account of his politics, to certain individuals, he having been a decided Federalist and in the habit of freely discussing political questions during Mr. Jefferson's administration. It was thought advisable that he should withdraw from Albany, and it was agreed between him and the President of Union College that the interests of both colleges should be committed to the latter." [11]

Only Provost Mason and the Columbia Trustees were displeased with this real estate substitute for a money grant. For years Columbia had been complaining bitterly because its huge land endowments in Vermont had vanished in the boundary settlements between the two States following the Revolution. Four petitions to an unsympathetic legislature and now, in 1814, this ungenerous gift of Dr. Hosack's mid-Manhattan botanical garden in place of such a grant as that "praiseworthy munificence to a kindred institution." [12] How unjust!

What good were these twenty acres, then three and a half miles out of town in the center of Manhattan Island? Dr. Hosack had bought them in order to raise "exotic species" and medicinal herbs for use in his teaching and for sale, but the venture hadn't paid. In 1810 the State had passed "An Act Promoting Medical Science . . ." which included a provision for paying $74,268.75 to Dr. Hosack for his garden and greenhouse, a sum to be raised, as usual, by the state's lottery managers.[13]

The New York State Board of Regents, which had been responsible for the gardens, had then turned them over to the struggling College of Physicians and Surgeons, which had less luck with them than had Dr. Hosack. The gardens were back in the hands of the Regents by 1814, and they were happy to find a taker for them, even such a reluctant one as Columbia College. "Thus, solely through the influence of the President of Union College, Columbia received that magnificent property [between 47th and 51st Streets, fronting on Fifth Avenue] which today forms its principal endowment." [14]

With the tactless Provost Mason out of Albany, Nott was now free to buttonhole, to compromise, to adjust his argument to win those legislators he had come to know so well. He, unlike Mason, had always held his tongue during the political rages which divided New Yorkers. Martling Men, Lewisites, DeWitt Clinton baiters, warmongers, frontiersmen, and city merchants, of all these cadres of the Republican and Federalist forces permanently encamped at Albany, Nott was now able to draw enough of them onto neutral ground to renew his hopes.

Two additional riders to the lottery Act were gracefully accepted by Nott and his lieutenants, including Senator Martin VanBuren, one granting special bank-stock-buying privileges to the new medical school "of the western district," and the other giving to the officers of the New-York Historical Society access to the records of the State. Hamilton College, it was also agreed, should be granted $40,000 rather than the $30,000 Judge Platt had said it needed so badly.

What magic Nott wove around these party-conscious, war-harried legislators on behalf of Union College will never be known; the "great court of honor," which was to become his new campus, must have been planted in poppy seed, for the final draft of the Literature Lottery Bill included $100,000 for the Ramée buildings. Just as successful must have been his plea for the talented indigent students already moving up through a state supported system of common schools: $50,000 was included for them in the bill and kept there at the insistence of Nott's friend, William A. Duer, Federalist Assemblyman from Dutchess County, and chairman of the Committee on Colleges and Academies. Twenty thousand dollars was also appropriated for apparatus and the library, and another $30,000 to cancel debts already con-tracted. The Union College share of the state's educational bounty was to be the giant's share.

If Senator Root's objections to the amended Bill the last day of March had seemed unexpectedly mild, his devious move on Wednesday afternoon the 13th of April was sheer double dealing. Eliphalet Nott had good reason to recall the drama now staged in the Senate Chamber:

> a dinner was given [that day] by the steamboat interests to which many of the friends of the bill were invited. The President of Union College, who had also been invited, apprehensive that some advantage might be taken by the enemies of the Bill in the afternoon session, declined the invitation. . . . On the assembling of the Senate in the afternoon, it was found that every opponent of the Bill was present, whereas many of its friends were absent at the dinner. . . . no sooner was this Bill returned from the [House] than General Root moved the postponement . . . until the month of May, before which time it was known the legislature would adjourn.
>
> . . . None of the prominent speakers friendly to the Bill were present. The President of the College, however, succeeded in getting several individuals to make short speeches against the motion. In the meantime a messenger was sent to the place where the dinner was given in order to inform the friends of the Bill there of the danger . . . and to call them to its rescue. The Senators to whom the appeal was made had the magnanimity to respond to this call, and, leaving their unfinished repast, hastened to the Senate chamber, gave their votes . . . and returned to resume the places they had left at the dinner table.

And so, on the afternoon of the 13th of April, 1814, Eliphalet Nott outmaneuvered General Erastus Root and won, at last, his great gamble, or his great "hazard," a semantic choice in terms now to become central in all Nott's planning. With the Lottery Act lumped together, finally, in a last minute rush of Assembly Bills, with those for the relief of heirs, a bridge over the Genesee River, "payment for entertaining Indians visiting the Seat of Government," and for a fireproof room for the clerk of Herkimer County, Eliphalet Nott also won for all but one of those institutions he had so widely befriended all they had asked for; Columbia College was not pleased with Dr. Hosack's Elgin Botanical Gardens, but then, why, in 1814 should it have rejoiced to receive an unproductive piece of real estate when its greatest rival for state favors had just been granted $200,000, with interest?

The opening statement of this "Act Instituting a Lottery for the Promotion of Literature, and for other purposes. . . ." passed on the afternoon of the 13th of April, 1814, is the real measure of Nott's success: "Whereas well regulated seminaries of learning are of immense importance to every country, and tend especially, by the diffusion of science and the promotion of morals, to defend and perpetuate the liberties of a free state: THEREFORE, be it enacted. . . ."; the paragraphs which follow listing the endowments to Union, Hamilton, Columbia, the medical colleges, and a Negro church and school, also represented his triumph over patriotic men who, once lured onto that neutral ground he prepared for them, were, at least momentarily, concerned about the real "liberties of a free state" which, Nott was certain, must ultimately be defined in its seminaries, and by its teachers of science and morals.

In winning so much for so many, however, Eliphalet Nott opened even wider the lid of that Pandora's Box he had unlocked in 1805. Lottery dollars would flow from it again to pay for so much of what Pandora's Ancient World inspired in Nott: his Ramée campus, to which Greece and Rome had contributed the ordered forms of its buildings, Athens' example of a state supported education for the talented poor which Assemblyman Elisha Williams had cited; and now this lottery itself, controlled, so the citizens of Greece and Rome had believed lotteries were controlled, not by men, but by the capricious gods.

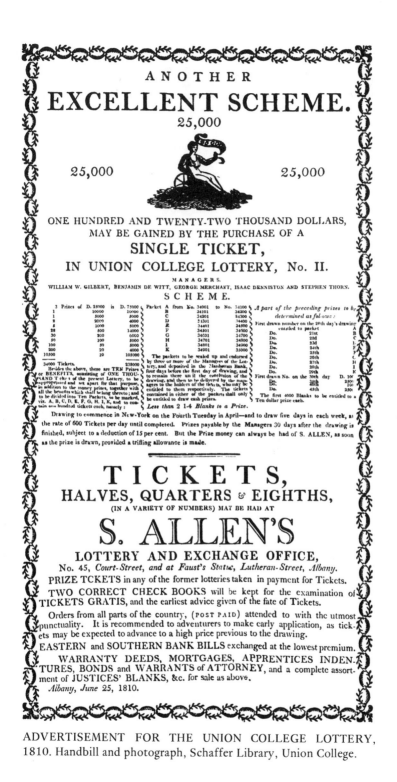

ADVERTISEMENT FOR THE UNION COLLEGE LOTTERY, 1810. Handbill and photograph, Schaffer Library, Union College.

ADVERTISEMENT FOR THE UNION COLLEGE LOTTERY, 1812. Kidder handbill, 1812, original in Harvard University Library.

Jabez Hammond believed Nott had won his great prize by virtue of his own special talents. "Certainly," Hammond wrote, "it is owing to his indefatigable exertions and matchless skill and address that a majority in favor of the Bill was obtained in both houses. His ingenuity in explaining away, and warding off objections, his skill in combining different and apparently conflicting interests, and above all, his profound knowledge of the human heart . . . rendered him almost irresistible . . . and secured the success of the great measure he advocated." [15]

There was a postscript to the Literature Lottery Act, an unexpected rider which to Nott, still the Christian Millenarian, must have seemed a revelation, proof that his gamble had been, in truth, a "hazard," and no gamble at all.

"No Bill before the Legislature," it was reported in the Session Laws for 1814, "excited greater interest and attention than this Act. Much credit is due to the unwearied exertions of the able and eloquent President of Union College in promoting its passage."

II

The great Lottery Act governed the Commencement exercises in July. One student orator made his theme, "The Necessity of Virtue and Public Spirit to a Free Government"; a second student spoke on "The Importance of a National University," an educational ideal with strong French overtones and a Jeffersonian blessing which could only be realized if there were publicly supported schools and colleges.

Eliphalet Nott's baccalaureate delivered Commencement Wednesday was the speech which, in Greek tragedy, would surely have brought messengers from Delphi with foreshadowings of grief. Without mentioning the Literature Lottery directly, Nott made it the subject of his address. Because collegians before the Civil War were more often students of morality first, and then students of the sciences and literature Nott felt impelled to rationalize for them and their parents the vast lottery enterprise he, his Trustees and the State had just joined to write into law.

The oblique approach, the euphemism, the elastic definition, Nott's increasing use of these sophists' devices show through an address which he announced was to be an attack on gambling and gamblers. He would not, he told his audience, "hold up to universal obloquy," everyone who takes part in a game of chance. Many of these are good men; the apology for such gamblers is "that they sin ignorantly," even as does the humane master of slaves, before whom he would speak of slavery "with utter detestation." [16]

In what ways, Nott asked his hearers, does the gambler sin? Because he unprofitably consumes time, because he misapplies property, because gambling "imparts no expansion or vigor to the mind," and because "gambling's influence on the affections, and passions, and heart is deleterious." Nott headed his list of gamblers with the card player, "an automaton, a living mummy, the mere mechanical member of a domestic gambling machine . . . [in him] envy rankles, jealousy corrodes, anger rages, and hope and fear alternately convulse the system."

And then, in one paragraph of this baccalaureate, as though it were an aside with which all right thinking men agreed Nott inserted the distinction he wished his hearers and the hosts of "adventurers" soon to be asked to buy lottery chances to make: they were not to think of themselves as gamblers, but rather, as buyers of hazards. The gambler challenges Natural Law, but the man who hazards only invites the operation of Natural Law because, in hazarding, he consciously serves God's purpose. If the hazard serves "some principle of public policy . . . if the transaction will, on the whole, be beneficial to the parties or the community," no crime is committed. The hazard, Nott pronounced, must "benefit society," the community "must be indemnified" by it, or else it becomes gambling, and so "the order of nature is reversed."

The rest of this baccalaureate was little better than an oratorical wax works of pleading wives and orphaned children, of gamblers who, blindly reversing the order of nature, earned for themselves the degradation God visited on them. The rationalization, of course, was both Christian and pagan, and there was comfort in it for Nott as well as for the thousands who were to flock to the "Fortunate Offices" for their six dollar tickets, or their half or their fractional shares in the Literature Lottery; they were "adventurers", hazarding, many of them, all they earned, or could borrow, or steal. What to the sceptics was word juggling was the ultimate rationalization which was to carry Eliphalet Nott, the Christian apologist, through the decades during which the Literature Lottery was to spread fortune and misery, and even suicide in ever widening circles from that "new and airy site" on which he envisaged the college he intended to make the glory of New York State.

CHAPTER 2

The "Grand Plan" takes shape

THE climate of Harvard, it has been said, favored the translation of its officers into marble busts. The "noble type," the Cambridge Man, was a President Kirkland, a President Josiah Quincy, the latter a man of probity, a no-nonsense man, a cautious reasoner, conservative, without affectation, kind, given to understatement, brimming with filial and paternal affection; briefly, a marble bust, or at least one marbleized.[1]

The President of Union College who moved with his students into new classrooms on an unfinished campus facing frontier America in September, 1814, was not the Harvard type. Where the Cambridge man resisted change in courses and methods of teaching, Nott proposed change and forgot method. His advice to a new instructor would have reversed the flow of the Charles had the President of Harvard given it:

> 'You are fond of Greek,' Nott said to young Tayler Lewis, '. . . it is a noble study . . . I care less for Greek than you do, and less for books as a means of educational discipline. But a college must have a wide curriculum, to be a varied or enlarged as circumstances may demand. All kinds of men and minds are needed. . . . go on, ride your own hobby, but do it becomingly; do not rail, as you are sometimes inclined to do, at the practical, the utilitarian, the scientific. . . .'[2]

Professor Tayler Lewis, who was to know Eliphalet Nott for almost fifty years, said of him, finally, what could hardly have been said of those who ruled in Cambridge: "To make men of energy, 'men of action,' was his favorite idea."[3] It was the Mohawk flowing east out of the cabin clearings, and the new town sites which glittered at the foot of Nistiquona Hill, not the Charles meandering by Harvard after having passed a dozen rustic Bostons.

Eliphalet Nott's student body was expanding at a rate far greater than that of any other college in America. Harvard and Yale were still graduating larger classes, but Union's fifty seniors who took degrees in 1816 were thirty-seven more than were graduated in 1805. Harvard, in 1816, graduated sixty men, only twelve more than received degrees in 1805, and Yale graduated a class of sixty-one, nineteen more than it had in the year Nott issued his call for progress in all things.[4] Princeton was losing ground, and Williams College, Union's closest neighbor to the east, was in despair.[5]

The new campus, unique in America, was new also in its promise to provide that "wide curriculum, to be enlarged or varied as circumstances demand." The state's recent tidal surge of financial support was based largely on Nott's democratic plan of education, on his backing of Common School Bills, and his program for instructing the talented indigent student for the greater glory of the state. These developments, a little frightening to marbleized conservatives, tinged with that levelling spirit New England expected of the New York breed, accounts in large part for this rapidly growing student body.

In 1815 a new and oddly confusing college "Laws" was issued, much of it a reprint of the "Laws of 1808"; its added pages, however, may have been agreed to after William Riggs, the Schenectady printer, had set up his type, for the body of these "laws" contained a restatement of the courses authorized eight years earlier, but then a second and different curriculum, listed as "The Courses of Study at Union College," appeared as an appendix on the inside of the back cover.

Here, in the new "Laws" of 1815 Union College first offered parallel courses of studies, a situation then unique in American education; here were parallel programs, one of them still heavily weighted with the classics and a second one designed for students, indigent or otherwise, who wanted practical courses rather than courses for scholars and "gentlemen." Here began, apparently, Eliphalet Nott's greatest break with academic tradition, one which was to culminate in his tradition shattering "Scientific Course" of 1827-1828.

The senior year in the "Laws of 1815" was again the chief concern of the President, and for those who elected the new program, the year was now to be given over wholly to the sciences. The Latin and Greek poets, for them, disappeared and even Homer was demoted to the junior class. "Stewart" and "Kames" were combined into a course in metaphysics and a new descriptive course called "Natural History" was scheduled as a series of third term lectures for them.

The junior class, as well as the senior, was to be taught Natural Philosophy and was to face not only an added course called "Fluxions," but was to study a textbook on trigonometry and spherics "printed especially for the use of the Junior class in Union College." Important, too, was the fact that French was once more offered, again as an elective for the student took it only following special arrangements with Nott.

The remaining "Laws of 1815" were much like those published in 1802 and 1808, with this exception: all authority was now officially centered in the President; faculty and students, courses and student discipline, all now responded to his will, and, from the evidence one suspects so, too, did his Trustees.

Princeton, four years later, had good reason to remember an innovating Eliphalet Nott as a veritable Pied Piper. The President of Union, whose obligations to this citadel of Presbyterian orthodoxy were many, agreed to fill the college pulpit during one of his trips to Philadelphia to sit with the Presbyterian General Assembly. President Ashbel Green, who had scrubbed out the last taints of liberalism remaining from the presidency of Samuel Stanhope Smith, must have seemed dour and hidebound to the Princeton undergraduates who, in the spring of 1819, listened to Nott's invitation to greatness. They heard, it was reported, "an eloquent discourse which greatly impressed them with his power as an orator and teacher." He must have been eloquent on that occasion, for when the fall term opened in Schenectady ten men presented their honorable dismissals from Princeton and entered Union College in order to become his students. [6]

For Eliphalet Nott the six years which followed the Literature Lottery grant of 1814 were years of grace during which he no longer had to keep his eye fixed to a telescope set up, one critic had said, for viewing "distant benefits." There were modest excitements: the move to Nistiquona Hill, family affairs, the financial chores of finding money to keep the college solvent until the State's lottery managers could dispose of earlier grants and so begin his drawings, a matter he had been assured they could put off for no more than the six years prescribed by law. These were also the years of those first crude "caloric" experiments which were to make Nott seem to his contemporaries an inventor "second only to Robert Fulton."

"Mr. Madison's War" had echoed north and west of the college. By the end of September, 1814, those students assigned to the hill had maneuvered among the paint pots and builders' debris to find their rooms as the remnants of 14,000 British troops under General Prevost found their way back into Canada from Platts-burg, intimidated by Commodore McDonough's naval victory on Lake Champlain. Schenectady, which had lost none of its Mohawk River sailors to British press gangs, did well by poling military and settlers' stuff west in its big Durham boats and returning, often, with ballasts of cobblestones for Schenectady pavements. "The Star Spangled Banner" was written that September, and the war died the day before Christmas with the signing of the Treaty of Ghent.

The next few years, optimists' years, were all new turnpikes, expanding paddle wheel fleets, the first waves of immigrants, booming foreign trade, easy credit and land, land, land for all users. Looking west from the windows of North and South Colleges students could see the sweep of the Mohawk Valley, soon to be the route of the Grand Erie Canal, "Clinton's Ditch," the greatest geographical and commercial treasure to be found in any of the United States. Promises of almost any dimension now seemed possible of fulfillment, even Jacques Ramée's Court of Honor which was to be Union College. It was simply a matter of time.

Nott, soon after the war, had his portrait painted, when the taste of success was fresher than it would ever be again. Ezra Ames, the cautious bank director and artist of Albany, saw a man about forty years old, obviously in command of himself, full of vigor, a ruddy face, a ship's prow of a nose, eyes hard for a boy to dodge, immaculately stocked, and gowned for learning.[7] Later artists, as Nott grew in fame to justify sitting for them, and then the photographers, were to see not only an aging man, but a man whose eyes and mouth lines said things too illusive for marble, or canvas, or, later, the camera's wink.

The Ames portrait to certain Schenectady county families was of the "yankeedoodler" of the recent Schenectady Common Lands exchange, but to his Trustees, to his students, and to a majority of the New York State Legislature, it was of a man unrivaled as the educator for the times. His baccalaureates and sermons delivered up to 1807 had been published three years later and had established him, according to his editor, as "decidedly the first on the catalogue of pulpit orators in this country."[8] The following year his reputation was such that both the *Edinburgh* and *Quarterly Reviews* joined him to their catalogue of distinguished Americans: Caesar Rodney, Justice Story, Rufus King, Bishop Hobart, DeWitt Clinton, Josiah Quincy and President Kirkland of Harvard, notables who had been asked for testimonials to the British magazines' virtues.[9]

In 1813 the Trustees of Transylvania University in Lexington, Kentucky, the "Athens of America," delegated Henry Clay and others as a committee to invite Nott to become its new President.[10] His distaste for sectarian quarrels, however, partly responsible for his turning down the flattering Park Street Church delegations from Boston, guaranteed his rejecting the offer from Kentucky, for Transylvania was then sickening from local Presbyterian controls.[11] In 1813 he had been in the midst of the literature lottery excitement; his future, so far as he was concerned, was committed. He had no time for what he was to call the "logomachies" of churchmen.[12]

"Year after year I have lived in the hope of a season of rest . . .," Nott wrote to his brother late in January, 1817. This same letter, however, suggests that talk of rest was ministerial rhetoric. Actually he was then very much the man of the Ames portrait: "I am connected with an extensive ecclesiastical body out of which there springs numerous obligations and duties," he wrote to the Reverend Samuel Nott whose circle had never expanded beyond the world of Jonathan Edwards and the Connecticut Valley. "Add to this several societies for benevolent religious purposes," he had continued, "add to this a college to govern, a class to instruct—a congregation to preach to—a

Legislature to visit—buildings to superintend—a new police to organize—a system of finance to arrange and a debt of near two hundred thousand dollars to provide for in these times of embarrassment—together with the concerns of a large family. . . . I begin to think" he had added, remembering, perhaps, the Reverend Samuel Nott's earlier strictures on his ambition, "that this hurry springs out of the Constitution of the World and that to him who will labour, no rest is to be found till he finds it in the grave." [13]

Eliphalet Nott, "first on the catalogue of pulpit orators," with dreams of building democracy's university, was now willing to labor even though the rewards of the Millennium he had been preaching were farther off than he had supposed. "Hurry" as he had said, was "of the Constitution of the World," and at forty the world had become, for him, full of satisfactions. Even though the wars of words within Christendom, "our Andover and Princeton logomachies. . . . ," of Congregational-Unitarian quarrels in New England, and Presbyterian disagreement along the Kentucky frontier, all proved to him that "the period of the millennium has not yet arrived," he hurried into their skirmishes and major battles as peacemaker.

"Brother Cumming," his letter to Samuel Nott reported, "is the same man that he has been and I fear that he will continue to be." The trial of Brother Hooper Cumming had climaxed the winter of 1816-1817 for Schenectady and for most of the Protestant denominations of New York State. Alas, poor Hooper! One too easily pictures Nott holding the skull of the Reverend Hooper Cumming as he philosophized, not on Yorick, but on Slander. A tragedy and a tragicomedy, the death of Hamilton and the unbelievable posturing of Hooper Cumming, until February, 1817 pastor of the First Presbyterian Church of Schenectady, gave Nott two of his memorable moments as an orator.

Cumming probably was deranged, but so attractively deranged that he had never lost a fanatically devoted following. As a plagiarist, "a man whose eloquence covered not a few of his own sins and other men's sermons," he had had an effrontery beyond belief; on one occasion he was said to have preached a Nott sermon as his own to an audience in which Nott himself was sitting. Frequent plagiarisms and intoxication forced his Schenectady congregation to dismiss him, a fact which did not deter the Third Presbyterian Church of Albany from making him its pastor-elect and from unsuccessfully requesting the Albany Presbytery, of which Nott was moderator, to set aside all plans for Cumming's trial.[14]

Nott opened the eagerly awaited preliminary trial of the Reverend John Chester, one of Cumming's accusers, with a speech on slander which was later declared to be "one of the most lucid and discriminating . . . and comprehensive, on that subject to be found in the language. As a literary essay it is worthy of a Foster. As a judicial utterance, it is worthy of a Marshall. . . ."[15]

When one considers the Nott who in his "Discourse" on the death of Hamilton used the calculated theatrical devices Brutus used to incite his audience, and then considers the Nott of the judicial pronouncement on slander one can believe his contemporaries' repeated claims for his power over men, for his knowledge of what moves and what quiets the heart. He had no public apathy to overcome this time. The opening speech at the trial of the Reverend John Chester was a cool, Olympian discourse on the nature of slander, of the motives which give rise to it, and the means by which it is circulated. Its closing paragraph, even without the calming, rational, knowing voice, is proof enough of Eliphalet Nott's range of expression; here he lifted a bitter church quarrel onto a plane above and beyond partisanship:

> Our first enquiry now is after truth; and we ought, with the solemnity that befits judges on character, and without favour or affection, to pronounce between this, our accused brother, and that Christian public to whom our judgment is to be returned. Till we have ascertained what is truth, and pronounced on it our duty is judicial merely; and we are not only not to conceal the truth ourselves, but as we expect to answer it to God, we are not to permit it to be perverted or concealed from others. This done, truth ascertained and declared, the door of forgiveness in Christ's house is always open, and the offender, how great so-ever his offense, may, by repentance and reformation, enter it.

The Reverend John Chester and then Mark Tucker, a former student of Nott's, were acquitted of slander, and Hooper Cumming, after trial and appeal, was left to go his own way, in company with a congregation which was not disturbed by the Presbytery's dismissal of him, "because of a partial derangement of mind." [16]

Life in Schenectady must have been duller with the gaudy Hooper Cumming gone. Eliphalet Nott and Professor Macauley took over his vacated pulpit for the next three years, until the divided congregation agreed to accept the Reverend Walter Monteith, who had been one of the three harried Union tutors during the building of North and South Colleges. [17] There were, however, the seasonal things to bring wonder and piety; the "year without a summer" had preceded the Cumming's scandal, and was a subject of conversation for decades. One imagines the letters home from Nistiquona Hill: June 9 [1816], "ice formed, sleighs were in use, and leaves fell from the trees"; June 17, "a blizzard left 12 to 18 inches of snow"; July 4, "ice formed as thick as window glass." [18]

II

Perhaps the general misery of that awful summer which swelled the stream of New Englanders moving west also spurred Eliphalet Nott to new interest in his iron castings, and grates, and flues. Certainly it was during these few years of grace following the 1814 lottery grant that Nott, the inventor, was born. The hours he was to give for the next quarter century to the sooty labor of his "heat experiments," were to him also his "play hours," as he wrote to a Nellie-nice Mark Tucker who, following the Hooper Cumming trial, constituted himself Nott's adviser and conscience.[19]

If Jacques Ramée's "Russian Stoves" had worked as well in North and South Colleges as they had in David Parish's mansion on the St. Lawrence, Nott might have found other uses for his "play hours" than in giving them up to "caloric." Ramée's parlor ovens, however, could not be put into every student's room, yet something had to be done to compete with the numbing cold that siphoned down the Mohawk Valley from Canada and the Great Lakes; a stove was needed which would be cheap, easy to operate, and, if possible, indestructible.

The Eliphalet Nott who had written an almanac, who had made notes on the Great Eclipse, and who was weighting the Union College curriculum with courses in the sciences was capable of the Yankee tinkering which produced "the coffin," that iron, four-legged rectangle of a stove built to defeat winter and the destructive genius of generations of students. Soon there was one in every student's room, and charges for chunk wood to feed them became regular items on term bills. "The coffin" was to become not only a source of heat, but of legends. These stoves were thrown down stairwells in moments of student excitement, and on more than one occasion they were poised on stair landings, ready to be dumped onto the heads of "townies" who dared to invade student precincts. Nott's "coffin" stoves endured, and for reasons beyond explaining, so too did the buildings in which they were stoked.

Winter then loomed far larger in men's lives than it does to those who now banish it by thermostat. Then there were the open fireplaces for warmth and for cooking, and thanks to Dr. Franklin, Count Rumford, and others who had developed them, wood-burning cast iron box stoves and oblong plate stoves for the kitchen, and for heating schoolhouses and other public buildings.

It is not surprising that the Yankee tinkerer and the humanitarian in Nott finally merged. What began as an off-hour search for a way to make winter bearable in his new college dormitories was to become a study of "caloric" for a higher end, one "turned to the account of the human family," as he now phrased it. [20] Out of this study, however, were to come coal-burning stove and boiler developments whose economic significance may justify those contemporary comments that Nott, the inventor, stood second only to Fulton. He had embarked, unknowingly, by the end of the War of 1812 on a second career as a manufacturer and exploiter of many patents, from those governing a "Fire-place and Chimney" issued in 1819, to those which covered boilers and machinery for his "S. S. Novelty," an anthracite coal-burning Hudson River boat which was to open up a new era in steam navigation. And, unknowingly, too, Nott, the inventor, soon began to introduce dangerous, and at times, almost ruinous financial complications into his own life as the President of Union College.

Criticism of the use to which he put his "play hours" began soon after "the coffins" were installed in the new dormitories. "It has been generally known in the vicinity of Union College," the editor of the Schenectady *Cabinet* reported in 1820, "that Dr. Nott has long been engaged in prosecuting an expensive course of experiments on heat, and it has as generally been believed that his time and money might have been more advantageously employed. In despite, however, of many failures and some derision, he has pertinaciously persisted for more than eight years, during which period it is understood about ten thousand dollars have, in this way, been expended."[21]

The editor of the *Cabinet* went on to congratulate Nott for having succeeded in giving the country its first dual-purpose stove, "a method of employing fire for culinary purposes in the kitchen as well as for warming the other apartments in a dwelling which combine cleanliness, economy, safety and elegance. . . ."

Nott's "Fire-place and Chimney," according to the *Cabinet*, "will displace the ordinary chimney and fire-place, and become the prevalent expedient for housewarming in all the colder districts of our country . . . fuel will become an item in the expense of a family of very inconsiderable amount . . . and considering the growing scarcity of *that article*, and the still greater scarcity of another, that is MONEY . . . I cannot but congratulate our neighbors in the north . . . of being able [now] to mitigate, within doors, the rigors of our climate. . . ."

Nott's work with grates and castings, however, had just begun. The editor of the *Cabinet* had suggested the direction it would take when he referred to the growing scarcity of fuel. America's fireplaces, stoves and expanding steamboat fleets were devouring the forests at an alarming rate, and Nott, who wrote to Mark Tucker that he would "deem it a happiness, should it yet be in my power to increase the comfort of the rich, and lighten the expenses of the poor, and stimulate the exertions of the industrious," was to find a dramatic solution to the fuel problem in his studies of "caloric" during the next decade. As for his critics, he told Tucker, who had complained about the uses to which he was putting his "play hours" and the money he now controlled, that the things he did with his leisure and his charity "are . . . between myself and God."[22]

III

The hurry of the world diverted the President of Union College while the four inefficient lottery managers for the State miscalculated and delayed the drawings of the Literature Lottery in their offices in the New York City Hall. Nott, with six years to wait for them to clear their wheels of lotteries granted prior to his, with six years to wait before he could continue the building of his Ramée campus and push forward his plans for expanding that "curriculum for the times" about which he had lectured young tutor Lewis, spent himself in a dozen ways.

Mrs. Nott, "the wealthy widow from Troy . . ." had been a semi-invalid for some time, and, in the winter of 1817, her husband confided to Samuel Nott he feared she would be "confined again for the winter." He, too, had "been quite sick"; this was the sort of lugubrious report, however, which seemed to be a regular part of his letters back to "Pisgah's Top," to the devoted and critical brother who shared a professional interest in mortality with him.

The Nott household by this time was probably gathered in one of the four "pediment ends" of the Ramée "colleges," although the Trustees had voted two years earlier to build a President's house, "as soon as the funds will permit." Joel Nott, the oldest son, was a Union College senior at this time, and Benjamin, if not John, was quite likely a student at the Schenectady Academy, reestablished in 1817 as a preparatory school for the college. Both John, bothered all his life by lameness and ill health, and Benjamin seem to have been academic laggards, for although John was only a year younger than Joel, and Benjamin less than three years younger, it was not until 1823 that the boys were graduated from Union.

There was also a new half-brother now, Howard Nott, a child in 1817, whose loyalties in this family must have been hard to establish, for he was not only much younger than Sarah, Joel, John, and Benjamin, but much younger, too, than his step-half-brother, Benjamin Tibbits, who had come into the household when his mother became the second Mrs. Nott, and who was also a senior at Union that year.

The gaiety in the President's house seems to have been of Sarah Maria's making. "Sally" was now 18 years old, "beautiful and interesting," according to a "Miss M." who met her in Boston a few years later. There was a rapport between Eliphalet Nott and his daughter, so much like her mother, the exciting and unpredictable Sarah Maria Benedict; it grew stronger each year as her brothers became the lesser beings to their father. The Nott of the Ames portrait may have had command of his Trustees, his college, and his legislative friends, but in his own household he belonged to Sarah Maria in a way no one but her mother had known. His letters to her at this time (she was then visiting in Boston) were gentle lessons in the joy of living:

> A seat vacant at the board, and at the altar, (he wrote in one of them,) reminds us of one we love, and awakens afresh each successive day the desire for her return. And still these days of absence bring with them, as they return, a source of consolation; for we remember that the morning sun rises not on us, till it has risen on you, and that the evening stars, before they are visible in our twilight have already been seen in yours.[23]

Whenever his life touched Sarah Maria's life, it took on aspects of love he showed only to her.

Table talk with this turmoil of children had to be controlled. There was no gossip, only talk of ideas and things, of books, music, philosophy, and always of religion, though Nott seemed to have taken the fear out of it for his children, for he talked about heaven as he talked about earth, and it was sometimes hard to tell where the boundaries of one stopped and the other began.[24]

Sometimes, too, the boundaries between those in the Nott household and many of the "young gentlemen" who occupied the student entries between the "pediment ends" of North and South Colleges must have seemed nearly invisible. With Joel Nott and his step-brother, Benjamin Tibbits sharing both worlds, with John and Benjamin Nott soon to follow them as students, and with Sally receiving the attentions of Alonzo Potter, senior in 1818, a Union College tutor in 1819, and her husband three years later, Eliphalet Nott was paterfamilias to their friends, and to most of the upperclassmen. Joel's roommate wrote back to Connecticut that the President "was a father to him," and boasted that he was wearing a shirt Joel had just given to him.[25] Professor Allen, of the earlier sheriff's courts and sentences to whipping, would not have approved of this "renovated and reorganized" college dominated completely now by a man for whom the parental system had come to mean all its name implied of affection as well as of obligation.

"Our College," Eliphalet Nott assured his brother in the spring of 1817, "is progressive . . . we have done much, but have much more to do. Two buildings four stories high and two hundred feet long are finished—together with a wing to each—two stories high and one hundred and seventy feet long—besides two houses for boarding, with outhouses." Among the latter was that "hospital for a professor" where Thomas Macauley may have been kept during the next year while he was "sinking under disease," probably that smallpox or cholera whose record of graduates on Nistiquona Hill over the next twenty years was written on the ranked headstones in the college cemetery then in the southeast corner of the campus.

One visitor, John Pintard, member of Tammany Hall, and a founder of the New-York Historical Society, after spending the night with the Notts in February, 1818, wrote to his daughter that the new colleges were each "as large as Nassau Hall," and that two more like them were to be built.[26] Schenectady, with its six thousand inhabitants in that year, was becoming famous for Union College as well as for the warehouses along the Binnekill and its western trade. Another visitor in 1818, John Duncan, the Scottish educator, looking at raw America with a foreigner's eyes, wrote that Schenectady's "principal claim to our notice arises from the proximity to Union College."[27] Although John Pintard had told his daughter that the city "has several pretty buildings which would not disfigure New York," Duncan was less kind; he blamed the Dutch for the Dorp's appearance, and dismissed the city as "somewhat ancient."

The college, however, impressed the Scotsman: "the distinguished talents and judicious administration of Dr. Nott have caused it to emerge from its obscurity, and it now takes precedence in the public opinion over many others of much older standing." What he could not comprehend was the report that the college "had received benefactions at different times to the amount of nearly 400,000 dollars, 90,000 sterling, and yet the President would permit the same professor to teach Belles Lettres and chemistry, "a combination of functions," Duncan wrote, "certainly sufficiently heterogeneous." He thought he detected the reason: "in the place of the endowment of Professorships, the greater part of this large sum has been expended on the college buildings and grounds." Duncan, the Scottish critic, was limited in his vision, and ignorant of the facts; the America of Eliphalet Nott eluded him.

Life on Nistiquona Hill expanded as this family of students grew and exploited the ever-renewing world of the undergraduate. The year the Literature Lottery was granted there were 160 "young gentlemen" in Stone College; six years later, in the midst of the first of those financial panics whose unpredictable cycles were to stun the nation, there were 255 students, many of them, according to the faculty report of that year, "unusually attentive to religion. . . ."

One reads Billy Lintot's page in the treasurer's record, headed "George K. Nichols (for son William B. Lintot, October, 1819 to April, 1820)," and a window opens on a world wonderful for what it had not yet become as well as for what it was: the October days were then shortening along the Mohawk Valley, and so the entries for lamp oil increase. Before the end of winter Billy was spending almost a dollar a month to keep his student lamp going. His Nott stove was rented at $3.00 for the winter, and "skates, shovel and tongs" cost him $1.70 more; wood for October was $2.00. Twelve weeks' board, "at the most expensive house," was $33.00. In December Billy Lintot was billed $1.25 "for wine, when unwell." He was billed $1.00 for paper and quills. A plaid cloak was charged at $8.00 and a new pair of pantaloons at $5.00.

The Schenectady tailors apparently had an importance in undergraduate life which they have long since lost. William Henry Seward, who venerated Eliphalet Nott from the time he entered Union as a callow freshman, testified that the bills he owed his tailor for keeping him up with the college Joneses were to blame for the serious break he had with his father, and for his running away from college for a period of schoolteaching in Georgia.

Lincoln's Secretary of State, looking backward to the Union College he had known between 1816 and 1820, wrote in his *Autobiography*, "I think I know of no institution where a manlier spirit prevailed among the undergraduates than that which distinguished the pupils of Dr. Nott."[28] Seward, who had never known Professor Benjamin Allen's inquisitorial courts, remembered that discipline was a private affair between a boy and his professor, or the President himself, and that if a boy had to be dismissed there was no fanfare announcing his disgrace.

Seward, recalling teachers and teaching, thought the college had permitted too much democracy: "the young, the dull, the backward, equally with the most mature and most astute," recited together, repeating the lessons memorized the night before, most of these "fragmentary tasks, while no volume or author was ever completed." Seward, however, was Phi Beta Kappa bright, and Nott's more tolerant prescription of a college prepared to train "all kinds of men and minds" for the brotherhood of Christians he then believed American education could produce was not for this intense young man.

Seward and his roommate, as juniors, decided they had to belong to the newly organized Phi Beta Kappa Society in which they were sure they would "acquire great secrets of science," and that they would "hold them in common with the great men of the country and the age," such men as "DeWitt Clinton, Chancellor Kent, and Dr. Nott."

The two boys gave up going to the college commons, stocked their dormitory room with provisions, rose at 3 A.M., "cooked and spread our own meals, washed our own dishes, and spent the whole time which we could save from prayers and recitations and the table, in severe study . . . need I say," Seward noted, "that we entered the great society without encountering the deadly blackball?"

Life on the hill then merged excitingly with the crosstides of state and national political life. Seward, as a senior, on behalf of the college "bucktails," those supporters of the Martin VanBuren branch of the New York Republicans arrayed against Governor DeWitt Clinton in 1820, delivered his first party speech before Vice President Daniel Tompkins, then running for governor against the overwhelmingly popular father of the Erie Canal; although Tompkins came up to the campus to hear his speech, Seward remembered that it "fell on stony ground," for Clinton was reelected.[29]

In 1820 the leading edge of that shadow which was to darken into the Civil War crossed the new campus. Before the national excitement over the admission of the Territory of Missouri into the Union and the Missouri Compromise which grew out of it, Nott's Northern and Southern students mingled simply enough as young Americans. Following this slavery compromise, however, a sense of separateness, according to Seward, created two college groups, increasingly at odds and soon organized to demonstrate their differences.

Nott, who, in his first baccalaureate in 1805 had challenged his young "adventurers" to test their common humanity by every device they could discover, instead of curbing the growing debate (Seward said the faculty "imprudently sanctioned it") allowed the Southerners to break away from the Philomathean Society, oldest of the two college literary groups, and set up an all-southern Delphian Society; in this way these Southerners would be forced to defend the institution of slavery and their new contention that the Southern way of life was superior to life in the North, not as a student rabble, but as responsible citizens governed by reason and the rules of debate.

Undergraduate ideas flowed vigorously and therapeutically. Seward, as a "bucktail" senior, tried to prove to his fellow members of the Adelphic Society that the Erie Canal then rapidly being extended west toward the Great Lakes and east toward the Hudson was "an impossibility, and that even if it should be successfully constructed, it would financially ruin the state." As a member of Phi Beta Kappa he took the negative on the question: "Ought the territory of Missouri to be admitted as a state without the proposed restriction?" and at Commencement that July he defended "The Integrity of the American Union."

Table talk in the Nott household could hardly have been more earnest or more wide ranging than were the debates on Saturday afternoons, on Anniversary days, and at Commencement in the halls of these undergraduate societies behind the pediment ends of the Ramée "colleges." Philomatheans, Adelphics, Delphians, and the members of that custodian of the secrets of science, Phi Beta Kappa, pronounced on the world and the universe:

> "Is the Growing Power of Russia dangerous to the Liberties of Europe?"
> "Can an Individual be Civilized?"
> "Is the Cultivation of a Military Spirit Beneficial to the United States?"
> "Was the Reformation the result of Natural Causes or the Special Interpretation of Divine Agency?"
> "Would it be Politic for the United States to assist the Southern Patriots in obtaining their Independence?"[30]

"Commencement in July, wrote Seward, "was signalized by an open feud between the Delphians, now known as the 'Southerners,' and the combined Philomatheans and Adelphics, now the Northern party. The class separated on the stage, and I think it was not until thirty years afterward that I received a kind recognition from any one of the seceders." [31]

If the darkening shadow of the slavery controversy embittered the Commencement exercises in 1820, there was a local but no less disturbing shadow cast over the Trustees' meeting which preceded it. The treasurer's report showed that the college was dangerously in debt. Nott's time of grace had run out; his plans for two more "buildings as large as Nassau Hall," a library, a steward's house and a President's house were still waiting for the lottery wheels to mix their mortar of dollars. In New York City the state lottery managers were deep in a scandal which would soon sweep across the new academic Court of Honor on Nistiquona Hill, across that "renovated and refounded Union College" which Nott had made a ward of New York State.

Henry Yates, junior State Senator and Mayor of Schenectady as well as Union College treasurer, was told by the Trustees, as the panic of 1819 spread ruin everywhere, to sell off the lots in the "military Grants" in western New York for what he could get for them and to mortgage the "gores and gussets" of the Schenectady Common Lands then held by the college. The following year he sold the last of the Union College share of the Garrison Lands at Fort Ticonderoga "beginning at a small elm tree marked 'C.C.U.C.G.W. 1812' " to William F. Pell for $2,964.50, about 300 acres on which the Pell Family a hundred years later began the restoration of the great fort on the headland between Lake Champlain and Lake George.

At the Trustees' meeting that July, in 1820, while William Henry Seward was rehearsing his Commencement oration on the integrity of the American Union, faculty salaries were reduced twenty percent below their prewar level, for by this time not even the combined talents of the President and his treasurer could alter what they then reported to the Board was "the depressed state of the finances."

The six years of grace had ended dismally. The lottery to date had produced nothing. The next year, at Commencement, the treasurer reported to the Board that Union College owed $135,602.11, and that the State had been able to pay in nothing more than a part of the interest on the $200,000 lottery granted in 1814. The Comptroller of the State of New York, Archibald McIntyre, long hamstrung by the incompetence of the lottery managers, sat for the last time as a Trustee in 1820, for that year an anti-Clinton Council of Appointment, following the defeat of Vice President Tompkins for the governorship, paid off political scores. Changes in the New York State political alignment not only immediately changed the state officers who sat on the Union College Board of Trustees, but, at this critical moment in New York State history, they produced political upheavals which altered the course of Nott's life.

The President of Union College had discovered during the preceding six years that somehow "bucktails" and Clintonians, "Martlingmen" and Lewisites, and a dying Federalism and a surging democracy were intricately involved in the future of his "Grand Plan," and that that future was not to be the simple unrolling of a scroll written in heaven. "A college," he had told tutor Lewis that year, "must have a wide curriculum, to be altered or varied as circumstances may demand"; those circumstances which bore on Union College he could no longer doubt, though shaped in heaven, were reshaped in Albany.

No messengers from Delphi arrived in Schenectady with the appropriate forewarnings. For Eliphalet Nott, however, and for the college the vast, tragic unfolding had begun; the political events, the panic of 1819, the lottery scandal, were as the first rings moving outward from the dropped stone toward a hidden shore. Those at Harvard who read the Greek dramatists, had they then been privy to the whole of Nott's life, would have thought the analogy, though overblown, at least descriptive.

CHAPTER 3

"A man divided"

ONE becomes aware, from the time the acknowledged and the "secret" lottery contracts were signed, that Eliphalet Nott, having accepted their conditions, is a man divided. In effect, he now becomes the protagonist of two plays, one, the Christian Morality in which he continues to act out the role of God's vicar, Eliphalet Nott, Doctor of Divinity, the President of Union College—a play whose traditional lines, however, seem at times unintelligible as the clamor of the play within the play drowns them out. In the inner play, more Greek than Christian, Nott declares his lottery contracts and all their fruits to be instruments of virtue, and so he challenges that Fate of the Attic stage which is concerned, not with a man's pretensions, but with his acts. As these two plays, from now on always interacting on each other, merge in their last and inevitable scene, their protagonist regains the human dimension, and Eliphalet Nott, stepping out of the Christian Morality, speaks, finally, as he lies dying the only words possible to a man who has heard the Furies.

"The plan," as Yates and McIntyre called it, was supported by Archibald McIntyre who, with good reasons for bitterness, had just been forced out of his office as Comptroller of New York State and because of that fact had just lost his seat on the Union College Board of Trustees. It was chiefly John Barentse Yates's plan and then, of necessity, it included his older brother, Henry Yates, Schenectady Mayor, State Senator, and treasurer of Union College, and Eliphalet Nott. Stage by stage "the plan" unfolded.[1]

On the 24th of July, 1822, the first objective was achieved when the President of Union and his treasurer filed in the office of the Mayor's cousin, John VanNess Yates, the Secretary of State,

ELIPHALET NOTT. Portrait by Ezra Ames, c.1820. Owned by the Old South Association, Boston, and on loan to Union College; photograph, Schaffer Library, Union College.

TICKETS IN THE SEVENTH CLASS, UNION COLLEGE LITERATURE LOTTERY, May 1822. Tickets and photograph, Schaffer Library, Union College.

their acceptance of an offer unique in the history of education. Nott had agreed that day, on behalf of his Trustees, to take over from the State of New York the sole management of the Literature Lottery. Five days later the strategy seemed complete when Nott and his treasurer signed a double contract embodying secret clauses with the new firm of Yates and McIntyre, lottery managers.

Jabez Hammond, the New York State political historian who knew all the men involved in the evolution of the plan, said that the agreement signed on the 29th of July was "one of the most important contracts, if so it might be called, that was ever made and executed in this community."[2] The estimation was justified in more ways than Hammond ever publicized, for out of that contract was to come a train of events which culminated in a bitter and spectacular legislative investigation of Union College and its President. Because of that contract the highest public officials of New York State who, during its existence, were also Trustees of the college, were to be faced with a threat so serious to their reputations as custodians of public funds that one of them, John C. Spencer, successively Secretary of State of New York, Secretary of War, and then Secretary of the Treasury of the United States, gave himself for more than a year to Nott's defense, and so indirectly to defending all of those who were in any way a party to the Yates and McIntyre agreements. The lid to Pandora's Box, on the 29th of July, 1822, opened wide.

The plan itself was the product of the political and economic aftermath of the War of 1812, the threatening collapse of the New York State lottery system, and especially of the ambitions of four unusual men, ambitions which proved to be beyond the powers of their contracts to limit.

Everywhere Nott looked, there, it seemed, stood another Yates. When Mayor and Senator Henry Yates became clerk of the Union College Board of Trustees in 1800, the year Eliphalet Nott was made a member of it, he came to meetings with his austere and humorless older brother Joseph, and his cousin John I. Yates, both of them charter Trustees of the college, each of whom had taken his turn as mayor of Schenectady, an office Henry himself occupied after them, from 1817 to 1824. Henry Yates was a mildly handsome man, obviously used to good living, his vivid blue eyes and strong nose seeming at odds with the slightly feminine cast of his face which he framed in deep sideburns, curled forward under his earlobes. Born in Schenectady in 1770, the treasurer of the college was three years older than its President. He had been a captain in the reluctant New York State militia during "Mr. Madison's war," had studied law in Albany with Abraham VanVechten, an antediluvian Federalist, and had then practiced his profession with his older brother Joseph in whose Front Street office in Schenectady he would have soon lost any vestiges of the Albany taint. The high Republican winds which blew through Front Street carried him into a Schenectady County judgeship, two terms in the New York Senate, and two terms on Governor Tompkins's all-powerful Council of Appointment, that archaic engine of party politics.

Henry Yates' brothers and cousins were always within easy reach. On the college faculty in 1822, the year "the plan" burgeoned into its green contracts, was a younger brother of the treasurer, Professor Andrew Yates, teacher of Moral Philosophy and Logic. The following year a nephew, John Austin Yates, was made a tutor; it was to be tutor John Austin Yates who, a quarter of a century later, as Professor Yates, would cry "Havoc!" in order to destroy the Eliphalet Nott who had hazarded far more than he knew when he signed the lottery contracts of the 29th of July, 1822.

Mayor and Senator Henry Yates, whose mind according to Jabez Hammond "may have been biased when he himself was not aware of it," had what John C. Spencer was to call during the bitter legislative investigations of Union College, "his connexions," all in surprisingly strategic positions. In 1822 Henry Yates joined his devoted younger brother, John B. Yates, Archibald McIntyre's partner in the firm of Yates and McIntyre, in signing the momentous lottery contract. Henry's older brother and law partner, Joseph, President of the Union College Board of Trustees and, that year, by virtue of the fortunes of the Republican Party the governor-elect of New York State, had agreed to become one of its sureties. The "House of Yates and McIntyre," as the members of the firm liked their partnership to be called, even as the House of Atreus, could invoke family powers.[3]

John Barentse Yates, fourteen years younger than his watchful and tolerant brother Henry, enjoyed the warmed silver spoon for most of his life. He was graduated by Union College two years before Eliphalet Nott became President: his brother Henry took him into his law office; Bucktail Republicans sent him to Congress for a term which ended in 1817. Because the family was devoted to Governor Tompkins, then retiring to the Vice Presidency of the United States, the Governor gave John Barentse Yates a midnight appointment as manager of the dormant New York State Literature Lottery, a political plum which, as soon as the older corruption-tainted Medical Science Lottery was completed, promised good eating.

This lottery managership seems to have reoriented the youngest of the Yates brothers; he refused to run again for Congress, and instead established a residence in New York City where the state's lottery managers had their headquarters. An impetuous and impatient man, however, he was not one for waiting. He had already invested heavily in lands south of Utica, within a mile of the route of the Erie Canal, and he now had time to see to his holdings personally. By 1818 he had established a mercantile business at Chittenango, bought a plaster mill, a grist mill, and become a manufacturer of "water lime." His finger on the pulse of this frontier country, he realized its life would flow along the great waterway only a half hour's walk from his village. Within a short time he became the promoter of a lateral canal connecting Chittenango with the Erie Canal and then the owner of a line of packet boats joining Yates country with Utica.[4]

By July 29th, 1822, the day the House of Yates and McIntyre signed its agreements with Union College and with Eliphalet Nott, John Barentse Yates had had his eye on the main chance for some time. Lawyer, merchant, miller, land speculator, canal boat operator, this least stable member of the ever-loyal Yates clan had by that year found his partners for the lottery adventure he proposed to Archibald McIntyre and Eliphalet Nott. Rumor in 1822 hinted that ex-Congressman Yates was overextended and in need of money.[5]

Archibald McIntyre, too, seems to have been financially embarrassed.[6] By the end of February, 1821, he had been driven out of the office of State Comptroller in an angry flurry of knife wielding by the bucktail Republican Council of Appointment, the majority of whose members were convinced he was to blame for the defeat of Vice President Tompkins for the governorship the year before. During the preceding fifteen years McIntyre, with his harried clerk's look, the faithful public servant who dotted his"I's" with decimal points, had managed to stay off the political spoils lists. Politicians of both parties knew him for the most competent financial officer in the State, master of the cobweb of war debts and overlapping lottery grants.

An excess of integrity, however, in the face of Tompkins's inflated claim for a payment of $250,000, the premium the war governor said he had earned in borrowing money to support the state's military efforts, ended McIntyre's unprecedented political honeymoon, as it ended Tompkins's hope to move back into the governor's mansion. Tompkins's bitter legislative supporters had the politicians' pleasure, however, of forcing McIntyre out of the comptroller's office, but in doing so they freed the most knowledgeable lottery expert in the State to find far greener pastures.

Six months after he turned the comptroller's office over to John Savage, his successor, Archibald McIntyre, "with his friend, John Yates, of New York," signed a three-year agreement with the directors of the Union Canal Company of Pennsylvania by which, as partners, they took over the long mismanaged lottery rights of a company struggling to operate the Delaware and Susquehanna Canal. Neither man needed to be convinced of the virtues of canal building. As early as 1816 McIntyre and William James, the Albany promoter, had signed a petition urging the legislature to vote for what its enemies were calling "Clinton's Ditch."

By 1822 John Barentse Yates's packet boats were already floating on Erie water. It was not, however, their old friendship or their interest in lotteries and canal financing which brought these strangely dissimilar men together in the "House of Yates and McIntyre": if their statements can be taken for something more than self-justification in the midst of much later crossfires of incrimination, they became partners, both declared, "with a view more speedily to realize the grants under which the (Literature) lotteries were established, when Union College was bankrupt, and without our success must have been hopeless of relief. . . ."[7]

It was Archibald McIntyre, his high, receding forehead shelving down to a heavy nose, his large, well spaced eyes creased at the corners, his mouth shaped for "no!" and a corona of thick, wavy hair reflecting the arch of eyebrows always at the question, who, "with Mr. Yates, suggested the plan," according to Eliphalet Nott, and "assisted us in the law. . . ."[8] The quadrumvirate of Nott, McIntyre, John B. Yates, and Henry Yates had come together at last to play their roles in as ingenious, and according to the enemies these men were all to make, as devious an arrangement for institutional and personal gambling as New York State had yet known.

The "Plan," to Eliphalet Nott, must have seemed to offer the brightest hazard of all those he had so far taken. "Archibald McIntyre, then a member of the senate of this state," according to a paragraph among the pounds of legal documents their contracts ultimately spawned, "and John B. Yates, a partner of his in the Pennsylvania lotteries, proposed to Eliphalet Nott to agree to the passage of an Act of similar purport and effect; and that to induce him to do this Archibald McIntyre offered in his own behalf, and in behalf of his partner, to contract for the whole of the said [literature] lottery, and to incur all the hazard and expense attending the sale and drawing of the tickets therein, to insure the college against the hazard of loss . . . which lottery . . . they could on the Vannini plan just introduced, complete in five or six years . . . and that at the request of Archibald McIntyre and John B. Yates, Eliphalet Nott, in behalf of the college, consented to cooperate in the procuring of the passage of the Act of April 5, 1822. . . ."[9]

As *Senator* McIntyre, sent back to Albany in 1821 "from the Middle District" embracing Fulton County and his home town of Broadalbin where his devotion to DeWitt Clinton and the Erie Canal meant votes, Archibald McIntyre was in a strong position to push the plan among politicians who had long respected his judgment. Senator Henry Yates could be counted on to quiet those who still resented McIntyre's refusal while Comptroller to pay ex-Governor Tompkins's outrageous broker's bill. And the moralists among the legislators, honest ones and those whose virtues were a matter of political expediency, would listen to the arguments of "The Doctor," as the clan of Yateses and Archibald McIntyre always referred to the President of Union College. Eliphalet Nott's pleas would be irresistible for the support of a heaven-sent scheme which would relieve the legislature of its obligation to see that the funds it had promised by the lottery grant of 1814 were at long last paid.

"The plan" seemed simplicity itself: press for a legislative Act "similar in purport and effect" to the Pennsylvania lottery law which gave to the Trustees of the Union Canal Company the entire management of the lottery granted to them, including the privilege of assigning their rights to others, as the canal company had just done to the new firm of Yates and McIntyre.

The timing was perfect. By 1822 the New York State Legislature had demonstrated how sick it was of the whole lottery business. Three years earlier a special committee of the Assembly, after hearing the ugly testimony of fraud and bribery in connection with the drawings then being so badly organized and run by the state-appointed managers, had prefaced its report with a statement which summed up the new attitude:

> The foundation of the lottery system is so radically vicious that your committee feel convinced that under no system of regulation that can be devised will it be possible for the legislature to adopt it as an efficacious source of revenue and at the same time divest it of all the evils of which it has hitherto proved so baneful a cause. . . . the only recommendation of the system of raising money by lottery, is the cheerfulness with which it is paid.[10]

Failures and defalcations among managers and sub-managers of the Medical Science Lottery still being run had cost the State far more than the $109,000 the committee cited. The Legislature, after listening to the litany of lottery evils reported by the committee had struck out angrily in the Lottery Act of 1819 which embodied dozens of stringent new regulations, mirrors of that world of hazard which Yates and McIntyre, and the President of Union College three years later were to claim as their own.

Eliphalet Nott had already made his distinction between gambling and hazarding: the gambler, "an automaton, a living mummy. . . ." one whom "envy rankles, jealousy corrodes. . . ." perverting the order of Nature to serve himself: he who hazards, however, Nott had declared, becomes the man of principle; in hazarding, such a man preserves the order of Nature, and so consciously serves God's purpose in a hazard whose outcome is God's will.

Gamblers, not hazarders, however, were the objects of those stringent new rules laid down by an outraged legislature in an act which the President of Union College must have debated in the dark of the night with that other self, the "Doctor" who accepted John Barentse Yates's "plan" to take over a system of financing "so radically vicious," the legislature was told, there were no regulations which could correct the evils.

Nott as well as the special committee on lotteries knew what those evils were: hundreds of unlicensed lottery offices across the State, "Fortunate Offices," as they were known, selling not only "guaranteed winners" to the credulous, but illegally insuring tickets "to suit the convenience of the Adventurer." Servants, laborers, and ill-paid clerks could place their earnings with such dealers, betting, or "insuring," that a particular ticket would (or would not) become a winner on a particular day or days during the drawing of the scheme for which the ticket was issued. Tickets could be rented from the dealers for some special day favored by the hopeful, or a dozen adventurers could share a six or eight dollar ticket. Tickets were sometimes forged. Bundles of "foreign" tickets from neighboring states were illegally sold by the New York dealers. State managers and sub-managers were known to have bought tickets for themselves, and then to have rigged the drums so that they, or their friends, were the winners. Tickets were often sold on prizes already drawn.[11]

Lottery fever produced scenes from which the moralists were recoiling in horror. The lottery arcades, one of them reported, were filled on the day of a drawing: "with loud imprecations and blasphemy, mingled with the scarcely audible whisper of profane, delirious and intoxicating joy, upon the announcement of a prize."[12] The reformers were filling the newspapers with case histories of insolvencies, frauds, larcenies, and robberies charged to those who frequented the Fortunate Offices; these, in turn, were said to be spreading intemperance and even to be driving their debt-ridden patrons to suicide.[13]

Nott, knowing these things, however, did not hesitate to take over as the manager of the Literature Lottery, a system "radically vicious," in order to raise the promised endowment that was to realize his own "Grand Plan" for Union College. Archibald McIntyre and John B. Yates he had known for years, and he had no reason to doubt that they, working, so they had assured him, for the same virtuous cause, would succeed where the State had failed.

Perhaps, too, the lottery fever burned in "The Doctor" himself. By the 8th of July, 1819, he had won $8500 in either the Medical Science or the Literature Lottery, in both of which he held tickets. The prize, according to an entry in an account book entitled "Dr. Nott's Private and Confidential Fund," was revealingly called "the nett [sic] avails of an investment made by the treasurer of Union College under the direction of the President." This "investment," Nott reported to the legislature four years later, "instead of being retained for individual use, by the purchaser and holder thereof, was gratuitously applied to the reduction of the debt of the Trustees."[14] Through seven lean years, until within a month of the time Nott himself became manager of the Literature Lottery, Henry Yates, "at the direction of the President," made many such investments, buying almost $500 worth of tickets in both the then state-run Medical Science and Literature Lotteries; the latter, at least, must have inspired confidence in the Union College treasurer, for its senior manager was his younger brother.[15]

Nott, apparently, unmoved by the grim revelations of the Baldwin trial of 1818 involving the honesty of some of the managers of the Medical Science Lottery or by the violent public and legislative reactions to it, continued to have cordial dealings with one of its managers, an Isaac Denniston, who was then supplying fruit and shade trees for the new campus, whose son was a student at Union, and who, during the trial itself was reported to have helped to rig a prize of $35,000.[16]

The two Notts, one the Christian moralist and the other the emerging "Doctor," optimist, and opportunist, made their compromise, and in the spring of 1822 the President of Union College, convinced of the sanctity of his mission, again helped to persuade a far less sympathetic legislature than he had known in 1814 to give him "our law," the Act of April Fifth, the lottery measure for which Archibald McIntyre and John and Henry Yates had persuaded him to lobby.

II

That act, "to limit the continuance of lotteries," was not only an admission of a costly state failure in public financing, but it also offered evidence of the strategy worked out by the quadrumvirate. The new state Constitution drafted the year before had flatly prohibited ever establishing another lottery. The Constitutional Convention of 1821, however, recognized that the old ones must drag out their course until the grants for which they were being run were honored. "Our law," took care of everything, as its preamble indicated, disarmingly suggesting how it was to be done:

> and *whereas*, it is believed that said lottery might be managed with greater economy and less hazard, by the institutions interested in its success, than it has hitherto been, or can hereafter be, by the state: and *whereas*, all that could be thus saved by greater economy in the management of said lottery, would go to diminish the loss of said institutions: *And whereas*, by such an arrangement the state would be relieved of the hazard of future losses: therefore,
>
> Be it enacted by the People of the State of New York . . . that it shall and may be lawful for the said institutions to assume conjointly, or to appoint one of their number to assume the supervision and direction of said lottery, and from time to time to appoint such and so many managers thereof, and other agents for the conducting of the same . . . and to make such contracts in relation to said lottery. . . ." [17]

Before the Act of April Fifth was passed Nott had already completed an essential step in implementing "the Plan" by making verbal agreements with Hamilton College, the College of Physicians and Surgeons, the Asbury African Church, and the New-York Historical Society to buy at discount all their rights under the Literature Lottery Grant of 1814. These institutions were quite willing to sell, for none of them wanted any part of the risks involved in this perilous proposal. Union College, in fact, must be the sole owner, supervisor and director of the Literature Lottery, if the full potential of Yates's and McIntyre's plan was to be realized. In order to make their control absolute, Nott and Senator Henry Yates also pledged their personal credit to pay off the other institutions, credit which, in 1822, so far as the President of Union College was concerned, may have been measured by the extent of his wife's estate. There is no reason to suppose, however, that Gertrude Nott objected, for her husband's arguments for action were beyond challenging, granted the moral premise on which he based them. Besides, a wife's estate, in 1822, was in her husband's hands.

Not even the legal language of legislators and lawyers and the Trustees of Union College could long hide the plan's audacity, or prevent a violent reaction to it by the New York State Board of Regents, once its politically sensitive members understood its real nature. By the end of July all but the last of its pieces seemed to be in place.

The second stage of the plan had not been completed until the college Trustees held their annual meeting at Commencement, a Board which was now weighted heavily with New York State officials: John V. N. Yates, Secretary of State, Supreme Court Justice Joseph C. Yates, then Governor-to-be, Samuel A. Talcott, the Attorney General, John Savage, the new Comptroller, and Benjamin Knower, the Secretary of the Treasury, were present.

The Board listened first to the faculty report: the college with 234 undergraduates enrolled, was growing. Professor Macauley, who had lived through the lean years, resigned and was given an honorary D.D. Nott's adopted son, Benjamin Tibbits, presented twelve volumes of the Vulgate in French to the library, and the President presented "Mathias's Account of the Four Monarchies," and a volume entitled "View of the World." Joel B. Nott, the scholar of the President's family, was appointed Professor of Chemistry, and Alonzo Potter, soon to be the husband of Sarah Maria Nott, was made "prospectively Professor of Natural Philosophy and Mathematics," with a salary of $1000 a year.

That July meeting in 1822 reminds one a little of Breughel's picture, "The Fall of Icarus," in which the great event appears off side, as one of many, a casual death, scarcely more worthy of attention than the dogs and the horses and that offshore ship coasting into a blue ocean.

The real business before the Trustees, so far as it concerned these Trustee-state officials, followed their action on Professor Macauley's resignation: the Board voted to accept the lottery burden the legislature had so willingly laid down in April. The Trustees then casually, or apparently so, gave to Eliphalet Nott unlimited authority to supervise the management of the lottery, now the college's chief asset. No action since the Trustees received their charter in 1795 was to have the repercussions which followed this simple transfer of the Board's authority to its President. The man and the Trustees, even as the captain and the crew of Breughel's ship, now headed into uncharted waters.

The Trustees next action was almost as significant; they voted to give the President what aid and comfort they could by transferring to their Schenectady members "and others who may be present" full authority to act for the Board, in the months between the annual July meetings. Interested members were now in easy call, particularly the Yateses.

The third stage of the plan so quickly completed following the Trustees' meeting, shows clearly that Nott had become the chief organizer of this quadrumvirate of new lottery managers. Five days following this meeting, the contract drawn by Nott and McIntyre for the actual conduct of the lottery by the House of Yates and McIntyre, was signed. A document as detailed and perhaps as devious as this one must have been in preparation long before the Trustees met, evidence that those who signed it knew their strength: "this indenture witnesseth that [Union College], for and in consideration of the sum of $276.090.14 to them in hand paid, or secured to be paid with interest" agreed to give to the firm of Yates and McIntyre the right "to the whole amount of tickets at their scheme price . ." in the Literature lottery.[18]

Calculations, over the months during which "the plan" was gestating, must have made for a mathematicians' holiday. The contract, of course, was the heart of it, and the key word in that contract was "Vannini." To McIntyre, the Yateses, and Nott, Vannini was to become known as "the mad Italian," but without him there would have been no contract, for it was his new system of lottery mathematics, leased by McIntyre and tested in Pennsylvania, which was at the base of the whole scheme to take over the state lotteries in New York in the name of Union College. Vannini's system revolutionized the part played by lottery managers; instead of drawings protracted for months, by what came to be called the "ternary system," or permutation plan, drawings could now be calculated in a matter of minutes. McIntyre, whose own genius for figures was affectionately remembered by his political friends, discovered he now controlled a margin of efficiency which guaranteed him success, a margin rooted in Vannini's mathematics which had been unknown to the state's managers.

In 1824 Yates and McIntyre published for the information of their "Adventurers" a broadside "Scheme and Explanation of the New System of Drawing Lotteries" which, for simplicity's sake, presented the "35 Number Lottery" in operation, though their actual "schemes" were far larger:

> The series 1,2,3 . . . . . to 1,2,35 will give 33 Tickets
> The series 1,3,4 . . . . . to 1,3,35 will give 32 Tickets
> The series 1,4,5 . . . . . to 1,4,35 will give 31 Tickets
> Continue in the same manner until you come to 1,34,35.
> The No.1 will then be repeated 33 times in the first series, 32 times in the second series, 31 times in the next; each of the 35 numbers will be repeated an equal number of times, giving a series in an arithmetical progression [to be divided by three] . . . . 6545 will be the No. of Tickets.

In the "35 Number Lottery" five ballots would be drawn from a wheel containing ballots numbered one through thirty-five. That lottery ticket bearing the first three of the numbers drawn won the first prize of $10,000; the second prize of $5000 went to the ticket bearing the 3rd, 4th, and 5th of the numbers drawn, the third prize of $1,310 to the ticket bearing 1st, 2nd and 4th of the numbers drawn, and so on, for the "10 prizes, with 3 Nos. on [the tickets], 300 Prizes with 2 Nos. on them,—and 2,175 prizes with 1 number on them." [19]

The "Vannini System" allowed Yates and McIntyre to draw a lottery in about fifteen minutes, as opposed to the older number-by-number drawings which sometimes took weeks to complete.

And so "the plan" grew, incubated by John Barentse Yates, who, at some point in the negotiations, ceased to be the senior manager of the Literature Lottery for the State, and who joined, instead, the now even more profitable operations of the "House of Yates and McIntyre." Nott, who claimed to have published an almanac as a young man, was an astute mathematician himself and was brought into the plan only on the strength of what he saw the new Vannini system promised.

The contract spelled out the details of that promise. In return for the right to sell all the tickets which the new Comptroller of New York State was still to certify must be sold in order to produce the money for which Nott had been waiting since 1815, Archibald McIntyre and John B. Yates in turn agreed to bear all the expenses of operation: they agreed not to sell tickets at the exorbitant advances on the scheme prices charged by the State's managers. They would "furnish a well lighted room for the drawings," pay the prizes, sell tickets for cash only, bank that cash at the direction of Nott, or his "board of managers," and furnish $70,000 in security for the faithful performance of the contract.

III

If Vannini had inspired what Nott called "our law," the "mad Italian" was indirectly the inspiration for that secret supplement to this agreement, one which could only have been written by that other Eliphalet Nott, the organizer, the man his lottery managers knew as "The Doctor." They reported later, during the chancery suits that were to bring them together as enemies, "that for the purpose of guarding against any knowledge of the second branch of the contract, the first has no reference or allusion to it. The first only [Nott] declared to be his intention to exhibit to the Board of Trustees, if called for." [20]

This supplement, this so-called "second branch of the contract," established the "President's Fund." Into it Yates and McIntyre agreed to siphon 2¼ percent of the money realized from the sale of all tickets under their agreement. Union College was to receive 8¾ percent on these sales until that final amount yet to be certified by the Comptroller was realized, leaving to Yates and McIntyre a profit of 4 percent, instead of the normal 5 percent which had customarily been retained by the managers for the State who, by law, had been directed to deduct 15 percent from their total sales to cover the sums granted, their operating costs, and their own profit. The Vannini System made this new arrangement possible.

Eliphalet Nott had his rationalizations for his "President's Fund". According to Yates and McIntyre, "the Doctor, who developed the draft of this branch of the contract, required that this form should be adopted, as he said, for safety, both to avoid an unnecessary publication of the actual amount that the colleges would receive from the lotteries, and so that a specific sum might be in his own hand to meet contingent losses, should any occur, and in order to render such aid as might become necessary without any formal call on the Board." [21] Nott, defending himself during the chancery suits twelve years later, unconvincingly denied the secret nature of his supplemental contract, and spoke only of its "cautious provisions and restrictions," as being necessary "for the greater security of Union College, inasmuch as neither John B. Yates nor Archibald McIntyre were, at the time, deemed to be responsible to any considerable amount." [22]

Nowhere, however, was the voice of the President of Union College less successful in drowning out the voice of "The Doctor" than in the denial of his secret agreements with his lottery managers. Writing to Archibald McIntyre three years later, at a time when disaster threatened them all, Nott, angry and frustrated by the behavior of the partners, admitted that "there is one man, and one man only interested in the Institutions who knew at the time what percentage we could have and be sure of our money."[23]

That "one man" was apparently William James (grandfather of Henry and William of far greater fame), the Albany merchant and promoter who was the only witness to the dual contract, and who seems to have been the "man of very great wealth" who, as Nott continued in his letter to McIntyre, "was desirous of embarking in the concern after our law was passed. . . ."

What the Trustees were not to be told was that Nott and McIntyre, who together seem to have worked out the details of both agreements, expected that over $100,000 would be deposited to Nott's credit as the nominal manager and supervisor of the Literature Lottery, moneys which, in fact, he was to use later as "The Doctor" in ways which his enemies were to say amounted to a betrayal of his trust as the President of Union College. The question his enemies were to ask was the inevitable one: did not the "President's Fund" belong to Union College? Nott's denial that it did then raised the corollary one: was it, then, a bribe, or more politely, an inducement on the part of Yates and McIntyre to get the cooperation of the President of Union College in a scheme to make a private enterprise of New York State's then failing lottery monopoly?

Neither of these questions concerned the members of the quadrumvirate on July 29, 1822. Their calculations had produced a completely agreeable situation. Yates and McIntyre, who insisted that Nott himself had drafted the supplemental contract, had good reason for keeping a secret which put Nott under as much obligation to them as they were under obligation to him. As for the President of Union College, his secret "President's Fund," born of great expectations, was to become as the waters of the sulphur spring emptying above Hans Groot's Kill in the college ravine where the rocks it touched were discolored, and the nose was offended, and those who drank it lived in hope of rewards its odors belied.

By the end of July, 1822, Archibald McIntyre, John Yates, and the Doctor had each taken his turn in completing the fortified circle of their new partnership. If Senator and Union College treasurer Henry Yates could now succeed in closing the last gap in it, not only would the Doctor insure the privacy without which his dual contract with the House of Yates and McIntyre and the tangle of verbal agreements which grew out of it must have been destroyed, but the Union College Board of Trustees would regain that corporate freedom which had been lost in 1805 to a New York State Board of Regents intent, so Nott was soon to declare, on destroying Union College itself.

A political coincidence, the conjoining of planets, God's will, whatever the agent, Senator Yates saw the opportunity and "suggested the measure" which, according to Eliphalet Nott, now took the Regents unaware.[24]

On January 9, 1823, Senator Yates presented an innocuously entitled bill to a committee of the Upper House: "An Act to amend an Act relative to the City of Schenectady."[25] This bill, actually a lethal blow aimed at the authority of the New York State Board of Regents, was what the irreverent would call a "sleeper," and, for the next five weeks it moved as such through both houses of the legislature, awakening neither Senators nor Assemblymen, and was enacted on February 14, 1823, a mere valentine of a law until the politicians who were also the Board of Regents got around to analyzing its provisions.

These were easily understood: The new State Constitution had cut back the number of Supreme Court Justices (who, by law, were also Trustees of Union College), from five to three. Ergo: by doing this the State had reduced the number of Union College Trustees from twenty-one to nineteen, and had done it unilaterally without consulting the college. And so, by virtue of the sanctity of contracts, the Union College—New York State agreement of 1805 was abrogated, Union College was again a free agent, and the Board of Regents was reduced to the role of "visitor," which might, if it wished, inquire about "matters of education and discipline," but nothing more.

Senator Yates, of course, had not mentioned the Board of Regents that January. He had asked only that the State renew its majority on the Board of the college at once by making his brother, Joseph C. Yates, the new Governor, and the Lieutenant-Governor Trustees in place of the two recently anatomized Supreme Court Justices, and, in a disarmingly phrased clause, that it also agree that all future vacancies among the Trustees "be filled as heretofore they have been filled: Provided [and what could have been more disarming] "the Board of Trustees of the college shall consent."[25]   All Union wanted, he assured the Senate committee, "was to be placed on the same footing as the other colleges are placed." The request seemed so reasonable no one had thought of objecting.

No "adventurer" in the Literature Lottery, however, was to gamble (the "Doctor" would have used the word "hazard") more on the turn of the drum than had Eliphalet Nott on the moccasined movement through the legislature of this amendment, attached to "An Act relative to the City of Schenectady"; it had slipped quietly enough between the aisles of both houses, and it had been hoped, would wait, invisible, until the next full Trustees' Meeting, dominated as it would be by Governor Yates and his bucktail Republican state officers who would "accept" it, and lodge it, a *fait accompli*, in the office of cousin John V. N. Yates, the Secretary of State. The Regents would, from that moment, be eliminated from the financial destinies of Union College, and from the concerns of the President and his treasurer, Henry Yates, in their operation of the Literature Lottery.

By March 24th, however, anguished cries of double dealing were echoing through both the Assembly and the Senate. Nott, years later, still obviously relishing the echoes of the battle the Board of Regents opened that month, told his Boswell, Professor Jonathan Pearson, that "the controversy with the Regents . . . was originally a political affair altogether and not aimed at Union College or himself. Judge Duer, [Chairman of the Regents] he told the sceptical professor, "was a political opponent of Governor Yates and Henry Yates, and for the purpose of attacking them, he attacked the college!. . . . the Doctor says that he wrote all the replies and conducted the whole controversy for Governor Yates and beat the opponents." [26]

The "controversy with the Regents," as Nott had called it, drew him at once into the internecine wars of New York State politics. By the end of April, 1823, he had turned a skirmish into a battle in defense of the sanctity of contracts, and of academic freedom for which he drafted the best political tacticians and legal brains in the State; essentially, he made them try again the famous Dartmouth College case in the name of Union College.

The Doctor's defense revolved around the one idea from which there could be no retreat: the Regents must be denied then and for the future so far as Union College was concerned, everything but the right to inquire "about . . . education and discipline." The defense must also prove that, contrary to the Regents' claim, Union College wanted a Board of Trustees dominated by the State's officers, and wanted them, furthermore, as protection against those very Regents who for the preceding eleven months had been spreading rumors about an "abuse of funds," preparatory, so Nott was certain, to "an attack on Union College . . . a fact well known," he reported, "to many persons in Albany and New York."[27]

Sovereignty, at this moment in the affairs of Union College, was a *sine qua non*. Nott and his Trustees' committee now publicly proclaimed that the State's contract with the college was, indeed, broken.

The legislature, Nott insisted, had agreed unanimously that the contract of 1805 no longer existed, and that it had offered a new contract at the request of Trustees who, he said, "having felt the good effects of the State on the concerns of the Board . . . were willing and desirous to preserve that influence," and who had gladly accepted the Governor and the Lieutenant-Governor as substitutes for the recently dematerialized two Supreme Court Justices. [28]

The Regents' cruelest offense Nott now declared in the sort of panegyric which had always moved his audiences, was against a college which had made the State its partner in education, a college which had placed its faith in the State's continuing aid, and on which, he proclaimed,

> professors have been supported-that library provided-that chemical and philosophical apparatus (inferior to none in America, it is believed) furnished; and on the faith of which grants the very ample site has been purchased and the entire buildings erected, in which a majority of the youth of the state, that are pursuing a collegiate education are and have been, from the time the appropriations were made, enjoying all the benefits and advantages those appropriations were intended to furnish—(not excepting the poor man's sons of promise, taken from their obscurity and educated free of expense, and returned to their country and their friends prepared in either of the professions, for an equal and honorable competition with sons of the wealthiest citizens, who had, from their infancy, been cradled in affluence).[29]

Nott stood firm on his high, constitutional ground. He cited judicial decisions on the inviolability of contracts, and triumphantly pointed to the Dartmouth College decision of 1819, citing Chief Justice Marshall's statement that by "a charter, an artificial, immortal being is created," coequal with any other beings, even the State itself which cannot unilaterally destroy a contract with men or the creatures of its charters.

On Wednesday, April 23rd, the rush toward adjournment on, the Assembly voted to have ALL the pertinent documents printed and referred to the next legislature, an arrangement which should have been satisfactory to the enemies of the Governor and to Nott, who foresaw a new legislature far more hostile to the Albany Regency, and so to Governor Yates, than the one about to adjourn. Even this, however, was not enough for the Board of Regents. The next morning, Thursday, a "Mr. Lynch, of Oneida" demanded that the House agree to the Regents' wish that the Attorney-General be asked to rule on the right of the Assembly to repeal Senator Yates's now notorious college act of February 14th. Its enemies were turning it into a mortal embarrassment to the Governor and to an Eliphalet Nott whose democratic ideas on education were thought to be a threat to the authority of the Regents.

That Thursday (Nott and his committee must have had fast courier service) the college, regretting that the Assembly had passed Mr. Lynch's motion, nevertheless proffered its reply to the Regents, insisting that the college's arguments, too, be printed and submitted in full. Nott declared that Senator Yates's act had not been hastily passed, that the Senator had acted the part of the honest broker.

The time had come for a showdown: these were constitutional questions which must be settled by unbiased, unimpeachable judges. Nott assured the legislators he had no objection to Mr. Lynch's motion; the greater question, however, was beyond the legislature's jurisdiction, and should go to the Chancellor, or to the Supreme Court justices.

Governor Yates, and those Trustees of Union who were also state officials, including the Attorney General, had remained discreetly silent. Nott's reports to the Regents and the legislature were signed by elected Trustees. Nott himself had spoken from Alpine heights, as a Moses from Sinai, lecturing the legislature on Constitutional law while below he could watch the tribal maneuvering of Clintonians, "High Mindeds," and the splintering groups of Regency Republicans preparing for the battle over presidential electors. The White House ambitions of George Crawford, John Quincy Adams, Henry Clay, and Andrew Jackson might so involve his enemies he would win the college case by default.

By Commencement Nott had bolstered his position with the lengthy judicial agreements of former Chief Justice Ambrose Spencer and Judge Jonas Platt, his old friend and the Hamilton College Trustee for whom he had included the Hamilton petition for lottery dollars with his own in 1814. Three of the most respected legal minds in the State, Thomas Addis Emmet, John Wells, and David Ogden concurred, adding that the Trustees had probably regained the right to fill all future vacancies on the Board, including even those seats now occupied by the officers of the State [30]

IV

The meeting that Commencement was attended by Chancellor James Kent, Governor Yates, and Lieutenant-Governor Erastus Root who, as Senator Root ten years earlier, had almost tricked Nott out of the approval of the Senate for his Lottery Act of 1814. Events, however, having moved the irascible General into the brigade of State's officers who were now Union College Trustees, dictated that Nott gratefully mark the change by awarding Erastus Root the Master of Arts degree at graduation.

The Trustees that July decided that the Adelphic Society might use "a small room adjoining their Hall for a mineralogical cabinet." The faculty reported it was concerned that 400 volumes, long on loan to the college, had recently been taken away by the Hartwick Academy of Oneida to whom they belonged, and the librarian informed the Board his only expense for the year was $1.50 spent for an account book.

Professor Alonzo Potter, Nott's new son-in-law and secretary to the faculty, reported that there were 209 students enrolled, twenty-five fewer than the preceding year. There was general pleasure, however, in the additions he noted which had been made to the "Philosophical and Chemical apparatus": "a Diamond," and "a magnetic machine; ... a machine for decomposing water, a Franklin point of platinia, a steamboiler for high pressure, Wallaston's Goniometer, a copper air funnel and holder, a rain gauge of copper, and six forms of crystals." Chemistry, now in the charge of Professor Joel Nott, was developing so rapidly, the board was told, "changes are needed to accommodate this department."

Politics and science found common ground that Commencement when the arch enemy of the Albany Regency, DeWitt Clinton, came to the campus and gave "a scientific discourse" to the Phi Beta Kappa Society. Nott himself had a father's pleasure in seeing his sons John and Benjamin each take his degree on Wednesday, John delivering an oration entitled "Death Preferable to a Life with Dishonour," and Benjamin a poem he called "The Power of Conscience."

It took the following year for the "Controversy with the Regents" to be drowned out in the strident cries of "King Caucus!" leveled at Governor Yates and the Regency Republicans by their political enemies. The Governor, who had probably been the chief target of the Regents' mandamus, was led to the slaughter by the Albany Regency itself, when his friends discovered they must have a sacrificial victim, one on whom they could heap the blame for their own lack of foresight in recognizing the strength of their opponents' demand that the legislature give to the people the right it then exercised to choose the electors for President.

In the hope of saving their own political skins the Regency allowed the governor's enemies to blame him for preventing an electors' bill from becoming law. Their desertion meant the end of Governor Yates's political career, for they did nothing to forward either the hopes he may have had for the Vice-Presidential nomination, or for a second term as Governor. For the "High Mindeds" and the "Coodies," and the friends of DeWitt Clinton, however, divide-and-conquer as a technique paid off, and, in the melee which followed, DeWitt Clinton, armed with the popular vote, became once more the Governor of New York State.

With the courage of one who has found sanctuary in the constitutions of the state and the nation, the President of Union College now magnanimously offered to accept, as he wrote, "any other and satisfactory substitute" for that "Act to amend an act relative to the City of Schenectady," which would be pleasing to the legislature; but a contract is a contract, he pointed out, and any substitute for Senator Yates's legislation which had returned to Union College its corporate freedom would have to be approved in Schenectady as well as in Albany. [31]

The new legislature, by its act of April 12, 1824, admitted defeat, or at least an impasse which, in a presidential year, was more than its members could cope with. Nott's and the Governor's enemies, however, had a last weak word. Union College was not to be denied the benefits of Senator Yates's measure, but, though the resident Trustees had already filed their acceptance of it, the Board was directed to do so again, and not "until February next." [32] From that time on, however, the Regents received only financial information about the use the college made of the money deposited in the "College Fund" by Yates and McIntyre; they were refused anything more "on the advice of the Honorable S. A. Talcott, then the Attorney General." [33] Of the "President's Fund" the Regents knew nothing.

Two weeks before the Legislature conceded defeat to the Doctor and his treasurer, the House of Yates and McIntrye had credited on their books payments amounting to $47,514.40 to the "College Fund"; $17,716.00 had been deposited to "the President's Fund," sums which had accumulated "in pursuance and fulfillment of the trusts . . . committed to them. . . . ," and on account of which, they said, "in or about the beginning of the month of April, eighteen hundred and twenty-three, [they] commenced the selling of tickets, upon a new method of drawing lotteries, called the *Vannini System.* . . ." [34]

If Eliphalet Nott thought at all about the fireball which had flamed "with the light of three suns" over Schenectady that spring of 1822 when John B. Yates suggested the lottery "plan" to him he may have felt it had actually been a sign of grace, considering the course of events since he had become the manager of the great "hazard." [35] As for Senator Henry Yates, his Valentine's Day Bill had closed the circle which bound him, his brother John, Archibald McIntyre, the President of Union College, and the Trustees including the chief officers of New York State, in a fateful enterprise. [36]

BOOK FOUR

The "Grand Plan"

CHAPTER I

"The Republic of the World"

No optimist of the Space Age could be more enamored of his galactic dreams than was the President of Union College of his own optimist's dreams when, on the Tuesday of Commencement Week, 1824, he shared with the members of the Union chapter of the Phi Beta Kappa Society and their guests his vision of the future, of a world perfected, not by any single act of God, but by the acts of men, not by way of ineffable mystery, but through the works of science. The millennial dream he had brought into the presidency with him twenty years earlier had, by 1824, evolved into a new pattern of hope; his was now a new focus: the night air seemed clearer and like the binary stars he saw through the college telescope, the landscape of the future resolved at last into its separate and describable points.

The many men who were the President of Union College: the "Doctor" to his lottery managers, "Old Prex," handsome and a giant presence to his students, the legislative floor-manager extraordinary to the Albany politicians, and the poet-father to Sarah Maria, his daughter, merged, that Tuesday, into the supreme optimist as he proceeded to thrill an audience which probably included Governor Yates, the Secretary of State, the Comptroller, and the Chief Justice who were then in Schenectady in their role of Union College Trustees. What the speaker said to his audience made the recent affairs of "bucktails" and Clintonians, of state electors and lotteries seem Lilliputian by comparison.

The open sesame to the wonderful world Nott conjured up for his listeners was the word "Means." To understand this ritual word of the church in the new definition Nott now gave it one must dissociate oneself from our age of scepticism. One must perform an act of the imagination, must recreate that climate of opinion in which Nott lived and acted from 1800 to the Civil War, those decades of seemingly endless frontiers when men were ignorant of Fermi, Einstein, Freud, James, and of Darwin, a less complex age which believed the atom and the unvierse were equally within the boundaries of the kingdom of God.

"If 'Means,' " Nott said to his audience of Christians who, in those decades, were also politicians, Erie Canal promoters, speculators in western lands, and the "young adventurers" now overcrowding his new classrooms devoted to "chymistry" and "the philosophical apparatus," "if 'Means' are the instruments in effecting man's *moral* renovation, then why should they not be such in effecting his *physical* renovation also?"[1]

If the President of a modern university should say to his students, "nuclear fission is the instrument in effecting man's *physical* renovation and why should it not be in effecting his moral renovation also?" he would be suggesting a no more radical use of the power of the atom than was Nott of the use by men of the power of God.

"Means" to Nott no longer meant only those devices of the church: attention to the Gospels, the formula of Baptism and those other Christian prescriptions by which men showed obedience to God. "Means" had now become the central word in his optimist's vocabulary: "Means" were now to be considered the instruments of the engineer, the dollars of the banker, a spreading democracy, highways to the West. "From misery as well as from guilt," he told his audience, "it is [man's], by the help of God, to accomplish his own deliverance and to work out his own salvation." Here was the synthesis of the moral world and the physical world America wanted: here was a Christianity sounding with timbrels and bugles to action, a clear, loud call "to work out" the renovation of this world. Earth, Nott had come to believe by 1824, must first be remade, its causes of misery eliminated, before man can expect the Millenium for which he must no longer wait, but which, in truth, he must earn.

Where then, lay the future? It belonged to free men weaving "the web of their own destiny." This was God's will, he said, and saying it was like slitting the winding sheets and stepping from a Calvinism which promised men only blind tomorrows. Nott was free at last of "Pisgah's Top," the school where his brother had taught him the fear of the Lord but not the wisdom of the Lord.

Knowledge, he told this college honor society in 1824, is power; it guarantees "a dominion extending with every extension of science, not only over animals, but over the elements, and brings Nature herself into greater and greater subjection." Science, to Nott, had become God speaking. As a natural philosopher, an astronomer, an investigator of "caloric," Nott spoke as a new prophet to the kind of men who were to bring to pass the new world he pictured for them as he now ranged from observations on interplanetary communication to speculation on the "true atomic theory."

"Nor ought the friends of science," he continued, "to remit their exertions until the most degraded tribes of earth shall have become regenerate, and shall stand forth each in his own Augustan Age. . . . until Attic wit and Athenian models shall everywhere appear; until Negroland shall have produced her own Granville Sharpe, Abyssinia her Milton, Thibet her Homer . . . until all that is gross, and vulgar, and revolting shall disappear, and not cities and provinces merely, or even empires, but the entire world shall exhibit through all its territories whatever is tasteful in art, recondite in science, or enchanting in eloquence and song." Not even in the midstream of his own eloquence did he call out the traditional landmarks of religion and the church; science marked the way into the future.

A college, he told the Phi Beta Kappa Society, "is the source and center of a mighty influence . . . not only over the scientific, but the unlettered public." Nor need his students fear that men have grasped all science has to reveal.

> Who knows, [he challenged them] but that some bolder and more fortunate experimenter is even now unsettling doctrines hitherto believed to be settled, and is displacing by solution from the ranks they occupy, not only potassium and sodium, but the entire kindred class of metallic bases? Who knows but that a more condensed heat brought to bear upon a crucible, or the electric stroke from some more powerful battery may not reveal to the sense of man some still simpler elements, more subtile [sic] combinations . . . nor will analysis have reached its utmost limits," he continued, "until all the elements which Omnipotence employs are known and named, and all the processes are revealed which perpetually succeed each other throughout the entire extent of a decaying and reviving universe.

"There was a time," he said, "when religion . . . saw in the everyday appearance of the heavens omens only of immediate dissolution (as did) Philosophy, too . . . by asserting that the solar system contained within itself a principle of destruction which was hastening its end by approaches which were visible." Eighteen years earlier Nott had made audiences shudder as he pictured a not too distant final dissolution, but "now," he said, "that time has gone by. . . . Science no longer supplied arguments against even that endurance of the earth . . ." which, as an enthusiastic young Millenarian he had once believed would end during his lifetime. Newton had assured men that the planets maintain their relative positions in a continually "readjusted system."

New achievements and motives for new efforts, he told his Phi Beta Kappa audience, will be found not only in astronomy: "the minimum of nature is as difficult of ascertainment as the maximum . . . perhaps as many wonders are yet concealed by nearness and minuteness as by distance and dimension . . . the internal structure of plants and minerals," he predicted, "shall become as familiar as their external aspects," and science will push on until "the true atomic theory shall be exhibited in experiment and verified by observation," until "visibility shall be imparted to elemental particles."

The "time may come," he predicted, as he looked into his optimist's crystal, "when rain, snow, and earthquakes, and tempests, and the various meteorological phenomena . . . shall be reduced to fixed and general laws; and their return, and duration, and degree shall be as capable of calculation as the ebbing of the tides, or the changes of the lunar phases."

Although he had at one time been convinced earth would be destroyed in a cataclysm of converging sun and planets and shattering meteors, by 1824 he saw a more cheerful prospect: "Man," he continued, "still looks upward with an eager eye, under the influence of a vague presentiment that the firmament above him contains something more than a mere orderly display of magnitude and motion, and that the orbs which roll in it may be the residence of some race of kindred spirits: spirits, it may be, whose acuter vision or more powerful glasses enable them to look down on us, regardful of our progress, eager to communicate their sympathies, and impatiently waiting for the time when our improved instruments shall enable us to recognize their signal, and to give back by telegraph from our sidereal watch-towers the signs of recognition."

"Who knows," he continued, "but some future and greater Herschel may construct an eyeglass of power to bring their habitations within our range of vision, and thus enable man to commence a correspondence with his sidereal neighbors? Who knows but that future generations, communicating with the nearest planets, and through them, with planets more remote, may effect an interchange of tidings, passed from world to world with the celerity of light, and carried as far as the sunbeam travels?"

The year before, in 1823, an eel three feet long had been the first living thing to pass east into the Hudson River from the new Erie Canal. Two weeks later, on October 8th, Governor Yates, the Mayor of Albany, and guests floated out of the locks below Stephen VanRensselaer's manor house, and into the river, the first travelers on a new highway still building that following July when Eliphalet Nott looked upward from the high ground above "Clinton's Ditch," five minutes walk from Union College, toward the "habitations . . ." of his "sidereal neighbors."

What an age to adventure in! "We have lived," he continued, "to see the lightning chained, and its dread stroke averted from the frail edifice . . . we have lived to see the ship made independent of the breeze . . . breasting the tempest by the impulse of steam . . . we have lived to see inland villages converted into ports of commerce, and inland products floating on artificial rivers traced by human hands, and connecting distant lakes with distant oceans."

"Who," he challenged his audience, "can set limits to science?" If, as he now believed, the scientist as well as the priest was an instrument of salvation there were no limits; nothing, then, must hinder the scientist, armed with divine means, in his work of renovating a world which could not progress morally until men had eliminated poverty and disease, as well as racial and social injustice.

Science, Nott pointed out, had recently produced the elements of a universal language, a sign language which was opening avenues to knowledge for the deaf and dumb, and which might, he prophesied, "be employed to remedy the more diffusive ills that have resulted from the confusion of tongues at Babel . . . this new language of the eye [may be] the only language which has any prospect of becoming universal."

Progress in medicine was there for all to see: "even hydrophobia is said to have yielded to surgical operation; and vaccination . . . has nearly removed the horrors of one of the most dreadful scourges of mankind . . ." "the maladies of the mind . . ." he declared, "are beginning to be better understood . . . no longer is the lunatic bound in chains . . . American physicians have contributed to juster views . . . to medical skill in Britain . . . is to be attributed that . . . increase in the average duration of human life. . . . so long as a disease remains to be healed," he now promised his young hearers, "or a pain to be relieved," there is work for the scientist to do. In time, he said, "the longevity of antediluvian man will return. Visionary or profane as we may deem it, the time approaches when the age of man shall be as *the age of a tree; and the inhabitants shall not say I am sick*."

Turning from visions of interplanetary communication and the earthly conquests of weather and disease, Nott looked into the future of nations: "In political as well as physical science," he told his audience, "a like progressive development is apparent: the new world," he said, "is in the midst of the sublime experiment of practical self-government, which will, in time, have its reactions in Asia and Europe". But, he warned, the great experiment will fail in America if the political scientist does not solve the problem of slavery.

Eliphalet Nott had taken his stand publicly on slavery as early as 1811 (he appears to have named his youngest son "Howard" for the English prison reform leader John Howard, and soon his first grandson would be called "Clarkson," perhaps for that Thomas Clarkson through whose efforts England had ended her slave trade). As the ugly controversy expanded Nott was to stand firm on his conviction: progress for America must include those political "means" which would free the Negro from his unnatural state of bondage.

Nott's Southern students, and his reputation as a man of affairs and an educator were drawing them in greater numbers to Union every year, were made to feel that the North bore a guilt even heavier than did the slave-owning South. "If the planter," he told his Phi Beta Kappa audience in 1824, "has long appeared in the odious character of *receiver of stolen men*, the trader of the North has long appeared in the still more odious character of *man-stealer* . . . in New England capital slave ships have been built . . . in New England, too, have stood the workshops in which those yokes and manacles have been forged that weighed on the limbs of the captive Negro during his passage to bondage." "The North and the South," he declared, "bear a joint iniquity . . . slavery in all its forms is odious, it is an evil gratuitous and unmixed . . . equally an evil to the slave, his master, and the state."

He did not stop with denunciation, but went on to prove his charges with the seemingly infallible argument: slavery (as he had said in denouncing gambling) "bespeaks an unnatural state of things . . . the balance of energies is disturbed." The day would come when slavery "will be disenthralled by the diffusion of science . . . it cannot stand," he assured his audience, "against the progress of society."

Not only will slavery for the sons of Cush go down before a society on the march, but so too will slavery for debtors. Enlightened statesmanship, Nott declared, "will wipe from the nation the reproach of making misfortune penal, and rendering to honest bankruptcy the retribution of imprisonment." Prisons, he promised, will become "disciplinary," not "retributive"; they "shall become retirements for contrition, and schools of virtue," and eventually, he proclaimed, "prevention" will be the goal of the penal system.

Progress is even wiping out the errors within religion itself, he now triumphantly told an audience representative of an America glad to have those scientific "means" it was already using to exploit the continent joined with those Christian means it traditionally employed when seeking heaven. By 1824 the President of Union College no longer saw the geography of the New Zion as coextensive with the boundaries of a United States singled out for special salvation. The New Zion of his vision was now a world state, and the role of the United States, he now believed, was to be that of the producer of the means, the energizer, whose men of science and whose wealth were essential to the task of Christianizing the earth.

Progress in religion, for Nott, was now a simple corollary to progress in the sciences. He prophesied, not uniformity of worship in the future, but "the mild and tranquil, and varied array of different Christian communities, advancing side by side toward heaven, and provoking one another on the way only to love and good works; . . . . who knows," he said, "but in the farther progress of Christian knowledge . . . that the unity of the church itself . . . *consists* [only] *in an inward oneness of spirit* . . . all combined and harmonized in one common system of benevolent exertion . . . by that celestial charity which . . . is the cement of society . . . which will transform the world itself into a theater of peace. . . ."

For "science," he continued, "is the handmaid of religion . . . and religion, in turn, to make man holy, must first make him wise. . . ; to the Bible science owes a mighty debt," he said, "political science . . . progress in the arts, all take their inspiration from it, and all acknowledge themselves limited by the mortality which only the promises of the Bible transcend."

"No elixir," he warned those who might presume to ignore the limitations of science "that will render man immortal remains by future analysis to be revealed. Nor is there any hope that synthetic chymistry [*sic*] will, in its progress, reverse the progress of final dissolution . . . let us," he stated at last, forever joining scientist and priest, church and laboratory, "hereafter connect Jerusalem with Athens; entwine the ivy of Parnassus around the cedar of Lebanon . . . yes: let us plant the banner of religion in the vestibule of science . . ."

One wonders if Ralph Waldo Emerson, thirteen years later, in his "American Scholar" address before the Phi Beta Kappa Chapter of Harvard sounded a call as welcome, or as challenging to his generation as was Nott's call to enter the "vestibule of science," to be progressive in all things," or one so radical as was Nott's call to make ready for a world "which will be Republican in government as well as in letters"?

Here, too, was more than the seer's view of the future. For Eliphalet Nott his Phi Beta Kappa address embraced a rationalization for all he had done, all he was hazarding; here, in the ends science could achieve were ends he did not need to confuse with those means he was then using to attain them. Here, too, was his old millenial dream rephrased now in the language of science. Here was the Christianity of his boyhood translated into the terminology of the chemist, the geologist, the political philosopher, and the humanitarian, the language of morality and miracle become interchangeable with the language of weights and measure.

Philosophy Hall that Tuesday must have been a hushed room as the President of Union College ceased speaking. What had the Doctor promised his audience? And America? and the world? Progress, always, and everywhere! Crime, disease, the storm, to be made as nothing by the men of science; a universal language to break down the barriers of prejudice and ignorance, and an Asia and an Africa as cultivated as ancient Greece and modern England. Wonders upon wonders to come out of those studies the fathers of his students remembered as Natural Philosophy and Natural History, of science become sophisticated in the new courses called "Chymistry," and Mineralogy, Botany, Hydrostatics, Fluxions, Magnetism, and Electricity. And there were even newer sciences to come, the President had said, which would discover "the true atomic theory," and which might eventually join the earth and the planets, and the whole cosmos as "sidereal neighbors."

Slavery would wither away, he had promised, as the scientists made it meaningless, and the nations would take down their barriers against each other as science made possible at last a "Republic of the world," where scientist, politician, and priest were the same man.

The class of 1824 had reason enough to agree with William Henry Seward, that august senior of the class of 1820 who had declared as he, too, looked back on his life at Union, "I find myself saying with inward pride and gratitude . . . I, too, am a pupil of Nott!"

CHAPTER 2

"The idea of a university"

THE year Nott climbed his prophet's mountain to view the future of the world, Union graduated the largest senior class of any college in America. Five years later, in 1829, only Jeremiah Day at Yale and Josiah Quincy, the then new President of Harvard, presided over larger American colleges.[1]

The best known college towns in the nation before the Civil War were Cambridge, Schenectady, and New Haven, and it was in them and in Charlottesville, Virginia, in the four years following Nott's panegyric to progress that the great contest for the minds of young Americans broke into the open, the forces of academic liberalism led by Thomas Jefferson, young Professor George Ticknor of Harvard, and Eliphalet Nott of Union, against whom the President and faculty of Yale College militantly arrayed themselves, along with the other reverencers of the classics, of the Trivium and Quadrivium which still dominated the college classroom.

Here, in three of these towns, the idea of the university in America was slowly generated, its feeder roots running east to Germany and France from Cambridge and Charlottesville, its tap root, however, plunging deep into American soil, as Eliphalet Nott of Schenectady developed his "Grand Plan" for Union College, his "university for the times."

This ideal of the University was the bond between the old ex-President of the United States and the new Smith Professor of Modern Languages at Harvard, and if there is any explanation for Eliphalet Nott's exclusion from the common cause these two men made at this time, it is that they could hardly imagine help for either Harvard or the new University of Virginia coming from another American college. Their visions, unlike Nott's, were transatlantic. Of these three men, however, Eliphalet Nott was chiefly responsible for permanently breaching the great wall of the then traditional American college curriculum, and for forcing an entrance at last into campus sanctuaries for students who would prepare themselves for life in the Nineteenth Century.

America is mirrored in many ways, but few of the reflections reveal the intellectual reach of the country and the tides of change better than the prosaic, unadorned college catalogues which today so dangerously confuse bewildered parents. In the 1820s these catalogues were equally useful, if unflattering, mirrors of the time. On one page, usually embodied in a pamphlet threateningly called the "Rules" or the "Laws," college authorities laid out the proven formula which had for generations made ministers, statesmen, and gentlemen, a rigid four-year course, rich enough in science to populate the philosophical societies and broad enough in the political ideas of Athens, of Rome, and of the approved Frenchmen and Englishmen of the Enlightenment to have enabled the Adamses, the Madisons, and Hamiltons of our colonial colleges to capitalize the legacy of the American Revolution.[2]

Seven self-styled "universities" existed in America in 1817 according to President Timothy Dwight; none of them, he believed, offering courses less rigid or fuller than the Yale curriculum. Dwight had pointed out in that year in a letter to Governor Nicholas of Virginia that "Cambridge, in Massachusetts, approximates nearer to the European standard than any of the rest; but even that," he added, "falls materially short." "In Yale College," the prideful old President incorrectly concluded, "there is probably more *science* taught than in any other seminary in the American Union; but probably less of *literature* than in the university at Cambridge."[3]

Timothy Dwight, militant Trinitarian and Federalist, then gave the Governor of Virginia a piece of advice which Nott would have applauded and which Jefferson, planning his new university on "the European standard" for an American Age of Reason would have dismissed:

> Will your Excellency pardon me for observing that, having lived more than thirty years in Yale College, and in every station included in its system, the experience forced upon me during this period has furnished

me with a complete conviction that the views concerning such an institution [as a university for Virginia] by men unacquainted with this subject except by speculation, and those of the first talents, are necessarily inadequate and erroneous.[4]

From Jefferson's international point of view the difference among the New England "seminaries" seemed hardly germane to his vast scheme. The only word in the Yale curriculum announcement of 1824 which would have stirred him was the word "optional," bracketed after the junior year offering of "Hebrew." With all that "optional" implied rather than with the named courses lay, so far as Jefferson was concerned, the core idea of a university.

The University at Charlottesville which opened its doors to 123 boys in 1825, was based, Jefferson wrote, "on the illimitable freedom of the human mind to explore and expose every subject susceptible of its contemplation."[5]

The contrast between the closed Yale curriculum of 1824 and the curriculum of options offered the next year at Charlottesville is the contrast between two Americas, one, still alive in Timothy Dwight's Calvinist mind, but withering in the public mind, and the other, an idealized America as rational as the classic Five Orders whose balanced, coordinated, and self-effacing elements produced the harmony of Jefferson's architectural masterpiece, "the academic village" at Charlottesville.

Jefferson's curriculum, unlike the one Nott was gestating, broke completely with the accepted and traditional four-year college course. His students were to be invited to travel academically as rapidly or as slowly as their powers permitted. Their time was to be spent in "exclusive application to those branches only which are to qualify them for the particular vocations to which they are destined."[6] There were to be no "courses" as Yale and Union knew them, but in their place eight "Schools" (Jefferson had wanted ten): "Schools" of Ancient Languages, Modern Languages, Mathematics, Natural Philosophy, Natural History, Anatomy and Medicine, Moral Philosophy, and Law. There were to be no traditional degrees, but only diplomas which were to be given on finishing the prescribed work of each school. Although the studies within a school were not optional, the student was to be invited to "listen to whatever he thinks may improve the condition of his mind."[7] Those not interested in diplomas could come as "university students" for whom there was "an uncontrolled choice in the lectures they shall choose." Entrance requirements seem to have been left to the judgment of the professor in charge of each school, though in general "we will require elementary qualifications only," Jefferson wrote to George Ticknor, "and sufficient age."[8]

If American boys had been inventions of the Enlightenment the University of Virginia would soon have emptied those "seminaries" of America which to Eliphalet Nott and Timothy Dwight were not subjects for speculation, but rather places crowded with boys for whom "The Illumination of the 13th of May," and the "Great Rebellion," were part of the academic facts of life, whose student rebellions in that order had shaken Union, and Harvard, and whose "Bread and Butter Riots" were soon to shake Yale to its foundations.

The University of Virginia came into being in 1825, and survived, but, as one biographer of Jefferson wrote, it remained for decades a place "dedicated to non-existent wants."[9] Jefferson's idealism "tended to eliminate the human fact of incentive." Both Dwight and Nott, however, knew from experience that the pursuit of learning for its own sake was not enough to populate an American college or university, a fact which Nott's radical elective curriculum, announced in 1828, was to take fully into account. By 1829 the enrollment at the University of Virginia had dropped to 120, three less than when it opened. Under its system of "uncontrolled choice," two-thirds of its students, during the first seventeen years remained for only one year of study. [10]

Europe, not America, was the source of George Ticknor's curriculum innovations, as it had been of Jefferson's, though unlike Jefferson whose university was designed to augment all things American, Ticknor's renovated Harvard was to augment freedom itself, that *Freiheit des Lehrens* and *Freiheit des Lernens* which permeated the Göttingen he and Edward Everett had attended. [11] Unfortunately, neither the majority of the Harvard faculty nor the Harvard students who rowdied in classrooms were generally ready for that declaration of independence from

American academic tradition so attractive to the rich, the well-traveled and the denationalized George Ticknor.

The newly appointed Smith Professor soon came to realize, however, that Harvard could not be a university in the Göttingen sense and certainly not a Charlottesville, but he believed, finally, enough reform was possible to correct the decaying morals of Harvard students and to allow Harvard to become at least "a respectable high school," to which, he wrote, "a young man may be safely sent to be prepared for the study of a profession." [12]

It took the "Great Rebellion" of 1823, after which forty-three Harvard seniors of a class of seventy were expelled, to move the Board of Overseers and the stiff machinery of committees to produce the new "Statutes" of 1825, a cheerless volume of thirteen chapters and 153 "Laws." Ticknor was disappointed; he had hoped Harvard would be reorganized by departments in which students could set their own pace; he had hoped to get rid of the traditional four classes, and to see degrees awarded after departmental examination . . . and he wanted, above all, the freedom he had known in Germany for students and professors to test their interests by sampling courses as they pleased. [13]

The faculty majority at Harvard, however, thought even those reforms granted were shockingly impractical. The new catalogue offered only a slight concession to the principle of course options, although Harvard did invite holders of college degrees won elsewhere to come to Cambridge as "Resident Graduates," where, for a fee of five dollars, they could rove among courses as university students were doing abroad, and as they had done at Union College since its chartering in 1795.

That rapport, however, which existed between Ticknor and Jefferson was conspicuously absent between this radical young Professor of Modern Languages and the majority of the Harvard faculty. Ten years after the new "Laws" were published Ticknor resigned his Smith Professorship to Henry Wadsworth Longfellow, satisfied that he had proved his own department in Harvard was worthy, at least, of the "good high school," the German "Gymnasium," for which by then he was willing to compromise his hope for a true university. [14]

The Göttingten-oriented Ticknor in 1826 was thirty-five years old; Thomas Jefferson was then eighty-three, waiting, with his friend John Adams, for July 4 that year, the appropriate day for the two greatest living Americans to die. Both the young Ticknor and the laureled Jefferson, internationalists by temperament and experience, wanted the best of the Europe they knew for America. Jefferson more than Ticknor had hoped to make European scholarship and academic freedom available at once in an America he mistakenly assumed was at last ready for its own Enlightenment. Both men, however, failed to assess the nature of boys and of the America courting exploitation.

II

The most successful of these three educational radicals was to be Eliphalet Nott, in 1826 fifty-two years old. The quadrangle of his travels was wholly American, and had its check points in Franklin (Connecticut), his boyhood home, Boston, Philadelphia, and Schenectady. He, too, was as ambitious as were Jefferson and Ticknor, but what he now wanted was the best of a science-regenerated America for the salvation of Europe and of the world. Here lay the drive behind the curriculum revolution he organized the year following Jefferson's death, a revolution which assumed neither an Age of Reason nor that America was ready for a university of classicists, philosophers, philologists, and scientists pursuing knowledge for its own sake, or for their own private ends.

Nott's educational revolution was won in his own generation largely because it articulated a common moral purpose for spiritual America and utilitarian America by offering parallel and equal college programs in science and in the humanities which combined their energies and so gave them an equal status: ministers, statesmen, and "gentlemen" in company with those science students who would exploit the physical world. All these students were, in Nott's thinking, to become bachelors of arts together, *frères sous les lois de Minerve.* . . .

> City Hall [Schenectady] : July 24th, 1827: Resolved that the faculty [of Union College] be authorized to arrange the studies in this institution as far as practicable in such a manner as to afford a choice between the ancient and modern languages and also between the branches abstract and scientific and branches practical and particular.

Few revolutions are announced with so unassuming a declaration as this one of the Union College Trustees. Jefferson's university, its program far better publicized, had adopted a Minerva seal in 1825. At Union in 1796 the motto beneath the head of that helmeted goddess had stated that under her laws: *we all become brothers.* For more than thirty years, while Jefferson had been "speculating," there had been a gradual curriculum evolution in Schenectady until the City Hall announcement of 1827 when Nott's rationale which presented science as the new Christian means to a perfected world finally opened to Minerva's pagan brotherhood of the wise a vast Christian membership.

Five years after Nott became President that arch conservative faculty sheriff, Benjamin Allen, had been ousted, and Nott had been left unfettered as an administrator. One remembers with what delight he reported soon after Allen's departure that he had engaged the man he believed was the most distinguished European scientist then in America, Professor Rudolph Hassler, the irascible Swiss astronomer and mathematician who "demonstrated and lectured," Nott had told his brother Samuel, "in the best European manner." To what degree Hassler indoctrinated Nott with German university ideals is unknown, but the two men were close friends throughout Hassler's stormy career with the United States Coast Survey; two of Hassler's mathematics texts which Nott had urged him to write were used in 1828 by those Union College Juniors and Seniors who elected the revolutionary new "Science Course" instituted in that year. [15]

Chemistry, offered in the first catalogue issued after Nott became President, continued to be taught by Professor Thomas Brownell, the year after Hassler's departure in 1811. Brownell began teaching at Union not as a scientist, but as a tutor of Greek and Latin. The year following Brownell's graduation, Nott arranged to have his young tutor visit Europe in 1809, to study not the classics, however, but the sciences; Brownell returned to Union with books and apparatus for his new courses in Chemistry and Mineralogy, and two years later, in 1811, these courses were being attended not only by undergraduates, but by "university students" who paid a course fee of twenty dollars each a year. [16]

Nor was Brownell the only faculty member to be turned from Greek, Latin, and Belles Lettres to the manipulation of figures and retorts. Thomas Macauley, who in 1806 was made Professor of Latin, five years later became Lecturer in Mathematics and Natural Philosophy; following the move to the new campus, in 1814, he was directed "to perform the mathematical and philosophical experiments."

Those first eclectic teachers of science at Union proved their devotion to their new courses in very real terms: Professor Macauley constructed much of his own apparatus which he gave to the college or sold to it on bargain terms: "mathematical instruments . . . a telescope . . . an electrical apparatus of a peculiar construction. . . ." [17]

Thomas Brownell, who resigned as Professor of Chemistry in 1819 to become Bishop of Connecticut, was long remembered at Union for the "Brownell Collection" of 2000 mineral specimens and for its detailed catalogue which he presented to the college on leaving. [18]

In spite of Nott's lottery involvements and the strange climate of hope and despair the lottery slowly spread over the campus, the idea of a science curriculum continued to grow. Although the President and the faculty, "owing to the depressed state of the finances," had had to take a twenty percent salary cut in 1820, the Committee on Chemical and Philosophical Apparatus reported to the Trustees that year that it had received "a suitable and seasonable supply" of equipment from Europe, and had bought "a useful machine for grinding glass."

Another faculty member, this time the President's oldest son, Joel, who had been made a tutor in Chemistry in 1820, went to Europe the next year for further study at college expense; while there he acquired a large science library and additional apparatus for which he billed the college on his return. He was immediately promoted to Lecturer in Chemistry and Mineralogy, and after Commencement in 1821, Joel Nott headed into the Indian country of Michigan "to make mineralogical examinations and a geological survey." [19]

Whether it was Eliphalet Nott himself, or Joel who published in 1825 a "Syllabus of Lectures on Chemistry in four parts" is not certain; Joel, however, by that year was the Professor of Chemistry, and used the little twenty-eight page pamphlet, printed in Schenectady, as his class text. [20]

Neither textbooks, college catalogues or "philosophical apparatus," however, reveal so well the steady growth of Nott's faith in science as the key to Grace and the New America as do his treasurer's records. In 1795 Union College spent 161 pounds for books "and those parts of a philosophical apparatus which can be obtained in America on good terms." In 1824 Henry Yates, the college treasurer, reported to the Trustees that the value of the classical library, the heart of the traditional curriculum, was $5,648.27; the value of the philosophical library and apparatus, however, had soared by that year to $14,114.82 1/2.

Over a period of two decades Eliphalet Nott had prepared his faculty and his Trustees to accept, finally, the great option, the dual curriculum of 1828 which offered his students their choice between the traditional courses girded with the classics, and a parallel course in the sciences for those who, he believed, would lead America in shaping "the Republic of the World."

"The Scientific Course," first published in the Union College catalogue for 1828, anticipated in the catalogue of 1815, must be considered one of the bench marks in the rising tide of American life. It successfully capitalized that word "option" which had held so much promise for Jefferson and Ticknor by offering Union College students a separate *but equal* science curriculum which led, as did the classics curriculum, to the bachelor of arts degree.

What at once shocked the older New England colleges about Nott's break with tradition was not any neglect of those upperclassmen who elected his classical option, or of his freshmen students, for they now received more of everything classical and less of things scientific than did the students in Cambridge; it was the omission of all classical studies after the Freshman year for those who elected the parallel Scientific Course, and the inclusion in that option of studies hardly suited to that bachelor's degree in the arts born of the trivium and the quadrivium of monastic scholars and medieval universities:

The *Scientific Course*:
Sophomore Class: First Term: Tytler's History; Arithmetic (Hasler, sic); Logic.
Second Term: Algebra—1st vol. Euler; Natural. Theology (Paley); Natural History (Ware).

Third Term: Jamieson's Rhetoric; Plane Geometry (Legendre); French or Spanish.

Junior Class: First Term: Blair's Lectures; Solid Geometry (Legendre); Algebra (Lacroix).

Second Term: Plane and Spherical Trigonometry, and the Applications (Hasler, *sic*); Natural Philosophy (Farrar's Mechanics); Descriptive Geometry and the Applications (Davies).

Third Term: Analytic Geometry (Biot); French or Spanish; Natural Philosophy (Farrar's Mechanics).

Senior Class: First Term: Differential and Integral Calculus (Boucharlot); Natural Philosophy, continued, Optics, etc. (Biot); Elements of Criticism (Kames).

Second Term: Astronomy (Biot); Moral Philosophy (Paley); Kames and Lectures on Chemistry.

Third Term: Anatomy or Blackstone; Physiology or Kent; Lectures on Elements of Criticism, Chemistry, Botany and Mineralogy.

Lectures During either Course on: Political Economy, Moral Philosophy and Evidences of Christianity, Rhetoric and Oratory, Natural Philosophy.

Here was academic innovation to shock traditionalists: one-third of this new curriculum was given over to science per se, thirty percent of it to mathematics and the rest to modern languages, social studies, law, English composition, and oratory. [21]

Professor Ticknor, if he read the Union College catalogue for 1828, may have applauded the modestly appended note to its announcement of the new scientific course, a note which concerned the method of instruction for all but freshmen: "[students]," it stated, "are divided into sections according to attainment, or choice of studies...." Perhaps Nott borrowed these important tenets of Ticknor's well-publicized proposals for Harvard reforms, but if so, he was also able to make them a permanent part of an academic revolution which his faculty never successfully rejected. [22]

These "branches abstract and scientific and branches practical and particular" changed the whole focus of college education for students who elected them. Nott's "Scientific Course," from which about one-third of the college was soon graduating as Bachelors of Arts, pointed his students directly toward the professions of engineering, medicine, law, mining, and those yet unnamed pursuits for which the studies of mathematics and science were to become, in the new age of steam, holier than writ.

III

A massive reaction against Nott, Jefferson, Ticknor, and the lesser innovators began in New Haven the year before Union College announced its "Parallel Scientific Course," and appeared the following year as the *Yale Report*, a cerebral curtain behind which gathered the classicists and those educational theorists who believed the colleges should be concerned solely with the disciplining of the mind and the building of character. President Day and the Yale faculty were justifiably alarmed at the forces laying siege to the ivied walls. [23]

By 1827 the infection of practicality reached the Corporation of Yale College, a member of which proposed in that year that "the dead languages" be dropped from the Yale curriculum. The solid bulk of the Yale faculty behind whom stood the ghosts of Ezra Stiles and Timothy Dwight rose in protest. The heresy was promptly dealt with in President Day's "A summary view of education in the college," the famous and reactionary *Yale Report*. [24]

President Day wrote as though his predecessors were at his elbow. A college, he insisted, must be concerned chiefly with the harmonious development of character and the discipline of the mind. To eliminate Greek and Latin from the curriculum was to destroy the symmetry of the traditional college course; it would be an invitation to barbarism, as the *Western Review* had insisted a few years earlier, a threat to civilization in America, as Lyman Beecher was to declare eight years later. [25] Changes in subject matter must be prayerfully considered, and made homeopathically. The university, as Jefferson and Ticknor thought of it, had no place in Day's prescriptions for Yale which he saw rather as an English college behind whose fences and walls the tested decencies were preserved. Eliphalet Nott's arguments for the largely classics-free "Scientific Course" were, if they were known in New Haven, ignored.

The *Yale Report*, aglow with the fervor of those defending academic tradition, intimidated many who might have experi-

mented with new courses and electives. It proved to be the vade
mecum of the "Yale Band" of young missionary-teachers who
fanned out of New Haven into the west to found Illinois College
and the institutions which developed from it, as well as those
conservatives who headed the new University of Missouri, the
University of Wisconsin, Hamilton, Lafayette, and Davidson
Colleges, and those other schools whose Yale leaders were to teach
in the long shadow of Timothy Dwight. [26]

Nott was an academic prophet without honor in his own day
save among those students who "adventured" with him, who sat
under him as he demolished the eighteenth-century world of Lord
Kames in his famous course based on his Lordship's *Elements of
Criticism*. Union College issued no reports. Nott made no speeches
in defense of his tradition-breaking curriculum. Not only was he
on the defensive as a challenger of tradition but, during those
years when Union was one of the three largest colleges in America,
Nott was constantly under attack as the governor of a veritable
Botany Bay, President of a college which, it was claimed, received
the rioters and the violators of the jail-house rules of the New
England colleges. [27]

The *Yale Report* he ignored. "The common sayings to our
disadvantage," he wrote to his son-in-law, Alonzo Potter, "though
undesirable, do not materially injure us. They do not prevent a
growing confidence in our institution," a modest observation
considering the fact that the nine-year-old, poverty stricken Union
College to which he had come in 1804 was, in 1828, one in
importance in the public mind with Harvard and Yale. [28]

As "the lottery permitted," Nott built. He and Union College
had reacted to the stimulation of life in the then most vital river
valley in the country, the one through which ran the Mohawk
River and the Erie Canal linking the seaboard and the frontier.
Jefferson's University at Charlottesville would have fared better in
the linden groves of Berlin or the bois of Paris, for it was not built
out of that experience with American education and American
boys which Timothy Dwight had written transcends all speculation on the subject. George Ticknor, trying to impose on Harvard
those two great freedoms he had discovered in Germany, the
freedom of learning and the freedom of teaching, had soon
discovered that Harvard was not ready for them.

Eliphalet Nott, however, coming to Union in 1804, had inherited a surprisingly untraditional curriculum born in the afterglow of the French Enlightenment; it was stimulated by New York's surging democracy of canal builders and pioneers, a Union College which had opened in 1795 with a French elective for admission, which had offered French as a four-year elective in place of Greek, a course in American History and American Constitutional History, and had invited "university students" to enroll only for those courses they chose to take. Nott never rejected this inheritance, but rather, he had conserved it, modified it, and developed it in the face of those New Englanders who looked on curriculum innovation as dangerously democratic. By the time he thrilled the Phi Beta Kappa Society at Union College in 1824 with his optimist's view of the progressive society he had transformed his curriculum to conform to his own changed world view; he had convinced himself that training in the physical and political sciences, not in the trivium, not in the theology of the Puritans, nor in speculative systems of thought, was the central concern of higher education in the America of his time. The philosophers and men of letters would come later, but the need of the times, he had told a questioning Mark Tucker in 1823, was for men of action; God, he had then said, had so inclined his soul, and so he would act and teach others to act. [29]

How well had he gauged his times? Two years after the "Scientific Course" was introduced and the *Yale Report* was published Union College graduated 96 students, Yale 71, Harvard 48, and Princeton 20. Ten years later the order was Yale 107, Union 105, Harvard 45, and Princeton 80 graduates. Not until the guns of Sumter, by which time Nott's radical curriculum of 1828 had become the common property of American educators and Nott and Union College were almost submerged in a sea of troubles, was the position of Union as one of the Big Three of American colleges challenged. Even in that year Union graduated 104 to Harvard's 115, Yale's 118, and Princeton's 85 Seniors. [30]

Eliphalet Nott's great educational option was seeded and nurtured by many of his own "young adventurers" who became educators. Thomas Brownell, student and tutor under Nott and then Bishop of Connecticut, opened Washington College, later Trinity, in 1823 with a program which included "university students" and a strong science curriculum. Francis Wayland, also Nott's student and a Union College tutor, went from Union to become President of Brown University in 1827 where his revolutionary reforms of the 1850s were extensions of those Nott had evolved, as Wayland repeatedly testified. [31] By 1845 thirty of Nott's boys had become Presidents of American colleges, including Leonard Woods of Bowdoin, Silas Totten of Trinity, and John H. Raymond, President in succession of Madison, Rochester, and Vassar Colleges. Henry Tappan, who was graduated from Union in 1825, tried hard during his stormy presidency of the University of Michigan in the 1850s to make it the Göttingen so dear to the young Ticknor. [32]

Credit and discredit have been indiscriminately assigned to Nott, Francis Wayland, to Jefferson, and to Ticknor for the supermarket nature of American higher education in the Twentieth Century. Those less well informed have heaped the blame on President Eliot of Harvard for inventing the elective system and for introducing it at Cambridge after the Civil War. [33]

Origins are significant only if the forces which generated them are understood. None of these early nineteenth-century college leaders, however, invented electives, or were the sole proprietors of the sciences. From Jefferson, Ticknor, and Nott to Eliot, each of them framed his plan of education to serve his own view of the world and of man's future.

Nott's educational reforms were those of one of the greatest optimists in an age of optimism, and they justify joining Nott with Jefferson as a leveler of those academic walls which had for so long shut students away from the changing life of the world. What the social historians have missed in evaluating Eliphalet Nott's place as an educational leader is the significance of his all-encompassing rationale for his elective "Scientific Course," (a rationale vital, however, only in his own generation), and the fact that he was the only college leader who awarded the traditional degree in the arts for achievement in those new studies designed, not for disciplining the mind, or for building character, but for men he saw taking up active roles in that new world into which his imagination and his optimism had carried him.

Professor Jonathan Pearson—still "Pinky Pearson" to Nott's "young gentlemen,"—on March 29, 1854, after reading in the New

York *Tribune* about President Wayland's "New System" at Brown, made an entry in his diary which belongs among the notes of the educational historians:

> For more than 30 years the 'New System' has been taught at Union in spirit and in fact; and of the 4000 young men who have been educated there under the eye of its venerable and well known President more than one third have never learned Latin or Greek enough to save a Freshman from the Dunce's block. Modern and living languages have been a substitute. There has been no compulsory course of study, but the young men have been perfectly free to choose such sciences & such languages as his taste or contemplated business in life dictated. Those purposing to study Theology have mostly chosen the 'Classical course'. Those looking forward to Law or Medicine, Agriculture, Manufacturing or Engineering, have pursued the 'Scientific', 'University', or 'Engineering Course' in which there are Modern languages, Mathematics, Physical and Natural Sciences. [34]

The college Merit Books in which are recorded the courses and grades of those 4000 young men confirm Professor Pearson's diary entry. They reveal also that at Union College there was far more of Ticknor's Göttingen than the young Harvard reformer was ever to see in Cambridge, for Nott's students were free to choose not only between the two great options, the Classical and the Scientific Courses, but they were also free to elect any combination of Classical and Scientific courses which their "taste or contemplated business in life dictated." [35]

The "branches abstract and scientific and branches practical and particular" are at the heart of our college and university catalogues today. Americans, whose eyes to European travelers before the Civil War seemed so steadily on the main chance, soon discovered that electives and scientific courses were increasingly useful in answering the question "How can I be successful?", the query which had supplanted the one so dear to colonial clergymen, "How can I be saved?" By the end of the Civil War, when the smokestacks of an industrial society were standing taller than haymows and the steeples of village churches, the bridge Nott believed he was building between the heaven-oriented America he had grown up in and the goods-and-chattels America of his last years had served the self-interest of his students well; the cosmos-embracing rationale on which he had based his ever widening and changing curriculum, however, could now be abandoned, for the students of the sciences, not God, it seemed, were manipulating the levers and throttles of power.

Nott had planned for men who, trained in the new sciences, would use their knowledge for ultimately moral purposes. In doing this he gave academic status to those who were to use their education for less exalted ends than his own. Following the Civil War young Americans were ready for the universities Jefferson and Ticknor had anticipated, prepared for them in part by an Eliphalet Nott whose vision of the future of the world and of its "sideral neighbors" they were anxious to realize, a new world in which the majority, however, failed to see themselves as he had, a brother-hood of men equally educated in the sciences and the humanities, under the laws of a Minerva few of them could any longer identify.

CHAPTER 3

"Kames"

LORD KAMES'S parting "Fare ye a weel, ye bitches," directed at his fellow judges of the Court of Sessions of Scotland, might well have included the President of Union College had the aging Scots jurist known what the Doctor was to do with his lordship's respected *Elements*, his exposition of Scottish "Common Sense" philosophy, psychology and aesthetics, as much as any other single text the molder of the thinking of American collegians between the American Revolution and the Civil War.

"As I expected," Nott was to tell class after class of his seniors, "Kames's philosophy is good for nothing!" And with that dictum he began loosening the keystone of the arch of Scottish rationalism through which he had earlier traveled as the student of those men of Princeton who had erected it on American soil. By 1828 his shattering statement, "I can safely affirm that [Man] is not a reasonable being," was shaking that keystone loose.

The title page of a surviving "Kames" notebook reads, "Instructions delivered to the Senior Class in Union College in 1828-9, by the Reverend Eliphalet Nott, D.D., LL.D., President, etc.-etc.-." [1] William Souls and Henry Baldwin, seniors that year, in becoming the joint keepers of this notebook became also members of a unique fraternity of American undergraduates whose meeting place was the shadow-filled third floor chapel room of South College where they and the Doctor interrogated and indicted the ghost of Henry Home, Lord Kames, author of *Elements of Criticism*, their textbook, and so often the object of scorn.

"There are many, I have no doubt, in this class, as there are in all classes, who cannot be persuaded to think. Them I could forward most by giving them longer lessons, but it has been my endeavor these twenty years since I have had the care of youth, to make men rather than great scholars." (Could a boy hope to become such a man as "Prex," a power wherever he was, power in his looks and force in his speaking?) "I shall not give you long lessons but shall lead you to exercise your own minds, in much thought. Seniors should act for themselves, and form them-selves . . . [here] you come to inquire into the principles of the mind, the causes of the emotions you have seen in it, and the manner in which it is moved."

This was the promise of "Kames"; it was to be a revelation and an initiation, a revelation of the mysteries of the heart and the mind, and an initiation into the world of the new "elect," those men of action capable of sharing Nott's vision of a "scientific" age.

"You are now approaching that period when you are about to enter the great world and if you would ever be men you must learn to be so now."

Nott quickly led his "young gentlemen" from the promise of the course to the first of its many challenges.

"Though nowise remarkable for their talents," Nott told the class of 1828, "yet men had gone on from [the last] class who will be great and have no small influence, and this in consequence of the manner in which they spent their Senior year . . . I shall be pleased to see you equal them. . . ."

Here, unitalicized, was their first lesson: stir the pride of those you would move. Before Lord Kames was brought in for his long agony, however, there were other equally basic and uncon-ventional preliminary lessons to be learned. There was the matter of reading:

"The folly of most people is that they read too much. You should read but little, and turn that to the best account . . I don't think it is as profitable to read many authors of excellence as to read one author many times . . . By this means you get imbued with his sentiments and see every thought. . . ."[2]

Nott, whose personal library shifted over the years from his own shelves onto those of his borrowers, believed in books only as goads to thinking and so to action. The Bible and Shakespeare, he announced, were his chief references for the study of character, and he constantly urged his students to treat them as such.

Next there was the matter of history and then the study of Belles Lettres, and "the more deep philosophy." "In reading history your object is to learn principles and to accustom yourself to thinking, to see how such a nation came to such a state, what causes lead to such events . . . dates and names you need not remember. . . ."

"In Belles Lettres choose one author for *style* and keep him constantly by your side and read him every day. . . ."[3]

To prepare the class for the thousand pages of Lord Kames's *Elements*, he charged its members to make an analysis of each of his Lordship's two volumes, not to write down everything they intended to remember;—"nothing," he assured them, "is easier than analysis . . . any man is capable of it." "Old Prex's"—"any man is capable of it" must have stiffened the backs of those for whom "the more deep philosophy" promised cerebration and its awesome consequences.

Nott's seniors were to find his constant injunction was to think, to analyze, and, finally, "to believe nothing merely because it is asserted by any author." Lord Kames's *Elements of Criticism*, framed in its eighteenth-century Scottish "common sense" doctrine, a system into which Kames had forced all literature and history, lost its sanctity in those afternoon sessions in South College. The rote teaching of the day, the recent *Yale Report*, with its emphasis on a classics-oriented education directed to preparing, not Americans, but young Athenians, was slowly set aside by Nott as he and his seniors went about their interrogation of the blasphemous Scottish jurist-philosopher whose ghost if it was present must have been amazed and shocked at Nott's substitution of inquiry for authority.

II

Henry Home, Lord Kames, died the year Washington's armies won their final victory. Henry Home and David Hume were cousins . . . that same David Hume against whom Nott had once preached anathemas for his philosophical nihilism. The Scottish judge and his historian-philosopher cousin were friends, but uneasy in their relationship, as one would expect of a Calvinist who believed with granite conviction in an objectively real world and of a skeptic who, with devastating logic, set aside the accepted cosmos of orderly systems, of a solid earth of rock and velvet, of bone and flesh, as mere fictions of fictional minds.[4]

Elements of Criticism, not *THE Elements of Criticism*, for Lord Kames insisted he was too modest for such an all-inclusive title, was published in three volumes in Edinburgh in 1762. Dugald Stewart, that equally rough-tongued Scottish judge, whose *Elements of the Philosophy of the Human Mind* was being read by Union College Seniors in 1796, thought his colleague had written a book "of infinite merit." Oliver Goldsmith is reported to have told Boswell he thought it "easier to write that book than to read it," and Samuel Johnson, that critic of critics, especially of Scotsmen, told his daily biographer that the *Elements* "was a pretty essay, though much of it chimerical."[5]

In 1785, the sixth edition was printed, the last to reflect the author's constant corrections and additions. By then the book had made its transit to America and was already a text at Princeton which, under President Witherspoon, the dour Edinburgher, had become the American citadel of the philosophers of Common Sense. "Kaims" [sic] as the *Elements* were called, was taught at Rhode Island College in 1783, borrowed, along with much of its curriculum, by President Manning, from the New Jersey College of which he was an alumnus. The first of at least thirty-one American versions of the *Elements* was printed in Boston in two volumes in 1796 and it was this edition which came to Union College in 1802 along with the delicate Jonathan Maxcy, who, moving to Schenectady from Rhode Island College, brought with him much of its curriculum as well as its strait jacket of authoritarian "laws."[6]

More than half a century later Nott's seniors were still taking "Kames," using a one-volume edition copyright in 1850, each chapter of which was preceded by "an analysis" prepared by Abraham Mills, its editor, and in which Kames's Latin and Italian quotations were given in translation. Lord Kames might well have protested even worse liberties could he have seen that Union College student's copy of the 1850 edition still on the library shelves, replete with marginal notes disputing his Lordship's conclusions, its back cover pages filled with lines from one of Byron's songs.

The Union College senior in 1802, however, who had performed his rote study of Kames under President Jonathan Maxcy belonged to the Eighteenth Century, to the world of George III to whom the *Elements* were dedicated, a work, so its author declared, designed to educate his readers "to early and virtuous discipline" as a support to an aristocratic government in politics and letters.

Fifty years later the student who was charged to make his own judgment on the *Elements* by Eliphalet Nott was studying under a man who, propelled by his own experiences, had himself made the transit from Kames's world of certainties deep into the Nineteenth Century. What made Nott's course the memorable experience it was for generations of Union College students was that they, too, were forced to make the same journey, and in doing it, were prepared, as few American college students were then prepared, to live in the decades of tension mounting toward the Civil War.

So Eliphalet Nott put Lord Kames on trial in Star Chamber sessions in the dark South College chapel room, and with him the concept of the rational man conditioned by Newtonian physics and nurtured on Lockean sensationalism. Each year for half a century Nott expanded there his role of prosecutor before a jury of Union College seniors.

"His recitations," Francis Wayland remembered, "were a pleasure which no student was willing to lose. We then began to feel ourselves men, and to form judgments for ourselves . . . I think I do not exaggerate when I say that attendance on Doctor Nott's course formed an era in the life of every one of his pupils."[7] Francis Wayland, who was later to carry Nott's curricular revolution to Brown University, was only seventeen years old when he was graduated in 1813, too young he said, "to apply his principles as I should a few years later."

Tayler Lewis, that irascible young classics tutor of 1821, remembered that the year before, when he was a senior, Nott's intention was to make his "young gentlemen" self-reliant, and to teach them "to distrust mere authority, where this stood in the place of independent investigation."[8]

Frederick Seward, son of Lincoln's Secretary of State, liked to tell of an Eliphalet Nott who seemed to him during his senior year in 1849, the "very embodiment of the Trustees . . . a stately figure" who won them all as he "analyzed man's emotions and passions," as he taught them, "how to control their emotions, and to control others, how to choose the modes of expression and the rules for the conduct of life . . . ," of the exciting talk that ran on until the five o'clock chapel bell broke its flow.[9] Seward remembered, too, "Little Kames," that "pocket pamphlet surreptitiously printed and circulated by the class [which contained] an abstract of each chapter. . . ." "Dr. Nott," Seward remembered, "knew of the practice, but never positively forbade it."

Three years later, another senior, David Murray, recalled that "rheumatism had crippled [Nott's] athletic frame, age had whitened his abundant locks," but that the old chapel room during "Kames" echoed to his "rich, sonorous voice. Nothing," Murray said, "dimmed the lustre of his intellect, or lessened the alertness of his powers." [10]

II

Kames was essentially a mechanist for whom the mind of man was a machine in which Deity has implanted certain intuitive guiding elements as data is implanted in those intricate twentieth-century "thinking" machines of man's invention which directs them to home on the stars or to frame the odds of a football pool. His lordship, believing in a Benevolent Deity, however, carefully compartmentalized his theology and his rational analysis. Kames, contrary to Locke and to his cousin David Hume, believed firmly in this implanted intuitive sense, and saw it as the mechanism which guarantees to man that what he perceives exists objectively, that it IS real, including his sense of human worth.

How then, does man arrive at his moral and aesthetic evaluations about this objectively real world which his sensory apparatus makes known to him? *Elements of Criticism*, and those American texts derived from it, offered their answers to American collegians for more than a century. If one will study the common nature of man, said Lord Kames, will analyze that vast, linked complexity reacting by way of its intuitive mechanism, one will discover as Hobbes had written earlier, "why we like unity in action, realism in character, and perpetuity in language." [11] In brief, such a study, or "analysis" will reveal the ways in which we come to know, and why we evaluate, or judge what we come to know on that ever ready scale of life which reads at one end "bad," and at the other end, "good."

Kames's scheme was rational; he used what he believed was "scientific method" to establish rules of reason for dealing with every possible psychological and aesthetic situation from the patterns of love, the why of our emotions and passions, to the correct attitude one should assume toward the varieties of literature, architecture, and music. The student who embraced "Kames" would be a man of correct tastes who knew the good from the bad, and who knew why he knew, because the reasons for his judgment were to be found in the book of nature as read by Kames and the Scottish rationalists of Edinburgh and Aberdeen.

Eliphalet Nott, however, building out of his own experience with men, stirred by the turbulence and crosscurrents of nineteenth-century American life, parted company with these eighteenth-century mechanists early in his career as a college teacher. What is the more remarkable about Nott's growing pragmatic attitudes is that he made them a vital part of his teaching long before Emerson's voice was to give the doctrine of individualism, self-reliance, and private judgment academic respectability.

And like Emerson who asked that no one become his guide to the new mysticism, who said, "I shall find it all out myself," so, too, did Nott, long before Emerson was seeking to avoid exposure to Leibnitz and Schelling, find it all out for himself by turning away from the safe companionship of the philosophers of Common Sense to a growing reliance on his own judgment.

> It is asserted, young gentlemen . . . that man is a *reasonable* being—but such is not the fact—and I make this remark that you may not go forth into the world with a wrong opinion upon this subject. After long experience and much reflection and intercourse with man I can safely affirm that he is not a reasonable being. [12]

With that statement Nott reduced Lord Kames's eighteenth-century landscape of external realities to a mirage, for with it he reduced man, the instrument for perceiving it, to the status, simply, of first and unique animal in the chain of living things. The horse, Nott told his seniors, exercises memory, and so, by definition, it reasons; the dog through his sense of smell, chooses, and so reasons. "Brutes" he told his classes, "then possess reason" but only in a calculable, inferior degree to man; "yet many men," he said, "might be found who possess less of reason than the elephant." The difference between brutes and man, he concluded, is then, simply one of degree; man is unique only in the possession of a moral sense.[13] Man's "reasoning," however, Nott declared, even when expressed in the collective judgment, the "common sense" of mankind, cannot be viewed as anything but a relative judgment.

There is no evidence that those classroom note takers were aware of the full import of Nott's conclusions as they carefully wrote out his argument for disposing of Kames's "real" world:

> Dr. Nott asked one, 'is the eternal world real or Ideal? What evidence have you that it exists?'
> Answer: 'The evidence of my senses.'
> Dr. Nott: 'What evidence do these senses give you? What in the first place is matter?'
> Answer: 'It is defined to be that which has length, breadth, and thickness, and which occupies space so that no two material substances at any one time be in the same part of space.'
> Dr. Nott: 'But why can't two material substances be at the same time in the same part of space? How do you know they can't?'
> Answer: 'Because they are solid.'
> Dr. Nott: 'How do you know that they are solid? How do you know that one cannot penetrate the other and both be at one time in one and the same place or the same part of space?'
> Answer: 'Because when I strike my hand for example against a board I find it solid; i.e., my fist cannot either penetrate or pass through it.'
> Dr. Nott: 'Then it is solid *quoad* fist. But suppose the board be made of glass and your fist of light. Your fist would find no difficulty in passing through; glass then is solid when *quoad* fist, but not *quoad* light; again suppose you should rush against a brazen door you would not be able to pass through it, but if your body were electricity it would not be stopped by the door, though it might be by some other substances as glass, etc., so that the door is solid *quoad* flesh and blood but not *quoad* electricity; at least this is all we know about it.'[14]

Kames's certainties about the objective reality of the things of his external world thus must have seemed less sure in the echo of Nott's "at least this is all we know about it."

Nott's next query, "What is matter?" and his answers were in the nature of an earthquake which shook Kames's landscape into rubble:

> Dr. Nott: 'What is matter? You see this book? Describe it. It is six inches long, four inches broad, and one inch thick; it is of a buff color and you might go on and describe the inside. Now six inches long is not a book nor is four inches broad a book nor one inch thick a book nor is the buff color a book nor are all these taken together a book; there is something which you have not described. What you have described are the properties of the book—and these alone can you see; now what is it you can't see?'
>
> Answer 'The essence of the book.'
>
> Dr. Nott: 'True. You can see properties of anything, whether externally or internally, but the essence you can never see. We know not what essences are. Are mind and matter essentially the same or are they different? We can't philosophically assert either that they are the same or that they are different.

Had Nott, by 1828, turned down Hume's road to skepticism? "We know not what the essences of mind and matter are," he said. "Motion," he told his seniors, "is only a relation between two or more bodies," and, "time," he concluded, "like motion, has no independent existence." [15]

Nott had come to see "reason" as one with muscle and passion, common to all animals, in man a mechanism capable of comprehending the properties of things, incapable of knowing of what they were the properties. And so man cannot know "fundamental nature," least of all his own. What is now of paramount importance to Nott is that, realizing this, he had come to believe that man must also recognize that as his knowledge increases through experience and by way of his scientific studies, he will sense new properties, new qualities in all he contemplates. As man the animal, he differs from other animals only in possessing a moral sense; as man, he differs from other men only in the degree of his sensitivity to the infinite variety of stimuli which produce his and their thinking, his and their concepts of properties and qualities. Believing these things, Nott could turn away from Kames's secure world of external realities and face a world in which a Christian, sustained by a faith which lay beyond rationality, could preach an overwhelming optimism to the Phi

Beta Kappa Society at Union College in 1824, and yet could face a world to be judged and rejudged from moment to moment on the basis of ever changing criteria.

So far as Nott was concerned the heart of Lord Kames's "analysis" was without a pulse by 1828.

> Whenever one begins to reason by analogy from matter to mind, [he told his seniors in that year], he goes wholly wrong. We often see a kind of resemblance but it does not hold true . . . as soon as a man begins to argue so, it is considered that all he says goes for nothing, for we know so little about the mind . . . such analogies as the author thinks he sees may serve well as an illustration, as an ornament, but as argument it is good for nothing.
>
> Learn to think for yourselves . . . become a man of mental muscle . . . believe nothing because it is asserted by any author.

"This is nonsense!" Nott exclaimed after he and his seniors had examined Lord Kames's mechanist's view of the way the mind operates, and his Lordship's conclusion as to the way the critic of literature and the fine arts must arrive at his judgments.

> Were the minds of Homer and Euclid and Newton mere gangways [he asked his Seniors], through which Idea drags Idea without leave or license from the owner of the brain?
>
> The train of ideas, if we must believe Kames, is varied by four causes, viz: the will, the tone of the mind, bluntness of perception, and order. Nonsense. The succession of ideas is indeed varied by these causes, but not by these alone. It is varied by passion, by experience and by a thousand other causes—example, a lover thinks most of love, a hungry man thinks most of roast beef. I can very well understand the eyes running over a landscape but not the landscape running through the eyes. [16]

Man, in Kames's view, is certainly not man in Nott's view. If Kames's view is true, "then," said Nott, "Newton was not an astronomer, nor was Euclid a mathematician, and there may yet be invented [a machine] for composing without human labor—for if such machines as this doctrine represents Newton and Euclid, be philosophers—as well may a polyglot be a linguist!" [17]

Only as an adult, he told the class of 1829, is man guided by reason as well as by passion, and then only when alone; as a child he is guided solely by instinct, as an old man by habit. "Young gentlemen, remember this truth . . . an argument founded upon sound reasoning will often fail . . . an argument founded on the feelings and prejudice of the public—*never*." [18]

"Old Prex" who had successfully manipulated legislators for many years to serve the purposes of education, was not counseling in the voice of Lord Kames.

> If you were an editor [he continued] you would not place your chief dependence on sound argument . . . depend on it, the merest trifle which would arouse the feelings or enlist the prejudices of the public would be more serviceable than whole pages of sound logic and close reasoning.

His lordship had designed the *Elements* for gentlemen, not for this occasionally Machiavellian American. "Slight impediments," Kames had written, "increase desire; insurmountable ones overcome it." Nott, master of the political gambit, by 1828, was ready to make a most un-Kamesian application of the principle:

> The skillful politician [he told his attentive seniors] may make use of it. *A* is desirous of obtaining a seat in the legislature, but there is in his neighborhood another individual, *B* whom he fears as an opponent; therefore, to get *B* out of his way, *A* by his secret influence has him nominated as a candidate for a seat in Congress. *B* is not desirous of going to Congress, but *A* cunningly casts impediments in his way—he pretends to oppose him and makes considerable noise about his unfitness for the office. *B* thinks to himself, 'since he makes such a violent opposition I WILL go in spite of him;' he exerts himself. *A* opposes. *B* redoubles his efforts and is elected, and *A* gains his object. [19]

III

One President of the United States, Chester Alan Arthur, six secretaries in the cabinets of various Presidents, fifteen United States Senators, eighty Congressmen, fourteen Governors of states, and brigades of lesser politicians had or were to make the "elements" of Dr. Nott their own; they modified them to suit their own visions of the good life, but when they, as Union College seniors, left their last lecture on "Kames," it was with the bias of Nott on them. [20]

The Doctor's "elements" were not taken from a textbook in the art of shaping public opinion; Lord Kames had included nothing so earthy as this:

> If [Nott said to his class] you are about to attempt to carry your point with an assembly of men you must first consider what sort of beings you have to deal with—if you were to address a college of Mathematicians your way to move them would be dry and mathematical illustrations. If you were sound you would necessarily succeed. If you address the bench or men accustomed to regular analysis, your argument must be arranged with perfect order and a clear train of thought—but as soon as you turn to the jury box, says you to yourself, 'I am now going to speak to a different kind of people—I must not talk so to them'—No! your sound argument and lucid reasoning would be beyond their comprehension—they would be lost.
>
> Now, if you have occasion to address a popular assembly, especially if they are excited and angry, you will be unable, by addressing the whole, to move them or to engage their serious attention or to make them follow your train of reasoning—but, if you call a single individual by name and address yourself to him alone his attention will be secured; you will then move him and soon the whole assembly.

The illustration which followed was out of Andrew Jackson's America, not Lord Kames's England:

> There was, a few years ago [the Doctor continued], a disturbance between the town and the students—a quarrel first commenced in town between two or three students and as many young men from the town—the alarm spread like wildfire through both college and town.
>
> The students upon the first news of the alarm, having armed themselves, rushed to the assistance of their fellows and dispersed all who had assembled—the students then returned to college. The citizens, enraged at what they supposed to be a violation of their rights, collected in great numbers before the gate of the college grounds—nearly all the inhabitants of the city had turned out—at least there were two or three thousand persons. I was at the gate, attempting to keep the citizens at bay, but could do nothing to move them for some time, it being so dark that I could not distinguish the features of any individual and the confusion was such that I could not distinguish a single familiar voice.
>
> At last, after I had tried to find somebody whom I knew—*well knowing* that this would answer my purpose, I heard someone call out, 'Yaup Ostrander!'—the name I never heard before, but this made no

difference. All that I wanted was to address myself to some one person so as to secure his attention. I was certain that I could move the whole multitude.

'Yaup Ostrander!' said I, 'hear a word of reason. It is so dark we cannot tell friends from foes. And we are first as likely to injure the one as the other. It is much better to wait until morning when we can see and then I will call on you and try whether we cannot settle the matter; if not, you have your remedy then as well as now and you will run no risk of hurting your friends.

'Zounds', said the man, 'the President is right. Let us leave this matter until morning and we'll then have our revenge more sure and with less danger to ourselves. Huzza boys, let us go!' The mob moved off simultaneously, huzzahing as they went. The next day according to promise, I called on the man whom I had addressed, but I found him to be a villain just escaped from prison.

Now this turned out exactly as I expected. It made no difference what person I addressed—you may rely on the principle in every case.[21]

Man feeling, man moved by the electric of his senses dominated the course.

"Dr. Nott does not approve of Kames's distinction between Passions and Emotions," recorded the note taker; the Doctor had told the class they were the same, differing only in degree. "Kames," he advised his seniors, "has not taken a very philosophical view [on the subject of the passions] ."

> . . . music [he told them] has various effects—it inclines people to love—wherever music is cultivated you may trace its effects upon the people—Italian music and French is effeminate; in Scotland they have sacred music, but it is not very refined in New York, it is not much cultivated there nor in the Southern States—but in New England the power of music is wonderfully displayed—it inclines the people decidedly toward matrimony. The people of New England generally marry young and many marry for love—half the matches proceed from attachments formed at singing school . . . to these singing schools is owing the surprising increase of the population in New England. . . .[22]

As the note takers industriously wrote perhaps Nott's mind swung back to those exciting months he had known as a young man in the Benedict household in Connecticut, and to the startlingly beautiful Benedict sisters . . . to the singing school at his

"Father Benedict's" church . . . to his marriage to Sarah Maria Benedict who still seemed so passionately alive in the daughter to whom he had written as though it were to her mother only, to a Maria "asleep," he had promised himself, "on Abraham's bosom."

Bachelors, he told his seniors, were almost impossible to find in New England, but in New York, without the singing school to fire the passions, they were everywhere; "I could recon [sic] up," he warned these young men, "50 within my acquaintance."

Bachelors in the South, however, were to be explained in terms of the ugly institution of slavery. The Southerners among the seniors, and Union College attracted more of them than were to be found in any other Northern college, must have bridled, or perhaps, thought themselves men indeed, when "Old Prex" said that:

> there the passions are vented on the loathsome objects, the slaves, and [the Southerners] look upon the white female as an angel or superior being; which is unfavorable to matrimony—she is worshipped and adored, but not loved and admired—no man would think of connecting himself to an angel, or a passionless being who could not sympathize with him in the affairs of life. Hence the song:
> Be an angel, my dear, in the morning,
> But oh, be a woman at night! [23]

"Old Prex" surely had undivided attention as he commented on love; in what other college in the America of these decades would the President wish, or dare, to discuss the intimate passions, or to inform his students on tested techniques guaranteed to win a woman's affections?

> If you wish to gain the affections of a young lady [he told the class of 1829], you must address her when she [is] in distress, whether real or imaginary: the tender passion [will] readily coalesce—if several young men should abide in a house together with several young ladies not very handsome and a series of afflictions should happen to them while the young men were there, if their hearts were kind they would pity them—they would endeavour to console them—they would infallibly begin to love them—and thus thousands of matches are formed that make those unacquainted with philosophy wonder. The fairest time for courtship is when a woman is in distress and a sagacious man would take such a time and always succeed. [24]

The Doctor may have smiled a little as he discussed the fairest time for courtship; the second Mrs. Nott, when newly widowed in 1807, was a prescription case, though modesty must have prevented him from citing it.

His lecture on sexual temperance may have caused some uneasiness in the class again, especially among his Southerners:

> Temperance [he told them], is universally necessary for the preservation of health. Intemperance of every species is ruinous, and none more so than the promiscous intercourse of the sexes—this practise universally hurts the constitution. I have carefully observed its effects. Of all the classes which have graduated more than ten years since there is not now one individual alive who was addicted to fornication while in college— they seldom, if ever, live to the age of thirty.[25]

The sentient man was central to the "Elements" of Eliphalet Nott. "You will see," he told these seniors, "in how many cases [in the matter of the passions] your author is guilty of gross inconsistencies."

Nott tried to follow Lord Kames chapter by chapter, but the "gross inconsistencies" of the "Analysis" and the "Synthesis" were obviously what held his and the class's attention, and these, in turn, led Nott up the highways of his personal experiences from which he drew constantly for illustration. The *Elements of Criticism* were often forgotten.

> there is a man in town whom some of you may know—Old Kelly—there is not perhaps a fact or circumstance that has happened since he was born which he does not recollect. He can tell you in an instant any chapter and verse he had ever read on anything which has been told him by whom and on what place. He is an excellent book of refference [sic] but he is a man of no great scope of intellect.[26]

The recollection about "Old Kelly" was part of Nott on the memory; here, as a probing psychologist, he adventured into areas his lordship had never trod. "I agree," he told the class of 1829, "with Gall and Spurzheim."[27] Physiognomy, pathognomy, zoonomy, cranioscopy, craniology, and phrenology, new names for new theories about the way man thinks, these and especially for Nott, craniology and phrenology, were the new European psychologies he considered worth observing, and which were then gaining American supporters.

In agreeing with Franz Gall and Johann Spurzheim, founders of phrenology, the latter a popular lecturer in America on the new "science," Nott subscribed to what he considered to be new proofs of individual differences, and so, by analogy, "proofs" that critical and aesthetic judgments, contrary to Kames, will always vary from individual to individual. According to the new phrenology, a man's "faculties," his innate mental powers, are strong or weak according to the size of that region of the brain occupied by the particular "faculty."

"Old Kelly" had a strong development of that area of his brain which could handle facts; Nott, on the other hand, had to admit he was weak in the matter of names. "I have never known any of my students by name," he confessed, although at one period, he told the class: "I know everyone by his walk; if I saw him standing at a distance I might not at first know him, but no sooner did he move than I knew him—in a class I always know a student by his number...."[28]

These new "sciences" fascinated the President. He recommended a phrenologist, J. S. Grimes, in 1840 to Professor Benjamin Silliman at Yale. In 1842 there were a number of demonstrations of "Animal Magnetism" at the college, during which a Professor Bonneville held sessions in hypnotism in which Nott and his son-in-law, Professor Alonzo Potter, participated. By this time Nott was "magnetizing" his servants, curing their toothaches, and experimenting with subjects who claimed to be able to read in a darkened room.[29]

Nott, trying to comprehend the symbolic language of Nature, was not afraid to "adventure" in any direction. The oddities he discussed with his seniors do not diminish his stature. In an age when we are beginning to suspect the porpoise may have things to say to us, Nott's challenges to Lord Kames explain in part why the senior class at Union was often a larger class than the senior class at Harvard and Yale and why, too, the conservative faculty members of those "colleges in the east," associated Union with that place of renegades, "Botany Bay."

> you have all heard of children born with the mark of a strawberry or such thing on their skin; in Connecticut I heard of a boy that had mud turtle arms.... enquiring into the matter I found that the mother in going over a bridge had accidentally trod on a mud turtle. The turtle put out its forefeet, and frightened the woman—her child had short arms of

this description—Now it seems established that snakes decoy birds—some indeed say that the old birds endeavouring to decoy the snake away from the young flies around the snake and at last through want of caution or anxiety to succeed in this attempt ventures too near and becomes a prey. But others insist the snake has a real power of charming. It is a fact at all events that some men have a power over serpents.[30]

Strawberry marks and mud turtle arms represented a newer psychology than Lord Kames had advanced, and suggest at least, an inhuman and non-benevolent aspect of Nature which Nott and the believers in animal magnetism were beginning to face.

Ghosts worked their way into "Kames" during a lecture on the nature of fear, and about them the Doctor spoke with becoming caution:

I doubt whether I do not somewhat believe in ghosts, and doubt whether any human being is entirely disenthralled from the belief, nor does a visit from the departed spirit appear at all an improbable act. But all I wonder at is that their visits aren't more frequent. The only reason why people don't believe in them is the utter want of evidence.[31]

The Doctor, however, did have first class evidence on the nature of fear which should have stirred any young American:

Nothing is more easy than to make men brave. In the War of 1812 the standing army though composed of the offscouring of the people became, as soon as disciplined in the service, perfectly dauntless, and would march fearlessly up to the cannons' mouth—The militia, on the contrary, though composed of far more worthy people would run at the first discharge.[32]

Nott then commented on the cowardice of the Russians when they faced the smaller army of Charles XII of Sweden, and added an observation which has overtones for the great grandsons of the students to whom he made the comment:

How different is the Russian now; statesmen and officers of genius know that they can make any people brave—no Russian will now run, or even waver and their officers know that in them they have an immovable phalanx. They may be overpowered and cut to pieces, but they cannot be otherwise conquered. . . .[33]

"Eloquence," the Doctor told the class, "is purely natural . . . when Excitement of feeling exists . . . you will find all eloquent from the little child to the decrepit old man." He admitted to his seniors that he hated what he called "the vexatious task of hearing you all speak one after the other," even though they did improve. He told them he had no faith in formal training in oratory; "I think," he said, "any training men may get of this sort generally spoils them, and at least does no good." [34]

Homer, Vergil, Shakespeare, Milton, Pope, Cowper, these are the only writers the note takers mentioned by name; others, no doubt, had anonymous lives behind the "etc., etc.," which terminate many of their entries. The President of Union College, however, was no enemy of the new writers; he simply saw the time of letters as a time to come; his America was still in its Homeric age, and he and his contemporaries, he believed, were still living lives others would chronicle.

Pope, the admired voice of Lord Kames's Eighteenth Century, bored him: "I have seldom read a hundred lines [of his translation of Homer] without being tired of the sameness of the rhyme." Joel Barlow's pretentious *Columbiad*, he wrote on another occasion, "is not for immortality . . . . . like [Timothy] Dwight's 'Conquest of Canaan', it is for the living age, not like Milton, for the ages to come. . . ." [35] Robertson, Gibbon, Hume, these were among the "many writers of excellent history," he declared. On the other hand he found few good writers of biography, "minuteness," he said, "renders [biography] tedious, or partiality excites disgust." [36]

Nott's seniors heard little from him about contemporary writers, novelists or poets. "a good novel," the Doctor said, "exhibits perfect freedom from every species of immoral tendency, together with the power of deeply interesting the feelings of the reader." [37] He apparently wanted in literature the best of two worlds; his authors would not violate the morality of the day, yet they would seek the "power of deeply interesting the feelings," a prescription for frustration which may well have helped to decide him to leave literature to others.

Scott's *Lady of the Lake*, and *Marmion* apparently fitted the two roles Nott prescribed for literature, though he never acted the censor, as well he might, when Union College students showed their enthusiasm for those romantic writers for whom morality was the lesser consideration. The precocious John

Howard Payne and Nott's special charge, in that first college
literary publication, *The Pastime*, of 1807, was loud in his praise
of Coleridge, Southey, Lamb, and Godwin; "the man of sentiment," the palpitating young editor had written, "the man of soul,
what can be more interesting, or more engaging than such lines as
[theirs]." [38] The romantic spirit found board, lodging, and tuition
at Union College sometime before it was welcome on most
campuses.

Well before Nott in 1824 publicly extolled those who search
for truth no matter where or in what guise it appears the society
libraries at Union were filling their shelves with Byron, Scott,
Coleridge, Shelley. By 1823 the Philomathean Society listed 166
novels in its catalogue, romanticists from Rousseau to Fenimore
Cooper, Mrs. Edgeworth, Breckenridge, and Washington Irving
(the latter's name preceded Nott's as one of the seven corre-
sponding members from New York State of the prestigious but
short lived "American Academy of Language and Belles Lettres,"
in 1821).[39]

The Union College *Student Album*, in 1827, praised Kant and
Schiller, and criticized Cooper's *Prairie* for not equalling in its
descriptions the German writer's "deeper and stronger pictures of
romance...."

"Passion alone can move." Around this dictum Nott built a
rhetoric for his students which was an open invitation to them to
test all writers of any school for what they had learned of man; he
meant it when he reiterated to class after class in "Kames": "learn
to think for yourselves ... believe nothing merely because it is
asserted by any author...." Under such instruction it is little
wonder that the writers of the romantic movement, anathema to
the Everetts and to such men as Andrews Norton of the *North
American Review,* only cautiously "noticed" by Professor Edward
Channing at Harvard, should have been welcome at Union, even
though "Old Prex" himself had no time and probably little taste
for the literary rebels who followed Coleridge.

IV

Neither literary rebellion, however, nor Lord Kames, dictated
the little textbook Nott published in 1836, "Help to Young

Writers," which he dedicated to the harried teachers of the Common Schools, to men and women who "struggle with the vacant, undisciplined mind," he wrote, "till they become exhausted and give up in despair." His pocket rhetoric is based firmly on his own analysis of human nature even though he borrowed a good deal from Dr. Hugh Blair's "Lectures on Rhetoric" (1783) to fill out its forty seven chapters. Nott informed the teachers who used his "Help to Young Writers" that they were to blame for their students' bad habit of "stringing together empty commonplaces and vapid declamations, of multiplying words and spreading out the matter thin, of composing in a stiff, artificial manner." The remedy, he announced, was to teach a boy to write "in a free, natural and simple style"; the object was to encourage an approach to composition as "lively, unfettered and natural" as youth itself.

Nott reserved for his seniors the full harvest of "his long experience and much reflection on Man." Animal magnetism, phrenology, prenatal influences leading to strawberry marks and turtle arms, threat of death by spontaneous combustion for heavy drinkers, topics which seem ridiculous now, in the 1820s were part of the ferment of the new century. These were peripheral things, however; what was vital was that Nott opened up all topics to every senior for examination and evaluation, including the nature of man himself.

The "elements" of Dr. Nott, unlike the *Elements* of Lord Kames, were in part the elements of a romanticist as well as of a pragmatist, of one who had glimpsed man ever reborn, striving to live in harmony with an ever-renewing world. Man, for Nott, was man living, man feeling, sensing, and so acting according to the rapport of his own being with a sentient creation within which he responds and grows as a child responds and grows within the living community.

Growth meant not suppression of the passions but a developing comprehension of their significance, and education meant learning to read the signs to which man's senses respond, perhaps, in time, responding even to signals from his planetary neighbors. Today's seniors might not elect "Kames," but the best of them would elect to sit under such a man as was Nott, a teacher for whom the orthodoxies of the day were topics for questioning and investigation, not the Sanskrit of received wisdom.

Nott, the prosecutor, in his last years on trial himself before the legislature of New York State because of the events which had made a storm of his life outside the classroom, finally so focused the evidence of his own experience on his Lordship's *Elements* that they were forgotten, and their author was left sitting in the dock to listen, instead, to the "Elements" of Dr. Nott.

CHAPTER 4

The "philosopher of caloric"

"The chapel was cold and no fire. The fellows attempted to scare the Old Doctor out of it, but he thought, 'It wouldn't become Seniors and philosophers to be afraid of a room which had nothing in it, not even caloric.' " Martin VanBuren Burt, Union College 1838, shivering as Nott continued his obsequies over the corpse of Lord Kames, may have reflected wryly on the "Old Doctor's" then nation-wide fame as an expert on "Caloric."[1]

If this senior course in "Kames" gave Eliphalet Nott his philosopher's forum, his "experiment room," located probably in the two-story arcaded wing running east from North College, gave him a laboratory where he amply proved to his generation what being a philosopher meant to one who had come at last to think of the work of the scientist as one with the work of the priest. The Christian's "means" and Eliphalet Nott's bright forge, and piles of cast iron stove plates were synonymous to him, if not to his critics who at first belittled his study of "caloric" as hardly befitting the minister and the President of Union College.

When, however, in 1820 the Lehigh Navigation and Mining Company dumped a load of its Pennsylvania "stone coal" somewhere on the campus with the hopeful injunction to Nott to do what he could to domesticate it, to make those Pennsylvania "black stones" a reasonable substitute for wood and soft coal in the stoves of the nation, the study of caloric became a philosopher's problem and Nott, as he contemplated the shining pile of intractable anthracite became, perhaps, the first of those scientist-educators to whom American industry learned to turn in its efforts to make nature both serviceable and profitable.[2]

Between 1820 and that time eighteen years later when young Martin Burt made his complaining journal entry two "caloric" revolutions took place in the American economy. The first was won on the American hearth, and the second beneath the walking beams of those boats which had inherited the "Clermont's" voracious appetite for wood, whose plumes of steam and smoke were waving in a new age of transportation. To both of these revolutions Nott contributed far more than those who took their fruits remember.

The first of those revolutions was recalled by a less forgetful editor of industrial history in 1872, a writer who knew the significance of the Nott Stove and that one device which made it unique, the most famous stove in America before the Civil War, the stove which gave the miners of anthracite coal their vast household market. "Indeed," this editor wrote, "three Americans, —Dr. Franklin, Count Rumford, and Dr. Eliphalet Nott of Union College—were pioneers in the invention and improvements, and the introduction of principles which are essential to the utility of any stove of whatever style now in common use in Europe or America."[3]

That one simple device which made Nott's name a household word in his generation emerged, however, from his "experimenting room" only after its inventor had labored there among his stove plates for at least a decade, giving his attention, he said, "not exclusively to stoves, but to those general principles of heat that have a bearing on most of the processes and comforts of human life."[4]

This humanitarian's generalization was a part of Nott's testy reply to one critic who had reported that Schenectady and Albany gossips thought the Doctor was wasting time and money on "caloric" which might better be spent on charity. Obviously in a state of heat himself at his critics, he replied with the quite human rationalization for his "experimenting" that he had taken up the study of "caloric" only after his "constitution gave way". Lifting and framing stove castings he had found more satisfying than "walking, riding, or kindred exercises."

But why stoves? America, in the first decades of the Nineteenth Century was still a nation of hearths, of buildings where chimneys and flues spread like ganglia to an infinite variety of fireplaces, of cast iron box stoves whose creators built to suit local needs and out of materials locally available: stone, brick, and cast iron plates whose decorations were often as intricate as snowflakes. These castings came from local forges, or more often from the iron foundries in New Jersey and Pennsylvania. By the time Nott set up his "experimenting room" these foundries were supplying plate in any wanted size to those stove makers lucky enough to be near the river ports and seaports. One has only to look at that menagerie of stoves which, during the Nineteenth Century, kept winterbound Americans close to their woodpiles, and, after Nott's success, their anthracite coal bins, to realize that here among the stove plates the blacksmith, the tinkerer, the artist hungry for surfaces to decorate, and the experimenter scheming on ways to use and to conserve fuel, particularly an ever scarcer wood supply, had challenging outlets for their ingenuity denied to them in an age of gas mains, power lines, and thermostats.

Nott's first stove, that oblong of cast iron known to his students as "the coffin," emerged from the experimenting room about 1815, his solution to the problem of how to shut winter out of the new dormitories on Nistiquona Hill. Wholly utilitarian, slab-sided, and decorated only with a "U.C." on its iron door, it was one in an ancient line of boxlike cast iron wood burners whose shapes reflected particular needs and purse limitations. The "coffin's" chief virtue lay in the fact that its castings were thick enough to withstand cannon balls, and so the vicissitudes of dormitory life. "Townies," invading the aristocratic precincts of North and South Colleges, were frequently confronted by a "coffin" poised on an upper stairway landing, an instrument of war which usually won a truce, if not a victory.

The fame of the President of Union College as an expert in "Caloric" spread following the granting of his first patent (February 3, 1819) for a "Fire-Place and Chimney."[5] He now joined the company of Benjamin Franklin and Count Rumford and the dozens of other stove experimenters before him who had worked at sophisticating the box stove with grates and flues designed to make them easier to use, more efficient, more ornamental, and capable, so it was generally claimed, of eliminating the smoke and soot which then begrimed the winter cities of the world.

Nott's "Fire-Place and Chimney" was advertised to be an improvement over other contenders in that it would serve both the cook and the householder. The Schenectady *Cabinet* in 1820, moved to defend the Doctor against his critics as well as to herald the virtues of the new "Fire-Place and Chimney," reported that, "It has been generally known in the vicinity of Schenectady that Dr. Nott has long been engaged in prosecuting an extensive course of experiments on heat, and it has generally been believed that his time and money might have been more advantageously employed. Despite, however, many failures and much derision, he has pertinaciously persisted for more than eight years, during which period it is understood about ten thousand dollars have in this way been expended."[6]

"The plan," the editor continued, "embraces every apartment from the kitchen to the garret. The soot is consumed as it is produced, and the fire is visible or concealed, as is preferred . . . the construction varies, being either plain and cheap for the convenience of the poor, or elegant and expensive for the accommodation of the rich. . . ."

The editor's candor had been echoed by the inventor of the "Fire-Place and Chimney" himself when, in his letter to the Reverend Mark Tucker, he had rationalized the uses to which he was putting his "play hours" as he had called them. "I shall deem it a happiness," he wrote, elevating the clanging which went on in the "experimenting room" into the pronouncement of the philosopher-humanitarian, "should it be in my power to increase the comfort of the rich, and lighten the expenses of the poor, and stimulate the exertions of the industrious."

The great opportunity to become, in fact, the benefactor of the poor, the rich, and the industrious was to come the year following the granting of his patent for the "Fire-Place and Chimney." Among the virtues of that wood burning "college model," the editor of the Schenectady *Cabinet* had noted, was the fact that fuel had become "an item of very considerable amount", and, he had added, "considering the scarcity of that article, and the still greater scarcity of another, that is MONEY. . . . I cannot but congratulate our neighbors in the north—of being able [now] to mitigate, within doors, the rigors of our climate."

Wood and charcoal, the chief fuel for the fireplaces and stoves of Americans, had seemed as much a natural right as the rivers which by the beginning of the Nineteenth Century were floating forests of logs to city markets. The fires which consumed them, however, lacked the regenerating grace of the spring rains which each year rose in such rivers as the Susquehanna, the Delaware, and the Hudson down which the loggers and raftsmen guided the winter's fuel of so many towns and cities. By the winter of 1820, when that load of "stone coal" was dumped close to Nott's "experimenting room," wood was selling in New York and Philadelphia for from fifteen to twenty dollars a ton.

Coal, the soft bituminous "sea coal" imported from England and Nova Scotia and brought north from Virginia from colonial times, was long the only substitute for wood; it was a dirty fuel for which generations of stove makers had devised their special grates and ingenious flues in order to make the "clean" fires they promised and seldom achieved.[7]

"Sea coal" was the fuel the city of Albany hoped someone would find when, in 1813, the City Fathers offered a thousand dollars for the discovery of "a coal mine within the distance of the navigable waters of the Hudson, of a strata not less than four feet in thickness."[8] There was real urgency behind their offer; not only was Albany worried, but so was every northern city, as the War of 1812 blocked all foreign trade, including that in "sea coal" which had long helped to keep the price of wood under control. In the winter of 1814 New York City alone consumed over 400,000 cords of wood and the price of it was up fifty percent over its pre-war cost.[9]

An even greater threat to the dwindling American woodpile were those rapidly increasing fleets of sidewheelers spawned in 1807 by Fulton's "Clermont," steamboats for whose voracious boilers the woodsmen were fast pushing the forests away from the river valleys and beyond the reach, economically as well as geographically, of ship operators and city householders.

Anthracite may have seemed to Tench Coxe, Alexander Hamilton's Assistant Secretary of the Treasury, one of the nation's great, untapped fuel resources, but who in 1794, or even twenty years later, could make a real fire with those black stones which seemed to pave the valleys of the Lackawaxen, the Schuylkill, the Delaware, and the streams which flowed into them? [10]

Anthracite *could* be made to burn, of course; its hardness and high ignition point, however, completely frustrated a nation which had always basked before wood fires a child could light. A few blacksmiths living in the anthracite valleys north of Philadelphia had made "stone coal" burn on forges supplied with a strong draught. As early as 1788 a Wilkes Barre tavern keeper, Jesse Fell, used anthracite successfully in his nailery. In a region where anthracite could often be picked out of the stream beds, where it shouldered its way above the top soil in open seams, it found users, but beyond the "stone coal" valleys little was heard of it, in part because of the almost insurmountable prejudice against it, and in part because the rock filled Schuylkill, the Laxawaxen, and the Lehigh rivers were still more barrier than transportation routes to the big seaboard markets.

If someone could only find a way to domesticate "stone coal," to make it tractable enough to compete with wood and "sea coal," those dormant anthracite mountains would soon spill their treasure into Pennsylvania riverboats afloat on streams cleared to get them to tidewater. No one, unfortunately, seemed able to do it, though grates and flues of every shape and size were tried. In 1808 Jesse Fell, that persistent Wilkes Barre tavern keeper, built a grate to use in open fireplaces which would burn "stone coal," provided one had the patience to ignite it, and could maintain the strong draught without which the fire soon died. Eight years later ovens and stoves which were said to burn anthracite were being made in Reading, Pennsylvania, but they were local products and did as little to spread the use of anthracite as did Oliver Evans's "Luminous Stove" of 1814, designed to burn "Lehigh Coal" but which seems to have functioned only on the pages of Dr. Mease's *Archives of Useful Knowledge*.[11]

The early grates for burning "stone coal" were too inefficient to overcome public prejudice. Only the pressing need of the smithies and foundries for fuel during the War of 1812 stimulated the Pennsylvania miners to attempt to move their anthracite beyond their own regions. In 1812 the first shipment of it, 220 tons, reached New York City, where it sold at twenty-five dollars a chaldron, sixty-four cents a bushel.[12] The demand by blacksmiths and foundries continued to grow, however; by 1817 it had justified making the Schuylkill River navigable, although the toll of twelve dollars per ton on shipments to Philadelphia did as much to frustrate the use of anthracite as did its unwillingness to burn.

By 1820 the Lehigh River, too, had been cleared enough to allow the renamed Lehigh Coal and Navigation Company to ship 364 tons of its "stone coal" to Philadelphia, "more than enough for family supply there" for the entire year. [13] Servants in the city, it was said, were being recommended because they were able to make "stone coal" burn. [14] With wood selling at from ten to fifteen dollars a ton, the slow burning anthracite, at $8.40 a ton, inevitably found some householders willing to try it. Philadelphia alone took over 100,000 tons of wood the year the operators of the Lehigh Coal and Navigation Company sent that historic load of anthracite down the Lehigh River to tidewater, around to the port of New York, up the Hudson to Albany, and then across the pine and sand plains to Schenectady, to be dumped on the campus of Union College. The operators of the Lehigh Company were taking the long chance, but it would be worth it if they could hope to redress the balance of coal production which in that year, 1820, saw the bituminous mines west of the Alleghenies produce 225,000 tons of "sea coal," or, "Pittsburgh Coal," while the anthracite mines east of the mountains produced a mere 4,065 tons. [15]

Six years later, on March 23, 1826, the Patent Office recorded the first of three patents granted that year to Eliphalet Nott of Schenectady, New York, covering devices "for the Evolution and Management of Heat." One suspects the load of "stone coal" sent to Schenectady in 1820 weathered for months untouched, for the intervening six years between its delivery to Nott's "experimenting room," and the creation there of his "Saracenic Stove" which began a new chapter in American economic history, continued those "times of embarrassment" about which Nott had begun to complain to his brother Samuel in 1817. By 1820 the country itself was in the grip of its first great financial panic, aftermath of the War of 1812 and of a speculators' orgy in land grabbing.

In 1820, not stoves nor the anthracite problems of the Lehigh Coal and Navigation Company, but the simple survival of the college must have fully occupied the self-proclaimed philosopher of caloric. For much of the next six years the "play hours" in the "experimenting room" could only have shrunk to minutes as the long dormant Literature Lottery was transformed into an octopus enterprise, and Nott, by 1822 its sole proprietor, endlessly conferred with his professional lottery managers and shielded their joint activities from inspection by the New York State Board of Regents. These were the years when Nott watched his college treasury and his private account rapidly fill with funds, and when, in his expanding optimism, he came to believe the cornucopia of his and the college's fortunes had barely been tipped.

When one recalls, too, that during the six years which passed before he announced the anthracite burning "Saracenic Stove" Nott was experimenting with that unconventional curriculum which he announced in 1827 as the "separate but equal Scientific Course," an academic innovation which in its way was to affect higher education in America as profoundly as his new stove affected the traditional ways of heating the homes and public buildings of the country, one is surprised that Nott found even the minutes to labor with Joe Horsfall, his pattern maker, at unlocking the energy of anthracite.[16]

During those six extraordinarily energized years in Nott's life the nation, too, seemed to be rushing headlong into an era which would demand whatever new sources of "caloric" and of spirit it could command: the Erie Canal was opened, the Missouri Compromise began to breed its slavery maelstrom, Russia claimed the Pacific Coast north of the 51st parallel, the federal power grew as the Supreme Court, in case after case, chiseled away at the granite walls of state sovereignty, and many of those forums of good men came into being to which Nott so wholeheartedly subscribed, which set the tone of the age, and measured its optimism and its inexperience: the Colonization Society, the American Sunday School Union, the Lyceum Movement, and, in February, 1826, the American Temperance Society to which Nott would later contribute some of its more awesome moments.

At last, however, on March 23, 1826, Eliphalet Nott's "Saracenic Stove" was patented. In a way it, too, was as much a response to the Christian optimism of the day as the lyceums, the societies and unions founded by those who hoped to bootstrap mankind into virtue, for its inventor, by having at last forced Pennsylvania's "stone coal" to give up its heat on his patented grates, believed he had begun to fulfill the larger humanitarian intention of his "play hours" to increase "the comfort of the rich and lighten the expenses of the poor, and stimulate the exertions of the industrious."

"I doubt if one instance can be found," D. G. Littlefield wrote in his *History of the Base Burning Stove*, "where, by the simple change of a part of a device, so entire a revolution was accomplished. [Eliphalet Nott] has shown us how to burn coal. He has laid down the true principles on which stoves must be constructed."[17]

"Heat evolution and management," the patent reads, "being the original rotary grate and floor for burning anthracite coal." A prosaic announcement for a revolution. The patent, one notices, is dated September 17, 1832, but it also back-dates Nott's "Saracenic Stove" six years, the original patent for which he surrendered in the latter year "on account of the defectiveness of the specifications on which it was founded. . . ." That "revolution," however, to which D. G. Littlefield referred had been won between 1820 and 1826. The years between 1826 and 1832 were years given to consolidating the victory, to developing the several "improvements" which finally produced that Nott Stove Ralph Waldo Emerson so envied his brother William who described it in 1831 "as the greatest comfort ever devised in the matter of heating rooms. . . ."[18]

The rotary grate was the revolutionary innovation, the heart of those "principles on which stoves must be constructed." By turning it, or rocking it gently, the dead ashes which, before Nott's movable grate, had slowly strangled the oxygen-hungry anthracite, were now dropped into an ash pit, and the burning coals were left free to feed on the all-important unimpeded draft.

"I wish to call the attention of the public to Dr. Nott's stove, or Compound Furnace for burning Lehigh, or other anthracite coal, or charcoal . . .," wrote Isaac Riggs, the Schenectady printer, in an encomium published in the Schenectady *Cabinet* on August 20, 1828. "I had one of these instruments put up in my printing room last winter and found it to exceed my most sanguine expectations. The room is 36 feet long and between 15 and 16 feet wide, with four windows fully exposed to the northwest. During the period it was in operation, I tested the quantity of coal (Lehigh) consumed in a given period and found that the consumption was half a ton in forty-two days and nights, with no more charcoal than was absolutely necessary to ignite it."

A wonderful thing to see, that first baseburner, its cast iron plates as gothic in their design as Horace Walpole's false ruins on Strawberry Hill. Its esthetic influence seemed almost as great in its time as was its charm for economy minded householders who could have traveled after 1832 from Albany to Schenectady in the "Gothic cars" of the pioneering Mohawk and Hudson Railroad, which borrowed "the architecture . . . of Dr. Nott's parlor stove" for its first passenger coaches.[19]

That baseburner of 1826 worked well *if . . .* if the user remembered to refill the head-high magazine above the rotary grate with "stone coal," and most especially if he remembered to close the magazine cover. If he didn't, gas, rising through the column of anthracite above the fire escaped, and, on occasion, exploded. The six new patents issued to Eliphalet Nott on January 29, 1832, under the single heading, "Stove for Anthracite Coal," were proof that improvements were needed in this earliest model which, though it worked well in the "experimenting room," could create havoc in the parlor.

I I

If a heedless opening of the magazine cover of those first Saracenic Stoves signalled danger of explosion to their owners, the arrangements for their manufacture and sale were equally signals of troubles to come to their inventor. The Saracenic Stove, with all its shortcomings, had promised to fulfill the fondest hopes of "the Doctor," and of the Pennsylvania anthracite mine operators. Nott held a patent on a basic development which, if he could control it, would give him command of an enormous market for his unique stove, a market for which the mine owners were ready to channel rivers and build canals to supply.

"H. Nott and Company," or, "The Union Furnace," was the immediate response to the golden possibilities of the new baseburner. It would have been franker to have called the new foundry "E. Nott and Company." There is little doubt that it was financed by the President of Union College from the time it was established in Albany, in 1827, at the junction of Washington and Central Avenues, until Howard and Benjamin Nott, his sons, were swept out of the management of the later Novelty Iron Works of New York City, offspring of "H. Nott and Co.," at the height of the "Jackson Depression" of the middle 1830s. [20]

When one notes that Howard Nott was under twenty years of age when "H. Nott and Company" was formed, and that he was the only child of Eliphalet Nott's second marriage, that his mother was the wealthy, fragile, and sometimes irascible Troy widow whose fortune had allowed her husband to indulge his interest in "caloric," whose estate had been among the guarantees of his signature on the lottery contracts he had negotiated, one feels that "H. Nott and Company" may have been an expedient solution to several problems for Nott as a father and husband as well as for Nott, the financier and inventor.

Howard's half-brother and partner, Benjamin Nott, was twenty-four years old when H. Nott and Company was established. Unlike the much younger Howard who seems never to have attended college, Benjamin was graduated from Union in 1823, after which he read law in the office of then Senator Martin VanBuren. [21] Benjamin, however, was hardly the student his own older brother Joel seems to have been. Joel, only two years older than Benjamin, had graduated six years earlier than did this second of the young foundry managers. These three Nott sons during the next decade, however, when their father's energies as the philosopher of caloric were at their peak, played their own hopeful and quixotic roles as their father's manufacturing and business agents as he proceeded to capitalize on those inventions which gave him an international fame.

How much the two young foundry operators really "managed" is impossible to know; there is little doubt, however, that "H. Nott and Company" soon became the largest maker of stoves in Albany; their "Union Furnace" alone was soon fabricating a 1000 tons of cast iron a year. [22] According to one capital district historian, Albany and Troy were to "owe their preeminence in the stove manufacture not a little to [Eliphalet Nott's] presence and counsel." [23]

"H. Nott and Company," their rapidly growing number of lessees, and the anthracite mine operators initially shared a common problem: How to overcome the decades of public hostility to "stone coal"? Nott's wide reputation among all classes of Americans as a preacher, as a man of vision, the President of tradition-shattering Union College was, no doubt, the new stove's best advertisement. If the "Doctor" said his rotary grate base-burner would fire anthracite, that was enough, or almost enough.

For the next two years, however, there were doubting Thomases to be convinced. The big forced draught furnaces of blacksmiths and foundries would burn anthracite; the constantly increasing shipments of "lump coal" proved it. The big problem before 1830, however, was to persuade householders to use anthracite. The bituminous "sea coal" fires whose smoke lay like a winter pall over Europe's cities, seemed to have grained their soot into the public thinking. All coal users were supposed to fall victim to "stove malaria". Gentlemen degenerated into "stove spitters," and the "smoke doctors," those mechanics who lived on faulty flues, were traditionally an expensive nuisance. [24]

Anthracite, however, could easily be proved to produce little smoke. Such encomiums as Isaac Riggs's, the Schenectady printer, were soon common in city and village newspapers. [25] Advertisements for the new stoves emphasized the money saving aspects of anthracite; "stone coal," in 1830, sold for $10.00 a ton in New York City, as against about $15.00 a cord for wood, and the price of coal continued to drop rapidly; by 1834 it was selling in the city for $7.50 a ton.

The Delaware and Hudson Coal Company was soon to monopolize the New York and New England market because of the shipping economies made possible by its new 180-mile-long canal to the Hudson River from Honesdale, close to its mines in Pennsylvania. The company had first to convince investors and New York State legislators that its product would actually burn before it could raise the capital to finish the canal, opened in December, 1828. [26] The Clerk of the New York State Senate earlier that year was "engaged to use [the company's hard coal] for one fire in that room". The directors sent a complimentary ton of its anthracite to Eliphalet Nott's friend and lottery supporter, Governor-elect Martin VanBuren, and, in order to convince visitors to its New York City office that its coal could sustain a fire, the directors installed an anthracite burning "apparatus in the kitchen of the company."[27]

As late as February, 1829, however, the Delaware and Hudson Coal Company had to rush its transportation manager, Horatio Allen, the importer of the company's "Stourbridge Lion," America's first steam locomotive, to the capitol at Albany in order to persuade skeptical legislators who were then debating a company canal bill, that its anthracite was really being burned in the new coal stoves. There was small irony for the President of Union College in the fact that it was Horatio Allen who defended the new stoves so successfully, for it was Allen's father, Professor Benjamin Allen, who had had to be dismissed from the faculty of Union twenty years earlier for exercising the discipline of an ill-tempered sheriff. For Benjamin and Joel Nott, however, Horatio Allen's hurried visit to Albany may also have offered a cousinly reunion, for Allen's mother and their mother were sisters. Considering the role the Delaware and Hudson Coal Company was later to play in the fortunes of H. Nott and Company this relationship becomes more than a casual matter.

If the statement of the directors of the Delaware and Hudson Coal Company is correct, that up to 1832 the chief consumers of their coal, their "Furnace Lump," were the "domestic users," then the statistics of anthracite production up to that year tell the amazing story of the swift conquest of the householders' market for this fuel, and of the remarkable success of Eliphalet Nott's first caloric revolution. From 1821 to 1827, the year H. Nott and Company was formed, the entire anthracite region produced only 79,000 tons of coal. By 1830 production had jumped to 234,790 tons. Two years later the Pennsylvania anthracite mines marketed 501,951 tons of "stone coal," exceeding in that year for the first time the Pennsylvania production of soft coal, a lead the anthracite mines held until the close of the Nineteenth Century.[28]

Although the expanding household market for anthracite became less important after 1832 than did the rapidly developing industrial market, "the stoves of Dr. Nott," according to Joel Munsell, the Albany historian and publisher, "received the preference wherever they were known," a statement he made in 1858, by which time anthracite had almost replaced wood in the stoves of city dwellers. Eliphalet Nott's rotary grate had proved, indeed, "that by the simple change of one part of a device . . . a revolution was accomplished."

If the miners in the valleys of the Lehigh, the Lackawaxen, the Schuylkill, and the Delaware had reason to rejoice, so, too, it would seem did the inventor of the Saracenic Stove. One can believe William Emerson's observation to his mother, in a letter he wrote on December 18, 1831, that "the Rev'd Prest. [of Union College] is said to be growing rich very fast by the sale of these patent stoves." [29] On Christmas day that same year Ralph Waldo Emerson wrote from Boston to William; after commenting on the "enormous price of fuel [wood] in New York," and noting that it was not quite so expensive in Boston, he observed, "I think I ought to have a Nott stove by your description of its beneficence." [30] There was no doubt the base-burner had conquered its market.

But Eliphalet Nott was soon to discover that his patents were less certain assets to him and to H. Nott and Company than they were to the anthracite producers. Two years after William Emerson's gossip that "the Rev'd Prest. was growing rich" H. Nott and Company was competing against Nott stoves being manufactured by foundries they had licensed in New York and Pennsylvania: the Hopewell Furnace, at Hopewell, Pennsylvania, turned out 5000 annually, the Windsor Furnace in Berks County, and a foundry in Reading are known to have sold stoves labeled "Nott's Patent." [31] And there were undoubtedly other licensed producers.

III

Brash lawlessness in the United States was never confined to the geographical frontier, and American frontiersmen had often either to call on their guns, or, if they were industrial pioneers, on their writs to protect their hard won gains. James Wilson of Poughkeepsie, New York, long known for his Franklin stoves and his cast iron wood burners, by 1833, and with little conscience, was producing stoves which were essentially Nott's rotary grate stove, and doing it not even "surreptitiously."

The suit which Nott brought against Wilson in the United States Court was, by agreement, submitted in October, 1833, to a

THE NOTT STOVE. The stove on loan to the
Schenectady Museum, Schenectady, New York;
photograph, Schaffer Library, Union College.

"MEN OF PROGRESS." Group portrait by Christian Schussele, 1862. Eliphalet Nott is the central figure of the five seated at the table. Photograph of the portrait, which as of 1962 hung in the White House, Schaffer Library, Union College.

group of distinguished New York jurists: Chancellor Kent, Chief Justice Ambrose Spencer, Mr. Justice Platt, and Mr. Justice Woodworth. As an action it was important, for on its outcome was established Nott's priority as the inventor of that basic stove element, the movable grate, which had made anthracite coal a household commodity. Others were later to claim that distinction, but the referees' award in the Wilson suit made it perfectly clear to whom the honor belonged. [32]

The question of priority, however, had remarkable vitality. Jordon L. Mott, after whom Mott Haven, New York, was named, patented a baseburner on May 30, 1832; because Eliphalet Nott's basic patent of 1826 was reissued on September 17, 1832 in order to correct certain specification defects in the earlier patent, Mott and members of his family persuaded themselves, as did several contemporary historians of American industry, that Mott's anthracite burning stoves preceded Eliphalet Nott's, an error which the history of the Saracenic Stove and the referees' "Award" in the Wilson suit should have made futile to entertain. By the time the Motts were indulging their vanity, however, the inventor of the rotary grate had more exciting and vital concerns to interest him than a controversy over priorities which the courts had settled.

One hopes the Doctor's sense of humor was up to enjoying the little irony which seated him next to Jordon L. Mott in Christian Schussele's famous painting, "Men of Progress," completed in 1862 and which now hangs in the White House; Mott himself paid for the canvas, and so for the privilege of joining a considerable company of American scientists and inventors. [33]

The Nott stove, thousands of them manufactured by H. Nott and Company, and the more thousands of these stoves made by pirating foundries, labeled "Nott's Patent," long "received the preference wherever they were known" in spite of the patent outlaws against whose raids the pre-Civil War inventor had little protection.

"Tomorrow, please God," John Pintard, President of the New-York Historical Society, wrote to his daughter Eliza, on January 28, 1832, "I shall attend church which is kept very warm by Nott's patent stoves which consume very little hard coal and give out a more powerful heat than any that have hitherto been invented." He noted that the Doctor's stoves had "been introduced into most of our churches and on a smaller scale in public offices. . . . [34]

The following year a Nott stove was taken, piece by piece, up Alpine paths to the Hospice of St. Bernard, in Switzerland, where, near the monastery, a poor grade of anthracite had just been discovered. "Dr. Nott's admirable stove," the report in the New York *American* stated, was "a complete success, . . . and the joy of the brethern knows no bounds." [35] Admirable the Doctor's stove was, but those who bought it frequently needed encouragement, as its inventor's letter, written to George Tibbets of Troy on November 4, 1835, indicates:

"As to the size you require—I can only say, that in the long run the large stoves are more economical than the small ones, because the coal itself is more perfectly consumed in them—If the question [you asked] respected your hall merely, a G.7. will be perfectly sufficient—But if you wish to produce an effect on the house, which is the wisest thing, then an N.7. will not be too large. In mild weather you can make a little fire in it—and in cold weather drive it & little or no fire will be required elsewhere— Indeed the true economy is to have no other fire—and it affords, too, the greatest comfort. On the whole if you have anyone who knows how to manage these stoves, you will not regret getting one—if you have not you will—they are the best, or the worst instrument, according as they are used—and if used right the trouble of using them is much less than that attending any other—" [36]

That the Doctor was not blind to the crotchets of his creation is echoed in his, "they are the best, or the worst instrument, according as they are used . . ."

The base-burner quickly found its way to an England so long soot stained by its "sea coal" fires, a fact shown in a comment by an English churchman who visited Schenectady in 1835, and who, after talking to Nott, sounded a Cassandra-like note on the Doctor's success as an inventor: "I was introduced to the President," this dour churchman wrote," a person known chiefly in Britain as the inventor of the stove which bears his name; . . . he was free to converse on subjects to which you led the way; but it was evident to me that his mind was filled with some engrossing care. One successful invention, like a prize in the lottery, often leads to ruin. His success with the stove may have led to other speculations; till he may find himself oppressed with the weight of world care, from which he would, but cannot disburden himself." [37]

This British churchman was more prescient than he knew. Gaiety, however, not sour prophecy, marked the supreme compliment Oliver Wendell Holmes paid the Doctor the next year, in his poem, "The Hot Season," a long burlesque on the events of a stifling June day:

> The gas light companies were mobbed,
> The bakers all were shot,
> The penny press began to talk
> Of lynching Dr. Nott;
> And all about the warehouse steps
> Were angry men in droves,
> Crashing and splintering through the doors
> To smash the patent stoves. [38]

By 1838 the Nott stove was as familiar a household object as a Windsor chair. James Fenimore Cooper in that year wrote in the last chapter of *Homeward Bound* about "some New York cockney who wandered from the crackling heat of his Nott stove," and so, presumably warmed by it to a poetic frenzy, looked out on the lower bay of New York and declaimed it to be the equal of the Bay of Naples. [39]

The Doctor's "patent stoves" had conquered their market. [40] Well before the financial panic of the mid-1830's destroyed H. Nott and Company, however, the doctor and his sons Joel, Benjamin, and Howard were deeply involved in a new enterprise, in what was to become Eliphalet Nott's second triumph as the philosopher of caloric, one that resulted in an achievement which many of his contemporaries were to agree placed him "second only to Robert Fulton" as the benefactor of the American economy. [41]

BOOK FIVE

*"Matters of Discovery, specific performance,
fraud account . . . ," 1828-1837*

CHAPTER I

The "House of Yates and McIntyre"

ELIPHALET NOTT'S life as the philosopher and the exploiter of "caloric" paralleled and depended upon his fifteen years as the grey eminence of the Literature Lottery. As this fief of hazards expanded it demanded of him a train of obligations, a *noblesse oblige* toward those involved in the lottery with him, as well as the talents of a Richelieu, before the State of New York, loud with moral outrage, closed that privileged domain. For fifteen years, however, Nott levied the Literature Lottery and then the Consolidated Lotteries for the "College Fund" and the "President's Fund," the latter a spreading pool of capital which buoyed his later career as a speculator in New York City and Long Island real estate, which floated his "S.S. Novelty," and which carried his sons Joel, Benjamin, and Howard Nott onto the shoals of the Jackson Depression. The path from his "experimenting room" seemed, during these years, to by-pass his President's office and end on the doorstep of the "House of Yates and McIntyre," that firm of lottery contractors who, in 1822, had persuaded him to become the superintendent of the last and the greatest of New York State's official gambling enterprises in the Nineteenth century.[1]

Archibald McIntyre, the ex-New York State Comptroller, and John B. Yates, speculator in western lands, and at one time one of the state appointed managers of lotteries, it will be recalled, had joined with the latter's elder brother Henry Yates, State Senator, Mayor of Schenectady, and Union College treasurer, and Eliphalet Nott in persuading the legislature to reestablish the New York State Literature Lottery of 1814 as a Union College enterprise wholly under their personal control. The "House of Yates and

McIntyre" had then been appointed by Nott as the contracting firm to raise the sums granted by the original lottery Act, subject always to Nott's supervision. The President of Union College had been given absolute authority by his Trustees to act in their name as he deemed best in any matter bearing on the successful exploitation of this munificent gift of the New York State law makers.

Archibald McIntyre, John Barentse Yates, Henry Yates, and Eliphalet Nott were thus drawn together by the lodestone of their ambitions, Nott to place Union College and himself among the agents to forward that manifest destiny he believed God had designed for the world, and more immediately, for America; the other three partners to exploit a cleverly conceived public lottery which, at first, had the sanction of the New York State Legislature and the social approval of most of their contemporaries. Given this unique opportunity, however, one which was to involve millions of dollars, these four men, restrained only by their individual codes of behavior, played dangerously for huge stakes.

Lottery tickets sold amazingly well that first year; five "classes" were offered to the public in 1823; the "adventurers" bought 99 percent of the tickets available, whole tickets, splits, and quarters, insured tickets, and group tickets. The conditions of the Union College contract seemed to be clearly established by the end of that year. The New York State Comptroller, John Savage, a graduate of Union College in 1799 and Archibald McIntyre's not so careful successor in that state office, had approved the annual amount of money the new managers figured they must raise in order to satisfy the 1814 lottery grants which, it was agreed, were as follows:

Union College	$ 226,476.19
Hamilton College	45,279.74
Asbury African Church	4,529.30
College of Physicians and Surgeons	33,971.58
New-York Historical Society	12,000.00

Senator Henry Yates and the Doctor, by borrowing on their own names, had bought out the rights of the other beneficiaries of the State's generosity at discount prices, and had thereby consolidated the Literature Lottery under their own control, something "the act to limit the continuance of lotteries" of April 5, 1822, had not contemplated. And there was the glossed over matter of the missing figures in the Milford and Owego Road Lottery of 1818 which Deputy Comptroller Ephraim Starr should have had when he calculated the amount of the lottery tickets drawn in the State in the five years before 1823. His erroneous figure of $1,679,000 was made the basis for calculating the amount of the tickets in the Literature Lottery which Yates and McIntyre could sell in any one year. A seemingly small matter, this, which the Doctor was to regret later. During these first pleasant months, however, the partners were fully occupied; they figured the sale of $4,492,800 worth of tickets would accomplish the purpose of the grant.[2] By the end of the year the "College Fund" was established on the books of the new firm, and into it was going 8¾ percent of the amount for which each "scheme" was to be sold; John B. Yates and Archibald McIntyre were taking four percent, and, by virtue of the second and secret clause of their contract with Union College, 2¼ percent was being credited to the "President's Fund." The "Madman Vannini," who had leased or sold his "ternary system" of lottery calculation to Yates and McIntyre, one which guaranteed to them a margin of safety new to lottery operators, was quiet for the moment, and the "Fortunate Offices" were flooded with "adventurers." Readers of the Schenectady *Cabinet*, on June 29, 1825, were promised that

Secor's Wheels of Fortune
　　No. 210 Broadway
　　　　and
　　No. 171 Chatham Street [New York City]
Contain all that is necessary to give Content. If $30,000, $20,000, $15,000, $10,000, $5,000 etc., etc., can give ease, comfort, pleasure, 'and all that sort of thing, and everything in the world,' you have only to call at Secor's to obtain the surest means of enjoying ease, comfort, pleasure, "and all that sort of thing."

CONTENT

Say, where is the man, be he ever so blest,
　　Who's not striving some scheme to invent,
That may give to his mind the sweet solace of rest,
　　And partake of the joys of Content?

And where is the man—but 'tis folly to ask
　　Who never had cause to repent
Of performing some ill-advised, burthensome task
　　While attempting to find sweet Content?

Content's all we ask, whether idiot's or scholar's,
　　'Tis the height of our wishes below,
And it may now be had for a very few dollars,
　　And all who wish it to Secor's must go!

The President of Union College knew well enough the ugly scenes that took place in the lottery arcades on drawing days, but he had found his own "content," his rationalization that these "adventurers" were hazarding, not gambling, that in so doing they were putting themselves in harmony with Natural Law by investing in a sanctified cause.

There had been a few practical adjustments in the contract during those first months of operations, though nothing to slow the march on "Secor's," and those other "Fortunate Offices" which now proliferated as Yates and McIntyre led America into the era of leviathan lotteries.

John B. Yates, impatient, sometimes choleric, his eye on financial horizons not shared with his partners, had no intention of limiting the House of Yates and McIntyre only to its professed objective of saving Union College from ruin. He wanted maneuvering room, as much freedom as possible to exploit those opportunities which always seem to find a gambler. He soon recognized the strait-jacket nature of those provisions of the firm's contract with Union College which stated that tickets must be sold for cash only, and that the money taken in through these sales must be deposited at once in a bank account subject "to the will of the treasurer of Union College," John's brother, one of Nott's newly appointed board of lottery managers. This board consisted of Henry Yates, and two voiceless handymen, Major Jonas Holland, the college registrar, and Joe Horsfall, Nott's pattern maker, and "experiment room" assistant. The board "made it possible for Nott to avoid publicly assuming the character of a manager of lotteries; by paying them token salaries they could have no claim "as managers of his President's Fund."[3]

John B. Yates's arguments for easing the contract burden had their appeal: If Nott would only allow tickets to be sold for credit he could be sure the lotteries would be run off in much less time than the ten or eleven years allowed for that purpose by the state comptroller. More urgent in Yates's speculator's mind was the need to allow the House of Yates and McIntyre "to keep and use the monies" derived from ticket sales rather than as required, "to deposit and continue the same in bank." Yates assured Nott they would all profit if he would only cooperate. The Doctor, perhaps guilelessly, agreed, though it should be noted that his acceptance of these contract changes was verbal. He also agreed to forego Yates and McIntyre's personal security bond for $70,000, insisting only that the money due the "College Fund" and the "President's Fund" be banked as soon as each drawing was completed. The new arrangement also freed Yates and McIntyre from the necessity of meeting fixed annual payments to the college.[4]

Optimism, even euphoria, echoed in the exchanges between the Doctor and his partners that first year when fewer than one percent of their tickets went unsold. In May, 1823, John B. Yates, then all cheerfulness, wrote to Nott from New York City that the first "scheme" had sold wonderfully, and that but for the fact that the New York-Albany boat was about to sail he would have inclosed their schedule for the next one: "Hitherto my most sanguine expectations," he continued, "have been realized. Unless some unforeseen, untoward circumstances occur, I have no doubt your change of the law will prove highly advantageous to you."[5]

The first drawing had taken place on May 20th; the city, Yates had told Nott, was full of talk about the new venture, and there were already enemies: "I find," he wrote, "Verplanck has attempted to stab my character. . . ."[6] But Nott, in 1823, was more than satisfied with the "reasonable views" of his new partners, and Gulian Verplanck, one of the political "high minded" Federalists, an enemy of the Yateses and the Albany Regency, had been dealt with when Verplanck's opposition in the legislature that February to the Valentine's Day college bill had come to nothing.

If John B. Yates had remained simply a lottery manager, and what Nott in 1823 had called the firm's "reasonable views" had continued, both the President of Union College and the college itself would have had wholly different histories. Wherever the road diverged which took the four partners so far afield from the route they had publicly declared they intended to travel, its high point came early in their association.

The Doctor had invited trouble by agreeing to the verbal revisions of the original contract with Yates and McIntyre. He had miscalculated their devotion to his own causes. So successful were the firm's operations in 1823 and 1824, however, that it soon found itself paying Union College more under the revised contract than it would have under their original agreement. John B. Yates had no taste for this generosity, and so he constantly pressed Nott for interest rebates on these additional sums.[7] By the end of August, 1824, Henry Yates of the divided loyalties was writing to his younger brother John, in New York City, that the Doctor was demanding payments to the "College Fund" and the "President's Fund," then mysteriously much in arrears, adding that Nott wished to put himself in a position "to bid defiance to any as to our conduct."[8] John Yates testily replied that certain aspects of the firm's ticket sales "were of no concern to the college," adding that their New York contract "is a drawback on us," and that the firm's books were open to inspection, and that so far as the Doctor was concerned, "what better statement does he want?"[9] If the college payments were in arrears, it was because John B. Yates was enjoying his new banker's privileges with them, and in ways which had little to do with Eliphalet Nott's concerns. What the Doctor wanted was undivided attention to the work of running off the Literature Lottery as speedily as possible, and respect for a contract which by virtue of its verbal revisions had now become a dangerously imprecise instrument.

Released from the strait-jacket of the original agreement, the House of Yates and McIntyre busied itself with its lucrative Pennsylvania grant, opening an office in Jersey City in 1823 under the management of the college treasurer's son, Henry Yates, Jr., and of A. J. Yates, the son of Professor Andrew Yates of Union College, for the sale of "foreign" tickets. Nott insisted this activity was intended to open the New York market to outsiders, all of which he declared "operated greatly to the injury of Union College."[10]

Nott's concessions to his lottery managers had allowed the partners to pile up large reserves of cash, most of which was earmarked for prizes to be paid as the various "classes" or "schemes" were run off. To John B. Yates, however, this short term capital seemed as charged with promise as a lottery ticket whose number has turned up in a dream. By the end of the firm's second year of operation he found a way to put this capital to work and so to offer himself as the rude model of the next century's investment banker.

II

Sponge thirsty for funds, William Hamilton Merritt arrived in Albany late in 1824 from Upper Canada. Merritt knew the Yates' sister, Eva (Mrs. W. J. Butler), who lived in St. Catherine's, on the Canadian side of the Niagara River; this was enough introduction to win John B. Yates's attention, and soon his enthusiasm for Merritt's plan to join Lake Erie and Lake Ontario by a twenty-eight-mile-long waterway which would bypass Niagara Falls, that Welland Canal which the Albany merchants had long discussed. [11]

With the Erie Canal and the Hudson River what could be more timely and more profitable than to extend the access to that settlers' empire of the Great Lakes country with a far more easily constructed waterway only a fraction of the length of Clinton's "Ditch"? Once committed to the idea, John B. Yates acted, as willing to hazard the security of that unbanked Union College money coming in from the "Fortunate Offices" as Nott had been willing to hazard the future of Union College on the lottery itself.

Merritt, John B. Yates decided, must not be allowed to set up a public subscription list. Instead, Yates promptly organized a group of his friends and together they bought up the whole stock offering. A few months later the new stockholders persuaded the Welland Canal directors to redesign the canal's "prism," to extend its depth from four to eight feet and to increase the capital stock from $160,000 to $800,000, half of which was to be offered in England, one quarter in Canada, and one quarter in New York. Again Yates acted: he and his friends took the $200,000 in new stock offered in New York, and an additional $100,000 of the stock reserved for Canadians.

What John B. Yates planned, however, had little to do with the unfolding events themselves. Those "adventurers" thronging into Secor's "Wheels of Fortune" offices were no more crestfallen when their tickets drew blanks than was Eliphalet Nott's lottery manager as he watched Canadians dump their shares of Welland Canal stock on the New York market. That year between the time when William Hamilton Merritt arrived in Albany with great expectations and the moment in January, 1826 when John B. Yates journeyed to Schenectady to tell the Doctor the shocking news that the House of Yates and McIntyre had no money left to pay off the prizes in the lottery scheme then being drawn must have been a shattering one. Instead of having been able to take his quick profit out of the market Yates had found himself called on to support it by buying up the rapidly falling Welland Canal shares. No bank would extend credit on them. Bad management, constant calls for funds, landslides, the need for special earth moving machinery, the letters from Canada had been constant reminders to Yates that he had made, possibly, a huge and ruinous miscalculation.

If that year seeded disaster for the House of Yates and McIntyre, it was also one of mounting disillusion for Eliphalet Nott. The partnership, all optimism in the beginning, seemed more and more to be held together by a contract Yates and McIntyre disregarded, or so it seemed to Nott, as it suited the growing ambitions of the firm which now included two additional junior Yateses. The contractors neglected the Literature Lottery when sales of their "foreign" tickets seemed more profitable; they complained that the New York contract was a burden, that the Doctor misinterpreted the verbal revisions to it, refusing to return to them what they argued were over-payments.

Nott was especially angered when, during the winter months of 1825, "someone," (and the inference was that it was his lottery contractors), tried to persuade the legislature to set up a consolidated lottery by joining the Albany Land Lottery and the Fever Hospital Lottery to the Literature Lottery, the latter the only one then being drawn, a move which technically could not be made without the permission of the Doctor as the superintendent of the Literature Lottery. Yates and McIntyre denied their part in the attempt which failed, but it left a residue of mistrust. [13]

Nott tried persuasion on every level he could think of to bring the firm, and particularly John B. Yates, back to those "reasonable views" of their obligations as he saw them. He tried to prove to Yates that the "House's" profit on its half share of the difference between scheme and selling price of tickets would amount to over $100,000, far more than the rebates of interest for which they had been harassing him. He argued that their use of unbanked money from ticket sales would be equally important to them . . . how nearly tragic it would be he did not yet know . . . and he pointed out the advantage he had given them by not insisting that they post the $70,000 bond called for in the original contract. [14]

His final appeal before the great crisis was a masterpiece of flattery, one which he might well have used as an illustration in a "Kames" lecture to his seniors on the nature of man and on how to manipulate it. Knowing John B. Yates's appetite for vast enterprises he concluded a letter to him in late February, 1825 with what purported to be private information:

> I have been maturing a national system of framing lottery classes and determining prizes, which, in my judgment, will displace the Vaninni system. That system is accurate but it is somewhat troublesome in the preparation of classes and it can never be understood by anybody but mathematicians. The system I have matured, has the same truth—greater simplicity—and will be intelligible to every dealer and adventurer. Its advantages are such, in my judgment, that it will be deemed of consequence to someone, should the U.S. institute lotteries, as well as in those states which shall hereafter institute them . . . after I have received the opinion of a few more men of science, I shall, if you wish, submit it to you and Mr. McI. before I say anything on the subject to any other person. [15]

If the "madman Vaninni's" ternary system had given Yates and McIntyre their economic advantage, the Doctor reasoned his "American System" would not only extend it, but would be "of consequence to someone" in the event of national lotteries, and who better than John B. Yates appreciated a special advantage? Nott's "American System" received a patent on September 9, 1825, signed by President John Q. Adams and Henry Clay, but from that time on nothing more is heard of it. From Yates and McIntyre's point of view the ternary system needed little improvement.

In a sense the Doctor's relations with Yates and McIntyre now took on the aspect of a lottery within a lottery, a hazard of schemes to win back from his partners what he now realized they were willing to take from him in vast gambling enterprises of their own, the Welland Canal involvement, and a dozen "foreign" lottery adventures made possible only by the banker's license he had too generously given them.

His own fears of being overwhelmed were crystallized at the Commencement meeting of his Board of Trustees in July, 1824, when Henry Yates, in his role as college treasurer, reported that Union had outstanding debts of $178,251.77. The ringing optimism of the President's Phi Beta Kappa speech that year had been in part a response to the happy auguries he had read into his contract with Yates and McIntyre. He had staked . . . "hazarded" would always be his word for it . . . his reputation on proving that he and they could do what the State of New York had failed to do: win from the Wheels of Fortune an estate equal to financing the predestined role he saw for himself and for Union College in the new America. His was the sanctified cause worthy of the sacrifices of thousands of "adventurers" in lottery tickets, sacrifices made in response to an unfolding manifest destiny to which Yates and McIntyre seemed increasingly heedless.

The lessons in human nature which Nott used to make his senior course in "Kames" the exciting event it was for his "young gentlemen" were now about to be demonstrated in his relations with his partners, men who dared to endanger his every hope for the future.

CHAPTER 2

"*Lottery No. 3, for 1825*"

IF there was small talk at first between the Doctor and John B. Yates about the college and about people that January 4, 1826, it was only an uncomfortable prelude. The Doctor and Henry Yates, the college treasurer, must have had some warning of what the latter's "much perturbed" younger brother John, had come to Schenectady to discuss: [The year just over? A very good one for the college: students were turning to Joel's "chymistry" course—a very large senior class—larger, the President believed, than any "in the colleges to the east." The "young gentlemen," though, had been restive, and the Schenectady Methodists were unforgiving] — perhaps the three men had yielded a moment's smile if Nott or his treasurer spoke of the letter the Schenectady *Cabinet* had published some months back: "a 'long Tom' cannon fixed to one of the college chimneys," the editor had written, "so that it will rake the church—those vile wretches, the students, are practising military tactics and preparing a battering ram against the church. . . ."[1] The Erie Canal? The Doctor may have suggested it would be a boon to his lottery agent's Chittenango property. . . .

There may have been no small talk at all; John Barentse Yates may have brushed aside all the amenities, and, characteristically, acted, confessing in aggrieved irritation his follies as the self-appointed banker for the Welland Canal Company which, at the moment, was no man's boon. The new canal had sponged up every dollar he had been able to raise of his own, from his friends, and to Archibald McIntyre's horror, for he seems not to have been consulted by his partner, from the now empty treasury of the "House," He may even have denied his Welland Canal gamble.[2] "Ruin," from whatever cause, was the one word these three men could exchange in complete understanding, for within two weeks

"Class No. Three, for 1825" of the Literature Lottery was to be drawn, the largest by far of any scheme yet to be offered to the public, with guaranteed prizes of hundreds of thousands of dollars which John Yates confessed the "House" could not possibly pay.[3]

No man, least of all John Barentse Yates, could admit to what he called his "temerarious speculations" without some attempt to justify himself. One must assume that rumors of a Welland Canal involvement had already reached Schenectady, for in the preceding August William James, that exacting Calvinist merchant-speculator of Albany, had "offered accommodation" to John Yates.[4]

The lottery contractor had at least two explanations to give for the shocking news he brought to Schenectady; "if" only the sales of lottery tickets in 1825 had equalled earlier sales, but floods of weak banknotes had come into the money market, and so a business depression had injured the "House"; in some schemes during the last year almost twenty percent of their tickets had gone begging.[5] If this explanation was not enough there was also what Archibald McIntyre called "the opposition which has sprung up," the mounting attacks in the press and in the legislature by growing numbers of moralists outraged by the always available stories of suicides, thefts, and alcoholism for which the lotteries were blamed. And especially there were the attacks of certain "malignant" New York ticket dealers who loudly complained of being cheated by the contractors for the Literature Lottery. Palmer Canfield of New York City was leading the pack with his petition to the legislature, charging Yates and McIntyre with denying tickets to vendors who did not cut the "House" in on their profits, with "giving the preference to out-of-state dealers," and with reporting to the State Comptroller that there were tickets unsold in "schemes" from which Canfield had been wholly excluded.[6]

Treasurer Henry Yates of Union College, always the loyal older brother to the man whose speculator's penchant he well knew, may have reviewed the "House's" payments under their dual contract with Nott: the last one received for the "College Fund" had been in April; there was still a balance of $57,000 due. The "President's Fund," however, had not been neglected; so far that concealed account had received over $48,000.[7]

If there were recriminations they were not heard beyond the room. "Lottery No. 3, for 1825" cast a rapidly advancing shadow which threatened to eclipse reputations and all hopes unless these three men could arrest it; this was the concern of the meeting.

J. B. Yates seems to have come to Schenectady prepared to deal with that immediate problem. Weeks after this meeting a letter was drafted by the "House" which bore, however, the earlier date line of "January 4, 1826," a letter which Nott later insisted was only a formality, "to embody in writing, the substance of what was proffered verbally by Mr. Yates . . . [and] accepted verbally by the President. . . ." This letter stated in the baldest terms the penalty Nott must pay for Yates's "temerarious speculations":

> It has become necessary that we should inform you, that such have been our losses, that we have no reasonable prospect of being able to pay the sum stipulated [sums owing to the "College Fund"] , or even to pay the prizes in the lottery now pending, unless we can procure immediate pecuniary assistance to a large amount. . . .
>
> In view of these circumstances, we have thought it our duty to propose to you that you and the treasurer should raise for our immediate benefit one hundred thousand dollars, together with such further sums as may be necessary to sustain our credit. . . .[8]

The letter was signed by both John B. Yates and Archibald McIntyre.

The Pandora's box Nott had opened twenty years earlier when he had traded the corporate independence of Union College to New York State in return for his first lottery grant must have seemed bottomless. In return for this extraordinary favor the "House" now agreed to put into writing their earlier verbal agreement with the Doctor which had substituted percentage payments on tickets sold in each lottery scheme in place of the fixed annual payments called for in the original dual contract.[9] If, however, this had been the only inducement held out to Nott to add to his many roles that of loan banker, John B. Yates would have been guilty of something akin to blackmail. According to the Doctor's later testimony there was another inducement discussed that memorable January day which was not mentioned in the firm's letter calling for one hundred thousand dollars.

If he could and would raise this money the Doctor recalled, John B. Yates held out to him a promise of new and greater profits for the "House," for the college and for the "President's Fund." John Yates, the Doctor also remembered, had stated that he "contemplated" a new bill to be submitted to the legislature which, if passed, would consolidate the Literature Lottery with the only other lotteries remaining to be run in New York State. The first was a lottery for a Fever Hospital for which New York City had paid the State $40,000 in 1823, and which Yates and McIntyre had purchased, and then the long dormant Albany Land Lottery which the "House" would buy if Nott agreed to the proposal, and the bill passed.[10] The advantages would be considerable: the two most important cities in the State would not have to wait for their money until the Literature Lottery had been run off, and their citizens, and perhaps the legislature, would feel a warmer attachment for lotteries *per se*. The college, too, could expect a still more rapid collection of its lottery endowment than it could without this consolidation with the New York City and Albany lotteries.[11]

This, at least, is the substance of what Nott insisted John Yates had offered on January 4th, 1826, in return for an immediate loan of $100,000 to pay the costs and prizes in "Lottery No. 3, for 1825," and "for further sums." What was actually said, however, then and later was lost in the clangor of charges and countercharges hammered out over the next eight years, first by Nott, then by Nott and the Union College Trustees against the House of Yates and McIntyre, and then by the "House" against Nott and his Trustees, a dissonance which grew out of the events of that January day in 1826 when John B. Yates projected ruin for them all. That was the day John Yates, the gambler, and Eliphalet Nott, the promoter of hazards, began their open contest of strength.

II

Taken separately, the two histories of that struggle, spun out in Chancery Court documents, present two pictures of honorable men defending themselves against what, to them, was the dishonesty and the devious self-aggrandizement of their opponents. The biographer of any one of these men from this point on, however, faces nearly impossible choices, for the harsh disagreements between Eliphalet Nott and the House of Yates and McIntyre were never resolved; in settling them out of Court by an expedient division of the huge sums of money at contest the moral issues themselves were never to be impartially judged; it is these unclarified issues which measure the character of the men involved. As one reads the dozen closely printed documents submitted to the Chancery Court in 1834–35 and the many letters and notes which both Nott and Yates and McIntyre were careful to exclude from their printed versions of the lottery history as each of them saw it, one enters a maze in which the greatest shock is not the discovery that there is no exit to it, but rather the awareness of what is happening to these partners and friends as events and ambitions forced them deeper into its strange alleys. [12]

Biography is, of necessity, narrative, and the essence of narrative is selection, editorial choosing, arranging, proportioning, and so judging. With a man's life, especially with such a man as Eliphalet Nott whose public commitments were to the highest ethical concepts of the nation, judgments on acts and commitments rooted in these two unresolved "histories" of the lotteries are at best presumptuous. How to keep them to a minimum?

Oddly, it is Yates and McIntyre who offer a working map of the lottery maze; in printing their bleakly titled pamphlet, "Examination of a Report Professing to be a Report of a Select Committee of the Trustees of Union College in Relation to the Pending Controversy with Yates and McIntyre," the lottery contractors placed, side by side, Nott's and his Trustees' "professed" version of the lottery history, and then their own. Although this "Examination" is the witness of angry men, it offers a guide, at least, for chronicling this incredible history. [13]

The two accounts, printed in parallel columns, agree only in their chronology, a chronology into which the Chancery Court "Documents" are divided. The "House" cited six so-called "periods," each of which was bounded by its own verbal and written contracts, or "stipulations," and its own lottery schemes and drawings.

Period by period, from 1822 on, one is drawn deeper and deeper into this shadowy maze of cross-purposes. From the first, Nott and his lottery contractors each claim they are taking huge risks for noble ends, ends, however, which in the acids of personal ambition and ever present fears of disaster, take on strange aspects, and finally, destroy their partnership. Behind each "period" of the lotteries' dreary arithmetic of owe and owing one sees the men themselves, Nott and the two Yateses and Archibald McIntyre, as each becomes the captive of the other in a prison of "accommodations" and revisions from which none of them can break out. In Nott's company one sees, too, the concerned men who signed that Trustees' report which was the subject of Yates and McIntyre's scornful "Examination": William L. Marcy, at the time of the Chancery suits Governor of New York State, United States Senator Silas Wright, and New York State Supreme Court Judge J. P. Cushman, men whose reputations along with those of their fellow Trustees as custodians of public funds, were equally in jeopardy with that of the President of Union College.

Charges and countercharges aside, the one fact, during this first "Period" on which Nott and Yates and McIntyre agreed, was the reality of "Lottery No. 3 for 1825." Nott recalled that "in full view of the danger [it posed,] he deliberately made up his mind to incur the personal sacrifices, and run the personal hazard necessary to prevent the failure of Yates and McIntyre and the consequent ruin which such failure must bring on the college." [14] Whatever the mode was by which he chose to put his decision into effect, the decision itself was perhaps the most important one he made as President of Union College. John B. Yates's record as the banker of the Welland Canal stems from it. On it rests the subsequent history of Union College and of Nott's multiple careers as the inventor "second only to Fulton," and the speculator worthy of standing with John B. Yates, though the Doctor might well have resented the comparison.

Nott turned at once for help to his one-time Albany parishioner, William James, the ruddy cheeked Scotch-Irish investor whose fortune at his death, was said to be second only to John Jacob Astor's. It was William James who, the preceding August, had offered John Yates an "accommodation," and who, in 1822, had witnessed the signing of the original contract between Yates and McIntyre and the college, and then its concealed supplement between the contractors and the Doctor. [15] It was again William James who had supplied the large sums Nott and Henry Yates had borrowed on their personal signatures to buy out the interest in the Literature Lottery then held by Hamilton College and the other grantees. Nott later assured Archibald McIntyre that James was that "man of very great wealth" who, knowing the advantage held by the lottery contractor who controlled the Vannini system of drawings, had wanted the Literature Lottery contract for himself. William James, "Merchant of Albany," founder of a famous American family, was in a very real sense the unrecorded fifth partner in the Literature Lottery enterprise.

On January 11, 1826 William James's "accommodation" of $100,000 was arranged, guaranteed again by Nott and his treasurer, and secured, as the deed noted, "by the new college edifices and all the houses standing on the premises" of the Ramée campus on Nistiquona Hill. William James's capital and his six and a half percent interest were safe. Nott could now hope, at least, that those "reasonable views" of the lottery operations would once again guide a very frightened Yates and McIntyre. [16]

So much for the "facts" on which Nott, J. B. Yates, and Archibald McIntyre could agree as to the events rising out of their crisis meeting on January 4th, 1826. The partners' "Examination" of 1835, however, belittled any Nott claim to sacrifices and hazards undertaken on their behalf. In doing so, however, they neglected the evidence of a letter Nott wrote to Henry Yates, the college treasurer, the day after the President had completed the negotiations with William James, a remarkable letter marked "confidential," one which, obviously, never found its way into the Chancery documents:

> You and I have such unlimited powers and have used them so boldly and so frequently without ever consulting the resident Trustees, who are a standing committee with powers on all emergencies, that I feel anxious in the first place to arm ourselves and prepare for our justification in case of the worst—and having done so to prevent the disaster contemplated—and if going even further than we have gone will prevent it—my advise is to go still further and to stick at nothing but impossibilities, for if we are able to show that we have gone into these varied and bold measures really to preserve and advance the interest of the concern trusted to us—whatever may be the result and however we may be charged with imprudence, our characters will not suffer—and this is what has chiefly given me uneasiness—and the more so as I know there are people who would make the worst use of our errors. [17]

"To arm ourselves and prepare for our justification . . . stick at nothing but impossibilities . . . show we have gone into these measures really to preserve and advance the interests of the concern trusted to us. . . ."; any hazard, Nott had decided, must be taken to achieve the sanctified end. Their characters were his chief concern, and these could not suffer if they were guarded by a carefully prepared "justification." Imbued with the certainties of the predestinarian, the President of Union College had elected to use his unlimited powers, use them as the man of action, unhampered by his "resident Trustees," and undismayed by the gamblers' follies of his lottery contractors. The conclusion of this letter, wonderfully irrelevant, suggests a cool nerve and the Yankee mind of its author: "Purchase for me," Nott added as an afterthought, "such a set of pencils as your brother's, of the best kind."

On January 17th, two days before "Literature Lottery No. 3 for 1825" was to be drawn, J. B. Yates, whose choice in pencils, at least, had pleased Nott, forwarded to the Doctor "package Number 727," containing fifteen lottery tickets on the pending scheme for which the Doctor paid $345, "the difference between the selling scheme price and the least sum it must draw. . . . ," an arrangement which cut the purchaser's hazard to a minimum. [18] If the Doctor had designed this purchase to test God's concern in the Literature Lottery he must have been disappointed for the wheel of fortune two days later emptied its treasure into other laps, and one of its richest prizes into the control of a man who seems to have been well placed to help Yates and McIntyre in their developing controversies with Nott.

On January 19, 1826 "Literature Lottery No.3, for 1825" was drawn, probably in the New York City office of the "House," at No. 164 Broadway in that "well lighted room" the contractors had agreed to furnish for these climactic occasions. As a "scheme" it dwarfed anything they had yet offered the public; it totaled almost $600,000 and its tickets sold for the unusually high price of forty dollars each, although most of the purchasers were share buyers, some owning as little as an eighth of a ticket. The lottery contractors were bitterly disappointed in ticket sales; over $104,000 worth remained unsold, a showing far worse than in any of the thirteen drawings already held. [19] They blamed the current business depression and the mounting attacks of enemy dealers and newspaper moralists. If Nott's $100,000 loan from William James was to bring the firm off without irreparable loss, a good proportion of the prize tickets would have had to be among those remaining undrawn from the wheel in which over $500,000 in prize numbers lay within the reach of the bare armed boy. Something may have gone wrong on drawing day, for it was not until four days later that the "Fortunate Offices" across the state could post the "numbers in Literature Lottery No.3, 1825: Nos. 17, 21, 7, 35, 6, and 31." [20]

If "package No. 727" had produced no evidence to encourage the predestinarian in Nott, one of the fateful numbers posted on January 23 suggested special providences of local origin: the winner of the $40,000 prize was the Honorable T. J. Oakley, "and others"; Oakley was the late Attorney General of New York State, and one of the most powerful men in state politics. According to Jabez Hammond, he was a Federalist turned Clintonian Democrat, "cool, sophistical," the son-in-law of a "political huckster" by the name of Robert Williams. [21] Whatever his connections and allegiances, he was to prove valuable to Yates and McIntyre the following May.

Four days after the drawing Archibald McIntyre, writing to the Doctor from the firm's New York City office, had nothing but heartfelt praise "for the prompt relief which you afforded us in our hour of difficulty and distress. We were . . . on the verge of ruin . . . ; I believe," he added, "that we are safe if we pursue a uniform and prudent course . . . we have had a lesson sufficiently appalling and distressing to keep us in very constant remembrance of it during life." [22]

His partner also wrote to Nott on the same day, but J. B. Yates had little time for confession of errors; he did admit that "our golden dreams for ourselves have vanished and with them all the imagined good I thought of doing with it. Still a comfortable competency is far from hopeless. . . ." Yates had his own reservoir of optimism, and for the time Eliphalet Nott was the surest source for keeping it replenished. "I am satisfied," Yates had continued, "if we are sustained six months, or at the farthest, for one year, we can save our friends, the college, and our reputations. . . ." Both partners included in these letters a new call on the Doctor for help, one which at the time seemed like an assurance that the firm's "reasonable views" had returned; "on mature reflection," John Yates had added, and this was the real burden of his letter, "I know that the presence of my brother, as treasurer of the college, during the whole time, to see to things and to aid, with all the energy he possesses, is positively necessary . . . Mr. McIntyre and I must now . . . both be often and long absent . . . we will need his active aid, and beside, the beneficial public effect it would have, that he is known to be here as the treasurer of the college. . . ."[23]

John B. Yates's out-of-town business, though he did not say so, would be largely concerned with Welland Canal affairs, and Archibald McIntyre, though he does not seem to have shared the fact with Nott, would often be occupied with an adventure of his own, a speculation involving more than 100,000 acres of Adirondack lands on which iron had been discovered, the site of what became the profitable MacIntyre [*sic*] Mine.[24] The presence of Henry Yates in the New York lottery office, "during the whole time to see to things" was to have a significance far beyond any Nott anticipated when he agreed to send the college treasurer to the contractors' office, where he was to remain "as the treasurer of Union College," cautioned, Nott declared later, to avoid any partnership connection.[25]

Henry Yates, still drawing his $1300 a year as treasurer and clerk to the Board of Trustees, his traveling expenses paid by the college, joined his brother and Archibald McIntyre in their office on lower Broadway about July first, not however, as the college's guardian angel over the affairs of the Literature Lottery, but as a full fledged partner in all the activities of the firm, an arrangement Nott was to declare was a shocking betrayal of the trust he had placed in him.

III

The bitterness of 1834 was a distillation of conflicts which, in 1826, were still in the making. Before he left for New York City that summer Henry Yates drew up the new lottery legislation his brother John had proposed earlier, a bill designed to consolidate the Fever Hospital and the Albany Land Lotteries with the college lottery. The partners and Nott and his treasurer had all agreed a Consolidated Lottery Bill would make for good public relations and that the consolidation would speed up the drawings of the Literature Lottery, a program Nott kept urging on the contractors largely to crowd "foreign" tickets out of the New York market.

On this much of the history of their new Consolidation Bill, passed April 13, 1826, both Nott and the "House" could agree in their Chancery suits; for the rest there was to be nothing but angry cries of deceit and extortion from Yates and McIntyre. The lottery contractors were to picture themselves as having been victimized by an Eliphalet Nott, who without telling them, "had in his own handwriting, made a few alterations in [the Bill] not very material, *except* in the substitution of the person having the *supervision and management of lotteries*, for the agent of the college. . . ."; in other words, the Doctor, both Yates and McIntyre insisted, substituted himself for Henry Yates, treasurer and clerk of the Board of Trustees, as the authority whose permission must be obtained by the lottery contractors for any plan they developed to reap the benefits of the new Consolidation Bill. Nott, they claimed, also "struck out a clause" which he thought might enable the contractors to purchase the Albany Lands Lottery "and mix them [the Albany Lottery tickets] with their tickets in the Fever Hospital."[26] Nott's object, the contractors bitterly noted, was to prevent them from acting without his express consent, "to influence their rights by a surreptitious act."[27]

April and May, 1826, had little of spring about them in the affairs of the Doctor and the House of Yates and McIntyre. The members of the latter, concerned about their "rights" under the new Consolidated Lottery Bill, now turned to T. J. Oakley, "one of the most eminent Counsel in the State," they reported, whose recent sharing of a large lottery prize may or may not have conditioned the fact that "he was unequivocally with us on this subject."[28] Oakley gave the contractors hope for the future by assuring them that the moment the Literature Lottery was completed they would be answerable only to the Attorney General and to the Comptroller of New York State, that Eliphalet Nott would then have no claim on the firm or voice in its affairs. Oakley especially agreed that the new act gave the "House" permission to run its Fever Hospital lottery concurrently with its drawings of the Literature Lottery, a point they were most anxious to determine. [29]

The lottery contractors had probably turned to Oakley soon after their second grim visit with Nott in Schenectady, in late April or early May. There had been much "warm altercation" that day, according to Yates and McIntyre's "Examination." There had been "great excitement on the part of J. B. Yates, and complaint of injustice . . . he hastily drew on a scrap of paper a memorandum of what he would do, and then threw it down, declaring that to be his final and unalterable position, and that it was made for peace sake. The Doctor examined and assented to it." The tensions during that session were apparently too much for Henry Yates, the college treasurer, "who remained out of the room during the negotiations, or rather, controversy. . . ." [30]

If the "Examination" is the true record of these events, then the Doctor's next moves were either the unethical ploys of an ambitious man, or they were the calculated moves of Lord Kames's scornful critic who saw men as less than his lordship's reasonable creatures, who taught the "young gentlemen" of Union College that man's passion-born ambitions could not be curbed by rational means. "Mr. [John] Yates," the "Examination" continued, "then made a fair copy [of the new agreement], but somewhat more explicit in its details and then left the room." The Doctor "then took up the original draft, wrote some explanations on it, and then endorsed his assent." Later examination of this draft, however, according to Yates and McIntyre, showed that the Doctor had "extended the college proportion" of the profits to be shared in the Consolidated Lottery drawings, twice inserting his own figures for this extension. This "fair copy," altered by Nott, was later signed for the contractors by Archibald McIntyre, its changed nature unknown to J. B. Yates, and, according to the "Examination," "wholly erroneous, founded on representations made by Doctor Nott, on which Mr. McIntyre confidingly relied. . . ." [31]

Nott's later testimony about the preparation of the new Consolidated Lottery contract, given to Governor Marcy, Senator Wright, and Judge J. P. Cushman in 1834, spoke only of "an interview," and that "terms of an arrangement satisfactory to the parties were settled, and presented in a written stipulation." [32] In its simplest terms that "second stipulation," however, controlled, and on the Doctor's terms, the division of profits which the new Consolidated Lottery Bill was expected to produce. John B. Yates's temper had flared, if the lottery firm's testimony in 1835 is credited, because the Doctor's "story about a prearranged mutual benefit by division of profit between the colleges and the contractors, if the law should be passed, is unfounded. We assert that there is no foundation for it." [33]

Wherever the "truth" lies, Nott, in 1826, by putting himself in a position to withhold permission to mix the land prizes of the Albany lottery with the money prizes of the Fever Hospital and Literature Lotteries, had extended his authority as "supervisor and manager" of the Literature Lottery to all of Yates and McIntyre's New York State lottery operations, and had thus cut himself in on the profits to be derived from the two lotteries which belonged wholly to Yates and McIntyre. As an exercise in strategy the Doctor's maneuvering was, if the facts are as the lottery firm reported them, much like his earlier generalship in the New York State Legislature which had won for him the State's lottery grants of 1805 and 1814.

Nott now held the upper hand, and in spite of the contractors' outrage, he refused to relax it. The terms he had won from them as his price for agreeing to the Consolidated Lottery Bill was the payment to his personal account of 6 31/100 percent of the gross amount of the money prizes in each scheme of the now to be combined lotteries after specified amounts had been drawn under the original Literature Lottery and Fever Hospital contracts. [34] "For risks taken and hazards run . . ." (a recurring phrase in all Nott's later statements defending his acts), the Doctor took this new levy from the "House," but as an individual; his rationale for this he made clear in his letter to Yates and McIntyre accepting the conditions of the "Second Stipulation": "this," he wrote, "I do the more cheerfully as the Trustees of the college are not made parties to the contract . . . and will not, therefore, be considered responsible for the hazard which may arise from proceedings had under it." [35]

The events of the spring and summer of 1826 severely damaged loyalties and friendships whose testing began three years earlier when Nott agreed to John B. Yates's plea to add the precarious role of loan banking to the firm's primary function of lottery contracting. The President, from that time on, was intent on controlling the New York State operations of the partners, and they, in turn, were equally intent on fighting what they were later to call "further imposition and burthen on the contractors" which were based, they claimed, on the Doctor's "illegal purpose" in altering the conditions of the Consolidated Lottery Bill of 1826. [36]

By July of that year each of these men was probing the still summer-green alleys of the maze their lottery association had created. John B. Yates was adventuring on tow-paths labeled "Welland Canal," Archibald McIntyre on trails pointing to the Adirondack fastness, and Henry Yates as an undeclared full-time partner of the "House" on the planked sidewalks of lower Broadway where, at No. 164, the contractors gathered to extend their lottery business into every state that would tolerate their operations. [37] Within a year they hoped to see the final drawing in the Literature Lottery, and so the end of the restraints put on them by the "Doctor," its "supervisor and manager." Events, however, were to prove such hopes as much subject to the whims of chance as had been the prize numbers in "Literature Lottery No.3 for 1825."

By July Eliphalet Nott's journey into the maze had allowed him to accumulate over $81,000 in principal and interest in his "President's Fund" and over $184,000 in principal and $49,000 in interest in the "College Fund," and ahead of him he could see ripening the fruits of the New York State Consolidated Lottery.

On July 4th, 1826 the Doctor was in Saratoga Springs where he offered prayers for the welfare of America on that fiftieth anniversary of national independence. The Union College cadets were "dined at the San Souci Hotel" where Major Jonas Holland read the Doctor's response to the town's welcome. [38] It was Major Holland who had just been given Henry Yates's duties as resident college treasurer and appointed Nott's keeper of the lottery records, the latter a task which Yates and McIntyre were later to declare the Major "knew no more about than he does about the Grand Lama of Tibet, or the Wandering Jew. . . ." [39]

Perhaps Nott would have offered prayers at the San Souci Hotel for Jefferson and John Adams, had he known that the two ex-Presidents, survivors of a more pristine America, were to die that day; he might even have phrased a private one for the impoverished Thomas Jefferson for whose aid the Virginia Legislature had reluctantly granted a lottery earlier that year, one which had been placed in the hands of the House of Yates and McIntyre. [40]

CHAPTER 3

"On a Magazine of Powder!"

PERHAPS a troubled conscience prompted Henry Yates on December 15, 1826 to write this revealing letter to the Doctor:

> My dear Sir—Yesterday I met a gentleman immediately from Providence, who informed me of the appointment of Dr. Wayland; I presume that immediate measures will be taken to employ or appoint another. . . . I have convinced John Austin [Yates] of the impropriety as it respects him at present. Brother Joseph's thoughtfulness on the subject of lotteries, is not new to me. He gives himself unnecessary trouble, and the evil exists only in his own imagination. It is, however, painful for me to think that the best part of my life, and the earnings of my earlier days have been hazarded for the promotion of the institution, and even now the sacrifice that I am making, should be construed to my own and your injury; that I, when risking the welfare of myself and family to the extent of what I have, should be supposed to anticipate in future some advantage, is not to be wondered at; but that you should, individually, astonishes me. I have never heard it intimated by anyone, and I believe it only rests in the mind of some evil persons, as what they or he would do in a similar situation.[1]

Professor Francis Wayland's imminent departure from Union for the presidency of Brown University meant the loss to the Doctor of a man as devoted to his own educational ideals, to his own conviction that, properly understood, the laws of political and economic life were one with the laws of the universe, as was the loss that year of his severe, Episcopalian son-in-law, Alonzo Potter, who, through Wayland's agency, had recently given up his Union College professorship to become an Episcopal rector in Boston. Something went out of Nott's life with the departure of both men, especially of Alonzo Potter and with him of the Potter household, of Maria, his daughter, and Clarkson, the small grandson. They and "Dr. Wayland" had provided a balance to the weight of Yateses, brothers and cousins, who surrounded Nott, to the "John Austin" of the college treasurer's letter, that "Rev. Johannes A. Yates" of the "catalogus" of 1828 whose frustrated ambition to take over Wayland's professorship of Mathematics and Natural Philosophy became a part of his and his family's growing bitterness toward Nott. Twenty-three years later it would be he who would open the floodgate of troubles on both the then aging President and his "curators," those Trustees soon to be spoken of by the embittered members of the "House" as the Doctor's "confederates."[2]

"Brother Joseph's [Ex-Governor Joseph C. Yates] thoughtfulness on the subject of lotteries . . . ," obviously written by Henry Yates in some impatience, reflected the wide-spread opposition to the lotteries Nott was constantly to join Yates and McIntyre in fighting in and out of the New York State Legislature over the next five years; such thinking was growing even among the Union College Trustees.

On November 7, 1827 the last drawing of the Literature Lottery took place; considering its tortuous history, the demise of this leviathan "hazard" was a quiet one. In Yates and McIntyre's table of "schemes" for the Consolidated Lottery it was "No.9" and included numbers in the Albany Land Lottery: $227,040 worth of tickets were offered to the "adventurers" from the sale of which the "College Fund" received $18,665.94 and the "President's Fund" $4,799.81.[3]

Between May 23, 1823 and November 10, 1827 there had been 31 "schemes," or "classes" drawn in the Literature Lottery and a total, according to Nott, of $4,948,597 in tickets had been offered, sales of which, presumably, entitled Union College to $443,002.23 plus interest at seven percent. On December 6th, 1827 in New York City, the Literature Lottery account was officially closed and the balance then due the college, $137,383.89, was provided for on August 1, 1828 in twenty-four notes, the last of which was dated December 1, 1831. The "President's Fund" was also settled at this time; at 2½ percent of sales it had accumulated $111,343.44 plus $20,378.48, in interest at seven percent, a sum for which, with the balance of the principal due, Yates and McIntyre gave the Doctor nine notes, the last of which was to be paid on January 1, 1832.[4]

In order to get this final settlement the Doctor had had to keep at both the Yateses and McIntyre throughout that summer. The partners had pleaded their "weight of engagements," of bank debts of over $200,000, of a Welland Canal involvement of $190,000; they did agree, however, that "affairs are evidently becoming brighter," and assured Nott that "we will be able to pay all. . . ."[5] John B. Yates even found time in one of these exchanges to arrange with the Doctor for as many of the latter's patent stoves, "as may be requisite to warm my factory in Chittenango."

An anxious Nott, on July 19, 1828, had pointed out in the last paragraph of a remarkably frank letter to Archibald McIntyre that "we owe above *one hundred thousand dollars* which is wanted and which we want to pay . . . you will allow," he told McIntyre,

> that I have gone to great lengths to sustain you in your embarrassments and now that they are drawing to a close you will not wonder that I am desirous of lessening my responsibilities as soon and as fast as it can be done with safety to yourselves, and especially as I have taken the course I have without the knowledge of the Board of Trustees or a single member thereof . . . you will justify me in pressing you to relieve me from this unpleasant situation as speedily as you can . . . I dare not do otherwise . . . any other course will be ruinous to us all.[6]

In the modified copy of this letter which was included in the printed Chancery Documents in 1835 Nott simply noted that he wanted to avoid "the appearance of neglect on my part. . . . I must be careful to avoid the appearance of evil."

If one accepts Yates and McIntyre's bitter Chancery Court indictment in 1835 of Nott's "management and supervision" of the Literature Lottery one discovers that the figures of this 1827-1828 settlement are all Nott's figures. The partners, in 1835, would call Nott's record "a pretended settlement," one made between a devious college President and a gulled Archibald McIntyre "as individuals," that McIntyre had had no authority from John B. Yates in 1828 to vary the conditions of the dual contract of 1822, and that Nott had had no authority from his Trustees to modify those contracts. The "House" was to claim Nott's final settlement of 1828 was inflated by $456,389, that it allowed for no rebates of interest due the "House," and that the firm, in the person of McIntyre, had guilelessly trusted Nott to prepare the settlement at a time when the affairs of the contractors were such as to make a careful review of their college accounts impracticable.[7] This battle of the bookkeepers, however, was not to be joined until six years later, by which time Nott, John and Henry Yates, and Archibald McIntyre had played out to a bitter end a relationship in which the fine Italian hand would have seemed a thing of callouses and blunt fingers.

II

Following the "settlement" of 1828 the Doctor continued as a partner in the operations of the "House" in everything but name. Instead of regaining their freedom to operate without him, as ex-Attorney General T. J. Oakley had assured them they would as soon as the Literature Lottery was closed, the contractors, with a grace which varied as drawings in their remaining Fever Hospital and Albany Land Lotteries varied, and their Contingent Residue drawings fluctuated, and as the Welland Canal affairs waxed and waned, continued to defer to the Doctor. His power over them was now rooted in his blandly titled "Second Written Stipulation," illegally wrung from the "House" in 1826, so its partners were to claim.

By September, 1828 there was no innocence left in their relationship with the Doctor. By that time the "House" recognized that he had become the firm's chief asset, and Nott, for his part, sure of his ability to gauge the self-interest of his fellow men, intended to hold tight rein on these lottery contractors who were still deep in debt to Union College and whose always perilous solvency they owed to him. The 6 31/100 percent on the gross amount of money prizes in the residue New York lotteries, payable to him, excluding the Fever Hospital Lottery, seemed to the Doctor to be a justifiable return for his continued cooperation in keeping the "House" solvent. In John B. Yates's letter to Nott at the end of September of that year there is even the covert suggestion of an actual partnership in the "House" for the President of Union College.

> You and my brother Henry, are the only persons to whom I speak with freedom, and with whom I confer, so that we may have the whole of our objects understood.
>
> You know that there is as much danger to our operations for the future, to give an impression that the college has received, or secured all its means originally intended to be given, as that there should be an impression that we are growing enormously wealthy. The latter is now out of the question, and men of business and reflection know it.
>
> I assure you, further, that the sooner a state of things is produced by which we mutually depend on each other, without the intervention of any third party, or person, the better. . . .
>
> We are now, as it were, situated on a MAGAZINE OF POWDER, with the torch in the hand of a man who is our friend today, but we know not how long, and he can blow us up when he pleases; and if anything happens to stop us, I am as well assured as I am of my existence, that no other lottery under the present grants will ever be drawn in the state of New York. . . .[8]

If Nott read this invitation to produce a state of things "by which we depend on each other . . ." as a partnership offer, he took no action. He obviously agreed, however, that future operations must not be jeopardized by too much good news.[9] William James's "torch" and its proximity to Yates and McIntyre's "MAGAZINE OF POWDER" may not have seemed as real a threat to the Doctor as J. B. Yates's own "foolish and temerarious" Welland Canal speculations to which Yates had confessed in this letter. William James as well as Henry Yates had been made Union College Trustees the preceding year, and William James as a member of its finance committee, would be quite unlikely to produce the explosion which would ruin the college which his son, Henry, was then attending. With Henry Yates in charge of its New York City offices, and all the partners "entered into a solemn written stipulation," as J. B. Yates had written, not to act without joint agreement, the Doctor had reason to think the "House" would be able to pay off its debt to the college, to his President's Fund, and to continue the new, wonderfully profitable arrangement with him for which he was prepared to continue to hazard and to risk "as an individual."

If he really knew the desperate situation now chronic with the contractors he was more the "adventurer" than he may have been willing to admit to himself. Yates and McIntyre owed the New York City and Albany banks $212,000 in short term loans, William James (that "firebrand," in the heated imagination of John B. Yates), had just refused to renew those notes of the "House" which he held, and Yates's Welland Canal gamble had become "a kind of cistern into which Eliphalet Nott poured credit at one end," according to one lottery historian, "while the Welland Canal Company siphoned it at the other." [10] The contractors' assets, on the other hand, to most of which they seldom referred, their profitable "foreign" lottery contracts, their large real estate investments in New York City and Philadelphia, and in a Welland Canal inefficiently building and yet to prove itself, were paper treasures unless the Doctor continued to hazard and pledge all the credit he could command. [11]

For a year and a half, from the close of the Literature Lottery until the close of the Fever Hospital Lottery on June 2, 1829, the Doctor responded again and again to Yates and McIntyre's often frantic calls for note indorsements to get them through their drawings. Desperately trying to quiet the clamor of banks for interest payments and loan cancellations, the "House" cut corners where it could. Finally, on January 13, 1829, the contractors decided to include the Doctor himself among their economies.

Their letter to him complained that to continue to pay him 6 31/100 percent of the gross schemes in their New York lotteries, an arrangement John B. Yates had protested violently when it was agreed to in 1826, "would be ruinous to us". The contractors now assured Nott that the "Second Written Stipulation" of that year had assumed that "all classes published would be sold," but that such had not been the case. Seldom could the "House" now sell more than half the tickets in a scheme, its members assured the Doctor, for the New York lotteries were again under violent attack. Better, they wrote, to give up the New York lotteries "than to go on with a hopeless prospect before us." [12]

Tight money, Palmer Canfield's unrelenting attacks, rumors of a pending Grand Jury investigation of lotteries in New York City, the hostility to lotteries as a moral evil of such men as "Brother Joseph," the ex-Governor and oldest of the Yates clan and president of the Union College Board of Trustees, and of Silas Wright, the New York State comptroller, such frustrations may, on days of poor drawings have made Yates and McIntyre look upon their New York contracts as a hopeless prospect, but there was a built-in silver lining: the drums which contained the tickets actually sold (perhaps only a half or a quarter of all the tickets scheduled to be sold in a scheme), spun off, as a result, fewer prizes. No matter how poor a showing their sales made on their ledgers, the "mad man" Vannini's ternary system guaranteed that the long-time odds were always with the "House." In an unguarded moment that next December, Archibald McIntyre confessed to Nott that "We cannot complain, and we ought not, for we find that at the end of every month, money has been made during the month." [13]

If the wheels were not currently generous, perhaps the Doctor would be: the firm would be greatly helped, it was argued that January, if he would agree to cancel the "Second Written Stipulation" of May 31, 1826, and substitute for it a new one to bear the same date, but one which would give the Doctor 6.31 percent "on the gross amount of tickets *actually* sold" instead of the same percentage on the total number of tickets *scheduled to be sold* in each scheme. The "House" also urged him to agree to take a just proportion of the Albany lands which the contractors had to buy in, and, also, to allow them to pay him his 6.31 percent on each drawing sixty days after it was completed instead of immediately after prizes were announced.

III

The President of Union College at this new juncture in the life of the great hazard, according to Yates and McIntyre's later "Examination," now fraudulently eliminated Union College itself as the beneficiary of their revised "Second Written Stipulation" through a device the lottery contractors did not become aware of, so they testified in 1835, until near the close of all the New York lotteries in 1833:

> The President [according to Yates and McIntyre's "Examination"] returned a draft for a new letter [or Stipulation] to be dated as the same day as the former one [May 31, 1826], which appeared to be much like the former one in every important particular, except the required variation, to which, only, Mr. McIntyre's attention was directed. This was copied by Mr. McIntyre, signed and sent. An important variation from the whole tenor of previous arrangements, contained in this letter, and its intended effect, by which Dr. Nott personally was substituted as the beneficiary, in consideration of his advances and responsibilities, in place of the college, was not observed by Mr. McIntyre; the other partners did not know it, and the fact of such a material variation remained undiscovered and unnoticed for a long time afterward. The object of this variation, and the surreptitious mode of its introduction, with the antedating of its commencement, are too apparent to leave a vestige of doubt, however strongly the committee [the Union College Finance Committee of 1831, consisting of William James, William L. Marcy, Judge, that year, of the New York State Supreme Court, and Eliphalet Nott] may indorse the profession of disinterested zeal for the welfare of the college. Further comment on it is unnecessary,—it speaks for itself. [14]

The Union College "Report" of 1834 on the lottery history states simply that the Doctor did not forward the substitute "Stipulation" requested by Yates and McIntyre on January 13, 1829, but that he did, "after some delay and much conversation, then transmit his further consent to a further drawing over of unsold tickets." [15]

Two "facts" *are* of record, however: the original "Second Written Stipulation" of May 31, 1826, *was* replaced during July 1829 by a substituted stipulation back dated to May 30, 1826, but dated, so the Doctor was to testify, "May *30*, 1826," to distinguish it from the agreement for which it was a substitute. This revised stipulation also declared that Nott's "consent and cooperation" were necessary to the execution of the Albany Land Lottery. It declared that Yates and McIntyre would require "a further continuance of the heavy personal responsibilities assumed on our behalf," and that in return for Nott's "responsibilities," undertaken in support of the "House," the contractors were to deposit to his credit 6.31 percent on the gross amount of tickets actually sold after June 2, 1829 in "the Contingent Residue," that huge reservoir of over $2,000,000 in unsold tickets carried over from the Literature Lottery and the Albany Land Lottery. These sales began before the closing of the Literature Lottery on November 7, 1827, and continued after the closing of the Fever Hospital Lottery on June 2, 1829.

John B. Yates, Henry Yates, and the two newest partners, James McIntyre and John Ely, Jr., were to claim they never saw this revised agreement; Archibald McIntyre would insist he had not been aware that Nott had substituted himself for the college as its beneficiary. All the contractors declared, in 1835, that this new stipulation which had been backdated to May 30, 1826 was deliberately framed by the Doctor in response to their letter of January 13, 1829, that it had been copied and then signed by a duped and innocent Archibald McIntyre on behalf of "the House, its object and surreptitious mode of its introduction ... too apparent to leave a vestige of doubt [as to its purpose]."

Whatever the motives and the mode of its introduction, the effect of this substituted stipulation is clear: with it the Doctor established his personal claim to 6 31/100 percent on the ticket sales of the Consolidated Lotteries and their residues of unsold tickets which were drawn following the Lottery Consolidation Act of 1826. By asserting this claim, and by laying down the conditions by which he established it, the Doctor was to meet the increasing resentment of Archibald McIntyre, the hot anger of John B. Yates, and the frustrated diplomacy of Henry Yates whose ingenuity had helped to create the maze to which he was finally to admit none of them could find an exit.

Until the middle of 1828 the Doctor had been able to keep what he chose of his contractual relations with Yates and McIntyre a secret. His Trustees, excepting Henry Yates and William James, whose interests to that time were, in part, his own, knew only that the Literature Lottery had endowed the college far beyond their expectations. By 1829, however, the Doctor's own affairs, his private commitments as the inventor and manufacturer of the rotary grate anthracite-burning stove, and as the scientific investigator now of new ways of using "stone coal," had grown on a scale with the private enterprises of his lottery contractors. His own need for capital by 1829 was hardly less than was theirs. To protect his source of the capital needed to finance his private hazards he seems to have secured it by making himself the beneficiary of the back dated "stipulation" of May 30, 1826, of a sum which, through January 1832 amounted to $197,717. [16]

He may also have been influenced in imposing his revised contract on the "House" by a letter from a frightened Henry Yates, who, on Independence Day of 1829 wrote to the Doctor that the Mechanics' and Farmers' Bank of Albany was about to bypass the "House" and to make a direct call on the college to cover the partners' obligations which Nott had guaranteed. In his letter the college treasurer assured the Doctor the contractors were in no position to meet the drafts. "The most I fear," Henry Yates wrote, "is the noise it may create . . . this will, I fear, create many speeches, if communicated to the directors. . . ." In a second letter on the same subject written on the same day the worried Henry Yates added, "you know Brother Joseph is always busy. . . ." [17]

To prepare the ground for that time of truth when his Trustees must realize what he had hazarded as their unrestricted agent, not only of his own reputation but of theirs as trust officers, and what he, as an individual, was continuing to risk, he told William James early in 1829, or so he reported to the Board of Trustees at the beginning of the Chancery Suits in 1834, "that the funds of the college would, probably, through his instrumentality, be more or less increased" by virtue of his private arrangements with Yates and McIntyre. "As life was uncertain," he said he had told William James (who had been his chief support in all the Literature Lottery hazards), the time had come for the Board to know of his plans to endow Union College out of the proceeds of his personal 6 31/100 percent return on the Consolidated Lottery schemes which Yates and McIntyre had run following the close of the Literature Lottery and were to continue to run as the huge backlog of unsold tickets were formed into new classes and sold. [19]

How accurate the Doctor's memory was cannot be known, for William James died in the cholera epidemic two years before the Board took the Doctor's testimony in 1834, but in July, 1829, the Trustees did appoint a Finance Committee made up of William James, William L. Marcy, and Nott himself to prepare the college to deal with its prospective good fortune, and to help Nott and Henry Yates (whose ambivalent role as a partner in the "House" as well as college treasurer was, presumably, not then known), "to continue and mature their Grand Plan." [20]

"The Grand Plan" itself which Nott revealed sometime in 1829 to the Finance Committee satisfied its members that the President had acted wisely and "with disinterested perseverance." With his personal lottery profits, after he had deducted that vague sum to be charged to "hazards run and risks taken," he told the committee he proposed to endow an "Institute of Science and Industry" to be established under the auspices of Union College, one which was to elevate the Rensselaer Institute program to collegiate level, where, initially, "manual labor at the discretion of the Board shall be combined with mental application by all members thereof, whether preparing for college, for becoming teachers of schools, or for any other profession or calling in life . . ."; his was to be an Institute whose development would, in time, allow its students to take equal standing with the students of Union College. [21]

Yates and McIntyre's comment in their "Examination" in 1835 on these moves of the Doctor's was to be one of cynical disbelief, disbelief then concurred in by Henry Yates himself: "What the President may have communicated to the Committee of Finance . . . we do not know but we do know that in his various reports to the Board of Trustees, he has never made a single frank statement. The language in relation to the sum in his hands is the language of ownership. What shall be left *after deductions for his philosophical and mechanical experiments* may be appropriated for the benefit of the college, 'or some kindred institution,' if he *wills* it, or for his own benefit, if that shall please him better. . . ." [22]

Yates and McIntyre, after reviewing all of the Doctor's self-justifications as they were presented in the Union College "Report" of 1834, concluded that, "We know that it is one of the rules of the Doctor, in all his controversies to proceed in the prudent course of *quietly* forestalling opinion. He acts on the maxim contained in one of his letters that it 'is more difficult to influence men after they have taken ground than before they have taken it. . . .'"

Whatever were these later views of the members of the "House" and of the Doctor they, as well as he, had, by the summer of 1829, secured the concessions they both wanted, their's essential to keep afloat the Welland Canal venture and a complex of investment gambles only one of which was the running off of the residue of tickets in the New York State lotteries. They had secured in the Doctor, so they then thought, a continuing source of short term capital without which the firm would have collapsed, and an unofficial partner whose influence with legislators, growing numbers of them his former pupils, was beyond price.

I V

If there had ever been exits to the lottery maze Archibald McIntyre, John and Henry Yates, and Eliphalet Nott had created they were wiped out in the explosion set off by a terse, one paragraph letter written from the New York office of the "House" on April 27, 1832: [23]

> My dear Sir—We have this morning had a short conversation, on the subject of our finances and future operations. It will be necessary for you to make up your mind, not to draw any more money from here (except the sum to be paid today). Probably, some of the partners will write to you more particularly as to the course we mean to pursue.
>
> Very truly your friend,
>
> Doctor Nott   H. Yates

If the total eclipse of the sun the Doctor had watched a quarter of a century earlier had failed to take place he would have been no more shaken than he was by this letter from Henry Yates. What had happened? The letter of explanation which Henry Yates had said the partners would "probably" forward, was sent the next day, signed by Henry Yates himself, and the two newest members of the "House," James McIntyre, Archibald McIntyre's brother, and John Ely, Jr.; as a rationale for the firm's action it must have appeared grotesque to the Doctor. His "calculations," the new partners declared, "in relation to the profits to be derived from the lotteries, however true in theory, have been proved wrong, when tested by actual experiment." [24] These "calculations" they added, doubtless explained why the original contractors were so often in arrears during the first three years of operations.

Next, and with what could only have seemed incredible effrontery, they told him that in view of the fact that the firm had paid him far more than his efforts on their behalf could possibly justify, the "House" would expect him "to continue [his] friendly aid" and "to relinquish any further claim on us." Their last payment, they said, "can only be considered as a gratuity, and never would be tolerated if known," presumably by the hot tempered John B. Yates.

These three partners then compounded injury, it must have seemed to the Doctor, when they informed him that they had decided, in view of the fact that the New York lotteries would end the last day of December, 1833, and that the original partners had lost so much, largely by their generosity "to the institutions for which you acted," to give the five percent on ticket sales Nott was then receiving to Archibald McIntyre and John B. Yates as "an extra allowance . . . to make them whole." [25] "We are," they concluded, "reverend sir, with the greatest respect, your obedient servants," and then their three signatures, John Ely, Jr. signing for James McIntyre, "he having severely strained his wrist by a fall from a horse."

The President of Union College was fifty-nine years old that year. The surge of his ambition had long seemed more than his strength could sustain; "his health," an undergraduate wrote the following June, "is visibly poor, and I should not be surprised if his death [is] shortly announced."

"As ill as I am and unwilling to contest anything, I am not so unwell as to submit to such an unexampled outrage," the Doctor replied at once to the incomprehensible letter from the "House." If his illness, possibly his "rheumatism," that capsule diagnosis of half the ills of the period, had raised ideas of an imminent death in his mind, Yates and McIntyre provided a better restorative than the hydropathy baths he had been taking. His letter to Henry Yates, headed "Way, 10th May 1832" was one of three letters he wrote that day, the other two addressed to Archibald McIntyre and to the "House" itself, each of them brimming with incredulity, charging a "strange delusion" to the three new partners, informing all the contractors that reflection should correct their mistaken thinking, and that he would expect their regular returns to be made by the time his short trip in search of health was over. There was no letter to John B. Yates.

Reflection, however, did no more than to harden the position the lottery contractors had, as a "House," elected to take. "The simple truth of the matter is this," the firm wrote in answer to the Doctor's three letters of May 10, "All the partners of the House have uniformly been very willing to sanction and give full effect to your views of the arrangements between us (except Mr. J. B. Yates) however contrary such acquiescence might be to what they considered their legal rights. . . ." This last official communication of the "House" to the Doctor in which there is anything left of the rapport which had for so long existed between them restated "the appalling and ruinous losses" Archibald McIntyre and J. B. Yates had suffered "in acquiring that knowledge and experience" which was necessary, so it was now claimed, to their later successes as lottery managers. [26]

The Doctor had little need to read between the lines for the real message of this excessively polite apology which also invited him to recognize that the payments made to him by the House for the "risks and hazards" he had run for them since the end of the Literature Lottery had no legal standing, that "they had been cheerfully given as a gratuity, to a meritorious and public spirited man, for a valuable public object. . . ." By May 15, 1832, however, the contractors were agreed the season of gratuities was over, that their payments to Nott would from then on go, instead, to Archibald McIntyre and John B. Yates, that the Doctor's "indisputable evidence" of his legal rights to which his letters had referred could not in any way "change the opinion of any of us. . . ." Their letter closed with assurances of the pain the partners felt at Nott's unfortunate misinterpretation of their action, and with the observation that a proper review on his part would put things "in a very different light."

The great "hazard," with its parade of "adventurers" marching as the Lord's army into the "Fortunate Offices" of Secor's, of Palmer Canfield's, into the Allens's, into the Philadelphia Arcade, silent there for the breathless moment when Destiny and the bare armed boy reached into the lottery drum for the unearned fortune, the great hazard, somehow, had lost its heavenly direction, and was about to become a public scandal.

Reflection on the part of the "House" and "a proper review" by the Doctor again only confirmed their collision course. The Doctor waited with mounting irritation through the remaining months of 1832 for scheme payments which were never made. He knew well enough who had plotted the break. In a last request, made on December 20, 1832, to Henry Yates for payments due under his "stipulations," he pointed out that his services to Yates and McIntyre "had been quite as great as that rendered during the same period by Mr. J. B. Yates, by whom I am informed, the discovery of a want of consideration was made . . ." [in return for Yates and McIntyre's payments to him]. The Doctor added with bitter sarcasm, "I say, trifling as the consideration I have rendered may be, it is, I believe, as great as that rendered by Mr. Yates, while visiting England, residing at Chittenango, and drawing on the House for funds to fill up his Welland Canal stock, which funds have been raised, as I can show by letters in my possession, to a great extent by myself . . . had [Yates and McIntyre] failed I should have been ruined, and if they succeed, honor and justice alike require that they should fulfill their stipulations." [27] If this final appeal did not awaken the "House" to its obligations, he then wrote, he was ready, "to come to legal issue, if necessary, to a vindication of my rights."

Concern for "my rights" triumphed, and, on the 25th of December, 1832, Eliphalet Nott laid his case before Silas Wright, then the New York State Comptroller, a Union College Trustee, and a member of the College Finance Committee. The next day, after having "cursorily examined the contract and the correspondence with Yates and McIntyre," the Comptroller wrote to the members of the "House," advising them of the wisdom of keeping to the letter of their contracts with Nott; Silas Wright pointed out that they had been able to carry the lotteries on so long only because of the legislature's faith in the President of Union College, and in the purpose of the lottery grants. The Comptroller noted a rumor of "impending litigation," and warned the contractors of the inevitable hostility of the public against them if the Doctor took them into court. [28]

Three weeks later, writing to Nott from Washington where by then he had gone as the new Senator from New York State, Silas Wright again told the Doctor it was his duty "to enforce the contract . . . to indemnify the community for the evil continued by your means;" he added that it was his wish, "that a just share of the responsibility of any steps you may take may rest on me." [29] In the eyes of Silas Wright, Nott was morally obliged to sue.

The "House" reacted at once. Henry Yates, still the peace-maker, still hopeful that "mature reflection" would convince Nott, sent him an outline of the position of the contractors. The Doctor's errors began, Yates informed him, with his interpretation of the original agreement of 1822, with his belief that he "retained rights besides those stipulated in the contract." "The House," on the contrary, had always believed, Henry Yates continued, that the Doctor's only legal function under that contract was to see that "the avails were received and from time to time paid over." "The President's Fund" had been intended only as a "contingent fund," to take care of emergencies; it had been seldom used for that purpose, however, but had remained in the Mohawk Bank "as an indemnity to you." The Oakley prize had been paid with funds raised in part privately by both Nott and himself, Henry Yates noted, and for that service Nott had "taken an instrument for an additional allowance," a personal profit which Yates had refused to share but which Nott had justified accepting on the grounds of "advances and personal responsibilities." [30]

Henry Yates admitted that his own involvement with the "House" had forced him to become a partner. The Consolidated Lottery Act of 1826, he pointed out, had created a new and major "error" in the Doctor's thinking,—the idea that he had a right to a share of the "House's" profits in their Albany Land operation in return for his agreement to the Consolidated Lottery Bill. This he might only have justified if he had not "negatived . . . every idea of a partnership . . .," and so avoided the responsibilities for failure as well as for success.

In spite of these "errors" in the Doctor's views, Henry Yates concluded, the firm had continued to pay him 6.31 percent on its ticket sales until July 15, 1830, when Mr. J. B. Yates had demanded an end of all payments to the Doctor of those "gratuities" which the then reportedly unprofitable New York State lotteries could not sustain. Instead, however, unknown to J. B. Yates, his partner, Archibald McIntyre, had sent the Doctor on that day a new contract which substituted a five percent payment on New York State sales. Under this new arrangement the firm had paid Nott $116,642.68, to which must be added the $81,033.74 paid to him under the earlier stipulation J. B. Yates believed he had himself terminated, plus $31,004.20 in Albany Lands yet to be paid, and some $200,000 due Union College "of interest on sums they were unable to pay." [31]

"Lately," Henry Yates added, "I ascertained the most unpleasant feelings evinced at the sums paid, after it was supposed we had desisted . . . ." There had been talk of demanding large repayments from the Doctor, but Henry Yates, hoping, he said, "to prevent unpleasant consequences," evolved the idea of turning over to the original partners the five percent payments then still being made to the Doctor. "I then thought it the only mode of doing justice . . ." he wrote, "and certain I am that you will think so on mature reflection."

No sooner had Henry Yates posted this letter than the firm received Silas Wright's pointed reminder of what he believed the "House" owed Nott and the community and with it the hint of legal action to come. Immediately Henry Yates, considerably agitated, wrote to Nott that he was sorry "to see Mr. McIntyre in such angry feelings, and such a determination . . . if the rumor the Comptroller speaks of comes from you rely on it, you have done wrong. . . ." [32]

The year 1832 ended with both the "House" and the Doctor angrily committed to defending their "rights." The "House," in replying to then Senator Silas Wright's cautionary letter, suggested that the Doctor, if he really intended to try the matter in court, had "chosen a most unfortunate time . . ." in view of the fact that the lotteries still had a full year to run. Nott, perhaps hoping that "mature reflection" might also serve the "House," agreed to postpone the issue until the drawings were concluded at the end of December, 1833.

Up to this point there was talk on both sides only of "rights." Fraud, extortion, duplicity, the ugly language of bitter men defending their purses and their public images, these words began to be heard at the end of the year of unproductive truce. Yates and McIntyre's later ironic statement in their "Examination" of 1835 that the Doctor had calculatedly taken "the prudent course of quietly forestalling opinion" was solely their judgment. The public, as Silas Wright had pointed out to the contractors, was against them—theirs was a dirty business. The public, the legislature, the highest officers of the State were, in the nature of things, behind Nott who, by the time he filed his first bill in Chancery against the "House," on May 26, 1834, had again taken a moral position against which any attack on him must appear an attack on virtue itself.

In his report to his Trustees at their Commencement meeting in July, 1833, the year before he filed his charges, Nott had mentioned the "President's Fund" as one "held in trust for the institutions interested therein". He dwelt especially on those "additional lottery avails" which were his by "special contract . . . for personal services rendered, hazards run and monies advanced." The principal part of these profits, he had then announced, had, with the approval of the Trustees' Finance Committee, already "been invested in real estate, situate for the most part in the city of New York, and on Long Island, or elsewhere, or in bonds and mortgages, or stocks of some sort, and the residue appropriated to repair and experiments." In addition and out of these profits, he had told the Board, he had purchased the "old college," repaired it, and was then holding it hopefully against the time when Yates and McIntyre, by honoring their contract with him, would make possible the opening of his long promised "Institute of Science." And he had then assured the Trustees, even though the contractors should fail him and the college, "still there is reason to hope that something handsome will eventually be realized from the investments aforesaid already made. . . ."

What the Board was not prepared for that July, however, was the Doctor's unauthorized legal maneuver by which he would couple the Trustees of Union College with himself as co-authors of the Chancery Bill he filed against the "House" the following May.

Although United States Senator Silas Wright had suggested that he wished to share the responsibility of whatever action the Doctor took against the lottery contractors, the Senator had not invited him to make Governor Marcy, New York Secretary of

State John A. Dix, Attorney General G. C. Bronson, State Treasurer Abraham Keyser, and Comptroller A. C. Flagg parties to what the Senator had assumed would be a private suit.

Either the Doctor had made the worst mistake of his career in filing this joint bill in Chancery, or he had out-generalled the five members of the "House," and by confronting them with so overwhelming a force had guaranteed their rapid recovery from the "strange delusion" which he believed had overcome them. He had also maneuvered his Trustees into a position from which they could not withdraw, for he had so entangled his acts as their agent, acts for which they were responsible to the State, with his own as the private banker of the "House" that a judgment against him must appear to be a judgment against them. In 1831 Silas Wright, then New York State Comptroller, had joined William James in what was then claimed to be a full review of Nott's lottery operations; they had concluded their report with the warmest praise for the Doctor's unselfish and wise management of an enterprise no Trustee, they declared, thought could be brought to a successful conclusion. [33] Governor Marcy, as the State Comptroller before Wright took that office, had approved the Lottery Consolidation Act of 1826 and the schedule of "Schemes" offered by the contractors. By 1834 he and then-Secretary of State Azariah Flagg and General Dix were themselves members of the Union College Finance Committee, and so especially committed to preserving their reputations as trust officers.

The Board's awareness of its growing involvement can be measured by the fact that the Governor and Senator Wright, as Trustee members of a "Select Committee" appointed to deal with the Yates and McIntyre controversy, noted in a report prepared and printed "for private circulation" in November, 1834, that Nott had, indeed, made his Trustees co-authors of his Chancery Bill; whether this strategic move of the Doctor's was actually made, however, on the advice of and with the consent of the Finance Committee is not clear. [34] In November, 1838, the Governor, then a member of the Trustees' committee which brought the lottery suits to their unexpected conclusion, particularly noted in the court record at that time that Eliphalet Nott had filed his joint bill four years earlier without the consent of the Trustees. Marcy, however, conspicuously omitted in 1838 to note the fact of his own and Senator Wright's earlier advice by which Eliphalet Nott, he said, "had been guided throughout . . . ." [35] Nott's suit against the contractors which at first had seemed a simple matter of clarifying "rights" in which the college had a large interest, soon became a serious liability for these members of the "Albany Regency," politicians fated to go down to political defeat in 1838 before the new and militant Whig party.

An additional complication for these politician-Trustees was the residue of bitterness which the Yates clan held against them as members of a political clique which ten years earlier had destroyed the public career of ex-Governor Joseph C. Yates, still chairman of the Union College Board of Trustees. The members of the "House," in answering the Doctor's first bill against them, would refer to these state officials as the Doctor's "confederates," and charge them with abetting him in his use of the State's lottery grants for private ends. [36]

The Doctor had set the stage for a drama of frightening improvisations.

CHAPTER 4

"Matters of Discovery, specific performance, fraud account . . ."

THE Doctor had his memories of Ballston Spa, the Saratoga County seat, the Iroquois's place of cures, whose medicinal waters bubbled out of sulphur-yellowed craters. It was in Ballston where Maria, his gay and elfin first wife, had died, she who had gone there so hopefully to find health. The sulphur waters followed their underground channels still farther south to rise again in "Captain Jack's" garden in the ravine of Hans Groot's Kill on the Union College campus. The Doctor's journey in May, 1834, to Ballston Spa and to Judge Esek Cowan's Court was, in its way, again a search for cures, for the New York State Chancery Court was still that legal haven where "Matters of discovery, specific performance, fraud account and the like are peculiarly cognizable and relievable."

The Doctor's bill as he filed it is missing, along with the later official Chancery Court records of the case. [The file drawer labeled "N" which would have included "Nott" in the crowded archives room of the County Court House in Albany is the one drawer the author could not locate.]

The official record, however, is not needed, for this history of the death of friendships is uncomfortably full because of another of those ironic turns which seem to mark Eliphalet Nott's career. In the archives of the college one comes upon copies of the later "amended bills" filed by the Doctor and the Trustees and by Yates and McIntyre, together with a number of manuscript "demurrers" and comments on the succeeding stages of the case written by complainants and defendants alike, a cluttered record of spiraling hostility, many items of which are inscribed "from the papers of John C. Spencer," then one of the counsel for the "House."

John Canfield Spencer was a Union College graduate, a Clintonian Democrat, long opposed to the Albany Regency. Five years earlier he had been a special prosecutor appointed to investigate the disappearance of William Morgan, abducted, so it was charged, by a Masonic order sworn to avenge itself on the man who had, presumably, published its secrets. Spencer in 1834 was at mid-point of an outstanding political career, a member of the short-lived anti-Masonic Party which was soon to merge with the Whig Party and to toll the knell of the Albany Regency. "Tall and slender . . . eyes fierce and quick rolling—a face bearing the lines of thought and an unpleasant character of sternness," he was a man notoriously short-tempered and unable to work with others, but with a reputation for an amazing grasp of the details of whatever occupied his attention. The irony lies in the fact that it was John Canfield Spencer who, twenty years later, was to be found as the crusading counsel for Eliphalet Nott, who was to defend his old teacher against those who had inherited the lottery contractors' bitterness against the college and its President.

Among the Spencer Papers, in the Union College Archives is that angry "Examination" Yates and McIntyre printed early in 1835 as a rebuttal to the Doctor's and to the Trustees' view of their still pending case which the "Select Committee" of the college Board had ordered to be printed the preceding November.

The "House" made its first countermove to the Doctor's bill on July 21, 1834, when it forwarded a letter to the college Trustees, then holding their annual commencement meeting, a letter designed, so the contractors wrote, "to correct any mistaken impressions" their President had created. [1] The Board must have been aghast for the contractors then informed the members that the "House" had paid Union College $837,285.13 which Yates and McIntyre said represented an overpayment on the original contract of more than $300,000, the result "of many errors and mistaken data in computation". To this overpayment must be added, they wrote, an additional $193,462.24 paid to the President, "and, as we are prepared to show, without compensation," a sum paid to him "for the benefit, and to be paid over to the funds of the college." The Trustees were then informed that the "House" would require a revision of all settlements made with it, "and a return of the excess beyond what the institutions were authorized to receive. . . ." The first step, the Board was told, was for it to return to the contractors those securities of the "House" it held, and which, according to the contractors, only represented collateral for sums they once owed and had since paid. The letter ended with an invitation to the Trustees to confer with the contractors in order "to adjust all differences," and with the added hope that any committee appointed to deal with the controversy would be made up "of the most disinterested and uncommited persons."

If the Doctor's bill to which he had joined his guard of New York State officials was designed to intimidate the House of Yates and McIntyre, the latter's demands for so appalling an accounting may have represented a similar strategy on the part of the contractors. In any event the reaction of the Board was immediate: the "select Committee" consisting of the Governor, Senator Wright, and John P. Cushman, a newly elected Trustee and then a well known Troy lawyer and railroad promoter, was appointed at once; its two state officials, however, could hardly have been called either "disinterested" or "uncommited".

This "Select Committee" apparently made no attempt to reply to Yates and McIntyre's letter calling for the return of alleged overpayments, and the contractors, sure in their own minds that they had found legal grounds for the recovery of almost half a million dollars from Union College, and obviously annoyed that the "Select Committee" showed "no desire," so they wrote in their later "Examination", "to attend to the object of the appointment . . . ," now filed their own bill in Chancery that August both for the purpose of forcing the Trustees to return what they claimed were illegally held securities belonging to the firm, securities then in danger, so they were convinced, of being sold by the Doctor.

On the 13th of August the Court ordered the college not to negotiate the securities the contractors claimed, an order which particularly satisfied John B. Yates, for among them was his bond and mortgage for his estate at Chittenango. Undoubtedly both the contractors, the Doctor and the Trustees' "Select Committee" were shocked as they viewed the unbridgeable gulf their opposing Chancery suits had opened. In any event, the late summer and fall months were taken by their respective counsel for reflection and the writing of those "Demurrers" with which they intended to clarify "rights," take their clients out of court, and quietly compromise their claims, an Indian summer of reflection all too short.

Among the Spencer Papers is the first of these "Demurrers," written on behalf of the "House" by their attorney, Benjamin F. Butler of Albany, whose Washington duties as Attorney General of the United States were occasionally to delay the prosecution of the suits. Butler's "Demurrer" is also the chief source of information about the Doctor's Bill of Complaint itself, a reply in which Butler proceeded to reduce to legal realities what he argued were the Doctor's pretensions to "rights."

"The controversy," Attorney-General Butler pointed out, "must be settled, not by appeals to the legal tribunals, but by those private discussions and arrangements in which opposing claims equally incapable, perhaps, of judicial cognizance, can be taken into account, and to which, for very obvious reasons, it is most fit that this whole subject be referred." [2] The Doctor's bill appeared to Butler "insufficient" on two major counts: the Trustees, he concluded, had no place in it; their interest, he asserted, in the activities of the House of Yates and McIntyre ended with the closing of the Literature Lottery in 1827; their President's arrangements with the "House" after that date were private and personal, made for a share of the lottery profits which resulted from the sale of then unsold lottery tickets, and of schemes in the Albany Land and Fever Hospital lotteries in which the college had no legal interest.

The Attorney General pointed out that the Doctor's declared intention to use an undetermined portion of his profits for the benefit of the college constituted nothing more than a "determination," and that whatever such sum might eventually be, the Doctor has arranged to put it into a special trust fund over which the Trustees would have no corporate control. If, however, the Trustees *could* prove they were properly joined with their President in his suit then they, and they alone as a corporate body, were entitled to all the money claimed, and the Doctor's cause would simply merge with the corporation's.

Butler's second major conclusion was that the Doctor's personal agreements, or "contracts" with the "House" were invalid because they contained no evidence that he had given a "sufficient consideration" in return for the share of the profit he claimed. Butler pointed out to the Court that "it is curious to observe how much the personal services and hazards of E. Nott . . . are increased in importance by the lapse of time. . . ."

Although Attorney General Butler had hoped to bring about those "private discussions and arrangements" to which he had referred, the Doctor would have none of them until he had had the last word on the subject of "rights." The Spencer Papers include a remarkable manuscript copy of the joint Trustee–Nott answer to Butler's arguments. [3] It was prepared by Marcus T. Reynalds, counsel for the college, an Albany lawyer as well known as Butler, a graduate of Union College as was John C. Spencer, but unlike him, full of humor and a master of scorn whose appearances in court were said to have crowded the chamber with Union College students preparing for law, intent on observing this thin-faced man with the high forehead, whose every move and whose "rich and copious diction" charmed all who observed him. "Please keep your seat, Mr. Reynalds" was always the quick response from every judge as Marcus Reynalds, a stickler for the amenities, would regularly struggle to overcome the handicap of a wooden leg in order to stand when he addressed the bench.

If Reynalds, speaking for the Trustees in the fall of 1834, had the idea that the Doctor's relations with Yates and McIntyre were wholly those of a man intent on serving only the college, he must have been shaken by the revealing editorial work Nott exercised on his reply as the Trustees' counsel, to Butler's "Demurrer." The Doctor agreed with Reynalds' argument that the original lottery contract between the college and the "House," signed in 1822, was never operative because the contractors at that time failed to post the $70,000 bond called for by the contract. There was no disagreement with Reynalds' argument that the lottery proceeded legally under the later verbal contracts and "stipulations," all of which were unquestionably valid, according to Reynalds, because the Trustees had not at any time limited their President's power to act in their name, a fact which, he concluded, correctly joined them with Nott in the action against Yates and McIntyre. All the profits of the "House" which Nott had made possible by agreeing to the Lottery Consolidation Bill of 1826, excepting only those rising from the Albany Land Lottery, were, Reynalds maintained, to be shared with the President on the basis of the several "stipulations" which grew out of that act, all of them binding.

When, however, Marcus Reynalds wrote that "the personal acts done and rights secured by E. Nott . . . were done and secured for the benefit of Union College . . . ," the statement was crossed out and restated in the Doctor's hand to read "secured (in furtherance of the interest and) for the benefit of Union College (as well as its President). . . ." When Reynalds wrote "no practical division, however, of the avails of this joint contract is contemplated . . . the [President] did not act with a view to individual emolument . . .," the Doctor revised this statement to read that the joint contract and all later ones "were made both in his individual and official capacity . . . the interests of the two were known and felt to be identified and that the acts done by the President were understood by him and by the college, to be done in behalf of both. . . ." When Reynalds wrote that, "His determination [is] to devote the entire proceeds to the benefit of the College . . .," the Doctor added the qualifying phrase, "to devote (directly or indirectly) the entire proceeds to the benefit of the College."

By the time the Doctor had finished his revision of Marcus Reynald's answer to Butler's "Demurrer" the Trustees had been made aware of their mistaken conclusions about the college's "rights" in the Nott-Yates and McIntyre "stipulations." Even as Yates and McIntyre had recently assured the Doctor that any payments to him under those "stipulations" must be considered as "gratuities," so, too, was the Doctor informing his Board that whatever sums came to it as the result of his "personal service and hazards run . . ." on behalf of the "House," those sums, too, were "gratuities" in the sense that the Trustees had only courtesy claim to them.

As a counter to Yates and McIntyre's position that the Doctor could not assume two roles, that of agent for his Trustees, and that of individual claimant, Reynalds pointedly noted the dual role assumed by Henry Yates, that of agent for the Trustees in their relations with the "House," and that of a full-fledged partner who shared all the profits of the firm, including those derived from its contract with Union College.

Marcus Reynald's significantly edited reply to Attorney General Butler's view of the "rights" involved in the controversy agreed with the Attorney General's only in one point: that Judge Cowan's court was no place for this dispute which "for obvious reasons," it was "most fit" to submit to private arbitration, and concluded that Eliphalet Nott and the Trustees "will not object to this mode of settlement provided an intelligent and impartial tribunal can be obtained. . . ." Unfortunately neither Attorney General Butler nor Marcus T. Reynalds nor their clients had offered the slightest concession in the matter of "rights." These were now conditioned, so far as the Doctor was concerned, by his recent speculator's involvements in Manhattan and Long Island real estate, his "caloric" experiments with the S. S. *Novelty*, and his "Grand Plan" for a Scientific Institute to be connected with the college, "rights" unshakably confirmed by his rationalization that they were sanctified, as he had argued the Literature Lottery had been sanctified, by the heaven-approved nature of his commitments. Any tribunal charged with arbitrating the fixed positions taken by John B. Yates and Eliphalet Nott in the fall of 1834 could, with as much hope of success, have untied the knot of King Gordius.

November and December of that year were months of out-of-court maneuvering during which an outraged John B. Yates tried and failed to persuade Governor Marcy and United States Senator Silas Wright, members of the Trustees' "Select Committee," to "enter into an examination of the whole subject with him." [4] Senator Wright, on one occasion told the lottery contractor that "the committee viewed itself as a party" to the Chancery suits, a revelation, certainly, of the consciousness of these Trustee-politicians of their personal involvement in the Doctor's lottery commitments. [5]

II

If for a moment during these two months there was a hint of an opening out of the lottery maze of which Judge Cowan's court was then the center, the Finance Committee of the college shut it abruptly on December 3 with a letter to Henry Yates which was guaranteed to increase the anger felt by the partners and so soon to overflow in their "Examination." General Dix and John P. Cushman, in the nerve tightening language of lawyers, pointed out to their ex-college treasurer that they had "recently learned that while acting in that capacity you became a partner in the firm of Yates and McIntyre, and interested in their profits. The committee conceive that among the rights acquired by the college, are those which have grown out of your proceedings . . . while employed and acting as the agent of Union College . . . ; we deem it our duty to apprize you that we claim these profits as rightly belonging to the college." [6] The Finance Committee then "respectfully" asked Henry Yates for a copy of his partnership agreement, "together with a statement of all your operations" under the agreement, and "a full and detailed account of all moneys, stock, and other property received by you from the profits of said co-partnership. . . ."

Henry Yates's wrath exploded in his reply four days later:

> Gentlemen: Your most singular communication was received by me. Astonished as I have been at the strange and preposterous positions heretofore assumed by the President of Union College in his various exhibits, I will not pretend to conceal the feelings of greater surprise at the tenor of that letter, and its only and evident object. . . . [7]

That "object," spelled out later by Archibald McIntyre, seemed clear to the partners. The Doctor intended to "forward his ulterior plans, and if Mr. Yates resists such a claim indignantly and successfully, to draw a parallel between his own case and that of Mr. H. Y. and screen himself from accountability on the same ground. . . ." [8] So far as the contractors were concerned, Eliphalet Nott had become a Machiavelli indeed.

Henry Yates, in his reply to the Finance Committee, angrily denied its right to inquire into what he contended were his private affairs. As to his duty to the college during his partnership in the "House," he informed the committee he was willing "to answer any charges which the most malignant ingenuity can devise." He declared that "the charges which your letter implies . . . should and perhaps may, shut the door against any hope of amicable adjustment."

General Dix and J. P. Cushman, as if to lock that door, next wrote to "Messrs Yates and McIntyre" that while "there is no one the committee would more cheerfully treat with than Mr. Butler . . . " the contractors were to understand that any negotiations "can only have respect to an amicable arrangement for securing those rights . . ." about which the committee's mind was "definitely made up." [9]

Two weeks later these two Trustees again wrote to Henry Yates, not, however, as fellow members of the same Board, but as lawyers wholly indifferent to that "violence of feeling" to which they were adding. Salt for open wounds was encrusted on their final paragraph:

> During this period of [your] co-partnership, the accounts of the college fell into great confusion; large amounts received remained unaccounted for, and material losses were otherwise sustained by the institution in consequence of the partnership transaction of said treasurer and agent with Yates and McIntyre. During this period also heavy responsibilities were assumed, and large amounts of money were furnished, in behalf of said college, to said treasurer and agent, which were employed by him as additional capital for carrying forward the business transactions of said firm. . . . [10]

The committee ended its letter with the hope that "reflection" would bring compliance with its requests for information, "and thus relieve the committee of the necessity of resorting. . . . to legal proceedings. . . ."

Henry Yates's response to the committee, as Nott's had been to the "House," was born of his outrage: "no further correspondence on the subject is proper"; he replied, "knowing that [the charges] are gratuitous and unfounded, I feel I would be wanting in justice to myself to continue any interchange of letters which has led to such unwarrantable and exceptionable language." [11]

Behind both the Select Committee's private *"Report"* and the contractors' "Examination" of it were the shadows of worried public men who had been forced to acknowledge that they, too, as Trustees of the funds involved in the controversy, were themselves now on trial. For such reasons as these both documents must be read as one document, for much of that "truth" presented so differently by Yates and McIntyre and by Eliphalet Nott and the Trustees of Union College must be recognized as the very special pleading of those who recorded it, a more revealing and valuable record of bitter and angry men than it is a trustworthy record of events.

III

Because Richard Lawrence's two shots, aimed at President Jackson on January 30, 1835, hung fire, Vice President Martin VanBuren had to wait another year to take possession of the White House, and an Albany Regency which drew much of its vigor from the political veins of the Vice President missed a transfusion it badly needed. Governor Marcy, General John A. Dix, Comptroller Azariah Flagg, and the other members of the harried Regency who were ex officio Union College Trustees, must have been especially concerned that spring with their unexpected role as the "confederates" in the countersuit now brought against the Board and Eliphalet Nott by the House of Yates and McIntyre, a suit in which the President of Union College was charged with extortion and fraud, and the Board with responsibility for his acts. The "Bucktail" leadership in the State Legislature was already deep in trouble, countering accusations of awards of bank charters for favored groups, of violating the banking laws by winking at the distribution of bank stocks to the party faithful. [12] John B. Yates, the angriest of the lottery contractors, and himself a legislator that year, made his one memorable speech in the Assembly when he demanded the repeal of the Regency supported law which required the chartering and the strict supervision of banks by the State. [13] John Yates, in 1835, wanted nothing more than to eliminate the President of Union College from his calculation, and to have access to uncontrolled banks more hospitable to his mercurial schemes of financing.

Neither proposals to compromise nor intimidation could take this test of reputations, of Trustee fidelity, out of court. Three new bills in Chancery were filed during 1835, the last harsh stanzas in the bitter antiphonal chorus with which the Trustees of Union College, Eliphalet Nott, and the partners of the House of

Yates and McIntyre closed the New York State Lotteries for the following century and a quarter. [11]

Attorney General Butler and John C. Spencer, both on retainers from Yates and McIntyre, remained off-stage until the last act. The "House" was now represented before the Court by two members of the Yates family; John VanNess Yates was their solicitor, Secretary of State under ex-Governor Joseph C. Yates, and a distant cousin to the four Yates brothers. He was a genial Albany lawyer who was reported to be "somewhat irregular in his habits and lax in his morals . . . on easy terms with all classes of citizens . . . especially among what was called the lower order of the community." [15] Charles Yates appeared as counselor, a fledgling member of the bar, a son of Henry Yates, who had been graduated from Union College five years earlier.

The Trustees hired as their solicitor Alonzo Christopher Paige, at fifteen a graduate of Williams College; he had abandoned theology for the law, joined the Schenectady bar in 1818 at a time when it consisted of three Yateses, and three outsiders, including himself. [16] The law, to Paige, was a science, and as the reporter for the Chancery Court of New York he had become widely known as a brilliant legal analyst. [17] Although he had served Schenectady as a Democratic legislator he had little liking for those professional politicians whom he saw as "trimmers," men "of intrigue and policy." Politics as a way of life repelled this imposing "old school" solicitor for the college who was later to serve Union as a Trustee for thirty years, a growing thorn in the side of an Eliphalet Nott who had little use for the straitjacket of a legal clause he could not edit.

The axle around which the wheel of argument ground was the mysterious "Second Written Stipulation", the original of which was dated May 31, 1826. It was this strange, often revised contract which had set the condition of payment to Nott for the consent he gave that year to the consolidation of the Literature Lottery with the then dormant Albany Land and Fever Hospital lotteries owned by Yates and McIntyre. The lottery partners had excoriated that agreement in their later "Examination," and in their August 1834 bill in Chancery, claiming also in the "Examination" that Nott's final revision of this stipulation made in 1830 had been fraudulently foisted on the "House," and was designed to substitute himself in place of the college as the beneficiary of the Consolidated Lottery contract.

The original "Second Stipulation," of 1826, and the retro-active version of it, dated May 30, 1826, were, indeed, valid contracts, according to Alonzo Paige, Samuel Woodruff, the Doctor's personal solicitor, and Marcus Reynalds. They were prepared, they assured the Court, to prove that the Doctor's "risks run and hazards taken" under those agreements for so many years to support the credit of Yates and McIntyre constituted a more than adequate compensation for all the "House" had paid to him, including the $300,000 the Doctor still claimed.

The attorneys for the college and the "impleaded" Doctor made one charge in their amended bill of January 6, 1835 which acted like a blast from a blacksmith's bellows: Henry Yates was here formally cited to the Court as a full-time partner of the "House," and so, by implication, guilty of betraying his trust as the agent of the Board sent by it to New York City to guard its lottery interests. With this charge Nott and his advisers publicly offered as a sacrifice the reputation of a man whose older brother Joseph, long chairman of the Board, had his own memories of a similar fate ten years earlier at the hands of the leaders of the Albany Regency. Henry Yates, even as the ex-governor had once been, was now in a vulnerable position. By 1835 he was a man who was widely known to have grown rich as one of the manipulators of the New York State lotteries, a system now in public disgrace.

If Henry Yates felt himself abused in this amended college bill, John Barentse Yates was appalled at the prospect it presented, for here the lawyers for Nott and the Board claimed that his domain at Chittenango, his mills, his canal basin, and farms, and his "Polytechny," of which his brother Andrew, ex-Professor of Moral Philosophy and Logic at Union, was principal, were all college property, transferred to its Trustees by his bond and mortgage, "taken as payment" from the "House" . . . so credited by the treasurer, and so charged by Yates and McIntyre on their account rendered, and so allowed in the subsequent settlement between the parties . . ." [18] Here was a present danger which above all others energized John Barentse Yates, the fear of losing his vast Chittenango lands. His claim that this bond and mortgage was given *pro tanto*, only as security for the debts of the "House" to the college was denied, the Trustees declared, in an earlier commitment by Henry Yates himself.

I V

The props and actors for this legal morality were now all in place: The "House," the Trustees and the Doctor had declared their "rights" before the Chancery Court, which could now embark in earnest on "matters of discovery, specific performance, fraud account, and the like . . . ," the stuff of drama in any age.

And "fraud account" had been now "discovered," according to Yates and McIntyre. In the amended bill they filed on May 16th Eliphalet Nott, Govenor Marcy, United States Senator Silas Wright, and Comptroller Azariah Flagg, members of the Finance Committee, and the other Board members again become the defendants, now brought on stage either as faithless custodians of the State's endowments, or as accessories to the general dishonesty. The contractors, especially Henry and John B. Yates, their own reputations and estates in jeopardy, had in the months since the Trustees and Nott presented their "amended" bill, discovered, they were sure, new evidence they believed would fasten on Eliphalet Nott the inescapable charge of fraud.

Fraud, discovered in the President of Union College, in a man with a national reputation as an educator and as a clergyman, in a college teacher who stood ten feet tall in the eyes of his students, becomes an awesome charge. John Barentse Yates had prepared it that spring, a new record on which the "House" now based its claims. He had forwarded his evidence to Albany sometime in the weeks before the lottery contractors filed their latest "amended Bill," addressed as an urgent "Memorandum for J. C. Spencer, Esq., Bement's Hotel, room No. 6." [19]

John Yates, on the basis of his new evidence, driven by his passionate desire to regain control of his Chittenango lands, had convinced himself that Eliphalet Nott had deliberately falsified the figures on which the original Literature Lottery contract was based, as well as the figures on which their angrily debated "Second Written Stipulation" had been framed. He had already convinced himself that the Doctor had driven the "House" to an unwise speed-up of their drawing of their lottery "schemes," and so into those financial reverses from which the Doctor had extricated them at little cost to himself, but at an enormous cost to the "House" through what John Yates had insisted were illegal verbal and written contract changes extorted from men who saw themselves as innocent and gullible public servants. His "Memorandum" to John C. Spencer, one of the attorneys for the "House," showed there was little room in his thinking that spring but for what he believed was his annihilating arithmetic.

John Yates, following a review of the Comptroller's records, was certain he had discovered in them proof of deliberate fraud on the part of the Doctor, proof which had long eluded him because, as he wrote to Spencer, "the contractors never felt themselves required to examine critically into the accuracy of the computation . . . this was left to Dr. Nott and was presumed accurate. . . ." [20]

In its baldest terms John Yates's "Memorandum" charged three gross "frauds" on the "House" by the Doctor which the contractors had already reviewed in their "Examination" and by which Nott had progressively swelled the amount Yates and McIntyre were legally supposed to sell in tickets for the benefit of Union College by $1,259,735. By a series of calculated deceptions, Yates purported now to prove, the Doctor had paved the way for extorting almost $200,000 from the House following the close of the Literature Lottery in 1827, and that, on the basis of these deceptions, the Doctor now expected the Chancery Court to support him in his illegal claim for an even greater sum.

This "Memorandum to J. C. Spencer, Esq.," brought to a climax the dozen years of contest between John Barentse Yates and Eliphalet Nott during which each had checked and counter-checked the other's response to the opportunities which the cornucopia of lottery dollars had opened to them. The final sentence of Yates's "Memorandum" distilled the hostility of that last year of association; "the above information," he wrote to Spencer, "fastens upon him as I think the charge of fraud, without the power to escape, in order to swell the proportion [of the profits he claimed]."

The attorneys for Yates and McIntyre lost no time in developing John Yates's damning arithmetic, and so in pursuing what they must now have believed was certain legal victory. Among the Spencer Papers is a note addressed to Alonzo Paige, solicitor for the Trustees, from Charles Yates, solicitor for the "House," in which this son of Henry Yates notified Paige that he intended to petition the Chancellor at once for the appointment of a receiver "of the estate and effects of said Trustees . . . at the capital, in Albany, 3rd Tuesday in April, at 10 o'clock in the forenoon," a counter, no doubt, to the rumor that the college was about to petition the Chancellor for a receivership for the "estate and effects of Yates and McIntyre." [21]

The confusion of issues, the legal kitchen middens of contracts, verbal agreements, and dubious "stipulations" left by the contractors and Eliphalet Nott as these men lost themselves in the lottery maze, were placed, finally, before Chancellor Reuben Walworth, defined, however, that September, 1835, by Yates and McIntyres' new charges of fraud and extortion, direct and implied. Point by point Samuel Woodruff, Alonzo Paige, and Marcus Reynalds now made their replies on which the life of the college and the good names of its President and its trust officers depended.

Yates and McIntyre's basic error, the attorneys for Nott and the college now argued, was in assuming that the Literature Lottery contract of 1822 had established a fixed yield and a fixed sale of tickets. [22] They insisted that the President of Union College, always "consulting" with the contractors, had "assumed" only that tickets to the amount of $4,492,000 could be sold; it was clearly understood by the "House" and by Nott, however, in 1822, that this assumed total might well change as new conditions arose. Yates and McIntyre must also be reminded that Union College had retained specific "rights" such as its share "in the profits arising from the loss of prize tickets," and "to all profits arising from the sale of tickets above their scheme price," as well as to "the interest on money held for the payment of prize tickets . . . and other incidental advantages." [23]

In addition to those peripheral "rights" established or implied by the contract of 1822, were the advantages to be derived from substantial contract changes, both verbal and written. The attorneys for Nott and the Trustees emphasized again and again their doctrine of the elastic contract, one in which the college retained all "rights," subject to the unrestricted supervision and revision of its agent, Eliphalet Nott.

As a further defense of their position, Nott and the college now took common ground against the "House" as to the college's share of the lottery profits. The Trustees entered their claim to "all avails" under all contracts involving the Literature Lottery as well as the Consolidated Lotteries to November 10, 1827, when the Literature Lottery drawings were completed. All subsequent profits rising from Nott's "individual agreements" with the "House" were now claimed jointly by the Board and by the President. This joint claim they justified on the basis of Nott's earlier commitments to the Trustees that all his "individual" verbal and written agreements with Yates and McIntyre were made always with the future of the college in mind. [24] The Board members, perhaps, thus hoped to absolve themselves from direct responsibility for Nott's relations with the contractors following the close of the Literature Lottery, and Nott, on his part, sought perhaps to justify keeping an as yet undetermined portion of those profits for his own use by committing a part of any settlement with the "House" to his already established trust fund, his personal endowment for the long promised Union College "Institute of Science and Industry."

CHAPTER 5

The Tri-Partite Agreement

IF the Chancery Court bills of 1834 and 1835 amended and summarized the confusing mathematics of hazard and gamble, of remembrance and assumption which eroded and then destroyed the vital partnership between Eliphalet Nott and the lottery contractors, they also presented barely recognizable portraits of the four men who had come together in such optimism in 1822 to create, perhaps, the most significant lottery adventure in American history. These bills reflected an Eliphalet Nott who had claimed the lottery began as the sanctified hazard, and who used its dollars like a Yankee trader, of a John and Henry Yates, and an Archibald McIntyre, all of the less exalted vision, who had used the lottery capital to create the Chittenango fief, to exploit the iron deposits of the Adirondacks, and to finance the Welland Canal.

Chancellor Reuben Walworth had long known these men who, rather than their contracts, were on trial. To what extent were the portraits they gave him of each other recognizable as the men who came, finally, into his courtroom in 1835? Had the lotteries, "that evil," Senator Silas Wright had written to Eliphalet Nott, "continued by your means," so marked the famous President of Union College that Samuel Woodruff, his solicitor, and the attorneys for the Trustees could not hope to erase the picture Yates and McIntyre had prepared for the Chancellor of a man who had willfully stooped to fraud and extortion in order to wring from them, from Union College, and from New York State, a fortune to which he had no legal claim?

Eliphalet Nott's Trustees, excepting Henry Yates, had supported their President before Chancellor Walworth without reservation in his claim to authority to contract with Yates and McIntyre on behalf of the Board in all matters bearing on the Literature Lottery. They had supported him in his contention that the "President's Fund," the fruit of his Supplemental Agreement made with Yates and McIntyre in 1822, was added to the original contract at his own insistence, "for supervision and management," and that, contrary to the contractors' claim, the "President's Fund" had never been considered a purely "contingent fund" set up to cover only emergencies or unexpected losses. [1]

But to whom, then, did the "President's Fund" really belong? The question becomes a camera lens, the images of the men it tries to define kept always in soft focus. In September 1835, Chancellor Walworth was told by the attorneys for Nott and the Board that that part of the "President's Fund" associated with the Literature Lottery was received by Nott "as the President and agent of Union College . . . to remain a contingent fund for meeting losses [which at the close of the Literature Lottery] was to be divided [with Hamilton College] *pro rata*. . . ." according to the interest each had in that lottery in 1822. [2] Both Azariah Flagg, Comptroller of New York State by 1835, and General John A. Dix, the Secretary of New York State, however, remembered a quite different conclusion. Both men, as long-time Trustees representing the State on the Board, recalled "that it was conceded by all, except Henry Yates, that this sum was Dr. Nott's, he saying all the time he intended to give it to the College, or some kindred institution . . . it was considered as belonging to him." [3] In addition "to this amount allowed for management," Azariah Flagg recalled, were the large sums the President had received from Yates and McIntyre "for risks, hazards and responsibilities" run for the contractors, sums Flagg recalled which were "conceded by the Trustees to belong to Dr. Nott." [4]

There seems little doubt that Nott himself thought of the "President's Fund" as his from the beginning, to be dealt with according to his own conscience, and that the new view expressed in the Chancery suits in 1835 represented the second thoughts of state officers and Trustees very much worried by their role as "confederates" of an Eliphalet Nott who was their agent, then being charged by Yates and McIntyre of defrauding the State and the college by having established the "President's Fund" secretly in order to siphon off for his own use hundreds of thousands of dollars.

The Trustees, again excepting Henry Yates, denied without reservation that September that there was anything "secret" about the "President's Fund," or that a "knowledge of its contents was intended to be kept from the Trustees."[5] Chancellor Walworth was left in no doubt about the character of Dr. Nott as they saw it. Their picture was of a man who had run infinite risks to save Yates and McIntyre from utter ruin. They pictured his services to the "House" as a complete justification for his "individual" claims against its members, and assured the Chancellor that anything in the contractors' Bill of Complaint "intended to insinuate that . . . Eliphalet Nott has at any time, or in any respect misled the said Yates and McIntyre, these defendants utterly deny all knowledge or belief of the truth of such insinuation, and unhesitatingly repel it."[6] In repelling these attacks on Nott, the Trustees of Union College also repelled any flanking attacks on themselves, all "that unlawful combination and confederacy" with which the contractors had charged them.

What did Yates and McIntyre ask the Chancellor to believe about the members of the "House"? They presented themselves to the Court as victims of fraud and extortion at the hands of a devious and scheming college president, supported by "confederates" among his Trustees. They presented themselves as victims of a misinformed public opinion, hounded by an unsympathetic legislature, fulfilling, for the sake of their devotion as patrons and graduates of Union College, a sequence of lottery contracts which had actually plunged them toward financial disaster, or so they claimed.

If one sees the history of the Literature and Consolidated lotteries through the eyes of the generation which outlawed them, as something partaking of the nature of an unfolding morality, one then has the choice of two "satans": in the script as John Barentse Yates wrote it, the Corrupter was Eliphalet Nott. To the President of Union College "Satan" was clearly John Yates, the destroyer of his "Grand Plan" for Union College, his "Institute of Science and Industry," as well as of that "individual" estate he saw as his due for the "hazards, risks, and responsibilities" he had undertaken on behalf of the contractors.

Nott's view of John B. Yates became his Trustees' view: It was Yates, the impatient gambler, they informed the Chancellor, who had insisted on those contract changes which gave him his speculator's use of Union College lottery money. They accused him of deliberately flooding the New York lottery market with "foreign tickets" as a retaliation for Nott's resistance to the claims of the "House" for rebates of interest paid to the college. [7] It was John Yates, they charged, who pretended falling ticket sales to win legislative sympathy, and, finally, who, in spite of astronomical profits, had been the leader in plans to cheat the college and its President of the full reward of their joint contracts. [8]

Henry Yates, for so long Union College Treasurer and Trustee, was characterized by them as the once confidential agent of the Board, a man who had deliberately betrayed the trust they had reposed in him by becoming a full-time partner in the "House," who had then left the records of the college treasurer's office in confusion, and who had manipulated his accounts while in New York City to increase the profits of the contractors. [9]

If Chancellor Walworth was expected to smell brimstone when John and Henry Yates were in view, apparently he was not expected to detect it in an Archibald McIntyre who for so long had acted as the peacemaker between his partners and an Eliphalet Nott increasingly on guard against the machinations of the Yateses. Although Archibald McIntyre had joined his partners in charging Nott with fraud, the picture of him one gathers from the amended bill filed in September 1835 by Nott and his Trustees, is of a man often unaware of his partners' betrayals of trust, or of the true state of their books of account.

What, finally, was to be the judgment of the Chancery Court on those "matters of discovery, specific performance, fraud account, and the like"? It could be for Yates and McIntyre the last harvest of their "temerarious speculations," and for Eliphalet Nott possibly the worst of that host of evils which had been crowding out of his Pandora's Box of lottery hazards for thirty years, and for many of the Trustees of Union College a politically explosive ruling on their performance as trust officers, as custodians of the State's grants to education.

In the late fall of 1835 Yates and McIntyre's objections to almost every position Nott and his Trustees had taken that

September were laid before Master in Chancery William T. Fondey; in a sweeping ruling he "allowed" almost every exception the contractors had taken to the College Bill. If Chancery Court action had ended here then there might well have begun a state-wide scandal of unmeasurable scope. On the following January 8, 1836, however, Chancellor Reuben Walworth listened as Marcus Reynalds fought the blanket denunciation of his and Samuel Woodruff's and Alonzo Paige's case for Nott and for the college. Defendants and claimants alike now enlisted their strongest spokesman. John C. Spencer appeared before the Chancellor for the "House," arguing in support of a legal victory his clients thought they had won before Master in Chancery Fondey. The latter had allowed at least seventy exceptions which had been taken by Yates and McIntyre, most of them challenges to Eliphalet Nott's record of his verbal exchanges and agreements with the contractors. Spencer knew that if Chancellor Walworth chose to support his Master in Chancery's basic conclusion that the President of Union College had no standing in these suits except as a Trustee, a single member of the corporation of the college, there would be the almost insurmountable burden for Nott and for the Board of reconstructing separate cases for new hearings before the Court of Errors as well as the expanding risks of ugly publicity.

II

If the actors in that day's drama, however, hoped for a quick resolution of its tensions they were disappointed. Why Chancellor Walworth delayed his ruling for months is not known. He was himself in a vulnerable position. He owed his Chancery Court appointment to Regency Democrats, some of whom, as Union College Trustees, were themselves defendants in these suits. He was, in fact, a defendant himself for, as Chancellor he, too, was a Union College Trustee, and a devoted one apparently for he had not missed a meeting of the Board since becoming Chancellor in 1828.

Reuben Hyde Walworth, though respected as a student of the law, was detested by a good many New York lawyers for his rudeness and querulousness on the bench, and for his tendency to base his judgments not on legal precedents but on a code of Presbyterian Calvinism.[10] If he saw the Literature Lottery, as had Nott, as a sanctified hazard which had been perverted by men willing to gamble with the Lord's bounty, he may well have hoped that with the passage of time there might come heaven-directed changes of heart, and so a willingness to compromise an issue ready-made for the Whig press and for those office-hungry Whig politicians who privately seconded Governor Marcy's unhappily phrased observation: "To the victor belongs the spoils." The later enmity of Thurlow Weed, king maker among Whigs, is reported to have killed Walworth's hopes for appointment to the Supreme Court of the United States, and finally, to the elimination of the Court of Chancery itself. [11]

Providence, from the Presbyterian point of view, decided the issue. Suddenly, on July 10, 1836, John Barentse Yates died at Chittenango. The directors of the Welland Canal, noting "the melancholy event," memorialized him that August "as its chief and most steady supporter," in the interests of which "neither his time, his talents, or his purse were refused." [12] The citizens of St. Catherines, Upper Canada, named a street in his honor. [13] Perhaps they knew nothing of their debt to Union College, where the death of John B. Yates may have been read by one man at least as he had once read the death of Hamilton, as God's warning to those who would interfere with divine purpose.

The legal confusion which might well have gone on to a climax before the legislature now ended quietly in the anticlimax of a settlement, off-stage, behind closed doors. If John Yates's death was a blow to Yates and McIntyre's cause, Chancellor Walworth's almost complete reversal of the ruling of Master in Chancery Fondey, which he announced sometime in late July, 1836, *nunc protunc*, as he signed it, to that January day when Marcus Reynalds and John C. Spencer had argued its failures and merits, must have left the surviving members of the "House" badly shaken (two partners were gone, for James McIntyre, too, had died in 1835). [14]

If the contractors were shaken, so, too, was John C. Spencer: in a memorandum written in his almost illegible hand and headed "Remarks on Chancellor's Opinion," he declared at one point that "Chancellor utterly mistakes the matter. . . ." Yates and

McIntyre's error, he told the partners, or their solicitor, Charles Yates, had been in bringing a suit against a corporation for "discovery." Spencer seems to have been incredulous in the face of the Chancellor's decision that "part of the prayer for specific relief is applicable to Dr. Nott, and the whole of the general prayer. . . ." Spencer looked on this key reversal of the Master in Chancery's earlier decision as simply bad law, or, in view of the timing of the decision, perhaps as expedient law. Whatever his personal opinion, he recommended to the surviving partners that they appeal [to the Court of Errors] almost all of Chancellor Walworth's ruling. [15]

With John Barentse Yates gone, however, the driving force of the partnership seems to have gone. Sometime before July 26, the date of the Commencement meeting of the Union College Trustees, Attorney General of the United States Benjamin Butler, Yates and McIntyre's senior counsel, suggested to unnamed members of the Board that the lottery contractors were ready to come to "an amicable compromise." The Board immediately appointed a committee made up of Nott, Governor Marcy, Senator Wright, Comptroller Flagg, and J. P. Cushman, "or any three of them, to adjust the whole subject."

Archibald McIntyre's bitter protest the following October, included in his "Statement of Account" made up for his attorneys then preparing for the "amicable compromise," was almost the last echo of the contractors' voices in the strange dialogue in which the history of the Literature Lottery is written. He and his partners are willing to make a settlement, he wrote, only "because, perhaps, compelled, under the circumstances, to do so. . . ." The partners agreed to waive their charge of "the improper additions" of over a million dollars in tickets made by the Doctor to the Literature Lottery contract of 1822 in order to end the controversy, insisting only that the College recognize as improper the Doctor's alleged addition to the figures used in settling the Trustees' lottery account in 1828 of "$413,186" in tickets, a sum added, McIntyre declared, by the Doctor in order "to swell the assumed remaining rights of the college" in the Consolidated Lotteries contracts. "The fraud," McIntyre wrote, "is as palpable as any that was ever presented to the consideration of an earthly tribunal for correction. . . ." He then added: "We cannot permit ourselves to believe that just men will insist, not only that we yield in the one instance, to injustice, to our injury . . . but [will] compel [us] also to admit the College as having rights . . . more than nine times what those rights were." [16]

The remaining partners, Archibald McIntyre, Henry Yates, John Ely, Jr., and, by July 1836, Archibald McIntyre, Jr., son of the deceased James McIntyre, finally agreed to end all litigation if the college would refund to them $141,063.59, a sum which included the amounts represented by John B. Yates's bond and mortgage on his estate at Chittenango still held by the college, the firm's debt to the College of Physicians and Surgeons, certain other securities, and their claimed overpayment to the "College Fund" and the "President's Fund" at the time of the Literature Lottery settlement in 1828, plus those reported overpayments made to Nott in his "individual account" with the "House" which the partners had arbitrarily shut off in the spring of 1832.

There was no compromise offered to the Doctor in Archibald McIntyre's "Statement." The contractors stood firm on their contention that the "extortions" which had already been paid to him were paid through him for the college, and that the additional sums he still claimed from them had been paid instead to Archibald McIntyre and John B. Yates by the newer partners in order "to compensate them for their losses under the contract of 1822," a "compensation" of over $132,000 taken from that stream of payments made to Nott which John B. Yates had once called the Doctor's "gratuities." [17]

Moralities should end with virtue triumphant and evil clearly delineated. The history of the Literature Lottery however, and of that Consolidated Lottery with which it was merged ends in bookkeeper's columns. The balances were decided by reference, not to that Christian code by which Eliphalet Nott had once judged Alexander Hamilton, but by reference to those mundane "compelling circumstances" which Archibald McIntyre declared had forced the members of the "House" to seek an "amicable compromise," a settlement which was finally framed as the "Tri-Partite Agreement," signed on July 27, 1837, but between the lines of which one still reads the unsettled charges and countercharges, the moral issues with which the accountants could not deal. [18]

There was little that was "amicable" about this Tri-Partite Agreement. In order to bring the Chancery suits to a close, the Trustees admitted an overpayment to the college by Yates and McIntyre of $94,477.47.[19] In order to correct this error they agreed to return John B. Yates's bond and mortgage on his Chittenango property, other securities claimed by the contractors, and to assume a debt of $20,000 the latter owed to the College of Physicians and Surgeons.

The President of Union College proved difficult. Secretary of State John A. Dix recalled many years later that "Dr. Nott assented [to the Tri-Partite settlement] with great reluctance." Instead of the additional $300,000 to which he insisted he was entitled, $150,000 was included in the agreement, to be paid to the Trustees, but in fact as an additional and final payment to him for those "risks, hazards, and responsibilities" he had translated over eleven years into his "President's Fund" of almost half a million dollars. "Dr. Nott," Secretary of State Dix recalled, "surrendered his own judgment to the earnest wish expressed by Mr. Flagg, Governor Marcy, Mr. Wright and myself, to put an end to what we believed would prove an unpleasant and protracted controversy."[20]

The State's chief officers, the leading Regency Democrats, had their way. It would be a mistake to argue that these men who dominated the Union College Board for so long could conceive of themselves as even minor villains in this unresolved Morality Play, but there can be little doubt that they had been made aware that they as Union College Trustees had delegated dangerous powers to their President, for the exercise of which hostile New York State Whigs and the public could well hold them accountable.

If the moral account remained unsettled the bookkeepers' accounts, seldom tallying, were finally "adjusted," and the profits of the great hazard were theoretically determined and listed for the private edification of those privileged to see them. Union College, it was agreed, had received on the Literature Lottery grant of 1814-1822 to the time of the "Settlement" with Yates and McIntyre in 1828, the gross sum of $542,468.22. The college retained, after buying out the interest in the lottery held by Hamilton College, the College of Physicians and Surgeons, the Asbury African Church, and the New-York Historical Society in

1822, and after repaying Yates and McIntyre a part of what the "House" had claimed as an overpayment, the net sum of $372,887.42. To this amount must be added the sum the college received on a later settlement with its President for its share of his profits on his "individual" contracts with Yates and McIntyre, $140,000, a ledger total, finally of $512,687.42. [21]

The "President's Fund" up to the time of the 1828 "Settlement" with the "House," had accumulated $133,069.83, to which one must add the $75,140.87 deposited in the Doctor's "red box" in the Mohawk Bank, his special profit for arranging the T. J. Oakley and the William James loans to the "House" in 1826. To these two amounts the bookkeepers added $338,000 for those later "responsibilities assumed on behalf of Yates and McIntyre." The only deduction from these sums was the $95,165.09 which Nott had turned over to the Trustees in part as a payment on his promised endowment for his long projected "Institute of Science and Industry." The great hazard, so far as the President of Union College was concerned, had given him a bookkeeper's profit of $451,045.61. [22]

These large sums, credited to both the college and to Eliphalet Nott, were, unfortunately, not bank balances, but were distributed in a vast array of investments in bonds and mortgages, real estate speculations, and in the notes of the "House" which made the later work of the college treasurer and the finance committees a labor of frustration until long after the Civil War.

For the Doctor, for John Barentse Yates, for Henry Yates, and for Archibald McIntyre the Tri-Partite Settlement of 1837 became a monument to the long-dying of the great gamble, or the great hazard, a semantic choice in labels which depends on whether your optimism stems from Eliphalet Nott's Calvinist New England, or from that speculator's America which bred the ambitions of the partners in the "House" of Yates and McIntyre, and of that quasi-partner they had always called "the Doctor," and, in anger and exasperation, "the old fox."

There are, finally, the tragic overtones of the dozen years in which Eliphalet Nott and the House of Yates and McIntyre exploited the New York State lotteries. What, in 1822, all four men had proclaimed was a dedicated enterprise, a true "hazard" within the meaning of Nott's definition of that word, had, by the end of 1833, run its course with Yates and McIntyre's last drawing outlawed as a common gamble by the society which had so long endorsed it.

As the "hazard" Eliphalet Nott had proclaimed the lottery to be it could only have succeeded if he, the members of the "House," and the officers of New York State charged with certifying it had conducted themselves as priests, not as men of the market place. When the often diametrically opposed evidence of the Chancery suits is examined, and one hears again the outraged voices of John Yates and Archibald McIntyre charging "the old fox" with deviously enriching himself at their expense and at the expense of Union College, one must also recall Nott's updating of his brother's Edwardsian Calvinism, his new faith that democracy and science, too, echo God's voice, that education, experimentation, and exploitation of the physical world were the Christian's "means" to promote the regeneration of mankind, essential steps in the return to Eden. Within the framework of such thinking a Literature Lottery, a "House of Yates and McIntyre," and Union College itself were expendable mechanisms to be used in achieving that divinely directed, "scientifically" certain end. Within the framework of such a ruthless optimism, this amalgam of Nott's ambition, of his religious inheritance, of his psychological insights into that ultimate maze, the human mind, the narrower self-interest of those about him who failed to share his vision of a perfectible world, made them, too, expendable. In a medieval society Eliphalet Nott might well have expressed this rationalization without compromising, as a sword-carrying Bishop, or a Hussite martyr; in the nineteenth-century America which had possessed him, however, there were no such simple ways to the New Jerusalem.

BOOK SIX

Profits, Steamboats, and the Higher Law,
1830-1845

CHAPTER I

Captain Neziah Bliss: Steamboats and Real Estate

> Warner, Class of 1826, says Nott had Joe Horsfall, his pattern maker, set to work to devise a stove [to extract gas from anthracite coal] : one night, about 11 Warner heard a rap on his door and Dr. Nott opening, beckoned him to come down to his study—on entering he saw no light—but in one corner of the room there was a new stove and issuing from a small orifice on the top a little blue flame about one inch long.
>
> The Dr. turned to Warner with gravity and said, 'What do you think of it?' Warner, with some difficulty repressing his laughter, answered, 'I think it equals the blue lights of Connecticut.' Without moving a muscle the Dr. said, 'You may go,' and from that time to this the stove was never more heard of. It took the Dr. this costly experiment to teach [him] that there is no illuminating gas in anthracite. . . .[1]

ENTRIES such as this one in "Pinky" Pearson's "Thinking Books" slow the rush of events in Nott's life with which Professor Jonathan Pearson was to become increasingly familiar; in this entry he reduced them to a pace he could follow and a dimension his antiquarian's mind could embrace.

Horatio Warner of the class of 1826, who was to remember his alma mater with the "Warner Prize" for seniors, one which coupled scholarship with moral character, gave Professor Pearson another gossipy entry which, if true, marks the starting point of the Doctor's second caloric revolution, and of those experiments and real estate speculations which led his enemies, in 1835, to petition the Chancery Court to appoint a receiver for "the estate and effects" of Union College.

> Warner (Pearson wrote), tells of Nott's experiments on steam while the former was in college. Nott found Warner in his room one day drawing a steam engine; Nott got interested, and asked Warner for the book he worked from; Warner said it was the Encyclopaedia, and that Joel Nott

had it. After vacation Nott took up the subject again, and had Warner make several drawings of a boiler to be heated by anthracite coal . . . the first two plans being unsuccessful, Warner kept, and still has in his diploma case. . . . Warner says that these were the first attempts which the Dr. made in his steam experiments which resulted in his spending 300,000 or 400,000 dollars for nothing.[2]

What Warner had recalled Pearson did not record until 1859, more than twenty years after the S.S. *Novelty* had made her historic run in 1836 from New York City to Albany, and Eliphalet Nott had been hailed as a benefactor of his country "second only to Fulton." If it was true, as Warner assured the keeper of the "Thinking Books" it was, that the Doctor's steam experiments were so costly, it was ignorance which led him to say they led to nothing, for the Doctor's second revolutionary application of "Caloric" in the 1830s became what both Warner and Pearson and others had failed to recognize, a bench mark in the expanding record of the American economy.

If the first two drawings Horatio Warner claimed he had made of the Doctor's boiler designed for steamboats were failures, those which followed opened, for their inventor, a new series of hazards which were soon to match in daring John Yates's Welland Canal gamble. A coal burning steamboat had been tried as early as 1816 by a Captain Roorback of the *Car of Neptune* who had hoped bituminous coal could be made to substitute for the pine knots becoming scarcer and scarcer as the paddle wheel fleets on the Hudson consumed the forests bordering the river.[3] Soft coal, however, was still too expensive east of the Alleghenies for the extravagant fires of steamboats, even though in 1819 the "Savannah" with "75 tons of coal and 25 cords of wood" undertook the first trans-Atlantic voyage; her bituminous coal supply soon gave out, however, and her return trip was made under sail, her performance having stirred little interest in her paddle wheel capabilities on either side of the Atlantic.[4]

In 1825 John Mowatt, the first operator on the Hudson of those safety towboats designed for passengers afraid to ride on the explosion-prone side-wheelers, tried to burn coal on the "Henry Eckford," but the lack of a sustained draught ended the experiment.[5] Three years later the directors of the Delaware and

Hudson Canal Company optimistically agreed that anthracite would soon become the "most favored article" in steamboat operation; already, they declared in their annual report that year, they had run a hundred-horsepower engine for twenty-four hours on hard coal.[6] Nothing was closer to the hearts of the anthracite mine owners than the opening of the steamboat and railroad market for the limitless supply of stone coal arching under the Allegheny hills. The Delaware and Hudson's directors, with their new canal running from their mines near Honesdale, Pennsylvania, to the Hudson River at Rondout, near Kingston, had agents canvassing coal users in New York and New England, trying to induce them to use anthracite. By 1832, the directors reported, they had spent $12,000 the preceding year on promotion. They noted particularly that three New York City ferries on the East River, and one on the North River, had been using anthracite for some time "with complete success," and then, in the forgetful manner of promoters, added that the use of anthracite in the paddle-wheelers was "still an experiment . . . susceptible of much improvement," but that the "attention of interested people guarantees that ere long [anthracite] will be the common fuel in steamboats."[7]

The race to turn stone coal into profits was on, and high on the list of those "interested people" was the President of Union College, whose rotary grate "Saracenic Stove" was already the joy of the anthracite miners. Perhaps it was Warner's not too well suppressed laughter which turned the Doctor in 1826 from his experiments with anthracite as a source of illuminating gas to the problems to be solved in building a practical anthracite-burning steamboat.

The Doctor had apparently recognized that the heart of the problem of successfully using anthracite for steamboat fuel lay in developing a boiler which would possess two so far unrealized virtues: maximum safety from those scalding explosions which made the slower trip on towboats so attractive to the apprehensive traveler, as well as a boiler which could be protected from early destruction over the raging heat of a live bed of anthracite coal. A secondary problem he also recognized was the need to find a way to burn anthracite in great enough quantities, and, as the Doctor's patent specifications later declared, "with such uniformity as to keep up an adequate supply of steam in fast boats . . ."[8] With speed the first concern of the boat operators in what, by 1830, had become a dangerous and highly competitive bid for record runs, partial success in burning anthracite in minehead pumping engines and wallowing ferryboats was not enough.

Sometime between Horatio Warner's senior year and 1828 the Doctor developed plans for a tubular boiler which held so much promise that Joel Nott, his oldest son and then Professor of Chemistry at Union, decided to desert his classroom and undertake a career as a promoter of his father's "caloric" inventions. It was also Joel who seems to have been the first to meet the visionary Captain Neziah Bliss of King's County, New York, self-styled "steamboat engineer," and a long-time navigator "on the western rivers." It was not long before Joel and the Captain decided to enter a steamboat in the Hudson River passenger trade, a boat which was also to become a floating "experiment room" for Joel's father.[9] Late in the fall of 1829, their then unnamed and unfinished boat was towed, probably from William Brown's shipyard at Hyde Park to a berth at the foot of Hamilton Street in Albany, where it spent the winter in the hands of Webster and Wells, a firm of joiners. [10]

Benjamin Nott, Joel's younger brother, recalled years later that it was not only Joel who had introduced his father to the "steamboat engineer," but that, contrary to Neziah Bliss, the new boat had been taken down the river by his brother and the captain in the spring of 1830, "to a shop on the North River side of New York City," where she had been equipped with only one engine, brought east from Pittsburg, and with boilers designed, not by his father but by the Captain himself. [11] At about this time Joel Nott disappears from the Munchausen history of the S.S. *Novelty*, then still unnamed, and the Doctor takes his son's place unwillingly, if Benjamin Nott is right, as the Captain's partner. [12] Joel and his then pregnant wife, Margaret, sailed at the end of August for England, encouraged to do so apparently by William James, his father's lottery adviser, with high hopes of capitalizing on his father's anthracite developments, including particularly the new tubular boilers for steamboats. Joel's letter sent from London to his mother-in-law, Mrs. Charles Cooper of Albany, announcing the birth of his daughter that November, ended with the comment that "all the engineers of eminence in England enter most warmly into my plans . . . Mr. Perkins pronounces the steam boiler the most perfect thing ever invented, and says he only hopes to live long enough to have a conversation with Father, who he thinks must be one of the greatest men. . . ." [13]

Captain Bliss, by 1830, thought so too, though years later he recalled the sequence of events up to this time quite differently. He and the Doctor, he insisted, had met in 1827 because the Doctor was then looking for a marine engineer "to join him on a large scale in the improvement of steam boilers and engines supposed to have been invented or discovered by him . . .". Their association, the captain later claimed, led to the building of the S.S. *Novelty* in 1829. [14] Here the captain's memory may have failed him, for he insisted that the new boat was constructed at the "Novelty Works" in New York City, at the foot of 12th Street, near the Dry Dock on the East River, on land, and in buildings purchased or erected by the captain himself for this purpose, "to enable Doctor Nott to have entire control of the application of his improvements in steam machinery; all these activities managed by the Captain, and in his name, . . . the pecuniary means furnished by Dr. Nott." It seems certain that the Novelty Works, however, were not operating until sometime in 1831, and that Captain Bliss may have preferred to forget what Benjamin Nott swore was true, that the boat Joel and the Captain had built, and then equipped "at a shop on the North River . . ." had failed on trials made in 1830 because the captain's own boilers were inadequate; Benjamin Nott declared his father "had always expressed his doubts of their success." [15]

II

"The Novelty Works," when that East River shipyard and foundry was established, became immediately the new capital of both the captain's and the Doctor's hopes. When the latter took over Joel Nott's interest in the new boat he insisted, according to Captain Bliss, "on carrying out his plans on an extensive scale." With an optimism rooted in part in his "President's Fund" of lottery dollars, he bought, through Neziah Bliss, the new foundry's site on "Burnt Mill Point," immediately south of Nicholas

Stuyvesant's "meadow," facing Bushwick on the opposite Long Island shore, leaving the title to the property, however, in the captain's name. [16] "I acted as agent for Dr. Nott," an embittered Neziah Bliss remembered twenty years later, "and under his general direction," his compensation for engineering services not definitely agreed upon. "I relied," the captain recalled, "on the vague and general promises of Dr. Nott . . . immense pecuniary advantages were expected to be derived from his discoveries and applied under my superintendence." [17]

From 1831 on, the "philosopher of caloric" in Nott, and the "marine engineer" in Captain Bliss were to alternate with the speculator in both men. The captain not only knew a good deal about poppet valves and the high pressure boilers he favored and had known on the western rivers, contrivances which may have been a part of the boat which failed him and Joel Nott in 1830, but he had visions, too, of great wealth to be made in Manhattan and Long Island real estate. He had found his ideal partner at last in the President of Union College, a man capable of visions on any scale.

The first fruit of their engineering partnership, however, was "Dr. Nott's new steamboat" the "South America," according to a reporter's misnomer in the Albany *Argus* on May 18, 1831. The Schenectady *Cabinet* a week later reported it was "a steam boat without a name, generally called Dr. Nott's boat". It arrived at the Albany docks "on Monday, May [. . . .], in 13 hours from New York City, a conveniently arranged boat," the *Argus* stated, "with a horizontal engine and an improved mode of producing steam." The new boat had eight boilers, four on each side, one set of which may have been fired by wood, and the other probably by anthracite. The boilers were the Doctor's this time, the first tubular boilers to be used successfully in steamboat navigation. [18] The traveling season was open, and on June 8th the new boat, by then called *The Novelty*, made her second run from New York City to Albany, Captain Peck at the wheel, a pilot "whose experience and urbanity well qualify him for the station." [19]

It was a springtime to be remembered. President Jackson's "trail of tears" was marked with milestones of Indian bodies, as thousands of them moved on forced marches to new homes west of the Mississippi River. William Lloyd Garrison's ringing abolitionist cry, "I will not retreat a single inch, and I will be heard," was still reverberating in the press, and would have been echoed, perhaps, even in that shipboard newspaper reported to be among the innovations on "Dr. Nott's new boat," for the Doctor, too, was known to be a strong anti-slavery man. That March, in Albany, the turnpike men were out-voted in the legislature by the promoters of the almost completed Mohawk and Hudson Railroad, innovators who had won a right-of-way into the heart of the city for their new mode of steam transportation. Earlier, in February, the Albany City Council had ordered the City Chamberlain to advertise a reward of $500 for the discovery of a coal mine within five miles of the Hudson River north of Poughkeepsie. America, that spring, was in motion, discarding old-fashioned things, her Indians, her voices of reason, her older modes of transportation, with equal enthusiasm for whatever promised greater profit, greater production and greater speed.

The *Novelty*, though new, failed to capitalize on the traveling season that year. On the 10th of June the Doctor appended a surprising note to his grandfatherly letter addressed to Clarkson Nott Potter, aged six, which explains why the S.S. *Novelty* disappeared from the Hudson until the next year:

> You must tell your father [the Rev. Alonzo Potter] that Captain Bliss's new Boat, on her first trip cracked the flanges of her tubes on one side—this is a great misfortune as I fear she will not be running again when he comes on—and the more so as the furnaces and the boilers exceeded the most sanguine expectations—but whether the manner of fastening the tubes will answer remains to be determined—and fears are entertained that the tubes attached by flanges will not stand and should they not a very serious loss will be incurred. . . . [20]

Clarkson may have been puzzled, but his father, who was preparing to give up a Boston parish and return to Union College as Professor of Rhetoric and Natural Philosophy, understood the Doctor's disappointment. The failure that June is explained by a brief note on the *Novelty* which appeared on July 8, 1836, in the Schenectady *Reflector and Democrat*:

> A few welded iron tubes [had been] procured at the factory of Mr. Pomeroy of Pittsfield as, however, a sufficient number could not be obtained, an attempt was made to procure copper tubes; but this having been found impracticable, Mr. Bliss next resorted to sheet iron riveted

tubes, and finally, after meeting with many discouragements, succeeded in finishing the boat, if not on the original plan, on one so nearly approximating thereto as to show, though it failed, that the original plan, could it have been executed, would have succeeded. Professor Nott having in the meantime gone to England and got the original boiler into use there, tubes were ordered, and it was intended by Mr. Bliss to refit said boat with boilers constructed on the original plan. But being disappointed in this, he resorted to the common flue boiler. . .

The S.S. *Novelty* was apparently returned that June to the expanding "Novelty Works" at the East River end of 12th Street, the new foundry and shipyard which was shortly to become also the headquarters of H. Nott and Company. Howard and Benjamin Nott were now business agents for their father in his steamboat activities as well as manufacturers of his "Saracenic Stove," and had made the move to Manhattan from Albany with the intention of expanding their stove operations to include the heavy casting and marine engine building which, until then, had been largely the monopoly of the Allaire Works, successors to the foundry established in Jersey City in 1816, by Robert Fulton. [21]

The *Novelty* was put up for major changes, all of them accompanied, Captain Bliss reported, with a good deal of argument between the Doctor and himself, for the captain had decided that the Doctor's prescription for "very small tubes" for his new boilers was wrong; Neziah Bliss, as the Doctor's marine superintendent, seems to have had his way in 1831. If he had come to have doubts about the Doctor's inventive genius, however, he recalled later he had extreme confidence in him in other matters.

III

One must imagine the Doctor and Captain Bliss, their arguments over "steam at high elasticity" and proper tube dimensions quiet for the moment, standing on the slip at Burnt Mill Point. The captain was thoroughly familiar with the sand hills of Bushwick on the opposite shore, an area of farms and tide-mills stretching along the East River north from the town of Brooklyn, embracing the new village of Williamsburg, and north of it, the market gardens of Greenpoint. Northeast of Williamsburg they could see the inlet of Newtown Creek which divided Greenpoint from Hunter Point, and the salt meadows and farmland that spread on north to the Hell Gate, where the East River channel divided, one branch swinging on east into Long Island Sound.

The captain's talk, however, was not of the wheeling gulls, nor of the romantic prospect of Brooklyn Heights and the white sails riding outside the United States Naval shipyard at Wallabout Bay which he and the Doctor could see to the southeast, across the East River. Captain Bliss had a full-blown case of speculator's fever, then the common infection, and his concern in 1831 seems to have been to pass it on to the Doctor. Brooklyn, he noted, was a boom town; Neziah Bliss, who already owned what he called "a block factory" in Bushwick, had seen Brooklyn's population swell from 5000 in 1820 to more than 20,000 by 1831. He had watched the land boom expand northward, the real estate speculators growing rich by cutting Bushwick farm acres into city lots at Williamsburg, profitably joined to New York City by Morrell's steam ferry. He had seen the magic performed by General Jeremiah Johnson's two-rod roadway recently opened between Wallabout Bay and the new ferry. He had seen Williamsburg swallow up the ancient town of Bushwick, then incorporate in 1827 with 114 citizens, and by 1831 attract an additional 2000 residents, most of them New York City commuters. Greenpoint and Hunter Point, a little to the north of Williamsburg, still farmland, were waiting for exploitation, and so, too, was Newtown Creek, which divided them and Queens and Kings Counties. Newtown Creek, the captain believed, was an exploiter's dream. For special and secret reasons he had decided to share it with the Doctor. There, across the East River, and one can imagine the sweep of the Captain's arm, was an opportunity to make a fortune on a scale to dwarf even the profits of a lottery. [23] His secret would wait, however, until he had sold his new partner on the virtues of a less hazardous speculation.

If Neziah Bliss had not made the sand hills and farmlands of Bushwick irresistibly attractive to the Doctor, he had only to face him north, point out the indentation in the Manhattan shoreline immediately above the "Novelty Works" known as "Stuyvesant's Cove" and reveal to him what the record only suggests he did, a plan which the Yankee in Nott must have admired. The Captain had information that thirty-five acres of the "Cove" were available, an area of meadow and swamp which was part of Peter Stuyvesant's huge "Bouerie Farm" of colonial days and which his descendants had cultivated and partly filled in. By 1831 Nicholas Stuyvesant was convinced further filling was too expensive, especially of those areas of the cove then only projected into the East River, underwater acres which the Corporation of New York City hoped to see transformed into new streets and taxable property, a process then slowly transforming the waterfronts of both the North and East Rivers. Labor and the cost of dirt and cartage to the "Cove" site, however, had become prohibitively high. [24]

Costs for fill might be too much for Nicholas Stuyvesant, but to developers who had the sand hills of Bushwick to level and other Long Island farmland to prepare for a townsite and only a short barge trip between the "Cove" and Greenpoint to transfer their fill, costs could well be low enough to justify buying the thirty-five acres of the "Cove" north of the Novelty Works; filling operations there could eventually create a housing subdivision of sixty acres, some five hundred city lots!

If the Doctor was not already infected, Captain Bliss had his secret revelation which may also have been his clinching argument for underwriting these dreams of real estate empire. Newtown Creek, dividing Greenpoint and Hunter's Point, was known to the Captain to be under consideration by the Federal Government as a possible site for an addition to the Navy Yard on Wallabout Bay. Hazard or gamble, the optimist in the President of Union College could not resist the infection. Captain Bliss later testified that when they purchased Hunter Point in 1834 the Doctor said that he had Union College funds to invest, and that, so far as Newtown Creek was concerned, he was confident the Government would be willing to pay a high price for the property adjoining it, "because the money would be applied to educational purposes." [25]

How long, actually, it took Neziah Bliss to involve the Doctor in these ambitious real estate speculations is not on record, but the evidence for his general argument lies in the sequence of land purchases the President of Union College and his "marine engineer" undertook in 1831 and 1832. On the 15th of April,

1831, they bought "the sand hill," thirty-five acres of the Mazerole Farm at Greenpoint, for $15,000; this was their first purchase in what was intended to be the site of their new town of 250 acres for which the Doctor was to furnish the money and which the Captain was to develop "for the joint and equal benefit of both." The next year, on May 19, the Captain agreed with Nicholas Stuyvesant to buy the "Cove" lands for $17,000, and with that purchase completed the following September, the Captain and the Doctor were ready to begin operations, "under a general understanding," the Captain remembered, "That [Nott] should supply the necessary funds to purchase the property and to improve and make it available. . . ." [26]

Unhappily for the new partnership, on May 10th, 1832, the "House" of Yates and McIntyre, much of whose cornucopia of lottery dollars had long been upturned into the Doctor's lap, suddenly tipped it to pour its thousands into the pockets of the lottery contractors themselves. How much of the Doctor's real estate hazard from that time on had been dangerously increased neither man could then know, for the Doctor was not yet aware of the extent of Yates and McIntyre's determination to dry up the flow of money into his "President's Fund," and, too, neither of them could have predicted the consequences of Andrew Jackson's growing annoyance with the Bank of the United States.

Captain Bliss, that May, executed his bond for $200,000 to the Doctor to cover his obligation to pay him half that sum in three years for what the Doctor had invested in the S.S. *Novelty*, and which, in case of forfeit, would give the Doctor sole ownership of their boat. The view, at least, for both men from Burnt Mill Point that spring of 1832 was an awesome spectacle. As their S.S. *Novelty*, lengthened and newly engineered largely according to the Captain's specifications, left her slip that April, the smoke from her four stacks as she sailed up the East River also measured their town-to-be at Greenpoint, their Navy Yard to be created at Newtown Creek, and a Stuyvesant Cove waiting for its land fill.

The development of this dream of acres, however, now had to wait on a hoped-for change in the Doctor's newly embittered relations with his lottery managers, as well as on his health which, by Commencement that July, had seemed so precarious to "Pinky" Pearson, and finally, on the star-crossed fortunes of the S.S. *Novelty* itself, though on April 28, 1832, "Dr. Nott's boat," as she had long been called, sailed north, "new and in the best of condition." [27]

CHAPTER 2

"*Coal mountains into gold mountains.*"

ONE suspects the *Novelty* at this juncture was more Captain Bliss's boat than she was the Doctor's. The changes made in her, however, had been designed to put the *Novelty* in a position to challenge the fleet of so-called "first class boats" then being used "for the convenience of passengers" between New York City and Albany, boats which could easily have outdistanced the original *Novelty*.

"Successful competition for the business of this noble river," according to a report in Silliman's *Journal* in 1833, meant speed and more speed: Fulton's *Clermont*, that "mill on a raft" of 1807, had churned north to Albany in thirty-six hours; the *Paragon* in 1820 had made the trip in twenty-seven hours; six years later the *New Philadelphia* cut the trip to twelve hours and twenty-three minutes, and on May 31, 1832, the *Novelty*, her four stacks unique among these "boats of the first class," made a record run down river to New York City in nine hours and forty-seven minutes and soon afterward in nine hours and eleven minutes. [1]

There was probably not much experimenting with anthracite furnaces during the *Novelty's* two years of competitive sailing, what with tight schedules of as many as twelve stops each way, six of them usually at wharf side. Although the newspapers treated the Hudson River boats as though they were race horses, there was already nostalgia for the old days of the tow-barges, "discontinued," according to one traveler, "to the regret of those who love quiet enjoyment, and whose nerves have not been inured to composure by frequent proximity to the moving power." [2]

Though the "*Novelty*" seems to have been in mechanical matters largely Bliss's boat at this time, the Doctor had paid, through H. Nott and Company, the accumulating costs of rebuilding her. Beginning in 1833, he personally battled the new and powerful Hudson River Association on her behalf, a confederation formed in the spring of that year, made up of the Troy, the Hudson River, and the North River lines, a self-constituted arbiter of sailing schedules.

In his two letters to the Association's directors who had barred the *Novelty* from the Association's timetable of sailings, the Doctor's indignation burned as hot as his draught-blown anthracite; he was conscious, he wrote first, "that monopolies are odious," a phrase, however, he tactfully crossed out in his final letter, and for which he substituted the statement that he was aware "that the number of boats on the river is large . . . ," but "that the demand for accommodation will soon overtake the supply." [3]

The Hudson River Association had offered the *Novelty's* owner a special contract which the Doctor had flatly rejected: he would not, he wrote, "start the *Novelty* between 10 and 11 o'clock with any other boat, however inferior which the directors may choose to associate with her and which they shall be at liberty to withdraw whenever it may suit their convenience . . .". The *Novelty*, he pointed out, "is a new boat and a popular boat . . . ," and had been running successfully on the river "before the foundation of the present association, and she cannot, therefore," he insisted, "by any couler [*sic*] of reason be at this time excluded from it." The capital investment in the *Novelty*, he wrote, "is so great I cannot afford to sacrifice it." He, too, he assured the directors, had "rights . . . and friends . . . ."

The Directors of the Hudson River Association were apparently intimidated by the Doctor's vehement claim to his "rights," or to "friends," or both, and so, during May, 1833, the *Novelty* was again on the river, under the command now of Captain Wiswall, as one of the boats of the Association's "10 o'clock line," alternating her sailings with the *"Champlain."* During that month she broke the northbound record, steaming from New York City to Albany in nine hours and forty-five minutes, including nine stops, a record she held for the rest of that summer.[4]

"Doctor Nott's boat . . . ," beginning that fall, could not have sailed into worse luck if she had carried the Ancient Mariner as a passenger. Competition between the paddle wheelers was becoming nearly ruinous as travelers shifted their favor. Races between boats developed, and the bursting of their pipes and boilers became a standard feature of the newspapers. Warnings of the coming Jackson Depression were noted by men like Philip Hone, late Mayor of New York City and a director of the Delaware and Hudson Canal Company, who reported in December "that stocks have fallen prodigiously."[5] The Hudson River Association cut fares from $3.00 to $2.00 at the height of the season the next year in order to meet the challenge of the new "People's Line." Within two years regulation was dead, and the paddle wheelers sailed on helter skelter schedules, packing their decks with as many as they could hold at fifty cents a head for the full trip up or down the river. Sometimes a clutch of boats would leave Albany, jammed with bargain hunting travelers, followed within minutes by a single vessel which had not made the docks in time, its decks empty.[6]

Between midsummer, 1834, and the following October the Doctor wrote to R. P. Hart of Troy, New York, President of the Rensselaer and Saratoga R. R. Company, in answer to an inquiry as to whether the S.S. *Novelty* was for sale: "The *Novelty*", the Doctor then assured his correspondent "was little injured and is repaired and ready for receiving her boilers and engines," testimony enough that she had met with some kind of accident.[7] Nowhere does the Doctor reveal the bargaining ethics others had criticized in him better than in this letter in which he tried to unburden himself of a now apparently damaged *Novelty*. "She had," he assured his inquirer, "but a single owner, but though there may be a lien on her by others, I have no doubt it will be well for the Association to purchase and for Mr. [Bliss] to sell the *Novelty*—if, indeed, he can sell her without too great a sacrifice. When I last saw him I advised him to get out of the business and he seemed quite disposed to do so—if he could consistently."

"Since I saw him a project has been got up for refitting the *Novelty* in such a manner as to render her a faster and more agreeable boat—and unless the suggestion contained in your letter shall eventuate in her purchase I have no doubt she will be so fitted up—this would be peculiarly satisfying to the pride of Mr. Bliss, and may induce him to prefer running her after she had been improved to selling her in her present state. I shall communicate with him on the subject and if desired shall be happy to be instrumental in bringing about a satisfactory and final arrangement.''

After the 3rd of October, however, neither the Association nor R. P. Hart of Troy were interested in buying the *Novelty*. On that date, bereft of her own power, loaded with a cargo of the Doctor's "Saracenic Stoves," and under tow, headed apparently for Albany and the refitting the Doctor had mentioned, she ran onto the shoals of the "Overslaugh" below the Capital, where she sank.[8] As for Captain Bliss, according to a report in the Schenectady *Democrat* sometime later,

> having met with so many disappointments, and his health in the meantime having failed, [he] though fully confident of the practicability of the original plan, was reluctantly induced to forego the prosecution of it himself, and to permit the whole concern to pass into other hands.[9]

On December 30, 1834, the Doctor exercised his right to take possession of the *Novelty*, and Neziah Bliss transferred her title to H. Nott and Company.

I I

> The period has now arrived (the New York *Journal of Commerce* reported on Monday, March 18, 1835) when anthracite will doubtlessly be extensively used as a fuel in steamboats. A steam ferry boat had been started in New York which has been fitted up with Dr. Nott's patent tubular anthracite coal boilers. This application of anthracite to the generation of steam in boats has been completely successful! Dr. Nott has been offered one hundred thousand dollars for his patent by the Messrs Stevens of New York, in the steamboat line, and this sum he has refused. The facts above stated are highly important to the anthracite coal regions. Dr. Nott deserves great credit for his enterprise and ingenuity. He will, in all probability, realize, together with a large portion of fame, the more substantial reward of a large fortune.[10]

By the 28th of March the stock in the Delaware and Hudson Canal Company had climbed to 122, "an advance of 34 percent in two weeks."[11]

Captain Bliss must have been convinced that he had been hasty in giving up his interest in the *Novelty* if he read the widely reprinted "letter from a gentleman in Philadelphia to a friend in Schuylkill County [Pa.]," written sometime early in April, following the run the *Essex* made "with a party of gentlemen on a trial excursion of forty or fifty miles upon the Hudson and in the Bay. . . .":

> I wrote . . . sometime ago on a contemplated invention by the learned and indefatigable Dr. Nott, of New York. . . . *Complete success* has attended the untiring labors of Dr. Nott . . . the *Essex* is now plying between New York and Jersey City, at the rate of 14 miles the hour. You will remark that this is a ferryboat, made for burden, and therefore, has nothing of the clipper about her. You may *infer*, therefore, what the speed of a *real model* for running must be—you will know all about this in the course of the next summer. The steamboat called the *Novelty* will bring out this wonderful experiment in all its grandeur and usefulness. [12]

The excited "gentleman from Philadelphia" then indulged himself in some glowing arithmetic: The *Essex* had burned two and a half tons of coal in twelve hours, therefore, a trip to Albany at fourteen miles an hour would consume four tons at a cost of about twenty dollars; the largest of the "North River Boats," he figured, would burn only seventy-five dollars worth of anthracite for the same trip, instead of the $375 in cord wood it was currently burning, a saving in an eight months season, at six trips a week, of about $19,200 in fuel alone. He was equally enthusiastic over the inevitable savings in labor costs: instead of the twelve firemen required on the largest of the North River boats, each of them paid at the rate of $20 per month, plus another ten dollars apiece for board, "Dr. Nott's invention requires, for the same boat, only four firemen," at a saving of $2,800 a season.

Not only the prospect of economy in the operation of "Dr. Nott's invention" stirred this reporter, but, he continued,

> this extraordinary man has so contrived his boilers as to superadd the great desideratum of *personal security*. Should a bursting of a boiler happen there will issue only a teapot of water, or a quantity so small as to endanger the life of no one. Then, again, all the dangers from sparks and from the ignition of the great bodies of wood . . . is effectively done away with. . . .

If the Doctor himself had written the final paragraph of this letter from "the gentleman from Philadelphia," he could not have summed up better his own faith that sanctity and profit had met once more in his new water tube boilers and furnaces:

> I always told you [the friend in Schuylkill County was informed] your coal regions were destined by *Providence* for greater ends than to furnish fuel for your parlor stoves and chambers. Already has Dr. Nott made a demand upon them for culinary purposes, and now, again, for the transporting of millions over the world, with all they deal in. . . .

The anthracite regions were kept posted about the Doctor's progress through the *Miners' Journal* of Pottsville, Pennsylvania, which quickly borrowed the Philadelphian's letter as it appeared in Poulson's *American Daily Advertiser*. The long awaited "prospect of transporting millions over the world, and all they deal in. . . ." seemed about to be realized by the mine operators on the eastern slopes of the Alleghenies.

There can be little doubt that it was a renewed partnership between the promoters of anthracite and the Doctor which had persuaded him to outfit the *Essex* with his water-tube boilers and furnaces, and then to a refitting of the *Novelty* for the third time. Shortly before Howard Nott signed his contract with the "Managers" of the Delaware and Hudson Canal Company on March 14, 1835, they had noted in their Board Minutes that

> there is no longer any reason to doubt the speedy adoption of anthracite coal as the fuel for generating steam in the boats in the North River. The experiments in which Dr. Nott has been engaged for several years have been brought to a satisfactory result, and arrangements are now making to start a passage boat of the first class on the North River, using Lackawanna coal under his patent Tubular Anthracite Coal Boilers. The boat is expected to be ready during the present season of navigation. [13]

The whistle of the *Essex* during March, 1835, served to sound the "open sesame" at last before the gates to that vast market for anthracite represented by the steamboat fleets of the world, and to justify the reported offer by the "Messrs Stevens" of the Hudson River Association of $100,000 for the Doctor's patent, issued on the 25th of April of that year "for Steamboilers and Furnaces." [14]

What, actually, had the Doctor finally accomplished? He had proved his small-bore multi-tube boilers were safer than the conventional great tanks of water sitting above their roaring pine-knot fires.

Tubular boilers, however, were not enough to explain the *Essex's* success. His new furnaces, too, were equally important. Steamboats commonly set their tank boilers on brick beds close to their hearths on which the pine wood fires were built. Heat was raised under them quickly and the flame was evenly distributed, usually through flues, but relatively soon the boiler and flue areas above the flames crusted and had to be replaced. The Doctor had finally solved the twin problems of fuel and boiler economy and efficiency by introducing anthracite, whose mysteries he well knew, as his source of "caloric." He developed a "molded brick" furnace or furnaces, set, not beneath his water-tube boilers, but between them, insulated from them by firebrick walls, and supplying the "caloric" to create steam in their water tubes through flues running from his furnace and controlled by dampers which gave a firm control over their water temperatures. [15] His anthracite hearths were controlled by forced air drafts combined with a supply of water vapor which fed the anthracite with enough additional oxygen to make his hearths, usually equipped with his rotary grates, as efficient as those which were burning up the forests of the river valleys.

In the *Essex*, then, he had finally joined a comparatively sophisticated combination of caloric developments, only two of them original, but, which taken together, became a new source of power; these justified the Phoenix-like reappearance of the *Novelty* in 1835, designed in collaboration with the Delaware and Hudson Canal Company, "to bring out this wonderful experiment in all its grandeur and usefulness."

The Doctor's confusion of commitments in 1835, however, and the nervous edging of the economy toward national disaster,—a year of "unparalleled high rates of labor, provisions and forages," according to the "managers" of the Delaware and Hudson Company,—seemed to have robbed the *Novelty* of the triumph which had been promised by the gentleman from Philadelphia for that summer. Howard Nott, the Doctor's son, was himself elected a "Manager" in October that year, and the following March joined his fellow managers in rewriting their contract with H. Nott and Company by adding a clause to it which may explain the Doctor's reported coolness to the offer of the "Messrs Stevens, of the old-line" for his boiler and furnace patents. In return for 1000 shares of Delaware and Hudson stock, worth then, at par, $100,000, H. Nott and Company agreed on March 1, 1836 to "run a steam passage boat on the North River using Lackawanna Coal, under Dr. Nott's patent Tubular Boilers, and with a speed equal that of any other boat on the river." [16]

The New York *American*, on June 22, 1836, carried the bare announcement that the *Novelty*, "using anthracite coal for fuel," would leave New York City for Albany the next day, Thursday, "at six o'clock a.m." The Albany *Evening Journal* carried the same notice that Thursday, adding the comment that it was doubtful if the Doctor's boat could equal the speed of the wood burning paddle wheelers.

By 6 A.M. Thursday morning, June 23, 1836, at least twenty-two were on board. Steam was up. Ezra Todd stood by the engines, and Captain G. E. Seymour, her new master, was waiting to pull away from the foot of Chambers Street. [17] Among the passengers were the "Managers" of the Delaware and Hudson Canal Company, including the ex-Mayor of New York City, Philip Hone, whose diary was to carry a record of this day's events. The Director of the Port of New York was also on board, as well as the famous D. B. Ogden whose reputation as a trial lawyer before the Supreme Court of the United States gave him special standing. Fortunately there was also a vigorous letter writer among them, perhaps the same "gentleman from Philadelphia," who had been on the *Essex* during her trial run that March. [18]

"The scene," according to the latter's ecstatic communication to the editor of the Philadelphia *Enquirer*, "was really a grand one. As the noble boat started from her moorings on the East River, a thrill of anxiety and mingled hope agitated the enterprising owners. But the harmonious working of the machinery, the onward motion of the boat, and the greetings of the multitude, with the complimentary ringing of the bells from numerous steamboats, which were responded to, made it an occasion for joy, . . . the result of the experiment was an absolute triumph." [19]

Never since Fulton succeeded (the editor of the Philadelphia *Enquirer* was then informed), has there been a greater victory in this department of science and of mind. It deserves a place in the volume of human benefits, alongside the achievement of the great man; and it will be placed there. Pennsylvania ought to be foremost in the acknowledgements of his discoveries. It strikes deep in her anthracite regions, and cannot fail in turning her coal mountains into gold mountains. Henceforth, the ocean will be the wide theatre for the consumption of the long hidden treasure. I predict that in 24 months from today, packets will be in motion to Liverpool, and Havre, and other places propelled by steam generated from anthracite coal; whilst rivers and bays and our own inland seas will be put in a foam by the flying, in all directions, of boats, under the impulse of that fuel which has, until lately, lain for ages undisturbed in the bosom of the mountains of Pennsylvania. . . . as to speed, the *Novelty* went 160 miles, blowing steam the whole way, in ten hours and twenty-seven minutes and, as is my conscientious opinion, could have performed it with ease in two hours less time.

The wind blew a gale from the west—the great extent of the upper works of the *Novelty* with her awnings all retarded her, and the tide against her, I may say, the whole of the way—or at least there was none in her favor—all goes to show what additional time might have been gained under a more favorable sky, and on the bosom of less turbulent and less opposing waters. . . .

Philip Hone, equally delighted with the performance of the *Novelty*, and a Pennsylvanian in his wish to see that state's anthracite mountains turned into solid dividends, wrote more objectively of that historic run to Albany: he gave the time as twelve hours, noted that "Dr. Nott has been engaged for several years in contriving machinery to accomplish this important object, and has now succeeded completely." [20] In much less detail than was used by the anonymous letter writer, Philip Hone then noted the facts which were closest to the hearts of his fellow "managers" of the Delaware and Hudson Canal Company:

The great desideratum was to contrive the means of igniting the coal, and producing a flame sufficient to create the steam. This has been effected by condensing hot air, which by injection into the bottom of the furnace accomplishes this object, and forces the flame into a chamber in which are a great number of iron tubes of the size of gun barrels, placed vertically. There are four of these furnaces. The quantity of coal consumed on this trip was about 20 tons (something less) which at $5 per ton amounts to $100. The same voyage would have consumed forty cords of pine wood, the present price of which is $8.00, making a difference of more than one-half. Dr. Nott, who was on board, has made experiments the result of which is, that the difference of expense on board the *Novelty* during one season will amount to $19,000. The *Erie* left New York an hour after us, and arrived two hours after our arrival, but she made the usual stops and we came directly on, so that their speed was nearly equal. The tide was against us all day, and there is a great freshet in the river. Dr. Nott has succeeded completely in this invention, which establishes the certainty that coal will succeed wood in our steamboats, and the Delaware and Hudson Company will hereafter be able to sell all the coal they can bring down the canal at an advanced price.

The New York City papers, the *Journal of Commerce*, the New York *American*, the New York *Herald* and the New York *Courier and Enquirer*, all reported on the Doctor's unqualifiedly successful demonstration that anthracite was, indeed, the fuel of the future. The editor of the *Herald*, on June 29th, headed his report, "New Era," and assured his readers that the Doctor's success "will cause a complete revolution in river, along shore, and even Atlantic navigation. It is confidently expected," he said, "that all trade between this country and Liverpool will soon be converted into steam lines of navigation." If so, he warned, "the handsome packet ships must seek employment elsewhere."

The encomiums in the New York *Courier and Enquirer*, also reprinted by the *Miners' Journal*, reached new heights of editorial "caloric":

> We invite the public's attention [to the "Card" signed by the *Novelty's* passengers] as announcing to the world an event, which to the people of the United States, is destined to prove only second to the grand discovery of Fulton himself. . . . it therefore may be truly said that if Fulton first applied the use of steam to boats—Nott has perpetuated it.

If the Doctor's success stimulated anthracite operators and big city editorial writers to visions of a revolution in water transportation, it excited a Schenectady commentator to high hopes for a revolution in railroad transportation:

> We are credibly informed [the Schenectady *Reflector and Democrat* reported] that the Utica and Schenectady Railroad Company have it in contemplation to try [the Doctor's] tubular boilers on their road . . . if the experiment succeeds, the railroad companies will be saved the expense of effecting insurance in buildings situated on the line of their roads, and the passengers will be able to travel with open windows, and with much more comfort than they do now.

The same writer had also seen "it announced in the New York papers that the Liverpool and New York Steam Navigation Company will construct their engine for the use of anthracite coal. A contract for a boat has already been made." [21]

III

Eliphalet Nott's new role of national benefactor, however, as the man who had capped the exploding costs of transportation, who had opened the ocean lanes to practical steam navigation, who had made "safety" a reality for the future on the North River boats, and so, hopefully, on all steamboats, needed more than the praises of the newspapers in order to sustain the role. His S.S. *Novelty*, "probably the longest boat in the world, [220 feet] . . . a floating palace . . . ," the safest, the most economical, and among the swiftest, within two weeks of her triumphant run to Albany on June 23, 1836, sailed into a slow turning maelstrom of events which the Doctor, in his moments of prophecy, had never foreseen.

Although the last advertisement for the Doctor's "New Line" appeared in the Albany *Argus* on August 20th, the *Novelty*, now an "opposition boat," continued in service until at least August 26th when the editor of the *Argus* published his thanks to Captain Seymour for delivering the New York City newspapers for the second time that month "in advance of the mail." The *Novelty* by now must have been especially galling to the directors of the Hudson River Association: anthracite coal for fuel, so clean, so economical, offered an advertising gambit they could not match;

here was a boat equipped with boilers proclaimed as the safest in marine use, capable of challenging the fastest of the "Old Line's" wood burners.

A "communication" to the *Argus* from "a party of 14 from New Jersey," who also arrived at Albany on the *Novelty* that August 26th, appeared in the paper the next day. If the Doctor had wanted a curtain speech to mark his final appearance as a steamboat entrepreneur he could hardly have improved on it:

> "An Elegant Trip Up the Hudson"
> We left New Jersey at 5 o'clock this morning and at 7 o'clock entered on the *Novelty*. In her at a rate of 17 miles an hour we reached the Highlands, and now at half past 5 p.m. we are two miles below Albany. This boat for neatness, pleasantness of arrangement, gentlemanly deportment of commander, order and propriety of table, and of attendants, surpasses any boat we have ever seen. The table furniture is elegant, and the cooking superior. The motion of the machinery easy, and from its horizontal action not subject to the unpleasant jar which is experienced on other boats. The annoyance from cinders and ashes is wholly avoided. We say unqualifiedly, we have never seen anything which can compare with this boat in all those respects which contribute to the comfort and pleasure of travellers. We must not forget the luxury of a fine soda fountain is had on board. While we would not detract from the merit of other boats, we say that it is evidently the best.

It was as though the young John Howard Payne, once the Doctor's precocious student, later the idol of the American and English stage, had walked off the boards to the thunderous applause of a Drury Lane audience, had torn up a long-run contract, and had then vanished from London. The S.S. *Novelty*, in mid-season, a marine sensation, now disappeared from the Hudson.

The only contemporary answer to the question, "What happened?" offered no satisfactory explanation. On September 7th the Albany *Argus* carried the following notice:

> *Novelty* has been purchased by the old-line of steamboats and has been withdrawn from the navigation of the river. We regret the circumstances, because it is of the highest importance to the travelling community both immediately as a matter of safety and economy, and remotely in reference to a supply of fuel that the experiment of burning anthracite coal should be fully tested.

The *Argus*, "regretted the circumstances . . . ," and what were these?

Benjamin Nott that April, in a "confidential" letter to Mayor Erastus Corning of Albany told Corning that H. Nott and Company "have sold out all its stock"; "what we intend to do," he had added, "You will of course see the propriety of my not writing." [22]

There seems little doubt that the *Novelty's* fate was one with the fate of Cornelius Vanderbilt's "People's Line" in 1834, and with unsavory Daniel Drew's revived "People's Line" shortly afterward, when the murderous rate wars between the "Old Line" [the Hudson River Association], and such astute rivals as Vanderbilt and Drew were solved by the Association by the simple and costly expedient of buying them out: Vanderbilt's boats for $100,000 plus $5000 for each of the ten years he agreed to stay off the river, and Daniel Drew, who is reported to have reinstituted the "People's Line" in order to blackmail the Association, for $50,000 plus $10,000 for each of the years he and his partners sailed their boats elsewhere. [23]

The New York *Herald*, on May 3, 1839, indignantly reviewing the monopoly's operation for the preceding four years, noted that "rivals have been removed by purchase, threat, or by running into them. . . . It is a curious fact," the writer noted, "that there are some steamboat captains now in this city (who have been bought off the North River line by the old monopoly company) who walk about the streets with their hands in their breeches pockets, and who are each receiving from $5,000 to $10,000 annually for staying in the city doing nothing. . . ."

Between 1835 and 1839, the *Herald* reported to an indifferent public, the Old Line had paid out over a quarter of a million dollars to buy off the competition in order to maintain its three dollar rate. Among its purchases was the S.S. *Novelty*, price not revealed.

The Albany *Argus* in 1836, and the New York *Herald* in 1839, might lament the abandonment of the public interest by those who controlled the monopoly and by those who sold out to them, but Eliphalet Nott was too much the "Doctor" of the Literature Lotteries, too much the practicing psychologist who taught his seniors how to manipulate the opportunistic nature of man to have any illusions that the S.S. *Novelty* alone could win against the Hudson River Association. That cartel wanted no threat to its rate control, and quite probably, no constant reminder to its patrons that there was a boat on the river whose water-tube boilers made its own boats obsolete, a "novelty" in boats whose use of anthracite was a challenge to its three dollar fare, as well as a challenge to those dealers in forests who had a vested interest in a now out-moded source of "caloric" for marine purposes.

By the end of November, 1836, H. Nott and Company, ostensible owners of the Novelty Works, were making their "second overture" to the Delaware and Hudson Canal Company in an attempt to stay in business. [24] If, they bargained, the Delaware and Hudson Canal Company's ' managers" would not press for collection of the notes due from H. Nott and Company that November and December, the Novelty Works would put "a new steamboat [significantly the word "new" is then crossed out in the draft of this "second overture"] on the North River, equipped with Dr. Nott's Patent Tubular Boilers and burning Lackawanna coal, to run from New York to Troy, or some point not short of Sing Sing . . . and to continue to run through the year 1837 . . ." H. Nott and Company promised further that, if their boat failed to run through 1837 the Delaware and Hudson Canal Company would no longer be bound to deliver to the Notts the 1000 shares of company stock according to the agreement of October 27, 1835.

This "second overture," however, seems to have been an academic exercise; by the end of 1836 the American economy was deflating too rapidly to save the Doctor's sons from bankruptcy. The following year the Delaware and Hudson Canal Company dropped Howard Nott from its Board of Managers, noting in the company's "Report" for 1837 that the year "was one of extraordinary and perhaps unparalleled difficulty . . . [with] pro-ductive labor and industry almost paralyzed, and business gen-erally brought down to a supply of the mere wants of the community."

The Jackson Depression altered the hopes of most Americans, including the Doctor's, as it dimmed the public memory of the S.S. *Novelty*. The name "H. Nott and Company" disappeared from the Novelty Iron Works sign over the sheds housing the stilled forges by the East River slip, and "Stillman, Allen and Company" took its place. The new managers were the Receivers of the tangible assets of the company, largely stove and engine castings.

If 1840 saw the first lifting of the economic pall for the nation, it also witnessed the last contemporary references to the S.S. *Novelty*. One of them occurs in Jonathan Pearson's "Thinking Books" and gives to the Doctor and to his by then legendary boat the dimensions of the folk tale into which Americans like to translate their villains and heroes:

> Dreadful accident! About half past 12 yesterday the steamboat *Novelty* blew up when opposite Hudson. Strange to tell not a single person was injured save the venerable Dr. Nott, owner and inventor of the improvements introduced into her machinery. He was thrown full five hundred feet into the air and entirely cloven in two . . . and one half falling in the city of Hudson and the other half in the village of Athens. These places are at war about their prospective rights to do honour to his remains by giving a public burial and placing a monument over the illustrious man . . . both claiming to have the venerable Dr. Nott. The cause of this melancholy accident is said to have been sheer carelessness—the Dr. sat across the safety valve at the moment of the explosion.

"Who," wrote the then new Professor of Chemistry and of Natural Philosophy at Union College, "made this lie?" [25]

Finally, on September 8, 1840, buried among more exciting matters in an Albany newspaper, was a notice one may read either as the real obituary of that strangely starred boat, or as an announcement of her rebirth:

> Steamboat *Eureka*, Captain Sherman, using boilers transferred from the *Novelty*, makes her first appearance. [26]

After 1840 neither the Monopoly, the "dislike of innovation," nor the willful rejection of boat builders bent on speed at the cost of safety could hold back the "New Era" in steam navigation promised by the editor of the New York *Herald* the week after the S.S. *Novelty* had pioneered the way. During 1840 Isaac Newton, long a director of the "Old Line," put two new boats "of the first class" on the Hudson, the *North River* and the *South America*, each of them designed to burn anthracite. [27]

The marine historian seldom mentions the sources of power used in the new boats; an occasional record, however, indicates the steady substitution of hard coal for wood. In 1846 the *Thomas Powell*, designed for anthracite furnaces, was put on the Newburgh-to-New York run; she was soon "a favorite of the public . . . and of more than average good speed." [28] The next year Isaac Newton added the *New World* to his fleet of North River boats, for a time the most glamorous boat on the Hudson; she "owed her source of power to the versatile Eliphalet Nott of Union College." [29] That anthracite as a fuel for steamboats was winning its way with little public notice, however, is testified to again in the records of the Delaware and Hudson Canal Company: in 1840 their annual "Report" declared that "complete success by this time [has] attended the use of anthracite in steamboats," and, twelve years later, in 1852, their "managers" noted that the year had seen "a rapidly increasing demand from sea-going steamers for 'Lackawanna' coal."

The Doctor's water-tube boilers and anthracite furnaces, costly to build and to maintain, had to wait for general use on the development of those "sea-going steamers" with their better engines, iron sheathing, strict safety inspections, and the screw propeller which made them truly competitive with sail in the decades following the Civil War. The S.S. *Novelty*, however, in 1836, had, indeed, opened the "New Era" in transportation. [30]

"VIEW OF THE CITY OF ALBANY, FROM THE OPPOSITE SIDE OF THE HUDSON RIVER." The steamer in the foreground may represent Nott's *S.S. Novelty.* Drawn and engraved by J. H. Hall for the *American Journal of Scientific and Useful Knowledge,* where it appeared in Vol. I, no. 1, 1835. Photograph, from this same illustration in *The Reflector and Schenectada* [sic] *Democrat* of 11 December, 1835, Schaffer Library, Union College.

ELIPHALET NOTT. Bust by Henry Kirke Brown. Owned by Union College;
photograph, Schaffer Library, Union College.

CHAPTER 3

"I am the oldest president in the United States."

Mr. C., "Dr., how long have you been at the head of Union
  College?"

Dr. N., "Thirty years. I am the oldest president in the United
  States, though I am not the oldest man in office. I
  cannot drop down anywhere in the Union without
  meeting some of my children."

"Mr. C." (Ira Clisby of the Class of 1815), in company with a
group of young lawyers, clergymen, and college tutors, had
persuaded the Doctor, who had been discovered relaxing at a
Saratoga hotel during the summer of 1833, to favor them with a
"conversation."[1] The Doctor obviously enjoyed this respite from
the angry exchanges of his Chancery suits, his arguments with
Captain Neziah Bliss, the cautious correspondence with the
Hudson River "Monopoly" over scheduled sailings for the S.S.
Novelty, and probably from Mrs. Notts's querulousness, "a
scolding helpmate," who, according to "Pinky" Pearson, a Union
College junior that year, "on many slight pretenses berates the
poor old man soundly with her unruly tongue."[2]

In any event, the "conversation" gave the Doctor free rein.
One meets, for a rare moment, the aging President as his "young
gentlemen" knew him, an anomaly to his contemporaries, as
radical in his thinking as the youngest of his hearers that summer's
day, a teacher whose unorthodoxies were rooted in a Christian
optimism which, however, blinded him with few illusions about
the world or his fellow men. The core of these comments seems
always to bear on the nature of man, on its malleability, and its
inconstancy, and on the fact that man is a creature ruled through
his emotions.

"Mr. C." began the dialogue with the cheerless remark that nearly half the members of the class of 1815 were dead. The Doctor, though mildly shocked, agreed that it was quite usual for many graduates to die soon after leaving college: "I can assign no other reason," he told his concerned hearers, "than the marked change which then takes place in the student's whole manner of living, diet, etc."

He then told the company that his "little anticipatory notes" about his students had been "generally fulfilled." Through suggestion, not by shows of authority, that was the way he managed them.

"Mr. C." next asked the question which marked some of them as novices preparing to be prudes and which allowed the Doctor to take them all into the area of his deepest convictions:

> *Mr. C.* We have been seeking amusement and profit by some exercises in elocution. Mr. G. and myself have been trying to read Shakespeare a little; but some gentlemen here have had some qualms of conscience as to the propriety of it, and have condemned the reading of Shakespeare as demoralizing. What is your opinion, sir?
>
> *Dr. N.* Why, as to that, I always say to my young men, "Gentlemen, if you wish to get a knowledge of the world and of human nature, read the Bible. The Bible is the first and the best book that can be studied for the exhibition of human character . . . if you will read other books, read Homer and Shakespeare. They come nearer, in my estimation, to Moses and Paul, in their delineations of human character than any other authors I am acquainted with. I have always taught my children to read them. . . .

"A knowledge of the world and of human nature . . . ," read the Bible for it, not as a theologian, but as a psychologist; study Homer's battlefields of maimed hopes, and the whims of heroes and double-dealing gods, and that dark world of cross purposes Shakespeare knew so well, and the wonderful make-believe of his comedies: "all these [authors] come nearer, in my estimation in their delineations of human character," the Doctor told this circle of young Americans, "than any other authors I am acquainted with." The Doctor had his own villains and his own battlefields that year, some of them within hailing distance of his hotel, for Chancellor Walworth's summer home was in Saratoga Springs, and

Chancery suits were known to be argued in his living room. The Doctor had no intention of letting "Mr. C." divert him:

> Ministers as a class, know less practically of human nature than any other class of men. As I belong to the fraternity, I can say this without prejudice. Men are reserved in the presence of a respectable clergyman. I might live in Schenectady, and discharge all my appropriate duties from year to year, and never hear an oath, nor see a man drunk; and if someone should ask me, 'What sort of a population do you have in Schenectady, Are they moral people? Do they swear? Do they get drunk? for aught I have seen or heard I might answer that this is after all a very decent world. There is very little vice in it. People have entirely left off the sin of profaners, and as to intemperance, there is very little of that.' But, I can put on my greatcoat and an old slouching hat, and in five minutes place myself amid the scenes of blasphemy and vice and misery which I could never have believed to exist had I not seen them. So a man may walk along Broadway and think to himself, 'What a fine place this is! How civil people are! What a decent and orderly and virtuous place New York is!' While at the same time within thirty yards of him are scenes of pollution and crime such as none but an eyewitness can imagine. I would have a minister see the world for himself. It is rotten to the core.

He was no stranger, in the summer of 1833, to New York City. Not the innocence of ministers, however, but the cynicism of lawyers was much on his mind, as he turned to a class of men, he told "Mr. C." and his friends, who "are brought into contact with dishonesty and villainy in their worst developments. . . .

> I have observed, in doing business with lawyers, that they are exceedingly hawk-eyed and jealous of everybody. The omission of a word or a letter in a will, they will scan with the closest scrutiny, and while I could see no use for any but the most concise and simple terms to express the wishes of the testator, a lawyer would be satisfied with nothing but the most precise and formal instrument, stuffed full with his legal caveats and technicalities.

One remembers the Doctor's cautious wording and rewording of his Yates and McIntyre contracts, of his own carefully imprecise "supplementary agreements" with his lottery contractors, and of his language of "legal ownership" by which he had established his own and his Trustees' claims to hundreds of thousands of dollars of lottery profits, all of it exercises in "caveats and technicalities."

In answer to "Mr. C's" question as to who was the more eloquent, ministers or lawyers, the Doctor had no hesitation in claiming the greatest eloquence for lawyers. Why?

> The superior influence of the things of sight over things of faith. The nearness of objects enhance their importance. The subjects on which the lawyer speaks come home to men's business and bosoms. Some present and immediate object is to be gained. The lawyer feels, and he aims to accomplish something. But ministers have plunged into the metaphysics of religion, and gone about to inculcate the peculiarities of a system, and have neither felt themselves, nor have been able to make others feel.

The lawyer "feels," and ministers do not. Lawyers deal in tangibles "that come home to men's business and bosoms." The clergy, walled off from the world by naivete and metaphysics, which the Doctor certainly was not, fail, he said, because they "want knowledge of human nature." Although the Doctor did not say it to this circle of young men in Saratoga Springs in the summer of 1833 there was little doubt that his own worldly successes stemmed from his ability to play the lawyer as well as the minister.

"Teach men to think and feel," he told his listeners, as he concluded what seems to have been a peroration on the two groups of men he knew best. As for formal instruction in how to become eloquent, however, he added, "I should about as soon teach a man to weep or to laugh, or to swallow, as to speak when he has anything to say."

"Mr. C." now turned this "conversation" which seems to have been anything but that, to the theatre where, he claimed, the tragedians generated eloquence at will. The Doctor, again emphasizing his arguments for naturalness and the eloquence of the heart, put "Mr. C's" tragedians into proper focus:

> Ah, the speaking in the theatre is all overacted. There is no nature in it. These actors, placed in a public assembly, and called upon to address men on some real and momentous occasion, would utterly fail to touch men's hearts while some plain countryman, who never learned a rule of

art, would find his way at once to the fountains of feeling and action within them. The secret of the influence which is felt in the acting in the theatre is not that it is natural. Let a real tragedy be acted, and let men believe that a real scene is before them, and the theatre would be deserted. No audience in this country could ever bear the presentation of a natural and real tragedy. Men go to the theatre to be amused.

"Mr. C.," however, was not to be put off: "Why is it," he asked the Doctor, "that when Kean appeared on the stage he engrossed all ears and eyes, and nothing else was seen or thought of but himself? The acting of Kean was just as irresistible as the whirlwind. He would take up an audience of three thousand in his fist, as it were, and carry them where he pleased, through every extreme of passion."

The Doctor's answer was the answer which "proved" his rule, a test of it that must have won the admiration of the listeners:

> Because these actors were great men. Cooke, as far as I have been able to learn (I never saw him . . . I once had an engagement to meet him in Philadelphia, but he was drunk at the time and disappointed me) was perfectly natural. So I suppose Kean to have been. So was Garrick, so was Talma. And the secret of these men was that they burst the bonds of art and histrionic trick, and stood before their audiences in their natural, untrammeled strength.

"Mr. C.," apparently convinced, then asked the Doctor if he had heard Webster?

> I have never heard him speak. I have had the pleasure of a slight personal acquaintance with him, and from what I know of him I should say he would have less power over the passions of men than Hamilton. He is a giant, and deals with great principles rather than passions.

The "conversation" then turned to consider what the Doctor thought of man in his most unnatural posture: man, the religious sectarian:

> *Dr. N.* I am disgusted and grieved with the religious controversies of the present age. The division of schools, old school and new school, and the polemical zeal with which the controversy is waged, are entirely foreign to the true spirit of Christianity. The Christianity of the age is, in my view, most unamiable. It has none of those lovely, mellow features which distinguish primitive Christianity. If Christianity as it

now exists should be propagated over the world, and thus the Millennium be introduced, we should need two or three millenniums before the world would be fit to live in.

The Doctor had always offered himself to his "young gentlemen" as a seeker, one to whom the spreading sectarianisms of the day marked the limitations of blinkered men. His sermons on the Resurrection were already well known to generations of Union College students; they offered no comfort to quarrelling Christians. Christ, for Eliphalet Nott, was, first, the historic carpenter of Nazareth, then the Son of God and, finally, the embodiment of Natural Law. The Doctor preached the literal Trinity when his hearers were capable of comprehending no more. He also preached the *idea* of Christ, an idea which he believed grew in dimension as men grew wise, until the Trinity became the unknowable, until one could accept as a way of life the unending challenge to comprehend Natural Law.

II

Others than "Mr. C." and his circle also knew a different Doctor Nott during these years of Chancery suits and caloric experiments, a man different, too, from the "Doctor" known to his lawyers, or to Captain Neziah Bliss.

Clarkson, his small grandson, had recently heard from Grandfather Nott about "Rattler," the new colt he had just bought, and was told by his grandfather to let his mother know that "John" and "Bill," the other horses, had been sold because there was no sense in keeping them as long as the Potters remained in Boston.[3] The sharp tongue of Gertrude Nott, his second wife, made an old man miss the happier voices of the Potter clan, and especially the companionnship of Maria Potter, Clarkson's mother, whose gaiety had always been a reminder of his household in those simpler days in Albany, when Joel and John and Benjamin were satellites to their sister Maria, and all of them made their orbits about the mother who seemed still with him when her daughter, Maria Potter, was in Schenectady.

Union College students knew the Doctor in a dozen revealing ways. Henry Wikoff, known later as "chevalier" Wikoff, the engaging mountebank, friend-to-be of Napoleon III, of the ballerina Fanny Elssler, and of the editor James Gordon Bennett, wrote in his *Reminiscenses of an Idler* of his arrival at Union College in 1831, after Yale had ordered him to leave New Haven:

> 'I know all about you [the Doctor had said] . . . you have recently been dismissed from Yale.'
>
> Though taken aback, I ventured to say, 'it was hard to lose my diploma for a single offense,' and I looked up appealingly. 'Your character is not of the best,' he returned. 'I fear you will be anything but a good example, and I have had bad fellows enough to deal with.' 'Depend on it, Mr. President,' I expostulated, 'if you will give me another chance, I will never cause you to regret it.' 'I have my doubts,' he said in his blunt way, 'but if you can pass I will admit you.'
>
> On the beginning of the term the good-hearted President summoned me to say that he had assigned my quarters in his immediate neighborhood, and meant to keep his eye on me. I knew of his infinite delight in detecting a delinquent, and he was said even to disguise himself at times for that purpose. It was not unlikely that I should put his dexterity to the test, for I discovered, to my horror, that no sooner were my troubles over than my love of frolic returned. . . . many a brisk drive had we [with his roommate, George Brisbane, brother of Albert Brisbane, the Fourierite] . . . when Dr. Nott was in bed, all the way to Albany . . . before a railway was thought of, and only for the sake of a good supper . . . it was forbidden fruit, and that, to thoughtless youth, was irresistible. . . . with all his dexterity and vigilance, the good old President had utterly failed to get me in his grip, and I am sure thought none the less of me for eluding him. We parted the best of friends . . . when he handed me my diploma with a *bene exeat*. I shall always revere his memory.[4]

"Pinky" Pearson in 1835, the year before he returned to the campus as a young tutor, saw the students' Doctor through the eyes of a hero worshipper:

> In the greatest of all studies [Pearson wrote in the first volume of his "Thinking Books"] the study of mankind, Dr. Nott has acquired wonderful knowledge. He can read human nature as a book. Among all his contemporaries he has no equal as a cunning manager and governor. His word is law in Union. His will is only to be known to be obeyed, not servilely but cheerfully. Of all my acquaintances in college I never yet knew a student who did not love the Doctor as a father.

The next year, however, the new tutor was a little shocked at one of the Doctor's "pithy sayings and wise remarks;" "Schenectady is the town," (he reported the Doctor as saying) "under the horse's tail." Pearson hastily added that the Doctor's observation alluded to the old "Dorp's" filthiness; "correct enough in truth," Pearson wrote, "but rather vulgar withal."

Gulliver to the Lilliputians was no more awesome than was the Doctor to his students on those memorable occasions when, seemingly from nowhere, he would loom up in the midst of one of the frequent town-gown fracases. The class of 1832 remembered what he did to their war plans, though he was in Albany when the members were mustered, and, defying the faculty, marched out to meet a gang of roughs.

Armed with guns, clubs, and pistols, the angry students were amazed to see the Doctor's carriage pull up in front of their forces, though how word had got to him in Albany no one knew. The class historian recalled that the Doctor entered "at once in sympathy" with their plans; he told them they were right, that it would be cowardly and degrading to submit; at the same time he told them there was a policy in war, and that he would espouse their cause if they would listen to his advice: "With ten of your party I can whip an army of roughs." The Doctor then picked ten leaders, and sent the arms and the rest of the boys back to their studies. He and his phalanx of ten students then marched off "to resist the stand of roughs."

The Doctor, facing the enemy, immediately called attention "to the smallness of his party." He pointed out to the townies that they should recognize the good in his boys, that "the foundations of the business world rests on their shoulders . . ." He went on to ridicule neighborhood quarrels, and to point to the value of peace and good order, and the childishness of throwing "brickbats and mud." "He won the mastery," according to the class historian; "the roughs set up a cheer . . . a bloodless victory was won."[5]

The heroics of these occasions no doubt grew in the telling, but to the great majority of his "young gentlemen" the Doctor was to remain always the man who could outsmart, out-talk, and out-finance any competition. He had broken out of the mold of the traditional college head: the theologian-scholar, the sectarian minister. The Doctor had become to most of his students the archetype of the successful American whose touch was Midas, and whose authority rested on his ability to deal with men who, as he loved to demonstrate, are moved by the unfathomable promptings of their human nature.

III

The Eliphalet Nott who had nothing but scorn for the anti-Shakespeare pieties of some of "Mr. C's" circle in 1833, who wrote of "Rattler" the colt to his grandson, who longed for the return of his daughter Maria as his warfare with the House of Yates and McIntyre opened in 1831, and who endured the sharp tongue of an ailing wife from whom, perhaps, he had found escape in his "experimenting room" on the campus, or in the less articulate clangor of the Novelty Iron Works, was no better prepared for the future which the Jackson Depression was to force upon him than was his grandson Clarkson for that straitjacket role of "Temperance Boy" his grandfather counseled him to accept.

On March 15, 1837, the then young Tutor Pearson summed up the tragic shift in the national life which accounted, in part, for the new attention he also declared the Doctor was beginning to give to his neglected professions of clergyman and of college president:

> 'Hard Times' is in everybody's mouth—but as to the cause all differ. 'Down with the banks!', 'away with your rags!' cry the Loco Focos. 'Metallic currency and easy times!' say the True Bentonians. The Jackson men curse the Monster, the opposition the Specie Circular. Some say the short crops and the influx of immigration cause the scarcity of provisions, and the great body of the people lay the 'Hard Times' at the doors of·the Speculators. Our banking system is corrupt. . . .

And again, on May 22nd:

> the 'pressure' reaches every village and hamlet and paralyzes every sort of business. The rich and the poor equally suffer or I might say the poor laborer is the chief sufferer for he is thrown out of employ and left to starve with his needy family. The New York merchants and mechanics are particularly great sufferers—nearly 22 large houses have fallen a sacrifice to the Gold Experiment of General Jackson and from this point the 'pressure' is moving northward through New England and shutting up the cotton mills and throwing hundreds of laborers out of work. . . .

Henry David Thoreau, when, ten years later, he closed the door on his cabin at Walden Pond, declared that he had "other lives to live," a remark Eliphalet Nott could well have made in 1837. The Concord pencil maker had deliberately turned away from an industrializing America because he had a vision of a simpler and so a better life in Concord. Eliphalet Nott, too, had seen Eden, but it had been defined for him in the smoke of foundries and paddle wheelers, a vision no less mystical than Thoreau's was to be! The Doctor, however, had embraced the America Thoreau was to reject, an America in which an unforeseen Jackson Depression was a just portion of its manifest destiny.

"Since his failure last fall," "Pinky" Pearson, the young custodian of the college's reputations and skeletons reported, the Doctor "seems to have entirely left his affairs in the hands of his sons and turned his attention more to the College and the pulpit. He has preached more within three months than in the preceding five years. The Doctor is mending his ways."[6]

The receding turmoil of the chancery suits, the current pressures of the Jackson Depression and all it meant in terms of the Doctor's collapsed hopes for his *S.S. Novelty*, for the future of the Novelty Iron Works, and so for an immediate expansion of his "Grand Plan" for the College, these things fell away as he again occupied the pulpits of his ministerial neighbors.

"I went to hear Dr. Nott preach yesterday morning," young George Wright wrote from Troy to his father on February 26, 1838. "I always thought that those who praised him, as some do, were enthusiastic in his favor from feelings of personal liking and friendship. But I was mistaken. Yesterday's effort, although his voice is broken and weak, convinced me that he is the greatest orator of his day. For sublimity of image Clay nor Webster will compare with him. Nor had I any conception of the power of oratory. The whole congregation listened with breathleass attention from the commencement to the close. . . . his sermon . . . was all *committed* to memory too which has a good effect. Even on the orator's artificial control of voice and emphasis, he surpassed all men that I have heard and I can imagine what he *must* have been, the most eloquent man in America."

The Wizard, and a spate of other undergraduate critics, however, were not so kind as they spread their anonymous broadsides around the campus. Much of the bad feeling was prompted by the Doctor's failure to materialize the "Octagon", as one author called it, and those other buildings of Jacques Ramée's monumental campus plan which the Doctor had yet to translate into brick and mortar.

> In all this young literary wonder-world,
> Of all the doctors, give me Doctor Nott;
> Lord! what a map of wisdom is unfurled,
> When he exposes all the wit he's got.
> *Non tibe sanum erat sinceput*!
> When you your present situation did accept
> And left the *holier* for the *fatter* spot;
> For then religion lifted up her voice and
> Wept.
> I think it had been better, had you kept
> The place you held before, for it behooves
> A man, a minister of God y-clept;
> To go to preaching, not to *making stoves*;
> To do your Master's business where he moves,
> And not to speculate on *steamboat stock*;
> Your pious heat, your own quick *silver* proves
> It's down to *zero*, hard as is rock.
>
> (*The Wizard*, Union College, 1838)

It was easy for these undergraduate editors of the *Wizard*, the *Vision*, the *Frying Pan*, the *Spyglass*, the *Insinuator*, and the *Crucible* to rhyme and pun at the Doctor's expense, for they had committed little to the Union College he had created and they understood less of the optimist's world he had formed out of the splintering Calvinism of his New England boyhood, the rationale of the Scottish philosophers of Common Sense and his own unorthodox convictions about the nature of man.

The keeper of the "Thinking Books" had his own charges to lodge against the Doctor that first year of the Jackson Depression:

> I don't like the arrangement of the college concerns. Doctor Nott is President, Treasurer, Director, Trustees, and all. He makes tutors, professors, and other officers. He pays salaries, and fixes them. In fine, he is Union College, or rather Union College is his! His private concern altogether. Nobody else has a thing to do except as he directs, merely as his agents.[7]

Tutor Pearson, by then, had joined the shifting opposition of faculty members still common to every campus. He had his reasons for pique, however: by that July the "pressure," as he had called the spreading financial panic, was threatening his own salary. College income was so low General Dix of the Finance Committee reported that the Board "may, at the present meeting reduce all [salaries]."

Feast and Famine had their chairs at the Trustees' meeting held during the 1837 Commencement. There had never been so many students: 347 were registered; 147 had entered during that year. Eight "had been removed by death . . . six by the epidemic." Only Yale, the third oldest college in America, was then larger. As to prospects, even Yale might well be envious, for, though Union College was momentarily embarrassed, its income would be unequaled very shortly, if the arrangements made with the Doctor at the Trustees' meeting that July turned out as both he and the Board had no doubt they would.

They agreed "a separate fund to be denominated Doctor Nott's 'Fund' "—should be set up by Jonas Holland, the treasurer who had succeeded Henry Yates of the divided loyalties. Into Doctor Nott's "Fund" were to go those sums which, it was then agreed, belonged to him following a pro rata division between him and the college of the fruits of his Consolidated Lotteries contracts with Yates and McIntyre, and of his real estate speculations at Stuyvesant's Cove involving land sales above 12th Street and along the East River, and at Bushwick and Hunter's Point on Long Island, speculations inspired by Captain Neziah Bliss while he was superintendent of the Novelty Iron Works. The pro rata division, it was understood that July, would give to the Trustees a bookkeepers' settlement of $140,000 for "the responsibilities assumed . . . in behalf of Yates and McIntyre" by Union College, and to the Doctor $338,000, sums which were paid to him in addition to the money paid both to the college and to the Doctor on the original Literature Lottery contract.[8]

One wonders what thoughts ran through Trustee Henry Yates's mind as he listened to the terms of this settlement. He, as a member of the Board, was present that day, as were Governor Marcy, General Dix, Azariah Flagg, and Chancellor Walworth, those state officials and long time Albany Regency members who had speeded the recent Chancery suits to their out-of-court settlement that year. Ex-treasurer Henry Yates could only have felt the normal satisfactions as the Finance Committee also announced that the assignees of H. Nott and Company, whose Novelty Iron Works' assets were then being liquidated, were soon to repay over $100,000 to the college which had been advanced out of its funds to the builders of the S.S. *Novelty.*

"In fine," Tutor Pearson now wrote of that "old prex" he had so revered as a senior, "he is Union College."

I V

If Union College was a projection of Eliphalet Nott the financier, by 1837 the college also reflected in other ways his last ten years of almost unbelievable activity, so much of which had taken place away from the campus. His son-in-law, Alonzo Potter, had returned to Schenectady in 1831, much to the Doctor's delight, for his daughter, his beloved Maria and her family, were again close by. From then on sober sided Alonzo Potter had acted as the Doctor's Vice President, the resident authority during the latter's many absences.

Alonzo Potter, his high brow and jut chin symbols of his scholarship and firm principles, "the only bookmaker among us," Pearson once commented, was far more the conventional educator than was his father-in-law. "since his return from Boston," Pearson recorded in 1833, "this new rigour began."[9] Under Potter's influence the reins of student discipline were drawn tighter: the "Dorp's" new dancing school was put off bounds, "supper parties" at Schenectady taverns were strictly forbidden, and the embryo fraternities, the first college social fraternities in America, were denounced as "secret societies" by the Doctor before a chapel audience on December 3, 1832, when he thundered that "the first young man who joins a secret society shall not remain in College one hour!" This declaration young Pearson believed would crush them; "we may now consider them . . . extinct in three years," he noted, but then he figured without allowing for the Doctor's elasticity in the face of an opposition he discovered he could not curb. Within the year the ban on secret societies was lifted, and Union College lived on to be hailed across the land as the "Mother of Fraternities."

Alonzo Potter, though he tried to reform "the lax discipline of class instruction," had, for the time being "found the task too Herculean. . . ." [10] The "Senatus Academici" of 1837: six tutors, one Adjunct Professor, five full Professors, and a President who had left day-to-day operations to them while he planned for the future—were, with their Trustees, still unaware of the widening gulf opening before them.

The Doctor in 1837, along with his countrymen, stood surrounded with their successes, no one quite believing that destiny was taking away what it had given. The unrestrained optimism, however, which had energized Eliphalet Nott and most of America from the beginning of the century, was now gathering itself as a great wave which meets the up-tilting shelf of the continent; it had begun to crest, dark and vast, arching toward the land, moved by other laws than the watchers understood, to break two decades later in the churning chaos of the Civil War.

"New Schools, new Professorships, new Scholarships . . . and an Observatory . . ."

THE spring of 1839, if only for a brief moment, may have seemed to the Doctor to have about it something of that spring of 1805 when, as the new President of a frontier college, he had been filled with plans to make of Union a better instrument to serve God's will than he had been able to make of his Albany pulpit. Spring was again in the March wind, and the Doctor was once more devising fresh plans for his college and for himself. The years since 1805 had been seed years for American humanitarians. All about him men were cultivating new causes, new formulas for perfecting themselves and their neighbors. He, too, had commited himself to such enthusiasms as the temperance movement, to working for a renewed respect for the Sabbath, to prison reform. The new Whig Governor of New York, William Henry Seward, once his pupil and still his devoted admirer, had now turned to him for advice on matters of public education. By the spring of 1839, outchallenging every other summons to the humanitarians was the strident and impassioned one to deal with slavery.

The Doctor was free at last of lotteries, of stove making, of steamboat monopolies, of "banks and brokers," as he had written to ex-Comptroller Azariah Flagg, who was now an ex-Trustee. He was, he thought, secure in a fortune which, in an ever progressing America, could only grow larger. He was ready now to turn his time and his energy to being a leader among humanitarians, and of being again the full-time President of Union College, that guiding presence on the campus his son-in-law, Professor, and Vice President Alonzo Potter, was fast becoming.

What he was not prepared for, however, was the tragedy which, on March 16, 1839, moved like the umbra of an eclipse over his and the Potter households: "an entire community was thrown into the deepest sympathy of grief by the death of his only daughter," Dr. Backus, pastor of the First Presbyterian Church of Schenectady, recalled. For her father it was a shattering event, for Maria had been her mother incarnate. "She had made his home so bright, so like it of old, when her mother was its gladness," Dr. Backus remembered, adding that "no one could mistake the potency in that ever to be remembered loving influence." [1]

"The blow fell upon all alike," her husband, Alonzo Potter, wrote to their close friend President Wayland at Brown, "it was not until about three minutes before she expired that I became really alarmed . . . so confident was the feeling of her physician . . . that he left her and went to the North College. Becoming disturbed, however, at her continued faintness, I sent for him, and though he returned immediately, all that was done seemed to have no effect on her pulse, and she sank [in] about four hours, after having given birth to her seventh child—her first daughter. . . . sometimes the thought rushes in on me that more, much more, might have been done to save her life. But I dare not entertain the thought: 'that way madness lies' ". [2]

Three days following Maria's death her father's thoughts turned back to Connecticut, to his older brother to whom he could speak of the magnitude of his grief:

> She was a very dear child [he wrote], and to me so needful in my old age. I had hoped she would attend my death-bed and close my eyes, but God has ordered otherwise. She was my strongest tie to earth, and it is broken . . . .She was a Christian of no common order, and was, I trust, ripe for heaven, whither I hope she has gone and whence I would not, if I could, recall her. I will go to her; she will not—and I rejoice that she will not—return to me. . . .
>
> What a mysterious Providence is the death of Maria! She has left seven children; all small, one an infant. . . . I am sure it is wise and merciful, and, though I cannot understand, I can trust the dispensation of my Heavenly Father. He will provide for these motherless children. He can sanctify this death to them, to me, to all. . . . Be that as it may, our work is nearly done. And, in looking back I can appropriate the words of the preacher, 'Vanity of vanities, all is vanity'. [3]

One measure of these two men, Maria's father and her husband, the Doctor and Professor Alonzo Potter whose expectations of succeeding his father-in-law as the President of Union College now began to wither, can be read in these letters they wrote following Maria's death. Professor Alonzo Potter, even in his grief, wrote in the scholarly literary periods which marked him as the academic man: "Life seems to me little more than a scene of broken vows and resolutions," he wrote to a former Boston parishioner, "and after all I have experienced of the uncertainty of and vanity of life, of the necessity there is in all of us for more grace, and of the sufficiency which we find in it for our support when we make it our trust, under such circumstances nothing is more amazing to me than that my affections should still revert so fondly to the world. . . ." [4]

"I will go to her," Maria's father had written in the simplicity of his grief; "she will not—and I rejoice that she will not—return to me. . . ." One suspects that Maria's death left so great a void in the Doctor's life that whatever thoughts he may have had of turning the presidency over to Alonzo Potter faded now as he sought to fill the void with new plans both as an educator and, because his energies outmatched his years, as a man of causes.

The Potter household of seven children was, for a time, broken up. Maria's cousin, Sarah Benedict, adopted the infant daughter, Maria Louisa; the four youngest boys went to live with another of Maria's relatives, the next oldest boy remained at a Troy boarding school, and Clarkson, a Union undergraduate that year, continued to live with his father.[5] Two years later Professor Alonzo Potter married Sarah Benedict, and the children were gathered together again in South College.[6]

For the Doctor, however, there was only a great loneliness. His second marriage had its rewards, but Gertrude Nott had been ill most of their years together. They had lost a child ten years after their marriage, and their son Howard, and Maria's three brothers, Joel, Benjamin, and John, each had their own orbits, circling close to or distantly from their father as they needed him.[7] Howard, soon after Maria's death and the confused affairs of H. Nott and Company were settled, came back to the college as Registrar. Joel and Benjamin, who had married into the wealthy

Cooper family of Albany, set themselves up as gentlemen farmers; and John Nott, the Reverend John Nott, lame, with a lurid reputation among Union College undergraduates as a philanderer, who had lived from 1830 to 1839 in his father's shadow as a tutor of rhetoric, became pastor of the Reformed Church of Rotterdam, New York, as well as Assistant Professor of Rhetoric at Union.[8]

If Maria Potter's death and the faltering economy were to have far reaching consequences for Eliphalet Nott, so, too, was the end of the sixteen years of dominance of the Albany Regency over New York State politics. The Jackson Depression changed not only the complexion of the government in Albany, but also the control of the Union College Board of Trustees. There could be no thought of retirement now for the Doctor, with new men to be shaped into useful Board members, to be brought into his designs for the college as he had once brought Governor Marcy, and other State officers, and their predecessors back through the years of the lotteries.

> Pedagogues, you know, claim an interest *ex-officio* in pupils they have trained up [so the Doctor wrote early in July, 1839, to Governor Seward, elected in the Whig landslide the preceding November] : and especially in those who share in the honors of those whose minds they have aided in forming—and the glory thus achieved is held in all orthodox schools to be a kind of common property to be divided between the teacher and the taught. . . . I have too much confidence in your filial piety toward your Alma Mater to suspect that you require, even to be put into remembrance. . . . the meeting of the Board of Trustees of which you are a member will be on the afternoon of the 23rd—I have desired to see you on some account, previous to the commencement—and if when you come to town you will come on the hill I will have a bed in keeping for you and it will give me pleasure to have you with us—tho, since the death of my daughter we are less able than before to make our friends happy as we are at board with the person who has taken Dr. Potter's house—but still we can make them comfortable.[9]

The State's chief officers continued to be, technically, a majority of the Board, and the Doctor, an expert in human relations, must have been especially glad it was Governor Seward he welcomed to "College Hall" during Commencement week.

II

That "matter of some account" the Doctor had wished to see the Governor about during July may well have concerned those conferences then being held in Albany during which Seward, the President of Union College [to whom the Governor regularly signed himself, "always, my dear sir, your obedient and docile pupil"], and the Rev. Dr. Luckey of the Methodist Church were then evolving a plan to get some 25,000 immigrant children, largely Irish Roman Catholics, off the New York City streets and into the schoolrooms, a generous humanitarian scheme which did little credit, however, to the Doctor's reputation as an astute judge of human behavior. [10]

It would be easy enough to write off their plan as a part of a cynical maneuver by that Whig king-maker, Thurlow Weed, who was then hoping to win over the crucial Irish vote in New York City, but, for Seward, the proposal he, his old teacher, and Dr. Luckey evolved was designed also to meet a genuine human need on the basis of a compromise reasonable men should accept. In their zeal to help these segregated and belittled immigrants the Doctor and the Governor both forgot, however, those senior class hours in "Kames," and what the Doctor taught there about the passions and man's bondage to them.

Their plan, considering the forces at work in New York City, was almost naive: "The children of foreigners," the Governor informed the Legislature in January, 1840,

> are too often deprived of the advantages of our systems of public education in consequence of prejudices arising from differences of language or religion. It ought never to be forgotten that the public welfare is as deeply concerned in their education as in that of our own children. I do not hesitate, therefore, to recommend the establishment of schools in which they may be instructed by teachers speaking the same language with themselves and professing the same faith. [11]

If the Governor, the President of Union College, and the Rev. Dr. Luckey had set out to stir up the American nativists and widen the religious differences which the alien immigrant tide of the preceding decade had already created, they could not have devised a better scheme. The Doctor, who scorned sectarians, and Dr. Luckey and the Governor were furiously accused of trying to use the State's Common School Fund in a plan to establish what would amount to State-supported parochial schools. Roman Catholic groups in New York City immediately petitioned the city's Common Council for a share of the State's school money then under the control of the Public School Society, a devoted charitable organization which had become a quasi-public Board of Education, its members solidly Protestant, their schools' curriculum and religious teaching anathema to the Irish immigrants.

The gap between Governor Seward's educational proposal and its effect on New York State voters is symbolized in two scenes, the first reported by a Whig office-seeker who, intruding on one of the strategy sessions preceding the Governor's message of 1840, "came one evening to the Governor's retired study in the wing of his house . . . and then retired abashed at finding there the stately form, venerable white head, and benignant face of the college President, and the active, black-clothed figure, keen gaze, and quick, practical utterance of the Methodist divine, both engaged in discussing themes, not of politics, but of philanthropy." [12]

Instead of discussions of philanthropy, however, the Common Council chamber in New York City was filled with outraged charges by the Democratic majority of political trickery to win Irish votes for Seward, and by urban Whigs and nativists of plots to use state money to alloy the Protestant purity of the city schools. The Democrats of the Common Council finally found a formula to save face with their Irish supporters by taking the high moral ground that to set up separate schools for foreigners would "violate . . . the very letter of our Constitution." [13] The fires the Governor and his old teacher and Dr. Luckey had ignited, however, were to burn dangerously for the two terms Seward was to serve in Albany, and were to account in considerable part for his then temporary retirement from politics. [14]

If Commencement in July, 1839 brought Governor Seward to the campus for the first time as a Union College Trustee, it also brought with him his new Secretary of State, John C. Spencer, who was also Superintendent of Common Schools and soon to be involved in the New York City school crisis the Doctor had helped to precipitate. Surely John Canfield Spencer, also one of the Doctor's old pupils, must have been impressed with the ironies posed by the confrontations in "College Hall" that afternoon. He had good reason to remember Chancellor Walworth who was there, and who had so surprisingly ruled against him on almost every position he had taken as one of the counsel for Yates and McIntyre against the Doctor and his Regency Trustees in the Chancery suits that had ended the bitter lottery controversy a few years earlier. Spencer must have wondered too, why Henry Yates was still present as a Trustee, that member of the "House" who, during the long lottery trials, had been excoriated by the Doctor and his fellow Board Members as the betrayer of his obligations as college treasurer and Clerk of the Board.

If there were fences to be mended so far as John C. Spencer was concerned, the Doctor had begun his work on them soon after the Whig victory. On February 6, 1839 he wrote to this new Secretary of New York State, making the same special claims on Spencer as his old student that he was to make the following July on the new Governor:

> It is the privilege of age to volunteer its counsel to the young—and the pedagogue, whether ungowned or gowned, always appropriates a share of the honors won by those who have been under his tuition. . . . I think I can trace the operations of a mind whose habits of analysis and combination, it is grateful to believe that I had some agency in forming—and the influence of which will I trust be felt in this community when I shall have ceased to have any further agency in the formation of the public mind. . . .[15]

The Doctor's letter to his new Whig Trustee was a model of his tactical methods; it ignored completely the recent alignment of Spencer as a counsel for the House of Yates and McIntyre against him and his Regency Trustees, as well as those dark charges of fraud which no court could settle. Instead, the Doctor now urged Spencer's attention to the glory which would redound to the political "Dynasty" that would dare to establish a "minister of public education. . . . it would confer," the Doctor informed his old pupil, "great benefits on the Republic." If this should seem impossible at the moment, the least Spencer should do would be to devote himself in his secondary office as the Superintendent of Common Schools, to "a Field . . . large and various enough to give occupation to your untiring mind. . . ."; the Doctor then closed his letter with the comment that if the Whigs were to retain office, "it will be because they identify their interests with the interests of *the people*. Between aristocracy and democracy there can be no question—make the people wise and good as you can and then go along with them and direct them. . . . ," a policy John C. Spencer must have recognized as one on which the Doctor spoke with authority. The "N.B." below the signature was no less typical of the Doctor; Joe Horsfall, his recent assistant in his "experimenting room," and a Robert Harvey, an employee of the Novelty Iron Works from which Howard and Benjamin Nott had been forced by the "hard times" to retire, were good Whigs, Spencer was told, and were now "applicants for office," though, the Doctor assured the new Secretary of State, "I never interfere in those matters."

After decades of a Board of Trustees he could direct, the majority of them long the Democratic leaders of the State government, there was now a new Board, made up not only of the Whig leaders who were its new majority, but of two newly elected members, Alonzo Paige and Jacob Lane. The former, as counsel for the Trustees in the Chancery suits, was quite aware of the Doctor's powers and determined, too, to resist them when he thought fit, a man who would prove to be a new type of Trustee, the corporation lawyer whose first loyalties were to institutions, not men.

III

By Commencement of 1839 Union College—the Doctor's college—(and it was then his by almost any test) was in a unique position. It was potentially the wealthiest college in America. Waiting for the end of what appeared to be only a temporary faltering of the economy, the Doctor could turn his mind again to university planning, for it was a Union College transforming itself into a University which more and more took hold of his imagination. Much had been done. He could point in 1839 to a curriculum uninhibited by the sectarian demands which were then seeding church dominated colleges across the nation, a curriculum which had grown in step with his almost Messianic conviction that America was a land destined to lead Europe, Africa, and Asia into a Christian Union, the Republic of the World. His formula for education could never be the academically conventional one of

Alonzo Potter; his university was to be a place for students of Natural Law, for men of action seeking through the sciences ways of releasing their fellow men from a physical and spiritual degradation forced on them by the cardinal sin of ignorance.

During the preceding ten years when he himself had acted rather than preached, Harvard had seemingly lost ground; its student body in 1839 was down to 216, fewer by 31 than were registered in the Harvard of 1829. Yale, cloistered, its sectarian curriculum producing those proliferators of church colleges, was the secure bastion of Protestant orthodoxy, then the largest college in America, with a student body of 411. Union, the youngest of this Big Three by 150 years, had been growing at a faster rate than Yale, however, increasing its student body from 218 in 1829 to 315 a decade later. [16] Princeton, almost destroyed by Presbyterian zealots, was only prevented from closing its doors in the 1830s by the salvaging operations of its alumni. [17]

The sectarianisms the Doctor had so deplored to "Mr. C." and his circle in 1833 were at the root of an intellectual retrogression then manifest on many American campuses, a retrogression which had almost wiped out the educational gains of the Enlightenment of the Revolutionary period. Union College, however, its name a measure of its loyalty to a more generous Christianity, had long been a better custodian of what it had inherited from that era than were the colleges dominated by their churches. Christian piety at Union had at least shared the rational scepticism of the Enlightenment, a union of sects dominated by the classic symbol on the College's Minerva seal.

The new Board present on Commencement Day 1839 had only to attend the graduating exercises to sense a changing land. It could be read in the titles of the addresses given by the graduating seniors, many of them no more than seventeen or eighteen, boys who now spoke gravely to their elders on subjects ranging from "Steam Power" to "Chivalry," from "Free Labor" to "The Votaries of Themis."

These "Young Gentlemen," many of whom were products of the Doctor's "Parallel but Equal Scientific Course," addressed themselves directly to the sciences, to such topics as "Saline Springs," "The Formation of Caves," "Anthropology," and "Lunar Inhabitation." They spoke on "Physiognomy" and

"Phrenology," those predecessors of psychology which had long held the Doctor's attention. They spoke on "Female Education"; there were travelogues on places to which these Byron-touched boys had never been; on the "Andes" and "The Pyrenees." And there were literary criticisms of Goethe and Schiller and of Washington Irving, the first two inspired no doubt by Professor Louis Tellkampff, of Göttingen, teacher of Latin, Modern Languages, and "Civil Polity", recommended that July for a full professorship and a salary which was to be no more than $1000 a year.

The new Board of Trustees, listening to the Commencement speakers that July of 1839, may have looked back nostalgically on their own commencements, when "abolition" was a subject for crackpots, when the White House had yet to know Jacksonian democracy, and the President of Union College, laboring over anthracite-burning stoves and steamboats, could proclaim himself the "Philosopher of Caloric."

At their afternoon meeting the New Board disposed of lesser college matters first: Professor Proudfit, teacher of Greek and Latin since 1818, was denied an advance in salary; unlike other faculty members, he had chosen to have it set by direct negotiation, not by the number of students in college; "too bad," the Trustees' Minutes noted, "that his determination is now different." Three honorary "A.B." degrees were awarded to seniors who had not graduated owing "to ill health or straitened circumstances". Professor Potter, the new Vice President, was added to the Library and Philosophical Apparatus Committee. The Doctor's interest had never been in books, so perhaps his son-in-law who saw the college in scholars' terms might do something about the library which, four years earlier, the Trustees had been told was "far behind the requisitions of the age."

With the treasurer's report the new Whig state officers were introduced to the Doctor's private world of real estate speculation and lottery account settlements: John C. Spencer, the new Secretary of State, knew their history. Alexander Holland, who had carried on the treasurer's duties for his father, Major Jonas Holland, who had died that year, listed the Doctor's and the college's holdings for the Board: one-half of Stuyvesant's Cove, the other half, mortgaged to the President by Captain Neziah Bliss, and now held by the college in trust for the Doctor until he and the Trustees should settle their lottery accounts with each other. The acting Treasurer also listed as college property one-half of 212 acres of "Hunter Point" on the Long Island side of the East River, and forty acres of mill site in the Village of Waterford about to be mortgaged to the college by Edward James, accountant for H. Nott and Company during their ownership of the Novelty Iron Works.

There was one foreshadowing and jarring note that afternoon: Hamilton College had sent in a claim to one-seventh of the Literature Lottery profits, a claim based on their treasurer's interpretation of the contract the Doctor had arranged with Hamilton in 1822 by which he had bought out Hamilton's share in the lottery grants. By 1839, Hamilton declared its share had grown to $50,000 plus the amount of notes covering money Hamilton had had to borrow from Union. Governor Seward, John C. Spencer, and the Doctor, as the new Finance Committee, were instructed to investigate the claim.

Perhaps the Doctor radiated some of the euphoria that July which had filled him in 1814, following the Legislature's granting of the Literature Lottery. As in 1814, the college again seemed to be on the verge of a great expansion. Patience, and the Board would have a fortune to be derived this time from the Doctor's Manhattan and Long Island real estate speculations and from the sums he had promised to donate from his personal profits in all his enterprises, to be used to forward the university ideas now occupying the Doctor's mind. If he could not yet found his "Institute of Science and Industry" proposed ten years earlier, he could prepare the way for developments which should be equally momentous.

To give substance to the Doctor's resurging optimism the new Finance Committee proposed that afternoon that the Board authorize it to apply to the Legislature for a special act to allow the college to receive funds from the Doctor and from other donors in order to establish "New Schools . . . new professorships . . . new scholarships . . . and an observatory . . ." to be associated with Union College, and, terminator of all mundane hopes, "a college cemetery." The Finance Committee was authorized to present the petition immediately. Every prospect justified it; the student body was growing rapidly, their President's reputation as an educator for the times was a commonplace in the nation's journals, and so soon as the temporary business collapse had passed, the great plans for new schools and professorships should be well within realization.

It was clear the Doctor still dominated his Trustees, and that he had successfully involved his new Board in his revitalized plans for a vastly enlarged Union College as he had been able to do in 1814 when he and his Board then saw visions of a new Union buoyed on lottery dollars. There was again the same optimism: Eliphalet Nott, "free of bankers and brokers," of stoves and steamboats, could look forward to filling the emptiness left by his daughter's death not only with the life of the college for which he believed he was again providing an unprecedented endowment, but also with those humanitarian activities with which American optimists hoped to bootstrap mankind into a better world.

CHAPTER 5

The Higher Law

Wayland, remember what I tell you. I may not live to see it, but you probably will. This is one of those questions that can never die. This agitation will spread from city to city, until it involves the whole country, and becomes the leading political question of the day! (Both he and I have lived to see the fulfillment of the prophecy.) [1]

FRANCIS WAYLAND, President of Brown, stopping over in Schenectady in 1834 to visit with "my old friend and instructor," had just come from New York City which was then echoing with the uproar of an anti-Abolitionist mob which had stoned Lewis Tappan, Abolitionist spokesman, broken up a Bowery Theater performance of "Metamora," and damaged two churches whose pastors were believed to harbor Abolitionist sentiments. [2]

Francis Wayland had assured his old teacher that so long as the Abolitionists worked on the principle that "the public mind" could only be influenced by appealing "to the passions" they could not expect "any mere police power" to protect them. The young College President from Providence, Rhode Island may have been remembering his hours in the Doctor's classroom where, as a senior, he had listened to him develop a psychology based on the dominance of the emotions.

Why then, if the Doctor himself condemned slavery, and he had been preaching against it since his Baccalaureate in 1811, did he not join the parade of Abolitionist leaders, and march with such men as William Lloyd Garrison, Arthur and Lewis Tappan, his friend Gerrit Smith, and Wendell Phillips? Why, if he knew so well how to move men in great and little causes, did the Doctor not ring the changes of the heart in the war on slavery?

In answering that question one must see the Doctor reacting to events, not in the order of their importance as the historian ranks them, but according to his own experience, moved by the expediencies and the cautions which then seemed vital to him.

In 1811 he had eulogized Howard, Clarkson, and Sharpe, the English anti-slavery leaders, before his Commencement audience and had declared that he would rather inherit Clarkson's fame, won for ridding England of the slave trade, than he would Caesar's. He had assured his hearers then that "Africa . . . will rise . . . if there be any truth in God." [3] By 1824 the Doctor was telling a Union College audience that the North as well as the South bore the iniquity of imposing slavery on America, that both Northern slave traders and Southern slave receivers were equally guilty of perpetuating "an unnatural state of things," that slavery, however, would eventually "be disenthralled by the diffusion of science. . . . it cannot stand," he had declared, "against the progress of society."[4]

A year later, in 1825, the Doctor was looking hopefully to the African Colonization movement as a possible way out of that "unnatural state of things" which both North and South then seemed anxious to find. "If this project of colonization is feasible," he wrote to John W. Taylor, a leader in the movement, "it should be seized on by the national authorities, and rendered efficacious to the fullest extent that is practicable. To keep our slaves in thralldom forever, if it were possible, is to entail wretchedness on them—to free them and retain them is to do the same."[5]

By 1834, however, as his reaction to Francis Wayland's report that year on the anti-Abolition riots in New York City showed, he was no longer counting on this reasoned solution to the slavery problem. But four years later, in defending his conservative pupil against those who then saw Wayland as a defender of slavery, he still spoke the humanist's hope: "It is an age of speculation as well as of action," he wrote, "but truth will receive benefit by discussion. It must be so with the question of temperance and liberty."[6]

Slavery, a dangerous shoal in 1839, lifting nearer the surface of the national life each year, had already set up its crosscurrents, as Governor Seward could remember from his own graduation of

1820, when the senior class had divided, North facing South, on the Commencement stage. Two of the seniors at the 1839 Commencement echoed the free states' side of a dialogue which was then being taken over by extremists for and against slavery: "African Colonization" as a topic that year could still bridge the widening gap between the seventy-seven Southerners who were a part of the student body, but "Abolition," the topic which followed it that day, for most of them and their slave-owning fathers, was now one for rising and angry voices.

The audience knew the Doctor's record as an anti-slavery man: he had long encouraged campus discussion of slavery, recommending always that reason and the rules of debate would make sense of an argument which the passions would destroy. Tutor Pearson in his *Journal* entry for June 9, 1837 noted the Doctor's simple solution for dealing with student slavery extremists:

> Lerow . . . formerly connected with Waterville coll. . . . where he made himself known by his violent abolition measures . . . tried the same game here but without success. When he applied to Dr. Nott for permission to form an abolition society, expecting a flat denial he was answered thus: 'Yes, my son, you may form that, as many societies in Coll. as you have a mind to.' From that day Lerow never had to attain notoriety in coll. and he became significant only because he was not opposed.

Truth, for the Doctor, was one with the "higher law," the Law of Nature, which he had preached since 1802 when he had justified the American Revolution as God's correction of an "unnatural state of things." He had invoked the "higher law" two years later when he had charged Alexander Hamilton and Aaron Burr with risking their lives by duelling, lives which were not theirs to jeopardize. He had promulgated it twenty years later when he had told the Phi Beta Kappa Society of Union College that the Laws of Nature, when understood and obeyed, would be seen to be the very constitution of the Republic of the World, of a society free of slavery, of disease, of poverty, and of ignorance.

Long before Senator William Henry Seward sought in 1850 to take the slavery problem out of the political arena by invoking the "Higher Law" on behalf of Negro liberty, Seward, Francis Wayland, and several thousand other Union College graduates who were to share the ever angrier debate that ended in Civil War had heard the Doctor expound this doctrine of the "Higher Law," though the phrase itself was Seward's to write on the public conscience.[7] Seward and Wayland, and all the Doctor's pupils had long heard him insist it was to that law that men must ultimately refer their acts as individuals and as citizens, as students, as scientists and politicians, and so as Christians. It was the reality of this "Higher Law" which, the Doctor taught, made so futile all final appeals to the passions or to mere human reason; these were limited instruments only, he had insisted, which if rightly used were but aids to the comprehension of Natural Law.

II

Although both slavery and intemperance had long been declared "unnatural," by the 1830s the crusade against alcohol seemed to many the greater cause; that enemy, temperance leaders were charging, destroyed not just the liberty of Negroes and the property rights of Southerners, but enslaved all men of every race and color it could trap. For the Doctor the cause of slavery was then degenerating into sectional, passion-bound issues less and less amenable to that rational argument and scientific examination which he then believed must be a prelude to its solution. The cause of temperance, on the other hand, seemed then to be ripe for just those talents and powers he had in abundance, and which, by 1837, were no longer confined to dealing with Chancery Court suits, or the stoves and steamboats of his career as the philosopher of caloric. Unlike the slaveholders, and those Northerners who lived on a slave economy, distillers and wine merchants, many of them the good men of their communities, as well as the ministers, politicians, and others in high and low places who drank, seemed ready to capitulate before the rational and scientific attack the Doctor believed he could mount against this more vulnerable enemy.

If the lotteries and the Chancery suits which grew out of them had revealed the Doctor as Shylock, as Machiavelli, or as the Banker-Politician-Educator Extraordinary and the chief benefactor of Union College, the temperance movement revealed him as he was remembered by the huge audiences that crusade could once recruit. Before the temperance movement was fragmented among the politicians, Eliphalet Nott won national and international fame in his attacks on that "unnatural state of things" which he was to contend led men to invite their own destruction by drinking the poisons of the distillery, the wine vats, and the brew house.

As an Albany pastor, the Rev. Eliphalet Nott had welcomed the casks of wine the young men of his parish had given him each New Year's Day. As the young President of Union College he had framed its laws to guarantee only that his students did not visit taverns without liberty; "to get drunk" they were told, was, among other evils, "a gross immorality." By 1815 the fine for bringing "spiritous liquor into the college" had been raised from the dollar it had been since 1802, to three dollars. Six years later such a crime was subject "to fine, admonition, or suspension". It was these flexible levels of punishment the intemperate student faced until the Civil War made the excitement of "taverns and groceries" and secret suppers at Given's Hotel only a glowing memory.

Temperance, until the mid-1830s, meant for the Doctor a drinker's respect for the "good friend" of the table. "The author of Christianity," he had told his graduating class in 1806, "came *eating and drinking.* . . . the first of that splendid series of miracles . . . was performed *at a marriage supper.*" He pointed out, however, that "nature has stamped on the very frame of man her *veto* against excess. . . ."

Not until temperance was caught up in the waves of revivalism which swept in and out of the frontier camp meetings in the 1820s and became a part of the oratory of Methodist and Baptist enthusiasts did the cause against alcohol find the vitality necessary to recruit a crusade. When intemperance was declared to be one of the major stumbling blocks to salvation it found hearers by the millions and supporters by the thousands. While the Doctor welcomed such revivalists to the campus in the 1820s as Asahel Nettleton, and those itinerant enthusiasts who followed him, he, himself "maintained a majestic calm of speech and deportment," it was reported, during the days of excitement which closed shops and classrooms, and moved students through various stages of "anxiety" into church membership; the Doctor knew well enough the evanescent nature of their emotionalism.[8] He did revise his "Resurrection Sermons" for them, but these were revisions only; he had no time for literary productions, he claimed, and no taste for the sort of "glowing Hibernian fervor" which had been offered by Professor Macauley around the bier of a deceased student during the height of the Nettleton revival.[9]

The Doctor took only a minor role in the rapidly expanding temperance movement of the 1820s. Perhaps he recognized how vulnerable he was to the attacks of those who opposed the pledges against "ardent spirits" that soon became as common as leaves wherever the proliferating temperance societies were organized. As the unrelenting promoter of the Literature and Consolidated Lotteries during the 1820s he was, in the eyes of many humanitarians, the promoter also of an evil linked inevitably with drunkenness and public disorder. The Doctor could protest Erie Canal traffic on the Sabbath, and such matters as flogging in the United States Navy, but to protest too strongly against those who sold and drank "ardent spirits" would have been to invite charges of inconsistency, even of hypocrisy, on the part of those who were incapable of discriminating between "hazard" and "gamble" as he had done in order to justify the Literature Lottery.

By the mid-30s the New York State lotteries had been outlawed, and the temperance movement had entered a new phase. By that time the Doctor was a supporter of Edward Cornelius Delavan of Albany, who had, almost single handed, established the New York State Temperance Society in 1829. Two years later, he and Delavan founded the "Schenectady City Society for the Promotion of Temperance" whose pledge asked no more of its members than that they abstain from all distilled liquors, "except as a medicine." [10] The Doctor mistakenly claimed in a letter to Mark Tucker the next year that the first temperance society in New York State was one founded two years earlier by the students of Union College, forgetting the vigorous "Billy Clark Society" of Saratoga, organized twenty years earlier. He pointed out in this same letter to his old student those principles on which he said he would operate "were I going throughout the land as an agent in the cause of temperance . . . I should adapt my measures, and modify my articles of association, everywhere," he said, "to the existing state of things. It is useless to go very far beyond public opinion. . . . change the state of society, enlighten public opinion, correct the public taste; and the dram shops will be closed, of course." [11] Until Cornelius Delavan re-educated him, the Doctor, too, was willing to tolerate, and probably to drink the wines of the marriage feast, as the champagnes and madeiras testified which were provided for the guests following the wedding in Albany in 1832 of his son Benjamin to Elizabeth Cooper. [12]

If John Barentse Yates by the mid-1830s was the villain in the Doctor's lottery schemes, Edward Cornelius Delavan became something akin to Chaucer's "Parfait Knecht" in the great temperance crusade in which the Doctor was to march in the years following Yates's death in 1836. With Delavan to prompt him the Doctor was not only to become a national and international figure in the expanding and changing temperance movement, but, with the Doctor to prompt Delavan, that wealthy and charitable man was to become the Doctor's chief supporter as a Union College Trustee. "Cornelius" Delavan, however, chief founder of the strongest state temperance society in the country, unlike the Doctor, was not content to continue to fight only against the use of "ardent spirits" with the variety of pledges which the state and local societies issued, that ran a gamut of permissiveness from agreements to be moderate in the use of distilled spirits, to rugged commitments "to avoid all that can intoxicate," from that "Kentucky Blue Ruin" of the frontier to the wines Delavan himself had once imported and sold as an Albany wine merchant.

By 1831 Delavan had put his large fortune to work to help to re-educate the nation, to make men believe that alcohol in any guise is the destroyer, waiting to ensnare the drinker of anything in which it is present: gin, whisky, brandy, wines of the table and the wines of the sacrament, down to the hard and soft ciders on which the politicians then floated to office. He financed the *Temperance Recorder* of that year, organ of the New York Temperance Society which, under his leadership, in 1835, published the new "teetotalers" position; from then on, it was to become also the Doctor's position.

> Our views [its editor wrote] with regard to pure wine are, that the Bible sanctions its moderate use—there can be no immorality in such use, under certain circumstances; but in our present condition with the fact that pure wine is fatal to the recovery of the drunkard, because it

intoxicates, often forms the appetite for stronger drinks in the temperate, and its use by the rich hinders the poor from uniting with temperance societies—that all, or nearly all, the wine in this country is a most vile compound; these are the reasons why we urge abstinence from all wine. [13]

If the Doctor had been cool at first to Cornelius Delavan's thrusts against the windmill of public apathy, disapproving of Delavan's violations of the Doctor's cardinal principle that "it is useless to go very far beyond public opinion," especially in this matter of the "Wine Question," he now allowed himself to be converted by the weight of evidence Delavan piled up in the pages of the *Recorder*, in pamphlets, and public appearances, that the wines of commerce were, in fact, poisons. [14]

When the Doctor coupled these revelations with a surprisingly scholarly examination of the variant meanings of the Hebrew word for "wine" as it was used in the Old and New Testaments he was ready to produce those "Ten Lectures on the Use of Intoxicating Liquors" which, first given before the Schenectady Temperance Society during the winter of 1838-39, were to put him in the van of the temperance army. By the time of his death almost thirty years later the Doctor had delivered the series in Boston, in New York City at the huge Broadway Tabernacle, in Philadelphia, in the legislative chamber in Albany, and before dozens of audiences elsewhere. The "Ten Lectures" were printed by Delavan in 1846 and distributed by the thousands throughout the United States, Canada, and England. During the next year temperance purists charged the Doctor with disrupting the temperance movement itself. The "Ten Lectures," however, outlasted the attackers, and appeared in new editions here and in England periodically until the Civil War eclipsed every lesser cause. [15]

III

The "Ten Lectures" were the Doctor epitomized. By 1838 he was ready to deal with temperance as he had with those earlier controversial public questions on which he had spoken out. Professor Tayler Lewis, in his introduction to the 1857 edition of the "Ten Lectures" wrote that, "few works have done more to place the cause of temperance on elevated, rational, and Scriptural grounds . . ." Certainly "elevated, and rational" the "Ten Lectures" were; with them their author tried to take the "Wine Question" out of the jurisdiction of the temperance societies, the wine merchants, and of the signers of those less than total abstinence pledges and to translate the question into an appeal to the "Higher Law." His surprise must have been considerable when he discovered that there were hard core "teetotalers" who disdained his peacemaking, whose reading of his "Ten Lectures" was that they were a subtle invitation to destroy the total abstinence movement.

Diversity of opinion, the Doctor assured his hearers, could only be harmonized by a rational examination of the evidence, a statement his following lectures, however, modified with all those appeals to the emotions over which the Doctor was as much a master as an Asahel Nettleton before a Camp Meeting. Lectures One and Two were appeals to the mind, but the heart and the viscera lay below it, and these, too, were the Doctor's targets. Even before he had concluded the first lecture he was probing for them as he massed the statistics of alcoholic consumption and then of the crime and disease linked to it. Analysis seemed suddenly to give way before the dreadful scene which must illustrate it, too powerful to be suppressed, for what had figures to offer when he had witnessed the death of a drunkard?

> But, oh! what a death-scene!. As if quickened by the presence of the King of Terrors, and the proximity of the world of spirits, his reason suddenly lighted up, and all his suspended faculties returned in their strength. But they returned only to give retribution a severer aspect, and to render the final catastrophe more instructive and more terrible. For though at intervals he seemed to pour his soul out in confession, and to implore forgiveness in the most thrilling accents, shame, remorse and despair were predominant and there was at times an awfulness in the paroxysms of his agony, which no words can describe, and which can be realized only by those who witnessed it. 'There,' said he, pointing to his glass and his bottle which he had caused to be placed by his death-bed, 'there is the cause of all my misery; that cup is the cup of wretchedness; and yet—fool that I have been!—I have drank it; drank it voluntarily even to its dregs. Oh, tell those miserable men once my companions, who dream of finding in inebriation oblivion to their miseries, as I have dreamed of this; tell them,—but it were vain to tell them—Oh! that they were present, that

they might see me, the dreadful sequel, and witness, in anticipation, the unutterable horrors of a drunkard's death.' Here his voice faltered—his eye fell upon the abhorred cup—and, as his spirit fled, a curse, half articulated, died away upon his quivering lip! [16]

The Doctor's alternations between history, statistics, and the charnel house during these lectures offer a textbook case of the Doctor's theory and practice as an orator; his seniors could have asked for no better examples of audience control in a period when there were no strictures against intemperance in the display of a speaker's emotion.

The third lecture was an exhaustive study of *Yayin*, the generic Hebrew term for all wines, of *Tirosh*, the new wine, the juice of the grape in the cluster, of *Ausis*, of *Sobbe*, of *Hamar*, and the wines that were "mockers": *Sheckar*, derived sometimes from the palm tree, and of *Mesech*, the mixed wines. The Doctor examined with care every text in which the term *Yayin* and its cognates occur; he was careful not to claim that there was no alcohol present in some of the "good" *Yayin* of the Bible, but only to plead that where it was present in sufficient quantity to "disturb the healthy action of the system," then was it to be avoided.

Here was the Doctor's answer to those who sold the "wines of commerce" which in almost every instance Edward Delavan had proved to be among the "mockers," modern duplicates of the condemned drugged and brandied wines of Bible days. In "Lecture No. 5" and "Lecture No. 6" the Doctor charged that the American public was, in most instances, not buying wine at all, but "extracts of logwood . . . sugar of lead . . . combined with New England rum, western whisky, sour beer, or even Newark cider, put up in wine casks, stamped Port, Champagne, or Madeira . . . the ingredients of which they are composed . . . collected and mingled, and their color and flavor imparted in some of those garrets above or caverns beneath the observations of men; caverns fitly called Hells; . . . I had a friend," he told his hearers, "who had been himself a wine dealer, . . . and I enquired of that friend as to the verity of those statements. His reply was, *'God Forgive what has passed in my own wine cellar, but the statements made are true, all true, I assure you,.'* "[17]

Although the Doctor then declared that "this friend has since gone to his last account," Cornelius Delavan must have recognized himself as the twin of the departed wine dealer.

Lectures Seven and Eight brought the series to its climax and completed the Doctor's examination of the "Wine Question." Above the analysis of chemists and the scholarship of Bible students were the ultimate sources of their knowledge. . . ; "the Books of Revelation and of Nature—of the Laws of God. When these are obeyed," he told his audience, "we are in harmony . . . when we disobey, at variance with His government." Intemperance must be recognized, finally, as the violation of this higher law; "hence," he proclaimed, "by the very ordination of God, habitual use defeats itself, for it impairs the sensibility on which it operates." [18] To prove his conclusion the Doctor here introduced his audience to what must have seemed to them and to him the ultimate in alcoholic horror, that final penalty the drunkard might be called upon to pay for his violation of the laws of Nature, "the end for those miserable beings who are, with increasing frequency, consumed by the slow and quenchless fires which the use of intoxicating liquors hath gradually kindled in the living fibres of their own bodies." He cited a Dr. Schofield's report of a young drunkard who he had found "roasted from the crown of his head to the soles of his feet," who had been discovered in a blacksmith's shop "standing erect in the midst of a widely extended silver-colored flame, bearing . . . exactly the appearance of the wick of a burning candle . . . . . it was purely a case of spontaneous combustion," a "fact," the Doctor declared, supported by Professor Benjamin Silliman of Yale, and duplicated in the records of the French *Dictionnaire Medicine*. [19]

The Doctor's lurid account of death by spontaneous combustion inspired, so it is reported, "a few grotesque experiments by the faculty of the old Bowdoin Medical School. One of them included the bleeding of a notorious Berwick sot whose blood was ignited and burned with a hard gem like flame before a cheering gallery of medics." [20]

To this *quod erat demonstrandum* there was little more to be added. Lectures Eight, Nine, and Ten were largely recapitulations of his central thesis that intemperance "reverses the order of nature." [20] The concluding moments of Lecture No. 8 must have left the Doctor's audiences limp, for in order to make graphic all he had said about the destruction alcohol worked on the human system, he displayed before their horrified eyes Dr. Thomas Sewall's recently completed drawings of the human stomach, commenting on each of them until he arrived at the seventh, representing "a stomach in which this progressive destruction is completed . . . it is the stomach of the maniac—the drunken maniac, as seen after death by delirium tremens. . . ."[21] Then, piling Pelion upon Ossa, he closed the lecture with a recital of the "Maniac's Plea," lines which he said "convey but a faint idea of the frightful ravings of a poor inebriate confined in an asylum," and "who thought himself sane and the friends who had placed him there deranged." The taste and the cultural range of the temperance audiences can be gauged to some extent by the popularity of this rhymed "phrenzy" of twenty-four stanzas written quite probably by the Doctor himself, stanzas which as they rolled from the lips of the President of Union College were also a witness to his own range as an orator. One stanza speaks for the whole poem:

> There! there again—that demon's there.
>   Crouching to make a fresh attack—
> See how his flaming eye-balls glare—
>   Thou fiend of fiends, what's bro't thee back
> Back in thy car? For whom? From where?
>   He smiles—he becons me to come—
> Where are those words thou'st written there?
>   "IN HELL THEY NEVER WANT FOR RUM!"
> In hell they never want for rum.
>   Not want for rum! Read that again—
> I feel the spell! haste, drive me down
>   Where rum is free! where revellers reign,
> And I can wear the drunkard's crown.[22]

Professor Tayler Lewis remembered "that these appeals were often overwhelming; . . . multitudes," he reported, "who had yielded to no other oratory were brought to range themselves on the side of temperance" following exposure to the Doctor's appeals to the mind, the heart, and by way of Dr. Sewall, to the viscera.[23]

The Doctor had to pay a price for his choice of crusades. Almost at once objections were raised by some medical authorities that Dr. Sewall's plates illustrating the effects of alcohol on the human stomach misrepresented those effects. The faculty of the Albany Medical College refused to hang the plates on their walls. [24] The Doctor, who continued to use them as the climax of his "Ten Lectures," joined Delavan and his supporters against a divided medical profession in defending them as at least useful representations of the progressive havoc alcohol wrecks on the stomach. Delavan's *Enquirer* carried the Doctor's letter written the next year urging that Sewall's plates be placed "in every district and Sunday School, as well as in every academy, lyceum, college, and temperance society throughout the length and breadth of this and every other land [including] the jails, courthouses, poorhouses and penitentiaries...," [25] a recommendation Delavan did his best to forward at his own expense.

When, however, the editor of the *Enquirer* carried his war against wine drinking to the communion table itself, and the Doctor backed him with letters to the *Enquirer*, and the New York *Observer* supporting Delavan's conclusion that the communion wines, too, were usually "mockers," the adulterated "wines of commerce," the unity of the temperance crusade, at least in New York State, was seriously threatened. The Rev. Dr. Backus, minister of the First Presbyterian Church of Schenectady, later a Union College Trustee, charged that both the Doctor and Cornelius Delavan had "the presumption to throw the firebrand into the churches, and [to] set the people of God to quarreling over the very emblems of the Redeemer's love." [26] Gerrit Smith, seldom temperate in his own opinions, went so far as to suggest that Christ, if he supplied an alcoholic wine at the wedding feast in Cana, did so out of ignorance that alcohol was a poison. [27]

In 1846 Delavan, at his own expense, printed the Doctor's "Ten Lectures" as the fourth number of the *Enquirer*, and sent copies of it broadside over America and England. If the Doctor, the next year, was made aware of the fact that his best efforts were not enough to make even the leaders of the temperance movement refrain from casting stones he eventually recognized that the movement itself was doomed as its leaders allowed it to become what, in 1855, he called "a political engine." He wrote to Delavan in that year that, because the politicians had captured it, the temperance crusade would lose its force "as a great moral power"; it would be no longer "a regulator of other movements," and would become, itself, a political party doomed "to share the fate of other political parties." [28]

Eliphalet Nott, that "renowned and venerable patriarch" of the temperance movement as he was called by the Executive Committee of the New York State Temperance Society in 1855, in that year distilled a wisdom from his experience few could then recognize; in a letter to Delavan criticizing Gerritt Smith's demand for laws and more laws to deal with both intemperance and slavery, he wrote that "under a despotic government his reasoning would be conclusive. Here the governed are the governors, and to secure the enactment of good laws, the law givers must first be educated." [29] Two years later he told Delavan that "the temperance effort must be suspended. There must be a pause, and much of the past forgotten. . . ." [30]

By then Eliphalet Nott was eighty-four years old, a weary veteran of the second lawyers' war to be waged against him and Union College. His years as a temperance crusader, however, had given him the friendship of "Cornelius" Delavan who, for the sake of the Doctor, became, himself, a Trustee of Union College in 1837, and who, twelve years later was thanked by the then embattled old President for taking "our beloved Alma Mater under your paternal care. . . ." [31] Both Chancellor Walworth and Edward C. Delavan with whom the Doctor had fought the war of the "Wine Question" were to become his supporters now in formulating the university plans with which the Doctor hoped to crown his career as an educator, as well as his allies in helping him to defend himself and the college against those new enemies who were waiting to march out of the returning shadows of the Literature Lottery.

CHAPTER 6

"This College rides, like a ship in full sail, majestic . . ."

"THIS afternoon I dropped into Mr. Brown's studio. His heads of Dr. Nott, Dr. Potter and others almost speak."[1] Governor Seward's casual visit to the sculptor James Brown of Albany about which he reported to Mrs. Seward in May, 1842 had confronted him with the busts of two men whose clay pallor spoke more of the grave in which each had a common professional interest than of the real world about which each had strong, and, especially where Union College was concerned, quite different views. Could they have harmonized these differences Union College might well have remained one of the Big Three of American higher education. The events of the next three years, unfortunately, ended Vice President Alonzo Potter's expectation that he would succeed his father-in-law in the presidency and gave to the Semi-Centennial celebration of 1845 its discordant overtones.

The Doctor and his son-in-law both spoke on July 22, 1845 before the greatest gathering of alumni and visitors the College or Schenectady had ever seen. In the grove to the east of the Semi-Centennial arch of fir boughs, surrounded by a thousand male dinner guests and what the New York *Tribune* called "that double row of flowers," their ladies, each said unphrased good-byes to the other, though few in the audience could have known of the cabal of ministers and laymen who had worked behind scenes to prevent the Vice President and Senior Professor from succeeding an aging Eliphalet Nott. The Semi-Centennial celebration was, for some, a shadow play of courtesies and speeches, a few of which touched obliquely on the differences which separated the Doctor from his son-in-law and which prevented Trustees and friends of the college from uniting to support it.[2]

The weather was perfect, and the day offered "a delightful oasis in the dreary waste of political, professional and commercial life . . . following the sweltering furnaces of the preceding weeks," according to the Albany Evening *Journal*.

For four hours there were odes, and music, and the lengthy addresses of the Senior Orator, the Rev. Joseph Sweetman of the class of 1797 and of Alonzo Potter, the junior orator, of the class of 1818. Dr. Sweetman, standing between two worlds, visualized the one he knew best, the Dorp Schenectady of his undergraduate days, its gable-ended houses standing on the edge of the western frontier of New York State. As old men will, he saw his college days as "times of honesty, of simplicity, of good feeling". He was concerned that "ye, of this day . . . ." might see things worse appear than he had known, things "more congenial with pride, more flattering to vanity, and more pressing with demands for needless, if not pernicious expenditures." He was eloquent about Union's part in leavening American society with the best of what, he said, was "kind, humane, and benevolent." Dr. Sweetman's remembering was all the Committee of Arrangements could have asked to set the tone of the day.[3]

Between this country minister's reminiscences and Vice President Alonzo Potter's junior oration Alfred B. Street's many stanza'd ode was sung. Written for the occasion by a then favorite American poet who held an honorary degree from the College, its last stanza is one with all those that preceded it:

> Let memory be baptised in light,
>> Care, cease thy dark and gloomy reign!
> Hail, day of splendor, fresh and bright!
>> Joy, swell thy loudest, merriest strain![4]

Vice President Alonzo Potter, that "bookmaker," according to an increasingly critical "Pinky" Pearson, had prepared a junior orator's speech which had little about it of either a junior's station or of that joy which Alfred B. Street had just hailed. One has only to look at the bust of the Doctor's son-in-law which seemed so near words to William Henry Seward to know that the junior orator would not be frivolous. His was the speech of the President he might have been had the Doctor resigned in his favor, a discourse which echoed more of Harvard and Yale than it did of the Union College Eliphalet Nott had created.

To the undergraduates in the audience he was "Old Potter," solid with learning, who had published on topics as widely separated as "Logarithms," "Trade Unions," and a list of the proper books for the spreading associations of young mechanics. His six sons and his daughter were also grandchildren of Eliphalet Nott whose grief at the death of their mother had had a more profound emotional effect on the Doctor than on an Alonzo Potter whose every moment was charged with "fire and energy," a phrase he so often used, that drive toward self-improvement about which he was constantly lecturing and writing.

Looking backward, the junior orator saw "giants": Washington, and the great men of the generation of the Revolution whose passing had been followed by decades during which, he assured his audience, "we see the insidious approaches of mediocrity".[5] The fashion to decry the present is as old as the prophets, and Alonzo Potter spoke to his audience not only as an Episcopal priest but as one of that new breed of Christian socialists who would attempt to take the gospel out of the pulpit and into the market place, into the factories, the city halls, and the legislatures, and so attempt to stem a "mediocrity" which, they were convinced, was in sharp contrast to an earlier age of virtue.[6]

The junior orator indicated that he was neither blind to nor unappreciative of the services to society of the scientists of the nation, among whom he especially noticed Joseph Henry whose work in electromagnetics while an instructor at the Albany Academy had made the telegraph possible. Oddly, he had no praises for his father-in-law, however, who had been so recently heralded for his labors as the "philospher of caloric."

The Semi-Centennial itself was Alonzo Potter's subject, and all it meant to a Union College whose presidency he had had the strongest possible reasons to think he was to assume. On at least five occasions he had turned down flattering offers within the Episcopal Church which he had already served as a priest from 1824 to 1831 as the Rector of St. Paul's Chapel in Boston. Although he had usually protested that his health was too poor to assume the bishoprics which he might have had in Massachusetts, Rhode Island, and Western New York, he had also pointed out "the peculiar and apparently imperative character of the duties with which I am charged here" which made leaving Union impossible.[7] Since 1838 he had been Vice President, acting for the Doctor during the latter's many absences from Schenectady, aware that his father-in-law believed his own retirement was imminent, that the latter ranked himself "as an old man" as he wrote to his brother Samuel in 1840, when he noted "that I must soon (I see it) resign an unfinished task."[8]

Not once in his speech did Alonzo Potter mention the name of Eliphalet Nott. Perhaps the junior orator was aware of the cabal which had been at work for several years in what one of them had called "a movement against Dr. Potter."[9]

The Vice President and Senior Professor may also have been shocked by the little resistance the Doctor had raised when he told him that May of the action of the Episcopal Diocese of Pennsylvania. "Where I expected the most determined and painful opposition, there is comparative resignation [to my going]," Alonzo Potter wrote to an old Boston friend.[10] A week later he cut his ties with the college to become the Bishop of Pennsylvania in response to what he insisted was the call of Providence to a higher office. Eliphalet Nott was to be left to finish his task alone, one for which he needed, however, health and youth, and the compliant Trustees of his first decades as President, and that time of optimism which preceded the Jackson Depression.

Alonzo Potter used the last part of his junior oration to unburden himself as a critic of the college. He let the shots fall as they would, and if the Doctor must receive some of them, so be it. If Union had already graduated in fifty years half as many men as Harvard had sent out in 200 years, it was to be explained as part of the phenomenal growth of the country over the preceding half century. He saw, however, serious flaws in Union College's development; "its library, apparatus and museum," he told his audience, "are wholly inadequate to the wants of such an institution." He was afraid Union might well become "moored on the great stream of human progress . . .". He referred to the danger to institutions which are directed solely by "active, practical minds. . . ."; that such institutions could only improve "in proportion as they combine the progressive and conservative spirits wisely together." The junior orator could hardly have spoken plainer.

"Hitherto," he continued, "we have trained our children too much as if what the world calls success were the grand end of life, and the most important boon that education can grant. Too often we have forgotten that all this vulgar and outward success can never fill up the vast desires of the human heart." Alonzo Potter then presented his ideal college president, a man, he said, whose concern it would be to see that "the soul was touched and tuned to finer issues," and in saying this he said nothing Eliphalet Nott would have denied, but which, in essence, separated these two men as philosophers of education, for Potter was for ends which could be served only by scholarship and libraries, for a religion, and so a life of forms as well as of piety. His father-in-law was for an education designed "for the heat and the work of the day," an education for pragmatists, lessons to be learned by doing, for a life to be fulfilled by acting purposefully in a democracy in which compromise with one's ideals in order to obtain goals limited by the nature of men could be the essence of wisdom. Alonzo Potter chose to leave Union in 1845 in response, he said, to the call of Providence to a higher office. Characteristically, his father-in-law had left his church in 1804 to become an educator, and for the same reason. The tragedy for Union College in its Semi-Centennial year was, indeed, that Eliphalet Nott and Alonzo Potter could not then have merged their "progressive and conservative spirits wisely together."

The new bishop's vision was, finally, of a Union College in which "the speculative and elegant culture of earlier days shall not come into violent and fatal collision with the positive and practical science of our own time." He spoke also for newer times; he told his audience that "the future of their *Alma Mater* is in *their* hands," that the day of one-man rule of a successful American college was over. He called for their aid in creating a college which would reflect "the essential condition of all excellence," a college, in fact, which, like the Harvard and Yale of 1845, would stand above and apart from the market place, the legislatures, the factories, and foundries Eliphalet Nott·had made a part of his own experience. "We can make energetic, practical men elsewhere," the junior orator told his fellow alumni. Only from a properly administered college devoted "to a high general education," he said, could the disciplined student emerge, prepared to create "a refined and elegant culture. . . ."

Young Professor Pearson, if he was in the audience that morning, may have remembered the Doctor's earlier comments "on the fitness of the various denominations of Christians for the wants of the people . . .": "Episcopalians," the old President had said, "are the rich, the fashionable, and the refined; Methodists for the lower classes, Baptists for the middle class," and, he had added with a nice catholicity, "Presbyterians are the whining hypocritical, and mean," an observation with which his son-in-law, within the wider meaning for him of that Semi-Centennial celebration, could only have concurred. [11]

II

Music, odes and, orations completed, Joel Nott reorganized the Alumni Procession on the West College green at two o'clock and, mounted on a white horse, led them up College Hill to the Pavilion tent erected in the grove east of North and South Colleges, passing first under the arch of fir boughs and the welcome woven into it in flowers: "Salvete, Filii Alumnae Matris," and the dates, "1795" and "1845."

Ex-Governor William Henry Seward, although a member of Chairman John C. Spencer's Dinner Committee, was not in Schenectady that day. His letter to the Committee of Correspondence however, left no doubt that the Union he regretted he could not be personally present to honor was memorable to him because he had been, he wrote, "a Pupil of Nott." To Thurlow Weed, five days later, he confided that he was afraid the Doctor "will think hard of me for leaving the Commencement. But it was best I go elsewhere. I thought that the loud drum beat would recall enough who will be indifferent hereafter, when I am zealous." [12]

Alonzo Potter had chosen that morning to announce that he had resigned as Vice President and Senior Professor; he had chosen to omit, as the junior orator, any reference to his father-in-law's achievements as that "venerable and venerated" President of the college, achievements which Spencer, Seward, Francis Wayland, and others had made the theme of their remarks either at the dinner or in their letters to the Committee which had arranged the huge celebration. He had gone to great lengths to picture a college which, unlike the Union College Eliphalet Nott had developed and was then projecting on an even larger scale, would, if Alonzo Potter had had his way, stand above the world "of wonderful activity and enterprise," a less democratic college, one more concerned with developing character and "an elegant culture," as he had phrased it, than with those scientific courses the Doctor had long emphasized and which he saw as ultimately an expression of Christian wisdom. Potter's college was not the Union its alumni were celebrating that afternoon, nor was the president of Potter's ideal college recognizable as his father-in-law, a fact which obviously disturbed one of the Doctor's old pupils, a Presbyterian colleague, a Trustee of the college, and quite possibly the voice of those who had organized to prevent Alonzo Potter from becoming the Doctor's successor.

"In conducting this Institution," the Reverend Mark Tucker, class of 1814, told the dinner gathering following the Fifth Regular Toast drunk in "Adam's Ale,":·

> We have been greatly relieved . . . by having as our President, for a good part of the time, one, a master spirit, who has watched over it with a sleepless eye, and in whom we have the fullest confidence; and, with reference to some of the predictions uttered today, in regard to the future prospects of the College, I feel constrained to say, that so long as the venerable President who has presided over it for four-fifths of its existence remains at its head, this prediction will be verified; . . . this College . . . now rides, like a ship in full sail, majestic, and tending to the haven of prosperity.[13]

Chancellor Reuben Walworth, whose decision for the Doctor in the Chancery suits in 1836 had once so annoyed John C. Spencer, immediately stood and offered the following sentiment: "Our Venerated and Venerable President—who understands the true secret of governing his students by teaching them to govern themselves."

The Doctor, still showing the effects of the rheumatic fever which had long bothered him and had made him more "venerable" in appearance than his seventy-two years justified, rose slowly, and, disclaiming any right to speak on the occasion, not being, he said, "a graduate of Union College myself . . . ," proceeded to demonstrate again those old tactical skills which had always led him onto higher ground in a potentially dangerous situation. If the presidency of Union College in 1845 was again an office that could divide those Protestant churches which, fifty years earlier, had seemingly buried their differences in order to establish a union of teachers and students and supporters free of sectarian bias, he did not acknowledge them, nor did he debate the nature of higher education which he had been defining for almost as long as the college was old, in a curriculum his one-time students had just been praising. Nor did he mention Alonzo Potter.

"I am going to repeat counsels I have given you," he told his hearers, and, in the security of that long successful formula, he repeated essentially what he had told the gathering of the Phi Beta Kappa Society and its guests in 1824. His theme was again a "renovated earth," the labor of men educated for the times, prepared to do the work of renovation which must be completed before there could be the moral regeneration of the race. He saw himself now as an old man: "My children," he told the hundreds of men present who could remember as college seniors those unorthodox views on the nature of man the Doctor had once opened to them, "with me life is waning to its close," as poor a prophecy as any he had ever made. If he could live again, he told them, "I would live better . . . from the outset I would frown upon vice." The new governor of New York State, his old friend ex-Senator Silas Wright, was in the audience, as were others who had shared the lottery years with him. There had been evils connected with that experience and he and they had acknowledged them. But the lotteries had produced forces which were still moving this "ship in full sail, majestic . . . tending to the haven of prosperity" which the Rev. Mark Tucker had invoked, and it was hardly a ship, the Doctor knew, for Alonzo Potter to pilot.

Since the death of Sarah Maria six years earlier there had been changes in the charts laid out for that voyage. There had been the lesser tragedy of the death of Maria's stepmother, Gertrude Tibbits Nott, so long ill and bedridden that her death in January, 1841, was a relief for her and for him. [14] He might well have smiled at the "venerables" and "venerateds" which had just been used to describe him, for his recent third marriage to Urania E. Sheldon, a schoolmistress from Utica, some twenty-five years his junior, had excited the gossips during the summer of 1842: "she is—rather young, and a pretty clever one" he had reported to his New York banker. "We may suppose," a neighboring minister had suggested, "that his youth has been renewed and hence qualified for greater application." [15] A member of the Tibbits family had gossiped that Professor Alonzo Potter had introduced his father-in-law to the attractive Miss Sheldon in the hope of getting his approval to her becoming the second Mrs. Potter; if so, the then Vice President bore no grudge, for he had married the Doctor and the Utica schoolmistress and shortly afterward had, himself, married Sarah Maria Potter's cousin. [16]

"Yes," the Doctor continued to the Semi-Centennial audience in those oratorical figures they expected, "though I were to exist no longer than those ephemera that sport away their hour in the sunbeams of the morning, even during that brief period I would rather soar with the eagle, and leave the record of my flight and fall among the stars, than creep the earth and lick the dust with the reptile, and, having done so, bed my body with my memory in the gutter." In brief, pragmatist that he was, the Doctor had acted. He and his son-in-law spoke a different speech, tuned to different eras, though for most of those older alumni present Eliphalet Nott on "ephemera" was still more exciting than the new bishop on higher education and what the junior orator had called ". . . the essential conditions of all excellence."

Since Maria's death the Doctor's flight had circled not only the college, and the men who seemed to him to be serving it, but the national causes of temperance and abolition. He had told young "Pinky" Pearson he was a "locofoco," but that increasingly cynical observer had noted in his journal that "he don't [sic] go with either party . . . thick with the one in power," [17] that the Doctor was, in fact, "a warm abolitionist" who had told him that "the emptyings are in the cask and it begins to work," that there would never be another slavery President, that "one party or another will come over and take the anti-slavery ground here at the North, and then will begin the Song of War!" [18] His solution for the problem of slavery in 1845 was "to let the South withdraw from the Union, if the slave states insisted." [19]

As the Doctor spoke that July to those who had been his "young gentlemen" he must have looked at John C. Spencer, the dinner chairman, with mixed emotions, for Spencer, too, had had his time of bitterness. Not only had he recently resigned from President Tyler's cabinet rather than join in the politically expedient program to annex Texas and so support the extension of slavery, but he had suffered the incredible events of 1842 when Philip Spencer, his son, briefly a student at Union, then a Navy midshipman, had, during a cruise of the *Somers*, and while his father was Secretary of War, been hanged from the yardarm, convicted by his fellow officers of planning mutiny. [20] The Doctor at the time had urged the Secretary not to resign his post, had visited him in Washington, and had cemented a friendship which was soon to become the most meaningful one of his later life.

As the "venerable" Doctor spoke he could see before him a microcosm of mid-nineteenth century America. Perhaps, as he spoke, he remembered another distinguished audience: five years earlier, on invitation, he had addressed the Congress of the United States, had delivered before both Houses, and the President, and his Cabinet, that sermon which never failed to move his hearers: "The Tomb! The Grave! The Resurrection!" [21] What was left to be done, he was convinced, must be done by the begetter of the unfinished business for which he was responsible, which had produced the Union College such men as Spencer, Seward, Wayland, and Governor Wright, if not his son-in-law that day, saw as worthy and as a projection of himself.

He spoke briefly. The solution of all problems, his, the college's, and the nation's, he concluded, was there for all to read, in the pages of the Bible. It was that simple, and that complex, and it was to the comprehension of this truth that men were to be educated. No one present, politician or sectarian, could have taken him to task for that revelation. If Alonzo Potter had meant to speak to those sectarians in Albany, Princeton, and elsewhere who had organized to keep him from the presidency of Union College, he did not hear his father-in-law reply for them. Between the new Bishop of Pennsylvania and the aging President of Union College there was far too much in common to separate them from each other for long. Sarah Maria and her sons and daughter bound the new Bishop and Eliphalet Nott in a family affection which was to be proof against even the machinations of the Reverend Samuel Miller's hostile churchmen and those new enemies of the Doctor's about to steal out of the lottery past. [22]

The speeches and toasts in "Adam's Ale" continued into the early evening. Governor Wright spoke his praises for the college and its President, then the Reverend Cyrus Mason spoke for New York University, "a child of Union College," he told his hearers. Bishop Doane of New Jersey spoke on higher education for women, and Dr. J. M. Wainwright, speaking for Harvard, said that Harvard's greatness was largely the fruit of Alumni loyalty and support. The new Bishop of Pennsylvania, responding to the Tenth Regular Toast, admitted that "accomplished scholarship has been a sort of mania with me," and charged his fellow alumni again with their responsibility to see Union's walls "crowded, absolutely crowded, with the accumulated learning of the past."

The Semi-Centennial dinner ended, finally, with an ode written for the occasion by Mrs. Sigourney ("the sweet singer of Hartford") and read by Joel Nott. The audience, following his delivery of the lines:

and see the sunset kindle with its touch of gold,
The hills rekindle, and illumine the grove. . . .
was awed, so the dinner committee reported later, "with the most gorgeous sunset man ever saw, (which) threw a golden stream of light through the grove." [23]

That evening the houses of the Doctor, of Professor Andrew Yates, and Professor Reed, Chairman of the Committee of Correspondence, were illuminated. There was a soiree, and, according to the New York *Tribune*, "a splendid balloon" was sent up near the Triumphal Arch. Union College had celebrated its Semi-Centennial, the most significant moment of which, however, had actually taken place off-stage that morning, when the Trustees embarked with the Doctor on a new course as fateful as had been the one they undertook with him when they accepted the provisions of the Lottery Act of 1822.

III

As the alumni and the corporation of the city of Schenectady exchanged greetings outside "College Hall" that morning of the great celebration, the Trustees, meeting inside, settled a unique account with their President. Henry Yates, their ex-treasurer and still a Trustee, not being present, they could unanimously agree to return to the Doctor as much of the Stuyvesant Cove and Hunter Point lands previously conveyed by him and by Captain Neziah Bliss to the college "as shall be necessary . . . to cancel any cash balance due the President . . . on a final settlement with him."

According to Alexander Holland's treasurer's report, the Doctor's personal advances to the college had begun with his transfer of $8500 he had himself won on a lottery ticket in 1819, and had continued through his transfer to the college of his portion of the Tri-Partite Settlement made with the House of Yates and McIntyre in 1837, to the sum total of which the treasurer had added interest to July 1, 1845, to produce a Trustees' debt to the Doctor of $366,177.63. Here, certainly, was academic financing unique from any point of view. Optimism, however, was as high that morning in "College Hall" as it was outside, on the West College Green.

"Eliphalet Nott, presiding . . ." was still the most significant entry in the Trustees' Minutes for July 22, 1845. Ex-Vice President Alonzo Potter could preach "excellence" and high scholarship, call for students to be cloistered behind walls of books; he could tell the alumni and the Trustees that day that, "practical men can be made elsewhere," but he could not tell this to his father-in-law.

As there was no one present at that Trustees' meeting who could remember the whole of the lottery history, so there was no one present who could comprehend the magnitude of the Doctor's career as an educator, who had the perspective to see that the Union College of 1845 was more than its unfinished Ramée campus, more than its Semi-Centennial speakers were to boast it was, more than its reported endowment, largely because the Doctor presided. What he had done since 1804, unadvertised, slowly and practically, to break the grip of classicists, of academic traditionalists, on the curriculum of the American college so that it might lead in the day-to-day work of physical and political, and so, ultimately, of moral world renovation as he saw it, was occasionally acknowledged: Francis Wayland was then becoming Eliphalet Nott extended as he strove to make of Brown a college for the times. New York University, still no University in fact, was "the child of Union College," according to Dr. Mason who spoke that afternoon; the Reverend Henry P. Tappan, organizer of the University of Michigan-to-be, who was to receive his degree of Doctor of Divinity from his alma mater later that day, had, according to his biographer "had his attention focused upon the problem of university ideals and university administration which for over sixty years were Eliphalet Nott's chief concern." [24]

The Doctor's vision in 1845 of a "University" to be financed by himself and his Trustees, was of a Union College constantly extending, embracing new faculties, laboratories, an expanding library and museum, where George Ticknor's two *freiheits*, his two freedoms, to teach and to learn, would be conditioned by the Doctor's Christian mystique of the renovated earth culminating in the spiritually reborn man. [25] His immediate plans, limited only by the state of the economy, called for an observatory to be built on the high ridge just south of the campus, new professorships, new scholarships, new "schools" yet to be defined, and what his students impatiently referred to as "the long promised Octagon," Ramée's "chappelle," which was to rise between North and South Colleges.

In 1845 the only handicap the Doctor might have acknowledged in maintaining Union's lead in his bid for university standing vis-à-vis Harvard, Yale, and those other colleges engaged in the academic reassessments then taking place, was the fact that he was seventy-two years old. The full length, life size portrait by Henry Inman, ordered by an alumni committee six years earlier, in the flush of the excitement attending the preparation for the Semi-Centennial celebration (a portrait finally paid for by the Doctor himself when no authorization for the picture could be found), [26] depicted a ruddy-cheeked, white maned chief justice for Minerva, standing before an imposing vista which included Ramée's open forum of a campus, complete to the last building. [27]

If, out of the lotteries, Union by 1845 had won its position as the richest, or potentially the richest, college in America, it had also gained its standing by that year as "the college for times" because the Doctor had also constructed, as John C. Spencer noted at the Semi-Centennial dinner, "a curriculum for the times." [28] That September the Doctor would continue that development by announcing an addition to the current work in the sciences, the establishment of new courses and a new department which were almost as revolutionary in their import as had been the announcement seventeen years earlier of the "Scientific Course." William M. Gillespie, A.M., was brought in that fall as the "Lecturer in Civil Engineering," and head of the new "Department of Civil Engineering," the first teacher of so mundane a subject who was to be recognized by an American college as having equal standing with its teachers of the classics.

The arrival of Professor Gillespie, diffident, a stammerer, a fine classical scholar himself, "proficient in French and German, and well versed in Old English literature," as well as in the engineering subjects he had studied in England and France for the preceding ten years, can be linked, probably, to the death three years earlier of Amos Eaton, founder of the Rensselear Institute in neighboring Troy.

On April 22, 1845, two months before Alonzo Potter resigned the Vice Presidency of Union, his father-in-law resigned the presidency of Eaton's then impoverished "common workshop for all." The Doctor had served as President of the Rensselear Institute since 1829, encouraging Eaton in his tireless efforts to make the fruits of scientific achievement available, first, to farmers and mechanics and then to that new breed of builders called up by the canal, turnpike, and railroad planners. The President of Union had seen Eaton's "Rensselaerian Plan" of learning by doing as achieving on an elementary level and for people the colleges did not reach a portion of that work he stated in 1828 he intended to magnify in his projected "Institute of Science and Industry," then waiting on the lottery for funds. Neither Eaton nor the Doctor had seen either the Troy school or the college in Schenectady as in any way in competition; the President of Union had sent a "professor" from John B. Yates's "Polytechny" in Chittenango to Eaton to prepare him to teach farm sciences to the lottery manager's neighbors and tenants. Eaton had lauded the Doctor's "discreet concern" as the Institute's President in 1835 in helping its staff to secure "for the school a reputation which will probably long survive its own dissolution." [29]

In 1839, sick and discouraged, Eaton had taken his concerns on the failing state of the Rensselaer Institute, no longer enjoying

Stephen VanRensselaer's bounty, to the Doctor. Although there was little correspondence between the two men, the Doctor's frequent presence in Troy, either on college business at the Farmer's Bank, where Mrs. Nott's brother, Hugh Peebles, was the Cashier, or visiting among her influential Tibbits relatives, gave both men every opportunity for discussing Eaton's complaints against the miserliness of Trojans, and his always compromising dependence on the patroon. These sources of funds the Doctor must have compared to the Literature Lottery, and probably with private thanksgiving that he had won an independence unknown to the struggling Eaton. The Doctor's work for the Rensselaer Institute was hailed by its founder again in 1840 in the latter's dedication of the eighth edition of his *North American Botany*: "he is entitled," Eaton then wrote, "to the first place in the memory of its teachers," who, with a number of the school's alumni, Eaton noted, had asked the author to join them in his tribute to the President of Union College.

With Eaton's death in 1842, however, the Rensselaer Institute lost its driving force. Stephen VanRenssealaer's sons were helpful with counsel, but seldom with money, and the Institute by 1845 seemed about to close. The Doctor's resignation as President of the Troy school that April and his parallel appointment of Professor Gillespie to his own faculty as "Lecturer in Civil Engineering," suggest that he had found the moment ripe to take advantage of Gillespie's availability to carry on the substance of Eaton's work, and at the same time to open up to Union College students in the sciences those courses in engineering and architecture his own grandson, Clarkson Potter, had had to go to Troy to find on an elementary level the year Amos Eaton died. [30]

To the new Bishop of Pennsylvania, Professor Gillespie's appointment the year of the Semi-Centennial celebration may have seemed one more reason for questioning the Doctor's curriculum making, for what kind of Bachelor of Arts was it who could count toward his degree such workaday courses as "surveying" and "Location of Roads (in the field)," as the building of Freeman's Bridge over the Mohawk River, and in such architectural exercises as "Construction in Stone, Wood, Iron, etc."? One wonders to what extent Alonzo Potter encouraged or discouraged Professor Gillespie in 1844 when the latter wrote to him of his hopes of making Union College "still more the nucleus of general science . . . to prove her willingness to keep pace with the higher aims of the utilizing spirit of the age." [31] The Doctor, who saw all subject matter as a divine discipline, could only have approved of Gillespie's new plans for work at Union in architecture which, Gillespie had written, "should be studied in its double character of a science and a fine art . . . ," a course in which there should be "ample scope for profitable comment, as with us there is such a wide field for improvement on our Grecian temples and ginger-bread Gothic style buildings." Professor Gillespie, in 1845, brought with his theodolites and surveying instruments and his years of university association abroad, a new sophistication and ideas of curriculum expansion thoroughly congenial to Eliphalet Nott.

IV

These years immediately following the Semi-Centennial celebration were as an Indian Summer in the Doctor's affairs, a brief span following the striking of Welch and Mann's circus tent which the Semi-Centennial Committee had hired for its "Pavilion". It was the last fair weather he was to know, a time during which he could survey his harvests and plan his final and, hopefully, his greatest planting, his "university for the times."

If, in some way, the Doctor, as a father, may have failed his sons as he believed they had failed him, he inspired in his grandsons the same affection mixed with awe he instilled in most of his students: "he always loved the companionship of the young," his grandson, later Judge Charles Cooper Nott of the Federal Court of Claims recalled, "and he seemed to yearn for the sports and pleasures of boyhood. I remember him at the age of seventy and upward, running with ardor and the speed of a boy to stop a runaway horse, and how, falling in the attempt and cutting his hand upon the sharp stones of the College terrace, the wound healed kindly in a few days as if it had been made in the flesh of a child." The Judge also recalled a picnic he and his classmate, Frederick Seward, were taken on by the Doctor, "to a new place of interest in the Helderberg hills . . . no one in the party was so young as my grandfather. He talked, laughed and jested; he scrambled up and down difficult places, and came back at night fresh and enthusiastic, and ready to start forth again on the morrow. There surely have been few persons who in childhood were so impressed with the grave responsibilities of age, and who in age had so much of the buoyancy and freshness of youth." [32]

The Nott household in South College then consisted of "Uranie," as the Doctor called his new, "pretty smart wife," the third, very young Mrs. Nott, and these grandsons coming and going with their college friends, always welcome, and Maria Louisa Potter, the granddaughter whose birth had been one with the death of her mother. Maria Louisa spent far more of her girlhood in her grandfather's house than she did in the bishop's, in Philadelphia.

Professor Jonathan Pearson, now more than ever "Pinky" of the glowing cheeks to his students in chemistry, and a constant visitor at the Notts, continued during these interim years to enter his Boswell observations in his "Thinking Books". Following the Semi-Centennial, "the doctor said . . ." begins more and more of these entries and soon, when they become star chamber revelations, the "Doctor" as a heading gives way to that hieroglyphic symbol the shocked recorder of secrets designed to look like a smoking Nott stove. Unlike Boswell, however, Baptist Professor Pearson came, finally, to war against his subject, although he always seemed ready to declare a truce long enough to record the Doctor's earthy estimates of people and events: the "Doctor" on politics, on abolition and total abstinence he always noted with the respect due a major actor by one who watched the scene from the wings. Until he became acting college treasurer in 1850 he knew only the gossip of faculty members and nervous Trustees about the Doctor's activities as the college Midas. For the brief interim following the Semi-Centennial celebration, however, the "Thinking Books" reflect simply the Doctor's Indian Summer, a time of elder statesmanship and things remembered for the old President.

Pearson was then apparently almost as much at home in the President's South College residence as were the grandsons, and the give and take of that forthright household echoes through his journal. Urania Nott, ex-schoolmistress of Utica, was obviously not in awe of her "venerable" husband, who, during one of

Pearson's visits in 1845, chided his new wife for her fondness for reading biographies. The "Thinking Books" recorded the exchange that December:

> The Doctor. I never read but one in my life, and that was about that Methodist man—you know, Urania, what's his name?
>
> Mrs. N. Wesley?
>
> The Doctor. Yes, Wesley. Folks read too much and think too little.
>
> Mrs. Nott. I never saw any man carry out that opinion but you,—I don't believe you ever read a book. I never saw you read any. I don't see how you got along in your younger days.
>
> The Doctor. I always have some by which I am reading. But I read slowly and thoroughly. . . .

"Pinky" Pearson then recorded their argument over who read what, an exchange which ended in the Doctor's declaration that he had no library any more; "folks," he announced, "have borrowed all away. I gave up long ago keeping any book, and out of revenge I never return any," a statement he reinforced in 1848 when he gave Pearson 206 volumes and pamphlets for the college Library.

The Doctor's own health, until the year following the Semi-Centennial, had defied those Yankee Cassandras of his youth who had prophesied an early death for him. In the fall of 1846, however, he went down before an overwhelming attack of "inflammatory rheumatism" which struck during a visit to his old pupil and then fellow Trustee, the Reverend Mark Tucker of Wethersfield, Connecticut. With great difficulty he was finally brought back to Schenectady, suddenly an old man in appearance, unable to walk, his face lined with suffering. He was taken a few months later to one of the popular "Hydropathic Institutes," this one located at Oyster Bay, Long Island. Here he apparently benefited from "the cold water cure," although he was jailed for several months in a mechanical wheel chair he learned to lever about the building. [33] Here also the other cure-seekers were astonished to see him and Urania driven through the grounds in an easily entered three-wheeled carriage which he brought back to the campus following what seems to have been his second trip to the Hydropathic Hospital in the fall of 1848. He had been so crippled during the preceding year that he had had to be carried into the Presbyterian Church for the Commencement exercises that July.

"Moses" joined the Nott household in 1847, the thirty year old escaped slave who had journeyed along the Underground Railroad from Talbot County, Maryland, to Troy, New York, and then to Schenectady where a local physician, Dr. Fonda, employed him until the crippled Eliphalet Nott needed the help the courtly, cheerful Moses Viney could give him. [34] Driving the little three-wheeled carriage, helping the ailing Doctor, "venerable" in appearance at last, carrying his messages about the campus and into town, "Moses" was to become even more of a campus character than "Old McKenny," the head janitor of the college buildings, or "Mr. Gonsaul," the steward of the Commons whose charge of $1.25 a week for board during the 1840s was considered gross profiteering.

If this Indian Summer of the Doctor's began to wane with his attack of inflammatory rheumatism in 1846 it was still the season for developing those new projects which were to bring Union College, "that ship in full sail, . . ." into the promised landfall. The first of these projects was his own, a promoter's scheme through which he expected to guarantee his family's security, and to produce those large contributions needed to complete the Ramée campus which gave such elegance and meaning to the portrait Henry Inman had painted of him. His second project was a corollary to the first, the new curriculum for Union College, scaled to University dimensions, the planning for which may have helped to crowd out the pain and annoyance of the physical disabilities his slowly receding illness had forced upon him.

V

On April 1, 1846 the Doctor in his role as real estate promoter, transferred to Richard Blydenburgh and Hezekiah Bradford of New York City that Stuyvesant Cove property recently reconveyed to him by the Trustees at their Semi-Centennial Board meeting. The "Cove," valued in 1845 on the college books at $70,000, was potentially of enormous value, but in 1846 much of it had yet to be transformed into saleable city lots. Still before these new partners was the problem of filling in the underwater land extending from the Cove's shore line to the eastern boundary of New York City, still only a northeast projection on the Corporation's maps, acreage-to-be, however, which the Doctor fully assumed was his by right of the city's prior grants to the Stuyvesant family. [35]

With this prospect before him, and plans still to be completed for the development of his even more valuable Hunter Point lands across the East River, the Doctor, in 1846, could face the ordeal of illness with greater equanimity. He was free, too, during his convalescence, to plan the new curriculum, "to adapt the same," according to the record of the Trustees' meeting which approved the final draft in 1849, "to the existing wants of the community," a curriculum which the Albany *Knickerbocker*, in August that year said was intended "to make the college more on the University system." [36]

On the 4th of September, 1847 the Doctor, in his wheel chair, propelled himself into the West College library room and informed the Trustees about the first stage of his sweeping academic plan to transform Union College. The Doctor announced that day that he and Edward C. Delavan would each give $10,000 "toward the erection of the seven principal buildings to be erected, in order to the entire completion of the original plan. . . . ." Their conditions were that the Board proceed at once to raise an additional $80,000 and to liquidate all outstanding college debts, a program the Doctor also promised he and his long-time partner in the temperance crusades would assist.

As a result of this offer a new Education Committee was immediately organized. The Doctor was made its chairman and to it were appointed ex-Chancellor Reuben Walworth, just made an elected Trustee, and Bishop Alonzo Potter, also a newly elected Trustee, the Reverend Mark Tucker, and Judge J. P. Cushman. The new assignment proved that the Bishop was now at least willing to compromise his less democratic views of the functions of higher education to accommodate his father-in-law's enthusiasm for "things utilitarian and scientific." At the Board's meeting the next year the new Education Committee reported that it was actively reviewing "the whole subject of education at Union College": what new professorships must be established, and what ones, "if any, may be abolished ". This last part of their study was quickly translated into seeds of rumor, tares the Doctor's enemies were soon to reap. The Committee announced it was also planning to improve the diplomas awarded to "University students in order better to describe the degree of attainment"; it also agreed to study the problem of faculty retirement and that of a fitting compensation for "Tutors" and "Fellows," two faculty categories which were to have new importance in a revitalized Union College.

Because of his continuing illness, his son-in-law was directed at this Trustees' meeting to act for the old President "On Commencement Day and at the Public Dinner . . . if he shall be too unwell. . . ." The Doctor, however, had finally set the stage for the climactic scene of his life.

On November 29, 1848 the Trustees met in special session in Albany, in the office of the Whig Secretary of State, Christopher Morgan, the Doctor again in the chair, to act on the developing plans of the Educational Committee, now called the "Committee on Reorganization." Governor Wright was dead, and the Democrats, split between "Barnburners" and "Hunkers," were out of office. Whig Governor John Young, in low favor with Thurlow Weed, and marking time until his Whig successor, Hamilton Fish, could be sworn in the following January, was present, however, with Attorney General Jordon and State Treasurer Alvah Hunt.

The new roster of professorships was completed, designed to carry out the committee's plan for a "more liberal provision for instruction in the application of science to the useful arts. . . ." The titles of the new professorships indicate that the Bishop and the Doctor had found common ground: the Bishop's successor in the chair of Moral Philosophy was also to be the new Vice President. There was to be a Professor of Ancient Languages and Literature; of Mathematics, Pure and Applied; of Natural Philosophy, Practical and Theoretical; of Natural History and of Chemistry; of French and Other Modern Languages and Literature; of Agricultural Chemistry and Chemistry applied to the Arts; of Civil and Topographical Engineering; of Ancient History and Philosophy; of Modern History; of Law and Civil Polity; and of Anatomy and Physiology. The new plan reflected the waters of the Rhine, those "freedoms" of the German student so dear to George Ticknor and to a Harvard still fumbling for them. Ticknor's *freiheit des Lernen* could be carried no further than the Doctor planned to carry it; the Committee of Reorganization recommended that November that "such a latitude of choice ought to be allowed the students in the departments of study . . . that the Honors of the Institution may be awarded in some form to every young man who shall distinguish himself by persevering and successful devotion to any liberal branch of knowledge."

The Doctor and his committee members must have felt an especial urgency to announce the new curriculum; it appeared in the college catalogue for 1848-1849 as a hope only, soon to be realized. In the year of the Union College Semi-Centennial celebration, they were fully aware, there were over one hundred colleges in the United States, and competition for students had become a pressing problem. Yale, in 1847, had publicized a new "Department of Philosophy and the Arts," open to all college graduates, "and others"; Harvard, in the same year established the Lawrence Scientific School on a gift of $50,000, a school limited, however, to the teaching of Science to undergraduates, much to the annoyance of President Edward Everett who had hoped to see the same broad "university system" established which was implicit in Eliphalet Nott's plan of reorganization. The Rensselaer Institute, in nearby Troy, under its vigorous new director, Benjamin Franklin Greene, was about to throw off its academy status, and to announce a three-year program to train "Civil Engineers, directors of works, superintendents of manufactories, professors of applied sciences, etc." [37] Yale and Harvard were belatedly opening their doors to the new studies, and Union, long "the college for the times," must continue to meet the challenge with an ever widening curriculum, "to be varied or enlarged as circumstances may demand," a radical educational principle with which the Doctor had startled his young classics tutor, Tayler Lewis, almost thirty years earlier.

That November meeting of the Trustees in 1848 heard a plan of expansion outlined which, if the Board could implement it, and could raise those seven Ramée buildings it had been challenged by the Doctor and Edward C. Delavan to build immediately, would create in Schenectady as much of a "University" as all but a few American collegians were prepared to attend before the Civil War. The 1848 Report of the Committee on Reorganization, signed by its chairman Reuben Walworth, and approved unanimously, was designed to produce the fulfillment of all the Doctor and his French architect, during that winter of 1813, had envisioned rising on Nistiquona Hill: Ramée's "Chappelle," and his "colleges," and their framing "pleasure grounds," open to the West, flung wide as Christopher Tunnard, the architectural historian was to write, "as if to express Dr. Nott's policy that education was not for the chosen few."

The "Grand Plan," however, so long ripening in the Doctor's mind, was still subject to hazards not even the Doctor, famous among his students for a more than ordinary wisdom, could have foreseen. He could not have anticipated, for instance, the outrage of John Austin Yates, Professor of Oriental Languages in Union College, a member of that Yates family whose hostility was not new to the Doctor, a teacher whose quarter of a century on the faculty was to be terminated "from and after the next commencement," presumably because Oriental Languages seemed to have little place "among the existing wants of the community." For the Doctor, his season of fair weather was over.

BOOK SEVEN

Maze Without Exit: 1845-1854

CHAPTER I

"Fiat justicia, ruat coelum"

THE scale of the drama about to be played out must be measured by the words of ex-Secretary of War and ex-Secretary of the Treasury John Canfield Spencer, who was drawn finally into its action, and into what, by 1853, had become one of the ugliest undercover battles for state and national reputations in the history of the New York State Legislature:

> This intricate, protracted, tedious, and extraordinary investigation . . . involves the character of some of the most distinguished and most able men of our State. The executive officers—the Governor, Lieutenant-Governor, Secretary of State, Comptroller, Attorney-General and Treasurer, are and for more than thirty years have been, by virtue of their respective offices, Trustees of Union College. Judicial officers of high rank, and other distinguished citizens, have been Trustees. If the charges brought forward are sustained, it is impossible to screen any of these trustees [and this would have included Spencer himself] from the charges of the most gross and culpable inattention to their duties, and ignorance of the fiscal affairs of the College; or a wilful and wicked abandonment of its rights and interests to the cupidity of its President.[1]

The majority of the Senate Committee which was to hear Spencer's overwhelming "Argument" in defense of the Doctor and of the vulnerable public men who had been or still were Union College Trustees, was to agree with him that, had the long ordeal proved the Doctor had fraudulently taken for himself nearly a million dollars belonging to Union College, as the accountant for the Senate Committee testified in 1853 he had, "numbers of those who have held the highest stations in the State and Federal governments must have forfeited all claims to the public confidence."[2]

No Trustee, however, at that Board meeting held in November, 1848, in Secretary of New York State Morgan's office, called to hear and to approve the ambitious program for new buildings and new professorships "on the university plan," the fulfillment of which was to be the culmination of Eliphalet Nott's career as the President of Union College, could have suspected the tragic consequences which were to follow the vote that day to dismiss their Professor of Oriental Languages, a member of that junta of Yateses long known to the Doctor. That vote accounts for as much subsequent Union College history as did the lost nail which was prelude to a lost kingdom.

Professor John Austin Yates, "a singular compound of good and bad," according to Jonathan Pearson, and holder of that seemingly outdated Professorship of Oriental Languages, had actually been in deep trouble himself during this period, guilty, it was said, of leading a double life, a charge which had become almost public property, and which resulted in serious accusations being lodged against him before the local Dutch Reformed Church which he served as a supply. His plans to marry an unnamed lady had apparently revealed activities which required him "to clear up his character," and which made him fearful of losing his faculty position, a fact which his chief accuser emphasized in a letter denouncing him to then Governor Hamilton Fish. The Governor was informed that "it is believed and asserted as coming from Professor Yates that after his union with this lady, his chief dependence for retaining his present post in College will be on your Excellency's influence and support." [3] The Governor was then told that he need only turn to "Dr. Nott, Chancellor Walworth, Dr. Sprague, Bishop Potter, etc.," for confirmation of the charges, and that so far as Professor Yates's pending marriage was concerned, "were this lady a sister of mine it would be infinitely preferable to follow her to her grave than to have her fall into such hands."

If the Professor of Oriental Languages had been without "connexions" he might well have remained a forgotten sacrifice to his own vagaries, but this particular faculty member, so popular with his students, was also a nephew of Trustee Henry Yates, ex-treasurer of Union College, ex-mayor of Schenectady, and ex-New York State Senator, charged long since by the Doctor and the Board with having betrayed their trust in him by becoming a secret member of the House of Yates and McIntyre, the Doctor's firm of lottery managers. Professor John Austin Yates was also a nephew of that late lottery partner, John Barentse Yates, who had been unrelentingly opposed to the Doctor's profitable role in the affairs of the "House," and whose step-daughter in 1829 had become Mrs. Professor John Austin Yates. The nephew's bitterness at losing his professorship, however, was but a portion of the flow from a family wellspring of hostility.

"An act of the Trustees," the Board declared in one of its later "Replies" to the violent charges soon to be made in the Assembly and then in the Senate against the Doctor and the Trustees "gave to an individual connected with the College great personal offense. This act was imputed to the President, though unjustly, for being sick at the time he was not even consulted concerning it. The aggrieved party threatened to retaliate by placing the College, through the influence of friends, under the ban of the Legislature."[4]

"Justitia et Veritas," two unidentified Union College seniors of the class of 1849, named Professor Yates as the agent who triggered the train of legislative investigation. In a bitter letter to the Albany *Daily Knickerbocker* on September 3 that year they wrote that, having called at the Professor's house the preceding July to ask for his signature on their diplomas, "he, in a faint voice, replied, that he was no longer connected with Union College, as his professorship had expired the day previous. I was dumb-struck, my friend burst into a copious flood of tears; . . . report says that Dr. Nott accused him of being instrumental in Mr. Pruyn's making the motion requiring Union College to make a full report of its concerns, etc., to the Legislature."[5]

John Austin Yates, in debt to the college for over $1000 in unpaid notes, as well as for "cow pasture, coal, ground to plant, books not returned to the library," in serious trouble with the congregation of his church, suffering from what his physician was said to have called "an alienation of the mind," reportedly having carried his burning brand to Robert H. Pruyn, Chairman of the Committee on Colleges, Academies, and Common Schools of the New York State Legislature, died suddenly on Sunday, August 26, 1849, "after ten hours illness, of cholera."

If he played the role of prologue to this tragedy now opening, the action he had begun was to be developed by his uncle, Henry Yates, by State Senator James W. Beekman, and their satellites who seemed willing to destroy the college in order to settle personal scores and serve political ambitions.

"It is notorious," John C. Spencer was to tell the last of the Senate Committees investigating Union College, "that Mr. [Henry] Yates and his connexions have been active in what I do not hesitate to call a vindictive persecution of Dr. Nott. It is well known that one of those connexions, from the commencement of your inquiries, has filled the columns of the filthiest and most abandoned newspaper in the State, with garbled and partial statements of facts in the case, with wholesale misrepresentations, with abuse of me for undertaking the defense of Dr. Nott, and with one continued stream, black with malignity, of the most outrageous calumny against that old man." [6]

On May 8, 1849, the Albany *Daily Knickerbocker* had expanded its campaign against the Doctor and the Trustees with an article headed "It Don't Pay." Its Irish editor, Hugh J. Hastings, called Union College "the celebrated absorbent," and demanded to know where over $300,000 in state endowments had gone. He charged that the Trustees had invested college funds "in worthless bank stock and valueless due bills," and demanded that the Assembly's commission appointed on April 11 to investigate the college's financial history, "before it leave this time-honored seminary . . . probe this fifty thousand dollar business to the bottom," a sum Hastings declared had been wasted on bad mortgages.

"Let us have the names of the individuals who owe this immense sum," the *Knickerbocker's* editor wrote, "and also a brief inventory of their uncles and their cousins. By becoming acquainted with a man's relations we can often account for the manner in which his bank book is kept."

"Uncles and cousins": from the beginning of the Doctor's ordeal, these included not only Yateses, but Beekmans and Sanderses, men whose Dutch blood mingled and followed the course of the Hudson and the Mohawk, joining families from New York City to Schenectady. James William Beekman, with ambitions to become governor of New York State, to be even richer than he was, and to restore the Beekman name to its seventeenth and eighteenth century preeminence, lived, when in Albany, with "Uncle Jacob," Jacobus G. Sanders, a member of the Union College Class of 1812. "Uncle Jacob's" devotion, in company with other Sanders nephews and supernumeraries, to the cause of destroying Eliphalet Nott deserves remembrance as a cruel backstairs charade whose performance, when publicized by Spencer, contributed to the closing of State Senator James W. Beekman's political career.[7] "There is no man who knows [the Sanderses]," John C. Spencer declared before the Senate's investigating committee, "who does not also know, that for many years no terms of vituperation against the President of Union College have been spared by the members of that family." Their enmity, according to Spencer, stemmed "from an old difficulty with the President about the purchase of some land of the college, and by a steady refusal of Dr. Nott to minister to the ambitions of one of the family to be a Trustee of the college."[8]

Enmities which took root in a harassed professor's pique, which spread into undrained cisterns of family grievances, could only have risen into massive bloom under the watchful and calculating husbandry of so righteous a citizen as James W. Beekman, the dedicated and philanthropic politician from the 8th ward of New York City. One can only account for the relentless and, on occasion, unscrupulous four-year campaign Beekman began to wage against Eliphalet Nott and Union College in the spring of 1849 by viewing this strong willed, arch conservative Dutch aristocrat in the light of his commitments in a time of violent change. He saw the northern states filling with a growing army of Abolitionists he hated, of Irish immigrants and Roman Catholics he feared, of radical Whigs like Thurlow Weed and William Henry Seward whom he saw as mortal enemies of the nation, of those temperance leaders who, like Edward C. Delavan and the Doctor himself, appeared to him as dangerous censors threatening the rites of the bottle as well as the free enterprise profits of his grog shop constituents.[9]

"The old fox," Uncle Jacob Sanders informed then Assemblyman Beekman on April 25, 1849, "has outwitted all pursuit at present." By this time Beekman seems to have fully accepted his role as the Doctor's harrier. He was now actively baying his quarry as a member of the "Pruyn Committee" which had been holding preliminary hearings through that month on what the Albany *Daily Knickerbocker* was calling "another Canal Bank iniquity." [10] On March 12th, on the motion of Assemblyman Robert H. Pruyn, Union College had been ordered to produce a "true statement of all the property owned by the said College . . . in what manner the said funds are invested . . . changes in investment . . . within the last ten years . . . to be verified by the oath of their President and Treasurer." Beckman soon took the lead in pressing the inquiry. It was Beekman who, later that month, persuaded the Assembly to extend the period of review from ten years to twenty-five years, and who, the next month, was trying to discover whether the college had any interest in the Novelty Iron Works, and was interviewing Charles Yates, Henry Yates's son, inquiring for a list of those Chancery Bills the "House of Yates and McIntyre" had filed against the Doctor and the Trustees in the 1830s. [11]

By the end of that April Chairman Pruyn, "with power to send for persons and papers" from Union College, had interviewed Archibald McIntyre and had been informed by him that the "House" had paid the college $800,000 as its share of the lottery profits, not $200,000 as the Trustees claimed. [12] The smell of scandal was in the air.

By the end of May the Albany *Daily Knickerbocker*, intoxicated with the odor, printed another of the diatribes against the Doctor and the Trustees which were to become its stock in trade for the next four years; this one, headed "Union College," stated that:

> Before the committee complete their labors, there will be a chapter about steamboats and patent stoves written, that will astonish the cocked hat of the oldest inhabitant. For years Union College has been as much a machine shop as a seminary of learning, and the number of piston rods about the house are almost equal to the students. The professors have studied the science of hot water so long that we fear some of them have got their foot into it.
>
> . . . in our opinion, the whole management has been for years as rotten as oranges three for a cent. [13]

The reaction at the college that spring to the demands of the legislature "to report forthwith to this House" had been immediate. The Doctor "on his own responsibility," had treasurer Alexander Holland prepare schedules of the State's land and lottery grants to Union, and of the college property then on the books. To this report, sworn to on April 5th, the Finance Committee, assuming that what their legislative enemies really wanted was a record of the Doctor's financial relations with the Trustees, had the treasurer append to his report a copy of the review of 1831 on those relations made by then Comptroller Silas Wright and Secretary of State John A. Dix, together with the statement that on two other occasions the Doctor's arrangements with the Board had been subject to "a special and searching examination."

At the July meeting of the Board, less tense because trustee Henry Yates did not appear, the Finance Committee was enlarged by the addition of State Treasurer Alvah Hunt and Comptroller Washington Hunt, office holders under Governor Hamilton Fish. Although these appointments must have seemed strategic moves from the Board's point of view, each of these men was a "Seward Whig," a part of Thurlow Weed's "*Journal* Clique" to which then Assemblyman James W. Beekman was uncompromisingly hostile.

Both the Schenectady *Cabinet* and the Albany *Argus* thought the Doctor's prompt reply to the legislature's demands that spring "places this institution beyond suspicion," a conclusion to which the *Daily Knickerbocker* on May 29 replied, "It don't [sic] do any such thing," adding that the Canal Bank had made an equally glowing report of its assets "only a few days before it shut pan on its stockholders, and paid its depositors two doughnuts on the dollar." The next day, the *Knickerbocker* returned to the attack with an editorial headed, "That Chapel," and wondered publicly if the Trustees still had what the writer said was some $50,000 or $60,000 raised to build it, "for the first hod full of mortar has not yet been mixed." The editor wondered if the Board had "swapped off" the chapel funds for Mohawk and Hudson Railroad Company stock, charging that it was "generally believed that at one time Union College owned about one-third of the whole enterprise." It was this rumor which Chairman Pruyn of the Assembly's investigating committee later declared was the immediate reason for the call by the Assembly for the college records, to see if, as the rumor had it, the stock ". . . purchased with [college] funds, was never owned by the college, but was the private property of the president," or whether "it was purchased with his own funds and at his own risk."

II

By the time the Trustees met at Commencement in 1849, their accusers' version of Union College's financial history was a matter of public record; the die had been cast, and there was no retrieving it. The Pruyn Committee, even as the *Daily Knickerbocker*, had not been impressed with Alexander Holland's, the Doctor's, and the Finance Committee's reply to the legislature that April, and so, in spite of the cholera scare, the committee, consisting of Chairman Robert Pruyn, J. W. Beekman, J. D. Button, Alonzo Johnson, and G. L. Disoway, journeyed to Schenectady on May 16th where, through May 26th, they "met in the apartments of the President," and where "very full explanations of the financial transactions of the college were made by the president and the treasurer, both being always present." The Doctor was no doubt still in his wheel chair with "Moses," the new servant who was then also a fugitive slave, close by, an affront, if Beekman was aware of "Moses," to a committeeman who, as a "Cotton Whig," was a militant supporter of fugitive slave law legislation.

Small lapses were probably beneath the notice of these earnest investigators; had they cared to, however, they might have leavened the charged atmosphere in the President's apartment with comments at the expense of "Uncle Jacob" Sanders's nephew, James W. Sanders, who, as Commissioner of Deeds, had recently affirmed that "Alexander Hamilton, [sic] treasurer of Union College being duly sworn . . . , had attested before him on April 5th that the College's reply "was just and true." [14]

The Pruyn Committee worked methodically through treasurer Alexander Holland's ledgers. When these records, going back as much as fifty years, seemed inadequate, the committee members probed the Doctor's memory. All investments, they noted, had long been made by a Trustees' Finance Committee, currently made up of the Doctor who was its chairman, Judge

Alonzo Paige, Edward C. Delavan, and the New York State Comptroller, then ex-Congressman Washington Hunt, a "Seward Whig," and soon to follow Hamilton Fish as Governor of New York.

The committee's probing on the next to the last day of their hearings produced what James W. Beekman was looking for, the account which Johnson's notes reported, "is the only one the college has of moneys received from lotteries under the legislative acts of 1814 and 1822, from Yates and McIntyre." Alexander Holland's books showed that the college had received, in all, $317,124.50, a sum less by almost a half million dollars than the $800,000 reported to Chairman Pruyn that April by Archibald McIntyre.

The Doctor and his treasurer were asked again how much the State had granted to Union College, to which Holland replied that the total was $358,112.13, a revised figure based on the lottery grants, subsidies, and real estate known as the "Military Lots." The treasurer's answer to "Question No. 3": "What sum (if any) was realized by Dr. Nott?" was recorded as "Does not know." To "Question No. 6": "What sum, if any, has been allowed to Dr. Nott, as his compensation for personal services and hazards?" the then wary treasurer answered, "The college has no account of any such allowances." "Question No. 7" probed suddenly to the wellspring of the Doctor's financial history: "Does not the President by virtue of a resolution of the Trustees of Union College, manage the property of the college as his own, inter-changeably, as occasion arises?" Alexander Holland must have been stunned, not only by all the question implied, but by the burden of responsibility he must assume in answering it.

"There are resolutions," he told these legislators, "authorizing him as chairman of the Finance Committee to direct the application of the funds." "A. Johnson's" notes then add that "in reply to the branch of the question demanding 'does he not use the funds of the college, etc.,' replies, 'he has never done so to my knowledge.' " One feels the tensions of this moment, the Doctor silent, in his wheel chair, this college treasurer bound by an inheritance of records and privileged information which perhaps no man, including the old President himself, could ever hope to explain. It is obvious in the light of this question, and of the corollary ones which followed, that the Chancery suits of the 1830s had settled nothing. There would now be an accounting before a less sympathetic court than the one Chancellor and still Trustee Reuben Walworth had sat on a quarter of a century earlier. Then Benjamin Franklin Butler, the Attorney General of the United States, and James Canfield Spencer, on behalf of the House of Yates and McIntyre, had raised the same issue when the Doctor's Trustees who were state officers, men like Secretary of State Dix, and Governor Marcy, had guided him to the safe haven of an out-of-court settlement, and had joined the whole Board of Trustees in sanctioning his claims to ownership of those lottery profits known as the "President's Fund."

Whatever thoughts went through the Doctor's mind were set aside as these legislators turned to him with their "Question No. 9: Do the Novelty Works stand on the register's books of the city of New York as the property of E. Nott or of Union College?," a surprising question, for one has not heard that the Doctor had any interest in that foundry and cradle of his S. S. *Novelty* since his sons Howard and Benjamin, its once nominal owners, had gone down in bankruptcy in 1836. The Doctor "was understood to reply, 'They stand in the name of E. Nott.' " [15]

The Committee then questioned him about Stuyvesant's Cove, loading its inquiries with hostile inferences. "Question No. 13: The Novelty Works being the private property of Dr. Nott, for what reason has that money [Yates and McIntyre's recent and final payment of $17,500 to Union College] been employed to enable Hezekiah Bradford to make a dock there?"

Denial and explanation: the money is in the hands of the college treasurer.

There were denials and explanations to cover a dozen questions implying dishonest or indiscreet use by the Doctor of his power, as Alonzo Johnson noted, "to direct the application of the funds as he may think fit," a power given to him, as the secretary of this legislative committee again pointedly noted, "by a resolution of the Trustees of Union College."

On the last day of these hearings the Pruyn Committee asked whether "Union College ever owned any railroad stock,' and (if any) in what company, and what has become of it?" Alexander Holland's reply that the college had never owned any railroad stock was, by this time, an anticlimax, for it was now clear why the Pruyn Committee had braved the dangers of cholera to come to Schenectady; James W. Beekman had gathered all he needed to write the majority report filed with the legislature the following year, on March 19, 1850.

Three days after the committee left Schenectady the Albany *Daily Knickerbocker*, commenting on the committee's visit, called on its readers to "fear God and do their duty . . . give us light, and stand from under." On May 30 its editor closed his comments on "That Chapel" by observing that "We have no objections to colleges becoming steam boiler shops, nor to presidents and divines connected with them becoming interested in steamboats, caravans and sore tailed monkeys,—we have no objection to their blowing the organ, all we are anxious about is, who pays for the wind. . . ."

III

For the Doctor there was to be a summer, a fall, and a winter of waiting. On the day the Pruyn Committee left Schenectady he wrote to Thurlow Weed, asking his advice on the wisdom of speaking or not speaking in his own defense before the committee's report was made. On June 2 Urania Nott, outraged at the Albany *Daily Knickerbocker's* penny-press stories, wrote to the Whig leader, begging him to take what action he could in defense of her husband whose calm resignation was incomprehensible to her. [16] In spite of the Doctor's and Urania's letters, however, the editor of the *Evening Journal* seems to have left the immediate defense of the Doctor to other papers such as the Schenectady *Cabinet* and the Albany *Argus*. [17]

Outwardly, the Doctor seemed serenity itself. On June 25, his seventy-sixth birthday, he invited the senior class to a "levee" at the President's house, a substitute for the "illumination" of all the campus buildings which they had planned. [18] Urania received roses, and the Doctor was presented "with a large, ripe orange of domestic growth, with stem and leaves attached." Congressman McKean of Saratoga County, sent his own portrait, "large as life and elegantly framed." When Urania and Bishop Potter could find no place to hang it, the Doctor settled the matter by telling them "to hang him in the library, where he should have been himself long ago." The faculty "and their ladies" arrived, and the Doctor seemed to everyone "to be in fine spirits, entertaining the groups who thronged about him with vivid delineations of the masterspirits of the last generation." One guest recalled that the Doctor praised Hamilton as greater than Webster, saying that "the greatest efforts of Hamilton have never been published."

When the Doctor was asked to speak he told his guests the secret of his longevity: "constant use of cold water baths . . . abstinence from all stimulants, both in food and drink," and pointed out to them that "man . . . is almost the only animal that outrages the plain and obvious laws of his nature." To his seniors he spoke of a coming judgment day, and charged them not to be absent "from the right hand of God" on that occasion, where he hoped to be found also. "Mr. McCoy of the Senior Class read passages from *Henry IV*, and then the speech of Adam in "As You Like It", ending

> my age is as a lusty winter,
> Frosty, but kindly.

Everyone agreed the whole speech was quite applicable to the Doctor.

While he waited for the Pruyn Committee to make its report, and suffered the roistering in the Albany *Daily Knickerbocker*, the less steady undergraduates attended "Dutch Fuddles" [country balls] "at the risk of a broken head," and meetings of the "Ugly Club," which were held in No. 26 South College, where the elect enjoyed "desperate fights and tremendous sprees" in their black painted room, in "an atmosphere redolent with the fumes of hot toddy and tobacco," all of it wonderfully and dangerously close to the Doctor's apartment in the north pediment end of South College. [19]

Waiting ended for Eliphalet Nott, finally, on March 19th, 1850, when four of the five members of the legislature's investigating committee, James W. Beekman, Dr. J. D. Button, Alonzo Johnson, and Gabriel Disoway, filed their majority report. The conclusions they drew were those the Doctor must have expected and dreaded, in substance, that he had used the funds of Union College "interchangeably with his own." The majority of the committee questioned the legality of the Trustees' transfer of Stuyvesant's Cove and the Hunter Point farm to the Doctor in 1845, and charged that his financial activities as apart from his campus duties, "were dangerous to the morals of the young, and to the Trustees who permitted it." [20]

James W. Beekman, Dr. Button, Alonzo Johnson, and Gabriel Disoway ended their summary with the damning conclusion that "Your committee have set forth a few, from among many cases of wrong management, and have established from an examination of these, the fact, which they are now constrained to report, that the financial condition of Union College is unsound and improper."

Gabriel Disoway had been finally pressed by Beekman into signing "any report you and the Doctor [J.D. Button] and Johnson can agree on"; "Fiat justicia, ruat coelum" ['let justice be done, though the heavens fall'] he had concluded his letter in which he assented to the wishes of the "cotton whig" Assemblyman from New York City. [21]

Chairman Robert H. Pruyn filed his minority report four days later; his position was the reverse of that taken by his fellow committeemen. [22] The Doctor's role, he said, as the supervisor of the lotteries, explained their success: "No one can examine the history of those complicated and immense operations without being satisfied that Union College owes all it has derived from them to its President, and that a Board of Trustees, with thrice the financial ability usually displayed by similar bodies, if it had undertaken their supervision, would have involved the college and themselves in ruin." The chairman agreed that the Trustees were blamable for having given far too much power to their President, although he assured the legislature that the Doctor's so-called "President's Fund" was quite legal, and that the Trustees had never claimed it. He noted too, that he was sure the transfer to the Doctor by the Trustees of the New York City and Long Island real estate was justified, inasmuch as it had been purchased by the Doctor out of his personal lottery profits. As to that Mohawk and Hudson railroad stock which had been the subject of so many rumors, it was the Doctor's stock, the chairman declared, and had never belonged to the college.

Assemblyman Beekman's majority report created a sense of outrage in Schenectady. Alexander Holland, on April 8th, appended to his annual treasurer's statement to the Legislature charges by him and the resident Trustees that the majority report of the Pruyn Committee was filled with "misstatements of facts, erroneous deductions, unfounded imputations and insinuations," and a point-by-point rebuttal designed to make clear the real objectives toward which Beekman was driving. [23] Holland accused the majority of the Pruyn Committee with deliberately perverting the record of the Doctor's lottery financing in order to make it appear that his "personal" contract with Yates and McIntyre having netted him, so Beekman had claimed, "nearly or quite a quarter of a million dollars," was "discreditable to the Trustees who had permitted it." What was to become the central issue of the legislature's investigation—the ownership of the "President's Fund"—was not yet spelled out, but Beekman's "imputations and insinuations" seemed quite clear. Alexander Holland was in no position to point out their political significance.

If the Assembly which, conveniently for Beekman, adjourned two days after the college's reply was filed, chose to take no action on the two reports submitted to it by the Pruyn Committee, the fact offered no guide line to James B. Sanders, Commissioner of Deeds, who had so recently attested that "Alexander Hamilton" was the treasurer of Union College. This nephew of "Uncle Jacob" Sanders and first cousin of now State Senator Beekman wrote a letter on April 25, 1850 to the latter, one which measures the flow of family hostility to the Doctor as well as the degree of influence both uncle and cousin appear to have had with their New York City "connexion":

My dear James;   April 25, 1850
    Enclosed I send you a copy of an article published this morning—it is an answer to an article which appeared in this week's Schenectady Sentinel, edited by Mr. Riggs—the paper which does the college

printing—the articles bear evidence of Nott's impress—and is aimed personally at you. . . . Dr. Nott evidently wants a newspaper controversy with you which I would by all means avoid, as it can lead to no good. I would not notice these attacks—but I would were I you gain all the information I could and let them hear from you next winter in the Senate. Dr. Nott evidently wishes to raise a fog—and false issue, and by that means escape the real question. I will from time to time send you what is published in this quarter. Mr. Watson the editor of the express [sic] [Albany Morning *Express*] has taken an interest in this matter and will no doubt answer the Sentinel's articles. The Sentinel promises to say more at another time.

The answer of Holland alias Nott was pretty generally circulated here. I was on the eve of sending you a copy sent me when Uncle Jacob said he would send his. . . .

I have written a hasty letter. Remember me to all, & believe me yours, etc.,

James B. Sanders

. . . . . Uncle Jacob joins me in my advice to you. [24]

Cousin Beekman followed the counsel of the two Sanderses exactly. By the middle of May the Doctor learned that Beekman was personally looking about Stuyvesant Cove, a mile or so below the Beekman country seat on the East River. Robert W. Lowber, the Doctor's new business agent, and from now on his second shadow, wrote to him that the new Senator had been asking questions of Hezekiah Bradford, then busy filling in the Doctor's underwater lots at the "Cove". Senator Beekman, Lowber informed the Doctor, had told Bradford that "you used the moneys of the College as your own, indiscriminately." Bradford, however, according to the Doctor's agent, had been cautioned "to say little or nothing." [25]

By Commencement that July, when the Trustees met in "Geological Hall," they and the Doctor were under a new attack by the Senator from New York City who, that April, had pushed a resolution through the Upper House which directed the Comptroller and the Attorney General "to examine further into the fiscal condition of Union College." No action, however, had yet been taken. State Comptroller Washington Hunt, who met as a Trustee with the Board in July, could hardly have thanked Beekman for the awkward position he had been crowded into as a member of the Administration called on to investigate himself as a

Union College Trustee and those other ex-officio Board members who, including the Governor, were Seward Whigs, and whose loss of character as Trustees of the State's educational funds could be turned into political capital. [26]

Since President Zachary Taylor's death early that July, and the inheritance of his office by Millard Fillmore, the "Accidental President," Senator Beekman's hopes for eliminating radical Whigs from the New York political scene had mounted, for word had come to Albany that Fillmore was determined to see the end of their power in the Whig party. Beekman had even been encouraged, should he continue "to speak out boldly for the Union," to expect "a distinguished" Federal appointment. [27]

Neither the State Comptroller nor the Attorney General apparently had much taste for the task Beekman's resolution had set for them, for neither of them had been heard from on the matter by Commencement time that year. Beekman himself, strongly influenced by "Uncle Jacob" Sanders, by then had plunged into those activities Democrats and Fillmore Whigs hoped would keep Governor Fish from succeeding Daniel S. Dickinson as United States Senator from New York. [28] He had also joined in the long fight for "Free Schools" which that year Horace Greeley helped wage and which, the latter wrote, he hoped Eliphalet Nott would join. [29] By this time, however, there was no committee table big enough to accommodate both Senator Beekman and the President of Union College.

Until the next April the Doctor and the Board had their reprieve, although it was quite apparent at Commencement in 1850 that Beekman's attacks, echoed by the newspapers, were hurting Union College. Ten years earlier, when Seward was Governor, and John C. Spencer was his Secretary of State, there were 315 undergraduates on the Hill; by July, 1850, the number had dropped to 224, with only 84 admitted during the year, a falling off no longer to be explained by the hard times of the Jackson Depression and its long aftermath. A Union College "on the University System" seemed more remote than ever, even though the Doctor that year turned over Mohawk Bank Stock, and a $20,000 bond and mortgage to the Board, to be used "for an observatory and other buildings" to be built as soon as others were generous, and his own contributions became productive. At that

July meeting he also persuaded a reluctant Board to rescind those "extraordinary powers" he had been given so long ago, powers which had enabled him to act as the Supervisor of the Literature Lottery, and, though he did not mention this, to accumulate his "President's Fund." Nor did he mention the new hazards he was then undertaking, not risks, but certainties, if his new advisers were right, and which, if successful, should end criticism of his financial operations as well as guarantee the success of his "university" plans. The fulfillment of these plans had suddenly become urgent as Columbia College supporters and ambitious Albanians began to discuss establishing a great national university in either New York City or at the State Capital. [30]

The Doctor must have missed "Moses" at this time, gone into Canada at the Doctor's expense, a "fugitive slave." The latter's owner had assured the Doctor's grandson, Clarkson N. Potter, who went south, following the passage of the Fugitive Slave Law in 1850 to negotiate the young Negro's freedom, that "Moses" could be bought for $1900. Although "Cotton Whigs" might approve his capture, the Doctor kept him in Canada until 1852, when his former owner, Richard Murphy of Talbot County, Maryland, reduced his price to $250, and "Moses," [freed] by Eliphalet Nott, came back to the campus and his duties as the Notts' doorman, driver of the three-wheeled sulky, and the Doctor's body servant until 1866 when he was the last mourner to leave the old President's grave.

"Moses" symbolized that side of Eliphalet Nott which embraced even Abolitionists and which could stun a temperance audience with his reading of the "Rum Maniac." The Doctor embodied a humanitarianism which Senator Beekman, speaking for a constituency of New York City ship owners, cotton traders, and liquor dealers, and out of his self-consciousness at being a Beekman, looked on with a growing distaste. Such men as the Notts and the Sewards he saw as destroying the America he was determined to preserve. The Beekman who was so soon to return to the attack on the Doctor and the Trustees of Union College, was, by contrast, the conservative good man, devoted even to such unpopular causes as "Free Schools," and public parks for New York City, and vaguely, to human rights so long as they were "nativist's" rights which excluded much that Irish Roman Catholics were demanding. His was a raw "Americanism," hostile to foreigners, to freedom for Negroes, and even to that un-American language corrupter, Noah Webster, against the introduction of whose dictionaries into New York's schools the Senator fought with the same devotion he was to give to destroying Eliphalet Nott, that other corrupter of youth, if one is to believe the majority report of the Pruyn Committee.

CHAPTER 2

"*A beautiful, speculative scheme*"

ONE issue, at least, was Senator Beekman's to order as he pleased. As chairman, now, of the "Committee on Literature" of the Upper House, he chose to wait until April 12, 1851, five days before the end of the legislative session, to train his artillery again on Union College. He began his attack in the Senate by sarcastically commenting on the "report of six printed lines to the Legislature" submitted by Alexander Holland the preceding April, and then set about to level the defense Holland had raised to the charges the majority of the Pruyn Committee had recently brought against the Doctor and the Trustees. [1]

By April 12, 1851, it was obvious Senator Beekman had examined the ledgers of the "House of Yates and McIntyre," where he had found figures which satisfied him that the Doctor and the Trustees of Union College had entered into agreements which were "entirely indefensible." The ink of his arithmetic was to spread now far beyond the Senate chamber:

> It is fair to state [Beekman assured his hearers] that none but an experienced accountant can unravel the intricacies of the money transactions of Union College. Your committee are satisfied that a critically correct balance sheet would show MORE ASTONISHING RESULTS than those now set forth. There is little doubt, then, that after the most liberal allowance for errors, the present balance against Union College, for which the Trustees of that institution are justly accountable, is very large, thus:
> —Received from the State, otherwise than by
> lotteries, granted previously to 1803 . . . [with]
> interest thereon for forty years .... $ 291,126.09
> —Received from Yates and McIntyre .... $ 802,323.28
> Interest thereon, as above $1,233,707.02
> —Funds received before the State grants
> were made .... $ 53,046.29
> Interest thereon for thirty years .... $ 111,397.20
>
> $2,491,599.88

The Senator at least was making a unique contribution to the history of American education: no college in the land had ever been charged with holding such wealth, or with having been so criminal in obtaining it. From his grand total the Senator then deducted credits he thought it proper to allow the college, the sum of $1,284,340.56, which included campus and buildings, the cost of operating the Literature Lottery, and the invested funds on the treasurer's books. The balance, $1,207,258.32, however, was unaccounted for, a balance which included the nearly half million dollars which Eliphalet Nott, with the sanction of his Trustees, claimed was his for "risks run and hazards taken" on behalf of Yates and McIntyre. This money, Senator Beekman now declared was, in fact, owing to Union College, a part of New York State's endowment of that institution.

The conditions of this second act of the legislative drama were now clearly stated; questions as to the ownership of railroad stock had faded into the cardinal issue: had the Trustees of Union College failed the State in preserving and husbanding its gifts to them, designed to be used solely for the purposes of education?

> It is extremely doubtful (Beekman concluded) how far the Trustees had the power to authorize their president either to claim as his own so large a portion of the avails of the lotteries as $111,343.44, or to permit him to use the college funds indiscriminately as his own while chairman of the finance committee, so as to bring them into debt to their president in the large sum [in 1845] of $366,177.63. . . . While professors' salaries were unpaid for two quarters at about the same time.

Senator Beekman ended his new charges that April with a call "for a legislative investigation in a thorough manner," and a request that a skilled accountant be employed by a new committee consisting of the Comptroller, the Attorney General, and the Reverend J. N. Campbell, a Regent of the University of the State of New York, to investigate both the college books and the books of Yates and McIntyre, "and to report an accurate balance sheet to the next legislature."

Behind this shattering attack was the Senator's intelligence corps of uncles and cousins, as well now as the headmaster of the Albany Academy, the Reverend Dr. William H. Campbell, who that February had tried unsuccessfully to supply the Senator with the Doctor's published comments on lotteries, and who had lamely concluded his letter by offering the information that a Union College student had recently been tried in Albany for stealing. Headmaster Campbell had then suggested that Senator Beekman write to him, asking if this story was true,—"this would free me," the Reverend headmaster wrote, "from the suspicions of the old fox, and would strengthen your cause. . . ." [2]

Three months later the head of the Albany Academy wrote again that he had been checking "the Doctor's acts and designs," reporting that local rumor had it the Senator's hostility to the Doctor stemmed from their disagreement over "up-town lots" [presumably in New York City], and concluded that the "Nott forces" hoped to prevent the appointment of an accountant, but that the chairman of the new commission to investigate Union College "will not be intimidated . . . and will report any dereliction on the part of the committee members to the Senate." [3]

"Your report," the Rev. Doctor Campbell then told Beekman, "has gone over the length and breadth of the land; I have myself sent out 3000 copies . . . ," a gratuitous kindness on the part of the man who would soon go to Rutgers College as its President, the New Jersey institution Beekman's father-in-law, the Rev. Dr. Phillip Milledoler, had once headed. Possibly the Senator's enthusiastic helper also thought he had found a way to make the "amende" for what, two years earlier, he had called the "betrayal" of the late Professor John Austin Yates.

On May 17 "Uncle Jacob" Sanders wrote to Beekman that his Senate charges against the college had "made quite an impression here [Albany], and in Schenectady. . . . Your friends in this quarter," Uncle Jacob promised, "will look out for you in this matter." [4] The Sanderses were apparently hoping the Senator was also looking out for them, too, for during that April the headmaster of the Academy had written to Beekman that the Chairman of the Investigating Committee, "is favorable to Mr. Sanders, but wants to know if he is reliable as an accountant. . . ." [5] Such an appointment, however, seems to have been too much for the Senator's hand picked commission to support. "Mr. Sanders" was by-passed, and on May 27th Levinus Vanderheyden, a public accountant from Troy, New York, undertook the labor of reporting "an accurate balance" of more than fifty years of Union College ledger keeping. The weight of that balance, Beekman believed, would sink forever the reputations of the President of Union College and of those "Seward Whigs" who were members of its Board of Trustees.

II

"Persons desirous of investigating a beautiful speculative scheme," the Albany *Morning Express* had advertised on May 10, 1851, were invited to call at the paper's office where they could pick up Senator Beekman's attack on Union College of April 12th, "left for distribution." With this notice, and the full report of the Senator's attack published by the *Express* two days earlier began a bitter series of countercharges by the College that the Senator and his supporters intended to deny the Doctor and the Trustees the elemental right to be heard in their own defense. "When, where, and by whom . . . ," the Trustees demanded of the editor of the *Express*, had they ever been approached by the Senator for their clarification of his charges? [6] Enough sympathetic Senate votes were available in late June to pass a resolution limiting the new Campbell Committee's authority, and defining its task. On July 3rd two new members were added to the committee, David Buel, and Philip S. VanRensselaer, both State Regents, and presumably unbiased, a counterbalance to the Rev. J. N. Campbell, its chairman, who was now rumored to be hostile to the Doctor. [7]

Again the old President and the Trustees waited, the latter enraged at Senator Beekman's tactics and the "flash press" exploitation of his charges. [8] The Doctor seemed all benignity as the political overtones jangled about him. The Board met in late June, not in Schenectady, but in Secretary of State Christopher Morgan's office in Albany where its members approved an angry reply to Senator Beekman, the publication of which, however, was suspended as it was being printed "at the instance of the President, who presumed that the Honorable Senator Beekman would, on the presentation of the memorial of the Trustees, make the *amende honorable*. . . ." [9]

Two other radical Whig officeholders, Washington Hunt, when he was State Comptroller, and his successor, Philo C. Fuller, had already declined to undertake the Union College investigation called for by the Senate at the beginning of the 1851 session; they had, each of them, been too busy, they claimed.[10] Comptroller Fuller was only able to escape serving on the new Investigating Committee when he lost his office in the fall elections that year to J. C. Wright, a Democrat. Whigs generally lost important posts that November, the result of a nation-wide reaction to the clamor of radical Abolitionists and "free soilers," and specifically to that unsettling doctrine United States Senator Seward had so recently proclaimed when he called on Americans to pose a "higher law" between the Constitution and those who would use the Constitution itself to guarantee the power of the slaveocracy. The radical Whig state officers of New York could hardly have regretted losing their ex officio seats on the Union College Board of Trustees, especially that recently elected United States Senator, Hamilton Fish, safely in Washington in spite of James W. Beekman's best efforts to deny him his new office.

The "amende honorable," however, never came from Beekman. Attorney General Chatfield, apparently aware of the Doctor's powers of persuasion, instructed Levinus Vanderheyden, the Investigating Committee's new accountant, "to admit no man to your confidence during the investigation, nor to disclose the state of the accounts to any person except the committee, until the report is drawn. We seek no advantage of Dr. Nott, nor do we intend to permit him to take the control of the investigation."[11]

The Trustees of the college at their July meeting in 1851 appointed their own committee of four, headed by ex-Chancellor Walworth, and including then State Treasurer Alvah Hunt, to meet with the Senate's commission and to assist with its investigation; these four men, however, as well as the Doctor, were *personae non grata*, and were never called on for help.

"Resignation of Dr. Nott," headlined a statement in the New York *Tribune* on August 9, a story copied from a Utica newspaper, and denied two days later by the *Tribune*: "We learn," the New York City paper reported, "that the resignation is . . . entirely without foundation . . . President Nott, we understand, has been improving in health for several years, and executes all his functions with the full vigor of his remarkable intellectual powers." The Doctor's vitality, as usual, seemed to return to him in his time of lawyers and subpoenas.

On September 12 he turned over all the college account books to Levinus Vanderheyden who took them back to the commission's office in Albany. Chancellor Walworth and the other "legal members" of the Board protested that these college records should never have left Schenectady, but the Doctor, claiming there was no formal resolution of the Trustees to that effect, wrote to the Chairman of the Investigating Commission that, "if there be anything wrong here, I am chiefly responsible for it, and shall hold myself in readiness to respond to any charge which may seem to be called for, even by an *ex parte* examination." [12]

Senator Beekman, the "uncles and the cousins," several members of Dr. J. N. Campbell's Investigating Commission, their accountant, Levinus Vanderheyden, and his assistant, Philip Ford, however, were now deeply committed to an ex parte examination which was to test even the Doctor's charity and his ability "to sound men," as Silas Burt, that observing Union college senior, had once put it.

On October 28 the "A. Johnson" whose notes as Secretary of the earlier Pruyn Committee had formed the basis of Beekman's Assembly charges, wrote to now Senator Beekman that the chairman of that first committee, Robert L. Pruyn, whom he had just seen in Albany, "coldly gave me his hand and said 'how do you do, sir,' and turned away. All well, if I have incurred the displeasure of a few of Dr. Nott's friends. I can only say it is not merited. I only regret we did not make a more thorough investigation [in 1849]. I honestly believe that there is no man in this State whose influence has been more injurious than Dr. Nott's. Instead of abusing us for what we did, he ought to be grateful for what we left undone." [13]

Between James W. Beekman and Levinus Vanderheyden, the work begun would be finished. On February 27, 1852, the Investigating Commission sent the accountant's preliminary report on his review of the college books to the Senate, a review completed, Vanderheyden testified, only down to 1820, though he drew on ledger figures entered as late as 1850. The gist of his report was that the Doctor was in debt to the college for $560,466.15. The figure, however, would undoubtedly change with the submission of the final balances which the accountant assured the Commission would be ready by the following September. [14]

"The question for us now to determine," Senator Beekman declared in the Upper House the next day, "is—shall [the accountants] go on?"[15] In flights of rhetoric and marine metaphor which spared neither Union College nor the emotions of his hearers the Senator depicted a self-aggrandizing Eliphalet Nott and a Board of Trustees who had allowed him to plunder the endowment funds which a humane New York State had entrusted to them:

> Floating upon the uncertain waters which encompass the Literary, like the Material World, there occurs here and there, alas! a college or an academy of learning. Some of these, like beacon fires, attract the wanderer, tempest tost, and blinded by the mists of ignorance, to an ark of safety—others show false lights, that they may prey, like wreckers, upon those who confide in them. Others again, happily still more rare, fitted out by the charity of the humane, and sent to cruize for the relief of the winter bitten mariner, vessels whose errand was to help out the weary end of the long voyage with timely provisions, have been known to turn pirates and to convert the very contributions entrusted to them, into means of sustaining their own wickedness—and to complete as plunderers an expedition which they began as missionaries.
>
> There exists in the State of New York an institution of learning, which claims to be almost independent of the State itself. For thirty years it has defied the Regents of the University, an August body to which was early entrusted the supervision of colleges and academies—It claims and for thirty years has claimed, to owe no allegiance and to be subject to no visitational powers, beyond its own Board of Trustees—It has set itself up as a high contracting party with the State and appeals to the Constitution of the United States, which guarantees the obligation of contracts, for its justification.

One recalls the letter Beekman received a week earlier from the Rev. W. H. Campbell in which the latter reviewed the Union College-Board of Regents controversy of 1823 and to which he had added the charge that the quarrel had then been manufactured by the Doctor and the Trustees in order "to get clear of the Regents," a conclusion the Senator had quickly made his own.

Now well posted on Yates and McIntyre's views of the Doctor's methods of financing, the Senator next pictured the members of the lottery firm as having lived in terror of the Doctor's exactions, of his threat to impose his own patented "American System" of lottery drawings on the "House," and of their outrage at the Doctor's duplicity in rearranging his contracts with them in order to swell his "President's Fund." "Annual visitations [by the regents] under these circumstances," the Senator charged, "might have been unpleasant to the Trustees, who had divested themselves of all power over the financial interests of their college." Beekman reviewed the growing debt of the Board to the Doctor, the "payment" to him of over $350,000 in Manhattan and Long Island real estate, and concluded that "the picture is complete . . . the 'financial committee' seem as much puzzled to know where the money has gone as ever countryman at a horse race, while gazing at the clever tricks of a thimble rigger, to know *where* the little joker is—."

The Senator, recalling his visit to the college as a member of the Pruyn Committee, made Shakespeare a fifth signer of that committee's majority report: "The Board of Trustees," Beekman now declared, "may well adopt the words of Sir John Falstaff, when he was telling of his adventure with the men in Buckram suits:

> These *four* [the Pruyn Committee majority] came all afront, and mainly thrust at me. I made me no more ado, but took all their *seven* points in my target, *thus*—but—as the devil would have it, three misbegotten knaves in Kendalgreen came at my back and let drive at me—for it was *so dark*, Hal, that thou couldst not see thy hand—

To which I would reply with Prince Henry—

> Why how couldst thou know these men in Kendalgreen, when it was so dark thou couldst not see thy hand?

Beekman now assured the Senate that the Trustees of Union College had plans to destroy him, that there was at that moment "lying stereotyped at the State Printers . . . a document which has as its object the extinction of this investigation by extinguishing me." The State Printer, who was Thurlow Weed, radical Whig and leader of the "Journal clique," had refused "to send a proof," claiming the document was confidential and private. The State Printer, Beekman now charged, "was disrespectful to the Legislature, to print a document which has not been accepted by it. . . ."

The Senator added a note of self-justification for his relentless pursuit of his quarry: "I was bound, in the words of one of my ancestors," he declared, "by mine oath, mine office, and mine honor to disclose [these findings] —Groping after the objects of my research, water muddied and blackened by the escaping animals, as cuttlefish conceal themselves when pursued, I have not been able to do more than indicate their retreats, and to exhibit a few specimens of the species." To this interesting zoological treatment of his sense of duty the Senator added his philosophical conclusions on lotteries and education in a curiously mixed metaphor which at least underscored his point: "Gambling and lotteries," he insisted, "are too nearly allied ever again to permit the fountains of knowledge to be filled by the wheel of chance." The fate of Union College, he was certain, proved his point, although his conclusion hardly followed it: "had the monies been applied as intended," he said, "instead of a barracklike range of 'stone houses,' with a vacant space between, where the observatory is to be, and a *fancy bond* of $20,000 to build it, we might have had a university of rank."

The Senator's knowledge of the Doctor's contributions as an educator, of the Trustees and the Doctor's plans for a Union College "on the university system," was as deficient as his knowledge of where the "observatory" was to go. "Its scholarship," Beekman continued, "rises no higher than that of any other little College in the land—and no well educated man names it in favorable comparison with Yale, or even with Brown University," a statement which would have surprised Francis Wayland, who as the President of Brown had borrowed so much from Eliphalet Nott of whom he was to say he owed more than to any other man. The Senator, a Columbia College graduate himself, failed to mention his own alma mater as a source of educated men, or to note that in New York State it was still behind Union College in enrollment and in the breadth of its curriculum. [16]

Senator Beekman, in that February, 1852, speech in the Senate never lifted his head above the ledgers of the House of Yates and McIntyre, or went beyond the gossip-gathering of the "uncles and the cousins." In his righteousness he never questioned his own motives for attempting to destroy the public image of the Doctor and of Union College.

Until the full Vanderheyden report was given to the Senate on March 1, 1853, the Doctor, too, "our cunning old prex," wore his own mantle of righteousness which he donned in every crisis of his life, certain that those who opposed him were passion blind to that "higher law" by which, he proclaimed, he tried to govern his acts. In Senator Beekman and Eliphalet Nott two Americas seemed to oppose each other, the one epitomized by the Senator's affection for his ancestors, for the past, for social evolution governed by property rights, the other America by the Doctor who assumed that ancestors and property rights were useful only as they served to bring about the one humane world he saw from his pulpit and his classroom. Both men were intent on implementing their convictions in the day-to-day world of the 1850s, and in doing this, both men put themselves on their collision course.

I I

The events of March and April, 1853, combined into a timetable of charges and countercharges made for melodrama. By March 4th the Campbell Committee, Judge David Buel and Philip Van Rensselaer dissenting, had sent Levinus Vanderheyden's report to the Senate "as a true and full exhibit of the pecuniary condition of Union College." According to these two minority members, the committee's chairman, the Rev. Dr. Campbell, and Comptroller J. C. Wright had not even read the report; the other majority member, Attorney General Chatfield, admitted he had only "cursorily examined the balance sheet." [17]

On March 12 the Trustees of the college sent an angry "memorial" to the Senate, protesting that they had never been consulted by Campbell's committee and concluding with the strongest possible plea for a new and impartial investigation which would allow the Board "to refute the calumnies" being circulated. [18]

On March 16th the Senate received an Olympian "Memorial" from the President of Union College which reviewed the failure of the recent Campbell Committee to visit the college or "to reexamine the proceedings already had". The Doctor called attention to his own voluntary suspension of the Trustees' reply to the Pruyn Committee charges, then to his release of the college books to Vanderheyden, and informed the Upper House that the Reverend Dr. Campbell had "promised to make a thorough examination himself," and that the Union College reply to the committee's findings "should be presented with their report to the Senate." [19] The Doctor declared he had hoped to remain mute "till the revelation of the tomb should have silenced calumny . . ." but the time had come, "in view of the *ex parte* and dishonest nature of the investigation to date," and "as an act of justice," the Doctor declared, "for the appointment of a new and impartial committee" before which both he and the Trustees could testify.

On Tuesday, March 22, Senator Beekman again took the floor of the crowded Senate chamber where, he said, he had expected to talk to empty seats, "because the Union College subject was so worn out." The Trustees' "end and aim," he declared, "was concealment and delay . . . ," their intention "to wipe out the correctness" of Vanderheyden's accounting by calling for a new committee, the same lawyer's device, he concluded, that had been once used to delay the impeachment before Parliament of Warren Hastings.

The Albany *Daily State Register* reported Beekman's speech in detail and noted especially that the Senator had declared his task was now done, that his claim that Union College "was a rotten institution" was now proved by the testimony of its own books. If the Senator believed the "Union College Affair" had served further to disillusion New York State voters with the irresponsible character of those Whig leaders who were also Trustees of that "rotten institution," then the political aspect of his task was complete, and now, with Vanderheyden's report, he need only sing the requiem.

Unfortunately for Senator James W. Beekman this easy and symmetrical victory was spoiled when Levinus Vanderheyden, two days later, stung by the "Memorial" of the Trustees which Thurlow Weed's Albany *Evening Journal* had published in full, replied to it in a letter which leveled new charges against the Doctor and Professor Jonathan Pearson, now acting treasurer of the college, charges which shocked readers across the state. [15] The President of Union College, Vanderheyden replied, had come to him privately and had tried to get him to alter the college accounts, and the acting treasurer, who had "borrowed" one of the college books from Vanderheyden the preceding summer, had returned it, so Vanderheyden now declared, "with an entire new account interpolated therein, filling several pages . . . changing the whole face of the result as to the President's account by making the college indebted to him over $200,000, instead of a balance of over $800,000 due from him."

For the next three days exchanges on the "Union College Affair" in the New York State Senate pushed even debates on Erie Canal financing into the background. On March 25th Beekman himself was charged with being on trial by Senator VanSchoonhoven, who assured the Upper House that "if Dr. Nott was found guiltless," the Senator from New York City would be dishonored. [21] As for the Doctor's "Memorial" to the Senate, that, VanSchoonhoven declared, was

> Modest, compact—beautiful, disinterested and beautiful—this document is the most appropriate that ever found its way into the archives of the Senate of New York. It is kindred to the eloquent words that eloquent old man has in years past uttered, which he had left as legacies to the classics of the language. [22]

The Albany *Daily Knickerbocker* had other ideas:

> The plug-muss which has grown out of Union College—Dr. Nott, the steamboat Novelty, patent stoves and Hudson bank stock—begins to grow interesting, if not sinful. [Vanderheyden] brings charges against Dr. Nott that should cover him with confusion and drive the financial officers of Union College into solitude and repentance. [23]

Hugh Hastings, editor of this paper with the largest circulation of any New York State journal north of New York City, claimed Vanderheyden's indictment of Acting Treasurer Pearson was damning, evidence enough that the acting treasurer had made new entries in the college books "changing the aspect of Dr. Nott's account one million dollars," and that it should cause the Legislature "to censure and punish."

On Saturday, March 26, John C. Spencer wrote to the editor of the Albany *Evening Journal* that the President of Union College, who was to preach in Albany the next day, would not answer Vanderheyden's charge, but that the Doctor and the

Trustees would, instead, confine their defense to the Senate, "the chosen ground of their accuser, J. W. Beekman." [24] The Doctor, Spencer concluded, had branded Levinus Vanderheyden's accusations "to be in all their length and breadth utterly, grossly and wilfully false," and then added "that he will try to force his libeler," and Vanderheyden's "confederates, if they can be found," to prove their charge before a jury. The Doctor had found his attorney in John Canfield Spencer.

The following Monday tempers flared in the Senate Chamber. Senator Beekman demanded that the college post a million dollar bond before the new committee, just appointed to reinvestigate the majority and minority reports of the preceding Campbell Committee, be permitted to begin its work. Senator VanSchoonhoven rose to call Beekman's charges "vile slanders," and Senator Taber demanded that the Speaker of the House give him time to get out of the chamber before the Senate voted on Beekman's motion to require the College to post the million dollar bond, a motion Taber said he "looked upon . . . as an unmitigated outrage, disreputable to the Senator who offered it." Beekman's only concession was to reduce the amount of the bond he demanded the Trustees post from $1,000,000 to $500,000, a substitute motion defeated by a fourteen to eight vote. [25] The new "Vanderbilt Committee," the third to be appointed by the New York State Legislature to investigate the financial history of Union College, was now free to begin hearings which would no longer exclude the testimony of either the Doctor or of the Board of Trustees.

Senator James W. Beekman, the "uncles and the cousins," and Levinus Vanderheyden, devoted to the truth of their biases would, for the first time, be forced to hear its revision in the Doctor's rationalizations and in John C. Spencer's momentous "Argument in the Defense of Dr. Nott" which he would soon present to the new Committee. Its members, Chairman John Vanderbilt, Judge Elisha Ward, and Nathaniel Jones, had drawn the least desirable legislative assignment of the session.

On April 8th, before the Vanderbilt Committee had organized for work, Beekman and Vanderheyden made their commitments doubly sure; the Senator petitioned the Upper House to append the accountant's affidavit charging fraud against Professor

Jonathan Pearson to the majority report of the Campbell Committee submitted the preceding March. Beekman also petitioned to have the affidavit of Captain Neziah Bliss attached to the Campbell Report, a detailed and hostile review by the Doctor's one-time superintendent of the Novelty Iron Works covering their joint Stuyvesant Cove and Hunter Point real estate investments, an affidavit in which Captain Bliss charged the Doctor with gross mismanagement in developing the S.S. *Novelty*, and gross profiteering in his real estate dealings with him and with the college. [26]

The Doctor and the Trustees for their part devoted their special meeting on April 27th to an exchange of confidence in each other which the Board, including New York State Treasurer Benjamin Welch, voted to have published as a handbill, and which Professor Pearson was authorized to print and distribute. The acting treasurer also gave the Board a detailed profit and loss statement designed to show the success of the Doctor as an academic financier. The Doctor advised the Trustees, at this meeting, to engage an attorney to defend their interests before the Vanderbilt Committee, and told them that he, too, would be represented by counsel.

III

During the spring and summer months as John C. Spencer labored on his "Argument in the Defense of Dr. Nott," the Doctor himself fulfilled all the demands of his role as the Nestor of college presidents. Francis and Theresa Pulzky, two among many Hungarian patriots then touring America, called on "Dr. Philalethes [sic] Nott . . . revered by his students as a father . . . and Mrs. Nott, an amiable and kind lady," who showed them "the beautiful view from her window, overlooking a fine garden laid out with reasonable taste by Professor Jackson." [27]

The Doctor had made himself a champion of Hungarian freedom during the spring of 1852 when he had urged the exiled patriot, General Louis Kossuth, to come to Schenectady. In his letter to the General, he had promised to gather an audience for him, that he would "call in the surrounding peasantry" for the occasion. [28] The word "peasantry" as it came from the Doctor's pen seems a strange choice for a Connecticut Yankee, but it must be remembered that he was now more than half a century removed from the simplicities of "Pisgah's Top," that hard Calvinist school of his boyhood. One suspects, however, that the "peasants" who gathered in Schenectady to hear the Doctor and the General talk on liberty and oppression on June 2, 1852, might not have cared for the medieval role assigned to them. [29]

The Doctor's last tie to the Connecticut of his boyhood had been broken that same spring when his older brother, the Reverend Samuel Nott, once the student of Jonathan Edwards the Younger, and then the Doctor's own teacher, died at the age of ninety-seven. He had been a New England conscience to his own parish for seventy-one years, and a conscience, too, to "young 'Liph'," whom the older brother had long seen as too ambitious, too ready to compromise his New England inheritance in order to get his way among "Yorkers", Americans who, the Reverend Samuel Nott had said, were a lesser breed.

The Doctor, now eighty years old himself, presided at the Commencement exercises on July 27, 1853, "with all his youthful vigor." "He now feels in the very prime of life," according to the reporter who wrote glowingly of the new Union College then in evidence, the new "Philosophical Hall" to be opened that fall with a department of Agricultural Chemistry designed as a part of a "super-graduate course for those who have completed the ordinary Bachelor's curriculum, and wish to enter upon higher and deeper departments of study." [30] Bishop Alonzo Potter's successor as Vice President and Professor of Moral Philosophy was now on the campus, the Reverend Dr. Laurens Perseus Hickok. The new Vice President, scholarly, popular with good students, had left the Auburn Theological Seminary in the hope of soon taking over the Union College presidency from a supposedly old and ailing Eliphalet Nott, but he had soon discovered that the Doctor's renewed vigor would postpone his hopes indefinitely. Dr. Hickok was also beginning to realize that the bonds of sympathy which had again yoked the aging President and Bishop Alonzo Potter, could never bind him, a closet scholar, to the commanding ancient whose career was then the subject of a New York State legislative investigation. [31]

The Doctor also acted as chairman of the Trustees' meeting that Commencement, a gathering from which Horatio Seymour, the new Democratic Governor, and the state officers who were, ex officio, Board members, were conspicuously absent. The registration was reported to be still dropping, down now to 189. The Trustees agreed that, in spite of their still unparalleled prospects, they had no choice but to retrench. Acting Treasurer Pearson had already discharged all but two of the College workmen, and the Doctor, he reported, had "with his characteristic generosity," agreed to buy the college's "disposable real estate" at "an increased price" in order to bolster a faltering income. The new buildings the public had been led to expect, the long promised chapel and the observatory, would have to be postponed. Pearson was ordered by the Board to see what could be salvaged from Benjamin Nott's defaulted bonds and mortgages of more than $6000. The Auditing Committee reported that it had begun its own review of the Doctor's relations with the lottery managers, Yates and McIntyre, and, the Trustees, following "some discussion and an explanation by Dr. Nott," agreed to table the matter until the new Senate Committee should finish its hearings.

As John Spencer, class of 1803, worked through the summer to put the history of those relations into the most favorable light he could, the Doctor, "keeping his business affairs to himself," as his agent, Robert Lowber, had so strongly advised him to do, may well have been reviewing his own off-stage activities as a Manhattan and Long Island real estate speculator.

I V

"Hazard" or "gamble," the drive to undertake new risks was as alive in the Doctor at eighty as it had been in the Yates and McIntyre days of secret contracts, verbal agreements, and their rewards of lottery dollars. During those earlier days he had leaned on the great rationalization: to "hazard," to adventure for the good cause was to serve God. From 1845 on, however, when he took Stuyvesant's Cove and the Hunter Point lands as payment against the huge bill of better than $350,000 he had presented to the Board in July that year, the Doctor seemed more and more to be leaning on the counsel and managerial services of a new breed of business agents. The great rationalization for the risks he and Henry Yates had run in the 1820's to keep the "House" of Yates and McIntyre solvent is absent in his correspondence with such men as Hezekiah Bradford and Richard Blydenburg, who, from 1846 to 1850, filled land, sold lots, and schemed to enrich themselves on his Stuyvesant Cove property.

By the time Senator Beekman had found his way to Hezekiah Bradford's "Cove" office in 1850 the Doctor had invested more than $500,000 in "money and paper" in Stuyvesant Cove alone, in what by that time the Doctor's newest business agent, Robert Wilson Lowber, was telling him had become a fraudulent operation.[32] Jonathan Pearson, years later, remembered the "Cove" as "a dismal place, stinking and foul," where "there are people who can be found to purchase little bits of ground . . . for $1600 and $2000 a piece."[33] In 1850, however, the most valuable portion of the Cove was still under water, land yet to be made, and whose extent depended on an exterior boundary line of New York City which had not yet been determined. By 1850 Richard Blydenburg and Hezekiah Bradford had taken for themselves some $180,000 by "encumbering" the property with various liens; Blydenburg, after appropriating $100,000, had sold his remaining interest to Bradford, whose one achievement had been to persuade the corporation of the City of New York to give the Cove owners "a grant of water front," wherever that might finally be in relation to the then undetermined East River boundary of the city. For the Doctor, however, those low tide mud flats extending into deep water appeared to be as full of potential profits as had his lottery contracts in 1822.

By the spring of 1850 the Doctor's "Cove" operations were, in fact, in considerable disarray. Over-extended, he was fearful of sudden calls from his creditors, including Stillman, Allen and Company, by 1850 the nominal owners of the "Novelty Works," which seems now to have become more brokerage house than machine shop. By June of that year, through a series of title conveyances, the Doctor was, himself, once more in full possession of Stuyvesant's Cove, shocked by the betrayal of Blydenburg and Bradford, but cheered with the plans of his new partners, Alexander Holland, the treasurer of Union College, and Robert W. Lowber, his new financial guide. By Commencement time the Doctor must have been doubly glad Senator Beekman's attention was focused elsewhere, for by then he had begun a series of court battles for title to those underwater lands at the "Cove" worth perhaps a million dollars. [34]

By the end of January, 1851, while the Senator, with the help of "Uncle Jacob" and Cousin James B. Sanders, was preparing even more violent charges against Union College, the Doctor was putting himself irrevocably into the hands of Robert Lowber, who, until the Doctor's death sixteen years later, seems always to have been within close reach. On the 30th of that month Lowber and Alexander Holland contracted to buy the "Cove" from the Doctor for $300,000, payable by July 1, 1853, and to pay off those "encumbrances" put on the property by Blydenburg and Bradford, to fill and prepare the land for sale, pay taxes, and credit the Doctor with one third of all lot sales above the purchase price, as well as to conduct the property suits the Doctor had recently begun. Captain Neziah Bliss, the Doctor's old partner in the days of the S.S. *Novelty* who, twenty years earlier had introduced him to the speculative possibilities of the "Cove" and Hunter Point, was to be asked to supply the enormous yardage of dirt needed to fill the deep basin between 13th and 16th streets, and Avenues B and C. [35]

For the Doctor the signing of this contract with these new partners seemed to put the development of the "Cove" on as sound a basis as were his arrangements for bringing his Long Island property south of Newtown Creek into the market, a problem he had solved the year before when it, too, was taken away from Blydenburg and Bradford and its management turned over to Charles Ely and Jonathan Crane, the latter a Schenectady twine manufacturer, inventor of the railroad turntable, and a fellow temperance worker. The future for the Doctor and for the college, excepting such part of it as Senator Beekman elected to usurp, seemed again to clear before him, pointing to the promised land he had been conjuring up since the first harvests of the lottery.

By the close of 1853 almost a half million dollars in Stuyvesant Cove water lots had been filled in and sold. Lowber had paid the Doctor over $200,000, and Alexander Holland, then still the college treasurer, had withdrawn as a partner in the "Cove" operation. By that fall both the Doctor and Lowber were convinced that they had only to wait for the official confirmation of that projected exterior eastern boundary line of New York City to make a huge windfall profit. [27] It was probably true that it was this prospect which had helped to jaundice Captain Neziah Bliss's testimony as to the Doctor's real estate profiteering, testimony which Senator Beekman had demanded be attached as an affidavit to the Campbell Committee's report to the Upper House that March, and which the Doctor's enemies had already widely publicized as proof of the Doctor's double dealing.

"Hazard" or "gamble," John C. Spencer, as he labored over his momentous "Argument" during that summer of 1853 was to be forced at last to redefine those terms for the old president in a secret confrontation the magnitude of which would have startled even Senator Beekman. And Beekman, that summer, had little doubt that Eliphalet Nott and his cooperating trustees were ruined men, waiting for their public damnation on the imminent confirmation by the Vanderbilt Committee of his charges that Union College had, for decades, been systematically plundered.

CHAPTER 3

"Plump contradictions . . ."

"IN this trying hour," the Alumni tribute to John Canfield Spencer was to read, "an eminent son of this institution stepped forth as the champion of our venerable father." [1] According to Levinus Vanderheyden's report in March, 1853, the Doctor sorely needed a champion, for the accountant had now "proved" to his own satisfaction, and to a majority of the Senate committee which had employed him, that Eliphalet Nott had taken $885,789.62 of Union College funds for his own use.

Bound up in Spencer's "voluntary and unsolicited efforts" as the Doctor's advocate before the Vanderbilt Committee were threads whose beginnings few would have remembered; the odd fact that twenty years earlier John C. Spencer had represented, not the college, but the House of Yates and McIntyre in its defense of the suit over the lottery profits brought against it by the Doctor; that he, as a Whig politician of national stature, had become aware of the extent to which the Trustees and their predecessors, including himself, were involved in the judgment soon to be made by the New York State Legislature on the Doctor's acts, and so on the acts of the Board. He was aware that should the Vanderheyden Report be accepted as the true account of the financial history of Union College and of the Trustees' relations with their President there would be no celebration of the Doctor's own semi-centennial the next year as the venerable father of a huge family of alumni, but rather there would be a tragic scandal, one which would shatter a father-image then second to none in America.

Knowing so much of the past, and most especially knowing the Doctor so well in his strength and his weakness, John C.

Spencer began to prepare the reply to Levinus Vanderheyden, that "Argument" which, he declared, was designed "to unravel the poisoned web which prejudice and skilful misrepresentation had woven." Spencer was sixty-seven in 1853, the year Levinus Vanderheyden's charges rocked the New York State Legislature, and crowded its Senate Chamber to hear Senator James W. Beekman's repeated obsequies over the corpse of Union College. The late Secretary of the Treasury and then of War, his LL.D. granted by his alma mater in 1849, had fought his last political fight in 1852 when he had campaigned for General Winfield Scott, the Whig candidate for President running against Franklin Pierce. Scott's defeat had been a triumph for those New York "cotton Whigs" who, like Beekman, saw it as a victory for them in their endless maneuvering in New York State to destroy Seward's political career and the power of the "Journal clique," among whom were men the Doctor had long claimed as intimate friends. With Abolitionists and "free soilers" curtailed, with conservative Americans breathing easier, with the Compromise of 1850 now securely the law of the North as well as of the South, Thurlow Weed, the disgusted editor of the Albany *Journal* had decided to "vacation" in Europe, John C. Spencer had withdrawn from politics to devote himself to his Albany legal practice and to such public services as the development of the Albany Hospital and the New York State Asylum for Idiots.

That he had been following the "Union College Affair" from the beginning, however, is clear from his correspondence. As early as January, 1849, at his request, Alexander Holland had sent him the laudatory report which Governor Silas Wright and William James, as Union College Trustees, had made in 1831 of the Doctor's lottery operations, and of the Doctor's commitment then to give an unnamed portion of his personal lottery profits to the college. [2]

In October, 1851, Spencer had "regretted" his inability to return a call made on him by Senator Beekman, at a time when the hue and cry of the Albany *Daily Knickerbocker* at the Trustees' heels was at its noisiest. [3] It was clear to him, by the time Vanderheyden's "Report" was given to the Senate on March 4, 1853, that the Beekman forces were determined to ruin the Doctor by methods as devious as any they had charged against him, by copy prepared for "a flash press," by the distribution of the Senator's ex parte legislative attacks on a nationwide basis, and by timing their committee reports so that they would be received by the Senate within a day or two of its adjournment, reports which neither the Doctor nor the Trustees could have an opportunity to examine. By the end of March the ex-Secretary of War and of the Treasury had decided to give "his voluntary and unsolicited efforts in the defense of their *Alma Mater*," as the Alumni resolution honoring him would read the next year, "and in the defense of their revered President . . . " a defense which was to become a legal tour de force, "performed with patience, perseverance, and great ability . . . without fee or reward."

During the following nine months Spencer either played the most cynical role of his legal career, publicly discrediting testimony which he privately believed valid, wilfully concealing the huge irregularity he came to believe he had discovered, or he played the role of a judge ruling beyond the mundane law, who justifies concealment to serve what he believed to be a higher law, in this instance to preserve the public image of Eliphalet Nott, and so to protect the reputations of the distinguished men who were and who had been the trust officers of Union College.

The tensions raised by the hearings which opened in Schenectady on August 4th are indicated in Spencer's own trial notes. Rumors of an "impeachment" were then in the air.[4] Attorney General Chatfield, acting "as one of the Trustees," on August 8th requested the Vanderbilt Committee to postpone Levinus Vanderheyden's testimony until the accountant could find counsel, which the latter was having great trouble in doing. It was Vanderheyden, the Doctor's attorney recorded, who assured the Attorney General that the "impeachment trial," apparently of Acting Treasurer Pearson for allegedly altering the college fund book, waited only on the completion of the Vanderbilt Committee's work.[5]

The Albany *Daily Knickerbocker* followed the hearings, as sarcastic toward Spencer's defense tactics as Spencer was toward the testimony of the Doctor's accusers. "Phi," the *Knickerbocker's* correspondent, lost no time in mounting the attack: "a beautiful and effective opening speech; the allusions to the time when nearly 50 years ago [Spencer] was under the fostering care of his *Alma Mater*, were touchingly pathetic. . . ."[6] The *Knickerbocker* was unrelenting during the two months of hearings, sparing neither Spencer nor the Trustees, nor the Doctor to whom "Phi" usually referred to as the "Financiering President," that head of Union College who must account, he said, for the neglect of its buildings and grounds, its library, its philosophical apparatus, and the small size of its freshmen classes. "Phi," whose researches into the facts of higher education were as incomplete as had been Senator Beekman's, harped on Union's failure to match the "new departments in science" then reportedly being opened at Harvard and Yale. The theme of the Knickerbocker articles was always: "Dr. Nott is a very dishonest man."[7]

Spencer's task was to prove that charge, now broadcast across the nation, untrue.[8] If, however, the Doctor was to stand free of all Senator Beekman and Levinus Vanderheyden had laid at his door, what must his attorney's tactics be? Spencer's decision is clear from the outset: to prove, first, the "malignity" of the Doctor's accusers, and then to prove that the evidence they brought against him was deliberately perverted to serve that "malignity," the axis around which the whole "Argument" must revolve. The result, "The Argument in the Defense of Dr. Nott . . . ," becomes as much a script for melodrama as were any of Senator Beekman's diatribes before the Assembly and then the Senate of the New York State Legislature.[9]

Four men: Beekman first, then Vanderheyden, then "Uncle Jacob" Sanders, and then Henry Yates, must be exhibited to the Vanderbilt Committee as a cabal:

Senator James W. Beekman: "triumphing in his unanswered calumnies of a defenseless old man and a venerable clergyman. . . ."

Levinus Vanderheyden, accountant, and self-appointed counsel to the Campbell Committee: "whose part in this drama was to furnish Beekman with the materials for his speeches and his efforts. As they have thus yoked themselves together, I propose to keep them in that mutually agreeable relation. . . ."[11]

"Uncle Jacob" Sanders: "[Senator Beekman's] near-connexion, [who] has done little else for three years but to busy himself in these matters and circulate the calumnious reports against Dr. Nott . . . [who] even ordered an edition of 1000 copies of the report of the [Campbell] Commission to be printed in a mutilated form . . . and which [Beekman] caused to be circulated . . . through the United States." [12]

Henry Yates: toward whom Senator Beekman's "partiality was exemplified . . . in his forbearance of the man who had been employed as the agent of the College, with a salary, to superintend and watch the movements of the [Literature Lottery] contractors, his brother, J. B. Yates, and A. McIntyre, and their associates . . . and who, instead of performing that duty . . . became their co-partner in the profits of the lotteries! [Beekman's] forbearance toward that gentleman was doubtless occasioned by their fellow feeling of animosity against Dr. Nott." [13]

It was as though the whole hive of troubles long since freed by the Literature Lottery had swarmed again. Vanderheyden's astounding account against the Doctor, according to Spencer, was based on the books of the "House of Yates and McIntyre," on those so-called secret contracts and agreements made by the Doctor with the lottery contractors thirty years earlier, and on the accumulation of that "President's Fund" which Levinus Vanderheyden indicated was the major portion of the nearly million dollars he and Senator Beekman finally claimed the Doctor owed to Union College. [14] This was a history Spencer knew better, perhaps, than Vanderheyden.

The first task Spencer undertook was to prove that the claims the old President had made "as an individual" against the lottery contractors in the 1830s, and to which he had then "impleaded" his Trustees without their knowledge, were, in fact, valid. To do this, however, he now had to recapitulate as his own the arguments of the attorneys for the Doctor and the Trustees as they had been developed in the 1830s during the Chancery suits.

To these arguments he now added a catalogue of accounting errors on Vanderheyden's part, errors which Spencer claimed were deliberate frauds, examples of forced balances, and contrived affidavits which, he told the investigating committee, proved overwhelmingly that the accountant and Senator Beekman had developed a "settled plan for stabbing in the back a man [Beekman] wished to destroy . . ." [15] Vanderheyden's bookkeeping methods, he told the Committee, were "utterly unintelligible . . . his credibility as a witness disproved," that he was "an unsafe witness . . . of insufficient moral force to restrain his passions," a claim Vanderheyden promptly countered by producing fifty citizens of Troy, his home town, to bear witness to his character. [16]

The "Argument in the Defense of Dr. Nott" finally moved onto new ground when Spencer faced the problem of explaining the Doctor's financial relations with the Trustees, a labor which meant he had been through a bookkeeper's nightmare of documents which even Spencer had to admit at times "afford little light. . . ." "Literary institutions," he told the Committee, "were never famous for strict bookkeeping; their officers have duties, and are engaged in pursuits of another character." [17] The burden of his defense was now to answer the fifth and last "Inquiry" posed by the New York State Senate in establishing the Vanderbilt Committee: "Has the President, or any other officer, participated in the profits of any lottery appropriated to Union College?" Levinus Vanderheyden's astounding balance against the Doctor, predicated largely on the latter's "appropriation" of so-called Union College lottery profits, was, according to Spencer, "one of the marvels of bookkeeping, calculated to astonish everyone"; it was a "fabricated, forced, and utterly unfounded account" which could never have existed "without the knowledge or suspicion of the Trustees."

So-called "loans" to the Doctor, his attorney declared, "were misnomers to cover any charge [Vanderheyden] has been able to rake up out of the rubbish of the years. . . ." Spencer then reviewed the accountant's report of half a century of so-called "losses" on routine real estate and stock investments, and successfully disposed of Vanderheyden's particular charge that the Doctor had sold stock to the college on one occasion in a bank which had closed its doors a month before the Trustees made the purchase. [18]

The books of the college which reflected the Doctor's transactions with the Trustees, Spencer now assured the Committee, "are no money accounts"; rather are they "a condensed view of the donations of Dr. Nott to the College, and of the changes which they assumed when converted into other property." [19] With this sweeping rationale the Doctor's attorney now proceeded to explain, as the Doctor had always explained, such investments as those which had gone into his "caloric" experiments, into the Novelty Iron Works, and especially, into the great land speculations at Stuyvesant Cove and Hunter Point. "The Argument in the Defense of Dr. Nott," like the *pièce bien fait* of the then contemporary French stage, was moving toward its well-made climax.

II

"Judge Ward has slept with Dr. Nott," an irritated Levinus Vanderheyden reported to Senator Beekman on October 6, 1853. The latter was unexpectedly preparing to return to private life, a politician "in fundamental disagreement with the dominant leaders of his party in New York State," according to his recent biographer. He was a bitter and frustrated man, no doubt, at finding himself, a Beekman, held up to public scorn and ridicule by such a master of those arts as John C. Spencer. [20] It had been charged in the Senate that if "Dr. Nott is found guiltless," his accuser would be dishonored, and the evidence was now mounting that Spencer, by some magic, was well on the way toward saving the Doctor whole. On the 3rd of October Chairman John Vanderbilt had written to the Senator, asking him to "attend before our committee and shed some light on this mystery of mysteries," an invitation Beekman accepted later that month, a tribute, certainly, to the depth of his convictions, for he knew that Spencer was hoping to pillory him.

Spencer assured the Vanderbilt Committee that he and the Doctor "rejoiced in the opportunity this at last afforded, of meeting this prime mover in the inquisitions against Dr. Nott face to face." Spencer's theme, the "malignity" of the old President's accusers was paramount. Beekman, he now declared, "has given us a rehash of the matter of his long and violent philippics in the Senate where there was no information or evidence to refute him. If he shall present a different appearance from that which he exhibited when marching out of the Senate Chamber, triumphing in his unanswered calumnies . . . the consequence will be of his own producing." [21]

Spencer, confronting Beekman, dealt first with the Senator's attempt to prove to the Vanderbilt Committee that the Union College Trustees, in 1849, had knowingly given him a printed version of the Chancery suit records of the 1830s from which they had intentionally omitted crucial Yates and McIntyre testimony. Spencer was able to show that this testimony had actually not been offered to the Chancery Court by the lottery managers until six months after the date on the so-called "fraudulent" document Beekman claimed had been given to him when he was a member of the Pruyn Committee.[22] Spencer noted the Vanderbilt Committee's "astonishment at this apparent evidence of deliberate deception and fraud, an impression which it was Mr. Beekman's design to make . . . but your astonishment," he added, "was still greater when I demonstrated that this foul charge was the coinage of Mr. Beekman's malevolence . . . this charge of deliberate fraud on the part of the officers of the college," Spencer declared, "and upon which so many charges in the Senate had been wrung, was exploded."

Senator Beekman was then questioned about his major charge that the lottery acts entitled Union College to all the profits arising, not only from the Literature Lottery, but from its President's share of the lotteries consolidated with it in 1826. This charge Spencer now claimed represented a "misconception" of the law, one which was even too much for Vanderheyden to support, for he, too, "utterly disclaimed those views of Mr. Beekman."[23] "It was on this frail basis," Spencer continued, "that [Beekman] sought to justify his charge, originally made in his report, that the College had received from Yates and McIntyre $850,000, very nearly the sum which the accountant has brought out in another way, seeming to have his eye fixed on his patron's original statement." "With the fall of the foundation falls the super-structure," Spencer assured the committee, and "thus terminated the pompous exhibition of Mr. Beekman, in the total overthrow of every one of his positions."[24]

In answer to an inquiry by a member of the committee as to "how a man of Mr. Beekman's intelligence could commit such a mistake," Spencer answered that "to a mind diseased, black would appear white and white appear black." He then reviewed the "animosities and calumnies" of the Senator's "near-connexions," of "Uncle Jacob" Sanders, and Henry Yates, and of Levinus Vanderheyden who, Spencer declared, had at last dropped "his character as an accountant, and come forth as the public accuser of Dr. Nott." [25]

In that role, Spencer now claimed, the accountant had joined Beekman in petitioning the Senate to add affidavits to Vanderheyden's Report of March 4, 1853, in which every charge was "not only false, but wilful and malignant." The Doctor's attorney reviewed, first, the letter from Captain Neziah Bliss in which the Captain stated that the Doctor had paid "a very trifling consideration" for the half of Stuyvesant Cove which the latter had bought outright in 1834, and nothing for the remaining half. Captain Bliss had claimed he had only loaned the bond and mortgage covering his half of the "Cove" to the Doctor so that the latter could raise money on it, and that the Doctor had then appropriated the assignment, and had later turned it over to the college at its unjustified face value of $75,225.32. [26]

Spencer, after cross-examining both Captain Bliss and then Edward James (son of William James, of Albany), the Doctor's business agent during the 1830s, told the Investigating Committee he was sure it must be apparent that the Captain's testimony was full of "plump contradictions," that the Captain's bond and mortgage, it was evident, had actually been given to cover his debts to the Doctor. By the time Spencer had finished examining Captain Neziah Bliss himself, the latter could only agree that "his mind was in such a state at that time that he knew very little of what he did." [27]

Spencer then turned to the charge of fraud Vanderheyden had leveled against Acting Treasurer Jonathan Pearson, to that statement in the Albany *Evening Journal* made the preceding March and repeated in Vanderheyden's affidavit, that Pearson had borrowed certain fund books of the college then in Vanderheyden's possession, and had returned them to the accountant so altered that they showed the college owed the Doctor as of January 1, 1853, $200,000 rather than that the Doctor owed the college over $850,000. "This charge," Spencer now assured the committee, "seems . . . to have been invented as a set-off to an anticipated attack on the accountant, for his own gross violation of the duty and propriety in tearing from a book of the College . . . a most important memorandum—keeping it from the officers of the college until the very close of this investigation." As for the charge itself against Pearson: Spencer declared Vanderheyden had himself asked Pearson to take the college books in question and to bring them up to date; this Pearson had done, and, in entering new and accurate balances, had fulfilled his duty.[28]

That equally serious charge of intimidation by the Doctor which Vanderheyden had published in two Albany papers, the *Evening Journal* and the *Register*, Spencer referred to only in a footnote to his record of the testimony of General George R. Davis, called by Vanderheyden to testify to the latter's competence as an accountant. The General admitted on the stand that he had asked Vanderheyden about his newspaper charge that the Doctor "had endeavored to induce [him] to alter the books of Union College." The accountant had admitted to the General that his "article was written under excitement, in consequence of a previous article that had been published in which the Doctor had charged him [Vanderheyden] substantially with perjury."

Spencer also quoted Vanderheyden's cloak and dagger accusation:

> The President met me by his appointment at the Troy House. He asked if we could not retire to a private place . . . I invited him to my house . . . he unfolded the object of his visit, which was to make sundry new entries in the books of the College . . . he continued in earnest labor with me until two o'clock the next morning, and, among other things, urged in substance, that, unless I yielded, a counter report would meet me in the Senate, charging me with falsehood in my statements. I declined his solicitations.[29]

The "sundry new entries" the Doctor had demanded Vanderheyden enter in the college books concerned the Doctor's claim to be the owner of the Stuyvesant Cove bond and mortgage which Captain Bliss had insisted had only been loaned by him to the Doctor. Spencer's comment on the General's testimony was that it proved the accountant had "coined an atrocious falsehood out of the interview with Dr. Nott."

On November 3, Levinus Vanderheyden, writing to Beekman, claimed that "Judge Vanderbilt is pro-Nott," and, writing again on

November 8, in almost desperate self-defense, declared, "I believe Dr. Nott the most guilty of men."[30] By this time, however, Senator Beekman had removed himself from political life, and by June of the next year he was on his way to Europe with his sick wife, out of hearing of the acclaims which were then greeting John C. Spencer's triumphant vindication of Eliphalet Nott, and of his exposure of Beekman's "foulest charges . . . caused by the ceaseless activity of the men who pursued [the Doctor] as if he were a wild beast, or a demon. . . ."[31]

The hearings of the Vanderbilt Committee ended in November with a summation by Spencer which was almost an epiphany. His tactical weapons: sarcasm, irony, proof of the malignancy of the Doctor's enemies, and of the contrived nature of their evidence, had seemed overwhelming to the Vanderbilt Committee and to the friends of the college. Levinus Vanderheyden's "monstrous account," Spencer had testified, was the result of a failure in character which he contrasted with the lustrous character of the Trustees, "these distinguished and very capable gentlemen, acting under the peculiar responsibilities of their stations and having reputations to maintain dearer to them than life. . . ."[32] Spencer had then cited the "lucid contrast" between Vanderheyden's report and the accounts of Union College funds drawn up by such Trustees as William James and Governor Silas Wright in 1831, by Governor Marcy, Silas Wright and John P. Cushman in 1834, and by General Dix and Judge Cushman in 1837: "their object," Spencer declared, "had no motive but the simple truth . . . and the discharge of duty."

Spencer's summary audit of the assets of Union College as of December, 1853, which he now gave to the Committee, offers a startling contrast to the one developed by the accountant for the earlier Campbell Committee:

"all [the Doctor] received from any transactions
growing out of the Literature Lottery . . . . $ 71,691.20 [plus]
"the sum . . . of sums received from the
(Consolidated Lotteries) . . . . $192,199.94 [plus]
". . . payments [for the Doctor] made to the
treasurer (on settlement of the Chancery
suits in 1837) $203,091.75
$466,982.89

"The whole of which," Spencer announced, "has been applied to purchases of property, and its improvement, for the College, so that in fact [the Doctor] has not realized a dollar, personally, from the receipts." To this total the Doctor's attorney then added "the balance of the President's Fund, after deducting expenses, $115,640.53, the whole of which has been transferred to the College, and from the beginning to the end, he has avowed the design of bestowing all these funds on the College." Of the grand total which Spencer then indicated had accrued to Union College from all the lotteries, the sum of $860,145.75, all but the principal sum of $277,522.33, paid to the college by Yates and McIntyre as its legal percentage from the returns of the Literature Lottery, had come to the Trustees as the sole result "of the wonderful devotion, the continued and indefatigable labors, and the sagacity of one man." [33]

As for the Doctor—and his attorney had saved the good tidings he had for the Vanderbilt Committee until the last—the Doctor, he was only now permitted to announce, had decided to give to Union College at once personal property to the value of $600,000: all that the college books showed the Trustees were still indebted to him for, plus the lands he owned at Stuyvesant Cove and Hunter Point. With this gift, to be known, Spencer informed the Committee, as the Nott Trust Deed, Union College would have assets of $1,023,720.18. "What a different view of results does this present," he declared, "from the Flemish statement of the accountant!" [34]

The "Argument in the Defense of Dr. Nott" concluded its golden arithmetic with a gloria to the Doctor:

> His whole life has been devoted to this one object [Union College], and all the fruits of his labors and hazards, which he had a right to appropriate to himself, and which almost any other man would have so appropriated—he has bestowed on this child of his affections and hopes. . . .
>
> For years he has submitted to private suspicion and public imputations, by persons who would not understand his purposes and plans, or who chose not to become acquainted with them. The newspapers have teemed with garbled and one-sided statements; the Senate Chamber has rung with the foulest charges, which reporters have transferred to the press . . . until a large part of this community has become saturated with prejudice.

He has, therefore, instructed me to prepare a full release to Union College, of all his claims to any pecuniary balance that may appear to belong to him on the books of the College. . . .

He has also instructed me to prepare a more formal conveyance confirmatory of that already executed, and vesting in Union College the immediate title in trust . . . of specific bonds and mortgages and contracts arising from the sale of the Stuyvesant Cove property and from the sale of lots in the tract consisting of the Hunter farm, and other land united therewith, by Dr. Nott, and Crane and Ely. . . . the whole amounting in value at this time, to at least $600,000. . . .

And here is the same KEY, to all the movements of Dr. Nott's life . . . it unlocks and explains his every act . . . it proclaims the reason and motive for the years of toil he has devoted, the rigid economy he has practiced, and the plans and schemes in which he has been engaged for fifty years. His own personal benefit, and that of his family, have been disregarded. Union College, the idol of his affections, of his hopes, and of his ambition, has been the sole, steady, and unvarying object of his ceaseless labors by day, and his anxious thoughts at night. . . .

Dr. Nott is a clergyman, and like his brethren, unacquainted with the modes and forms of business transactions; he is not an accountant; his mind looks to general plans and great results. . . . you will, I doubt not, bear your testimony to the pervading integrity and honesty of purpose, and the noble disinterestedness which have marked his whole administration of the affairs of Union College, and which entitle him to the highest credit and honor, and to the lasting gratitude of all friends of education, and of the amelioration of our race.[35]

The majority of the members of the Vanderbilt Committee, on December 30, 1853, reported their judgment on the Doctor's "integrity and honesty of purpose. . . ."[36] They dismissed Levinus Vanderheyden as unreliable; "false items," they declared, "were introduced into his accounts, and his balances are evidently forced." Vanderheyden's interpretation of the Yates and McIntyre records was dismissed, the accountant for the Senate committee having "misconceived the whole nature of the transaction." Earlier Trustees' Reports, particularly that of William James and Silas Wright, were "no small source of gratification" to the committee. The Doctor, it was unanimously agreed, was entitled to the "President's Fund," and so to Stuyvesant Cove and Hunter Point, which Spencer had emphasized, represented mere conversions in form of the Doctor's long intended gift to Union College. The

Committee agreed there was no justification whatsoever for the final and appalling sum of $946,826.83, the last amended total charged against the Doctor by the Campbell Committee's accountant, although Chairman Vanderbilt was undecided about the assignment of certain minor balances. The fact that the Committee was not in complete agreement on details did not prevent it from unanimously echoing John C. Spencer's praises of the Doctor, and his excoriation of the accountant for the latter's unsupported charges against Acting Treasurer Pearson for attempted "mutilation" of the college books, and of those charges of attempts by the old President to persuade the accountant to commit forgery.

"The just announced Nott Trust Fund," the Committee declared, "satisfactorily explains the design and object of Dr. Nott in all the somewhat complicated transactions in which we have been engaged. . . ." Nathaniel Jones and Judge Elisha Ward concluded their majority report in praises for the Doctor almost as fulsome as those John C. Spencer had used to close his "Argument":

> We should do injustice to him and to our own feelings, if we were to omit the declaration that in our judgment not only the great prosperity of Union College, but its very existence during periods of great calamity, are owing almost exclusively to his lifelong efforts, sacrifices and hazards in its behalf. He has been and is a public benefactor in promoting the great cause of education, on which our institutions, our property, our security, and our liberty depend. . . . we who have been required by official duty, and upon our high responsibilities, to scrutinize the conduct of the individual who has furnished such an example, may not shrink from the obligation of manfully avowing our disinterested and conscientious convictions.[37]

John C. Spencer had won his case. The fires an embittered Professor John Austin Yates had kindled in 1849 were out, or so it seemed. Senator James W. Beekman, and the "uncles and cousins" were publicly discredited, theirs the guilt, according to the majority report of the Vanderbilt Committee, of "individual hostility seeking its gratification by misrepresentations." For John C. Spencer, the paramount object of his months of labor had been achieved: his own honor and the honor of his fellow Trustees, "these distinguished and very capable gentlemen. . . . having reputations to maintain dearer to them than life," as he had phrased it, had been saved untarnished.

III

Behind closed doors, however, during the time Spencer was presenting his "Argument in the Defense of Dr. Nott" before the Vanderbilt Committee, events had taken place which, in retrospect, one can only view as culminating in a deception on John C. Spencer's part of the same order of magnitude as were the charges lodged against the Doctor by Levinus Vanderheyden and Senator James W. Beekman. What, in effect, Spencer appears to have decided privately, and in collaboration with unnamed friends of the Doctor's, was that Levinus Vanderheyden's bill against the President of Union College, although deliberately and "maliciously" inflated, was essentially correct.

> During the Senate investigations [the Doctor's] attorney and friends found it necessary in order to obtain a favorable decision that he should deed [his property] in trust, to Coll. [sic] at once. This was a bitter pill and persisted in with great pertinacity until finally J. C. Spencer, with a withering look and a tone of thunder said to him, 'Sir, you have not a shadow of right to that property. Your title to it is not worth a straw.' This produced the desired effect: the [Nott Trust Deed] was drawn up by J.C.S. in connection with Judge [Alonzo] Paige of this city.[38]

Jonathan Pearson, then the Acting Treasurer of the college, and from whose diary this revealing exchange is quoted, and who was himself then being threatened with legislative impeachment, wrote again.

> The first weakening of confidence in our management took place during the late investigation of the Senate Committees; and the final report was only made favorable to us by the fact that the Nott Trust Deed was made out and it was thought that this at least would be a salve for all previous bad management and ought to shield us from an unfavorable report.[39]

How to explain what must have been an extraordinary scene between Eliphalet Nott and John C. Spencer, between the "cunning old prex," young Silas Burt had referred to, and his dour, meticulous, and embittered attorney, scarred by the public scandal of his son's death? The thoughts of the old President about the property he had been forced to deed at once to the college is revealed by a document in the Union College Archives, a letter of no special importance, on the reverse of which, however, is written in the Doctor's hand, "Hunter Farm belongs to me . . . it is my property!"; underneath this statement is written in an unknown hand, "Deadly influence! Fade into classical silence."[40]

So far as the Doctor's title to the lottery profits which had gone into the "President's Fund" and so into Stuyvesant Cove and Hunter Point is concerned, one recalls Spencer's conviction, advanced during the Chancery suits of the 1830s, that the Doctor had no claims against the lottery contractors *as an individual.* What took place during Spencer's stormy and secret interviews with the Doctor during the period of the Vanderbilt Committee hearings suggests that nothing had occurred on that central issue to change his mind; obviously, however, it was not a conviction he could share with the Vanderbilt Committee.

If, however, this had been Spencer's only reservation about the Doctor as a "financiering president," it need not have moved the latter who had resisted it successfully ever since Trustees William James and Silas Wright had sanctioned his claims to the "President's Fund." The "bitter pill" which Spencer demanded that the Doctor swallow as though it were a purge had been compounded by a discovery Spencer believed he had made as he had reviewed the Trustees' *Minutes* and the treasurer's records involving that remarkable "settlement" of the Doctor's claims against the college made by the Board at its meeting held during the Semi-Centennial celebration in 1845.

Again one hears the voice of Jonathan Pearson who, as acting treasurer, was as close as any of the actors in this drama to the events which motivated it. Seven years after the Doctor's triumphant vindication by his attorney before the Vanderbilt Committee, Professor Pearson wrote in his diary:

> In 1845, when Cove and Hunter Property were deeded to Nott there was standing an unsettled account between Nott and Union College which Nott settled 'in his own way' without authority of the Board; J. C. Spencer, uncovering these facts, told Judge [Alonzo] Paige he coerced him [Nott] to give back a deed of the property to Union College! Property was advertised as worth $610,000 [in 1853], but in fact its real worth at that time was not above $180,000. . . .[41]

What Spencer believed he had uncovered was that Alexander Holland, following that Semi-Centennial Trustees' Meeting, had executed to Dr. Nott, and in the name of the Board, deeds to both Stuyvesant Cove and Hunter Point without the Board's authorization. Spencer and the Doctor's friends, believing they had discovered an irregularity to which they gave no name, had become convinced that Stuyvesant Cove and Hunter Point had been lost to the college by a strategem the nature of which, if Levinus Vanderheyden and James W. Beekman had become aware of it, could have been described in such terms of scandal neither the Board nor the Doctor could have hoped to counter them.[42]

In the face of this potentially dangerous development Spencer's strategy in 1853 had become an extension of his rationale of the converted donations by which he justified the uses to which the Doctor had put his "President's Fund". Stuyvesant Cove and Hunter Point must be returned to the College at once, reconverted again, and by whatever device would put the transfer in the best possible light. The result of Spencer's tactic was recorded by Acting Treasurer Pearson, when he wrote of that closed door scene which, he reported, "had the desired effect": the Doctor's unwilling capitulation to Spencer's "coercion," and the drawing up of the Nott Trust Deed which the Vanderbilt Committee then declared "satisfactorily explains the design and object of Dr. Nott. . . ."

With the Doctor's vindication made public with the filing of the Vanderbilt Committee's Report on January 4, 1854, the newspapers of the State quickly took up his praises. Henry J. Raymond, editor of the New York *Times*, a loyal Seward Whig and a political rival of Beekman's among the ward politicians of New York City, filled the better part of a page of his paper with a review of the long lottery history; he extolled the Nott Trust Deed as a fitting climax to the Doctor's brilliant record as a financier. Raymond particularly scored those who still insisted on claiming that the Doctor's gift of $600,000 to Union College was, in fact, the payment of a debt:

> The only motive which [the Doctor's] persecutors can have in still insisting that this is the discharge of a *debt*, and not a *donation*, is to blacken his character, torture the last years of his long, useful, and honored life, and throw a cloud of suspicion upon his integrity in after

ages. His own conscious purity of purpose will foil the most malignant part of their object; and the noble friendship of John C. Spencer has defeated the rest.[43]

Thurlow Weed reprinted the entire Vanderbilt Committee Report on the pages of the Albany *Evening Journal*, and included an editorial in which he sharply criticized Vanderheyden's "many . . . perversions of fact," and warmly praised the Doctor's attorney for his complete and convincing vindication of his client.[44]

Hugh Hastings, the editor of the Albany *Daily Knickerbocker*, after he had examined Spencer's "Argument," reported to his readers that he recognized his journal was undoubtedly that "filthiest and most abandoned newspaper in the state" to which Spencer had referred. The editor said he could understand Spencer's outrage, for "no other newspaper in the State had had the courage to show up the rottenness of Union College . . . we have charged Dr. Nott with making improper use of the funds of the College," Hastings unrelentingly declared, "and we have fortified our charges with a mass of statistics that would have driven a less influential man out of society . . . [Spencer's] report seems 'made to order,' and looks very much as if it had been licked into shape by the inventor of the steamboat *Novelty*." [45]

Ex-Senator James W. Beekman's letter, written on December 8, 1853, was his last effort to blunt the effect of Spencer's "Argument." That Spencer was to have his triumph and the Doctor his vindication must have seemed clear even then to this uncompromisingly conservative and self-righteous man. For Beekman there was only the solace of his journey to Europe and of his personal conviction that the outcome of the four years of the investigation of the affairs of Union College was less honorable to John C. Spencer than it was to himself. Perhaps Jonathan Pearson's comment on Beekman in his role as the Doctor's prosecutor is as charitable and as close to a just approximation of its true nature as one can come: "his mind poisoned," Pearson wrote, "by the wily insinuations of the plausible Professor (now gone before the High Tribunal)," Beekman began the investigation "with honest intentions, but what at first had been a just desire for the truth became in the end an intense determination to conquer and to make true his many harsh and astounding statements."[46]

Spencer's victory must, for him, have had a leaven of ashes. There is no doubt that Beekman's supporters were soon convinced that the Doctor's attorney had won at a price. In spite of the legal compromises Spencer believed he was forced to make on behalf of the Trustees and the Doctor, especially of the suppression of evidence which, if he had seen it, Beekman would have seized on as proof of his own charges, Spencer seems never to have lost his affection for the old President. Having long been a student of the Doctor's "financeering," as well as a member of his Board of Trustees, he may have understood that the Doctor's modes of doing business were a reflection of that long held belief he proclaimed as a teacher, that man becomes an unstable, emotional being when confronted with whatever challenges his self-interest. If Spencer remembered this conclusion he did not debate it, but fought to protect the Doctor from his own misjudgments, not only for the sake of those Trustees whose reputations were bound up with the old President's, but because he may have believed, himself, what he told the Vanderbilt Committee was, ultimately, the explanation for all the Doctor had undertaken . . . the Doctor's conviction that in acting he was serving Union College, "the idol of his affections," a cause which transcended the lesser, mundane legal code. The "Argument in the Defense of Dr. Nott" fails to cite a "higher law" for its support, but Spencer, even as Seward, seemed to have been willing to invoke it when he felt the courts were inadequate to deal justly with the acts of extraordinary men. As students of "Kames," the mark of the Doctor was on both men.

Two deaths soon followed the Doctor's vindication, deaths which should have finally sealed the entrances and the exits of that financial maze which had extended from the Literature and Consolidated Lotteries. Henry Yates, the ex-treasurer of Union College, died during March, 1854 at his home, the "Kane Mansion" in Albany, "of paralysis." According to one newspaper obituary "he was perhaps the wealthiest man in the State outside of the city of New York," worth $2,000,000, owner of most of the 1000 islands in the St. Lawrence River, and, as a member of the House of Yates and McIntyre, the source of his wealth, of some 80,000 acres in Louisiana, title to which had been confirmed by the Louisiana Legislature just before his death.[47]

One year later, on May 17, 1855, John C. Spencer died. Two months after his death Charles P. Sanders wrote to his cousin, ex-Senator James W. Beekman, that "the Nott affair is died [sic] away,—buried perhaps with John C. Spencer who died a month ago [sic] —the papers say his illness was brought on by a to [sic] close application in vindicating the cause of Dr. Nott—this we don't believe one word of—the cause will one day come right—so your uncle says." [48]

A grateful Board of Trustees entered their testimonial to John C. Spencer in their Minutes for July 25, 1854; because he had "volunteered his services in vindicating the President and the Trustees of Union College from the calumnies which had been long and industriously circulated about them," the Board authorized the resident Trustees to procure "a marble bust, or full length portrait . . . to be placed alongside the portrait of the President in one of the public rooms."

CHAPTER 4

"In the tenth lustrum of his presidency"

Whereas, we, the Alumni of Union College, would establish some suitable and permanent memorial to the virtues of our illustrious President—therefore:

Resolved, That we will order to be executed, and at the earliest practicable day to be erected on the College grounds, a Statue in marble of Eliphalet Nott. . ." [1]

Late Tuesday afternoon, July 25, 1854, was, for the old Doctor, a time to rest. He had made his address to the nearly one thousand alumni who had gathered after lunch in the First Presbyterian Church of Schenectady for the double purpose of celebrating his fifty years as the President of their alma mater, and of his vindication before the New York State Legislature in the face of those charges his enemies had brought against him. For Doctor Frank Hamilton, of the class of 1830, the Alumni meeting offered an opportunity to speak for all of Eliphalet Nott's "young gentlemen," who, boys and old men, had waited in the church following the Doctor's slow departure, "leaning on the arm of a gentleman, and moving with difficulty." "Venerable . . . illustrious . . . a truly *great man* . . . in the tenth lustrum of his presidency . . . ," the Alumni encomiums were to be as full as apparently was the Union College treasury. Dr. Hamilton's proposal for a statue of the Doctor was for a tribute which, he said, "could only feebly symbolize his virtues."

"Dr. Nott," he had assured Bishop Potter, the chairman of the Alumni meeting, "has not waited until his own decease would render his property valueless to himself, but with a generosity as noble and disinterested as it is singular, he has made and executed this munificent bequest [the Nott Trust Deed] to be used and enjoyed by us during his own life . . . [so] let us erect at once" Dr. Hamilton had concluded," "a statue in marble, pure, white, and immaculate as the character of the good man whose beloved form it will represent, and to receive whose blessings we are now all, and probably for the last time, gathered here together."

To procure the statue, a committee was appointed consisting of "the Hon. John C. Spencer, the Hon. W. W. Campbell, the Hon. Alonzo C. Paige, and the Hon. W. H. VanSchoonhoven," to whom Dr. Hamilton then offered, that evening, to become the first of ten persons to subscribe one hundred dollars each, or the first of twenty to subscribe fifty dollars each toward this marble memorial to Eliphalet Nott to cost from $10,000 to $15,000 and which, it was agreed, might appropriately be placed in front of the proposed "Graduates Hall," the new name for the long promised "Octagon."

For Jonathan Pearson, now Treasurer Pearson, July 25, 1854, had been a day to live through. "Where," he had asked in late April, "is the $2000 to come from to pay for the dinner?" Inasmuch as there were then three committees preparing for the celebration, one each appointed by the Trustees, the faculty and the graduates, "nothing is done," he lamented, as he carried on most of the work himself, mailing out several thousand invitations, arranging catering and music, and rhetorically asking on the pages of his journal, "Must Dr. Nott pay for his own jubilee?"[2]

For the Doctor, however, the day was, indeed, a jubilee, paid for with fifty years of the sort of "adventuring" he had urged on his seniors in his first baccalaureate. What was done was done, and it had been done with his eyes always on the future. There had been many reasons for not looking backward, not wanting a history of Union College prepared: "what is there to write?" he had asked Pearson the preceding March, "there is not anything worth knowing which is not already known . . . it is a small business to be raking in the dust and rubbish of the past."[3] He had burned the journal he had kept all his life when he married Urania Sheldon a dozen years earlier. At eighty-one he was as ready to hazard for the future as he had been at thirty-one, a future whose horizons and landscapes he had described to the huge audience of Alumni, Trustees, and State officials who had filled the church that jubilee day.

"The exercises of the morning," Professor Tayler Lewis remembered, "closed with Dr. Wayland's address," an earnest, occasionally eloquent outline of "The System of Collegiate Education in Our Age and Country." Francis Wayland, the President of Brown, answering the Doctor's invitation to speak that day, had replied that, "your wish . . . is a command . . . I have no more right to disobey than when, a thoughtless boy, I sat at your feet. . . ."[4] He had told the audience that morning he had come at the summons of one "to whom I owe more than to any other living man," and, as he spoke on education which "comprehends," he had said, "every interest of humanity," he seemed to be outlining for the Doctor, who had sat directly behind him on the rostrum, that system of education designed for the times which Wayland had long observed in operation at Union, and which in 1850 he had modified and introduced at Brown in the hope it would produce badly needed endowments and new students.[5]

As that "Nestor of American teachers," as Wayland had called him, listened that morning to his eloquent apprentice, he heard, especially in one paragraph, an echo of all he had been teaching generations of Union College men about the purposes of education, the ultimate meaning of the motto on their Minerva Seal:

> When our systems of education [Wayland told his audience] shall look with as kindly an eye on the mechanic as the lawyer, on the manufacturer and merchant as the minister; when every artisan, performing his process with a knowledge of the laws by which it is governed, shall be transformed from an unthinking laborer into a practical philosopher; and when the benign principles of Christianity shall imbue the whole mass of our people with the spirit of universal love, then, and not until then, shall we illustrate to the nations the blessings of republican and Christian institutions.[6]

Education for the times, the transformation of men into "practical philosophers," this had been the object of every break the Doctor had made with the classical curriculum and the rote teaching of the New England colleges. His "Scientific Course," that monumental "elective" which was to be more his monument than Dr. Hamilton's shadow of a statue, his rough formulations of a philosophy which looked toward William James, the philosopher of pragmatism, and away from Lord Kames, that Isaac Newton of the mind, these, too, were his achievements, along with those stove and steamboat patents which had made anthracite coal a national treasure.

Professor Tayler Lewis, who had come back to his alma mater to fill the place left by the forced retirement of John Austin Yates in 1849, remembered the Doctor as he had come into the church that afternoon:

> his locks were white as snow. His gait had grown feeble, feebler indeed than it would have been but for the rheumatic seizure of several years before, so that he walked now with difficulty. His face, within a few years, had grown more full of lines and furrows. His frame was thinner, his carriage less erect, and his general appearance that of a man on whom years were working their accustomed changes. His eye, however, was still bright . . . his voice, though less strong than in other days, was yet clear and distinct, so that few, in the stilled and expectant audience, failed fully to apprehend his lowest-toned enunciations. His address, which was somewhat over an hour long, showed no sign of mental decay. It was given *memoriter*, as his life-long custom had been . . . . there were passages in it worthy to rank with the productions of his palmier days. . . ."[7]

Few that July afternoon had been present in 1805, when the Doctor had hailed his first senior class as "young adventurers." Fifty years later perhaps half his students thought of themselves as Abolitionists, boys avid for the Civil War six years distant, some of them boys whose grandfathers had heard the Doctor's "Discourse on the Death of Alexander Hamilton," delivered to the citizens of Albany in 1804, grandfathers who had fought at Oriskany and Saratoga. The life of the College and of the nation seemed to telescope as the old President looked down, for the last time, he believed, on such a gathering as this one which had responded to the circulars sent out by his penny-worried treasurer.

"Fifty years ago . . . I stood for the first time . . . where the college edifices now stand . . . the same range of western hills, the same intervening, luxuriant flats, and the same quiet river then met the eye."[8]

Fifty years ago: "some forty students, scattered over the village of Schenectady, meeting for educational purposes in what is now a cabinet maker's shop, was the whole of Union College."

Fifty years ago: "chemistry was little known; steam as a motive power on the land or on the water, was less known; and electricity, though disarmed of its terrors, had been applied to no useful purpose. Then, to visit Albany, and do business and return, usually required three days; New York often three weeks, and Buffalo six."

In 1804, in the country west of the Mohawk Valley, the Doctor reminded his hearers, "the ploughshare had scarcely disturbed the soil . . . [there] the warwhoop echoed, and over all the inland waters the bark canoe floated in token of the red man's sovereignty." West and East, America had then been largely a land of handcrafts.

The Doctor, characteristically, spent little time in "raking in the dust and rubbish of the past" except to mention, as though he were reading from their tombstones, the names of the dead who were notable in his own pantheon: "JAY, CLINTON, HAMIL-TON . . . statesmen of imperishable memory; . . . the ingenious FULTON . . . the unhonored and forgotten FITCH, the real and the unrivaled author of steamboat navigation . . . ," and a catalogue of Trustees and faculty with whom he had served as President. What was important to him, however, was the record of "progress" man had made in the intervening fifty years, proved by the rise of new towns and cities, by the application of power to the work of hands, by man's improved understanding of those natural laws whose comprehension the Doctor had so long believed was the measure of progress.

"Progression," he proclaimed that afternoon, "indeed is everywhere apparent . . . we stand at the mere vestibule of the era of human improvement." The young Millennialist of 1804 had, by 1824, already disappeared in the practical philosopher; he was by then telling a Union College audience that earth might well be man's home for "hundreds of thousands of years to come." He had, by 1824, come to believe that man's Christian duty was not only to prepare to die, but first, to do what he could to transform earth into that Republic of the World it must become before there could be a Millennium. He had been eloquent before the Phi Beta Kappa Society a quarter of a century earlier, charging its members to comprehend the true meaning of the Gospel word "means"; in his then new, optimist's vocabulary, he had proclaimed that man, through education, "could, by the help of God . . . accomplish his own deliverance . . . work out his own salvation."

At eight-one, looking through the same glass, he saw the same vision, modified by the abrasions of thirty years:

> The first pages only, [he now told his hearers] in the history of man's doings on earth, have as yet been written. The residue remains to be filled, triumphs to be achieved during the days and years and ages of his predicted, glorious future. Nor will the last page in that forthcoming volume be inscribed until the action of fire, and flood, and storm, as well as steam and lightning, shall be understood and controlled; till the husbandman shall be able to protect his harvest field against the desolations of the hail storm; the seaman to elude the violence of the tempest; and the chemist, with his furnace and his crucible, to effect those changes in the form and qualities of bodies which God now effects with so much ease, and in a manner to us so incomprehensible, in his own vast laboratory; till oppression shall cease, misery be alleviated, peace restored, and the reign of Immanuel established in every realm, and among every race in this sin-cursed earth . . . . this progress of science, this improvement in the physical, is but the preparation and the prelude to the still more glorious improvement in the moral condition of men.[9]

With these words this "Nestor of American Teachers" epitomized the transformation of the eighteenth-century Calvinism of his brother's Connecticut church into that Christian dynamism he had long articulated as the practical philosopher, a dynamism which he and his fellow Christian optimists had come to believe represented a new order of Christian wisdom. Religion was to be viewed as a power to be channeled through the lives of educated men, to be made manifest in "this progress of science, this improvement in the physical." Here was the best answer to the Calvinist's awful question, "How am I to be saved?" This question, however, in these new times of less exalted vision, optimistic Americans were more and more translating into the question, "How can I become rich?" and were clamoring to answer in part by way of those practical and elective college courses which the Doctor had pioneered, and to which the new

Union College of "Super-graduate courses" to be supported by the just announced Nott Trust Deed was to be dedicated.

The triumphs of science in America, the old President proclaimed in 1854, were the triumphs of "Mind: free, educated, Christian mind," triumphs which began, he proclaimed, with the Pilgrims' flight "to savage hordes and forest wilds." The new era of political liberty, however, he now declared, had its origins in the American Revolution:

"Suddenly . . . individual opinion, aggregated, formed public opinion; which opinion, legalized and called into action, formed a new element in the government of nations, an element destined to absorb all other elements, and to become itself the governing principle of the race." [10] In America, as he had said in 1801, on the twenty-fifth anniversary of American independence, the world first heard the voice of God in the voice of a people. Since then, the Doctor had become convinced, it was the nation's manifest destiny to give world-wide meaning to the democratic principle. It was the manifest duty of American educators to develop those specific and practical courses for the America destined to realize the triumph of democracy.

His audience, listening to him with the awe reserved for the very old whose remarks may be born of unearthly wisdom, heard him add that "when more fully enlightened by science and sanctified by grace, [democracy] shall, in its strength and in its universality, be fully enthroned . . . at the utterance of that voice, thrones will crumble, dynasties be changed, armies be disbanded, oppression cease, and a bloodless revolution carried around the world."

The voice of manifest destiny seldom spoke more clearly than in the voice of "old man eloquent . . . . old prex . . . our cunning old prex," when he cited its works in the discovery of California gold, and pointed out its significance:

> By making a lodgment on the Pacific we have acquired the position, by the discovery of exhaustless mineral wealth we shall soon have accumulated the capital, and by a further and more skillful application of the elements of nature to the arts, we shall have secured the leisure requisite to the execution of the high office assured us in the providence of God—the office of cooperating with him in extending Freedom and

Christianity not only to the shores of the Pacific, but to the nations that lie beyond that boundary.[11]

In that one paragraph of his jubilee address the Doctor mapped the direction he had taken in his own life as the President of Union College: the pursuit of wealth in order to accumulate the capital necessary to implement his and, he was sure, God's plans. Between the optimist's role he had elected for himself and for the college, and its realization, however, was the dark dichotomy, bound by the reality of man's unstable nature which the Doctor had made the subject of what was, by 1854, probably, the most popular senior course in an American college. Now, at eighty-one, it was obvious he had not been defeated in his hope to see the chasm bridged between two inharmonious worlds, the one, of his own vision in which "progression . . . was everywhere apparent," the other of a world passion-bound in which the America of 1854 seemed to be erupting toward civil war.

The Doctor was politic enough not to raise the question of slavery before this audience, even though it was well known where he stood on the question of that "fearful incubus" as he had called it, that "very appropriate punishment" for "a young and fertile country . . . for the crime of inventing it." "For, if slavery is to be indefinitely extended," he had written to Francis Wayland that March, "it were better to be out of the Union than in it."[12] Revealingly, one of his old students reported that "the newspaper . . . the *Emancipator* . . . though ordered and paid for by the respected and venerable President . . . , was always, at his request directed and mailed to Mr. Holland, the Register, whose office was across the hall, opposite the room of the President."[13] In 1854 Union College as well as the country was a camp divided, and the Doctor had taken again to that higher ground from which he could view the struggle, not simply as the struggle for the freedom of black Americans, but as a vaster struggle "extending . . . not only to the shores of the Pacific, but to the nations which lie beyond that boundary."

There was one shift in the Doctor's thinking, revealed during this jubilee address, perhaps only apparent to a listener who had heard his Millennialist's message in his first years at Union. It was as though, for a moment, he had allowed his Bible to become one book only among many books devoted to the Gods of all faiths and of other times:

> Next to religion [he said], and as auxiliary to it, favor the cause of science. There is a mistaken view of duty which frowns on the study of nature lest its teachings should contradict the teachings of revelation. Truth is no less truth, when revealed in sunbeams from the firmament above, or exhumed from darkness amid the folds of the fossiliferous rocks below, than when inscribed on earth's surface, by the pen of the historian on scrolls of parchment, or transferred to marble by the chisel of the sculptor. Whatever God teaches, it cannot be profane for men to learn.
>
> No matter in what direction or to what extent inquiries after truth are prosecuted, from each the answer returned will be the same. From the strata embedded in the depths of the earth, from the blossoming flowers on its surface, as well as from the suns that burn and stars that glitter in the firmament above it, a voice, everywhere alike, is heard to say, 'God is here, and here, and here.'[14]

It was as though the Doctor was now reading of "Truth" by some evanescent, transcendental light. Perhaps he was, and perhaps his strictures on the Christian's duties were to be read by his initiates in the same light:

> "Go then," (he said), "and with the Bible in your hand, and the love of God in your hearts, study nature everywhere—deeply, fearlessly. And thus studying it, you will find that the teachings of Greece are the same as of Palestine—of Athens as of Jerusalem . . . that Ida and Olympus, no less than Carmel and Tabor, testify of God."[15]

In a sense here was not only the conclusion of his address, but the summit of his life as an educator, the true climax of a jubilee which was a testimony to what the Doctor, in his farthest reaching, believed was within man's grasp. The Doctor as idealist and prophet, had come at last to the boundary of his own vision, and in doing it, had outdistanced himself as a man, limited, as were other men whose moral goals, he had taught his seniors, were too often lost sight of, whose vision was blinkered by the passions and the ambitions of the moment.

The Doctor ended his address that afternoon of his Semi-Centennial, as he had his address in 1824, with a prophecy; this time, however, it was the vision of an old man, looking now past the world, past the planets and their sidereal neighbors, to a transcendental mystery, disarmingly framed in the symbols his hearers expected him to use:

> We shall see the sign of the Son of Man coming in the clouds of heaven. . . . we shall see the graves open, the dead rise, and judgment set. We shall hear the final sentence, and witness the final separation; hear the wail of lost spirits, and the song of triumph that will break from redeemed lips. [16]

To what extent he spoke in the metaphors of his profession, letting them stand as dramatic props, as Jonathan Edwards had once used the symbols of terror before his Enfield congregation, is impossible to say. The Doctor was eighty-one, and to describe the life of the spirit as he saw it there was still only the inexact language of men.

As the old president slowly left the church to the cheers of his students of half a century Dr. Hamilton was preparing the resolution to authorize his statue, "in marble, pure, white, and immaculate as the character of the good man whose beloved form it will represent."

That evening, according to the New York *Times*, there was "a large and jovial assembly of old classmates in the old college building." The Doctor, entering "a little after eight, helped by Bishop Potter, received about 1000 well-wishers. . . . Ice cream and sandwiches and ebony waiters, shoved about carelessly by rollicking lads," gave the West College its own jubilee, where, on display were two huge stone reliefs, " 'The Sculptures of Nineveh' . . . exhumed by an old graduate," and recently added to the college museum. [17] The reception in West College may have ended in a medley of special reminiscence, for it was to be the last time Union men would gather in the handsome building Philip Hooker had designed fifty years earlier, and in which the Doctor had begun his presidency. At the Board meeting that morning "West College" had been sold again to the City of Schenectady to be used this time as the central building in the city's just established free school system.

II

The Doctor's jubilee was tempered the next day by two meetings on the campus which, in spirit, had as little in common as most men believed did the teachings of Greece and Palestine to which the Doctor had referred in his Semi-Centennial address. At the first of them Wendell Phillips was the speaker, the man whose oratory on behalf of freedom for slaves was as visceral in its appeal as was William Lloyd Garrison's press; Phillips, whose cry, "Eternal vigilance is the price of liberty" was then stirring audiences as had Seward's call to accept the jurisdiction of the "Higher Law." Phillips had had to be smuggled into the annual meeting of the Literary Societies of the college. An enthusiastic member reported:

> It was done on the sly, the President and officers having ignored any knowledge of his advent to Schenectady. . . . he deserved the Doctorate at the hands of the Trustees for his performance . . . [but] he will wait long before he or anyone of kindred sentiments will receive such a blessing at their hands. Mr. Delavan and perhaps a few others are fearless and liberal enough to bestow such an honor, but policy or something else, will hem them all in . . . [they] will keep their gifts within the sacred circle of conservatism, or selfishness, a long time to come . . . [theirs] is a policy of 'titala me, titalabo te'. . . .[18]

As Wendell Phillips was moving his young audience with his attack on slavery, the Trustees were meeting again in "Geological Hall". This was the second of an almost unprecedented three-day gathering of the Board, for the Doctor's jubilee was, in part, their own; they, too, would have had a bitter Commencement if the charges made in the New York State Legislature against their President had been sustained. Governor Horatio Seymour was now present, as well as the Doctor's strongest supporters, Edward C. Delavan, Chancellor Reuben Walworth, and James Brown, of Brown Brothers, international bankers, whose daughter had married Howard Potter, the Doctor's grandson. If the old Doctor had enemies among the Trustees that day they declared themselves only in resisting the speed with which the Doctor seemed ready to put the provisions of the Nott Trust Deed into effect. How many members of the Board knew of that ultimatum John C. Spencer had recently given the Doctor in order to prevent what might well have become a legislative impeachment of the college officers is beyond knowing, though, according to the Doctor's critic, the Reverend J. N. Campbell, many of them did know.

The Nott Trust Deed itself had been sanctioned earlier by John C. Spencer, Judge Alonzo Paige, and the other "legal members" only when the Doctor had agreed to the corollary provisions of the Trustees' "Deed of Acceptance" with which it was coupled. By this latter deed the Doctor, in return for the full Board's reaffirmation of his title to Stuyvesant's Cove and Hunter Point, had released the college from every other claim of indebtedness he held against it. [19] This done, the Doctor, in response to Spencer's secret "coercion," had deeded back to the college that "munificent and gratuitous gift" which, in one form or another, he had intended, he had often declared, to include in his will.

III

The Nott Trust Deed, approved by the full Board that morning, was, in its provisions, the Doctor's final testament in his belief that "progression . . . is everywhere apparent." The Manhattan and Long Island real estate from which its income was expected to flow appeared to be a foreordained source of a full treasury. The Trust Deed's carefully evolved "university" provisions were, seemingly, an assurance of the final realization of the Doctor's "Grand Plan" for a Union College worthy of its Ramée campus. The crown of all his efforts for education, so far as the Doctor was concerned, lay in the provisions of the Nott Trust Deed "for the higher course of study," which, he wrote in an appendix to his jubilee address, "is about to be established." "When this is done," he had declared, "the requisite provision, it is thought, to a great extent, will have been made for meeting the wants of the country and the age in which we live."

"The Nott Trust Deed . . . from Eliphalet Nott and Wife . . . ," after restating the conditions under which the Doctor's accounts with his Trustees were settled, and listing in two appendices the specific real estate securities it transferred to the college, presented its "course of education . . . and a system of government" over which the Doctor, even when absent in felicity, hoped to remain the pater familias. [20] For his lifetime he retained the right to manage the yet undeveloped Hunter Point lands, "in order to place the property . . . in the most advantageous position for sale or lease." The income from both Stuyvesant Cove and Hunter Point was to be used exclusively to support thirteen specific "trusts," each of which was to be a boundary mark outlining a new Union College, "on the university system":

First: the income from $225,000 of the Fund was to be set aside to maintain nine professorships at $1500 each a year.

Second: Six Assistant Professorships were to be established on the income from $60,000, their holders to receive $600 each a year.

Third: An astronomical observatory was to be established "on grounds to be conveyed by the said Eliphalet Nott" and to be built and maintained on an endowment from the fund of $60,000.

Fourth: Another $20,000 was to be set aside to establish and maintain, "sixty Auxiliary Scholarships . . . in two classes: First Class Scholars . . . to receive Ten Dollars for each college term," and "Second Class Scholars . . . to receive Twelve Dollars each term," payment in both cases to be made "to the most deserving among those receiving or requiring material aid in the prosecution of their studies. . . ." These "Auxiliary Scholarships" were designed for those "University" students who wanted specific courses without the obligation to take a degree.

Fifth: Sixty Prize Scholarships were to be established with an endowment of $60,000, the income to be used to reward undergraduates in the "Third and Fourth Classes" of scholarship payments, $15 a year to be paid to men in the Third Class, and $18 a year to those in the Fourth Class. That graduate work was foremost in the Doctor's mind is proved by his provision that twelve Union College students who, each year, had been elected Prize Scholars, and who then chose to become resident graduate students, were eligible to further payments of $24 a term, to be paid to them for at least three years of additional graduate study.

Sixth: Nine Prize Scholarships for Graduates or Fellows were to be set up on the income of $45,000, the holders of which were to receive $300 each a year.

Seventh: The Fund was to set aside $20,000 to maintain a college cemetery on land to be given by the Doctor.

Eighth: "Philosophical, Mathematical, and Chemical Apparatus" was to be provided from an endowment of $10,000.

Ninth: Textbooks were to be purchased from the income of $5000.

Tenth: An "Eclectic Library" was to be maintained for graduate and undergraduate students on the income of $30,000 set aside for this purpose.

Eleventh: The "Geological and Mineral Cabinet" especially for Fossil and Mineral Specimens of the United States and State of New York" was to be supported by an endowment of $5000.

Twelfth: A "Cabinet of Historical Medals, Coins, Maps, Paintings, and other Historical Memorials," was to be maintained on the interest of $5000.

Thirteenth: A "Lecture Fund," established and maintained on the interest of $10,000, was to be devoted especially to lectures "on the dangers and duties of youth . . . the development and preservation of the physical, intellectual and moral constitution of man, and the preservation of health, and on the laws of life. . . ."

A "Miscellaneous Fund" was to be established with any residue income, to be used to pay administration expenses of the "Visitors" of the Nott Trust, to pay any deficiencies in any of the specific allotments, or to increase the number of professorships, or the salaries of those already established.

The Nott Trust was to be managed by six "Visitors," who "during their natural lives" were to be the Doctor, his wife Eurania, his son-in-law Bishop Alonzo Potter, the Doctor's son, the Reverend John Nott, long in poor health, and about to take a parish in Goldsboro, North Carolina, and two other Trustees, Judge W. W. Campbell, class of 1827, and R. M. Blatchford, class of 1815, the latter to be one of Lincoln's chief financial agents during the Civil War, and then ambassador to Italy. The "Visitors," excluding the Doctor, were to be paid $200 a year, and Urania Nott, if she survived the Doctor, was to be given the use of a campus house for her lifetime.

A "Nott Professor" when elected, was to be "earnestly recommended" to avoid tobacco, and was to be prohibited from the use "of spiritous liquors of any kind as a beverage". Assistant Nott Professors were to have less leeway, for they were specifically prohibited "the use of tobacco in any form." Graduate students holding Prize Scholarships would be expected to sign the same pledge as that signed by Assistant Professors, in addition to which they must be unmarried, reside in College and be prepared to assume tutorial duties for which they would be paid from the Miscellaneous Fund. Undergraduate Prize Scholars must also sign the tobacco and liquor pledges, and must agree not to join any college society without the permission of the President, and must promise to attend Sunday church exercises.

The Nott Trust, as had Union College, was, in the Doctor's mind, to draw its greatest strength from that "Parental Government" which had always placed him at the center of Union College life. Anyone in any way connected with the Fund would be expected to sustain his "system of reporting delinquencies by the Professors and other officers of College, . . . and of privately dismissing from College, with the least possible injury to the offender. . . ." In this provision for the continuation of the system of parental government the Nott Trust was revealed as a foundation prepared in a time when colleges dealt with boys. In its innovating provisions, however, for "Auxiliary" and graduate students it was a new kind of trust, and the Union College it envisioned anticipated those post-Civil War universities in which the pursuit of Truth, as the Doctor had envisioned it, would wind from Greece to Palestine, and so, by extension, out into the modern world.

IV

For the brief moment of the Doctor's jubilee, before the Civil War had become a certainty, before the short but disastrous depression of 1857 worked havoc among the perennial speculators, Eliphalet Nott seemed to have fulfilled that "Grand Plan" which he had begun to formulate as early as 1813 when he had persuaded the New York State Legislature to endow Union College from the proceeds of the Literature Lottery. The Legislature had then made the grant out of "respect to the increasing population and future exigencies of this great and flourishing state . . . to a seminary in which so many of the youths of [the] state are to be educated and with whose glory the glory of the republic is so intimately connected." The Doctor's argument in 1813 had been that the educated man would exalt the state and the republic. From 1824 on the Doctor's goal for the educated man had widened as he gave up his Millennialist's reading of the Book of Revelations as a useful calendar and became the practical philosopher, equally the priest and the teacher who read in the laws of nature and the vocabulary of science the hope of the world.

The Doctor had claimed no "firsts," only that what he did as an educator was done always in response to the needs of the America of his time. Others had tried, less successfully, to satisfy it on a more heroic scale: Jefferson at the University of Virginia, Ticknor at Harvard, both men hopeful of transplanting the European university into an America unprepared for it; Dr. Mathews, with his grandiose and weakly financed University of the City of New York; Peirce and Agassiz and their group of scientists planning for a great national university at Albany. Henry Tappan and Francis Wayland were both disciples of the Doctor's, the former perennially hopeful of introducing the German university into Michigan and into New York City, and always brought up against the hard fact that Americans still believed that democrats and scholars were, somehow, mutually hostile. Wayland was balked by an increasingly unsympathetic faculty at Brown in his attempt to build there on the curriculum reforms, the pattern of electives, and scholarship incentives he had known so long at Union.

Where others, however, lacked the Doctor's talent for compromise, where they were insensitive to the country's state of readiness for their educational innovations, the Doctor was always prepared to compromise, and worldly enough to take only the new ground he was sure he could hold. When Harvard in 1846, under Edward Everett, its new President, began planning its ambitious "Scientific School" for graduate courses in the humanities and sciences, its advocates had to settle for the elimination of all non-scientific work and a small beginning with advanced work in chemistry. When even more conservative Yale, supported by a new President, Thomas Woolsey, planned, in 1847, to add a graduate Department of Philosophy and the Arts, it recognized a need the Doctor had long tried to fill at Union, by opening its doors to "University students." Where Harvard and Yale, however, expected to leave their traditional undergraduate colleges untouched, the Doctor was prepared to reorganize the college itself, to expand from it, reaching out with his "eclectic library," an augmented faculty, a widened humanities and science curriculum, a new analytic chemistry laboratory, an expanded Department of Engineering, an observatory, all combined into a "University System" designed for strictly American participation, to serve not only scholars, but especially those who wanted advanced education, with or without advanced degrees, to make them more effective citizens in every walk of American life.[21]

By July, 1854, the evolution of the Doctor's "Grand Plan" seemed complete, and its realization within reach. The Nott Trust Deed was in the hands of Trustees who had approved all its provisions. The Union College catalogue for 1853-1854 had announced a three-year graduate course "to secure as thorough and complete scholarship in General Literature and Science as may be obtained at any European University," a program which, the announcement had added, "the growth of our Nation begins loudly to demand."

Neither the Doctor nor his Trustees, however, had planned, or could plan, in relation to many other national demands, the chief of which was then being raised by such radical anti-slavery men as Wendell Phillips. While the Doctor, Bishop Potter, and the Resident Trustees were resolving themselves into a committee that Commencement of 1854 to revise the undergraduate curriculum and "to prepare a course for resident graduates," Wendell Phillips was proposing measures leading to civil war at a meeting of the Union College Literary Societies to which he had had to be brought "on the sly."

BOOK EIGHT

"Sous les Lois de Minerve Nous Devenons Tous Frères"

CHAPTER I

"*The future is his world . . .*"

THE "past he regards not," Professor Jonathan Pearson wrote in 1854, a few months before the Doctor's Semi-Centennial celebration was to see so bright an old man's sunset, starred at its close by his huge "gift" to the College. The "future is his world," the new college treasurer continued, "in which are all his plans for the good of the college . . . he is now working for the year 1900."[1] A student poem, "The Money King," read at Commencement that year, spoke of the Doctor as a man who:

Gives with a hand still potent to enforce
His well—aimed bounty and direct his purse
One such as this is near this sacred spot,
You all do know him: I shall name him Nott.[2]

One must see the widely heralded Nott Trust Deed for what it actually was, in essence, the last and the largest of those "converted donations" which John C. Spencer had so recently persuaded the Vanderbilt Committee of the New York State Senate the Doctor had always intended for the use of Union College. Its productive funds were the bonds and mortgages covering those immensely valuable lands at Stuyvesant Cove on Manhattan Island and at Hunter and Green Points on Long Island, the latter divided by Newtown Creek, and bounded on the west by the East River.

Not an ambiguously worded dual contract this time, such as the Doctor had signed in 1822 with the men who formed the "House of Yates and McIntyre," but a multi-colored map of Stuyvesant Cove, drawn to serve the real estate ambitions of the Doctor and his business agents in the late 1840s now becomes the significant document in that expansion and final explosion of a speculator's bubble remarkable for its dimensions and the long range consequences of its collapse.

As with the lotteries contracts, the Stuyvesant Cove map posited a prize, if the hazard (or the gamble) the Doctor accepted in buying the property paid off. One sees on this map two linked and rough triangles of land embracing some fourteen city blocks of filled and unfilled New York City real estate whose boundaries ran from 13th Street and Avenue A northeast on a hypotenuse along a now expunged "Stuyvesant Street" to a line deep into the East River called "proposed exterior street." This "Exterior Street," convincing only on a map, was then as legally unstable as the tides which covered it; this underwater boundary line ran south to 14th Street (possibly to 13th Street) where it joined the base of the second and larger triangle which ran west again to Avenue C, then jogged south to 13th Street, west one block, then north again to 14th Street, and so west, finally, to Avenue A, the point of beginning.[3]

The prize, if it should be won, was this yet-to-be-filled-in-land represented on the Doctor's map by the smaller of the two triangles, an area labeled "C" and outlined in yellow, representing city blocks still awash and whose ownership depended on a final decision by the Court as to the rights of those who claimed up to that "proposed exterior street." The Doctor's already legally established holdings (Area "A" and "B" on his map) were then bounded on the east by Tompkins Street, and included the thirty-five acres of filled and unfilled land he and Captain Neziah Bliss had bought jointly from the Stuyvesant heirs in 1832 for $17,500.

With this map in mind one must imagine the Doctor during January, 1851, poring over its double triangles with his newest business partners, Alexander Holland, then still the treasurer of Union College, and Robert Wilson Lowber, "descendant of the privileged barons of Denmark." The latter was the son of John Lowber, the attorney to the resident agent of that vast tract of western New York lands owned by the Holland Land Company.[4] Robert Wilson Lowber had probably come into the Doctor's life in 1838, when, at twenty-four years of age, a veteran of two fur trapping and Indian fighting expeditions into the trans-Mississippi wilderness, he was searching for new outlets for his promoter's talents.[5] If Lowber's offer to the Doctor in that year to push subscriptions in New York City for the much talked about "octogon" for Union College was a prelude to a plan to exploit the Doctor's Manhattan and Long Island real estate, it was one which had to be postponed, for Lowber was to spend the following four years in Europe on land business for the New York City Farmers' Loan and Trust Company, dealing successfully with the Rothschilds, the officials of Hope and Company, and the head of the Bank of England who marveled at the competence of this American agent "who looked like a boy." Before his return to New York in 1845, Robert Wilson Lowber's stature was such that he had been presented to Queen Victoria, Louis Philippe at Versailles, and King William of Holland.

By 1849, when then Assemblyman James William Beekman and his "connections" were pillorying the old President and his Trustees before the New York State Legislature the Doctor may well have been glad to be unburdened of a series of private speculations by so competent an agent as Robert W. Lowber, who during the preceding four years had been an exploiter himself of a lead pipe patent, his own manufacturing plant on Water Street near the East River headquarters of the Doctor's Novelty Iron Works. In that year Lowber apparently became the Doctor's confidential business agent; the next year, according to his biographer, he was reported to have gone to Cuba to look after the Doctor's investment in the Cobra Copper mine, "which he disposed of to English interests." [6]

Perhaps the poet of the "Money King" had had unknown sources of information about the Doctor's private hazards; in any event there were soon others which involved Robert W. Lowber; "in 1850, and 1851," his biographer reported, "he investigated and managed [for the Doctor] the business of the Perkiomen Copper Mine, with General Cadwallader and Mr. McAllister, of Philadelphia, disposing of Dr. Nott's interest to them in 1852."

Here is a brief glimpse into a private world of hazards the Doctor seems to have hidden both from Beekman and the Senate accountant, Levinus Vanderheyden, where hundreds of thousands of dollars seem to have been involved, sums which, by 1857, were converted into campus gossip by those then waiting for the Doctor's death, and the outcome of Robert W. Lowber's first attack on the Nott Trust Deed.

In January, 1851, however, the map of Stuyvesant Cove was central in the planning of both the Doctor and his two new business agents, Lowber and Alexander Holland. The latter had long been responsible not only for the college books, but for the Doctor's private accounts, and, in this dual role, had arranged the reduction of the college's so-called debt to its President in 1845 by transfering both the Manhattan and Long Island real estate from the college to the Doctor, that "unauthorized" transfer of property the knowledge of which John C. Spencer had secretly used in 1853 to force the Doctor's immediate transfer back to the college of those bonds and mortgages which were then attached to the Nott Trust Deed.

For $300,000 plus one-third of the profit from the sales of the remaining "Cove" lots the Doctor in 1851 had agreed to transfer the "Cove" to Lowber and Holland who, in turn, contracted to fill in the water lots, dock and bulkhead the water front, conduct all legal actions initiated against the Doctor's title, especially to his claims to Area "C," that real estate prize of submerged land yet to be awarded by the courts, and to pay off those "encumbrances" of some $200,000 laid on the property by Richard F. Blydenburg and Hezekiah Bradford, the Doctor's first agents at the "Cove." [7]

By 1851 the Doctor had already had to take out an injunction against the City of New York and a certain "Thayer and Flagg" to prevent them from cancelling his claims to that underwater triangle of land. August Belmont "and others" would soon begin a suit against the Doctor's additional claim to property north of 16th Street, a suit which would be joined to the Doctor's action against the City of New York.[8] For the Doctor, and for Lowber and Holland, however, the gamble for the possession of this contested Manhattan real estate seemed worth any long drawn out court action; Lowber, an expert in the intricacies of land titles, in 1851 was certain the courts would decide in the Doctor's favor.

If this first contract between the Doctor and his new agents was prelude to legal contests which, in their conclusion, would destroy John C. Spencer's "Defense" of the Doctor and of his Trustees of the lottery era, it was also the prelude to another, and perhaps the greatest of the Doctor's private hazards. As a corollary to establishing this new contract for the development of the "Cove," the Doctor's preceding agents, Blydenburg and Bradford, had had to be discharged. As a part of his settlement with these two men who, Lowber assured the Doctor, had long abused his faith in them, the old President appears to have taken over their joint ownership of a 999-year lease on the Bristol Copper Mine, a clumsily worked rich ore pocket located at the south end of Zach's Mountain, in Bristol, Connecticut.[9]

With Lowber's help, the Doctor, by January, 1851, found himself in possession of a copper mine which Professor Benjamin Silliman, Yale College's noted chemist and geologist, and others had pronounced perhaps the richest copper deposit in the world.[10] The Doctor, in taking over the mine, apparently hoped to recover the more than $400,000 which Vice President Hickok of Union College later assured the college treasurer the old President had already invested in it during its operation by Blydenburg and Bradford.[11] With Lowber always in the background as adviser, the Bristol mine, however, remained only a peripheral concern for the Doctor for the next four years, its operations now in charge of Daniel Sheldon, the third Mrs. Nott's nephew, a new speculation to be left waiting at Zach's Mountain for its final two years of blue-sky development.

On January 30, 1851, the Lowber-Holland-Nott contract for developing the "Cove" was signed. Captain Neziah Bliss now emerged from the Doctor's past in the role of a sub-contractor with Jonathan Crane, the Doctor's agent at Hunter Point, both men scheduled to supply land fill for lots between Avenues "B" and "C," from 13th Street to 16th Street.[12] One can only marvel at this juncture at "old Prex's" vitality. He was still sure that all his speculations, like Antonio's caravels, would soon dock at their Rialto, and all the great plans of fifty years would be realized in these new hazards, with wealth enough, following his own death, to protect a lame and sickly John Nott, his widow Eurania, and to endow a Union College which, its Ramée buildings completed, would then crown Nistiquona Hill, become at last the great democratic university he intended it to be. The Nott Trust Deed would guarantee it all.

"Dr. Nott cares less for the past than for the future in which he is so busy fabricating a monument to his name that will be enduring," the new treasurer of Union College wrote on March 28, 1854.[13] "Pinky" Pearson, from boyhood one of the Doctor's "young gentlemen," had no knowledge at this time of the elaborate legal charade John C. Spencer had just conducted before the Vanderbilt Committee of the New York State Legislature in defense of the old President. Nor was he privy then to the Doctor's private world of speculation.

II

By December 1, 1853, when a second Stuyvesant Cove contract with Robert Lowber was signed, the future, as the Doctor had conceived it, had suddenly become less his to shape. By then he had had to bow to John C. Spencer's will in the creation of the Nott Trust Deed. By then, as a part of his settlement with Union College which so sharply curtailed his freedom as a "financeering president," he had been forced to conclude this new contract with his agent, Robert Lowber, one which for the first time carefully delineated the remaining "Cove" lands, the "encumbrances" on them, the suits pending in relation to the ownership of sections of them, a new contract which listed specifically those "Cove" bonds and mortgages which, like it or not, a few weeks later became a portion of his "donation" to Union College. [14]

At the heart of this second contract with Lowber and later, of the Nott Trust Deed itself, were three very special bonds and mortgages given earlier to the Doctor by Robert Lowber, representing $90,000, a part of the latter's promise, in 1853, to pay the Doctor $412,000 for what had remained of the "Cove" in 1851. These three securities were no ordinary ones, but were to bring the Doctor, too old and sick to defend himself, to judgment, finally, before his Board of Trustees. These mortgages covered in part underwater lots from 15th Street to 17th Street, land lying east of Avenue B to that mysterious, still underwater "proposed exterior street" which Nott and Lowber were expecting would become the eastern boundary of New York City. These mortgages were subject first, however, to the settlement of a suit begun by James Thayer and William Flagg in which they claimed ownership of these lots. They were also subject to that impatiently waited decision of the Superior Court which would decide the fate of Area "C" on the "Cove" map, that triangle of land the partners had conservatively valued at $135,000.

These key mortgages given to the Doctor by Lowber were placed on December 1, 1853 in escrow with John C. Spencer himself, who agreed to deliver them to the treasurer of Union College whenever the court decided in the Doctor's favor, a foregone conclusion, so far as the Doctor and his agent were concerned.[15] Spencer's hand in framing this second Lowber agreement is seen as clearly as it is seen in the framing of the Nott Trust Deed and the Union College release to the Doctor, signed three weeks later when, tired and sick, the ex-Secretary of the Treasury and of War climaxed his legal career by presenting the aged Eliphalet Nott to the New York State Legislature not only as the Nestor of American educators, but also as its Maecenas.

If Spencer had lived he might have been able to order the events which now followed. Given the hidden risks, however, built into the Nott Trust Deed, the problems of a Maecenas so soon without funds, of a very old college President who could not give up his office because of his entanglement in the web of his own speculations, perhaps even a John C. Spencer would have been overwhelmed. The father-image of the Doctor which Spencer had perpetuated by his widely distributed "Argument" had seemed secure; the intricate details of its shoring up were Spencer's fabrications, including particularly that significant reorganizing in 1853 of the Doctor's relations with Robert Wilson Lowber, including the funding of the Nott Trust itself.

Following Spencer's death so soon after the Doctor's Semi-Centennial celebration, however, that elaborate shoring began to give way. Three men, Professor Jonathan Pearson, appointed Union College treasurer in July, 1854 to succeed Alexander Holland, Judge Alonzo C. Paige, College attorney during the Chancery suits of the 1830s, and soon to be Chairman of the Board of Trustees, and scholarly Laurens Perseus Hickok, drafted by the Doctor from the Auburn Theological Seminary to take the place of Alonzo Potter as his Vice President, and presumably to be his successor as President, these men now became the chief actors as well as the increasingly impatient death watch during the Doctor's last, shattering "adventure" as a speculator.

The campus office of the new treasurer soon became a veritable gazebo for Trustees and faculty anxious to look out on what so many of them began to think, fearfully, was a dying enterprise. Here, among Treasurer Pearson's ledgers, Vice President Hickok, Vice President in name only, spoke out, frustrated, determined to force the now reluctant Doctor and the Trustees to honor his personal contract with them as he saw it. Here Professor Isaac Jackson ("Captain Jack") and Professor Tayler Lewis, whose salary complaints and newspaper controversies so worried the Doctor, Professor Gillespie and Professor Joy, and others, spoke frankly, took sides, and waited for the Nott Trust Deed to perform its promised miracles. Would it really renew the boy-and-time worn dormitories, their own run-down "pediment" houses, their classrooms, the library which had been theirs and Bishop Alonzo Potter's everlasting embarrassment?

For the increasingly isolated old President it was, perhaps, one more misfortune that the man closest to him during the final overwhelming of his plans should be precise, economizing, unimaginative Jonathan Pearson, who, tuned to an orderly, daily pattern of living, reflected on the pages of his Journal only the decimal and ledger realities he saw. They were shocking enough, however, to blind so parochial a diarist to the golden future foreseen by that octogenarian optimist who, from 1854 until his death now dominates the pages of Jonathan Pearson's "Thinking Books."

> Nott good naturedly complained this morning of my hard-headedness and obstinacy, laid down the following rules of an agent: that he may act contrary to the known wishes of his principal for his principal's benefit within the limits of his responsibility, that is, up to the amount of his own property, which must go to make up any losses that may accrue from his departure from said principal's orders!!! Also, that I have a right and that it is proper for me to obey his directions even if contrary to known rules so long as I suppose him responsible for the consequences and answerable to the Trustees.
>
> I dissented *in toto* from Nott's reasoning and advocated strict construction of the law and firm obedience to written or known rules of business. Came away as before unconvinced and grieved to see such one-sided, unsound advice given.[16]

The Doctor, as Pearson saw him in the spring of 1855, seemed less and less a subject for translating into that marble statue the alumni had voted the preceding July. Two months after this Journal entry, the new treasurer disapprovingly quoted the Doctor again:

"Pearson, I've no patience with such little, pitiful dickering as you exhibit, running to this gentleman and that for permission to do a thing which I know just as much about and a great deal more than they. Where would the College have been if I had done so 30 years ago?"

Pearson, obviously nettled, reported in his Journal he had told the Doctor that inasmuch as the latter had now resigned the plenary powers he had held from 1822 until 1849, "you are now to me no more than any other Trustee, having no separate and isolated authority."

To the old President, looking at his one-time pupil, almost forty years his junior, now a very proper bookkeeper, there was no reply which, in 1855, would have explained his lifetime of compromises and hazards. Pearson, in recording the Doctor's second rhetorical question, would have had to be his biographer to attempt an answer to it:

> Where would college have been if I had acted on your little, tuppenny policy and stopped to run to this Trustee and that for authority to see if the laws would allow me to act? . . . . I could never be trammeled by your rules and laws.[17]
>
> A strange character! [the new treasurer wrote that spring] a curious bundle of good qualities and defects! Humble and yet self-conceited! Shrinking from display and yet none more susceptible of praise and flattery! Just in many cases but greedy for credit even when due to another! Yielding yet opinionated, and obstinate to rule and direct in his own way. Intensely avaricious for money for a good object as he thinks—but entirely without order or system in making and managing it, rushing headlong into wild speculations and scarcely ever taking the longer, safer and surer methods of acquiring money![18]

By 1855 the Doctor had lost the allies of his youth: Timothy Dwight of Yale, President Samuel Smith of Princeton, and the movers and shakers of the New York scene when he was "superintending" the New York State lotteries, such men as William James, Governors DeWitt Clinton, Marcy and Wright, and those other Trustees who believed in him, and could be persuaded to accept those hazards his optimism had translated and still translated into certainties.

> rumors and much gossip are rife in our little circle in college [Jonathan Pearson noted the following February], thus [Nott] is head and ears under debt, and notes for himself and others hang over him to a frightful [extent], and if by hook and crook he clears himself, it will only be by the skin of his teeth, leaving little property or nothing of value . . . whether all this be true or only half of it what a spectacle for a man . . . of his office! Would it not be called imbecility in any other man thus to coquet with fortune and rashly hazard all upon the wildest of all possible speculations?

Within two years, from the signing of the Nott Trust Deed, to that February of 1856 when Pearson's office was buzzing with new rumors, the Lord's will as the Doctor had hoped it would manifest itself, and the reality of events had become alarmingly different.

III

The college treasurer's entries now began to reflect the Doctor's renewed enthusiasm for his Bristol Copper Mine, a speculation beyond the control of Pearson's "tuppeny policy" and Judge Paige's inhibiting regard for corporate niceties.

> [Nott] goes soon to Bristol, Conn., where he has a copper mine . . . a subject of some interest to him, inasmuch as it is a kind of lottery in which he apparently delights as of old. The rumor is that a rich vein has just been discovered in it. Doubtful! . . . it would be no good to ask him for information. . ." [19]

A month later, on August 26, 1855 the old President's increasingly disapproving Boswell reported that the Doctor had said to him:

> 'There's plenty of copper there if it can only be got out!' In the vacation he had a committee of Benjamin Silliman Jr., a Mr. Whitney [James Dana Whitney] and a foreign miner to examine the state and prospects of his mine . . . tis said he is trying to sell out to an advantage. Silliman asserts that the Dr. has spent more than $500,000. If so he will hardly see his money again. [20]

The treasurer's opinion of the Bristol Copper Mine is plain enough. He knew very little, in 1855, of the history of the Doctor's involvement in this most unacademic adventure, one which had been based on an enthusiastic survey made by Professor Silliman, Sr., during the 1840s. Jonathan Pearson, however, little by little, patched together the story of that involvement, reducing it, somehow, from the dignity of history to a caricature, a script for sad comedy, a story of an old man senilely destroying himself.

"Prof. S. [Silliman], the mineralogist," according to the skeptical Vice-President Hickok, had told the latter's nephew, Laurens Perseus Seelye, the "facts" behind the Doctor's half million dollar investment: Professor Benjamin Silliman, as Pearson recorded Hickok's story, knew all:

> Finally [Nott] met young Ben Silliman [Jr.] and told him if he would raise $60,000 he should take charge of the mine. B.S. canvassed the town [New Haven] for the money. Some took a $1000 worth of the stock, some took more—all his friends were appealed to and in the meantime [Nott] went to N. H. and preached. The people wondered that so old a man could have such vigor and power to speak so well at his age; they concluded that so good and wise a man must know what was in the mine and the stock was taken at once. At the end of two years the whole concern burst up—all was spent and N. [Nott] must have known from his long experience of the mine that it was good for nothing and that the money B.S. was raising would all be lost! . . . 'it was horrible,' says he, 'to see that old man act in such a manner.'[21]

Just for a moment, in this almost unrelieved picture of miscalculations, one sees the Doctor, "that fine looking old gentleman," who, another historian of Bristol reported, stopped one day at a farm house near the mine site to ask for directions. The farmer, an Englishman, and a share holder in mine at this time, was away, but his wife and young son hurriedly cleared a farm wagon, "a rug or piece of carpet was spread, and lastly an arm chair was placed in the wagon. Thus comfortably, Dr. Nott was taken by William Smith to view his mining possessions in Bristol," a trip during which the boy was so awed by the Doctor's lecture on the virtues of study and college that he became himself a student at, and finally, with the help of the Nott Trust Fund, a graduate of Union College in the class of 1863.[22]

The Bristol historian also noted that, "under the direction of Professor Silliman [Jr.] the most extravagant schemes and experiments of a costly nature, were indulged in, the Professor being a fine theorist but a very poor practical miner. Hundreds of thousands of dollars, from first to last, were poured into the mine, and, as the longest purse has a bottom, so in this case the bottom of the purse was reached . . . although an income of $2000 a month above necessary expenses was being received by the mine up to its closing." [23]

By the end of 1857 this collapse of the Doctor's last and greatest hope for another fortune was but one of a seemingly endless catalogue of business failures across the country. The causes have yet to be fairly allocated between the tariff reductions of that year, the overexpansion of industry, of real estate development, and of a decrease in California gold production, all of it one with that undisciplined enthusiasm for hazard or gamble which neither the Doctor nor other Americans like him had had tempered by that earlier economic collapse in the black year of 1837.

Jonathan Pearson's visitors each now bore the old President's crippling losses in his own way. On January 12, 1858, the day the papers, according to the "Thinking Books," announced the failure of the Bristol Copper Mine, Judge Paige dropped in to tell the treasurer that R. M. Blatchford, a fellow Trustee, had told him the Doctor "has lost all." James Dana Whitney, later State geologist of California, a stockholder in the Bristol Company and the Doctor's adviser in the mine's operation, complained to Pearson that the Doctor had not followed his advice, that Benjamin Silliman, Jr., was extravagant and without any mining experience, the proof of which was that he had cost the Doctor over $200,000 in the two years Silliman was connected with the company, and had left the Doctor burdened with the company's debts. [24]

Robert Lowber, a year later, then no longer the Doctor's agent, and with his own overwhelming bill to add to those already eclipsing the Doctor's optimism, gave Jonathan Pearson the final accounting of the disaster at Bristol:

> Up to 1857, $730,000 went into the Bristol Copper Mine, and after that under Silliman's management $140,000 more. . . . I found that out

myself & Dr. Nott could not believe it. In 1857 he might have sold the mine out for $250,000 & I urged him to do it, but Silliman and Woolsey persuaded him that by making a stock company with a nominal capital of $500,000 of which they would take $70,000 he might make something like $400,000 out of it. [25]

Vice President Hickok, James Dana Whitney, and Robert Lowber, each with his prejudices, had his own explanation for the failure at Bristol; Lowber, who, of these three men, knew the Doctor as a financier best, would have agreed with Whitney that the old President seemed to put his faith in those who promised most. Lowber, however, had also known, as they watched the collapse at Bristol, that a decision of far greater consequence to the Doctor's hopes had also been generating in New York City at the same time.

At the General Term of the Superior Court in November, 1857, it was decided that the underwater land extending east from Tompkins Street to that "proposed exterior street" embodied in that smaller of the two triangles on the Doctor's map of Stuyvesant's Cove, was not his. [26] With this decision a powder train of events was now fired leading straight to that magazine of long concealed evidence John C. Spencer had kept from destroying the Doctor during the recent New York State legislative investigations.

By denying the validity of the Doctor's claim to that triangle of land which he, Robert Lowber, and Alexander Holland, as college treasurer, had framed in yellow in 1851 on their map of the "Cove," the Court, in 1857, exposed the Nott Trust Deed itself to attack, and, perhaps, to destruction by the Doctor's creditors. For them, because of the collapse of the Bristol Copper Mine speculation, that last of the Doctor's incredible catalogue of private hazards, there was now no other possible source of credit left than this "gift" to Union College, against which they soon came to believe they could enter claims they could force the Trustees of Union to honor. That shoring which had supported John C. Spencer's elaborate "Argument . . . in Defense of Dr. Nott" in 1853 was about to collapse.

Robert Lowber, an enigma to Jonathan Pearson, a villain to Judge Alonzo Paige, and, so far as an appalled Eliphalet Nott was concerned, his alter ego in these last years of dubious financial history, had offered the Doctor two opportunities for money relief during 1856. If, argued Lowber at that time, the Doctor could persuade his Trustees to release to him two of those three very special bonds and mortgages placed in escrow, first with John C. Spencer and later transferred, so Lowber was to claim, without the latter's permission, to the Board of Trustees, the lands for which they were security could then be sold at enormous profit, in spite of the cloud still on their title.

What the college treasurer did not then know was that Union College held the "Cove" securities, according to Lowber's later testimony, not as owner of them, but only as custodian of them until the court decided whether or not the Doctor held title to those valuable, though still under water blocks of Manhattan real estate, east of Tompkins Street. If the Doctor's title was finally disallowed, however, Lowber, according to his two contracts with the Doctor, could then demand the return of securities which, he claimed, were his, rather than the property of Union College.

At this juncture of events in February, 1856, neither Eliphalet Nott nor Robert Lowber were concerned by anything so seemingly certain as this then pending court decision. Lowber's first deal, according to the keeper of the "Thinking Books," was completed in March, 1856, when one of the "Cove" bonds and mortgages was transferred to the Doctor, at his request, by the Finance Committee, and then by him to his agent who, according to Pearson, had sold the East River block involved "to a gas company [the Manhattan Gas Light Company] who seemed to have no fear of a suit or a defective title. . . ." "The question arises," Pearson noted, "what is the true reason for this transaction . . . the truth is . . . the exchange is needed in order to meet [Nott's] financial necessities. . . ." [27]

By the time the Manhattan Gas Light Company sale was completed the Doctor and his agent were buoyed by the fact that "Judge Hoffman favored Dr. Nott's view, [that he held title to the acres he claimed] and [had] decided the cause mainly in conformity thereto at Special Term . . ." The fact that the case had then gone on appeal to a higher court had in no way slowed up Lowber's rush to get rid of more of these still disputed underwater lands.

By the end of 1856 Lowber had a second and an even more profitable deal arranged. The Doctor, according to Judge Paige, Chairman of the Board, convened a meeting of the Finance Committee on December 12th that year from which the Judge was absent, a meeting which authorized a substitution of securities similar to the one the Doctor had arranged the preceding March. In spite of the fact that one member of this Committee, Bradford R. Wood, withdrew his signature from the certificate of transfer the next day, the Doctor had lost no time in using it to clear the way for Lowber to consummate this second sale involving "Cove" lands the debt ridden President was now hazarding the Superior Court would award to him. [28] By March, 1857, the Doctor's agent had completed the sale of the block between 16th and 17th Streets, Avenue C and Avenue D, to the City of New York, to be used for "an Uptown Market," a highly profitable transaction which netted the sellers $196,000, one which, "in order to get the thing done," Lowber later told Pearson, he had had to pay $27,000 in bribes.[29]

The true cost of these two "Cove" land deals is not to be measured in the temporary financial relief they gave the octogenarian President of Union College. The real accounting began at last as the Doctor's creditors started their searches for whatever crumbs were left on the shelves of his nearly bare cupboard of assets.

Robert Lowber, on December 15, 1857, was the first to reach for what could be taken. On that day he and the Doctor revised their contract of 1853. In order to stave off worse, a direct claim against the Nott Trust Deed, the Doctor signed over to his now ex-agent any remaining interest he retained in Stuyvesant Cove, or in any other real estate in which he and Lowber had had a joint concern, including the later highly successful Bald Mountain Lime Works near Greenwich, Washington County, New York.[30] In return for this abject admission of bankruptcy, Lowber, who seems to have been able to maintain his own solvency in this year of financial panic, agreed to pay some $50,000 on their joint debt of over $150,000 owed to Stillman, Allen and Company, so long the Doctor's bankers and the successors to his Novelty Iron Works, *provided* the courts sustained the Doctor's claims to land north of 17th Street.

The key clause in this last contract, however, stated again that should Robert Lowber decide not to appeal the recent Superior Court decision which had denied Judge Hoffman's support of the Doctor's claim to the disputed lands at Stuyvesant's Cove, those bonds and mortgages covering that property should be returned to Lowber. Here was the slow fuse the Doctor never imagined would be allowed to run until it ignited those explosive issues John C. Spencer had presumably buried forever in 1853, for those bonds and mortgages were now no longer his to return; they had become capital assets of the Nott Trust Deed, or so his Trustees believed.

The final catalogue of the financial disasters visited on the Doctor was recorded in February, 1859, by Jonathan Pearson who, in his role as college Cassandra, carefully set down the list given to him by Jonathan Crane, by then a bankrupt himself, a man convinced he, too, had been badly used by the Doctor in the latter's manipulation of Stuyvesant Cove and Hunter Point securities:

Losses on the S.S.Novelty:	$300,000
Losses from R.B.'s [Richard Blydenburg] management at Stuyvesant Cove:	70,000
Losses in the Bristol Copper Mine:	300,000
Losses in the Bristol Copper Mine machinery:	60,000
	$730,000

An embittered Jonathan Crane then added other information which Pearson recorded in shocked surprise:

Losses on Rev. Calvin Pepper, wild schemes	$ 20,000
Losses: H. Nott and Company . . . "Canada Lands"	80,000
Perkiomen Copper Mine	120,000
"N.C. Gold Mine"	145,000
Bald Mountain Lime Works	120,000
	$485,000

To this grand total of collapsed hazards amounting to $1,215,000, a Treasurer Pearson then suffering through the college's day-to-day poverty added his own comment: "These are by no means all his [Nott's] losses, if C. [Crane] is right . . . [the

Doctor] got the money from lotteries, Cove property, and sale to Crane and Ely of Hunter Point." [31]

As the storm gathered, Eliphalet Nott Potter was to remember his grandfather's "serenity" in the face of his losses about which faculty members and Trustees gossiped in the treasurer's office:[32]

> "Tutor M. [Millard] tells me [Pearson noted] that Nott told him he had lost $300,000[in the Bristol Mine] . . . on the other hand Lowber says he has made $500,000! How these two statements are to be reconciled is more than I know." [33]
>
> "Professor Gillespie says Bald Mountain Lime Works a complete failure . . . so ends the brilliant bubble, the toil of a life . . ." [34]
>
> "Vice-President Hickok says . . . Cove property is gone . . ."

On another occasion, the Vice President, after describing what he said was the Doctor's failure to keep faith with Jonathan Crane, told Pearson: "I have it from undoubted authority that C.N.P. [Clarkson Nott Potter, then the Doctor's attorney] said to him, 'Grandfather, you are not fit to do business, for if you deal with an honest man you will cheat his eyes out; and if you deal with a rogue, you are so credulous that he will cheat your eyes out!" [35]

The Doctor's oldest son, lame, dependent Professor John Nott, so often the butt of ribald campus jokes, bitter himself that his father's failure seemed to threaten his own security, exclaimed one day in the treasurer's office, "What a history would the minute recital of [father's] money transactions make!" [36] Finally Judge Alonzo Paige, toward the end of March, 1858, came to Pearson with the news "that he had been informed by one of the family that in a few days executions will be had by our sheriff of $40,000 against [the Doctor] . . . that he had given Clarkson Nott Potter a bill of sale of his household property to save it from the above executions . . . that he has lost *all*, and has nothing to live on save his salary and the income of $15,000 settled upon Mrs. Nott by Robert Lowber." [37]

The Doctor himself was becoming isolated more and more, not only from his Trustees, but from John, Joel, and Benjamin Nott, his three sons by Maria who made their bitterness plain at losing the inheritances to which they had adjusted their expectations for so long. His older faculty, too, saw their own prospects as "Nott Professors" jeopardized. His Vice President, Laurens Hickok, was fearful of exercising authority to which the old President clung, still hopeful of passing a reborn Union College on to his son-in-law, Bishop Alonzo Potter, to whom he turned in this year of bankruptcy and confessed the things he might have reserved for his daughter Maria, had she lived.

In January, 1858, he wrote to the Bishop that he hoped to see him live "to superintend what I have done . . . and left undone," a statement which might well have alarmed Vice President Hickok, had he known of it. [38] In June he wrote again to the Bishop who was then in England, that the failure of Stillman, Allen and Company had "blighted" his fortunes, and that he was then "disciplining his mind into submission" to the Lord's will. [39] By December the Doctor, writing once more, confessed to his son-in-law that he was fearful the latter's increasing ill health would keep them separated in what the Doctor confessed was his "time of increasing loneliness," when, as he reviewed the past, he saw so much he wished could be undone. [40]

Now eighty-five, the Doctor "still had the pluck of middle age," however, according to Jonathan Pearson, by this time wholly disenchanted by the wreck of the old President's fortunes. This he blamed wholly on what he reported in August was the great flaw in the Doctor's character: life, as the Doctor saw it, was a lottery "in which," according to Pearson, "there were a thousand blanks to one prize." The Doctor had had his rationale for so hazardous a way of life, but if Pearson, or Judge Paige, or the Judge's supporters on the Board of Trustees, had ever comprehended that rationale, they had long since discounted it and discounted, too, the Doctor's prayerful hazarding as only heedless gambling.

At Commencement in 1858 the Alumni Association was able, at least, to dedicate the foundation of Graduates' Hall, a building designed by Edward Tuckerman Potter, the old President's grandson, and which, to the Doctor, had become the black rock of Mecca, the goal, the touchstone of what was left of his life. Judge Harris, a member of the Board of Trustees, had welcomed the Doctor to the temporary platform at the construction site, presenting him to the crowd of townspeople and graduates as the parent of all Union College men. "Let the building rise," the Judge had proclaimed, "massive and grand, comely and beautiful in its proportions . . . let the building rise . . . and let it be a gathering place for the great and ever-increasing brotherhood of Union." If the energy which had produced the great hole in the center of the campus soon ran out, it flared at least in the Judge's memory as he recalled that other tribute to idealism embodied in the college seal of 1795: *Sous les lois de Minerve nous devenons tous frères*, he had recited in closing.[41]

Following the Judge's dedication, "a leaden box containing the charter of the college, a catalogue of former alumni, the portraits of the President and faculty, and a view of the Hall to be erected" was placed in a cornerstone, plus "a large grasshopper who happened at the moment to leap on the spot."

Perhaps the old president had been re-energized by the prospect of seeing the monumental "Octogon" come into being; in any event, the New York *Tribune* on February 20, 1859, reported that "the venerable Dr. Nott . . . has so far recovered from his recent illness that he walks out with more ease than at any previous time within the last ten years. He now walks a quarter of a mile (from South to North College and back) with one cane, while he formerly required two."

By the end of May, however, the Doctor was again a complete invalid, victim of a paralytic stroke. Jonathan Pearson, still shaken and confused by his then recent discovery of what he recorded in his journal was the Doctor's "secret contract with Lowber," noted on May 22, 1859, that he had met "Ann Carr, his nurse in his former sickness ten years ago . . . she judges him in a dangerous case and past recovery."

For weeks rumors welled up in the college treasurer's office like the bubbles in the sulphur spring in "Capt. Jack's" garden. Professor William Gillespie's, "he cannot long survive" was everyone's theme. Nurse Carr reported, "His nature has changed." On another occasion Pearson was amazed to find the Doctor lucid enough to demand details on the Trustees' management of the Hunter Point lands which he had given up under pressure from the Board the preceding March.[42] Rumor raced through the campus that the President was about to be baptized in the Roman Catholic Church, and that Bishop Hughes was on the way up from New York City to perform the ceremony.[43] Pearson reported that the

Doctor, hovered over constantly by Eurania Nott, nurse Carr, and Moses, the ex-slave who had thankfully made the Doctor his new master, was troubled that "Ben and Joel Nott . . . fail to visit him." [44] There was talk that as soon as the paralyzed President's death was announced Dr. Hickok would immediately discharge all the old college servants. [45]

On June 16 Pearson reported, "Dr. Nott is taken out to ride (10:30). Three weeks since yesterday, he told Moses, his colored man, that he should not live three weeks." On the 17th the college treasurer saw him "brought out and placed in his three wheeled chair on the walk along the South Colonnade, where he was rolled backward and forward for some minutes. It was a sad sight! Poor old man! His dim eyes are almost lustreless and sightless, sunken and rayless! His strength is no more than an infant's—one hand alone can be moved—his voice is feeble and indistinct—his mind wandering—his thoughts incoherent—still they run upon college matters."

On June 25, to Jonathan Pearson's amazement, the Doctor was alert enough to demand he bring him the seniors' diplomas, a hundred of which he then laboriously signed; "his best day," the Treasurer noted.

So many problems for the Doctor and for the college would have had simpler resolutions if the stricken President's prediction made to Moses in June, 1859, that he had only three weeks to live had been fulfilled. "I cannot die before my time" he had said, however, on another occasion. His "time," clocked now by an old man's relentless vitality, running on until his death six years later, was enough to allow lesser men to fill volumes of lawyers' briefs and the pages of Jonathan Pearson's "Thinking Books" with a record of human failures which was to appall that devoted, meticulous servant of the Trustees, a man whose optimism, measured by the Doctor's, reached no further than to hopes for good weather.

CHAPTER 2

"Munificent donation," or "magnificent humbug"?

COMMENCEMENT that July, following the Doctor's stroke, saw Vice President Hickok presiding in place of the President, absent from the platform for the first time in more than fifty years.[1] The Doctor's relations with his Vice President were at their lowest ebb; the faculty and Trustees had taken their stand as pro-Hickok or pro-Nott.[2] Professors Gillespie, Jackson, and Foster now thought the Vice President unsuitable to succeed the Doctor: too brusque, too rude, they agreed, too much the closet philospher. The Vice President's new book, *Rational Cosmology*, seemed too much "tinged with German Philosophy," according to some of the "old school Presbyterians," Episcopalians, and Dutch Reformed members of the Board, "excepting Judge Paige," according to Pearson.[3]

The Literary Societies had no entertainment that Commencement, their members still outraged at the Reverend Dr. Backus's refusal, two years earlier, to allow their speaker, a Professor of Theology at Harvard (probably the Reverend George Edward Ellis), to air his Unitarian views from the pulpit of the First Presbyterian Church of Schenectady. Unless they could choose their own speakers, the Societies chose to have none. Radical thinking seemed to be in the air; one newspaper account of the occasion reported that "free thought is gaining ground [here] . . . ."[4]

The Doctor also missed the meeting of the Board of Trustees that July. Governor Edwin Morgan, however, was present, the Republican protégé of Thurlow Weed, and with him had come his Secretary of State, the State Treasurer, and the State Comptroller. Three years earlier the Doctor had thought the election of a

Republican President would be the prelude to national disaster; better a divided country than one at war, he had argued in 1856, a position he had given up by 1860, however, when, casting his last ballot, he voted the Republican ticket, "even though he calls himself a Democrat," a disapproving Jonathan Pearson recorded that November.

In spite of the disasters which were building up off-stage, both nationally and within the borders of the campus, the college itself was growing rapidly again; from a registration of 200 the year of the Doctor's Semi-Centennial celebration, the student body by 1859 had increased to 330. Vice President Hickok awarded seventy-five Bachelor of Arts degrees that July, fourteen of them to students in the "Scientific Course," plus four degrees in "Civil Engineering," a new degree category the Board had established two years earlier. Once again Union College stood with Harvard and Yale, each of the latter the next year graduating only a few more men than did Union. There was a widespread belief now that the Schenectady college had unlimited funds for scholarships, that it was developing a unique "university curriculum," especially in its new departments of Civil Engineering and Analytic Chemistry, each of which then offered, perhaps, the most sophisticated laboratory experience to be found in America.[5] News of the Nott Trust Deed, that "munificent donation" to Union College, had had its effect on enrollment.

The Trustees at their meeting that July voted to refer the threatening Lowber problem back to its Finance Committee, and, in closing, approved a resolution of sympathy to be sent to the Doctor "in his present affliction." The Alumni gathering that afternoon "made arrangements . . . for the completion of Alumni Hall" to whose gaping foundation the old President was usually wheeled on his good days. The college treasurer recalled that the Doctor, following one such visit, had assured him that they had been looking at "the greatest foundation since the Colosseum" and that he thought Pearson should "write a puff" about it at once.[6]

As the one foundation, however, waited for its walls and roof to be raised Robert Lowber and Judge Paige each prepared, in his own way, to dismantle the ramparts of that legal structure John C. Spencer had erected at such cost to protect the Nott Trust Deed and so the reputations of the officers of Union College who had shared with the Doctor the "risks and hazards" of the lottery years.

"Lowber intends to prove," Pearson wrote in his diary on September 28, 1860, "that the Doctor's Deed [to Union College] was a pure gift while at the time he owed Lowber $46,000 . . . we, therefore, are to show that it was for a valuable consideration and to do so we must specify the items of indebtedness of Dr. Nott to Union College. This opens the old lottery transactions and Dr. Nott's gains thereby, as well as the unsettled accounts between him and Union College." Spencer, in 1853, had called the Nott Trust Deed that "munificent donation"; Judge Paige, in 1860, was determined to prove it was "the magnificent humbug."

One thinks of Urania Nott that August telling the college treasurer that no matter who won the pending suit her husband's character would be "ruined," and of the Doctor trying to quiet her fears with the comment that the legal maneuvering "is all a lawyer's way of doing things," and of Pearson then reassuring them both that it was his opinion the suit would, in the end, be compromised.[7] How much of Judge Paige's answer to the Lowber suit was fully comprehended by the tired and sick old man the Judge was to claim was quite incompetent to understand or to manage his affairs is beyond knowing.[8] The Doctor's own fear of its consequences, however, is clear enough.

Pearson reported a strange meeting held in his office at the end of that August when Alexander Holland, his predecessor as treasurer as well as the Doctor's partner for a short time in the exploitation of the "Cove," Robert Lowber, Robert Potter, the Doctor's grandson, and the Doctor himself were present. The Doctor, Pearson noted, had asked ex-treasurer Alexander Holland to examine the Trustees' Minutes for the year 1845 "to see whether the Trustees authorized the treasurer to deed away to Dr. Nott the Stuyvesant Cove property in payment of a balance which Dr. Nott claimed from Union College."[9]

Pearson reported he had then told the group the Trustees' resolutions had given no such authority, and that Holland had replied he believed his authority for transferring the "Cove" to the Doctor "came from a sort of confirmation the following year. . . ."[10] The whole purpose of the meeting, Pearson was sure, was to use the Doctor "for the supply of testimony to Lowber against Union College." One thinks of this meeting, not in Pearson's truncated report of it, but as it brought into focus the whole history of the Doctor's career as a speculator as well as the particular moment in that history whose meaning John C. Spencer had chosen, in 1853, to refer to a higher law, but which Judge Paige was now to explain in terms of fraud and intent to deceive.

Knowing this history, Judge Paige, by October, 1860, chose to reverse the judgments he and his predecessors had made at various stages of the Doctor's financial career. To protect the Nott Trust Deed from the attack of the Doctor's creditors Judge Paige now elected to destroy Spencer's painstakingly created image of the Doctor, an image the Judge had earlier chosen to sustain, and so to destroy Spencer's defense of those Trustees who for more than thirty years had supported the Doctor's soaring optimism as a financier and educator. The Judge and his supporters on the Board, in 1860, made again the choice Spencer had had to make seven years earlier between the Doctor's long professed intentions as the President of Union College and his acts as its agent. By condemning the settlements and judgments of the past, however, Paige was now able to establish the legal grounds for his premise, stated before a Judge Willards, the court-appointed referee that October, that the Nott Trust Deed was, and had always been, in fact, no donation, but the Doctor's payment of his long outstanding debt to Union College, and that such being the fact, the Nott Trust Deed was beyond the reach of Robert Lowber, or any other creditor of a now bankrupt and confused Eliphalet Nott.

To what extent *could* Robert Lowber hope to implicate the old President in fraud? Pearson, on November 10, 1860, recorded a conversation he had held with the Doctor's ex-agent which had completely shocked him. Lowber had assured him that he had paid the Doctor over $13,000 in interest on those controversial "Cove" bonds and mortgages then held in escrow by Trustee James Brown. Pearson had replied that he had received no more than $7000 of this money from the President.

"We instructed Brown to take the interest," the college treasurer recorded he had then told Lowber, "and not doing so, he is liable to us for it." Lowber's reply was that Brown had never received the instructions.

"Yes he did," Pearson told Lowber, "I sealed them up and sent the sealed package to Brown by Dr. Nott."

"I tell you again," Lowber was reported to have said, "I *know* they were never delivered to Brown."

"Then," Pearson replied, "you make out Dr. Nott a rogue, breaking faith with college by abstracting an important paper, to the detriment of the college."

On November 13 the appalled college treasurer reported that Judge Paige thought "the seals were broken by Brown and the [Trustees'] letter of instructions handed to Dr. Nott to get [Trustee] Bradford R. Wood's name thereto, and [it] was never handed back to [Brown] but instead, the instructions of Dr. Nott." The Reverend Dr. Backus, also a Trustee, according to Pearson, refused to believe Judge Paige's story. If true, it put the Doctor in the hands of a Robert Lowber intent, so Pearson was sure, on "intimidating Dr. Nott and his friends on the Board so as to accomplish other schemes of plunder from college." The old President, once the master of the compromise, had, it seemed to Jonathan Pearson, overreached himself in his desperation to prevent the revelation of matters long concealed.

If Lowber possessed information which could frighten the Doctor, whose mind according to the college treasurer "was a mere caos [sic] without memory or method or any power of recollection . . . ," Judge Paige had now found those special sources of information which might well be used to spoil Lowber's plans for breaking the Nott Trust Deed. To the Judge's own personal knowledge of the negotiations which had left the Doctor in the possession of his "President's Fund" at the end of the Chancery Court lottery suits of the 1830s the Judge now added the huge store of notes and memoranda John C. Spencer had built up during the New York State Legislature's investigation of the Doctor's career. Pearson had persuaded the Doctor that September to place these records in the College Archives. Step by step the Judge had been able to review more than thirty years of a history which, re-aligned to meet new needs, was to be turned now into a blanket indictment of the Eliphalet Nott whom Spencer was reported to have exhausted himself in defending.

James Brown's "to whom am I to pay the $40,000?" claimed by both Lowber and Union College, and the key to the whole controversy, produced at last this twofold answer from Judge

Paige: first, that entire sum belonged to the Nott Trust Deed because James Brown had illegally cancelled college securities, not on the Trustees' directions, but on the directions of one not authorized to give them. The Judge did not name the Doctor.[11]

The Judge's second argument for the college's ownership of the $40,000 was the result of two positions the Judge took in relation to the President's acts as a promoter. The Judge now contended that neither Stuyvesant Cove nor Hunter Point had ever belonged to the Doctor. The Trustees' Minutes for 1845 proved to Paige's satisfaction that Alexander Holland *had* illegally transferred those properties to the President without the sanction of the Trustees' Finance Committee which, Paige then concluded, had never discovered that the college, in fact, was then, or had ever been in debt to the Doctor.[12] These conclusions which Spencer himself had come to believe but which he had not revealed to the legislative investigators of 1853, then led Judge Paige into a corollary review of the history of the Doctor's "President's Fund" which the Judge now decided, had never, in spite of past Trustees' commitments to the contrary, belonged to the old President, a position which echoed the Doctor's enemies. This same conclusion had been at the heart of the testimony of Yates and McIntyre, the Doctor's lottery managers, during the Chancery suits a quarter of a century earlier, and of Senator James Beekman's violent attacks on the Doctor before the New York State Legislature in 1852 and 1853.[13]

Judge Paige then informed the Court that Union College was, as of the date of his answer to the Brown-Lowber suits, now claiming the "President's Fund" as a debt the Doctor still owed Union College, plus the huge sums accumulated in what had later been called "Dr. Nott's Fund." Then the Judge assured the Court that, contrary to popular belief in the "vindication" of the Doctor's acts by John C. Spencer in 1853, "the Doctor's debts to Union College exceed the whole value of all the bonds and mortgages, and securities, and all the other property, real and personal, assigned and conveyed to this defendant by the said Trust Deed of Eliphalet Nott."[14] The financial structure which Spencer with Paige's help had erected, was now a ruin.

Professor Pearson had been right in the prophecy he had made to Eurania and the Doctor: the Lowber suit was compromised that November. Lowber, temporarily defeated by Judge Paige's stand, accepted $15,000 of the $40,000 he had expected to win, Judge Paige insisting that Trustee James Brown was still liable to the college for the whole sum, that the College's loss was due solely to the Doctor's "imbecile meddling." [15] Not until the Trustees that December agreed to drop all charges against James Brown, then "temporarily in England," would the firm of Brown Brothers permit the distribution of the money that hapless Trustee had been holding for so long.

I I

If Judge Paige thought he had had the last word on the matter, however, he figured without Robert Lowber's fixed conviction that the Nott Trust Deed was what Spencer, in 1853, had declared it to be, the Doctor's "munificent donation" to Union College. Having profitably swept the Doctor's financial cupboard bare (he boasted to Pearson that the only reason he had compromised the suit was because the Doctor had more than compensated him for his loss by turning over to him the latter's interest in the increasingly profitable Bald Mountain Lime Works) Lowber laid plans for a flanking attack on the Nott Trust. [16] If the college would not permit him to exploit, as manager, the Hunter Point property, now the Nott Trust's chief asset, he intended to use every legal device he could to break the trust itself in order to collect the approximately $200,000 he eventually declared the Doctor owed him. [17]

During June, 1862, a Moses Taylor opened a creditor's suit against Eliphalet Nott to collect on a debt of the Doctor's he said he had purchased from Lowber in 1855. [18] On July 10, 1862, the Court awarded Moses Taylor $37,109.62, a judgment against the Doctor which was immediately given to the sheriff of Schenectady County to collect. The sheriff soon reported that Eliphalet Nott was wholly without property to satisfy the judgment. [19] Taylor's next step was to begin a creditor's suit against the Trustees of Union College and Eliphalet Nott in which he charged, as had Lowber, that the Nott Trust Deed, as the Doctor's "free gift" to the college, was subject to the prior claims of the Doctor's creditors. With the Court's judgment that the Doctor was in fact in

Moses Taylor's debt now on record, Lowber and Taylor were confident the Nott Trust could be forced to satisfy that judgment, and if that could be done, then the way would be open for anyone who thought he had a case against the Doctor to bring suit against the college.[20]

Judge Paige's answer to Moses Taylor was that Taylor and Lowber were acting "collusively to and with each other [by] . . . devising a fictitious claim against Eliphalet Nott," the intent of which "was to defraud Union College."[21] At no point would Alonzo Paige concede that he or any other Trustee had ever known of any contracts or agreements made between the Doctor and his ex-agent which could in any way have conditioned the college's possession of the Nott Trust Deed, a conclusion Robert Lowber was to exhaust himself in trying to refute in a litigation which was to drag on until 1875, nine years after the Doctor's death and seven years following the death of Judge Paige.[22]

Death of referees, mistrials, and postponements persuaded Lowber by 1875 that there was no hope that Union College would honor the commitments John C. Spencer had once made on behalf of Eliphalet Nott before the New York State Legislature. Robert Lowber, insolvent, discouraged that the Supreme Court's referee in 1875 had finally ruled that the Nott Trust Deed had, indeed, been the payment of a debt the Doctor had owed Union College, was finally persuaded not to appeal the case again by Clarkson Nott Potter, the Doctor's grandson. To end the matter Lowber agreed in that year to accept $10,000 as a final settlement of all his claims against the Nott Trust, and so to bring to a close a financial history whose interpretation must lie, at last, not in Trustees' Minutes and Court records, but in those blurred and interlined passages written in the mind by men who were moved, as the Doctor had so often pointed out to his senior "young gentlemen," as much by the compulsion of their passions as by their reason.[23]

One finds the Doctor himself in a lonely and very human moment in his year of crisis in a letter he wrote to his grandson Clarkson Potter a few months before Judge Paige was to level the fortifications John C. Spencer had erected to protect the Doctor's reputation:

"Few and evil have my days been," the bankrupt old man wrote to a grandson who, he then said, had given him "the greatest affection" of all the children of his "dear, departed Maria." [24] By the end of that year it may have been clear to the Doctor that his lifelong theological distinction between the words "hazard" and "gamble" was, in fact, his own distinction, a revelation which in those times when his mind was "not a caos" [sic], left him with no more than the hope of the Puritan Notts from whom he had descended that his intentions, at least, might win him the forgiveness of the unpredictable God for whom in his optimism he had presumed to speak.

Perhaps Judge Paige's reversal of Spencer's conclusions, stated in the latter's "Argument in the Defense of Dr. Nott," had all been just "a lawyer's way of doing things," as the Doctor had once said to comfort Urania, but one suspects that if the old President's mind had not been so confused during the last years of the Nott Trust suits, Judge Paige might have observed the depth of the wound the Doctor had received, a mortal hurt even Robert Lowber was constrained to point out to the Trustees in 1871. Still protesting the Board's position that the Doctor's acts as a "financiering president" had constituted a legal fraud against Union College, he called the members' attention to the warm praises of the Trustees of 1853 for Spencer's vindication of the Doctor in the face of the "malice" of the Doctor's detractors. By the Board's denial, after 1860, of all that John C. Spencer had successfully established in the Doctor's defense, its members had "wounded and mortified him," Lowber wrote, "beyond any adequate expression of mine." [25]

CHAPTER 3

"I cannot die before my time"

RESOLVED: That the cashier [of the Mohawk Bank in Schenectady] be requested to have the new $25 plate engraved in steel, with the portrait of Dr. Nott on the $10, according to a model presented to this Board. The additional charge for Dr. Nott is $100.

The bank's resolution of September 12, 1855, was fulfilled the following January when its "new issue of fives and tens" was ready, "the latter containing a portrait of the Rev. Dr. Nott" [". . . and very good-looking, too," one commentator reported]. [1]

Portraits, even as College catalogues and Trustees' minutes, are the much edited likenesses of their originals. For the Doctor in 1856 his appearance "on the $10" spoke clearly of the successful man of action he had intended to be, even as the Union College catalogue issue in 1852 reflected the "University" he intended Union College should become. Within three years, however, the man represented on "the $10" and the "University" promised by the Union College catalogues had been irreparably changed in the heat generated by personal misjudgments, personal antipathies and old enmities, and national economic collapse. By the summer of 1859 the Doctor's career as the Maecenas and the Nestor of American educators was over, and a semi-invalid and intimidated old man, no longer in control of events, began to move slowly off stage in the keeping, chiefly, of Judge Paige, Jonathan Pearson, Urania Nott, Nurse Carr, and a Moses Viney who, of all those closest to him, expected the least.

Events and people now reached the Doctor largely as Urania permitted: "he says he is completely under 'Uranie's' thumb now, and has to do just as she says," Jonathan Pearson reported a year after the Doctor's first stroke. [2] For Urania there was a relief of preparing the new President's House for occupancy, trips to New York City for wallpaper and furnishings, as Pearson fretted over Eurania's peremptory directions in connection with it, and of the fact that the donors' gift for its construction was far from enough to complete the building.[3] On July 3, 1861, just short of three months following the opening of the Civil War, the Notts moved into the big, square, cool residence on the south edge of the campus, "much too near the highway," according to the college treasurer.[4]

Beneath its windows the senior classes gathered during those last years to serenade "old Prex," to bring him a birthday or Commencement gift of flowers, and, when possible, to get his autograph on their copies of the motto he had adopted years earlier, and which Pearson regularly ran off for him on the College "Zincophile Press":

Perseverantia vincit omnia nec non et in gloriam ducit—Vita brevis, cursis gloriae Sempiternus

The Civil War which had finally come drained the classrooms, cutting the enrollment at Union from 437 in 1860 to 219 in 1865. It loomed for the old President in his times of clarity as the just retribution both the North and the South must endure for having instituted and perpetuated slavery. His last public prayer, delivered quaveringly in the Schenectady Presbyterian Church on Thanksgiving Day, 1860, was a plea for help for a nation seemingly ready to destroy itself.[5]

The black man had long had an advocate in the Doctor who, however, had been no leader in the fight against slavery in the manner of a Garrison or Gerrit Smith. Such Abolitionists were extremists, and the Doctor was always the man of compromises. He had hoped at one time the North and South would join in an African repatriation movement; by 1850 he saw the only hope in avoiding civil war in a divided America, the South going its own way as an independent nation. By 1860, however, he had become convinced, along with Seward whom he had earlier urged to run for the Senate, that the Union must be preserved, "that that odious bondage may have to be swept away in blood," as he told one correspondent.[6] His plan for preserving the Union, "developed in connection with several eminent statesmen . . . for abolishing slavery without civil convulsion or considerable disturbance to Southern interests," failed to get attention, it was reported, because of the opposition of the extreme Abolitionists.[7]

Compromise, staple of the Doctor's nature, became almost a parody of itself when, a few months before his first paralytic stroke, he had had to solve the problem posed by David Rossel, a boy many believed to be a Negro and who had applied for entrance to the junior class from "Central College," Ohio. Southern and Northern students organized for and against his admission. Vice President Hickok refused to act and turned the explosive problem over to the Trustees who then turned it back to the Doctor. The excited student committees met with the old President, who told them that while he saw no reason for barring a student because of his color, he would welcome a vote by the junior class, and that, for the sake of peace, Rossel would be barred "if a respectable minority oppose him."[8]

Behind scenes, however, the Doctor manipulated, and in a way the college treasurer characterized as "puerile"; "with great secrecy," Pearson wrote, "Nott had Professor Chandler [head of the Analytical Chemistry Department] examine Rossel's hair under the microscope to see if he is really an Indian and not a Negro."[9] A few days later David Rossel appeared in class according to one of the Northern juniors, "and continued thereafter without objection; . . . it was said he furnished evidence to our opponents that he was of French and Indian extraction." [10]

The blood bath which was to shrink registration and to take the life of Professor Elias Peissner, the college's young and brilliant German scholar, at Chancellorsville, seemed to crowd everything else from the now invalid old man's mind: "What is the state of the country?" was the question he asked most visitors. To Jonathan Pearson who called on the Notts almost every day, the question was asked again and again, when it could be asked: " Pearson,' says he, 'I am troubled about the country. But do your duty and take care of things. " [11]

Two of the Doctor's grandsons, Charles Cooper Nott, son of Joel, and General Robert B. Potter, son of Maria, fought throughout the war. Another grandson, Eliphalet Nott, Jr., son of Howard, and a doctor, escaped military service by joining a New Jersey insurance club which paid out $200 to provide a substitute for each of its members who was drafted.[12] "What is astonishing to all his friends," the college treasurer wrote following one of his visits to the Doctor in May, 1863, "his sons Benjamin and Joel never come nigh him. What a set of heathen must they be who cannot forego their imaginary injuries and visit a poor, invalid father." [13] Three months earlier Dr. Swits's homeopathic treatments had failed to prevent a second stroke, and again it was agreed by those who shared rumors in the college treasurer's office that the Doctor was "nearing the end."

Before two more destroying strokes in 1864 robbed him of his memory, the Doctor seemed to relive his first years in New York; he would tell Pearson of his "Court Church" in Albany, and of the Dutch Albanians' suspicions of Yankee interlopers like himself. He spoke of the wolves that attacked travelers on the Cherry Valley turnpike he had been among the first to use in 1795, and he spoke often of his boyhood in Connecticut, and told Pearson he had once thought of being a physician until the sights and sounds of sickrooms and the failure of his fellow townsman, Dr. Perkins, to effect cures with his "Metallic Tractors" disenchanted him. Once he recalled John Howard Payne, that phenomenal boy actor and student at Union during the first years of his presidency, whose song "Home, Sweet Home" had had its beginnings in the boy's nostalgic poem "Home, Dear Home," written while he was a resident of West College, or then "Stone College," long before the Erie Canal became its noisy eastern boundary. [14]

Following the second stroke of January, 1863, there was little left but the diminished form of the Doctor and within it only enough vitality to let him lay his hands on the hands of those who were allowed to see him briefly, and to permit him to ask again, "What is the state of the country?" William Henry Seward wrote from Washington to inquire about him. Urania answered for her husband, as she did all the letters that arrived from those who now wrote to an Eliphalet Nott neither Judge Paige nor Jonathan Pearson nor an embittered Vice President Hickok, nor the cliques of professors and tutors who drifted in and out of the treasurer's office, could any longer see above the debris of the old President's collapsed fortunes and hopes for a Union College "on the University plan."

Jonathan Pearson during these last years spoke out of sympathy for what age and sickness had done to the man in whose shadow he had made his professional life, but he was relentless in putting the blame on the dying President for the college's decline, for its buildings in disrepair or hopelessly inadequate for the college's needs, and for what he considered its low state of scholarship.[15] Francis Wayland, on the other hand, writing from Rhode Island in 1861, spoke of the Doctor as "his guide . . . and counselor."[16] Seward kept the portrait of his old teacher and adviser above the door of his Washington office, and boasted that "I, too, am a pupil of Nott." To the public, beyond the college and beyond Schenectady, Eliphalet Nott had become firmly one with those great American "Men of Progress" whom the artist Schussele had memorialized in December, 1862, in that huge canvas in which he had placed the Doctor in the company of such men of action as Robert Fulton, Eli Whitney, and S.F.B. Morse.

The old man's seeming awareness of the death watch of his friends and enemies was clear enough in his "I cannot die before my time." Both Francis Wayland and Bishop Alonzo Potter died in 1865, by which time Urania was able to make the Doctor only briefly aware of their going. On April 19 of that year the frail old man could hear the cannonading which echoed across the valley every half-hour as the faculty and students joined the mourners' parade up State Street as it marked the assassination of Abraham Lincoln, and the near-assassinations of William Henry Seward and his son Frederick.

Commencement that July, held in Dr. Backus's "illy ventilated" church, echoed "but little of the sublime, soul stirring eloquence" which one newspaper man seemed to expect in that year as the armies of the North and the South drifted home, the one to its parades, the other to the shambles left by the war. The best of the student orations, the reporter declared, was S. B. Rossiter's "A Profound Philosophy, the Want of the Age." The climax of the exercises that day, "clear, beautiful, exceedingly warm . . . ," was the awarding of a Doctor of Laws degree to Lieutenant General U. S. Grant, "the entire audience rose from their seats, and gave three deafening cheers."[17]

The Trustees met in "Geology Hall" that afternoon, in the "neat and commodious chapel" on the first floor of one of the two new buildings the Doctor had been able to add to the Ramée campus. There was no clock tower on "Geology Hall" as the old President had wanted, but the building housed the "Wheatley

Collection" of minerals and shells, reputedly "the finest cabinet in the world" and given to the college by Edward C. Delavan, the Doctor's warm supporter on the Board, that Atlas of the Temperance Movement who had long carried the weight of financing the New York State Temperance Society. [18]

Vice President Hickok attended the meeting "by courtesy," nominally in charge of the college, always aware of the pressure of opposition against him, of the Doctor's old and now defeated hope that Bishop Potter would follow him as President, aware, in July, 1865, of the rising hopes of a half dozen new candidates for the office. The faculty and the Vice President each submitted briefs that day defining their different conclusions as to what should be the powers of the President. Whoever was to succeed to that office, everyone realized, would walk in the shadow of a man he would not be allowed to emulate.

Clarkson Nott Potter moved that his grandfather's system of "Parental Government" be made the official rule for college discipline in the future, that, following his grandfather, future Presidents and faculty members share all administrative problems, each of them to exercise one vote, excepting tutors, and the President to cast the deciding vote when there was a tie.

The ill feeling among the faculty and the growing discord among the Trustees could be measured in the position papers submitted by the faculty and the Vice President, and especially by Judge Paige's reaction to those proposals of Clarkson Potter designed to set up a more democratic administration. The Judge agreed to the proposals themselves, but insisted that credit for them be given to the Reverend Dr. Backus. The matter of credit for the measures was put to a vote, which the Judge lost; the new procedures were then passed as "the resolutions of Mr. Potter."

Clark B. Cochrane, a Trustee ally of Judge Paige, then had the temerity to propose that the Board proceed at once to elect a new President, forgetting the Board's resolution of 1861 that the use of the Doctor's name "amply compensates the College" for retaining him in office. The vote on Cochrane's motion indicated some of the members of the two camps into which the Trustees had divided: the "noes" were registered by the Doctor's grandson, by Judge W. W. Campbell, James Brown, the Reverend Ebenezer Halley, Edward C. Delavan, and R. M. Blatchford; the "ayes" by

Judge Paige, the Reverend J. J. VanVechten, then chairman of the Board, Clark Cochrane, and that arch conservative Presbyterian minister, the Reverend Dr. Backus.

Before the Board adjourned it appointed a special committee to prepare a memorial statement in honor of the late Bishop Potter, and agreed to offer the Potter family a plot in the college section of the new Vale Cemetery recently developed just south of the campus.

On the "Hill," in his new house, the Doctor had been placed in an easy chair that Commencement where the nameless reporter who had attended the morning's exercises saw him "calmly awaiting his summons to another world, and giving what advice he was able to his old students and friends . . . he grasped our hand, and in feeble accents said, 'God bless you; be faithful unto death; live for God and your country, and all will be well.' We were so fortunate as to get his autograph. For a long time past he has not been able to sign his name and Mrs. Nott told us this would in all probability be his last autograph. It was through her efforts and assistance that an effort was made to obtain it . . ."

For the Doctor, from that Commencement until his death six months later, what the Board did, what Vice President Hickok said, what Jonathan Pearson wrote, what Robert Lowber demanded and Judge Paige denied, what, finally, confronted the two Unions whose existence to 1865 his own life had paralleled and for each of which the future that year balanced on the apex of unresolved events, all faded into the shadow of dying. Urania had been requested by Francis Wayland in 1862, two years before his own death, to record what the man he had called the Nestor of American educators might reveal of divine matters, presumably increasingly clear to him as his bonds to the living dissolved.[19] Although Bishop Potter and Wayland himself had settled such problems before the Doctor's time ran out, Urania seems to have fulfilled her task as she "rocked him to sleep in a specially prepared cradle, singing such nursery songs to him as 'Hush, my dear, be still and slumber.' "[20] Her report of what she heard comes to us by way of the Doctor's great grandaughter, Mariette Thompson, who recorded for the Potter family the nostalgic tales told to her by her own mother, Maria, Bishop Potter's daughter, tales "of Grandfather Nott . . . who wore a big hat with a cockade, like Napoleon, drove in a three-wheeled carriage invented by himself, and when at table . . . would not allow the conversation to fall into petty, local gossip." [21]

"When he was practically dying," Maria Potter told her daughter, "his wife wanted to collect some beautiful words or sentences to pass on to the family and to his admirers. Kneeling beside him one day she said, 'All is light before you, dear, isn't it?' Grandfather answered, 'No, dark.' "

"Mama liked the uncompromising, shattering truth of this answer." [22]

On Monday, January 29, 1866, at 3 A.M., time for the Doctor ran out.

CHAPTER 4

"All eventually will come right"

AN EPILOGUE
I: Aftermath

THE consequences of a man's dying usually concern so few; for those who immediately survived Eliphalet Nott, however, there was the work of "sorting out from the rubbish of the past," as he had characterized the task of the biographer, what seemed to them significant.

The funeral on the bitterly cold, snow-blurred Friday of February 2, 1866, reassembled all that could be gathered together of the public image of the Doctor which John C. Spencer had presented to the New York State Legislature in 1853:

> Attired in a full length and beautiful white merino robe with flowing tassels, covering a white linen robe with standing collar, the corpse was handsomely laid out in the eastern reception room of his late residence.
>
> Today his shriveled frame, his extremely emaciated countenance and his generally worn appearance bespoke little of what he was in his prime.
>
> Shortly after nine o'clock this morning, the remains were placed by the attending undertakers in a magnificent rosewood coffin, lined with white silk and elaborately studded with silver, on the lid of which was engraved:
>
> Eliphalet Nott, D.D., LL.D.
> Born June 25,1773
> Died January 29, 1866 [1]

The chief pallbearers were his old friends among the Trustees: ex-Chancellor Reuben Walworth, Edward C. Delavan, R. M. Blatchford, the ex-Minister to Rome, W. W. Campbell, ex-Judge of the New York State Supreme Court, and Thomas Hillhouse, the

State Comptroller. Professors Jackson, Lewis, Foster, and Acting President Laurens Hickok, the last four once the Doctor's "young gentlemen," represented his faculty, united for this moment.

Dr. J. Trumbull Backus delivered the funeral tribute before some 2000 mourners in the First Presbyterian Church, a eulogy "eloquent and deserved" it was reported by the New York *Herald*, "consisting of a sketch of his great powers as a man, a minister, an educator, and as the President of a great and opulent institution of learning . . . the greatest and wealthiest of any in the State of New York."[2] Nothing, however, the Reverend Dr. Backus said that day pleased the editor of the Troy *Daily Whig*, who lost no time in castigating his eulogy as "too trivial and commonplace an effort for the great occasion . . . ," and damned the Schenectady *Union*, "an insignificant rush-light of a newspaper . . ." for defending so poor an effort: "the coldest tribute to the memory of a great man that ever emanated from the pulpit."[3] The Troy editor, as were so many others, was looking ahead to the coming contest over the election of the Doctor's successor: "as for the bucolic Schenectady print," he wrote, "and its asinine editor, we can only say that both are serving a good purpose in the championing of Dr. Backus."[4]

The New York City, Albany, and Schenectady newspapers carried memorial and biographical sketches of Eliphalet Nott which were piously contemporary in their omission of those things that did not square with the public image of the towering parental President of Union College. In its entirety, they agreed, the college was a projection of his will and his personality, its alumni the practical men of action they were because of him, their college rich beyond all others because of his genius in which had been synthesized the man of God and the scientist-inventor.

The New York *Herald*, however, on February 2, 1866, concluded its article, "The Funeral of Dr. Nott," with a jarring note on the subject Dr. Hickok had thought was closed when he accepted the Vice Presidency in 1852:

> The canvass for the succession to the Presidency has already begun, and promises to be an acrimonious contest. Among the candidates are Rev. Dr. Hickok, Acting-President, Reverend Dr. Henry C. Potter, of Troy (son of the late Bishop Potter of Pennsylvania); Rev. Dr. Bacchus

[sic] ; Rev. John Nott, D.D.; Rev. Duncan Kennedy of Troy; Dr. Sprague of Albany; Isaac W. Jackson, LL.D.; Hon. Charles R. Ingalls; and the Hon. David L. Seymour, of Troy.[5]

The preceding January at a meeting of the Finance Committee held in Governor Reuben Fenton's office in Albany its members, including Judge Paige and Dr. Backus, agreed only that the Vice President should "administer the government of Union College until the next meeting of the Board." Nothing was said about the succession, a subject which by then had divided faculty and Trustees, and had already alienated many alumni.[6] Jonathan Pearson had characterized the expectant Laurens Hickok the preceding year as "a dreadful talker! Words!, Words!, Words! A good, honest man with many qualifications for his office . . . he has a strange want of tact . . . no power to conciliate and make friends, but without thought or knowing he steps on people's toes and then wonders why they cry out."[7] The Trustee opposition against Dr. Hickok was summed up by the college treasurer when he wrote that "Mr. Delevan says Mr. James Brown of N. Y. (who might give $25,000) says 'Not one cent while that man is at the head of it.' Mr. D. says no important contributions can be obtained from Dr. Nott's friends whilst we have our present head."[8]

On March first, at the first full meeting of the Board following the Doctor's death, one attended by the Governor and four other ex-offico Trustees, the matter of the succession was settled, but not without those who had been closest to the Doctor registering their disapproval. Ex-Chancellor Reuben Walworth's proposal that the election be by ballot was defeated by the pro-Hickok forces, and with that defeat the election of the Vice-President was assured, for only his hard-core opponents were ready for the bitter exchanges and the publicity which would have been generated in the campaigning for any of the other candidates. Five of the Trustees, however, were willing to make their opposition plain: F. C. Barlow, the then Secretary of State, E. C. Delavan, James Brown, R. M. Blatchford, and the Doctor's grandson, Clarkson Nott Potter.

For Laurens Perseus Hickok, however, his victory was to be a Pyrrhic one, as his two years of faculty-Trustee disagreements preceding his resignation were to prove. For Union College, "that great and opulent institution of learning," the years of "adventuring" it had known under the Doctor were over. With shocking rapidity Union lost its national stature, lost its rank as the peer of Harvard and Yale, and the leadership it had held in forwarding the great educational changes of the Nott decades. From a total registration of 437 in 1860 Union's student body shrank to 89 in 1872, and the college continued until the end of the century in often desperate straits to find the means to continue to function, leaderless in the sense that Eliphalet Nott was a leader, "enfeebled," as Judge Comstock was to inform the Board, by the decisions of its Trustees who chose to husband the Nott Trust Fund rather than to convert its assets when it was possible to do so into a working capital devoted to building the democratic "university for the times" to which Eliphalet Nott had committed them.

II

Ironically, all did eventually "come right," as Charles Sanders had promised it would to Senator James W. Beekman, the Doctor's chief enemy during the New York State Legislature's investigation of Union College, but not until the college itself had been almost destroyed by its Trustees' handling of the assets of the Nott Trust.[9] The story of the events which led to the final "conversion" of the Doctor's lottery fortune begins with a question Judge Alonzo Paige never allowed himself to consider: if Robert Lowber's claims against the Doctor had been met, not by Judge Paige's destruction of John C. Spencer's defense of the Doctor as the college's agent, but by compromises which would have left Spencer's elaborately contrived image of the Doctor unimpaired, would such compromising have lost the Nott Trust Fund to Union College? One has only to read the record of the Nott Trust as it was administered in the years immediately following the Doctor's death in 1866 to discover the surprising answer.

By 1868 the college's share of the Hunter Point lands, then embodied in the Hunter Point Trust, had increased in value, it was reported, to a point sufficient, if it had been sold and reinvested for income, to fulfill the provisions of the Nott Trust Deed. [10] Instead, the Trustees elected to join other certificate holders of the recently established Hunter Point Trust in making long term improvements in the property, a course of action they financed out of other Union College capital funds. This financing, however, resulted in starving the day-to-day operations of the college to such an extent that, by 1874, the Trustees were forced to seek a legal method of restoring the working capital by withdrawing $250,000 from the Nott Trust assets, by then estimated to be worth more than $900,000. [11]

In May that year Judge George F. Comstock, a Union alumnus, was asked by the Trustees to formulate a legal rule for transferring the needed funds from the Nott Trust to the College account, a task which the Judge fulfilled in a manner which outraged some members of the Board. Although Judge Comstock agreed that the Trustees could legally reimburse themselves for their expenditures at Hunter Point, by then amounting to over $100,000, he added the gratuitous information that the Long Island properties had by then so far grown in value that "they greatly exceed the anticipation of the author of the [Nott] Trust . . . [that these lands] were then capable of yielding income far in excess of the specific annual demands made by the Trust conveyance." [12] The Judge further annoyed certain vulnerable members of the Board by pointing out that the assets of the Nott Trust could have been converted long since into income-producing securities which would have financed all of the Doctor's "Nott Professorships and scholarships" and those other programs he had embodied in the Nott Trust Deed.

If, however, the Trustees chose "to enfeeble the College," as Judge Comstock phrased it in his unwelcome opinion, in order to gamble that Hunter Point would increase in value, that was their choice, although the Judge declared it was also his opinion that the Board was legally responsible for its failure to administer the Nott Trust Deed so that it could fulfill the purposes for which Eliphalet Nott created it. [13]

Behind the acrimonious debates which followed the Judge's opinion and which did much to weaken every aspect of Union College life until the last of the Hunter Point lands were sold in 1897, were such charges as those of Howard Potter, the Doctor's grandson, against the Reverend J. T. Backus and Judge Platt Potter, two Trustees who were guilty, he insisted, "of seizing the choicest Long Island City lots for their individual accounts," and then of having permitted Union College to pay their proportion of the taxes and maintenance charges. [14]

The year-to-year sale of Hunter Point lands, soon the heart of Long Island City, as the area was known from the mid-1850s, helped only to meet the most pressing operating expenses of the college for almost thirty years of shrinking enrollment and vacillating administrations and educational policies. While Harvard and Yale and the new state universities were becoming in fact the universities Eliphalet Nott had prophetically envisaged, Union College, during the tenure of the four frustrated Presidents who followed the Doctor, shrank in national influence and in the esteem of its alumni. [15] A few years before 1900 the Trustees considered abandoning the Ramée campus in Schenectady for a site offered to them by the City of Albany, a plan of desperation defeated only by the sale of the remaining Long Island City lots for $300,000, the last and the greatest money prize of the Doctor's many hazards. [16]

EPILOGUE II: The Apotheosis

Beginning with the eulogy to the Doctor prepared for the Board for its Commencement Meeting in 1866, John C. Spencer's work of image making began again. The Reverend Dr. Backus prepared the Board's tribute, noting inaccurately that the Doctor, as a student, had taken his B.A. and M.A. under Jonathan Maxcy, at Brown. Then, as though Judge Paige had never spoken, he continued:

> That [Eliphalet Nott] might replenish [the College's] exhausted resources he submitted to pursuits and liabilities which were repugnant to his tastes as they were detrimental to his professional freedom and comfort. And though success has ultimately crowned his exertions, and the College is, through him, munificently endowed, our greatest obligation to him in this respect is for the unexampled courage, patience, and meekness with which he endured the misapprehension and sacrifice thus incurred. . . .
>
> The remarkable development of his inventive faculty with the scientific researches and experiments which are now a part of his

reputation were necessitated by the exigencies of the Institution, and however beneficent the result of these distinguished labors, however worthy of admiration he was for these evidences of varied capacity, to his honor be it recorded that all was intended to subserve his loftier aim, to do his utmost for the melioration of mankind.

What the Reverend J. T. Backus wrote as the Board's memorial to its late President has been repeated on public occasions ever since, modified, illustrated out of memory and by invention, repeated by those sincerely and warmly in love with the Eliphalet Nott they re-created, often out of their need for him, chiefly to sound their calls to return to the lost world of colleges "parentally" disciplined, where all education was conditioned, presumably, by moral and ethical ends.

In 1876 the *Memoirs of Eliphalet Nott*, by Cornelius VanSantvoord and Tayler Lewis, was published, written chiefly "for the sons of the College who regarded their old instructor with veneration, gratitude, and love." The *Memoirs* more than fulfilled its purpose; it is a gentle biographical piety which has long been the source of much that has been written about Eliphalet Nott; it is a storehouse of letters and reminiscenses, especially for what Professor Lewis recalled of the Doctor's ministerial and temperance activities. The book's omissions and errors, however, served only to create a picture of a venerable college president-who-never-was, to forward the apotheosis of Eliphalet Nott and so to remove him from the exciting, opportunistic, hazarding, and gambling world of those "practical men" he loved above all others.

The "Octogon," later "Alumni Hall," whose foundations the Doctor had seen as the greatest since the Colosseum was built, became, finally, the Nott-Potter Memorial, for the completion of which Howard and Clarkson Nott Potter, his grandsons, gave $50,000, and to which the Trustees, at their meeting on June 23, 1879, agreed to associate the name of Bishop Alonzo Potter. Five years earlier it had been decided to surmount the then still missing iron dome "by a bronze statue of Dr. Nott, which has been given by some friends of Dr. Nott at an expense of $30,000 . . ." As the Nott-Potter Memorial, the building was finally completed as a library and art gallery, characterized by Jonathan Pearson as "this huge piece of folly and extravagance . . . a mere show building ostensibly for books for which it is entirely unfitted . . . but really for pictures, etc., a mere museum." The bronze statue of the Doctor, if paid for, has yet to be put in place.

In 1895 Union College celebrated its Centennial, an occasion of brave self-congratulation, when its graduating class of forty-nine represented renewed vitality since 1872, when eighteen were graduated. The Doctor was then the subject of the major speech on Alumni Day. Judge G. F. Danforth, of the class of 1840, spoke of him as

> not merely an Instructor, Confined to Books; he was not an Author; he did not compose Treatises; he was an Educator, Standing for Ideals, in Politics, in Religion, in all Things which Concerned Men. Though by Profession a Clergyman Devoted to his Calling, he was an Exception to the Criticism that Clergyman Understand the least and take the Worst Measure of Human Affairs of all Mankind that can Write and Read. In his Lecture-room the two Foundations were as Parts to the Whole. He therefore Inculcated High Aims, and when he Died left a Marked Impress upon the Times.

The oracular capitalizations of Judge Danforth's remarks were devised to make them a fitting compliment to the portrait of the Doctor by Ezra Ames with which Andrew VanVankren Raymond, the new President of the College in 1895, chose, in 1907, to introduce his three-volume *History of Union University*.

In January, 1904, President Raymond had suggested to the Trustees the appropriateness of celebrating the hundredth anniversary of Dr. Nott's presidency, and on September 29 that year the College gathered in the Nott-Potter Memorial, the huge, full-length Inman portrait of the Doctor behind the speakers' seats, the portrait of Bishop Potter facing that of his father-in-law from the south entrance, and portraits of Jonathan Edwards the Younger, the second President of Union, and of Francis Wayland, the Doctor's chief agent in the transmission of his liberating ideas as to curriculum and discipline, facing each other from the east and west sides of the Italianate-Gothic building which would have made Joseph Jaques Ramée wonder at the taste of the generation which had ordered it.

President Raymond, who had graduated nine years after the Doctor's death, in his address, emphasized the fact that the latter's fame lived in the memory of those who knew him as a personality of enormous power and effectiveness in his own time, but that his was a greatness which had left none of the "accessories . . . that cause some names to be written large in history. . . ." There were formal addresses by Frederick W. Seward, by the Doctor's grandson, the Right Rev. Henry Codman Potter, and Judson S. Landon, of the New York State Supreme Court.

The Doctor's apotheosis, accelerated by the *Memoirs* of 1876, was completed at the celebration of this Centennial of his presidency in 1904. Frederick Seward, the son of Lincoln's Secretary of State, a member of the class of 1849, whose memory of the Doctor went back to his childhood days when the then vigorous President had been one of his father's chief advisers, told his audience that the Doctor was "a man welcome everywhere, and that men turned to him as a matter of course for consultation about matters of church or state."

To Frederick Seward, in 1904, the Doctor's "old age was the epitome of all his past experience. . . . Dr. Nott, in his green old age was at his wisest and best," a conclusion few of the Doctor's faculty or Trustees would have privately accepted. When Seward recalled the Doctor he had himself known he remembered an overwhelming personality, "benign . . . the genial host . . . always cheerful and interesting," a man who saw lessons in everything. Seward, as did most of the Doctor's pupils, remembered chiefly the President's exciting "analysis of human emotions and passions," and his practicality. Beyond his own memory of the Doctor, however, was the Doctor he, too, viewed through the pages of the *Memoirs*, the man who, he told his audience, "will be enshrined in the memory of all who knew him," a conclusion which would have brought a variety of disagreement from Jonathan Pearson, and Judge Paige, the members of the House of Yates and McIntyre, from Captain Neziah Bliss, Jonathan Crane, from Senator James W. Beckman, and even from the Doctor's sons, Joel and Benjamin.

The Reverend Henry Codman Potter, soon to be Bishop of the New York Episcopal Diocese, the Doctor's grandson, and a member of the Class of 1841, was amusingly cavalier about the Doctor's nominal Presbyterian allegiance; he spoke of his emotional evocations in the pulpit, characterizing his grandfather's preaching as the sort of highly colored eloquence suited to the taste of a less sophisticated age. The grandson's easy, vernacular stories, his cool Christianity, would have shocked the Doctor, however, whose view from the pulpit, as Tayler Lewis had written, "was one of deep solemnity."

"We turn from our more bustling and eager time," the Bishop-to-be continued, "its stage crowded with so many and such unresting figures, to that calm and stately presence of an hundred years ago, and we own the image of a King of Men. Great Teacher, Great Ruler, and most of all in his life and work, in the pulpit, on the platform, and in the street, Great Preacher of Eternal Love and Righteousness. All Hail!"

The "All Hail!" needed only the Doctor's $30,000 bronze statue standing on the iron dome above his grandson's head to give the scene its touch of Rome.

Judge Landon's speech, "Dr. Nott, the Educator," fixed for his audience the picture of the Doctor as the noble teacher, aware from the first year of his presidency that in America alone the experiment in democracy could and would be tried, that his task was so to change education that the experiment must succeed. To do this, according to Judge Landon, of the class of 1855, the Doctor "filled his mind with wisdom rather than learning, and wrought out in his own brain more than the textbook could teach."

"The eye of his soul," Judge Landon declared in a rhetoric more reminiscent of the Doctor's age, "clarified the eye of his body, and he beheld the celestial light which irradiates the works of nature . . . ," a vision the Judge feared his own generation might well be guilty of denying, if not of destroying.

Judge Landon and his fellow speakers addressed their audience in the language of eulogy, which is not to say they spoke dishonestly, but only that they spoke the litany of occasion, and in doing it they helped to invoke the apotheosized figure of a man too remote, too large, too awesome ever to have been *en rapport* with ten generations of boys who had honored him as "old Prex, cunning old Prex," the man who could outsmart politicians, steamboat operators, lottery dealers, real estate promoters, and, joy to behold, their own assaults on the citadels he commanded, in and out of the classroom.

As the man and his world receded and the father-image took "the Doctor's" place the State of Connecticut helped to preserve the hard facts of his childhood by accepting the site of the Nott homestead in New Ashford, purchased in 1933 by the Union College Alumni Association, and by naming a section of the east-west road that passes it "The Eliphalet Nott Highway." Four years earlier Frank Parker Day, in his inaugural address as the eleventh President of Union College, invoked the apotheosized Doctor as "the genius of the place," and prayed that the Doctor's "mantle" would fall on him. What President Day yearned for was "a spiritual integrating force" which would make all teachers and all students the humanists the Doctor had wished them to be. President Day's hope, to be fulfilled, however, would have required a college-wide acceptance of Eliphalet Nott's faith that, politically, the voice of the people *is* the voice of God, and that, scientifically, the language of mathematicians and physicists is the language of Natural Law, immutable and divine. The financial collapse in 1929 made President Day's invocation to the Eliphalet Nott of his imagination at least a poignant one.

In 1944 Dixon Ryan Fox, President Day's successor at Union, in an address before the Newcomen Society which he called "Dr. Nott and the American Spirit," reviewed the Doctor's career in the more clarifying words of the historian. His sources, however, were still the bowdlerized records arranged by VanSantvoord and Lewis and the sentimentalities recalled by the Doctor's students, and by those who had for so long made him an image for public viewing.

President Fox, nevertheless, understanding more of the history of nineteenth-century America than had his predecessors, saw something of the paradox the Doctor's educational philosophy had posed for succeeding generations. As education in America, especially in the sciences whose teaching Eliphalet Nott had done so much to liberate, led to an increasing control over nature, increasing production of goods, and an increasing material prosperity, it had also led Americans into a regard for their material successes as ends and not means; this, to the Doctor, would have seemed idolatrous.

President Fox described modern education as essentially empirical. He, as had Frank Parker Day, saw little moral content in contemporary education, and saw the new technologies as "dangerous" when they were undisciplined by moral laws. He wrote and spoke of Union College as "the balanced college," however, one equally devoted to the study of the sciences and the humanities, as though Union had actually preserved Eliphalet Nott's rationale for the study of both the sciences and the liberal arts as humanistic studies. As a historian Dixon Ryan Fox sensed, in 1944, the paradox of his position as the President of a Union College which, without the Doctor's energizing, transcendental faith, or one equally meaningful to later generations of students and faculty, could resolve itself only into imbalance and new contradictions.

College presidents in the twentieth century may envy Eliphalet Nott what seem to have been his certainties. Those of them who recall him, however, still invoke the image of a man who never was the Doctor. "Old Prex, cunning old Prex," who taught more than four thousand Union College alumni, and through them countless thousands of others, will elude all of us until we are willing to comprehend the whole man and the changing nature of the College he created and re-created, with all those "evils maintained" by his means. Those who invoke the Eliphalet Nott of the mythmakers do themselves and him no honor when they ask to wear his mantle, for on them it must be as the king's new clothes, invisible.

Notes

BOOK ONE

1. New Ashford to "Pisgah's Top"

1. Charles Van Santvoord, *Memoirs of Eliphalet Nott, D.D., LL.D., for sixty-two years President of Union College* With contributions and revisions by Professor Tayler Lewis of Union College (New York, 1876), p. 126. Hereafter, Van Santvoord, *Memoirs*.

2. Van Wyck Brooks, *The Flowering of New England, 1815–1865* (Cleveland, 1946), p. 34.

3. Ezekiel Webster to Daniel Webster. Boston (September 15, 1805), Daniel Webster Papers, Dartmouth College, Hanover, N. H.

4. Brooks, *Flowering of New England.*, p. 12.

5. W. W. Campbell, *Annals of Tryon County, or, the Border Warfare of New York during the Revolution* (New York, 1831).

6. Eliphalet Nott, *A Discourse on the Death of Alexander Hamilton.* Delivered in the North Dutch Church in Albany, July 29, 1804, 4th ed. (Boston, 1805). Library of Congress, Moore Pamphlets, LXIV No. 6.

7. Sidney Sherwood, *The University of the State of New York: History of Higher Education in the State of New York*, U. S. Bureau of Education, Circular of Information No. 3, 1900 (Washington, D. C., 1900), p. 205.

8. Van Santvoord, *Memoirs*, p. 124.

9. Ralph Trumbull, "Ancestry of Dr. Nott," in MS, Alumni Office, Union College. Trumbull questions the Nathan Hale and Tapping Reeve connections.

10. Nott Family Bible. A single page from this Bible, owned by the Connecticut State Library at Hartford contains the vital statistics of the family of Stephen Nott, father of Eliphalet Nott.

11. Samuel Nott, *Autobiography*, in MS. Deposited in the Congregational Church Library, Hartford, Connecticut. Presented to "The Memorial Hall Estate by his grandchildren, Harriet Newell, Sarah Maria, and Samuel Nott, July 11, 1888." p. 107.

12. Van Santvoord, *Memoirs*, p. 13.

13. *Ibid.*, p. 13.

14. Samuel Nott, *Autobiography*, pp. 7-25.

15. *Ibid.*, p. 9.

16. *Ibid.*, p. 9.

17. *Ibid.*, p. 17.

18. *Ibid.*, p. 7.

19. *Ibid.*, p. 18.

20. *Ibid.*, p. 18.
21. *Ibid.*, p. 18.
22. *Ibid.*, p. 18.
23. *Ibid.*, p. 25.
24. Samuel Nott, Death Record, Nott Family Bible.
25. Samuel Nott, *Autobiography*, p. 25.
26. Samuel Nott, *Ibid.*, p. 25.
27. Samuel Nott, *Autobiography*, p. 48. The record of the Nott family residences during this period is confusing. Although the *Autobiography* indicates 1772 as the date for the removal to Ashford, Ellen J. Larned in her *History of Windham County, Connecticut*, II (Worcester, 1880), 23-24 states that Stephen Nott signed the covenant which brought the Rev. Ebenezer Martin from Canada Parish to the new Westford Meeting in Ashford Township. This covenant was signed in 1768.
28. Nott Family Bible, "Births."
29. Van Santvoord, *Memoirs*, p. 19.
30. *Ibid.*, p. 19.
31. Van Santvoord, *Memoirs*, p. 377.
32. *Ibid.*, p. 18.
33. Frank Hunter Potter, *The Alonzo Potter Family* (Privately printed, 1923), p. 6.
34. Van Santvoord, *Memoirs*, pp. 21-22.
35. *Ibid.*, p. 231.
36. *Ibid.*, p. 18.
37. Samuel Nott, *Autobiography*, p. 107.
38. Van Santvoord, *Memoirs*, p. 24.
39. Samuel Nott, *Autobiography*, p. 72.
40. *Ibid.*, p. 83.
4l. Leonard Bacon ed., *Contributions to the Ecclesiastical History of Connecticut* (New Haven, Conn., 1861), pp. 323, 325.
42. *Ibid.*, p. 338.
43. Samuel Nott, *Autobiography*, p. 95.
44. *Records of the Congregational Church of Franklin, Connecticut, 1718-1860* (Hartford, Conn., 1938), p. 7.
45. Samuel Nott, *Autobiography*, p. 98.
46. *Ibid.*, p. 94.
47. *Ibid.*, p. 268.
48. *Ibid.*, p. 274.
49. *Ibid.*, p. 274.
50. *Ibid.*, p. 275.
51. *Ibid.*, p. 142.
52. *Ibid.*, p. 142.
53. Eliphalet Nott to Henry Barnard. (January 1861), *The American Journal of Education*, new ser., XIII (March, 1863), pp. 132-134.
54. Samuel Nott, *Autobiography*, p. 98.
55. Sarah M. Nott, " 'Laws for my Pupils', of my Grandfather Samuel Nott, D.D., who died in Franklin," (November 17, 1882). Copy in the Union College Archives.
56. Samuel Nott, *Autobiography*, Chapter 13. Eliphalet Nott probably taught at two district schools in Franklin Township, one on Pautapaug Road, and the other at Lord's Bridge. (See: Alfred Nevins and others eds., *Encyclopedia of the Presbyterian Church in the United States of America* (Philadelphia, 1884.), pp. 581-582.
57. Franklin (Conn.) Church Record (1718-1932) in MS. p. 131.

58. Samuel Nott, *Autobiography*, p. 98.
59. Franklin Church Record, November 13, 1795. p. 136.
60. *Ibid.*, December 16, 1795, p. 138.
61. Samuel Nott, *Autobiography*, Chapter 12.

2. The *"Principal Instructor"* of Plainfield Academy

1. Ellen D. Larned, *History of Windham County, Connecticut* (Worcester, Mass. 1880), II, p. 329.
2. *Ibid.*, p. 328.
3. R. M. Bayles, *History of Windham County, Connecticut* (New York, 1889), p. 457; Larned, *Windham County*, II, pp. 321-323.
4. Raymond, *Union University*, I, (New York, 1907), p. 296.
5. Bayles, *Windham County*, p. 458.
6. *Ibid.*, p. 457.
7. Eliphalet Nott to Henry Barnard. (January, 1861). *The American Journal of Education*, new ser. 111, (March, 1863), pp. 132-134.
8. Norwich (Conn.) *Packet*, XXI, No. 1070 (September 18, 1794); No. 1071 (September 25, 1794).
9. *Ibid.*, No. 1074 (October 16, 1794); repeated in No. 1077 (November 6, 1794).
10. J. H. French, *Gazetteer of the State of New York* (Syracuse, N.Y., 1860) p. 703n; W. B. Sprague, *Annals of the American Pulpit*, I, (New York, 1857), p. 682.
11. Irving Mark, *Agrarian Conflicts in Colonial New York*, 1711-1775 (New York, 1940) p. 48.
12. Sprague, I, p. 685.
13. Williston Walker, *The Congregationalists* (New York, 1894), p. 287.
14. *Ibid.*, p. 287.
15. *Ibid.*, p. 320.
16. *Congregational Church Records*, Plainfield, Conn., 1793-1803.
17. Plainfield (Conn.) *JOURNAL*, February 23, 1871.
18. Van Santvoord, *Memoirs*, p. 37. In a letter to the writer, dated September 19, 1949, Miss Marion Brown, in charge of Special Collections, Brown University, stated that the Corporation records showed only the granting of the Honorary Master of Arts degree by vote of the Fellows on September 2, 1795, and the conferring of the degree on September 5, 1795, at the Commencement exercises held at that time. She further stated that the University has no record of any examination given to the candidates for the Honorary Master of Arts degree.
   Inasmuch as Professor Tayler Lewis, who collaborated with Dr. Van Santvoord in writing the *Memoirs*, knew President Nott well, it is reasonable to suppose he may have had information about Nott's education which is no longer available.
19. Eliphalet Nott to Henry Barnard. (January, 1861). *American Journal of Education*, new ser., XIII (March, 1863), p. 133.
20. Samuel Nott, *Autobiography*, Chapter XIII.
21. Van Santvoord, *Memoirs*, p. 41.
22. *Ibid.*, p. 41.
23. *Narrative of the Missions to the New Settlements*, published by the Trustees of the General Association of Connecticut, 1795, p. 19. (See the letter addressed to the Association of October 20, 1794, signed by 20 petitioners.)
24. *Ibid.*, 1797, p. 6.

25. Leonard Bacon ed., *Contributions to the Ecclesiastical History of Connecticut* (New Haven, Conn., 1861.), p. 176.

26. *Narrative of the Missions to the New Settlements*, 1797.

27. Jonathan Pearson, Diary, vol. 7 (June 20, 1860), Union College Archives.

28. Samuel Nott, *Autobiography*, Chapter XII.

3. *"Is This the Way to Zion?"*

1. Van Santvoord, *Memoirs*, pp. 54-55. Lewis, (New York, 1876), pp. 54-55.

2. Paul D. Evans, "The Frontier Pushed Westward," *History of the State of New York*, V (New York, 1934), Chapter 5.

3. Codman Hislop, *The Mohawk* (New York, 1948), pp. 211–231.

4. Eliphalet Nott, "Address at the Cherry Valley Endowment Drive," in Van Santvoord, pp. 42-43.

5. F. W. Halsey, *The Old New York Frontier* (New York, 1901), p. 342.

6. Trustees' Minutes, Cherry Valley Presbyterian Church, Cherry Valley, New York (September 5, 1796).

7. Van Santvoord, *Memoirs*, p. 47.

8. Halsey, Chapter 6.

9. Van Santvoord, *Memoirs*, p. 55.

10. Eliphalet Nott, *Federal Money, Being a Sketch of the Money of Account of United America. By Eliphalet Nott, A.M., Principal of Cherry Valley Academy. First Edition. For the use of schools.* (Cooperstown: Printed by Elihu Phnney [sic] for the author. M,DCC,XCVII). This copy, possibly unique, is in the Union College Archives.

11. Van Santvoord, *Memoirs*, p. 89.

12. Albany (N.Y.) First Presbyterian Church. Trustees' Minutes (July 13, 1798).

13. Van Santvoord, *Memoirs*, p. 55.

14. *Ibid.*, p. 55.

15. Codman Hislop, *Albany: Dutch, English and American* (Albany, 1936). pp. 207-235.

16. G. R. Howell and J. Tenney, *Bicentennial History of Albany and History of the County of Albany, N.Y., from 1609 to 1886.* (Albany, 1886), pp. 469-470.

17. A. V. V. Raymond, *Union University* I (New York, 1907), p. 307.

18. Dixon Ryan Fox, *Decline of Aristocracy in the Politics of New York* (New York, 1919), p. 3.

19. Albany First Presbyterian Church, Trustees' Minutes, (November 5, 1798).

20. Van Santvoord, *Memoirs*, p. 109.

21. Eliphalet Nott to Dr. Vine Utley. (n.d.), in Van Santvoord, p. 378.

22. *Ibid.*, p. 67.

23. Gorham A. Worth, *Random Recollections of Albany from 1800 to 1803* (Albany, 1866), pp. 74-77.

24. Van Santvoord, *Memoirs*, p. 236.

25. O. Turner, *History of the Pioneer Settlement of the Phelps and Gorham Purchase* (Rochester, N.Y., 1852), p. 193.

26. Eliphalet Nott, *A Discourse, delivered in the Presbyterian Church, in Albany, the Fourth of July, A.D. 1801, at the celebration of the twenty-fifth anniversary of American Independence.* (Albany, 1801.)

27. Howell and Tenney, *Bi-centennial*, p. 673.

28. Van Santvoord, *Memoirs*, p. 88.

29. Reverend John Blair Smith to James Moyes, (April 8, 1797). Union College Archives.

4. *The Pastor of the "Court Church"*

1. Van Santvoord, *Memoirs*, pp. 78-80.
2. Cuyler Reynalds, *Albany Chronicles* (Albany, 1906), p. 392.
3. Van Santvoord, *Memoirs*, p. 81.
4. J. B. Smith to Eliphalet Nott. August 8, 1799. (New-York Historical Society).
5. Lewis Sebring, *Dirck Romeyn*, MS., Union College library.
6. Reverend J. B. Johnson to the Reverend Alexander Proudfit. (September 19, 1801), New-York Historical Society.
7. "Agreement for the Organization of a College in Schenectady, 1785." MS., Union College Archives.
8. Reverend J. R. Hardenberg to Dirck Romeyn. (January 12, 1785), Romeyn Papers, Union College Archives.
9. Letter fragment, unsigned (October 8, 1801), Union College Archives.
10. W. C. Bronson, *Brown University* (Providence, 1914), p. 26.
11. A. V. V. Raymond, *Union University*, I (N.Y. 1907) p. 158.
12. Rhode Island College, "Laws of 1793," Archives of Brown University.
13. Bronson, *Brown University*, p. 149.
14. Van Santvoord, *Memoirs*, p. 149.
15. J. B. Smith to Eliphalet Nott, (August 8, 1799), New-York Historical Society. Photostat in Union College Archives.
16. O. W. Elsbree, *Rise of the Missionary Spirit in America, 1790-1815* (Williamsport, Pa. 1928), pp. 129-130.
17. *Ibid.*, pp. 128-129.
18. *Ibid.*, pp. 128-129.
19. *New York Missionary Magazine*, (1800), pp. 286-291.
20. Eliphalet Nott, *The Resurrection of Christ, a series of discourses*, Tayler Lewis, ed., (New York, 1872)
21. *Ibid.*, iii.
22. G. A. Worth, *Random Recollections of Albany* (Albany, 1866), pp. 74-77.
23. Eliphalet Nott, *Resurrection Sermons* (New York, 1872) pp. 129-131.
24. *Ibid.*, p. 122.
25. *Ibid.*, p. 122.
26. *Ibid.*, p. 107.
27. Worth, *Recollections*, p. 77.
28. Eliphalet Nott, *Miscellaneous Sermons* (Schenectady, 1810), p. 40.
29. Frank Hunter Potter, *The Alonzo Potter Family* (Privately Printed, Concord, N. H., 1923), p. 5
30. Nott, *Miscellaneous Sermons*, pp. 80-81.
31. *Ibid.*, p. 82.
32. Reverend J. T. Backus, *Funeral of the Rev. Dr. Nott*, pamphlet (N.Y. 1866).
33. John Howard Payne, *The Pastime*, vol. II, no. 1 (May 4, 1808), p. 8. Union College Archives.

5. *Schenectady via Weehawken*

1. William Coleman, A Collection of the Facts and Documents, Relative to the Death of Major-General Alexander Hamilton (New York, 1804) (reprinted by Houghton, Mifflin Co., Boston and New York, 1904), p. 61.
2. Eliphalet Nott, *A discourse delivered in the North Dutch Church, in the city of Albany, occasioned by the ever to be lamented death of General Alexander Hamilton,*

July 29, 1804. (Albany, 1804). "Appendix," giving will of Hamilton, his reasons for meeting Burr, and Bishop Moore's and Dr. Mason's account of his death: [33] –40. (In Union College Archives). For the various editions of this discourse, see Bibliography.

3. Raymond, *Union University,* 1, p. 299.

4. G. F. Danforth, *Union College Centennial Anniversary* (New York, 1897), p. 308.

5. Van Santvoord, *Memoirs,* p. 101.

6. John Kirby to Daniel Rogers. (August 15, 1804). Union College Archives.

7. Van Santvoord, *Memoirs,* p. 103.

BOOK TWO

1. President Nott and the White Moth of Hope

1. Van Santvoord, *Memoirs,* p. 65. Recently (August 17, 1968), in a letter from my colleague Professor Gordon A. Silber, was the following note on his work in trying to unravel the mystery of the origin of the French motto of the Union College seal:

My efforts to find the source of the 1796 seal with its French motto convinces me that the ideal of brotherhood, the symbol of Minerva, and the phraseology of the motto itself are completely typical of 18th century French free-masonry. Some of those taking active part in the steps which led to the founding of the college were masons. (For example, of the Committee of Seven appointed August 19, 1794 by the Trustees of the [Schenectady] Academy to develop plans for the new college, Jeremiah and Stephan Van Rensselaer, were members of the Masters Lodge, Albany, and Joseph C. Yates and [tutor] John Taylor were members of St. George's Lodge, Schenectady.) Whether it will be possible to establish a masonic element in the founding of the college seems to me to be problematical at this point.

See also: S. B. Fortenbaugh, "Adventures in the Skin Trade," Union College *Symposium,* Vol. 8, No. 4 (Winter, 1969/70), pp. 30-34.

2. I. Mark, *Agrarian Conflicts in Colonial New York.* (New York, 1940), p. 45n.

3. G. R. Howell and J. Tenney, *Bicentennial History of Albany* (New York, 1886) pp. 523-528.

4. Codman Hislop, "The Ghost College that Came to Life," *American Heritage* (Spring, 1952), pp. 29-31

5. J. R. Hardenbergh to Dirck Romeyn, (January 12, 1785), Union College Archives.

6. A. V. V. Raymond, *Union University,* New York I, (1907), p. 30.

7. H. Glen to Dirck Romeyn, (February 25, 1787), Union College Archives.

8. H. Glen to Dirck Romeyn, (March 30, 1786), Union College Archives.

9. Dirck VanIngen to H. Glen, (March 18, 1786), Union College Archives.

10. Raymond, *Union University,* pp. 34-35.

11. John Sanders, *History of Schenectady County* (Albany, 1879), pp. 46-57-151.

12. Robert Yates, a cousin of Mayor Yates, and a brother of his fellow trustee, John I. Yates, had set the pattern of the Yates' political thinking: he had been a radical Republican pamphleteer, a member of the New York Provincial Congress, of the New York Council of Safety, and had served on the committee which had drafted the first state constitution. He had also been a Clintonian delegate from New York to the convention which drafted the United States Constitution, leaving Philadelphia in disgust, however, before the work was completed. Under the patronage of Governor Clinton he

had risen to the place of Chief Justice of the New York State Supreme Court. He served Union College as a charter trustee until his death in 1801. J. Sanders, *Ibid.*, pp. 151-152.

13. Van Santvoord, *Memoirs*, pp. 114-115.

14. Trustees' Minutes, August 24, 1804.

15. Trustees' Minutes, May 3, 1803.

16. Raymond, *Union University*, I, p. 136.

17. A. C. Flick ed., *New York State History* (New York 1934), VI, Chapter 11.

18. Van Santvoord, *Memoirs*, pp. 91-92.

19. Raymond, *Union University*, I, p. 155.

20. Alumni Records, Union College Alumni Office.

21. John M. Mason to D. D. Tompkins, (February 25, 1805):
"Union College appears to be the reigning favorite" [for legislative favor] " . . . on the other hand, there is little reason why she should monopolize it . . ."; the Reverend J. M. Mason, pastor of the Cedar Street Presbyterian Church of New York City, the following year became editor of the *Christian's Magazine*, and in 1811, Provost of Columbia College. (W. B. Sprague, *Annals of the American Pulpit* IV (New York, 1856), pp. 1-4). Eleven years earlier Dr. Nicholas Romayne [sic] wrote from New York City to his nephew Dirck Romeyn that the Trustees of Columbia College hoped to prevent the establishment of a college in Schenectady, and that General Philip Schuyler "was directly opposed to the interests of Schenectada [sic]"; the plan of those who supported Columbia was to get enough towns to bid for the "college to the northward" to make a grant to any one of them politically inexpedient. Nicholas Romayne to Dirck Romeyn. (April 3, 1792), Union College Archives.

22. An Act for the Endowment of Union College," New York State Session Laws (1805), paragraphs 11 and 12.

23. Raymond, *Union University*, I, p. 136.

24. Thomas Davis, Jr., *Chronicles of the Hopkins Grammar School 1660-1935* (New Haven, Conn., 1938), p. 261.

25. Sidney Sherwood, *The University of the State of New York* (Washington, D.C., 1900), p. 63.

26. *Ibid.*, p. 24.

27. See Book I, Chap. IV, above.

28. Raymond, *Union University*, I, p. 136.

29. Eliphalet Nott to Stephen VanRensselaer. (*ca.* Feb. 1805), Union College Archives.

30. Raymond, I, *Union University*, p. 136.

31. *Ibid.*, p. 136.

32. *Ibid.*, p. 139.

33. Howell and Tenney, *History of Albany*, p. 444.

34. D. S. Alexander, *A Political History of the State of New York*, I (New York, 1906), Chapter XIII. pp. 688-689.

35. Jabez Hammond, *A Political History of New York*, I Albany, N.Y., 1892), pp. 123-124.

36. Raymond, I, *Union University*, p. 137.

37. *Ibid.*, p. 137.

38. Trustees' Minutes, July 17, 1805.

39. New York State Session Laws, (1805), paragraph 13.

40. Union University, Catalogue of the Officers and Alumni. . . . 1797-1884. (Albany, 1884), vii.

41. John M. Mason to D. D. Tompkins. (February 25, 1805), Union College Archives.

2. *"Novelties Worse than Paine!"*

1. Austin A. Yates, *Schenectady County* (New York, 1902), p. 130.
2. Timothy Dwight, *Travels in New England and New York*, II, (London, 1823), p. 464.
3. Yates, *Schenectady County*, p. 121.
4. Timothy Dwight, *Travels*, p. 464.
5. Lewis Sebring, *Dirck Romeyn, 1744-1804* (1938), Ms., Union College Library, p. 140.
6. G. S. Roberts, *Old Schenectady* (Schenectady, N.Y., n.d.), p. 108.
7. Yates, *Schenectady County*, p. 139.
8. Samuel Nott to Eliphalet Nott. (September 18, 1806), Union College Archives.
9. *New York Missionary Magazine* (1800), pp. 286-291.
10. A. M. Hamilton, *The Intimate Life of Alexander Hamilton*, (New York, 1910), p. 334.
11. Eliphalet Nott, *Counsels to Young Men on the Formation of Character . . .* (New York, 1842), p. 13. Further references to this 1805 Baccalaureate will be to this title and edition.
12. *Ibid.*, p. 14
13. *Ibid.*, p. 15
14. *Ibid.*, p. 19.
15. Trustees' Minutes, November 16, 1802.
16. Ernst Cassirer, *The Philosophy of the Enlightenment* (Boston, 1951), Chapters 3 and 4.
17. Eliphalet Nott, *Discourse . . . on the death of . . . Alexander Hamilton* (Albany, 1804).
18. Woodbridge Riley, *American Thought* (New York, 1915), p. 130.

3. *"The Purposes of Minerva and of God."*

1. James Fenimore Cooper, "The Eclipse," *Putnam's Magazine*, (September 1869).
2. Eliphalet Nott to Miss Catherine Putnam. (June 1806). A copy of this letter was found by Chester A. Hartnagel, Union, 1898, in a copy of Andrew Newell's *Darkness at Noon* in the New York State Library. See also: Eliphalet Nott to Reverend Samuel Miller, October 6, 1806, and reprinted in the *Monthly Anthology and Boston Review*, vol. IV (January 1807), pp. 55-56. Also: Miss Maria [Hull?] to Mrs. Eliza McLellan, June 15, 1806. Union College Archives.
3. Cooper, "The Eclipse."
4. Eliphalet Nott to Miss Catherine Putnam, *op. cit.*
5. Eliphalet Nott, *A sermon preached before the General Assembly of the Presbyterian Church in the United States of America; by appointment of their standing committee of missions, May 19, 1806* (Philadelphia, 1806). The sermon was reprinted two years later by S. Dole, Newburyport. [Mass.?]
6. Richard Hofstadter and Walter P. Metzger, *The Development of Academic Freedom in the United States* (New York, 1955), p. 187.
7. See Book I, Chap. 2.

8. François de la Fontainerie, *French Liberalism and Education in the Eighteenth Century* (New York, 1932), p. 44.

9. Allen O. Hanson, *Liberalism and American Education in the Eighteenth Century* (New York, 1926).

10. Union College By-Laws (December 9, 1795), Union College Trustees Minutes.

11. John Seaman to Eliphalet Nott. (July 29, 1806), in Willis Hanson, *The Early Life of Payne* (Boston, 1913), p. 77.

12. S. T. Noble, *A History of American Education* (New York, 1938), p. 234.

13. Charles E. Cunningham, *Timothy Dwight, 1752–1817* (New York, 1942), p. 197 ff.

14. E. E. Beardsley, *History of the Episcopal Church in Connecticut*, II (New York, 1868), vol. II, pp. 190–195; Eliphalet Nott to Samuel Nott. (April 14, 1810), in Van Santvoord, *Memoirs*, p. 123.

4. *"The Illumination of the 13th of May."*

1. W. T. Hanson, Jr., *Early Life of John Howard Payne* (Boston, 1913), pp. 58, 92.

2. A. J. Weise, *Troy's 100 Years* (Troy, N. Y., 1891), p. 50.

3. Van Santvoord, *Memoirs*, p. 199.

4. Eliphalet Nott, *The Resurrection of Christ . . . .* with introduction by Tayler Lewis (New York, 1872), p. 155.

5. Hanson, *Early Life*, p. 78.

6. *Ibid.*, pp. 78–80. John Howard Payne, in a letter to his sister, gives the following college routine for this period:
"to each duty the bell warns us to be punctual.
5, Rise.
½p5, Prayers; after which the classes retire with their several instructors to their particular recitation rooms.
8, Breakfast.
half past nine to eleven, study in rooms.
11, Recitation.
12. Recitation.
1, Dinner, recreation till 2.
2 to 4, Study in rooms.
4, Recitation.
5. Prayers.
½p.5, Tea. Recreation till 7.
7 to 9, Study in rooms. 9 to 11, devoted to anything which is agreeable in the rooms.
Not a light must be be seen, under a severe penalty, after eleven; and after seven no student is allowed to be out of rooms, under a like restriction.
A professor is constantly visiting the rooms, to see the laws fulfilled. They are as vigilant as they are severe."

7. Faculty Minutes, December 16, 1806.

8. *Ibid.*

9. Faculty Minutes, December 17, 1807.

10. Eliphalet Nott to Samuel Smith. (March 9, 1807), MacLean *Mss.*, Princeton University Archives.

11. Union College, "Notice to Parents," signed "B. Allen, Sec." (1807).

12. Trustees' Minutes, September 21, 1809.

13. In a less than enthusiastic letter that fall, Nott introduced Allen to President Kirkland, at Harvard, suggesting to Kirkland that the "new classical school" then contemplated for Boston would be a suitable place "for proving the talents of Professor Allen . . . . he will be governed by your advice." (Eliphalet Nott to President Kirkland. [October 4, 1809] , Harvard University Archives, Alumni Room.)

5. *"We shall not be hereafter what heretofore we have been."*

1. Eliphalet Nott to the Rev. Samuel Nott (April 14, 1810) in Van Santvoord, *Memoirs*, p. 123.

2. Professor Jonathan Pearson, Diary. Entries for October 11, 12, 13, and 14, 1841. Union College Archives.

3. Professor E.S.C. Smith, "Rudolph Hassler," *Union Worthies*, No. 13, (Union College, 1958).

4. L. C. Hatch, *History of Bowdoin College* (Portland, Me., 1927), p. 36.

5. Henry K. Rowe, *History of the Andover Theological Seminary* (Newton, Mass., 1933), pp. 2, 116.

6. Samuel Miller, Jr., *Life of Samuel Miller* (Philadelphia, 1869), 1, p. 239.

7. Eliphalet Nott to Hugh Peebles (*ca.* 1812). Union College Archives.

8. DeWitt Clinton, "Journal Made on Canal Survey," *MS.*, Montgomery County (N.Y.) Historical Society.

9. Sources for the statements involving David Parrish and Joseph Jacques Ramée: Ramée's "Grand Plan" of 1812–1813 for Union College will be found in Codman Hislop and Harold A. Larrabee, "Joseph Jacques Ramée and the Building of North and South Colleges," Union College *Alumni Monthly* (February, 1938), pp. 112–127; and in Christopher Tunnard, "Minerva's Union," *Architectural Review* (February, 1947), pp. 57–62.

10. Eliphalet Nott loans to U. C., Union College Treasurer's Report, 1811. Levinus Vanderheyden, testimony (August, 1853), *ms*, Union College Archives.

11. John Sanders to Jonathan Pearson. (May 2, 1880), Union College Archives.

12. Pearson *Diary*, September 28, 1856.

13. Union College Treasurer's Report, April 27, 1853.

14. Ramée, however, had made his impression; he is known to have designed the gardens, at least, if not the graceful, peristyled manor house for the sister of James O. Duane, a Trustee member of the college site committee, as well as a city house for the patroon, Stephen VanRensselaer, whose brothers were active Board members. See: Hislop and Larrabee, "J. J. Ramée," p. 123.

BOOK THREE

1. *The Lottery Act*

1. Peter Van Schaik to Peter Van Schaik, Jr., March 5, 1814. Union College Archives. The Van Schaiks were cousins of Herman Melville; see: Carter Davidson, "Herman Melville and Union College," *MS.* (n.d.), Union College Library.

2. Eliphalet Nott to the Reverend Samuel Nott. April 19, 1814. Union College Archives.

3. Journal, New York State Assembly (37th Session), February 4, 1814.

4. *Ibid.*, February 2, 1814.

5. *Journal*, New York State Senate (37th Session), March 28, 1814.

6. Claire Klein, "Columbia and the Elgin Botanic Garden Property," Columbia University *Quarterly*, Vol. XXXI (December, 1939), pp. 277–297. See also Addison Brown, *Elgin Botanical Garden*, (Lancaster, Pa., 1908).

7. Reverend John M. Mason to DeWitt Clinton, March 1, 1810, in Jacob Van Vechten, *Memoirs of John M. Mason, D.D.* (New York, 1856).

8. A.V.V. Raymond, *Union University* (New York, 1907), 1, pp. 148–150.

9. Jabez Hammond, *History of Political Parties in the State of New York*, 1 (Albany, 1842), p. 373.

10. Raymond, *Union University*, 1, p. 150.

11. *Ibid.*, p. 151.

12. *A History of Columbia University*, (New York, 1904), pp. 101–102.

13. Archibald McIntyre, Memorandum Book, March 12, 1810 (New York Public Library).

14. Sidney Sherwood, *The University of the State of New York*, United States Bureau of Education, No. 28, Circular of Information No. 3 (Washington, 1900), p. 207.

15. Hammond, *Political History*, I, pp. 373–374.

16. Eliphalet Nott, *Counsels to Young Men* (No. X) 2nd ed. (New York, 1842).

2. The "Grand Plan" takes shape

1. Van Wyck Brooks, *The Flowering of New England, 1815–1865* (Cleveland, Ohio, 1946). pp. 36–37.

2. A.V.V. Raymond, *Union University*, I (New York, 1907), pp. 155–156.

3. *Ibid.*, p. 156.

4. Graduate Statistics, Union College Alumni Office.

5. L. W. Spring, *Williams College* (Boston, 1917), p. 108.

6. John MacLean, *History of the College of New Jersey*, II (Philadelphia, 1877), pp. 184–185.

7. Eliphalet Nott: The Ames Portrait is in the Union College Collection.

8. Eliphalet Nott, *Miscellaneous Works* (Schenectady, 1810).

9. Union College *Concordiensis*, January 15, 1896.

10. Robert and Johanna Peter, *Transylvannia University, its origin, rise, decline and fall*, Filson Club Publications (Louisville, Ky., 1896), No. 11. Two years later John B. Romeyn, Nott's successor as minister of the First Presbyterian Church, Albany, was offered the presidency of Transylvannia. See: Robert Stuart to J. B. Romeyn. June 13, 1815, Union College Archives.

11. George P. Schmidt, *The Old Time College President* (New York, 1930) p. 218.

12. Eliphalet Nott to the Rev. Samuel Nott. January 20, 1817, Union College Archives.

13. *Ibid.*

14. Van Santvoord, *Memoirs*, pp. 216–219.

15. Eliphalet Nott, "On Slander," the opening speech by Nott as the Moderator at the trials of the Rev. John Chester and Mr. Mark Tucker in the case of the Rev. Hooper Cumming. February 18, 1817, Union College Archives. This date is in conflict with the reported dates of these trials in Joel Munsell's *Annals of Albany*, VI (Albany, N.Y., 1855), pp. 227–229.

16. Van Santvoord, *Memoirs*, p. 218.

17. John Sanders, *Early History of Schenectady* (Albany, 1879), p. 265.

18. Schenectady *Gazette*, August 22, 1959.

19. Van Santvoord, *Memoirs*, p. 239.

20. *Ibid.*, p. 239.

21. Schenectady *Cabinet*, November 22, 1820.

22. Van Santvoord, *Memoirs*, p. 239.

23. *Ibid.*, p. 206.

24. Raymond, *Union University*, I, p. 268.

25. W. M. Adams (U.C. 1816) to Lucius Bacon. July 29, 1814, Union College Archives.

26. Eliza Noel Pintard Davidson ed., *Letters from John Pintard to his Daughter, Eliza Noel Pintard, 1816–1833.*, I (New York, 1941), pp. 111, 176, 309.

27. John M. Duncan, *Travel through part of the United States and Canada in 1818 and 1819*, II (New York, 1823), pp. 3–5.

28. William Henry Seward, *Autobiography of William Henry Seward* (New York, 1877), p. 31.

29. *Ibid.*, pp. 35–36.

30. Minutes, Phi Beta Kappa Society, 1817–1820, Union College Archives.

31. Seward, *Autobiography*, p. 47.

3. *"A man divided"*

1. The records of Nott's relations with the House of Yates and McIntyre, as a lottery firm, are to be found chiefly in the printed *Documents Relative to the Dispute Between the Trustees of Union College and Yates and McIntyre*. References to them in these pages will be to this collection, by particular document, by paragraph number, or page number, and will be cited here as *Documents*. Unless otherwise indicated, the letters individually cited will be found in the college archives. For John B. Yates's authorship of "The Plan," see footnote 23, below.

2. Jabez D. Hammond, *The History of Political Parties in the State of New York . . . to December, 1840*, II (Albany, 1842), p. 93.

3. Hugh G. H. Aiken, "Yates and McIntyre: Lottery Managers," *Journal of Economic History* XIII (Winter, 1953). A useful review of the operations of the firm, limited by the fact that data used here was not then available to its author.

4. John E. Smith ed., *Our Country and Its People* (Boston, 1899), pp. 401–402. See also John Sanders, *Centennial Address Relating to the Early History of Schenectady* (Albany, 1879), pp. 152–155.

5. *Documents*. No. 12, para. 495.

6. *Ibid.* See also: *History of Montgomery and Fulton Counties, N.Y.* (New York, 1878).

7. *Ibid.*

8. Eliphalet Nott to Archibald McIntyre, February 1, 1826. Union College Archives.

9. *Documents*, "In Chancery: 'The Joint and Several Answers of the Trustees of Union College . . .' " p. 5.

10. *Report of the Select Committee on Lotteries*, April 6, 1819. (Albany, 1819).

11. A. Franklin Ross, "History of Lotteries in New York State," *Magazine of History*, vol. 5, no. 4 (February-June, 1907), pp. 219–220.

12. *A brief Survey of the Great Extent and Evil Tendencies of the Lottery System, as Existing in the United States.* (Philadelphia, 1833).

13. Ross, "Lotteries," p. 323.

14. *The Whole of the Documentary Evidence, relative to the controversy between the Regents of the University and the Trustees of Union College* (Schenectady, 1823), p. 7

15. *Appleton's Cyclopaedia of American Biography, VI,* (New York, 1889), p. 638.

16. Ross, "Lotteries," p. 265.

17. A.V.V. Raymond, *Union University,* 1 (New York, 1907), pp. 545–547.

18. *Documents,* No. 12, para. 29, "Original Contract with Yates and McIntyre." See also *Documents,* No. 10 (Trustees of Union College and Eliphalet Nott, vs. Yates and McIntyre, et al, Sept. 8, 1835, para. 27.).

19. For a full review of the operation of the Vannini, or "Ternary System," see Thomas Doyle, *Five Years in a Lottery Office* (Boston, 1841). Also, *Explanation of the permutation plan of lottery, and rules for constructing such a lottery; together with refutations of the charges raised . . . against the system. As also, some remarks addressed to the public by Yates and McIntyre, in relation to their rights as assignees of the New York Lotteries* (New York, 1832).

20. *Documents:* "Examination of a Report professing to be a report of a select committee of the Trustees of Union College, in relation to the pending controversy with Yates and McIntyre.—Printed by order of the Committee of Finance, to whom the same was referred at a meeting of the Board Nov. 24, 1834." p. 19.

21. *Ibid.,* p. 19.

22. *Documents,* para. 18, "In Chancery . . ." p. 4. See also Eliphalet Nott to Archibald McIntyre, Feb. 1, 1826 (Union College Archives). "There is one man, and only one interested in the institutions, who knew at the time what percentage we could have and be sure of our money . . . ." The "one man" was apparently William James, confidant of the four men who signed the dual contract, and the only witness to it.

23. Eliphalet Nott to Archibald McIntyre. Feb. 1, 1826. "To speak plainly, there were other offers made to me besides that of yours . . . and one man of very great wealth was desirous of embarking in the concern after our law was passed—I got rid of everything as I determined that you and Mr. Yates, who had suggested the plan and assisted us in the law, should have the benefit of the contract . . . ." The "one man" was probably William James.

24. *Documents,* "Controversy between the Regents of the University and the Trustees of Union College," 1823, p. 31.

25. "An Act to Amend an act entitled 'An Act relative to the City of Schenectady,' " passed in Febraury 1823. New York State Session Laws, 1823, p. 31.

26. Pearson Diary, May 5, 1860. Union College Archives.

27. *Documents.* p. 50.

28. *Ibid.,* p. 29.

29. *Ibid.,* p. 25.

30. *Assembly Document,* No. 213 (1849), p. 49.

31. *Ibid.,* p. 81.

32. *Session Laws,* 1824, p. 302.

33. *Assembly Document,* No. 213 (1849), p. 30.

34. *Documents* ("In Chancery" 1834), paragraph 17a.

35. S. W. Jones, Diary, Schenectady Historical Society, p. 33.

36. Significantly, Henry Yates and William James were the first elected trustees to join the Board (1827) since the college gave up its corporate independence in 1805.

BOOK FOUR

1. *"The Republic of the World"*

1. Eliphalet Nott, *Counsels to Young Men . . . . Being addresses principally delivered at the Anniversary Commencements of Union College.* No. XX (New York, 1842).

2. *"The idea of a university"*

1. R. F. Butts, *The College Charts Its Course* (New York, 1939), p. 137.
2. Richard Hofstadter and C. DeWitt Hardy, *The Development and Scope of Higher Education in the United States* (New York, 1952), p. 11.
3. H. B. Adams, *Thomas Jefferson and the University of Virginia.* U.S. Bureau of Education, Circular of Information No. 1, 1888 (Washington, D.C., 1888), p. 77. Adams, writing on pp. 130–131 of the University of Virginia's influence on Francis Wayland's reforms at Brown University, was apparently unfamiliar with Eliphalet Nott's influence on Wayland.
4. *Ibid.*, p. 77.
5. A. J. Nock, *Jefferson* (New York, 1926), p. 318.
6. Adams, *Jefferson*, p. 124.
7. *Ibid.*, p. 124.
8. *Ibid.*, p. 124.
9. Nock, *Jefferson*, p. 319.
10. P. A. Bruce, *A History of the University of Virginia,* II, (New York, 1920), p. 73.
11. Van Wyck Brooks, *The Flowering of New England* (Cleveland, 1946) pp. 72–88.
12. George Ticknor, *Life, Letters, and Journals,* 1, (Boston, 1876), p. 356.
13. Samuel Eliot Morison, *Three Centuries of Harvard* (Cambridge, 1936), pp. 231–232.
14. Ticknor, *Life, Letters, and Journals,* I, p. 357.
15. Eliphalet Nott to Rudolph Hassler. May 10, 1828, Union College Archives.
16. Union College Trustees' Minutes, July 24, 1811.
17. *Ibid.*, July 24, 1819.
18. *Ibid.*, July 27, 1819.
19. Albany (N.Y.) *Gazette and Daily Advertiser,* July 28, 1821.
20. E. W. Rice, "A List of 73 items by and about Eliphalet Nott," *Union University Quarterly* (November, 1904), p. 206.
21. "Squire Whipple and Union College," *Union Worthies,* No. 4, Union College, 1949, p. 6; Harold A. Larrabee, "Electives Before Eliot," Harvard *Alumni Bulletin,* vol. 42, no. 26 (April, 1942), pp. 894–895.
22. Francis Wayland, who was graduated from Union in 1813, and who, after four years as a tutor under Nott from 1817 to 1821, then spent four years in Boston as pastor of the First Baptist Chruch, may well have preached the virtues of Ticknor's Harvard reforms on his return to Schenectady as Professor of Mathematics and Natural Philosophy in 1826. See: Theodore R. Crane, *Francis Wayland and Brown University 1796–1841* (unpublished Harvard doctoral thesis, 1951), Summary, p. 5.
23. The new Rensselaer School in Troy, New York, had sent out a shock wave which even stirred the Massachusetts legislature in 1825 to investigate the possibility of establishing similar schools or colleges of science in that state. (Ethel M. McAllister,

Amos Eaton, Scientist and Educator 1776–1842 [Philadelphia, 1941], p. 375.) Nott, who saw the graduates of his new "Scientific Courses" as true bachelors of the arts, had had nothing but encouragement for men like Amos Eaton who made no pretensions about preparing scholars and gentlemen, but who had organized his Rensselaer School in 1824 in order to qualify teachers "for instructing the sons and daughters of farmers and mechanics . . . in the application of experimental chemistry, philosophy and natural history to agriculture, domestic economy, the arts and manufacturing." (*Ibid.*, p. 368.) The year Union College offered its Scientific Course Nott accepted the presidency of the Rensselaer School, and, according to Eaton in 1840, "was entitled to the first place in the memory of its teachers." (*Ibid.*, p. 241; Amos Eaton to Eliphalet Nott. April 21, 1840.)

From the point of view of the Yale conservatives the new Amherst Institute, too, was infected. Amherst, trinitarian, un-ivied, and unchartered in 1824, had been befriended by Nott that year when, out of patience with Yale, Williams, and Brown—colleges whose partisans were opposing the chartering of the new college—he granted Union degrees to seven Amherst seniors. (Union College Bill Book, July 27, 1824: "Dr. Sundry students entering from Amherst Institution," p. 89. Four of them paid the six dollar "President's Fee"; two who didn't pay were carried over to "the doomsday book.") Three years later Amherst, hoping for more students and financial support, tried to capitalize the spreading enthusiasm for the classics-free program by proposing a parallel course which included modern languages, English literature, "Mechanical Philosophy," and the physical sciences, designed, as was Amos Eaton's curriculum, "to show the relations to the more useful arts and trades." (L. F. Snow, *The College Curriculum in the United States*, (New York, 1907), p. 158.) There was no thought at Amherst, however, of granting the bachelor of arts degree for such studies, and the plan was soon buried by the faculty traditionalists.

Professor Ticknor's Harvard reforms were echoed in the plans of President James Marsh of the University of Vermont who hoped his Green Mountain students would profit by a four department arrangement which placed classical and modern languages and literature on a par with the sciences. President Marsh's students were to select any two of his departments and would have, if all had gone well, received the bachelor's degree for completing the prescribed work. Unlike the slow and solid growth of the idea of electives, however, and of the belief in the equality of the sciences and the arts under Nott, President Marsh's borrowed ideas were imposed on an unwilling faculty in the hope of bolstering the fortunes of a struggling college by opening its doors to students whose preparation would not admit them to such "hard" colleges as Union where the Freshmen year for all students was still a time of Athenians and Romans. Vermonters were no more ready for Marsh's German university ideas than was Harvard for Ticknor's, and the plan withered away for lack of support. (R. F. Butts, *The College Charts Its Course* [New York, 1939], p. 136.)

The Rensselaer School idea flowed west as well as east, and Hobart College, challenged perhaps by the "Polytechny" at Chittenango, tried briefly to establish a separate course at its opening in 1825 for students who wanted to by-pass the ancient world and to get on with what the Hobart innovators called "the practical business of life . . . without passing through a tedious course of classical studies." Here, too, there was to be only the "English diploma" for "the farmers and mechanics of the community" who took the new curriculum. Hobart made its short-lived concessions to democracy and utility as had the other lesser innovators, in the hope, largely of recruiting students. (*Ibid.*, p. 135.)

The "Polytechny" at Chittenango had close Union College ties as did the Rensselaer School which it resembled; not only did it take Professor Andrew Yates from Nott's faculty in 1825 to become its first principal, but the "Polytechny" was founded and financed by one of Nott's lottery managers, John B. Yates, brother of the new school's principal. (L. M. Hammond, *History of Madison County (N.Y.)* [Syracuse, 1872], p. 675.) To his dreams of lottery empire John Yates had added plans for a technical school on his expanding estate near Utica, plans which complicated the increasingly tangled and bitter relations between him and the President of Union. Nott, following the introduction of his own parallel "Scientific Course," immediately began planning for an astronomical observatory and a new "Institute of Science." (*Reply* of the Trustees of Union College to the charges brought before the Assembly of New York, March 19, 1850; and before the Senate, on the 12th of April, 1851, by the Hon. J. W. Beekman [Albany, 1853], pp. 32-33.) Nott's plans for his scientific school and Yates's ambitions for his "Polytechny," unfortunately, were both powered by the same spinning lottery wheels.

24. R. F. Butts, *College*, pp. 118–125.

25. *Ibid.*, p. 117.

26. Bureau of Education, Circular of Information No. 2, 1893. No. 14, *History of Education in Connecticut*, pp. 159-161.

27. Nott claimed "he had an arrangement with the President of Yale College by which they exchanged students" in order to give them a second chance (see J. C. Griffin, "Reminiscences," Union College *Concordiensis*, vol. 33 (February 19, 1910, pp. 13-14.) He seldom turned down a boy expelled from other colleges if he believed he could "reform" him. His reputation on this score was legendary. The rebels of Yale's "Conic Sections" riot, however, were not given sanctuary at Union (Eliphalet Nott to Alonzo Potter. (ca. 1830), in *Van Santvoord, Memoirs*, p. 155). "We have always refused young men revolting from government elsewhere," he added in this letter to his son-in-law, then in Boston and very much worried about the "Botony Bay" charges being leveled at Union.

28. Van Santvoord, *Memoirs*, p. 154.

29. *Ibid.*, p. 240.

30. Alumni records of the several colleges.

31. Van Santvoord, *Memoirs*, pp. 238-239.

32. Edward E. Hale, "Union Men in Education," Supplement, *Union Alumni Monthly* (March 1921).

33. Harold A. Larrabee, "Electives before Eliot," Harvard Alumni *Bulletin*, V. 42, no. 26, (April 1940), pp. 893–897.

34. Jonathan Pearson, Diary, (March 29, 1854), Union College Archives.

35. The B. A. degree was granted by Union College for completion of the Scientific Course. Nott's full stature as an educator has been denied him unwittingly by the historians of American education who have too long accepted an error made by Professor Tayler Lewis, co-author of the *Memoirs of Eliphalet Nott* (1876). On pages 155-156 Lewis stated that "the design (of the "Scientific Course") . . . was to enable young men who desired to pursue studies such as the modern languages, or others that might fit them for practical life, to do so without attending to the classics, or following the full course of collegiate study . . . they might remain in college for what period they chose, receiving when they left a certificate of the branches they had studied, and the time they had devoted to the pursuit, but not receiving the regular diploma which they alone were entitled to who had fairly and fully completed the classical course."

Professor Lewis was right in his statement only in so far as it bears on the part-time "University students." The Merit Books of Union College, however, which list all students, the courses they took and the grades they received demonstrate conclusively that students who elected the full course of studies prescribed in the "Scientific Course," and who completed the four-year curriculum were graduated as bachelors of arts from the time the new course was instituted.

The *Memoirs* were written ten years after Nott died at the age of ninety-three. Professor Lewis did not return to Union College until 1849, almost thirty years after he had left it as a young tutor of the classics. He was temperamentally opposed to all the "Scientific Course" represented . . . one remembers he confessed that Nott had had to caution him against his tirades against the sciences and things utilitarian during his year at Union as a young tutor in the classics in 1821. It is possible he may have recalled the "university student" (who had been welcome at Union since its chartering in 1795) as one with those who took the Scientific Course. From Squire Whipple, class of 1830, famous builder of bridges, on until Union began to award the degree of Civil Engineer in 1854, the Union Alumni Catalogue lists many distinguished engineers and scientists whose studies while undergraduates failed to include enough Greek and Latin, as Professor Pearson's diary noted, "to save a Freshman from the Dunce's block." They were all graduated, however, Bachelor of Arts.

What, in fact, developed was an elective system under which students were not required to confine themselves rigidly to either of the great options, whose mixed schedules of modern languages, the classics and the sciences would seem quite familiar in the conservative liberal arts college of the mid-Twentieth Century.

3. *"Kames"*

1. "Instructions Delivered to the Senior Class in Union College, Schenectady, in 1828–29, by the Reverend Eliphalet Nott, D.D., LL.D., President. Copied from notes taken by William Soul and Henry Baldwin, Junior members of said class." Notebook in the Union College Archives. S&B will indicate future references to these notes. See also: Abraham G. Lansing (Union, 1833), "Dr. Eliphalet Nott's Lectures to the Senior Class, 1832." Notebook in the Union College Archives.

2. S & B., p. 4.

3. S & B., p. 6.

4. Alexander Tytler, *Memoirs of the Life and Writings of the Honorable Henry Home of Kames*, 2nd ed. (Edinburgh, 1814). There is an excellent sketch of the life of Lord Kames in Helen W. Randall's *The Critical Theory of Lord Kames* (Northampton, 1944). See also *Dictionary of National Biography*, IX, pp. 1127-28.

5. Randall, *Kames*, p. 72.

6. Randall, *Kames*, appendix F, "A List of Editions of the *Elements of Criticism*, pp. 137-139; also pp. 85-86.

7. Van Santvoord, *Memoirs*, pp. 234-35.

8. Van Santvoord, *Memoirs*, p. 133.

9. A. V. V. Raymond, *Union University*, I (New York, 1907), p. 270.

10. Raymond, *Union University*, p. 301.

11. Lord Kames (Henry Home), *Elements of Criticism*, with the author's last corrections and additions, I, First American from the seventh London edition (Boston, 1796), pp. 21-22. This edition was used at Union at least until 1819 when the third American edition from the eighth London edition was purchased by the college. References will be to the 1796 edition. See also: Gordon McKenzie, "Lord Kames and the Mechanist Tradition," University of California *Publication in English*, XIV (1943), pp. 93-121.

12. Lansing, Notebook, pp. 2-3.

13. *Ibid.*, pp. 8-9.

14. S & B., pp. 52-53.

15. *Ibid.*, pp. 53-54.
16. S & B., p. 65.
17. S & B., p. 64.
18. Lansing, Notebook, p. 14.
19. Lansing, Notebook, p. 15.
20. Edwin G. Condé, "Union College, Maker of Men," Union College *Alumni Monthly* (Supplement), II (December 1920), p. 3.
21. S & B., pp. 18–19.
22. S & B., pp. 23–24.
23. S & B., pp. 24–25.
24. S & B., p. 27.
25. S & B., pp. 49-50.
26. S & B., pp. 40-41.
27. S & B., p. 41.
28. S & B., p. 41; see Eliphalet Nott to Benjamin Silliman, November 28, 1840, on "phrenology"; also F. R. Moore (Union 1843) to Reverend W. W. Nind [?], May 30, 1842, in Union College Archives.
29. Jonathan Pearson, Diary, IV, January 6-8, 1842.
30. S & B., pp. 69–70.
31. S & B., p. 35; see Dr. Nott's interest in the "Rapping Girls" in Albany in 1850: Syracuse (N.Y.) *Standard*, May 23, 1850.
32. S & B., p. 34.
33. S & B., p. 34
34. S & B., p. 94.
35. Eliphalet Nott to the Reverend S. G. Olmstead, March 3, 1855.
36. Eliphalet Nott, *First Lessons in Composition: or a help to young writers.* 6th ed. (New York, 1848) An edition titled, "Help to Young Writers" (1836), is in the New York State Library, Albany, New York.
37. Nott, *First Lessons,* p. 103.
38. John Howard Payne, editor, *The Pastime,* published while he was a student at Union College in 1807. Issue for Saturday, February 28, 1807, p. 16. The *Pastime* was probably the first undergraduate publication in an American college. See: Ernest Earnest, *Academic Procession* (New York 1953), p. 95.
39. A. W. Read, "The Membership in Proposed American Academies," *American Literature,* vol. 7 (1935), pp. 145–165. The New York State members of the "American Academy of Language and Belles Lettres" (1821) were: General John Armstrong, DeWitt Clinton, James Kent, Washington Irving, Eliphalet Nott, John W. Taylor, James R. Wilson.

4. The "philosopher of caloric"

1. Martin Van Buren Burt (Union, 1838), Diary, owned by Mr. and Mrs. Richard Wright, 311 Montgomery Street, Syracuse, N.Y.
2. William John Keep, "History of Heating Apparatus," (presented to the Business Historical Library at Harvard University by Helen E. Keep); microfilm at Union College, p. 284. William Keep graduated from Union College in 1865, became an expert metallurgist, and was for many years an engineer with the Michigan Stove Company. His manuscript history of the development of stoves in America is one of the most valuable and accurate sources of information on the subject. In 1865 Dr. Nott gave him what seems to have been his experimental model of the Saracenic Stove; it was tagged and left

at the college until 1893 when it was claimed by Mr. Keep and later exhibited at the Chicago World's Fair. It is now in the Henry Ford collection at Dearborn, Michigan.

3. *The Great Industries of the United States* (Hartford, Conn., 1872), p. 442. (A compilation).

4. Eliphalet Nott to the Reverend Mark Tucker, n.d., in Van Santvoord *Memoirs*, p. 239.

5. W. J. Keep, quoted in the Union College *Alumni Monthly*, by the editor, C. N. Waldron; here appears a complete list of Eliphalet Nott's patents, the first of which is dated February 3, 1819. Union College *Alumni Monthly*, Vol. 18 (1928–1929), pp. 15-17.

6. Schenectady *Cabinet*, November 22, 1820.

7. H. N. Evenson, *The First Century and a Quarter of the American Coal Industry* (Pittsburg, 1942). A very full history and statistical study of both the bituminous and anthracite production in America.

8. G. R. Howell and J. Tenney eds., *The Bicentennial History of Albany, N. Y.* (New York 1886), p. 470.

9. New York State Assembly Journal, March 7, 1814, p. 238.

10. H. N. Evenson, *Coal Industry*, p. 141.

11. *Ibid.*, p. 601.

12. *Ibid.*, p. 144.

13. *Ibid.*, p. 149.

14. *Miners' Journal* (Pottsville, Pa.) February 13, 1833.

15. H. N. Evenson, *Coal Industry*, pp. 429-431 (Table 20).

16. Jonathan Pearson, Diary, April 27, 1859.

17. D. G. Littlefield, *History of the Base Burning Stove* (1859) (pamphlet) quoted in W. J. Keep, "Heating Apparatus," pp. 266–267. Keep notes the continuing high regard for Nott's stove even though Keep himself felt Nott's ideas were outmoded in the decade before the Civil War: "In 1854, Mr. Littlefield tells us, he saw Dr. Nott's stove and became so impressed by it that he abandoned his own ideas and constructed a stove according to Dr. Nott's ideas which he called 'The Railroad Coal Burner', and which was made on royalties by Erastus Corning and Co. of Albany, New York. This stove was patented March 21, 1856" (p. 287).

18. R. L. Rusk, *The Letters of Ralph Waldo Emerson*, I (New York, 1939), p. 342.

19. Austin A. Yates, *Schenectady County, New York: Its History to the Close of the Nineteenth Century* (New York, 1902), pp. 166–167. See also S. Roberts, *Old Schenectady*, (Schenectady, n.d.,), p. 151: "The rolling stock of the road in 1839, consisted of 24 coaches called "gothic," with a seating capacity of twenty passengers each. These cost about $800 each. There were fifteen other coaches for passengers of a plainer style."

20. Howell and Tenney eds., *Bicentennial History*, p. 567.

21. See file, "Benjamin Nott, Union 1823," in Union Alumni Office.

22. Joel Munsell, *Annals of Albany*, IX (Albany, 1858), pp. 267–268: entry headed "Notes from the newspapers, 1833."

23. Howell and Tenney eds., *Bicentennial History*, section titled "History of Schenectady." p. 134.

24. Douglas Cain to the author, July 15, 1964.

25. Advertisement, Benedict and Roby: "The subscribers, agents for Messrs Nott & Co., offer for sale at their store a generous assortment of Anthracite Stoves, constructed on the principles laid down by Dr. Nott. . . . at from 30 to 45 dollars each." The Albany *Argus*, March 20, 1830; Advertisement of H. Nott and Company, "of the Union

Furnace. . . . manufacturers of Dr. Nott's Patent stoves and grates, for burning anthracite coal. . . ." The Schenectady *Cabinet*, May 18, 1831; in 1832 a second-hand stove (Dr. Nott's Patent) was sold by the executor of the estate of William James, one used "in the office of the testator," for twenty-eight dollars; the Schenectady *Whig* for June 15, 1834, carried a long paragraph describing in glowing terms the advantages of Dr. Nott's "New Bake Stove . . . which bids fair to succeed the common stove for culinary purposes . . . its superiority consists . . . in its taking not a quarter of the fuel [of the older stoves]." In 1839, three years after Howard and Benjamin Nott had lost control of H. Nott and Company, Stratton and Seymour, as their successors, were advertising "Dr. Nott's Patent Compound Spiculated Brick . . . the ultimatum of all inventions for the burning of anthracite coal; they are designed especially for Nott's coal stoves, and when used in them form a solid and durable furnace and air chamber . . . which radiates a quick and powerful heat, and gives to these stoves advantages no other coal stove possesses. A great variety of new and beautiful patterns, combining the above improvements, with Nott's new and splendid radiators, and now offered to the public. Those persons now having Nott's stoves in use can have either, or both the durable brick and radiators applied to them. . . ." New York *Commercial Advertiser*, October 14, 1839. Another advertisement by Stratton and Seymour for the "Saracenic Stove with Radiators . . . to be used in Halls, Reading and Assembly Rooms, Stores, etc., where but little pipe can be used. . . ." appeared in the New York *Morning Herald*, October 23, 1839.

For changing coal prices, see: H. N. Evenson, *Coal Industry*, and the *Miners' Journal* (Pottsville, Pa.), February 14, 1835.

26. *A Century of Progress: The History of the Delaware and Hudson Company, 1823–1923* (Albany, 1925), p. 61.

27. *Ibid.*, pp. 41-42.

28. H. N. Evenson, *Coal Industry*, pp. 429–430 (Table 20).

29. R. L. Rusk, ed., *Letters. . . . of Ralph Waldo Emerson*, I (N. Y. 1939), p. 342.

30. *Ibid.*, p. 105.

31. J. L. Bishop, *Early American Manufacturers*, II (Philadelphia, 1868), p. 371; see also Earl J. Heydinger (Hopewell Village National Historic Site) to "Stove History Department," Union College (March 14, 1960), and reply of "Professor F. L. Bronner of our Stove History Department" [sic], Eliphalet Nott file, Union College Alumni Office.

32. Award of the Referees, in the suit of Eliphalet Nott Against James Wilson, in the Court of the United States, May 28, 1834, and signed: A. Spencer, John Woodworth, Joseph Curtis.

33. Dinah Brown, *The New York Times Magazine*, March 11, 1962, p. 78. The article includes the Schussele picture, and an identification of the nineteen "Men of Progress" he represented in his canvas.

34. Dorothy C. Barck, ed., *Letters from John Pintard to His Daughter, Eliza Noel Pintard Davidson*, IV (New York, 1941, pp. 8, 13.

35. "Dr. Nott's stove in the Hospice of St. Bernard," from the New York *American*, reprinted by the Albany Daily *Argus*, July 15, 1833.

36. Eliphalet Nott to George Tibbets, November 4, 1835. Union College Archives.

37. Andrew Reed, D.D., and James Metheson, D.D., *Narrative of the Visit to the American Churches by the Deputation from the Congregational Union of England and Wales* (New York, 1835), p. 651.

38. Oliver Wendell Holmes, *Poems* (Boston, 1836). "The Hot Season" was the last poem in the collection, "arranged," the author noted in his preface, "according to the dignity of the subject."

39. Professor Patrick Kilburn to the author, September, 1970.

40. Captain Marryat, touring Canada and the United States in 1837, wrote in his *Diary in America* (New York, 1839), following a visit to the Union College campus: "I had of course heard of Professor [sic] Nott . . . Professor Nott who governed by moral influence and paternal sway, and who had written so largely on stoves and anthracite coal . . . with Professor Nott I had a rather hot argument about anthracite coal, and then escaped before he was cool again. . . . Seriously speaking, Professor Nott is a very clever man, and I suspect this college will turn out more clever men than any other in the Union." (p. 40).

41. Joseph Henry, writing from the Smithsonian Institution on November 14, 1873, said Dr. Nott, "was a man of original thought and of no ordinary inventive power as is evinced by his investigations and inventions in regard to the best means of burning anthracite coal; and in referring to this I may say he was a benefactor of his country by what he taught and the facilities he rendered in the general introduction as an article of domestic fuel, of this refractory but invaluable product." Van Santvoord, *Memoirs*, pp. 376–377.

BOOK FIVE

1. The "House of Yates and McIntyre"

1. The story of the "House of Yates and McIntyre" is developed by Hugh G. Aitken in "Yates and McIntyre, Lottery Managers," *Journal of Economic History* (Winter, 1953). New, essential relationships between Eliphalet Nott and his partners in the New York lotteries continue to emerge, however, as one reads the unprinted correspondence and the voluminous Chancery Court records of the controversies which finally took these men to law in 1834 as bitter enemies. Citations to the court records, and to the several "defenses" printed by the college, by Nott, and by the defendants will be referred to as *Documents* (Union College library number UH_2/ID637).

2. Aitken, "Lottery Managers," pp. 43–44.

3. *Documents*, "The answer of the Trustees of Union College . . . impleaded with Eliphalet Nott . . .," p. 4.

4. *Ibid.*, p. 5.

5. *Documents:* see "No. 12," para. 64 ("No. 12" is a printed and indexed documentary history of the controversy, so numbered and bound in UH_2/ID637). One must be careful to balance these printed documents against correspondence both sides to the controversy were glad to omit from the printed record.

6. *Ibid.*, para. 65.

7. The first evidence that Nott had miscalculated the purposes of his partners developed over the procedure by which the firm was to pay the $322,256.81 due Union College. Yates and McIntyre had originally agreed to pay the sum in ten annual installments, with interest, but the verbally revised contract changed all that; inasmuch as the drawings were now to be concluded in less than ten years, the partners decided to pay into the "College Fund" 8¾ percent and into the "President's Fund" 2¼ percent on the *actual selling price* of the tickets sold in each scheme. The firm, according to Nott, was still to be liable for interest on this money until paid; the only rebates on this interest Yates and McIntyre were to be entitled to were on installments made in anticipation of "schemes" yet to be drawn. John B. Yates especially objected to Nott's

construction of this part of the revised contract (see *Documents,* No. 10, "Joint answer of the Trustees and Eliphalet Nott . . ." paras. 40–41).

Nott's contract concessions were made to encourage Yates and McIntyre to run off the Literature Lottery as rapidly as possible, and with the largest possible profit margins. The original contract restricted the firm to selling tickets at no more than 22 percent advance on the scheme price until within four days of the scheduled drawing, without Nott's permission. The revised contract specifically noted that all extra profits rising from the difference between the scheme price and the actual selling price was to be divided between the college and Yates and McIntyre. Nott even proposed a profit making device which Yates and McIntyre later claimed they reluctantly accepted: tickets could be sold to the amount only of the calculated value of the scheme: Nott concluded that if the firm made up its official schedule for each scheme, first deducting its 15 percent management fee from the sum represented on each scheme for prizes, this percentage "could then be drawn over, and if so, we might divide such advantage between the college and ourselves." (See: *Documents,* "Examination of a Report said to be a report of a select committee of the Trustees of Union College. . . ." p. 26.)

8. H. Yates to J. B. Yates. August 26, 1824, Union College Archives.

9. J. B. Yates to H. Yates. September 1, 1824. Union College Archives.

10. *Documents,* "In Chancery. The joint and several answers of the Trustees of Union College . . . and Eliphalet Nott. . . .," p. 9. para. 41. Nott later explained the sale of "foreign tickets" had been unknown to him, although it had been authorized by Henry Yates, the college treasurer.

11. John Sanders, *Early History of Schenectady,* (Albany, 1879), p. 156. The Welland Canal activity of John B. Yates is given in detail by Hugh G. Aitken in his article in the *Economic Journal* already cited. See also J. P. Merritt, *Biography of the Hon. William Hamilton Merritt* (St. Catherines, Ontario, Canada 1875), and Hugh G. J. Aitken, *W. H. Merritt and the Welland Canal Company* (Harvard University, Ph.D. dissertion, 1951).

12. Aitken, "Lottery Managers," p. 46.

13. *Documents,* "In Chancery. The answer of the Trustees of Union College . . . impleaded with Eliphalet Nott. . . .," p. 7.

14. *Documents,* see "No. 12," Eliphalet Nott to J. B. Yates. (February 27, 1825), paras. 73-78.

15. *Ibid.,* para. 78.

2. *"Lottery No. 3, for 1825"*

1. Schenectady *Cabinet,* vol. XV, No. 767 (March 23, 1825).

2. Archibald McIntyre to Eliphalet Nott, (February 6, 1826), Union College Archives.

3. *Documents,* No. 12, para. 80. Yates and McIntyre to Eliphalet Nott, (January 4, 1826). See: Introduction to Footnotes, preceding chapter. Union College Library, call no. UH_2/ID 637; the twelve documents bound under this call number hereafter referred to as *Documents.*

4. William James to John B. Yates. (August 20, 1825). Union College Archives.

5. Jabez Hammond, *The History of Political Parties in the State of New York,* II (1842), p. 274.

6. Palmer Canfield, *Petition to the New York State Legislature* (August, 1824), New York Public Library, Pamphlet, *Circular Concerning Lotteries.*

7. *Documents,* No. 12, paras. 228a and 229a-229b; also No. 9, p. 6. Union College Library, call no. UH_2/ID 637.

8. *Ibid.*, No. 12, para. 80.

9. *Ibid.*, No. 12, First written Stipulation, January 24, 1826, paras. 94–95. Future disagreements were seeded in the final paragraph of this "Stipulation" in which the matter of "contingent residue" of unsold tickets, subject to a new contract, was cited as "verbally settled between the parties. . . ."

10. *Ibid.*, No. 12, para. 82.

11. *Ibid.*, No. 11, "Examination of a Report Professing to be a report of a Select Committee of the Trustees of Union College in relation to the Pending Controversy with Yates and McIntyre," printed by order of the Committee of Finance, to whom the same was referred at a meeting of the Board, Nov. 24, 1834. "Mr. H. Yates proposed, for the sake of conciliation, to unite with the Albany people, and aid in procuring the law for their relief. He drew the act . . . ," p. 36.

12. *Documents Relating to the Union College Lottery Controversy*, 12 pamphlets. Union College Library, call No. UH₂/ID637.

13. *Documents*, No. 11. Hereafter referred to as "Examination. . . ."

14. *Documents*, No. 12, para. 82.

15. William James to John B. Yates, (August 20, 1825), Union College Archives.

16. Eliphalet Nott to Archibald McIntyre. (February 1, 1826); see also Archibald McIntyre to Eliphalet Nott. (February 6, 1826). James returned the college's securities to Henry Yates, December 4, 1832. Union College Archives.

17. Eliphalet Nott to Henry Yates, Jr., (January 12, 1826), Union College Archives.

18. John B. Yates to Eliphalet Nott. (January 17, 1826), *Documents*, para. 83.

19. *Documents*, No. 12, para. 118.

20. Lottery broadside, "J. J. Lansing office, 47 State Street, Albany, N.Y., January 23, 1826." New-York Historical Society (SY/1826/34).

21. Hammond, *History*, I, pp. 427, 507.

22. Archibald McIntyre to Eliphalet Nott. (January 23, 1826), *Documents*, No. 12, para. 86.

23. John B. Yates to Eliphalet Nott. (January 23, 1826), *Documents*, No. 12, para. 90.

24. H. K. Hockschild, *The MacIntyre Mine* (Adirondack Museum, Blue Mountain Lake, N.Y., 1962), p. 3. McIntyre, during the winter of 1826, kept Lewis Elijah, the Indian guide who had discovered the iron deposit which was to become the profitable MacIntyre [sic] Mine, incommunicado, in New York City, in order to prevent the mine's location from leaking out.

25. *Documents*, No. 12, para. 92; see also "Joint Answer of the Trustees . . . and Eliphalet Nott . . .," pp. 11, 29, in *Documents*, No. 10.

26. *Ibid.*, No. 10, p. 36.

27. *Ibid.*, No. 10, p. 37; Yates and McIntyre also noted: "We have since learned with some surprise that the President boasts that he procured it to be stricken out." p. 36.

28. *Ibid.*, No. 10, p. 36.

29. "Case submitted for the opinion of Thomas J. Oakley, Esq., in May, 1826," signed by Oakley May 11, 1826. Union College Archives. Here Yates and McIntyre review the history of the Literature Lottery Act of 1822, the Fever Hospital Act of 1823 (by which the State was compensated for its losses in the earlier failure of N. Judah, New York City lottery dealer, by a payment of $40,000 by New York City in return for the grant), and the Albany Land Lottery. Among Yates and McIntyre's queries presented to Oakley were the following: 1) What are the firm's "relative rights" under the Consolidated Bill of 1826 *vis à vis* the "literary institutions," i.e., Union College? 2) Can

the "literary institutions" have the benefits of the new bill without the assent of Yates and McIntyre, who are the sole proprietors of the Fever Hospital and Albany Land Lotteries? 3) If the Literature Lottery is completed before any land and money prizes are mixed will its grantees have any further authority over Yates and McIntyre? 4) If the Literature Lottery is completed before the time allowed by the State has run out can its grantees still prohibit the drawing of the Fever Hospital lottery? A separate opinion was requested on the problem which was especially bothering the contractors: Does not the Consolidated Lottery Bill, they asked, permit the drawing of the Fever Hospital grant *concurrently* with the drawing of the Literature Lottery and the Albany Land Lottery?

To this last query T. J. Oakley agreed that the new law declared that "no arrangement shall be made under that act which shall prevent the closing of all existing grants. Within that time Yates and McIntyre and the grantees of the Literature Lottery could at their discretion mix the prizes . . . the only ground on which they *must* meet." It is here, of course, that Nott's substitution of his own name for that of Henry Yates as the person who will agree or not to the mixing of prizes (as indicated in the Consolidated Lottery Bill) became vital to Yates and McIntyre.

30. "Examination," p. 37.

31. *Ibid.*, p. 38.

32. *Documents*, No. 6, "Report of a Select Committee of the Trustees of Union College in Relation to the Pending Controversy with Yates and McIntyre. Printed by the Committee on Finance, to whom the same was referred at a meeting of the Board, Nov. 24, 1834," p. 3.

33. *Documents*, No. 10, "In Chancery, The Joint and Several Answers of the Trustees of Union College . . . and Eliphalet Nott . . . to the Bill of Complaint . . . ," filed September 18, 1835., p. 13. Here Nott testifies that the provisions of the "second stipulation . . . were examined with great care and deliberation, especially by A. McIntyre. . . ."

34. "Documents," No. 12, para. 111.

35. *Ibid.*, Eliphalet Nott to Yates and McIntyre. (June 10, 1826), para. 117.

36. "Examination," p. 37.

37. The firm of Yates and McIntyre promoted lotteries in New Jersey, Pennsylvania, Delaware, Rhode Island, North and South Carolina, Virginia, and the District of Columbia before the moral outrage of the 1830s began to curtail their operations. See J. S. Ezell, *Fortune's Merry Wheel*, (Cambridge, Mass., 1960), Chapter xi, pp. 204-230.

38. N. B. Sylvester, *History of Saratoga County* (New York, 1878), p. 120.

39. "Examination," p. 32.

40. Ezell, pp. 170–171. This lottery, run off after Jefferson's death, proved to be a failure.

3. *"On a Magazine of Powder!"*

1. *Documents*, No. 12: Henry Yates to Eliphalet Nott, (December 15, 1826), para. 119.

2. *Ibid.*, No. 8, "In Chancery . . .: Yates and McIntyre vs. Trustees of Union College and Eliphalet Nott, (August 12, 1834)," para. 32a.

3. *Ibid.*, No. 12: "Summary: Literature and Land Lottery Consolidated, 2nd Period," para. 170.

4. *Ibid.*, No. 12: para. 229.

5. *Ibid.*, No. 12: John B. Yates to Eliphalet Nott, (September 26, 1828), para. 178.

6. Eliphalet Nott to Archibald McIntyre, (July 19, 1828). See draft as printed in *Documents*, No. 12: paras. 172-176; also draft of this date, differing in essentials, in Union College Archives.

7. *Documents*, No. 8, p. 26, paras. 33-34.

8. *Ibid.*, No. 12: John B. Yates to Eliphalet Nott. (September 29, 1834), paras. 187-191; also para. 217.

9. *Ibid.*, No. 12: paras. 396-98; 402-6; 408-11. See W. H. Seward *Autobiography*, F. W. Seward, ed., (New York, 1877) (February 6, 1831), p. 179.

10. H. Aitken, "Yates and McIntyre Lottery Managers," *Journal of Economic History* (Winter, 1953), p. 40.

11. *Documents*, No. 12: John B. Yates to Eliphalet Nott. ("Received Nov. 28, 1828"), para. 220; also para. 127.

12. *Ibid.*, No. 12: Yates and McIntyre to Eliphalet Nott. (January 13, 1829), paras. 232-239.

13. *Ibid.*, No. 12: Archibald McIntyre to Eliphalet Nott. (December 22, 1829), para. 307.

14. *Documents*, No. 7: "The Examination," 1835, pp. 41-42.

15. *Ibid.*, p. 41.

16. *Documents*, No. 12: Archibald McIntyre to Eliphalet Nott. (February 15, 1832), para. 476; see Nott's revised figures, paras. 483-484.

17. *Ibid.*, No. 12: Henry Yates to Eliphalet Nott. (July 4, 1829), paras. 254-255.

18. *Documents*, No. 10: p. 28, para. 137.

19. *Ibid.*, No. 12, para. 265.

20. *Ibid.*, No. 12, paras. 266-268.

21. New York State Legislature: Act of April 3, 1831, Chap. 273, p. 342; also *Documents* No. 12, para. 439.

22. *Documents*, No. 7: "The Examination," p. 42.

23. *Documents*, No. 12, 27, April 1832.

24. *Ibid.*, April 28, 1832.

25. Yates and McIntyre, on July 15, 1830, forwarded what, in the *Documents*, is termed the "Fifth Written Stipulation," a new agreement whereby the "House" was to pay Nott five percent instead of the previous 6 31/100 percent of the gross amount of lottery tickets sold, payment to be made ninety days after the drawing of each class, and a payment in Albany Lands of one-half "of those that may fall into our hands," instead of the previous land payment of 6 31/100 percent of the Albany property Yates and McIntyre had had to take from winners.

Nott later declared that he did not reply to this letter containing the "Fifth Stipulation" and that the "Fourth Stipulation" was never given up. (*Documents*, No. 12, para. 380.) Nott declared his agreement to accept the five percent return and to permit it to be paid ninety days after the drawing was a verbal one made with Mr. McIntyre, and that the "Fifth Stipulation" included the unwarranted change in the Albany Land payments. (*Documents*, No. 12, para. 374.)

26. *Documents*, No. 12, May 15, 1832.

27. *Ibid.*, December 20, 1832.

28. *Ibid.*, Silas Wright to Yates and McIntyre. (December 26, 1832).

29. *Ibid.*, Silas Wright to Eliphalet Nott. (January 15, 1833).

30. *Ibid.*, Henry Yates to Eliphalet Nott. (December 31, 1832).

31. Eliphalet Nott, "MS. No. 27," Union College Archives. (See: Folder: "Lotteries-Accounts and Statements, 1804–1830"): Here, in a memorandum in Nott's hand, are his figures for the Union College–Yates and McIntyre settlement of August 1, 1828. His explanation of special payments to the "President's Fund" to this date are revealing:

"for payment of the prize in 'No. 3 for 1825' ... in consideration of personal responsibilities to be assumed by the President and Treasurer of Union College in order to sustain the contractors in the furtherance of their contract ... balance taken by the President as per special stipulation for responsibilities assumed on behalf of managers ... $75,140.87. ... notes above referred to [including $62,243.02 Nott then reported as belonging to Union College] ... are deposited in the Mohawk Bank (in a red box) as the property of the President of Union College."

32. *Documents*, No. 12, Henry Yates to Eliphalet Nott, (January 2, 1833).

33. Union College Trustees' *Minutes*, July 31, 1831; see also J. C. Spencer's *Argument* (Albany, N. Y., 1853), Appendix XXI, pp. 36-44.

34. *Documents*, No. 6, "Report of a Select Committee. . . ." (November 24, 1834), p. 11.

35. Spencer, *Argument*, Appendix, XXVII (November 15, 1838), p. 50.

36. *Documents*, No. 8, "In Chancery ... Archibald McIntyre (etc.) vs. Union College Trustees ... and Eliphalet Nott ... ," (filed August 12, 1834), paras. 34c, 34d, 35.

4. *"Matters of Discovery, specific performance, fraud account . . ."*

1. *Documents*, No. 7; "Examination," pp. 4–6.

2. "Demurrer," Yates and McIntyre's reply to the Nott-Union College Bill in Chancery. (May 26, 1834), (n.d.) Union College Archives, p. 47.

3. Eliphalet Nott-Union College answer to Yates and McIntyre's "Demurrer," Fall, 1834, by M. T. Reynalds. Union College Archives.

4. "Examination," p. 7.

5. *Ibid.*, p. 3.

6. *Ibid.*, December 3, 1834, pp. 11–12.

7. *Ibid.*, December 7, 1834, pp. 11–12.

8. "Questions for Counsel," in the handwriting of Archibald McIntyre, (1834), para. 36, Union College Archives.

9. "Examination," December 19, 1834, pp. 12–13.

10. *Ibid.*, January 6, 1835, pp. 12–13.

11. *Ibid.*, January 19, 1835, p. 5.

12. Jabez Hammond, *The History of Political Parties in the State of New York*, II, (New York, 1842). See this volume for the record of a reporter personally associated with this political history.

13. Hammond, *History*, II, p. 448.

14. The "amended bill" of January 6, 1835 is included as "No. 9" in *Documents*; Yates and McIntyres' answer to it of May 16, 1835 is here derived from Nott's and the Trustees' reply to their bill; dated September 8, 1835, this last bill filed in the Chancery Court Suits, is included as "No. 10" in *Documents*.

15. Hammond, *History*, II, p. 430.

16. David McAdam, *History of the Bench and Bar of New York*, I (New York, 1897), p. 439.

17. Alonzo Paige, *Reports of the Cases in the Court of Chancery*, 2 vols. (New York, 1830–1848). The Literature Lottery suits are not mentioned.

18. *Documents*, No. 9, January 6, 1835, para. 23.

19. "Memorandum for Mr. Spencer," (n.d.), Union College Archives.

20. *Ibid*: The Comptroller's books, according to John B. Yates, showed that Nott in 1822 had illegally added two large sums not intended by the Comptroller to be included

in the figures on which the computation of tickets still to be drawn in the Literature Lottery, $4,492,800, had been determined. This figure, Yates assured Spencer, had first been incorrectly inflated by $143,344 in tickets to cover two "schemes" the Comptroller had neglected to include in his accounts of drawings held by the State's managers over the preceding five years. To this first "extortion" Yates then charged that Nott had added another $660,000 to cover the value of those tickets which had been drawn in the Owego Lottery of 1817, but which had been omitted in the Comptroller's accounts. The Doctor, if Yates's "Memorandum" was correct, had padded the figures the lottery contractors had trustingly accepted as the basis for determining the Literature Lottery contract of 1822 by $803,344.

If this had been the end of the so-called extortion by Nott one suspects the contractors would have accepted it, for they, too, stood to profit by the sale of those unauthorized tickets. John Yates's outrage, however, peaked to boiling when he reviewed the effect of this so-called fraud of 1822 on what he assured Spencer was the even worse extortion of 1826, when Nott and Yates and McIntyre consolidated the Literature Lottery with the Albany Land Lottery and the Fever Hospital Lottery owned by the "House." Their "second written stipulation," signed on May 30, 1826, had established the "rights" of Union College, and of the contractors in the future profits of the consolidated lotteries, and from the contractors' point of view, had turned into an evil not to be tolerated: its whole arithmetic was false, according to Yates, for it had been constructed in large part on the basis of these inflated figures the Doctor had supplied in 1822.

Under the "Second Written Stipulation" of 1826, Yates pointed out to Spencer, the profits from the consolidated lotteries were to be divided pro rata—according to the interest the "House" and the college each had in their respective lotteries. Because Nott, it was claimed, had distorted the college's interest by almost a million dollars in 1822, the contractors had paid the college 6 31/100 percent interest on the lottery profits after 1826, when, in fact, the college should have received no more than 3 percent to November 10, 1827, when the Literature Lottery drawings were completed, and the college's interests in the affairs of Yates and McIntyre were at an end, or so Yates and Oakley had believed.

John B. Yates reviewed what he reported to Spencer was Nott's illegal maneuvering for advantage in 1828, when, according to Yates, he inflated the figures he used then to settle the Literature Lottery contract by $456,391, a deception which, joined to those the Doctor had already practised, swelled the unauthorized sale of tickets for the benefit of Union College to a grand total of $1,259,735. By this series of "extortions" which had progressively increased the obligations of the "House," "it appears," Yates declared to Spencer, "that an attempt was made [by Nott] to arrange proportions for [his] future operations under the privilege of the Albany Law [The Consolidated Lottery Act of 1826] pursuant to what the Doctor calls a verbal arrangement. . . ."

Yates's innocuous phrase, "a verbal arrangement" pointed directly to the heart of the Chancery Suits, to that elastic "Second Written Stipulation" which in 1829 and again in 1830 was reborn and rewritten by the Doctor, a monument to sharp practice, if Yates is to be believed. By having arranged the "proportions" Nott was able to force the contractors to pay him 6 31/100 percent on the profits on their own lotteries when, Yates wrote in the Memorandum, Nott's profits, on a final accounting, "should have been, perhaps, no more than one or two percent." On the strength of this rewritten and backdated "Second Stipulation" of May 31, 1826, the Doctor, according to the contractors, had not only substituted himself for the college as the beneficiary, but was now suing them for the recovery of an additional large sum [Nott estimated it at $300,000] to be paid to him "in his individual capacity."

21. In Chancery . . . Yates and McIntyre vs. Union College and Eliphalet Nott. ms. (April 17, 1835), Union College Archives.

22. *Documents*, No. 10, para. 23.

23. *Ibid.*, para. 26.

24. *Ibid.*, para. 101.

5. *The Tri-Partite Agreement*

1. *Documents*, paras. 120 and 124.

2. *Ibid.*, para. 20.

3. John C. Spencer, *Argument*, (Albany, 1853), "Appendix," p. 67.

4. *Ibid.*, "Appendix," p. 73.

5. *Documents*, No. 10, para. 18.

6. *Ibid.*, para. 164.

7. *Ibid.*, para. 41.

8. *Ibid.*, para. 84.

9. *Ibid.*, para. 105; also Spencer, *Argument*, "Appendix," p. 98.

10. Richard B. Morris, "Reuben Hyde Walworth," *Dictionary of American Biography*, XIX (1936), pp. 406–07.

11. *Ibid.*

12. Tribute to the Hon. J. B. Yates, Daily Albany *Argus*, August 31, 1836.

13. J. B Merritt, *Biography of William Hamilton Merritt* (St. Catherines, Ontario, Canada, 1875), p. 162.

14. Reuben Walworth, "At a court of Chancery held for the State of New York at the City of Albany on the 8th day of January, one thousand eight hundred and thirty six." The Chancellor's ruling, made following John B. Yates's death on July 10, 1836, is so attested by James Porter, Register of the Chancery Court, Union College Archives.

15. J. C. Spencer, "Remarks on Chancellor's Opinion," Union College Archives.

16. Archibald McIntyre, "Statement of October 12, 1836," J. C. Spencer Papers, Union College Archives.

17. *Ibid.*, last page.

18. Spencer, *Argument*, "Appendix," pp. 51–88.

19. In 1833 Attorney General Bronson declared that the Owego Lottery was improperly allowed in the Deputy-Comptroller's certificate of 1823; see Spencer, *Argument*, "Appendix," p. 49.

20. *Ibid.*, p. 68, para. 296.

21. *Ibid.*, pp. 91–94; also p. 48.

22. *Ibid.*, p. 48.

BOOK SIX

1. *Captain Neziah Bliss: Steamboats and Real Estate*

1. Jonathan Pearson. *Diary* (April 27, 1859), Union College Archives.

2. *Ibid.*, April 27, 1859.

3. Cuyler Reynolds, *Albany Chronicles* (Albany, 1906), p. 425.

4. J. H. Morrison, *History of American Steam Navigation* reprint ed. (New York, 1958), pp. 407–408; Ralph N. Hill, *Sidewheeler Saga* (New York, 1953), p. 84.

5. *One Hundred Years of Progress of the United States* (Hartford, Conn., 1877), p. 241.

6. *History of the Delaware and Hudson Company* (Albany, 1925), pp. 41–42.

7. *Ibid.*, pp. 71–72.

8. Eliphalet Nott, "Steam Boilers and Furnaces for Boats," U. S. Patent Office, April 22, 1835; also, "Steam Generator," March 9, 1836. See: Union College Archives for subject heading "Dr. Nott's Inventions," for miscellaneous drawings and patents, specifications, etc., for stoves, boilers, and steam engines.

9. Benjamin Nott, testimony, New York State Legislative Investigation into the affairs of Union College, 1849–1853, given on September, 14, 1853. Union College Archives.

10. Albany *Argus*, December 11, 1829, speaks of "an unfinished boat . . . at the foot of Hamilton Street . . . built at Hyde Park by William Brown, and [it] has a round stem [sic] . . ."; Morrison, *American Steam Navigation*, p. 53, states that the boat was built by Chauncey Goodrich, at Hyde Park, N. Y.

11. Benjamin Nott, Testimony (September 14, 1853).

12. *Ibid.*

13. Joel B. Nott to Mrs. Charles Cooper, London. (November, 20, 1830). Union College Archives; Joel Nott, after notifying Joseph C. Yates of his plan to take a leave of absence from the College, sailed for England with his family on the 24th of August 1830.

14. Neziah Bliss, Testimony, New York State Investigation into the affairs of Union College: *Senate Document* No. 68, April 8, 1853, pp. 3–9.

15. Benjamin Nott, Testimony (September 14, 1853).

16. Neziah Bliss, Testimony, *Senate Document* No. 68, p. 4.

17. *Ibid.*, p. 4.

18. D. L. Buckman, *Old Steamboat Days on the Hudson* (New York, 1907), p. 54. *Appleton's Cyclopedia* (Vol. V., p. 673) states that John Stevens "patented the multi-tubular boiler" in 1803, and, according to the same source (Vol. 11, p. 364), that R. L. Stevens developed the "first marine tubular steam boiler" in 1831, "and was among the first to use anthracite coal." Again, the same source notes, however, (Vol. 11, p. 364) that John Erickson developed the tubular steam boiler about 1827. There seems little doubt that Nott was experimenting with anthracite for marine use as early as 1826, and that by 1831 his experiments with hard coal were well enough known to prompt Thurlow Weed to write that Nott's success with anthracite on steamboats "had opened ocean travel to steam navigation . . . ." See: Thurlow Weed, *Autobiography*, I (1884), p. 387.

19. James Brewster, "Eliphalet Nott as a Steamboat Owner and Builder," Union College Alumni *Monthly*, vol. 24 (1936), pp. 48–52. Much new material relating to the "Novelty" has become available since Brewster wrote his article.

20. Eliphalet Nott to Clarkson Nott Potter. (June 10, 1831), Union College Archives.

21. "Howard Nott and Company, Stove Mfgs.," according to the New York City *Directory* for 1831–1832, was located at 235 Water Street; the *Directory* for 1833–34 lists the company as being at 242 Water Street; in 1838–1839 their address is listed as "Twelfth, n. Dry Dock," which is also the address given for the "novelty works." The "Novelty Works" is first listed in the New York City *Directory* for 1833–1834, under the heading for "Thomas B. Stillman" who succeeded Captain Neziah Bliss as Eliphalet Nott's superintendent. By 1839 the *Directory* lists "Thomas B. Stillman, novelty works, 12th; house, 101 Avenue D," and for 1842–1843, "Stillman & Co., steam engine mfgs., and Iron Foundryers, Novelty Works, foot of 12th & 13th sts., on the East River, office 242 Water St." In the Directory for 1843–1844 the listing is for Thomas B. Stillman, with whom are associated R. M. Stratton and Charles B. Seymour.

22. Neziah Bliss, Testimony, *N. Y. State, Senate Document No. 68*, (April 8, 1853), p. 5.

23. H. R. Stiles, in the *Memorial History of the City of New York*, (ed. by J. Grant Wilson), N.Y. 1893, 4 vols. vol. IV. pp. 1–26; also H. R. Stiles, *A History of the City of Brooklyn*, II (Brooklyn, 1863), pp. 410–411. See also E. L. Armbruster, *Brooklyn's Eastern District* (Brooklyn, 1942) pp. 38–199.

24. Neziah Bliss, Senate *Document No. 68*, p. 10; see also: *Stuyvesant Cove, Report and Documents*, 1825–1831 (N.Y. 1832).

25. J. C. Spencer, *Argument*, (Albany, 1853), "Appendix," p. 74.

26. *Ibid.*, "Appendix," pp. 75–76; see also, *Senate Document No. 68*, p. 13.

27. Albany *Argus*, April 28, 1832; see also: Eliphalet Nott to the Directors of the Hudson River Association, (n.d.) *ca.* spring, 1833, Union College Archives.

2. *"Coal mountains into gold mountains."*

1. W. C. Redfield, "Notice of American Steamboats," *American Journal of Science*, XXIII (1833), p. 317.

2. *Ibid.*, 317.

3. Eliphalet Nott to the Directors of the Hudson River Association (spring, 1833), two rough drafts for letters in the Union College Archives.

4. James Brewster, "Eliphalet Nott as a Steamboat Owner and Builder," Union College *Alumni Monthly*, vol. 24 (1936), p. 50.

5. *History of the Delaware and Hudson Company* (Albany, 1925), p. 97.

6. G. Howell and J. Tenney eds., *History of the County of Albany* (New York, 1886), p. 489.

7. Eliphalet Nott to R. P. Hart. (October 9, 1834) Union College Archives.

8. Cuyler Reynolds, *Albany Chronicles* (Albany, 1906), p. 512.

9. E. M. Stone, "The Novelty," *Reflector and Democrat*, Schenectady, July 8, 1836.

10. Miners' *Journal* (Pottsville, Pa.), March 28, 1835, reprinted the article on the *Essex* as it appeared in the *Journal of Commerce* on March 18, 1835.

11. Miners' *Journal*, March 28, 1835.

12. *Ibid.*, April 18, 1835. Copied from Poulson's American *Daily Advertiser*, April 11, 1835.

13. Delaware and Hudson Canal Company: Company "Reports," 1835, p. 6n.

14. United States Patent Office: April 22, 1835, "Steamboilers and Furnaces for Boats"; March 9, 1836, "Steam Generator." Drawings and specifications for these developments are in the Union College Archives, prepared by Edward James. Edward James testified in 1853 that he had been long employed by Dr. Nott in preparing his papers for patents, and that he had been "in charge of the business of H. Nott and Company," presumably in the capacity of an accountant. (see Edward James's testimony before the New York State Legislative Committee investigating the affairs of Union College: J. C. Spencer, *Argument* (Albany, 1853), "Appendix," p. 39.)

15. Fox's Brick Moulder: Patent for this moulder was bought by Nott in 1831. Union College Archives.

16. Delaware and Hudson Canal Company: "Reports," March 1, 1836, p. 7.

17. F. E. Dayton, *Steamboat Days on the Hudson* (New York, 1925), p. 382; Albany *Evening Journal*, June 24, 1836.

18. New York *American*, June 29, 1836.

19. Miners' *Journal*, (Pottsville, Pa.) July 2, 1836. The Miners' *Journal* reprinted this letter as "From the Phila. *Enquirer*, N.Y., June 15, 1836." This same letter,

however, appears in the New York *American* on June 29, 1836, where it is offered as a first-hand account of the *Novelty's* trip of June 23, 1836, "by a writer of the Philadelphia *Enquirer*, who was also a passenger. . . ."

20. Allan Nevins ed., Philip Hone, *Diary of Philip Hone, 1780–1851*. 2 V. (New York, 1927), Entry for June 23, 1836.

21. Schenectady *Reflector and Democrat*, July 8, 1836.

22. Benjamin Nott to Erastus Corning. (April 4, 1836), Union College Archives.

23. Wheaton J. Lane, *Commodore Vanderbilt* (New York, 1942), p. 60. An excellent review of the operations of the Hudson River Association and its competitors.

24. H. Nott and Co., "Second Overture" to Delaware and Hudson Canal Co. (November, 1836), Union College Archives.

25. Jonathan Pearson, Diary. (March 31, 1840), Union College Archives.

26. Cuyler Reynolds, *Albany Chronicles* (Albany, 1906), p. 541.

27. D. L. Buchman, *Old Steamboat Days on the Hudson River* (New York, 1907), p. 55.

28. John H. Morrison, *History of American Steam Navigation* (New York, 1958), p. 159.

29. Ralph N. Hill, *Sidewheeler Saga* (New York, 1953), p. 101.

30. Research has not turned up an authenticated picture of the S.S. *Novelty*, although the gallery of pictures of Hudson River steamboats in the nineteenth century is a particularly full one. In the Schenectady *Reflector and Democrat* for December 11, 1835, however, is a "View of the City of Albany, from the Opposite Side of the Hudson River," by J. H. Hall, a well-known Albany engraver of woodcuts, in which is depicted a steamboat which fits the descriptions of the *Novelty* as she sailed the river at this time; she was a boat "with four sets of boilers (placed over the paddle wheel guards) . . . and carries also four chimneys," according to W. C. Redfield, the English engineer whose article, "Notice of American Steamboats," appeared in Benjamin Silliman's *American Journal of Science* in 1833, vol. 23. Owing to her horizontal engines there were no walking beams, as there were on two other Hudson River boats which carried four stacks: The *Champlain* (*ca.* 1831–1840) and the *Francis W. Skiddy* (*ca.* 1849–1851): See H. C. Brown, *The Lordly Hudson* (New York, 1937), p. 331.

3. "I am the oldest president in the United States."

1. Edwin David Sanborne ed., "Opinions of the Late Dr. Nott Respecting Books, Studies, and Orators," *Atlantic Monthly*, vol. 20 (1867). Reprinted as a supplement to the Union College Alumni *Monthly*, March, 1933, with a foreword by Codman Hislop and H. A. Larrabee. "Mr. C." has been identified as Ira Clisby of the Union College Class of 1815: see Jonathan Pearson, Diary, vol. 4, pp. 410, 421; also, Van Santvoord, *Memoirs*, p. 249.

2. Jonathan Pearson, Diary. (October 28, 1833), Union College Archives.

3. Eliphalet Nott to Clarkson Nott Potter. (June 10, 1831), Union College Archives.

4. Henry Wikoff, *Reminiscences of an Idler* (New York, 1880), pp. 21–22.

5. C. E. West, *An Address on the Fiftieth Anniversary of the Class of 1832*. Brooklyn, N. Y., 1882, pp. 29–30.

6. Jonathan Pearson, Diary. (March 24, 1837).

7. *Ibid.*, January 17, 1837.

8. J. C. Spencer, *Argument in the Defense of Dr. Nott*, (Albany, 1853), "Appendix," XXV, p. 48.

9. Jonathan Pearson, Diary. (January 30, 1833).

10. C. E. West, *An Address at the Fiftieth Anniversary of the Class of 1832.* Brooklyn, N.Y., 1882, p. 34. Union College Alumni files.

4. "New Schools, new Professorships, new Scholarships . . . and an Observatory . . ."

1. Rev. J. T. Backus, "Funeral Discourse for Eliphalet Nott," (1866), p. 4. Union College Archives.

2. M. A. DeWolfe Howe, *Memoirs of the Life and Services of the Rt. Rev. Alonzo Potter, DD., LL.D., Bishop of the Protestant Episcopal Church in the Diocese of Pennsylvania* (Philadelphia, 1871), p. 90.

3. Eliphalet Nott to Reverend Samuel Nott. (March 19, 1839), Union College Archives.

4. Howe, *Memoirs*, p. 92.

5. *Ibid.*, pp. 92–93, 98.

6. *Ibid.*, p. 98.

7. Van Santvoord, *Memoirs, passim.*

8. Joel B. Nott, married to Margaret Taylor, adopted daughter of Lieutenant Governor John Taylor and daughter of Dr. Charles D. Cooper of Albany, following his return from London sometime before April 6, 1836, when the Albany newspapers note that he and his associates had opened subscription books for "The Albany Tunnel Company." He appears to have established himself first in Bethlehem, N.Y., where he was known as "Judge Nott"; he was apparently active in Albany County politics, and appears frequently on the college treasurer's books as a borrower of college funds and as a representative in real estate transactions for his father and for Bishop Alonzo Potter. See his "Obituary," New York *World*, May 24, 1878, which reviews his intimate association with New York City politics after the Civil War.

The Reverend John Nott's reputation among undergraduates is given highly imaginative treatment by the student editors of the *Crucible* in January, 1841, and in the *Insinuator* for 1840, as well as in Pearson's Diary on many occasions (see "John Nott," Pearson Diary index).

Howard Nott, who, with his half-brother, Benjamin Nott, had lost control of the Novelty Iron Works in December, 1836, remained as College Registrar from 1839 through 1843; he, too, seems to have become a gentleman farmer following his mother's death in 1842, when he appears to have moved to Rexford Flats, in Saratoga County, New York.

9. Eliphalet Nott to Governor W. H. Seward. (July 6, 1839), Union College Archives.

10. W. H. Seward, *Autobiography* (New York, 1891), pp. 460–461. See also: E. E. Hale, Jr., *William Henry Seward* (Philadelphia, 1910), pp. 144–148.

11. Hale, *Seward*, p. 145; also John E. W. Pratt, "Governor Seward and the New York City School Controversy, 1840–1842," *New York State History*, XLII, No. 4, (October, 1961), p. 356.

12. Seward, *Autobiography*, p. 461.

13. Pratt, *Seward*, p. 356.

14. *Ibid.*, p. 362.

15. Eliphalet Nott to John C. Spencer. (Feb. 6, 1839), Union College Archives.

16. U. C. Trustees' Minutes, 1839. Figures for the registration in American colleges for 1839 are frequently reprinted from the *American Quarterly Register*, XIII (August,

1840), and can be considered only approximately correct. The *Register* lists the number at Union as 286, when the correct count is 315; R. F. Butts, in *The College Charts Its Course*, (New York, 1907), lists the colleges in 1839 in terms of their enrollment as follows: Yale, 411, Union, 286 [sic]; Virginia, 247; Princeton, 237; Harvard, 216.

17. T. W. Wertenbaker, *Princeton, 1746–1896* (Princeton, 1946). Princeton offers a classic example of a vigorous institution almost destroyed by sectarian enthusiasts who, in the 1830s, elected to take it out of the main stream of American life. See: Wertenbaker, Chapter 7.

5. *The Higher Law*

1. Van Santvoord, *Memoirs*, p. 214.

2. R. B. Nye, *Fettered Freedom, Civil Liberties and the Slavery Controversy, 1830–60.* (East Lansing, Mich., 1949), p. 164.

3. Eliphalet Nott, *Counsels to Young Men*, 2nd ed. (New York, 1842), p. 85.

4. *Ibid.*, pp. 294–297.

5. Eliphalet Nott to John W. Taylor. (November 30, 1825), Union College Archives.

6. Van Santvoord, *Memoirs*, p. 213.

7. Senator William Henry Seward, speech in the U. S. Senate (March 11, 1850), denouncing the Compromise of 1850, in which he called for recognition of a "higher law" than that of the Constitution.

8. Van Santvoord, *Memoirs*, p. 227.

9. *Ibid.*, p. 228.

10. G. R. Howell and J. Tenney, *Bicentennial History of Albany* (New York, 1886), p. 117.

11. Van Santvoord, *Memoirs*, p. 181.

12. William Cooper to Mrs. Joel B. Nott, then in London, England. (1832), Union College Archives.

13. John A. Krout, *The Origins of Prohibition* (New York, 1925), p. 158.

14. *Ibid.*, 163–164.

15. Eliphalet Nott, *Ten Lectures on the Use of Intoxicating Liquors*, The *Enquirer* (ed. Edward C. Delavan), vol. 1, No. 4 (August, 1846).

16. *Ibid.*, p. 149.

17. *Ibid.*, "Lecture No. 6," p. 167.

18. *Ibid.*, p. 169.

19. *Ibid.*, p. 170.

20. Professor Herbert Brown of Bowdoin College to Professor Harold A. Larrabee, and quoted by him in a letter to the author, August 25, 1970. See also Herbert Brown, *The Sentimental Novel in America* (Durham, N.C., 1940), p. 221, n. 89.

21. Eliphalet Nott, *Ten Lectures*, p. 174. See also, Krout, *Prohibition*, p. 229, n. 10 and Van Santvoord, *Memoirs*, pp. 185–188.

22. *Ibid.*, pp. 174–175.

23. Van Santvoord, *Memoirs*, p. 184.

24. *Ibid.*, pp. 184, 187.

25. Eliphalet Nott to Edward C. Delavan. (June 6, 1842), in Delavan's *Enquirer*, vol. 1, No. 2; see also *The Enquirer*, vol. 1, No. 3, for Nott-Delavan correspondence on the Albany Medical College dispute.

26. Reverend J. T. Backus to Reverend John Clancy of Charlton, N.Y. (December 29, 1841), Union College Archives.

27. Ralph V. Harlow, *Gerrit Smith* (New York, 1939), p. 78.

28. Eliphalet Nott to Edward C. Delavan. (August 14, 1855) in Van Santvoord, *Memoirs*, p. 189.

29. Eliphalet Nott to Edward C. Delavan. (September 17, 1855) in Van Santvoord, *Memoirs*, p. 334.

30. Eliphalet Nott to Edward C. Delavan. (n.d. though probably early in 1857) in Van Santvoord, *Memoirs*, p. 336.

31. Eliphalet Nott to Edward C. Delavan. (May 25, 1849 [?]), Union College Archives.

6. *"This College rides, like a ship in full sail, majestic . . ."*

1. W. H. Seward to his wife (May 24, 1842), in, *Autobiography*, (New York., 1891), p. 605.

2. *The First Semi-Centennial Anniversary of Union College. Celebrated July 22, 1845* (Albany, 1845), 186 pp.

3. *Ibid.*, p. 21.

4. *Ibid.*, p. 38.

5. *Ibid.*, p. 47.

6. E. D. Baltzell, *Philadelphia Gentleman* (New York, 1958), pp. 231–232; 234–236; see also Dixon Wexter, *Saga of American Society* (New York, 1937).

7. M. A. DeWolfe Howe, *Memoirs of Alonzo Potter* (Philadelphia, 1871), pp. 85, 97.

8. Van Santvoord, *Memoirs*, p. 242.

9. The Reverend Duncan Kennedy to the Reverend Samuel Miller. Albany, N.Y. (January 25, 1844), Princeton University Archives.

10. Howe, *Memoirs . . . Potter*, p. 111.

11. Jonathan Pearson, Diary. (January 6, 1843), Union College Archives.

12. W. H. Seward to Thurlow Weed, Auburn, N.Y. (July 27, 1845), in *Autobiography*, p. 754. See W. H. Seward's sketch of the life of Eliphalet Nott which prefaces the English edition to Nott's *Lectures on Temperance*, 1863, and reprinted in Edward C. Delevan's *Temperance Essays*, 1865, No. 15.

13. *The First Semi-Centennial Anniversary*, p. 90.

14. Gertrude Tibbits Nott died at Schenectady, N.Y., January 5, 1841, D.A.R. *Bible Records*, Vol. 8, pp. 164–165; see also Van Santvoord, *Memoirs*, p. 275.

15. The Reverend Daniel Stewart (Ballston Spa., N.Y.) to the Reverend John Clancy. (August 23, 1842), Union College Archives.

16. Sarah B. Tibbits to the author. (Feb. 23, 1938).

17. Jonathan Pearson, Diary. (March 23–26, 1842).

18. *Ibid.*, Dec. 31, 1844.

19. *Ibid.*, Jan. 15, 1845.

20. Eliphalet Nott to J. C. Spencer. (Dec. 18, 1842); see also: *Dictionary of American Biography*, XVII, p. 450.

21. Daily Albany *Argus*, January 10, 1840; see also *Union College Magazine*, vol. X (June, 1872), pp. 36–41.

22. Eliphalet Nott to Alonzo Potter. (October 5, 1845) in answer to the latter's request for information on the Doctor's methods for handling difficult church situations. Van Santvoord, *Memoirs*, pp. 305–309. See also Howe *Memoirs . . . of Alonzo Potter*, (Phil., 1871), for the record of the warm personal relationship which continued between the two men until Alonzo Potter's death on July 4, 1865.

23. *The First Semi-Centennial Anniversary*, p. 158.

24. Charles M. Perry, *Henry Philip Tappan* (Ann Arbor, Mich., 1933), p. 70.

25. The idea of the "University" in pre-Civil War America is well developed by Frederick Rudolph in *The American College and University* (New York, 1962); he concludes by saying that "as in its people, its geography, its churches, its economic institutions, the United States in its universities was to reveal a remarkable diversity that would encompass differences in wealth, leadership, public influence, regional needs."

26. Jonathan Pearson, Diary. (April 22, 1854).

27. An alumni committee, in 1839, employed Henry Inman to do a full-length portrait of Eliphalet Nott which was accepted as "a perfect delineation . . . of . . . one whose name is so interwoven with the literature and science of our country . . . ." In 1846 another committee of alumni, consisting of T. C. Reed, William Henry Seward, and John C. Spencer were soliciting their fellow alumni to contribute the still unpaid balance of $700 due on the original bill of $1000; the committee underscored their request by pointing out that the artist had been dead for some time and that his widow and children "are in circumstances of great destitution." As Pearson noted in his journal on April 22, 1854, the Doctor himself finally settled the account.

28. Following the Commencement of 1852 the Syracuse (N.Y.) *Tribune* commented on the new "super-graduate course for those who have completed the ordinary bachelor's curriculum, and who wish to enter upon higher and deeper departments of study . . ."; the Union College catalogue for that year listed six departments "intended for the instruction of those who wish to continue after the expiration of the usual four years' course, whether graduates of Union or other colleges":

Agricultural Chemistry and Chemistry applied to the arts, *in extenso*;

The Higher Mathematics and Astronomy—Theoretical and Practical;

The higher Calculus of Engineering;

Language and the Philosophy of Language;

History and the Philosophy of History;

Comprehensive Metaphysics.

Union College advertised, in 1852, what was probably the first graduate training, per se, to be offered by an American college; in 1853 the catalogue announced that the "Graduate's Department will consist of at least five Professors, giving more comprehensive instruction than the College course anywhere permits, in Natural Science, Mathematics and Astronomy, Ancient Philology and Literature, History and Metaphysics; and designed for a three-year course, to secure as thorough and complete scholarship in General Literature and Science as may be obtained at any European University." The next year Union graduated Masters of Arts *in course*, and might well have gone on to the fulfillment of the promises of the catalogue of 1853 but for Nott's financial failures after 1855 and the mismanagement of the Nott Trust Deed following the Civil War which doomed the program. See also Book Eight, chapter two, note 5.

29. E. M. McAllister, *Amos Eaton: Scientist and Educator* (Philadelphia, 1941), p. 460.

30. Rensselaer Polytechnic Institute, Catalogue of Graduates: Clarkson Nott Potter received the only "C.E. (Rens. Inst.)" granted for the year 1842–1843.

31. William M. Gillespie to Alonzo Potter. (September, 1844). On December 4, 1846, however, the Doctor wrote to President Edward Everett of Harvard supporting Professor Gillespie's candidacy for the Rumford Professorship. After high praise for Gillespie's work as Professor of Civil Engineering at Union, President Nott added the revealing information that Gillespie's religious opinions, unwelcome among some at Union, would be in favor in Boston and at Harvard. Eliphalet Nott to President Edward Everett. (December 4, 1846), Harvard University Archives.

32. Van Santvoord, *Memoirs*, p. 232.

33. S. H. DeKroyft, *A Place in Thy Memory* (dedicated to "Mrs. Rev. Doctor E. Nott", N.Y., 1868) pp. 119–120; see also pp. 155–162 for Mrs. DeKroyft's report of a visit to the Notts in Schenectady, and the Doctor's 76th Birthday gathering.

34. Union College *Centennial Souvenir, 1895*, p. 13. Also, *Union College Garnet (Centennial Number)*, 1896, pp. 207–208.

35. The complex, dismal history of the litigations in which Stuyvesant Cove involved Eliphalet Nott, Union College, and their agents can be read in a series of printed court records beginning in 1860:

1. James Brown *against* the Trustees of Union College, Robert W. Lowber, and Percy R. Pyne; Supreme Court of New York, N.Y. 1860.

2. *Answer* of the Trustees, and the Opinion of Judge Hoffman (*in re* James Brown, above). Schenectady, 1860.

3. The Trustees of Union College . . . *against* Robert W. Lowber and Elizabeth, his wife, impleaded with Moses Taylor, and others, *Amended Answer.* Supreme Court of New York, 1862.

4. As above: *Amended Answer* of Defendant, Moses Taylor. New York Supreme Court. N.Y. 1862.

5. Moses Taylor *against* the Trustees of Union College . . . and Eliphalet Nott, defendants. *Pleadings.* N.Y. 1864.

6. Robert W. Lowber, "To the Finance Committee of the Board of Trustees of Union College, on the claims of Robert W. Lowber." N.Y. 1871.

These documents are bound and indexed as "UH2/LU583 vol. II, Stuyvesant Cove," in the Union College Library.

36. Albany *Knickerbocker*, August 28, 1849; in an article from Schenectady, signed "Veritas."

37. Palmer C. Ricketts, *History of Rennselaer Polytechnic Institute, 1824-1914.* 3rd ed. (New York, 1934).

BOOK SEVEN

1. *"Fiat justicia, ruat coelum"*

1. J. C. Spencer, *Argument in Defense of Dr. Nott, against the charges of L. Vanderheyden and James W. Beekman; presented before the Committee of the Senate, appointed to investigate certain pecuniary affairs of Union College . . . with principal documents*, etc. (Albany, 1853), p. 1. Hereafter referred to as *Argument*.

2. New York State Senate Document No. 5 (January 3, 1854). Report of the majority of the investigating committee in relation to the affairs of Union College, p. 16.

3. J. P. Fisher to Governor Hamilton Fish. (February 10, 1849), Hamilton Fish Papers, Library of Congress.

4. Reply of the Union College Trustees to Senate Document No. 71 (April 12, 1851), dated March 12, 1853, pp. 26–27.

5. Albany *Daily Knickerbocker*, September 3, 1849 (clipping in Pearson's scrapbook, vol. 1, p. 23. Union College Archives); see also "Veritas" to the same paper, August 23, 1849, noting Professor John Austin˙Yates's recent death: "his connection with college, and being a resident in the community rendered him the bitter object of that *one* whose hatred and envy fell upon Rev. Hooper Cumming until he *too* was

compelled to seek refuge among strangers and die of a broken heart . . . . about one year since it was talked of . . . that a great change was to take place in the affairs of Union College; but how is it? The *bubble* has broken, the new faculty be elected, or rather the old ones reinstated, but the Trustees through the influence of President Nott, as I believe, failed to reelect Dr. Yates . . . . ," *Ibid.*, p. 23; see also A. Holland to J. A. Yates. (July 27, 1849): his professorship "vacated" in November, 1848. Union College Archives.

6. Spencer, *Argument*, pp. 58–59.

7. Edward F. Delancey, *Memoir of J. W. Beekman* (New York, 1877), p. 14.

8. Spencer, *Argument*, p. 97.

9. Philip L. White, *The Beekmans of New York, in Politics and Commerce, 1647–1877* (New York, 1956), pp. 575–616.

10. Albany *Daily Knickerbocker*, May 29, 1849.

11. White, *Beekmans*, p. 608; R. H. Pruyn to J. W. Beekman. (April 28, 1849), Beekman Papers, New-York Historical Society.

12. *Ibid.*

13. Albany *Daily Knickerbocker*, May 29, 1849.

14. N. Y. State Assembly Document No. 146, March 19, 1850, pp. 33–39.

15. The actual ownership of the Novelty Iron Works at this time is difficult to determine. On July 12, 1843, the Doctor wrote to his banker, G. A. Worth (City Bank of New York), "In order to simplify my account at your bank I wish to separate what belongs to the Novelty Works from what belongs to another . . . ." Howard Potter, his grandson, was employed by the Novelty Iron Works in the 1850s; this son of Bishop Alonzo Potter married the daughter of James Brown, head of the banking firm of Brown Brothers, who had taken over the Novelty Iron Works from H. Nott and Company in 1836; following his marriage, Howard Potter left the Novelty Iron Works for employment in his father-in-law's New York City offices. (*The Alonzo Potter Family*, Privately printed, Concord, N.H., 1923, p. 17.) On August 20, 1851, Robert M. Stratton gave an affidavit that he was a member of the firm of Stillman, Allen and Company "owners and proprietors of the Novelty Iron Works . . . ." (Reply, Union College Trustees, to charges . . . brought . . . by J. W. Beekman, p. 9.) See also the paper jacket binding the deeds involving the Novelty Iron Works; this jacket is undated, but in the hand of Eliphalet Nott:

"Title Deeds of Novelty Works from Nicholas Stuyvesant to Neziah Bliss—of whom I purchased 3/4 as will be seen by titles in another package—the other 4th Mr. Bliss sold to Benjamin Tibbits of whom I purchased that 4th." Union College Archives.

16. Eliphalet Nott to Thurlow Weed. (May 26, 1849); Eurania E. Nott to Thurlow Weed. (June 2, 1849). Union College Archives.

17. The Albany *Evening Journal*, through March, 1850, mentions only Joel B. Nott's polite controversy with John C. Spencer on the matter of perpetual leaseholds, a subject then exciting the anti-renters in their disputes with the Van Rensselaers. Joel Nott was an Assemblyman from the second district of Albany County, and made a strong speech denouncing the perpetual lease-hold doctrine. John C. Spencer, in a letter to the *Journal*, took exception to Joel Nott's sources on which he based his arguments. Albany *Evening Journal*, March 22, 1850.

18. S. H. DeKroyft, *A Place in Thy Memory* (New York, 1868), p. 155.

19. Union College *Scroll*, vol. 1, No. 3 (May, 1850).

20. Assembly Document No. 146, March 19, 1850, p. 7.

21. Gabriel P. Disoway to John W. Beekman (March 18, 1850), Senate Document No. 71, April 12, 1851, p. 9.

22. Assembly Document No. 147, March 23, 1850.

23. *New York State Assembly Document No. 190*, April 8, 1850: Annual Report of the Trustees of Union College for the collegiate year ending July, 1849, p. 3.

24. James B. Sanders to James W. Beekman, (April 25, 1850), Beekman Papers, New-York Historical Society.

25. Robert W. Lowber to Eliphalet Nott. (May 11, 1850), Union College Archives.

26. White, *Beekmans*, p. 593.

27. *Ibid.*, pp. 595–596.

28. *Ibid.*, pp. 596–600.

29. Horace Greeley to "Friend C.".: [W. L. Crandall, editor of the Syracuse *Journal*, Secretary of the Free School Convention called for July 10, 1850, at Syracuse?] T. E. Finnegan, ed., *Free Schools, A Documentary History of the Free School Movement in New York State* (Albany, 1921), p. 348. On June 13 Crandall forwarded to Beekman a list of those invited to the convention, among whom was the President of Union College. Considering that the Doctor thought of himself as one of the prime movers in establishing the principle of free education in New York State, it is odd that he seems to have made no response to Crandall's invitation. Alonzo Potter, the Doctor's son-in-law, however, wrote to Crandall, urging the convention to consider that Free Schools were "as much for the interest of capital as for labor," an argument he considered irresistible. *Ibid.*, p. 347.

30. Richard J. Storrs, *The Beginnings of Graduate Education in America* (Chicago, 1953), Chapter VII, pp. 67–74. The Doctor and the Board must have looked on the plans of this distinguished group of scientists as highly competitive; among the group was Louis Agassiz and Benjamin Pierce, B. A. Gould, and J. D. Whitney, all associated with Harvard, James Hall, Albany paleontologist, and others, who, by 1851, had elaborate plans for a great national university, to be established under New York State patronage at Albany. By 1852, however, the project began its eventual collapse; Francis Wayland, Alonzo Potter, and T. Romeyn Beck, theoretically backers of the project, were accused in that year of opposing its more liberal provisions (J. D. Whitney labeled them "the *Old Fogies* . . ."); the fact that these three men were all Union College men, aware of the university plans developing in Schenectady, may have lessened their enthusiasm for a graduate school too much like the one the Doctor had been planning for some years. At Union there might be some chance on the part of the academic conservatives to restrain scientific inquiry; under Agassiz and his friends there were no subjects, as Potter believed there were, which it would be immoral to investigate. (*Ibid.*, p. 73.) If the "Old Fogies" thought to control inquiry at Union, however, they were to be shocked at the spirit of free inquiry the Doctor was to express in his speech at the semi-centennial celebration of his presidency in 1854.

2. *"A beautiful, speculative scheme"*

1. *Report of the Committee on Literature on the Conditions of Union College*, April 12, 1851. Senate Document No. 71, 1851. The members of the committee were J. W. Beekman, chairman, T. B. Carroll, and Samuel Miller.

2. W. H. Campbell to J. W. Beekman (February 3, 1851), Beekman Papers, New-York Historical Society.

3. W. H. Campbell to J. W. Beekman (May 14, 1851), Beekman Papers, New-York Historical Society.

4. J. G. Sanders to J. W. Beekman (May 17, 1851), Beekman Papers, New-York Historical Society.

5. W. H. Campbell to J. W. Beekman (April 16, 1851), Beekman Papers, New-York Historical Society.

6. *Reply of the Trustees . . . to charges brought on the 12th of April, 1851* (Albany, 1853), p. 5. See *Documents*, Union College Archives, VH2/ID637.

7. J. C. Spencer, "Argument . . . ," (New York, 1853), pp. 7–8.

8. Schenectady *Cabinet*, April 23, 1851: Union College has had "enemies both secret and open for thirty years . . . aided by anonymous pamphlets and a flash press . . . ."

9. *Reply of the Trustees*, p. 6.

10. *Report of the Comptroller in answer to a resolution of the Senate relative to Union College* (February 7, 1851), Senate Document No. 26, 1851.

11. Levinus Vanderheyden, letter to the Albany *Evening Journal*, March 24, 1853, citing Attorney General Chatfield's instructions to him, dated June 8, 1851.

12. *Reply of the Trustees*, pp. 2–3; Eliphalet Nott to Reverend J. N. Campbell. (September 12, 1851), Union College Archives.

13. A. Johnson to J. W. Beekman (October 28, 1851), Beekman Papers, New-York Historical Society.

14. *Report of the Commission on Union College* (February 27, 1852), Senate Document No. 40, 1852; see also *Statement of the Accountant*, Senate Document No. 58, 1852.

15. J. W. Beekman, "Speech delivered in the Senate, Saturday, February 28, 1852." Beekman Papers, New-York Historical Society.

16. In 1850 a statistical report listed Union College as first in New York State with an enrollment of 268; Hamilton College, 158; University of New York, 151; Columbia College 130; Madison University, 127. (Union College *Scroll*, 1850, p. 14.)

17. *Report of the Majority of the Commissioners to examine the affairs of Union College*, Senate Document No. 41 (March 4, 1853), p. 3; see also, *Report of the Minority of the Commissioners . . . , ibid.*, pp. 4–5.

18. *Ibid.*, Senate Document No. 41, Appendix, "Memorial of the Trustees of Union College, to the Hon. the Senate of the State of New-York" (March 12, 1853), p. 235.

19. *Ibid.*, Senate Document No. 41, Appendix, "Memorial of the President of Union College to the Honorable, the Senate of New-York" (March 16, 1853), pp. 236–239.

20. "Union College—Heavy Charges against Its Officers," Albany Daily *Knickerbocker* (?), clipping in Jonathan Pearson's Scrapbook (Union College Archives), p. 77.

21. Albany *Evening Journal*, March 26, 1853.

22. Albany *Daily State Register*, March 28, 1853.

23. "Union College—Heavy Charges against Its Officers," Albany *Daily Knickerbocker* (?), clipping in Jonathan Pearson's Scrapbook (Union College Archives), p. 77.

24. John C. Spencer to the Editor of the Albany *Evening Journal*, ca. March 28, 1853, and published in the *Journal* at that time; from a clipping in Jonathan Pearson's Scrapbook, Union College Archives.

25. Albany, *Daily State Register*, March 28, 1853.

26. "Resolution of Mr. Beekman on the petition of Levinus Vanderheyden, Neziah Bliss, and Joseph D. Monell."; transmitted to the New York State Senate April 8, 1853, and thereafter designated as Senate Document No. 68 (1853).

27. Francis and Theresa Pulzky, *White, Red and Black: Sketches of American Society* (Redfield, N.Y., 1853), Vol. 2, p. 221. This record would indicate the Notts were then living at the north end of North College.

28. Eliphalet Nott to General Louis Kossuth (May [?] 1852), U. C. Archives.

29. "Liberty and Oppression," a part of a *MS.* speech with this title, apparently by Eliphalet Nott, dated June 2, 1852, is in the Union College Archives.

30. Jonathan Pearson Scrapbooks, Vol. 4, p. 19, Union College Archives. Quoted from a newspaper clipping bearing the date July 27, 1853.

31. The growing controversy over the succession to the presidency of Union College is reflected in *The Correspondence between Dr. Nott and Dr. Hickok in reference to The Appointment of the latter as Vice-President, etc., of Union College and his Letter of Acceptance, and the action thereon of the Board of Trustees* (Schenectady, 1859).

32. Robert W. Lowber, *To the Finance Committee of the Board of Trustees of Union College on the claims of Robert W. Lowber* (New York, 1871), pp. 6–7. Here is a detailed outline of Eliphalet Nott's exploitation of Stuyvesant's Cove, and of Lowber's defense of his complicated contracts with the Doctor and the Trustees; here also is the controversial history of Nott Trust Fund financing which led, after 1859, to a repudiation by the Union College Finance Committee, and those Trustees who supported it, of the agreements between the Doctor and the Board on which the Nott Trust Fund was established, and the repudiation of those legal positions on which John C. Spencer had based his "Argument in the Defense of Eliphalet Nott" in 1853. R. W. Lowber's "Letter" of 1871 to the Trustees, and the various suits in which Lowber's Stuyvesant Cove operations with the Doctor involved the Board are contained in a volume labeled "Union College-Stuyvesant Cove" (UH2/L U583/v.2) Union College Archives; also, Robert W. Lowber to Eliphalet Nott. (May 31, 1850), Union College Archives.

33. Jonathan Pearson, Diary. (August 20, 1860).

34. *Ibid.,* July 25, 1859. "Lowber asserts from his own knowledge that Dr. N. has received $1,000,000 from the Cove property first and last."

35. Lowber, *To the Finance Committee,* pp. 9–11.

3. *"Plump contradictions . . ."*

1. *The Celebration of the Fiftieth Anniversary of Dr. Nott's Presidency of Union College, July 25, 1854* (Schenectady, G. Y. Vandebogert, 1854), p. 102.

2. Alexander Holland to John C. Spencer. (January, 1849), Union College Archives.

3. John C. Spencer to James W. Beekman. (October 10, 1851), Beekman Papers, New-York Historical Society.

4. John C. Spencer, holograph notes. (August 9, 1853), Union College Archives.

5. *Ibid.*

6. Albany *Daily Knickerbocker,* August 9, 1853.

7. *Ibid.,* August 11–12–15–17–22, 1853; on August 22 the *Knickerbocker* made its comparison of Union with Harvard and Yale, and offered its conclusion that the Doctor was "a very dishonest man."

8. The Board of Trustees had appointed Platt Potter, late partner of Judge Alonzo Paige, to represent them at the Vanderbilt Committee hearings. Both he and Spencer held not only their political sympathies in common, but also their common interest in developing public support for humane care for the insane. Platt Potter became Judge of the New York Supreme Court in 1857, and in 1865 a Trustee of Union College.

9. Spencer, *Argument.* (Albany, 1853).

10. *Ibid.,* pp. 93–94.

11. *Ibid.,* p. 98.

12. *Ibid.*, p. 96.
13. *Ibid.*, p. 97.
14. Vanderbilt Committee Report, January 4, 1854 (Senate Document No. 5), p. 16.
15. Spencer, *Argument*, pp. 14–15.
16. *Ibid.*, pp. 15–16; see L. Vanderheyden to James W. Beekman. (November 2, 1853), Beekman Papers, New-York Historical Society; Vanderheyden told Beekman that the Vanderbilt Committee, following this testimony to Vanderheyden's reliability, then rebuked the Doctor's attorney.
17. *Ibid.*, p. 4.
18. Spencer, *Argument*, pp. 103–104. Vanderheyden had charged the Trustees had bought $5000 in Hudson (N.Y.) Bank stock in August, 1819, one month after the Hudson Bank had failed. Spencer assured the Vanderbilt Committee this stock had been bought by the Doctor as a routine investment of college funds, in a stock declared legal for such investment by the New York State Legislature, and that the transfer of the stock to the Trustees in August 1819 was merely the legal assignment to them of their own property.
19. *Ibid.*, p. 89.
20. Levinus Vanderheyden to James W. Beekman. (October 6, 1853), Beekman Papers, New-York Historical Society; P. L. White, *The Beekmans of New York, in Politics and Commerce, 1647–1877* (New York, 1956), pp. 615–616.
21. Spencer, *Argument*, 1853, pp. 93–94.
22. Beekman's charge, made earlier in the Senate, was proof, so far as Spencer was concerned, of "Mr. Beekman's design . . ." to prove "deliberate fraud and deception" on the part of the officers of the college.

Beekman charged that the "officers" had given him a pamphlet called "Chancery Documents" during the hearings of the Pruyn Committee in 1849, and that among them was a copy of a Yates and McIntyre Bill, purportedly sworn to on August 4, 1834. Beekman then produced a printed copy of the same bill, also sworn to on August 4, 1834, but containing "whole pages" of important testimony omitted in the pamphlet given to him by the college.

Spencer answered Beekman's charge of a deliberate attempt to deceive the Pruyn Committee by showing that the pamphlet copy of the Yates and McIntyre Bill given to the Pruyn Committee in 1849 was printed on November 22, 1834, as proved by the letter of that date, signed by Jonas Holland, then college treasurer, which preceded the pamphlet copy of the bill. Spencer than showed that the printed copy of this bill, so different from the one given the Pruyn Committee by the college, was actually an amended Yates and McIntyre bill filed six months later, on May 16, 1835; Spencer then claimed that Beekman knew these facts, that he had admitted he was familiar with both the college's and the Doctor's answer to this amended bill of May 16, 1835, and so could not have confused the original with the amended bill. "Thus," Spencer concluded, "this charge of deliberate fraud on the part of the officers of the college, and upon which so many changes had been rung in the Senate, was exploded." (Spencer, *Argument*, pp. 94–95.)

Beekman, in a letter to the Vanderbilt Committee on December 8, 1853, challenged Spencer's explanation: both the college pamphlet, and the Yates and McIntyre *amended* bill, though quite different, actually bore the same date, August 12, 1834, "and the same *jurat*." This being so, Beekman then claimed, it then followed that both documents should correspond, "ought [the college pamphlet Bill] not be a copy of that Bill to which its date and *jurat* precisely correspond—Here, my dear Sir, is Mr. Spencer's special pleading—so unfair that I trust you will not refuse to examine the documents before you credit the 'explosion' of my testimony." (Beekman Papers, New-York Historical Society).

23. Spencer, *Argument*, pp. 95–96.

24. *Ibid.*, p. 96.

25. *Ibid.*, pp. 96–97.

26. *Ibid.*, pp. 99–100.

27. *Ibid.*, pp. 99.

28. *Ibid.*, pp. 104–105.

29. *Ibid.*, *"Documents*, etc." No. XLIV, P. 90, note (a).

30. Levinus Vanderheyden to James W. Beekman (November 3, 1853). In this letter Vanderheyden also tells Beekman he plans to "memorialize" the Senate to demand that the Vanderbilt Committee report on *all* the testimony. He also says that the Doctor has upset the plans of a Judge Parmalee to run for the Senate from the Schenectady-Albany districts, and that the Judge is now prepared to help Vanderheyden. In his letter of November 8, 1853 Vanderheyden tells Beekman he believes the Comptroller [J. C. Wright] and others have "befogged" several of the members of the committee. (Beekman Papers, New-York Historical Society).

31. Spencer, *Argument*, p. 111.

32. *Ibid.*, p. 108.

33. *Ibid.*, pp. 109–110.

34. *Ibid.*, p. 110.

35. *Ibid.*, p. 113.

36. *Report of the majority of the Investigating Committee in relation to the affairs of Union College*. Senate Document No. 5. January 3, 1854. This report was signed on December 30, 1853, by Nathaniel Jones and Elisha Ward. The Committee was unanimous in its opinion that the "President's Fund" was legally the property of Dr. Nott (p. 10).

37. *Ibid.*, p. 26.

38. Jonathan Pearson, Diary (November 30, 1857). Union College Archives.

39. *Ibid.*, August 4, 1857.

40. Eliphalet Nott to   ?, rough draft dated May 25, 1849. Union College Archives.

41. Jonathan Pearson, Diary (February 15, 1860).

42. *Moses Taylor, Plaintiff, against The Trustees of Union College . . . and Eliphalet Nott, Defendants. PLEADINGS.* New York State Supreme Court, May 26, 1863. Union College Archives (UH/LU583/V.2).

"this defendant [Union College] further answering states, that without any final settlement between the said finance committee and Eliphalet Nott, having been previously made, and without any cash balance having been previously found by said committee to be due by this defendant . . . [Stuyvesant Cove and Hunter Point] deeds . . . were executed and delivered by the said treasurer of this defendant, to the said Eliphalet Nott . . . without any authority from defendant, and were therefore void, and conveyed no title to the premises therein described, to the said Eliphalet Nott, and that under and by virtue of said deeds the said Nott acquired no legal or equitable interest in the said premises" (pp. 5–6).

43. "Union College and Dr. Nott," *New York Daily Times*, January 7, 1854.

44. Albany *Evening Journal*, January 14, 1854.

45. Albany *Daily Knickerbocker*, December 7, 1853.

46. Pearson, Diaries (March 15, 1854).

47. Austin A. Yates, *Schenectady County* (New York, 1902), pp. 142–143; also Pearson's scrapbook, Vol. IV, p. 47, a newspaper clipping dated Albany, March 20, 1854, Union College Archives.

48. Charles P. Sanders to James W. Beekman. (July 21, 1855), Beekman Papers, New-York Historical Society;

On December 22, 1854, Jonathan Pearson wrote to the Doctor, then in New York City, that "Mr. Spencer . . . is a very sick man, and I think has some doubts how it will go with him." The Acting Treasurer, just back from a visit to Spencer, told the Doctor that his attorney "takes an interest in the college, its reputation, success, and inquired particularly about you." (Union College Letter Books.)

4. *"In the tenth lustrum of his presidency"*

1. *The Celebration of the Fiftieth Anniversary of Dr. Nott's Presidency of Union College*, July 25, 1854, Schenectady: G. Y. Vandebogert, 1854, pp. 110–111.

2. Jonathan Pearson, Diary (April 21, 1854); also June 29, 1854. Union College Archives.

3. *Ibid*., March 23, 1854.

4. Francis Wayland to Eliphalet Nott. (May 22, 1854), Brown University Archives.

5. T. R. Crane, *Francis Wayland: Political Economist as Educator* (Providence, R. I., 1962), pp. 37–41; see also Professor Jonathan Pearson's comment that Brown's "new system . . . has been taught at Union in spirit and in fact . . . for more than thirty years. . . . ," Jonathan Pearson's Diary. (March 29, 1854).

6. *Ibid*., p. 45.

7. Van Santvoord, *Memoirs*, p. 323.

8. *The Celebration of the Fiftieth Anniversary of Dr. Nott's Presidency*, pp. 55–79.

9. *Ibid*., pp. 64–65.

10. *Ibid*., pp. 60–61.

11. *Ibid*., p. 66.

12. Eliphalet Nott to Francis Wayland. (March 21, 1854), Van Santvoord, *Memoirs*, p. 320.

13. Horace Dresser to *New York Daily Times*, July 26, 1854. In Jonathan Pearson's Scrapbook, No. 1, p. 23.

14. *The Celebration of the Fiftieth Anniversary of Dr. Nott's Presidency*, p. 70.

15. *Ibid*., p. 70.

16. *Ibid*., p. 76.

17. *New York Daily Times*, "from Schenectady, July 27, 1854." Jonathan Pearson's Scrapbook, No. IV, p. 23.

18. Horace Dresser to *New York Daily Times*. (July 26, 1854), Jonathan Pearson's Scrapbook, No. 1, p. 23.

19. Trustees Minutes, July 25, 1854.

20. *Trust Deed from Eliphalet Nott and Wife, to the Trustees of Union College*. Executed on January 28, 1854, Union College Library.

21. For an excellent treatment of the development of graduate education in America, see: R. J. Storrs, *The Beginnings of Graduate Education in America* (Chicago, 1953). The Nott contribution to this history would undoubtedly have loomed larger if the author had had access to the Nott material at Union College.

BOOK EIGHT

1. *"The future is his world . . ."*

1. Jonathan Pearson, *Diary*, (March 23, 1854), Union College Archives.

2. *New York Daily Times*, July 26, 1854.

3. "James Brown against the Trustees of Union College of the Town of Schenectady, Eliphalet Nott, Robert W. Lowber and Percy R. Pyne." New York Supreme Court, City and County of New York, June 9, 1859. Map interleaved between page 10 and page 11. Union College Archives, LH2/LU583/v. 2.

4. *History and Biography of Washington County, and the Town of Queensbury, N. Y.* (Chicago, Ill. 1894), pp. 236–241.

5. Union College Letter Books, (December 17, 1838). Union College Archives.

6. *History and Biography of Washington County, and the Town of Queensbury, N. Y.* (1894), p. 239. Queensbury, N. Y.

7. "James Brown against the Trustees of Union College," p. 2; see also Robert W. Lowber, "To the Finance Committee of the Board of Trustees of Union College on the Claims of Robert W. Lowber" (New York 1871), pp. 9–10. Union College Archives, LH2/LU583/v. 2.

8. Lowber, "To the Finance Committee," pp. 7-8, 16–21.

9. Milo L. Norton, "Copper Mines in Bristol," in *Bristol, Connecticut, or "New Cambridge,"* (1907), pp. 440–441.

10. Epaphroditus Peck, *A History of Bristol, Connecticut*, (Hartford, 1932), pp. 136–137; see also M. L. Norton, *op. cit.*, p. 440.

11. Jonathan Pearson, Diary, (December 6, 1858), Union College Archives.

12. Lowber, "To the Finance Committee of Union College," pp. 13–14.

13. Jonathan Pearson to the Reverend Samuel Nott. Wareham, Massachusetts, (March 28, 1854). Union College Archives.

14. Lowber, "To the Finance Committee of Union College," pp. 19-26.

15. *Ibid.*, pp. 22-24.

16. Jonathan Pearson, Diary, (March 24, 1855).

17. *Ibid.*, May 14, 1855; March 15, 1855.

18. *Ibid.*, February 21, 1856.

19. *Ibid.*, August 14, 1855.

20. *Ibid.*, September 26, 1855; see: Professors B. Silliman, Jr., and J. D. Whitney, "Report of the Examination of the Bristol Copper Mine in Bristol, Conn.," (New Haven, 1855).

21. *Ibid.*, December 6, 1858.

22. M. L. Norton, *op. cit.* p. 243.

23. M. L. Norton, *op. cit.* p. 441.

24. Jonathan Pearson, Diary, (May 1, 1858).

25. *Ibid.*, July 25, 1859.

26. Lowber, "To the Finance Committee of Union College," p. 42; see also "James Brown against the Trustees of Union College . . . *et al*; Answer of the Trustees of Union College and the Opinion of Justice Hoffman," pp. 44–45 (1859–1860). These actions are bound in a single volume in the Union College Archives, UH2/LU583/v. 2.

27. "Trustees of Union College . . . against Robert W. Lowber, and Elizabeth, his wife, impleaded with Moses Taylor and others." Amended Answer of Moses Taylor, in the Supreme Court, County of New York, 1862, pp. 32–33. Bound as in No. 26 above.

28. Jonathan Pearson, Diary: entries for December 11-12-13-15-16, 1856. See also "Union College vs. James Brown. . . ." p. 48. ("Answer of the Trustees. . . . .")

29. Jonathan Pearson, Diary, (March 24, 1860). For the college's version of this transaction, see: "James Brown against the Trustees of Union College, *et al.* . . . Answer of the Trustees . . .", 1860, pp. 48–50. For Robert W. Lowber's Defense, see: Lowber, "To the Finance Committee of Union College. . . . ," 1871, pp. 57–63. New York City's interest in this real estate is described in the New York *Tribune*, February 13, 1857; see also New York *Tribune*, November 14, 1856, for Judge Hoffman's decision for Nott in 1856 at Special Term, and the issue for August 17, 1857, for Lowber's own history of the transaction, and the *Tribune's* scathing review of it.

30. Lowber, "To the Finance Committee of Union College . . . ," pp. 53–55. For Nott's association with Lowber in the Bald Mountain Lime Works (1852–1857, see: *History and biography of Washington County, and the Town of Queensbury, N. Y.* (Chicago, 1894), pp. 239–240; also: Crisfield Johnson, *History of Washington County* (Philadelphia, Pa., 1878), pp. 91–92.

31. Jonathan Pearson, Diary, (February 2, 1859).

32. *The Alonzo Potter Family* (Concord, N. H., 1923), p. 44.

33. Jonathan Pearson, Diary, (January 7, 1858).

34. *Ibid.*, January 9, 1858.

35. *Ibid.*, November 28, 1857.

36. *Ibid.*, January 18, 1858. See John Nott's "Testimonial" for a Dr. Lighthill's cure of his lifelong deafness: New York *Journal*, February 19, 1864.

37. *Ibid.*, March 29, 1858.

38. Eliphalet Nott to Alonzo Potter (January 25, 1858), Union College Archives. (Microfilm from original in the Philadelphia Academy.)

39. Eliphalet Nott to Alonzo Potter (June 10, 1858), Union College Archives. (Microfilm, as above.)

40. Eliphalet Nott to Alonzo Potter (December 4, 1858), Union College Archives. (Microfilm, as above.)

41. Jonathan Pearson, Scrapbook No. 4, pp. 27–29, Union College Archives. "Graduates' Hall" was here estimated to cost $20,000. The account noted that some $3000 to $4000 had been subscribed before the dedication, that books were opened afterward for further subscriptions, and that Senator W. H. Seward pledged $250, R. M. Blatchford and Judge Lott $500 each, and Judge Ira Harris, who laid the cornerstone, $100.

42. Jonathan Pearson, *Diary*, (March 3, 1859). Pearson reports here in his journal, that Nott gave up "his agency" in Hunter Point at this time only under pressure from Chancellor Reuben Walworth. For Pearson's report on his visit to the property and the Board's "Hunter Point Trust" arrangements, see the Diary entries for April 1 through April 9, 1859.

43. *Ibid.*, June 6, 1859.

44. *Ibid.*, June 7, 1859.

45. *Ibid.*, June 7, 1859.

2. *"Munificent donation," or "magnificent humbug"?*

1. Jonathan Pearson, Scrapbooks, vol. IV, p. 32: a newspaper clipping probably from the Schenectady *Cabinet* (n.d.), Union College Archives.

2. Jonathan Pearson, Diary, (June 27, 1859, August 3, 1860), Union College Archives.

3. *Ibid.* (May 23, 1859). Pearson's diary from 1858 until Nott's death, is filled entries dealing with Vice President Hickok's difficulties with Nott and the latter's friends on the Board over the limits of Hickok's authority and his right to succeed to the

presidency, and with the feuding between Hickok and his supporters and those faculty members who distrusted his scholarship, and who hoped to see some way found to block his succession to Nott's office.

4. Jonathan Pearson, Scrapbooks, Vol. IV, p. 32.

5. For a study of this phase of Nott's university planning, see Professor L. K. Bacon's paper, "History of Early Chemical Education at Union College," Union College Archives, and his article, "A Precursor of the American Chemical Society—Chandler and the Society at Union," *Chymia, Annual Studies on the History of Chemistry* (1965).

6. Jonathan Pearson, Diary (June 17, 1859).

7. *Ibid.* (August 14, 1860).

8. Robert W. Lowber, "To the Finance Committee of Union College on the claims of Robert W. Lowber." (New York 1871), p. 73. Union College Archives, call number UH2/LU583/v. 2.

9. Jonathan Pearson, Diary (August 25, 1860).

10. The record which follows is taken from the Trustees' Minutes for 1845–1848:

July 22, 1845: Alexander Holland, Union College Treasurer, read to the Board the full account of its indebtedness to Eliphalet Nott. The proposal to settle that indebtedness by transferring Stuyvesant Cove and Hunter Point to the President was referred to the Finance Committee.

July 21-22, 1846: The Minutes of the preceding meeting of July 22, 1845 were read and approved, and the Treasurer's report for 1846 was read and referred to the Finance Committee "to be recorded when approved by them". This latter report had noted the transfer of Stuyvesant's Cove and Hunter Point to the Doctor in settlement of the college's obligation to him, and had pointed out that there remained a cash balance due the President of $41,340.57.

July 27, 1847: A. C. Paige in the chair: "the Minutes of the last meeting read and approved."

July 28, 1847: Although the contents of the report are not noted, the Finance Committee's report *was read and accepted*. Judge Paige was present at the reading.

July 28, 1848: The recorded treasurer's report noted that a balance of $41,340.57 was still owed to the President, "as per settlement of lottery claims with Finance Committee." (See their report, Minutes, 1846, p. 214.)

A review of this record, however, must include Jonathan Pearson's observation made on April 25, 1859: "this tampering with the book of Minutes is no new thing with [Nott] . . . he has time and again tinkered them and caused to be inserted matters that the Board never heard of until they were seen there . . . matters, too, of the gravest import . . ."

11. "Answer of Union College . . . to James Brown, *et al.*," 1860, pp. 5–6.

12. *Ibid.*, pp. 22–23. The unanswerable question now arises: did Judge Paige, whose probity Pearson declared was of the highest order, choose to forget his personal knowledge of the acts of the Trustees and Finance Committee from 1845 on, for he was a member of the Board through these years, or had there, indeed, been "tinkering" (as Pearson called it) with the Minutes by the President? If the treasurer's report for 1848, prepared by Alexander Holland, is correct, then both John C. Spencer and Judge Alonzo Paige based their conclusion on the corollary one the Judge was to cite next, that the "President's Fund" itself had never, in fact, belonged to the Doctor, a conclusion Spencer himself held and which he had put forward during the Chancery suits of the 1830s, but one which Spencer had reversed during his defense of the Doctor in 1853 before the Vanderbilt Committee of the New York State Senate.

13. *Ibid.*, pp. 26–27.

14. *Ibid.*, pp. 26–27.

15. Jonathan Pearson, Diary (November 2, 1860).

16. *Ibid.*, November 10, 1860.

17. Platt Potter, *A Condensed History of the Trust Created by Statute, April 14, 1860, commonly called "The Hunter Point Trust", and of its incident "The Nott Trust"; and also, of the acts of administration by the Trustees of Union College* (June 1882), Union College Archives.

18. *Moses Taylor, against the Trustees of Union College, in the Town of Schenectady, and Eliphalet Nott,* N. Y. State Supreme Court, February 4, 1863 (New York, 1864), pp. 1–2. Bound with copies of other suits involving the Nott Trust Deed in Union College Archives, UH2/LU583/v. 2.

19. *Ibid.*

20. *Ibid.* See also preliminary actions: *The Trustees of Union College, in the Town of Schenectady, in the State of New York, against Robert W. Lowber and Elizabeth, his wife, impleaded with Moses Taylor and others, Defendants. Amended Answer of Robert W. Lowber,* July 19, 1862 (New York, 1862).
—Same as above: *Amended Answer of Defendant, Moses Taylor,* Sept. 12, 1862. Both of these reports are bound as above, n. 18.

21. *Ibid. Answer of the Trustees of Union College . . .* in the complaint of Moses Taylor, May 26, 1863, pp. 19–20.

22. Lowber, "To the Finance Committee of Union College . . . ," *passim.*

23. "Union College / The Case of the Trustees of Union College Against Robert W. Lowber Decided in Favor of the College." Syracuse *Journal,* October 5, 1875; Platt Potter, *A Condensed History of the Trust Created by Statute,* April 14, 1860. . . . ," pp. 34-38; see also "Controversial Documents" Hunter Point Trust, including charges of Howard Potter and defense of their acts by J. T. Backus and Platt Potter, UH2/OU58.

24. Eliphalet Nott to Clarkson N. Potter (June 25, 1860), Union College Archives.

25. Lowber, "To the Finance Committee of Union College," p. 73. Lowber, in his letter to the Finance Committee in 1871, also noted, "the obloquy and reproach heaped upon Dr. Nott and myself by one closely allied with you in your official relations with Union College. During their progress [the Lowber-Nott Cove developments] I often warned Dr. Nott of the secret influences at work to ruin him and disgrace him, to weaken his influence in the affairs of the college, and to keep within himself the control of his fiscal affairs." p. 74. Lowber ended his long communication with a glowing tribute to the Doctor: "all that is gracious and benignant in human memory will rest upon his name forever. . . ." Lowber concluded by saying that, "the suit brought by me to enforce my claims and my defense to those brought by the college had his approval, and I am sure that were he alive today he would earnestly urge their settlement by the College" (p. 75).

3. *"I cannot die before my time"*

1. See also the Schenectady *Reflector,* January 11, 1856 for confirmation that this ten dollar banknote was issued. Frank J. Manheim, an instructor at Union College in 1938, discovered this banknote reference, reported that he had seen the note himself, although it can no longer be found in the historical collections of the Mohawk Bank.

2. Jonathan Pearson, Diary (May 18, 1860), Union College Archives.

3. Trustees' Minutes, July 22, 1857: "Mrs. Harriet Douglas Cruger and her brother of New York City, because of their high regard for Eliphalet Nott, engaged to build the President's House, provided the Board will guarantee that the Notts will be allowed to occupy it during their lifetime." By 1863 they had paid in $5000 for its construction

(Minutes, July 23, 1863); during July 1866, the Trustees agreed to repay Eurania Nott all she had personally put into the new house. (Minutes, July 25, 1866.) See also: Mrs. Eliphalet Nott to Jonathan Pearson, (January 9, 1861), Union College Archives.

4. Jonathan Pearson, Diary (May 30, 1857).

5. Van Santvoord, *Memoirs*, p. 349.

6. Eliphalet Nott to the Reverend Dr. Alden. (December 3, 1860) Union College Archives.

7. "Eliphalet Nott," in *The American Portrait Gallery, with Biographical Sketches* (New York, n.d.).

8. New York *Tribune*, "Equal Rights at Union College," January 26, 1859; here, in a letter signed "Junior," the correspondent said that his class, by a majority of ten, had admitted "a colored person." "Junior," however, noted that the class had agreed to Rossels's admission only after he had sworn that he was of Indian and French extraction. See Jonathan Pearson, Scrapbook, Vol. 4, p. 33, Union College Archives; also New York *Tribune*, February 7, 1859, and Rhode Island *Pendulum*, February 5, 1859.

9. Jonathan Pearson, Diary, (January 22-26-27, 1859).

10. A. V. V. Raymond, *Union University* (New York, 1907) 1, p. 311.

11. Jonathan Pearson, Diary, (February 27, 1864).

12. Eliphalet Nott, Jr., to Mrs. Howard Nott, August 24, 1864, Union College Archives.

13. Jonathan Pearson, Diary (May 14, 1863); For an obituary of Joel Nott, see New York *World*, May 24, 1878; here also is an account of Joel's long association with New York City politics and politicians.

14. Notes by an unknown reporter (February 13, 1865), Union College Archives; see also Willis Hanson, *Early Life of John Howard Payne* (Boston, 1913).

15. Jonathan Pearson, Diary, *passim*. From the beginning of the R. W. Lowber suits against the Nott Trust Deed, the college treasurer seems to have been convinced that Nott deliberately abandonned the college interests and his professional life as an educator for the excitements of the market place and the hope of personal profits as well as profit for the college. There is no indication that Pearson was ever aware of Nott's theological rationale for his activities as a financier and as the "philosopher of caloric."

16. Francis Wayland to Eliphalet Nott (September 17, 1861), Brown University Archives.

17. Jonathan Pearson, Scrapbooks, Vol. 4, p. 80. Unnamed newspaper, a clipping of August, 1865.

18. Trustees' Minutes, July 27, 1858. The cost to Delavan was $10,000. See his deed of gift, this date; also Trustees' Minutes, July 24, 1866.

19. Francis Wayland to Urania Nott (January 18, 1862), Brown University Archives.

20. Reverend Leander Hall, *Half Century of the Class of 1856* (1906), pp. 11-15, in Union College Archives.

21. Frank Hunter Potter, *The Alonzo Potter Family* (Concord, N. H., 1923). (The incident referred to is quoted by Potter from Mariette Thompson's *Brought Up Abroad* (a MS. biography), pp. 52-53.

22. That Eliphalet Nott had had other moments when his optimist's view of a world moving toward perfection had flagged is attested by the following quotation from the 1872 edition of his *Resurrection Sermons* (No. X, p. 147, edited by Tayler Lewis). Although the sermon cannot be dated it was obviously one in that series on the Resurrection which so moved his audiences when he was the young pastor of the "Court Church" in Albany, sermons which, revised, he continued to use during his years as the President of Union College:

"All the present population gone; not one remaining who knew, or loves, or thinks of us, or who has ever heard our names. The shrubs we set have died; the trees we planted have mouldered. Every ornament has been effaced. The very dome has fallen in, and the column that supported it lies in ruins—ruins over which the ox browses, the tent is spread, or on which the soldier's foot profanely tramples. Those things that were have become as though they had never been."

4. *"All eventually will come right"*

1. New York *Herald*, "from Schenectady, February 2, 1866." In Jonathan Pearson's Scrapbooks, Vol. 4, p. 65. Union College Archives.

2. J. Trumbull Backus, D.D., "Address at the funeral of the Rev. Dr. Nott, Schenectady, February 2, 1866, in the Presbyterian Church." (New York, 1866), Union College Archives.

3. Troy (New York) *Daily Whig*, "The Nott Eulogy," February 7, 1866. Jonathan Pearson, Scrapbooks, Vol. 4, p. 65.

4. Austin A. Yates, *Schenectady County, New York, Its history to the close of the 19th Century* (New York, 1902), pp. 447–448. The political rivalries which may have motivated some of the Troy editor's attack are noted here.

5. New York *Herald*, "The Funeral of Dr. Nott," Jonathan Pearson, Scrapbooks, vol. 4, p. 65.

6. Jonathan Pearson, Diary (September 28, 1863); The alienation of the alumni "is one of the worst evils Nott's administration has entailed upon us . . . ."

7. Jonathan Pearson, Diary (April 1, 1864).

8. *Ibid.*, April 18, 1864; see also L. P. Hickok to his nephew Julius Seelye. (March, 1866), Union College Archives, describing his 17 to 5 election by the Board.

9. "An Abused Trust," New York *Atlas*, March 16, 1867. Here, in a detailed review of the legal positions Judge Paige had taken in defense of the Nott Trust Fund, the writer in the *Atlas* offered a "revelation" of the "Facts" in connection with the transfer of the Nott Trust to Union College in 1853–1854. The *Atlas's* writer cited Eliphalet Nott's "defalcation" in relation to his financial dealing with the college, and then continued with a further revelation of what was claimed to be the current manipulation of the Hunter Point lands for the benefit of members of the Board of Trustees. James Annable, Mrs. Nott's nephew "and favorite relatives of the late President of Union College," and other "speculative friends," were charged with milking the property, with "huckstering" in the sale of valuable lots.

10. "Opinion of Judge George F. Comstock, June 1, 1874," transcribed on the pages of the Minutes of the Union College Finance Committee for 1874, pp. 212-217.

11. *Ibid.*, p. 213.

12. *Ibid.*, pp. 207–208.

13. *Ibid.*, pp. 215–217.

14. Union College Documents (UH2/OU58): "Controversial Documents," No. 5, "Statement for Trustees of U.C.," Howard Potter; see Platt Potter and J. T. Backus's defense, Nos. 8-9-10.

15. "Union University": Organized in 1873 under the leadership of the Doctor's grandson, Eliphalet Nott Potter, President of the college for twelve years of almost continual dissension. The object was to bring together the Albany Medical College, the Albany Law School, the Dudley Observatory, and Union College,

"to form Union University, their relation to the College as the nucleus to be similar to that subsisting between Harvard, Yale, or Columbia, and the related schools of Law, Medicine, etc., with the proviso that each institution reserves all its legal rights, and its corporate independence, and its location in fact, and so with each board and faculty. . . . each is bound to advance the well-being of each. . . . their mutual relations are to be adjusted as experience ripens, and advantageous results are evidently dependent on further development under the general conception of the University idea."

The history of Union College, however, from Eliphalet Nott's death until the sale of the last of the Hunter Point property in 1897, was such that there was little opportunity for so loosely formed and permissive an organization as that of "Union University" to grow. The great private university foundation envisioned by those who, with Agassiz in the early 1850s, had planned for the University of Albany, has yet to come into being, though the potentials exist in the Capital district of New York State for the joining of its private educational institutions and libraries and museums, into a true "Union University" capable of justifying even the optimism of an Eliphalet Nott. The ceremonial "Union University" which exists today, with its Chancellor who is also the President of Union College, its symbolically common graduating exercises, and its University Board of Governors, could yet become that "University for the times" Dr. Nott had hoped to create out of the State's bounty of lottery dollars. See: A. V. V. Raymond, *Union University*, I (1907), Chapter XXIX, pp. 435–443. See also: George E. Peterson, *The New England College in the Age of the University* (Amherst, 1964). Note this author's treatment of the idea that the post-Civil War colleges were justifying themselves as the educators of "the whole man," a task left to them by the increasingly impersonal, specializing, permissive universities. See also his review of the trial by the Union College Trustees of President E. N. Potter, pp. 100–108, 227–228.

16. Raymond, *Union University*, p. 407. See also: Henry Hope Reed, Jr., "The Affluent Legend of Hunter's Point," New York *Herald-Tribune* (magazine section) July 21, 1963. See also: "Merged Traffic Courts to Shift to Long Island City," in the Long Island City *Star-Journal*, April 19, 1961. In order to prevent the reversion of this land to Union College in 1961, when the Queens County courts were moved into the new Criminal Courts Building, Long Island City decided to move the Long Island City District Municipal Court, the Long Island City Magistrate's Court and Municipal Term from their rented quarters into the old Court House.

"Nott Avenue" as a Long Island City street name seems to have been first used on the map issued by G. W. and B. Colton, New York, 1866. It then paralleled 12th Avenue to the north and ran east-west for six blocks to Jackson Avenue. By 1888 it had crossed the Dutch Kill's Canal and had been extended east of Calvary Cemetery Avenue by three blocks.

By 1941 the name was bracketed with the name "44th Drive," a street then ending at Jackson Avenue. (Hagstrom Company, N. Y., 1941.) The Hagstrom Map of 1958 shows only "44th Drive," although it does show an "Annable Street," named for Mrs. Nott's nephew, manager in residence at Hunter Point for some years.

A Bibliographical Essay

I

WHEN Frank Parker Day, the eleventh President of Union College, and the author decided in 1932 to collaborate that year on writing the life of Eliphalet Nott, President Day said, "I'll buy a four-drawer file, and we'll go to work." That empty file was only a symbol of dozens to come, for thirty-five years ago Union College was seemingly without archives. The College, however, was no academic Topsy which had "just grow'd," for there was then even a massive three-volume *Union University*, published in 1907, to prove not only the College's legitimacy but its considerable accomplishments; and there was the *Memoirs of Eliphalet Nott, D.D., LL.D.* published in 1876. It was obvious, however, that both these loyal efforts were designed for the blazer-and-boater alumni of our decades of sensibility, both works compounded of carefully winnowed Trustees' Minutes, public records, bowdlerized correspondence, and the protective reminiscences of those who were concerned with creating an "image" of a college and of a man worthy of their patronage and their praises rather than for those concerned with a meaningful history or a meaningful "life" of one of the most remarkable college presidents in American educational history.

That empty file which Dr. Day purchased in 1932 was also a symbol of an institutional myopia which Union had long shared with all but a few American colleges whose roots, as do Union's, run deep into the soil of American life. Textbooks in American history weighed on our library shelves, and our history faculty kept their dates with the approved events, too often, however, insensitive to the record of American life written in the nature of the very buildings which housed them and their students and to the responses to American life of their own active and vocal trustees, presidents, faculty, and alumni who for more than 150 years have mirrored the American experience with an immediacy and an impact the record of which would have given life and excitement to the teaching of any course in American history with which it had been integrated.

It has taken more than thirty years to fill that file President Day had so hopefully purchased, and the dozens of other files which now stand with it in what are the still growing archives of Union College. President Day himself has now become a part of that record, as have his two successors, Presidents Dixon Ryan Fox and Carter Davidson, along with the complex and illuminating history of the way one American college reacted to war and depression, technological change and social upheaval, to trustee and faculty wisdom and blindness. These men, gone now, were themselves keenly aware of the teaching potential slowly developing in the vast array of long-scattered official documents, letters, diaries, and other bibliographical materials without which this biographer of Eliphalet Nott would have had to repeat the established pieties.

Hopefully the realization will come to Trustees and curriculum makers that the colleges themselves, not only Union College, but dozens of others, with their human, their educational, their economic, and their architectural history, with their changing responses to their regions and to the nation, are an untapped source for learning experiences which, when developed and made an appropriate part of the curriculum, will not only enlarge and make far more meaningful an undergraduate's four years on his campus, but will make him a better alumnus, and a better trustee, should he aspire to assume such a responsibility.

To those who may still think the records which reflect the life of an American college reflect too parochial a history to justify the scholarly attention of its faculty and students the author recommends a close reading of the bibliographical essays which conclude two recent studies of American educational history: Frederick Rudolph's *The American College and University: A History* (New York, 1962), and George E. Peterson's *The New England College in the Age of the University* (Amherst, 1964).

II

1. *The Union College Collection*:

From shoe boxes, unsorted piles of letters, documents, and ledgers gathered, until 1935, in the attic under the dome of the Nott-Potter Memorial, and from the attic of the Old Chapel of Union College came the material which, with the Trustees Minutes dating back to the founding of the Schenectady Academy in 1785, and with the records of the Union College Treasurer's office, now form the central collection of the Union College archives, housed at last in an appropriate vault and reading room in the Schaffer Library.

An unfortunately still separate but important collection of alumni, Trustee, and faculty biographical data and photographic material is in the keeping of the Alumni Secretary in Lamont House.

While the Union College collection is by no means fully catalogued much has been done by way of alphabetical, topical, and chronological indexing as library staff could be spared to do it, but the records on deposit at Union College of almost two centuries of Schenectady Academy and Union College history, of Schenectady town, city, and county history, and of the regional history of the Mohawk Valley and of the Capital District of New York State, has presented an archival task which still waits on additional professional help which can only be supplied by a Board of Trustees and its faculty advisors aware that their archives are, relatively, as significant as their laboratories.

2. *Manuscripts and Other Unpublished Material Prepared by Eliphalet Nott*:

Eliphalet Nott destroyed the journal he claimed he had kept until his third marriage in 1842. His sermons and occasional speeches which were in manuscript following his death, as well as his personal correspondence then in the possession of the third Mrs. Nott, were "arranged with [her] skillful hand" and then turned over to Charles VanSantvoord who, with Professor Tayler Lewis, prepared the *Memoirs of Dr. Nott*, published in 1876. (See: Introduction, *Memoirs of Dr. Nott*.) What was the nature of that lost material can be known only through the still further arranged and edited sampling of it which appears in the *Memoirs*. Much of this material which had been in Professor Lewis's custody was destroyed, it was reported, following his death.

An occasional letter bearing on personal matters has turned up among the papers of a few of Eliphalet Nott's many descendants, and these letters, and the names of those who have generously lent them, are noted in the appropriate chapter bibliographies. The considerable bulk of the Nott correspondence now gathered in the Union College archives bears almost exclusively on the affairs of the College and on those legal controversies and business concerns of Nott's which so intimately involved the College. The onion-skin letter books of the treasurers of Union College before the Civil War are a huge storehouse of Nott material; their smudged pages, kept in the decades of crude transfer processes (the "Zincophile Press"), are now an invitation to blindness.

Eliphalet Nott, in his own failure to expand much of his thinking into published form, made good his assertion that he believed his was an age for action; the age of literature, he told his associates, was in the future for which he and his generation must pave the way. There seem to be no complete surviving manuscript sermons, and only a few rough drafts or excerpts of his occasional speeches. His opening address at the church trial of the Reverend Hooper Cumming, entitled "On Slander," dated February 18, 1817, is in the Union College archives. There is also a fragment in the same collection of what appears to be a speech on liberty and oppression, prepared apparently for the occasion of General Louis Kossuth's visit to Schenectady in 1852. Unfortunately there are only student notes to tell us of Nott's famous course his seniors knew as "Kames." Although he had been often asked to publish those lectures which to his "young gentlemen" had seemed so "practical," nothing Eliphalet Nott himself prepared for this memorable course is known to have survived.

3. *Manuscript Records Bearing on Eliphalet Nott now at Union College*:

The fifteen-volume journal (the "Thinking Books") kept by Jonathan Pearson from 1832 through 1875, begun before his entrance as a Union College freshman and continued during most of his fifty years of association with Union as a student, faculty member, librarian, and treasurer, constitutes the single most intimate view we have of Eliphalet Nott and Union College for these critical years. Pearson's shifting reaction to Nott must be weighed with care, for it was governed by the clash of two quite different personalities. While each man tried to assess the other honestly, their differing intellectual and imaginative ranges too often led them to judgments which other evidence either modifies or cancels.

Professor and Treasurer Jonathan Pearson also kept a series of scrapbooks which he filled with a miscellaneous collection of newspaper clippings, college publications, student broadsides, and public notices which are invaluable in following Nott's career. These scrapbooks are only haphazardly indexed.

The *Minutes* of the Board of Trustees which are complete from the chartering of the College can be read as official history; if read, however, without the illumination of those other source documents and letters which were brought into the archives as this biography developed, the Trustees' *Minutes* are simply officialese masking significant developments.

The *Minutes* of the Faculty for the years of Nott's presidency are largely records of course attendance, discipline measures, and faculty lists of seniors recommended for graduation. Nott's relations with his tutors and professors were almost as "parental" as they were with his students, and decisions concerning curricular changes and College government were Nott's decisions, made only occasionally after consultation with the Trustees, or the faculty.

4. *Manuscript Material Bearing Directly on Eliphalet Nott as the "Philosopher of Caloric": The evolution of the Nott stove and the "S. S. Novelty".*

The development of the Nott stove is reported in detail by William John Keep of the Union College Class of 1865, in his "History of Heating Apparatus," written during his years as an engineer for the Michigan Stove Company; this manuscript review of stove development in America is now in the library of the Harvard Business School; a microfilm copy is in the Schaffer Library at Union College.

The manuscript diary kept by Professor Jonathan Pearson also contains extensive references to Nott's stove, the S.S.

Novelty, and to the Novelty Iron Works. Because Nott's affairs and College affairs are inextricably joined one finds frequent references to purchases and services Nott required as an inventor and the exploiter of his inventions throughout the pages of the Union College Letter Books.

The *Minutes* of the Managers of the Delaware and Hudson Company for the years Eliphalet Nott and his son, Howard, were associated with them in the development of the ferry boat *Essex* and the S.S. *Novelty* reveal much about the economic factors which spurred and then ended Nott's career as a steamboat developer.

Many of the patents issued to Eliphalet Nott, drawings for his stoves and steamboat boilers, grates, and machinery, and the specifications describing them are in the Union College Archives.

5. *Manuscript Records Involving Nott as the Superintendent of the Literature Lottery, in the Chancery Court Suits, and the New York State Legislative Investigations which Grew out of his Career as a Lottery Entrepreneur*:

The huge bulk of this material is in the Union College Archives where, in time, it will be fully catalogued. These records, so far as the author of this biography is concerned, were as an unknown country, the extent of which no one could have anticipated when he began his work. The author makes no pretense that he has mapped even its major paths without error, for here is the terrain which Nott's enemies said was so full of hazards it exhausted and then took the life of John Canfield Spencer who, as the apologist and the attorney for Eliphalet Nott, spent his last days in the old President's defense.

6. *Manuscript Material Bearing on Eliphalet Nott as a Mine Operator and Real Estate Speculator*

The day-to-day operations of the Bristol Copper Mine are recorded in the manuscript reports of the mine's managers now in the archives of the Connecticut State Library, Hartford, Connecticut; there is a photostat copy of these reports in the Union College Archives. Much of what we know about Nott's relations with the Bristol Copper Mine and with the Bald Mountain lime operation in Washington County, New York, is to be found in the references to them in the Pearson Diaries.

Nott as a real estate speculator at Stuyvesant Cove and at Hunter Point is reflected in the *Minutes* of the Union College Board of Trustees, in the Pearson diary, and in the letter and document files in the Union College Archives. Here also are the extensive records of the College agent for the Hunter Point Trust, consisting largely of the transactions involving sales of land and the improvements the Trust undertook at Hunter Point. (See: Book VIII, Chapters 1-2-4.)

Bibliography

ON ELIPHALET NOTT

Manuscripts

AT UNION COLLEGE, SCHENECTADY, N. Y.

"Bristol Copper Mine (Bristol, Conn.) Operational Record." Copy from the Connecticut State Library, Hartford, Conn. Union College Library.

Dailey, William N. P. "Rev. Eliphalet Nott, D.D. LLD. President of Union College 1804-1866: A Sketch of His Life." Copy, original for nomination of Dr. Nott to the Hall of Fame, June 29,1929. Union College Alumni Office.

————, "Eliphalet Nott: Data submitted to support nomination of Nott to the Hall of Fame of New York University, "April 20, 1939. Union College Library.

"Dr. Eliphalet Nott's Lectures to the Senior Class, 1832," "Professor Potter's Classification of Knowledge," "The Warning." Student notebook belonging to two members of the class of 1833, John Erwin and A. G. Lansing. Union College Library.

"Dr. Nott's Inventions." A miscellaneous group of drawings and specifications covering Dr. Nott's stoves and boilers. Union College Library.

"Dr. Nott's Private and Confidential Fund." Treasurer's record. Union College Library.

Hollister, S. D. Letter of May 12, 1913, to Waldron [Charles] re Dr. Nott's three-wheeled carriage. Union College Alumni Office.

"Hope." Fragment of an essay. Union College Library.

"Instructions Delivered to the Senior Class in Union College, Schenectady, N.Y., in 1828-29, by the Rev. Eliphalet Nott . . . President. Copied from Notes Taken by Wm. Soul and Henry Baldwin, Jun . . . Members of said Class . . . 1829." Union College Library.

"Liberty and Oppression" [title supplied], June 2, 1852. Union College Library.

Nott, Samuel [1754–1852]. "Extracts from the Autobiography of the Rev. Samuel Nott (b.1754 d.1852) . . . that Relate to
1. His brother, the Rev. Eliphalet Nott . . .
2. His son, the Rev. Samuel Nott, Jr . . .
3. His boyhood, especially references to his parents, comp. by Ralph Trumbull, Schenectady, 1932." Union College Library. (Complete manuscript of the autobiography is deposited in the library of the Connecticut Congregational House, Hartford, Conn.)

Nott, Sarah M. " 'Laws for My Pupils' of My Grandfather, Sam'l Nott, D.D., Who Died in Franklin." November 17, 1882. Union College Library.

Palmer, Thomas. "Diary or Daily Journal." Vol. I, August 20, 1843– September 30, 1844; Vol. II, October 1, 1844–May 4, 1846; Vol. III, May 5, 1846–December 21, 1847; Vol. IV, Jan. 1, 1852–December 31, 1853. Union College Library.

"Poetic Outburst." Fragment, n.d. Union College Library.

Spencer, John C. Papers, Union College Library.

Trumbull, Ralph. "Ancestry of Dr. Nott." N.d. Union College Library.

"Union College Faculty Minutes," 1799____. Union College Library.

"Union College Letter Books," ca. 1820–1870. Union College Library.

Union College Merit Books [title varies]. Union College Library.

Union College Treasurer's Books. Union College Library.

Union College "Board of Trustees' Minutes," 1795____, Union College Library.

Yates, John B. "Memorandum for Mr. Spencer, Esq." Union College Library.

AT OTHER LOCATIONS

Albany (N.Y.) First Presbyterian Church Trustees' Minutes.

Beck, T. Romeyn. Letters. New York State Library, Albany, N.Y.

Beekman Papers. New-York Historical Society, New York City.

Benedict, Rev. Joel. Papers. Plainfield (Conn.) Congregational Church.

Burt, Martin Van Buren. Diary. Owned by Mr. and Mrs. Richard Wright, 311 Montgomery Street, Syracuse, N.Y.

Cherry Valley Presbyterian Church Records, 1796. Otsego County National Bank, Cherry Valley, N.Y.

Correspondence of Howard Townsend to his mother, Mrs. Isaac Townsend, Albany, N.Y., 1841–1844. New-York Historical Society, New York City.

Eaton, Amos, Collection. New York State Library, Albany, N.Y.

Fish, Hamilton. Papers. Collections of the Library of Congress, Washington, D.C.

Franklin (Conn.) Congregational Church Papers, 1718–1932.

Jones, Samuel W. Diary, 1821–1855. Schenectady County Historical Society, Schenectady, N.Y.

Keep, William J. "History of Heating Apparatus." Baker Library, Harvard University Graduate School of Business Administration, Cambridge, Mass. Microfilm in Union College Library.

McIntyre, Archibald. Memorandum Book. New York Public Library, New York City.

MacLean Papers. Princeton University, Princeton, N.J.

Mills, Mariette Thompson. "Brought Up Abroad." (Noted in Potter, Frank H., *The Alonzo Potter Family*. Privately printed, 1923.)

Missionary Society of Connecticut. Papers. Congregational Church House, Hartford, and Connecticut State Library, Hartford.

Nott Family Bible. One page containing vital statistics in the Connecticut State Library, Hartford.

Nott, Samuel. "Autobiography." Congregational Church Library, Hartford.

Paige, Harriet Bower. Diary. 8 vols. Schenectady County Historical Society, Schenectady, N.Y.

Plainfield (Conn.) Congregational Church Records, 1793–1803. Plainfield, Conn.

Romeyn, Theodoric (Dirck). Papers. New York Public Library, New York City.

Wayland, Francis. Papers. Brown University, Providence, R. I.

Pictorial Materials

PORTRAITS OF ELIPHALET NOTT

At Union College

(A recent study of the material is found in Feigenbaum, Rita F., "The Early Portraits of Union College 1800–1850." M.A. thesis, 1967. Union College Library.)

Ezra Ames portrait painted c. 1820, owned by the Old South Association, Boston, and on loan to Union College, is mentioned in two letters and two articles:

> Unsigned letter of December 1, 1930, to Dr. Frank Parker Day, Union College Alumni Office.
>
> McKibben, F. P., letter of October 19, 1922, to Charles N. Waldron. Notice of this letter, Union College Alumni Office.
>
> "Mrs. LeRoy J. Weed Locates Portrait of Dr. Nott," [title supplied] *Union Alumni Monthly* (Schenectady, N.Y.) 20:133 (March 1931).
>
> [Reproduction of] *Union Alumni Monthly* (Schenectady, N.Y.) 21:[60] (January 1932).

Other Nott portraits at Union College are: an Ezra Ames of 1828; an Ezra Ames, previous to 1842; a Henry Inman of 1839; an unknown artist's, undated; a plaster bust by Henry Kirke Brown; Mrs. Augustus Fox mural, Schenectady, N.Y., Union College, Sigma Phi Society.

At Other Locations

Ezra Ames oil from life, circa 1814. Albany, N.Y., Albany Institute of History and Art.

Christian Schussele oil "Men of Progress," as of 1862. Washington, D.C., the West Wing of the White House.

John F. Weir, Oil, 1888, New York City, The University Club of New York City.

The Nott portraits are mentioned in:

"The Heroic Portrait," [Inman] *Union Alumni Monthly* (Schenectady, N.Y.) 3:97 (February 1914).

"More Portraits," *Union Alumni Monthly* (Schenectady, N.Y.) 28:257–258 (July–August 1939).

ELIPHALET NOTT DAGUERREOTYPES AND OTHER PICTORIAL REPRESENTATIONS.

Churchill, R. E., of Albany, N.Y., photograph. Union College Alumni Office.

Classbook of 1868, photograph; and classbook of 1884, photograph. Union College Alumni Office.

Evans, O. B., of Buffalo, N.Y., daguerreotype. Advertisement of his lithographic copy, January 4, 1856, and W. H. Seward's testimonial letter, "Pearson Scrapbooks," 3:389, 399. Union College Library.

Frick Art Reference Library, photograph. Union College Alumni Office.

Hislop, Codman, photograph, circa 1860–1863. Dorset, Vermont.

Mohawk Bank Note [$10.00] likeness referred to in the *Schenectady Reflector*, January 11, 1856, p. 2.

The Parthenon (Schenectady, N.Y., Union College) photograph for *The Parthenon* from an engraving by Asher B. Durand from the oil by Ezra Ames. Union College Alumni Office.

"Pearson Diary" (MS), mention of photograph of E. Nott and Mrs. Nott in entry for April 23, 1855. Union College Library.

Photograph included in a letter from Dr. Nott to W. W. Crannell, February 10, 1854. Union College Library.

Ripley, "Believe It or Not," cartoon featuring E. Nott, in *Union Alumni Monthly* (Union College, Schenectady, N.Y.) 28:163 (April 1939).

Sartain, John, engraving. Photograph of the engraving appears on endpapers of Jaffe, Bernard, *Men of Science in America: The Story of American Science Told Through the Lives and Achievements of Twenty Outstanding Men from Earliest Colonial Times to the Present Day*, rev. ed. New York: Simon and Schuster, 1958.

University Club portrait in photographic reproduction, *Union Alumni Monthly* (Schenectady, N.Y.) 28:78-79 (January 1939).

Valois, E., New York City, photograph. Union College Alumni Office.

Various poses in photographs taken at various times, photographers unidentified. Union College Alumni Office and Union College Library.

Walker, John, photograph of the Schussele painting. In "American Masters in the National Gallery," *National Geographic Magazine* 94:295-324 (September 1948).

DR. NOTT'S GRAVE

Photograph. Union College Alumni Office.

NOTT, URANIA E.

Photograph, "taken in the fifties or before." Small card photo, the gift of Mrs. K. C. Colwell of Wyoming, Ill. Union College Library.

Published materials

WORKS BY ELIPHALET NOTT

"Account of an Eclipse," *The Port Folio*, Fourth Series, 5:29-32 (January 1818).

An Address, Delivered to the Candidates for the Baccalaureate in Union College, at the Anniversary Commencement, 30 July 1806. Cambridge: W. Hilliard, 1806.

An Address, Delivered to the Candidates for the Baccalaureate, in Union College, at the Anniversary Commencement, July 30, 1806. Schenectady: John L. Stevenson, n.d.

––––––– in *The Addresses, Delivered to the Candidates for the Baccalaureate at the Anniversary Commencements in Union College* . . . Schenectady: Riggs & Stevens, 1814.

––––––– in *Miscellaneous Works.* Schenectady: Wm. J. M'Cartee, printed by Ryer Schermerhorn, 1810.

––––––– [Review of] in *The Christian's Magazine: Designed To Promote the Knowledge and Influence of Evangelical Truth and Order*, 1: 112-119, 2nd ed. [1806].

An Address, Delivered to the Candidates for the Baccalaureate, in Union College, at the Anniversary Commencement, July 29, 1807. Albany: Printed by Websters and Skinner, at their bookstore, in the Whitehouse, corner of State and Pearl streets, 1807.

"Address to the Alumni of Union College at their Celebration of the Fiftieth Anniversary of his Presidency, July 25, 1854," in *The Celebration of the Fiftieth Anniversary of Dr. Nott's Presidency of Union College, July 25, 1854.* Schenectady: G. Y. Vandebogert, 1854, pp. [53]–79.

The Addresses, Delivered to the Candidates for the Baccalaurate at the Anniversary Commencements in Union College . . . Schenectady: Riggs & Stevens, 1814.

Almanac [?] "Letter from Rev. Eliphalet Nott, D.D., Dated Jan. 1861," in "Schools as They Were Sixty Years Ago," *American Journal of Education*, 13:132–144 (March 1863).

"American Lottery: Or System of Arithmetical Chances: Being a Method of Designating, with Despatch and Impartiality certain [Numb] ers as Prizes to the Exclusion of Certain Other Numbers Similarly Situated, according to Uniform and Intelligible Rules, and yet in such a Manner that the Result Shall neither be Subject to Human____or Human Control," [Patent]. Union College Library.

Analysis of Hexameter. Attributed to Nott in contemporary manuscript note above caption-title, in "Catalogue of Books in the Union College Library," compiled (about 1858?); n.p., n.d. Consulted at the Beinecke Rare Book and Manuscript Library, Yale University, New Haven, Conn. [Kingsley Miscellaneous Pamphlets, v.22, no. 4].

"Astronomical Part by 'Gabriel Goodweather' " [?], *Phinney's Calendar: Or Western Almanack For the Year of Our Lord 1798* . . . Elihu Phinney [1798–].

————in Severance, Frank H. "The Story of Phinney's Western Almanack." *Buffalo Historical Society Publications*, 24:343–358 (1920).

The Correspondence between Dr. Nott & Dr. Hickok in Reference to the Appointment of the Latter as Vice-President &C., of Union College, and his Letter of Acceptance, and the Action Thereon of the Board of Trustees. Schenectady, N.Y.: Cyrus Thayer, 1859.

Counsels to Young Men on the Formation of Character, and the Principles which Lead to Success and Happiness in Life: Being Addresses Principally Delivered at the Anniversary Commencements in Union College. New York: Harper & Brothers, 1860 [c.1840] [eds. : 1841, 1842, 1850, 1855, 1856].

"Curious Observations on Light, during the Late Total Eclipse of the Sun. From a Letter of the Rev. Eliphalet Nott, D.D., President of Union College, to the Rev. Samuel Miller, D.D. Dated Schenectady, October 6, 1806, and Communicated by the Learned Writer to Dr. Mitchell," *Monthly Anthology and Boston Review*, 4: 55–56 (January 1807).

A Discourse Delivered in the North Dutch Church, in the City of Albany, Occasioned by the ever to be Lamented Death of General Alexander

Hamilton, By Eliphalet Nott . . . Albany: Printed by C. R. and G. Webster, 1804. "Appendix," giving the will of Hamilton, his reasons for meeting Burr, and Bishop Moore's and Dr. Mason's accounts of his death, p.[33]-40.

A Discourse Delivered in the North Dutch Church, in the City of Albany Occasioned by the Ever To Be Lamented Death of General Hamilton, July 29, 1804. By Eliphalet Nott, A.M. Pastor of the Presbyterian Church in Said City. Published by Request. [2nd ed.?] Albany: Printed by Charles R. and George Webster, at their Bookstore, corner of State and Pearl Streets, 1804.

A Discourse Delivered in the North Dutch Church in the City of Albany. Occasioned by the Ever To Be Lamented Death of General Alexander Hamilton. Hanover: Moses Davis, 1804.

A Discourse, Delivered in the North Dutch Church, in the City of Albany, Occasioned by the Ever to be Lamented Death of General Alexander Hamilton, July 29, 1804. By Eliphalet Nott . . . 3rd ed. Salem: Printed by J. Cushing, 1804.

A Discourse Delivered in the North Dutch Church, in the City of Albany, Occasioned by the Ever To Be Lamented Death of General Alexander Hamilton, July 29, 1804 . . . Stockbridge: Re-printed by Heman Willard, Sept. 1804.

A Discourse, Delivered in the City of Albany, Occasioned by the . . . *Death of Gen. Alexander Hamilton, July 29, 1804. By Eliphalet Nott* . . . *To which is added, a paper, Written by Gen. Hamilton: containing, his Motives and Reflections on the Causes that have Led to This Fatal Catastrophe. Also—His Will, Bishop Moore's Letter, and a Letter by the Rev. Mr. Mason.* Greenfield, Mass.: J. Denio, 1805.

A Discourse, on the Death of Gen. Alexander Hamilton, Delivered in the North Dutch Church of Albany, July 29, 1804 . . . 4th ed. Boston: Printed by David Carlisle, 1805.

A Discourse on the Death of General Alexander Hamilton, Delivered in the North Dutch Church of Albany, July 29, 1804. By Eliphalet Nott . . . *Also as an Appendix, His Address, Delivered to the Candidates for the Baccalaureate, at Union College.* Augusta [Me.] : Printed by Peter Edes & Son, 1805.

A Discourse, Delivered in the North Dutch Church, in the City of Albany, Occasioned by the Ever to Be Lamented Death of Gen. Alexander Hamilton, July 29, 1804 . . . 3rd ed. Albany: Websters and Skinner, 1806.

A Discourse Occasioned by the Death of General Alexander Hamilton, Delivered in the North Dutch Church, in the City of Albany, July 29, 1804. By Rev. Eliphalet Nott, D.D. Schenectady: Re-published by G. Y. Van Debogart, 1853.

_____ in Coleman, William. *A Collection of the Facts and Documents, Relative to the Death of Major-General Alexander Hamilton, with Comments: Together with the Various Orations, Sermons, and Eulogies, that have been Published or Written on His Life and Character* . . . New York: Hopkins and Seymour, 1804, p. 104–131 [Reprinted by Houghton, Mifflin and Company, 1904, pp. 108–137].

_____in Nott, Eliphalet. *Miscellaneous Works*. Schenectady: Wm. M'Cartee, 1810.

_____ in Williston, Ebenezer Bancroft, comp. *Eloquence of the United States*. Middletown, Conn: E. & H. Clark, 1827, v. 5, p. [207]–229.

_____as "Nott, (E.), Lijkrede, naar 2 Samuel 1:19b., gehouden in de Holl. kerk in de stad Albany, ter gelegenheid van den altoos betreurensw. dood van Alexander Hamilton, op den 29en Julij 1804." Uit het Eng. vert. door S. A. BUDDINGH. *Amst.,van Bakkenes en Veenhuysen. (L. van Bakkenes en Co.)*1836. [Was in N.Y. State Library, destroyed by 1913 fire.] From *Alphabetische Naamlijst Van Boeken, Plaat en Kaartwerken* . . . Amsterdam: C. L. Brinkman, 1858, p. 483.

_____in Fish, Henry Clay. *Pulpit Eloquence of the Nineteenth Century: being supplementary to the History and Repository of Pulpit Eloquence, Deceased Divines; and containing Discourses of Eminent Living Ministers in Europe and America, with Sketches Biographical and Descriptive* . . . New York: M. W. Dodd, 1857; Dodd & Mead, 1874, p. 378–393.

_____in Hillard, George S. *The Sixth Reader: Consisting of Extracts in Prose and Verse, with Biographical and Critical Notices of the Authors, for the use of Advanced Classes in Public and Private Schools* . . . Boston: Brewer and Tileston; Philadelphia: Martin and Randall, 1863, p. 321–323.

_____in Johnston, Alexander ed. *Representative American Orations to Illustrate American Political History*, 3 vols, New York and London: G. P. Putnam's Sons, 1844, vol. 1, p. 117–128.

_____in Raymond, Andrew Van Vranken. *Union University: Its History, Influence, Characteristics and Equipment, With the Lives and Works of Its Founders, Benefactors, Officers, Regents, Faculty, and the Achievements of Its Alumni*. New York: Lewis Publishing Co., 1907, vol. I, p. 113–132.

A Discourse Delivered in the Presbyterian Church, in Albany, the Fourth of July, A.D., 1801: At the Celebration of the Twenty-Fifth Anniversary of American Independence . . . Albany: Charles R. and George Webster, 1801.

_____in *Miscellaneous Works*. Schenectady: Wm. J. M'Cartee, printed by Ryer Schermerhorn, 1810.

A Discourse, Delivered in the Presbyterian Church, in the City of Albany, before the Ladies' Society, for the Relief of Distressed Women and Children, March 18, 1804 . . . Albany: Charles R. and George Webster [?1804]; "Appendix, by a Friend [obituary Mrs. Sally Nott]" p. [37]-39.

Federal Money: Being a Sketch of the Money of Account of united America, by Eliphalet Nott, A.M. . . . *Principal of Cherry-Valley Academy. First Edition, For the Use of Schools.* Cooperstown: Printed by Elihu Phnney [sic] for the author, M,DCC,XCVII.

First Lessons in English Composition: Or, a Help to Young Writers, 6th ed. New-York: Saxton & Miles, 1846.

"Gambling," in *Atkinson's Casket or Gems of Literature, Wit and Sentiment.* no. 2, February 1833, p. 71.

"Gospel Charity," in Lyman, Asa, ed. *The American Reader Containing Elegant Selections in Prose and Poetry: Designed for the Improvement of Youth in the Art of Reading and Speaking with Propriety and Beauty, and for the Cultivation of a Correct Moral Taste,* . . . 2nd ed. Portland, Maine, 1811, p. 252-256.

"Lectures on Temperance Delivered at Schenectady, N.Y. at the Request of the Schenectady Temperance Society . . . during the Winter of 1838-1839," *The Enquirer Devoted to Free Discussion as to the Proper Use of Alcoholic Poisons.* (Albany, N.Y.) 1:[147]-180 (August 1846).

————— *The Enquirer* . . . vol. 1, no. 4, bound with plates, p. [147]- 180 (August 1846).

Lectures on Temperance. Albany: E. H. Pease & Co., 1847.

Lectures on Temperance: with an Introduction by Tayler Lewis . . . Amasa McCoy, ed. New York: Sheldon, Blakeman & Co.; Boston: Gould & Lincoln; Chicago: S. C. Griggs & Company; London: Trubner & Co., 1857.

————— [reviewed in] *North American Review,* 85:572-573 (October 1857).

Lectures on Temperance, by Eliphalet Nott . . . *with an Introduction, by Tayler Lewis* . . . *edited by Amasa McCoy* . . . Hamilton, C. W., A. M. Moffat & Co., 1858.

Lectures on Bible Temperance, with an Introduction by Tayler Lewis. English edition. London: Trubner & Co., 1863.

————— *A Review of Dr. Nott's Lectures on Biblical Temperance: from the "Alliance News," June 1863.* Manchester: Printed at the *Guardian* Offices, n.d.

Lectures on Biblical Temperance, 2nd English ed., People's Edition. London: Trubner & Co., 1866.

—————[a planned appendix for] in Stuart Moses. *Scriptural View of the Wine-Question in a Letter to the Rev. Dr. Nott* . . . New-York: Leavitt, Trow & Company, 1848.

_____[excerpts] in Delavan, Edward C. *Temperance Essays and Selections from Different Authors . . . also a Treatise on Tobacco, by General John H. Cocke, . . .* Albany: 1865, p. [28], [30], 135-136.

Miscellaneous Works . . . With an appendix. Schenectady: Wm. J. M'Cartee; Ryer Schermerhorn, printer, 1810.

[Contents:] A Discourse Delivered . . . the Fourth of July, 1801.

A Discourse Delivered . . . in Albany to the Ladies'
    Society for the Relief . . . March 18, 1804.

A Discourse . . . Occasioned by the . . . Death of
    General Alexander Hamilton, July 29, 1804.

A Sermon Preached before the General Assembly . . .
    May 19, 1806 . . .

Baccalaureate Addresses, 1805, 1806, 1807.

A Star in the East: a Sermon . . . Feb. 26, 1809 . . . by
    the Rev. Claudius Buchanan . .

_____[reviewed in] *The Literary and Philosophical Repertory: Embracing Discoveries and Improvements in the Physical Sciences; the Liberal and Fine Arts; Essays Moral and Religious: Occasional Notices and Reviews of New Publications; and Articles of Miscellaneous Intelligence.* Edited by a Number of Gentlemen. Middlebury, Vt.: 1:[1]-34 (April, 1812); 1:118-137 (November, 1812).

"Noble Sentiments," *American Penny Magazine and Family Newspaper,* 1:420-421 (August 9, 1845).

"On Card Playing," in Welles, E. G., comp. *The Orator's Guide: Or Rules for Speaking and Composing: From the best Authorities.* Philadelphia: G. L. Austin, 1822, p. 70-75.

"On the Power and Influence of an Individual," in Welles, E. G., comp. *The Orator's Guide: Or Rules . . .* Philadelphia: G. L. Austin, 1822. p. 68-70.

"On Slander," [title supplied] in "Moderator's Address," *Official Documents of the Presbytery of Albany Exhibiting the Trials of the Rev. John Chester and Mr. Mark Tucker: Together with the Whole Case of the Rev. Hooper Cumming.* Schenectady: Henry Stevens & Co., 1818, p. 19-25.

_____[mentioned] in Munsell, Joel. *The Annals of Albany,* Albany: J. Munsell, 1855, v. 6, p. 229.

"Oration on Duelling," in Lyman, Asa, ed. *The American Reader Containing Elegant Selections in Prose and Poetry: Designed for the Improvement of Youth in the Art of Reading and Speaking with Propriety and Beauty, and for the Cultivation of a Correct Moral Taste, . . .* 2nd ed. Portland, Me.: 1811, p. 208-217.

"Parental Duties," *Germantown* (Pa.) *Telegraph,* November 12, 1845, p. 1, col. 6.

"President Nott's Address," in *The First Semi-Centennial Anniversary of Union College, Celebrated July 22, 1845*. Albany: W. C. Little and Co.; Schenectady: I. Riggs, 1845, p. 92–97.

The Resurrection of Christ. A Series of Discourses . . . with an Introduction, and Notes by Tayler Lewis. New York: Scribner, Armstrong & Co., 1872.

"The Savior," *Atkinson's Casket or Gems of Literature, Wit and Sentiment*, no. 4, April 1832, p. 180.

"Sentiments of Eliphalet Nott, D.D., on Duelling," in Sabine, Lorenzo. *Notes on Duels and Duelling, Alphabetically Arranged, with a Preliminary Historical Essay*. Boston: Crosby, Nichols and Company, 1859, p. 360.

"Sermon by the Rev. Dr. Nott, President of Union College," [delivered in South Dutch Church, New York City] *New York Daily Tribune*, January 23, 1854.

A Sermon Preached before the General Assembly of the Presbyterian Church in the United States of America: by Appointment of their Standing Committee of Missions, May 19, 1806 . . . Philadelphia, Jane Aitken, 1806.

"Seventeen Letters Patent." Union College Library.

————in Keep, William J. "Dr. Nott the Inventor," *Union University Quarterly*, 1:249–252 (February 1905).

[Nott?] *Syllabus of a Course of Lectures on Chemistry: in Four Parts*, pt. 1, Schenectady, N.Y.: I. Riggs, 1825.

Tribute to the Memory of Mrs. Mary L. Sprague, Wife of W. B. Sprague, Pastor of the Second Presbyterian Church in Albany. Albany: Packard and Van Benthuysen, printers, 1837.

Trust Deed, from Eliphalet Nott and Wife, to the Trustees of Union College. [n.p., n.d.].

"What Hath God Wrought? A Narrative of the Revival of Religion within the Bounds of the Presbytery of Albany in the Year 1820," *Albany N.Y. Presbyterian Church Pamphlets*, 2nd ed. Philadelphia; S. Probasco, [?1821].

What Hath God Wrought? A Narrative of the Revival of Religion, Within the Bounds of the Presbytery of Albany, in the Year 1820, 2nd ed. Philadelphia: S. Probasco, n.d. [Copy in the Union College Library.]

WORKS BY OTHER WRITERS

Articles and Reviews

"An Abstract of the Laws of Union College (Under President Nott, 1840)," "Laws of Union College, Under President Webster, 1890. Unabridged," *The Concordiensis* (Schenectady,), 14:[47]–48 (1890).

"An Abused Trust," *Atlas* (New York), March 16, 1867.

Aitken, Hugh G. J. "Yates and McIntyre: Lottery Managers," *The Journal of Economic History*, 13:36–57 (Winter 1953).

Alexander, Robert C. "The Wisdom of Dr. Nott: Chips from the Lecture Book of the Great Educator." *The Concordiensis*, January 18, 1893, p. [3]–6; February 1, 1893, p. [3]–6; Febraury 15, 1893, p. [1]–5.

Alumnus. "Reminiscences of Eliphalet Nott, D.D. LL.D.," *Union College Magazine* (Schenectady), 10:36–41 (June 1872).

"Anecdote of Dr. Nott, of Union College," *Harbinger, Devoted to Social and Political Progress*, 4:90 (January 16, 1847).

Banks, H. S. "Reminiscences and Studies of the Class of 1829, Union College," *The Concordiensis*, 14:[141]–143 (May 1891).

Beugge, Walter J. "Mother of Fraternities," *Brooklyn Central* (Central Branch, Brooklyn and Queens Y.M.C.A.), March 3, 1933, p. 5–6, 22–23.

Bischoff, Al. "Nott Started as President at 31," *The Concordiensis*, October 20, 1931, p. 1, 3.

"Botany Bay," *Union Alumni Monthly* (Schenectady), 27:178–179 (April 1938).

Brewster, James. "Eliphalet Nott as a Steamboat Owner and Shipbuilder," *Union Alumni Monthly*, 24:48–53 (December 1934).

"A Brief Memoir of the Reverend Dr. Nott [from the Parthenon Magazine of Union College]," *North American Magazine*, 2:220–222 (August 1833).

Cavert, Samuel M. "A Glimpse into Union's Past," *The Garnet* (Schenectady), 1910, p. 9–13.

"Centenary," *Union Alumni Monthly*. 4:25–27 (December 1914).

"A Centennial," *Union Alumni Monthly*, 3:33–36.

"College Commencements. Union College. The Semi-Centennial of Dr. Nott's Presidency," *The New York Times*, July 28, 1854.

"College Rules in 1818: Strict Discipline During the Early Administration of Dr. Nott," *The Concordiensis*, April 18, 1901, p. 6–7.

Cowley, W. H. "Two Gentlemen of Union," *American Scientist*, Summer 1940, p. [69]–73.

Cruikshank, J. C. "Reminiscences of the Class Graduating at Union College, Schenectady, 1834," *The Concordiensis*, 13:78–80 (March 1890).

[Dailey, William N. P.] W.N.P.D. "Antiquarian," *Union Alumni Monthly*, 6:67–68 (December 1916).

Davidson, Carter, "Three Eras of Higher Education," *Journal of Higher Education*, 19:289–294 (June 1948).

Day, Frank Parker. "Eliphalet Nott," *School and Society*, 29:625–632 (May 1929).

"The Days of '46," *Union Alumni Monthly*, 18:101–104 (February 1929).

"Dr. Holmes Scores One on Dr. Nott," *The Concordiensis*, January 16, 1895, p. 12.

"Dr. Nott," *New York Tribune*, January 31, 1866.

"Dr. Nott Again," *Union Alumni Monthly*, 17:100-101 (February 1928).

"Dr. Nott on the Ministry," *The Concordiensis*, April 20, 1901, p. 5.

"Dr. Nott or the Students of Union College," *Union College Magazine*, 11:67-71 (November 1872).

"Dr. Nott, the Educator," *Union Alumni Monthly*, 16:222-223 (June 1927).

"Dr. Nott, The Inventor," *The Garnet*, 1894, p. 173-175.

"Dr. Nott the Inventor," *Union Alumni Monthly*, 18:15-17 (November 1928).

"Dr. Nott's Opinion on Library Hours," [title supplied] *Union Alumni Monthly*, 27:52 (December 1937).

"Dr. Nott's 76th Birth Day," *Union College Magazine*, 12:[3]-7 (November 1873).

"E. Nott's Chariot" [title supplied], illustrated, *Union Alumni Monthly*, 9:[255] (July-August 1920) and 18:[1] (November 1928).

"Editorial" [on courses], *The Concordiensis*, 14:74 (January 1891).

Edwards, Wakeman W. "A Reminiscence," *The Concordiensis*, 12:74-76 (February 1889).

"Eliphalet Again," *Union Alumni Monthly*, 22:4-5 (November 1932).

"Eliphalet Nott," *The Concordiensis*, February 13, 1909, p. 9.

"Eliphalet Nott," by A. C. S. *The Fascicle: or Little Bundle of Thoughts* (Wilbraham, Mass., published by the Young Ladies' Literary Society of the Wesleyan Academy), 1846, p. 22-26.

"Eliphalet Nott," *Hartford Pearl and Literary Gazette* (Hartford, Conn.), 4:[131-14 (August 27, 1834).

"Eliphalet Nott, D.D.," *American Literary Magazine*, 4:523-528 (March 1849).

"Eliphalet Nott, D.D. LL.D. 1804-1866," *The Garnet*, 1936, p. 26.

"Eliphalet Nott, D.D. LL.D: Abridged from The Parthenon," *American Magazine of Useful and Entertaining Knowledge*, 3:317-318 (May 1837).

Eliphalet Nott Highway. "Facsimile of an act of the Connecticut Legislature," *Union Alumni Monthly*, v. 22, cover illustration April 1933.

"[Fiftieth] Anniversary of Dr. Nott's Presidency," *New-York Daily Tribune*, 27 July, 1854.

"Fifty Years Ago," *The Garnet*, 1899, p. 146.

"First Fifty Years," *The Garnet*, 1895, p. 175-183; "Second Fifty Years," *The Garnet*, 1895 p. 184-189.

"Flashlight on Science," *The Scranton Republican* (Scranton, Pa.), March 26, 1925.

Flint, Timothy. "Original Papers," *The Athenaeum: Journal of English and Foreign Literature, Science, and the Fine Arts*, September 19, 1835, p. 714-716.

Flint, Weston. "Our Washington Letter," *The Concordiensis*, January 16, 1895, p. [3]-4.

Giffin, N. C. "Eliphalet Nott, D.D. LL.D. Reminiscences," *The Concordiensis*, February 9, 1910, p. 13; February 16, 1910, p. 13; March 16, 1910, p. 12.

Gray, John G. "A Disciple of Dr. Nott," *The Concordiensis*, April 12, 1893, p. [3]-5.

Green, Andrew Heatley. "Eliphalet Nott, " *The Concordiensis*, November 2, 1892, p. 17.

H[ale] E[dward] E. "First Lessons in English Composition: or a Help to Young Writers by E. Nott, D.D.," [title supplied] *Union Alumni Monthly*, 19:235-236 (June 1930).

"*Harper's Magazine*, June 1855," [excerpt] *The Concordiensis*. Commencement Number, 1892, p. 175.

Hislop, Codman, " 'A Loud and Awful Warning' : Eliphalet Nott on the Death of Alexander Hamilton," *New-York Historical Society Quarterly*, 40:5-19 (January 1956).

————, "The S. S. Novelty," *New-York Historical Society Quarterly*, 49:327-340 (October 1965).

————, and Harold A. Larrabee, eds. "Opinions of the Late Dr. Nott Respecting Books, Studies and Orators," *Union Alumni Monthly*, supplement March 1933.

Hitchcock, O. B. "Concerning Dr. Nott," *The Concordiensis*, January 15, 1896, p. 15.

Holmes, Oliver Wendell. "The Hot Season," *Union Alumni Monthly*, 21:270 (July-August 1932).

Hulbert, E. M. "Copper Mining in Connecticut," *Connecticut Quarterly: An Illustrated Magazine, Devoted to the Literature, History and Picturesque Features of Connecticut*, 3:[23]-32.

"In Memory of Dr. Nott," *The Concordiensis*, April 7, 1906, p. 9.

"The Inaugural Response of Doctor Potter," *Union College Magazine* 11:75-81 (November 1872).

Johnston, George A. "A Page from the History of the Past," *The Concordiensis*, February 27, 1895, p. [3]-4.

Jones, Leonard Chester, "Dr. Nott and the Fundamentalists," *Union Alumni Monthly*, 16:69-70 (January 1927).

Landon, Judson S. "Dr. Nott the Educator," *Union University Quarterly*, 1:143-152 (November 1904).

Lansing, Gertrude, ed. *Three Addresses Delivered at Ashford, Connecticut, October 21, 1933*. Litchfield, Conn.: The Enquirer Press [1934]. "Opening Address by Rev. George C. Chappell on the Site of Birthplace of Eliphalet Nott"; "An Address by Dr. Edward Ellery Presenting to the

State of Connecticut the Memorial Boulder and Tablet, a Gift of the Connecticut Alumni of Union College in Memory of Eliphalet Nott, President of Union College 1804-1866"; "An Address by Governor Cross accepting for the State of Connecticut the Monument and Park and Dedicating the Eliphalet Nott Memorial Highway near Warrenville, Connecticut."

Larrabee, Harold A. *Dr. Nott's Duel: Some Shots in the Dark at Union's History.* Privately printed, 1939.

————, "Electives Before Eliot," *Harvard Alumni Bulletin,* 42:[893]-897 (April 26, 1940).

"The Lasting Influence of Dr. Nott," *The Garnet,* 1896, p. 198-202.

"Legend of Dr. Nott," *The Garnet,* 1899, p. 150.

[Lewis, Tayler.] "Dr. Nott," [copied from the *New York Tribune]* *Schenectady Daily Union* (Schenectady, N.Y.), January 31, 1866, p. 2.

"A Life of Seward," *Union Alumni Monthly,* 1:14-15 (January 1912).

"The Lottery in College Edification," *The Concordiensis,* December 1889, p. 14.

"Memorabilia," *Union Alumni Monthly,* 1:24-26 (January 1912).

"Memorial of Dr. Nott," [re the affairs of Union College] *New York State Senate Journal,* 25 March 1853.

"Minerva and the Greeks," *Union Alumni Monthly,* 29:59-61 (January 1940).

"Miss Helen E. Keep Gives Mr. Ford a Dr. Nott Stove," [title supplied] *Union Alumni Monthly,* 21:35 (December 1931).

"Moses," *The Garnet,* 1896, p. 207-208.

"Moses Viney," *The Concordiensis,* January 15, 1909, p. [5]-6.

"Moses Viney," *The Garnet,* 1910, p. 279-284.

"Nott on the Eclipse of 1806," [title supplied] *Union Alumni Monthly,* 1:15 (January 1912).

Nott Memorial Number, Union University Quarterly, 1:[121]-252 (November 1904). [The speeches of Frederick W. Seward, Rt. Rev. Henry C. Potter, Judson S. Landon, Dr. Horace B. Silliman, Judge Charles C. Nott, David Murray, Dr. Nelson Millard, Dr. Sheldon Jackson, Samuel R. Thayer, and President Andrew V. V. Raymond].

"Nott's Lectures," *Meliora: a Quarterly Review of Social Science in its Ethical, Economical, and Ameliorative Aspects,* 6:150.

"Nott's Presidency," [title supplied] *Union Alumni Monthly,* 29:28 (December 1939).

"Nott Memorial Highway," [title supplied] *Union Alumni Monthly,* 22:107 (February 1933).

"Nott Stove," [title supplied] *Union University Quarterly,* 4:182-183 (November 1907).

"Now I Axe You," [cartoon] *The Concordiensis*, February 23, 1929, p. 5.

An Old Alumnus. "From Dr. Nott," *The Garnet*, 1898, p. 161.

"The Old Nott Elm," *The Concordiensis*, January 21, 1908, p. 11.

"Our Mothers," *Union Alumni Monthly*, 4:106-107 (February 1915).

Parker, Robert B., Jr. "Spirit of Hallowe'en Neglected at Union," *The Concordiensis*. October 23, 1928, p. 3.

"The Payne Gate," *Union Alumni Monthly*, 1:1-7 (November 1911).

Peck, Luther W. "Nott's Lectures on Temperance," *Methodist Quarterly Review*, (Fourth series vol. 10) 40:441-452, July 1858.

Phelps, Egbert. "Recollections of Eliphalet Nott," *Western Monthly*, 4:35-43 (July 1870).

"Phi Beta Kappa," *Union Alumni Monthly*, 3:146-148 (April 1914).

Pratt, John W. "Governor Seward and the New York School Controversy, 1840-1842: A Milestone in the Advance of Nonsectarian Public Education," *New York History*, 42:351-364 (October 1961).

"President Nott," *The Concordiensis* October 15, 1902, p. 11-12.

"President Nott's Discipline," *The Concordiensis*, February 3, 1904, p. 7.

"Presidential Lectures," *Union Alumni Monthly*, 10:69-70 (January 1921).

"The Presidents of Union College," *The Concordiensis*, April 29, 1903, p. [5]-7.

"A Reminiscence of Dr. Nott," *The Concordiensis*, 9:51 (February 1886).

"Resolution on Dr. Nott," *New York State Senate Journal*, February 1, 1866.

"Rev. Eliphalet Nott, D.D. LL.D.," *Union College Magazine*, 2:94-98 (March 1862).

"Revered President Extolled," *The Concordiensis*, October 1, 1904, p. [5]-9.

Rice, Alexander H. "Reminiscences: the Hon. Alexander H. Rice '49, Ex-Governor of Massachusetts Writes of the Days of Dr. Nott," *The Concordiensis*, November 21, 1894, p. [3]-6.

Rice, Edwin W. "A Nott Bibliography," *Union University Quarterly*, 1:206-210 (November 1904).

[Richmond, Charles Alexander.] "Richmond Speaks on 'Payne at Union,'" *The Concordiensis*, May 8, 1923, p. 1, 2, 3.

Ripton, B. H. [report of Dean Ripton's address to the Men's Club of the First Reformed Church] "Dr. Nott Lived Too Many Years," [?Schenectady, N.Y.] newspaper clipping, n.d.[? 1933], Union College Alumni Office.

Roberts, George S. "A Connecticut Educator's Influence on Union College: The Constitution State Contributes Many of America's Ablest Educationists—Story of the Distinguished Nott Family Told." *Connecticut Magazine*, 9:[549]-554 (1905).

Rotundo, Joseph. "Eliphalet Nott," *Union Alumni Monthly*, 21:74-79 (January 1932).

[Sanborn, E. D., ed.] "Opinions of the Late Dr. Nott Respecting Books, Studies, and Orators," *Atlantic Monthly*, 20:527–532 (November 1867).

Scott, W. "Great American College Presidents. 1. Eliphalet Nott of Union College," *The People: Issued in the Interest of Free, Universal, and Equal Education*. 10:[1]–3 (March-May 1908).

"Situation of Union College," *The Concordiensis*, May 1887, p. 106–107.

Stillman, William J. "Dr. Nott of Union College," [*Autobiography of a Journalist*, by William James Stillman. 2 vols. 1901. Houghton, Mifflin & Co. . . .] *The Living Age*, 230:[61]–64 (Supplement July 6, 1901).

————, "Union in the Forties," *The Concordiensis*, February 28, 1900, p. [5]–6.

Strong, Edwin Atson. "A Great Teacher," *Union Alumni Monthly*, 2:69–73 (January 1913).

"Temperance," *Union College Magazine*, 10:17–18 (June 1872).

"That Lottery," *Union Alumni Monthly*, 2:154–155 (March 1913).

Townsend, F. DeP. "The History of Union College," *The Garnet*, 1920, p. 179–181.

"The Union College Lottery," *The Concordiensis*, October 24, 1894, p. [3]–6.

"Union College: Organization and Early History," *The Garnet*, 1884, p. 20–26.

"Union Eighty Years Ago," *Union Alumni Monthly*, 27:16–17 (November 1937).

"Union in 1802," *Union Alumni Monthly*, 15:53–58 (December 1925).

Van Schaick, John, Jr. "The College Life of Secretary Seward at Union," *The Concordiensis*, March 19, 1892, p. 108–112.

"Venerable Men," *Union Alumni Monthly*, 1:17–18 (January 1912).

"View of the City of Albany," [? with the *S.S. Novelty*] *American Journal of Scientific and Useful Knowledge*, Vol. 1, no. 1, 1835.

[Waldron, Charles N.] "Minutes of the Last Meeting," *Union Alumni Monthly*, 27:212 (May 1938).

————, " 'Twas Here the Old Alumni Sat,' " *Union Alumni Monthly*, 29:58 (January 1940).

Weeks, D. R. "Dr. Nott and the Trustees," *Union Alumni Monthly*, 18:79–81 (January 1929).

[Wells, William] "Union College," *Scribner's Monthly*, 12:229–241 (June 1876).

Books

Addison, Daniel Dulany. *The Clergy in American Life and Letters*. New York: The Macmillan Company, 1900.

Award of the Referees, in the Suit of Eliphalet Nott against James Wilson in the Court of the United States [printed document dated May 28, 1834, 4 p.]. In Union College Library.

Backus, J. Trumbull. *Address at the Funeral of the Rev. Dr. Nott, Schenectady, February 2, 1866, in the Presbyterian Church, by the Pastor.* New York: Wynkoop & Hallenbeck, 1866.

Buttre, Lillian C. *The American Portrait Gallery with Biographical Sketches of Presidents, Statesmen, Military and Naval Heroes, Clergymen, Authors, Poets, Etc., Etc.,* New York: J. C. Buttre [ca 1877].

The Centennial Celebration at Cherry Valley, Otsego Co., N.Y., July 4th, 1840: The Addresses of William W. Campbell and Gov. W. H. Seward, with Letters, Toasts, &c., &c. New York: Taylor & Clement, 1840.

Cherrington, Ernest H. *The Evolution of Prohibition in the United States of America.* Westerville, Ohio: The American Issue Press [1920] p. 86.

Delaware and Hudson Canal Company. *Annual Reports* for the years 1831, 1832, 1834-1845 [consulted at the Boston Public Library].

DeKroyft, Mrs. Helen (Aldrich). *A Place in Thy Memory . . . by Mrs. S. H. DeKroyft.* New York: J. F. Trow, 1856.

Documents Relating to the Union College Lottery Controversy [title supplied] twelve reports bound in one volume:

    1. "The Whole of the Documentary Evidence, Relative to the Controversy between the Regents of the University, and the Trustees of Union College." Schenectady: Cabinet Printing-House, 1823.

    2. "To the Regents of the University of the State of New-York," "Supplement," "Appendix," "Reply of the Trustees of Union College, to the Opinion of the Attorney-General." N.p., n.d.

    3. "Appendix, Opinion of the Late Chief Justice Spencer, Opinion of Messrs. Emmet, Wells, and Ogden, Opinion of the Late Chancellor Kent." N.p., n.d.

    4. "Documents: Relative to the Dispute between the Trustees of Union College and Yates and McIntyre." N.p., n.d.

    5. "Remarks on the Foregoing Communication from A. McIntyre and J. B. Yates, to the Board of Trustees of Union College." N.p., n.d.

    6. "Report of a Select Committee of the Trustees of Union College, in Relation to the Pending Controversy with Yates & M'Intyre." N.p., 1834.

    7. "Examination of a Report Professing to Be a Report of a Select Committee of the Trustees of Union College, in Relation to the Pending Controversy with Yates and M'Intyre." N.p., 1834.

8. "In Chancery, Before the Chancellor: Archibald M'Intyre, John B. Yates . . . vs the Trustees of Union College." N.p., n.d.

9. "In Chancery: The Answer of the Trustees . . . to the Bill of Complaint of Archibald McIntyre." N.p., n.d.

10. "In Chancery: The Joint and Several Answers of the Trustees of Union College . . . to the Bill of Complaint . . ." N.p., n.d.

11. "In Chancery: Before the Vice Chancellor of the Fourth Circuit." N.p., n.d.

12. "Documents." N.p., n.d.

Duyckinck, Evert A., and George L. Duyckinck. "Union College," *Cyclopedia of American Literature: Embracing Personal and Critical Notices of Authors, and Selections from Their Writings, from the Earliest Period to the Present Day: with Portraits, Autographs, and Other Illustrations.* New York: Charles Scribner, 1855, V. II, p. 194-197.

———. [same] *Edited to Date by M. Laird Simons.* 2 vol. Philadelphia: Wm. Rutter & Co., [1875] and republished Detroit: Gale Research Co., 1965, V. I, p. 917-922.

Fowler, Philomen H. *Historical Sketch of Presbyterianism within the Bounds of the Synod of Central New York. Prepared and Published at the Request of the Synod. By P. H. Fowler, D.D. The Presbyterian Element in our National Life and History. An Address Delivered before the Synod of Central New York at Watertown, October 18th, 1876, by Professor J. W. Mears, D.D.* Utica, N.Y.: Curtiss & Childs, 1877, p. 618-624.

Fox, Dixon Ryan. *Dr. Eliphalet Nott (1773-1866) and the American Spirit.* A Newcomen Address. [Princeton, printed at the University Press] 1944.

Griffin, Edward Dorr. *Extracts of Missionary Sermons, Preached in America, by Drs. Griffin, Nott, Morse, and Miller* . . . London, [?1812] .

Hough, Franklin B. *Historical and Statistical Record of the University of the State of New York During the Century from 1784 to 1884 . . . with an Introductory Sketch by David Murray* . . . Albany: Weed, Parsons & Company, Printers, 1885, p. 155-159.

"Journal of the Meetings of the Board of Regents of the University of the State of New York," v. 1, July 17, 1787-March 29, 1810 [typed transcript of an original record, office of the Commissioner of Education, Albany, N.Y.] .

Lippard, George. *Paul Ardenheim The Monk of Wissahikon.* Philadelphia: T. B. Peterson [date of 1848 assigned, edition uncertain], p. 425; and letter regarding it from Roger P. Butterfield to James Brewster, September 26, 1932, in Union College Library.

Littlefield, D. G. *A History of the Improvements Applicable to the Base Burning or Horizontal Draught Stove, from the Original Invention by M. Delesme in 1680, to the Present Time, and the Base Burning Stove as* an *Engine of Combustion, Compared with Other Stoves. By the Inventor of the Railway Coal Burner, Parlor Furnace, &c. Erastus Corning & Co., Agents.* Albany: C. Van Benthuysen, Printer, 1859. [Pamphlet, Baker Library, Harvard University Graduate School of Business Administration; copy at Union College Library].

Marryat, Frederick. *A Diary in America, with Remarks on its Institutions.* Philadelphia: Carey and Hart, 1839, p. 40.

―――. [same, review of] *The Knickerbocker, or New-York Monthly Magazine,* 14: 280–283 (September 1839).

New York Edison Company. Claim of title to Tompkins Street land and referring to "conditions of the grant by the City to Eliphalet Nott, . . ." p. 76. In *Calendar of the Commissioners of the Sinking Fund of the City of New York.* "Dock Department," No. 158, p. 74–82 (January 28, 1931).

New York State Legislature. *Reports of the Investigation by the New York [State] Legislature into the Affairs of Union College and Dr. Nott as Trustee of Certain Funds of the College, 1850–1854* [title supplied]. N.p., n.d. Eight reports bound in one volume:

1. "State of New-York. No. 146. In Assembly, Mar. 19, 1850. Report of the majority of the Select Committee, Appointed to Investigate the Affairs of Union College."

2. "State of New-York. No. 147. In Assembly, Mar. 23, 1850. Report of Mr. Pruyn, constituting the minority of the Committee on Colleges, &c., of Assembly, 1849, on Affairs of Union College."

3. "The Trustees of Union College, to the Commissioners Appointed to Examine the Charges made by Mr. Beekman. Reply of the Trustees of Union College, to the Charges Brought before the Senate on the 12th of April, 1851, by the Hon. James W. Beekman."

4. "State of New-York. No. 190. In Assembly, April 18, 1850. Annual report of the trustees on Union College for the Collegiate year ending July, 1849."

5. "State of New-York. No. 71. In Senate, April 12, 1851. Report of the committee on literature on the condition of Union College."

6. "State of New-York. No. 41. In Senate, March 4, 1853. Report of the majority of the commissioners to examine the affairs of Union College."

7. "State of New-York. No. 5. In Senate, January 31, 1854. Report of the majority of the investigating committee in relation to the affairs of Union College."

8. "Trust Deed, from Eliphalet Nott and Wife, to the Trustees of Union College."

Peirce, Josephine H. *Fire on the Hearth: the Evolution and Romance of the Heating-Stove, with 145 Illustrations from Photographs and Drawings Showing an Amazing Variety of Heating Devices; also Entertaining Anecdotes, excerpts from old Diaries and other Papers, alluring Advertisements and interesting bits of Information pertaining to their Manufacture and Uses. Introduction by Robert W. G. Vail* Springfield, Mass: Pond-Ekberg Company, 1951, p. 99, 126–131.

Rice, Roswell. "Acrostic on Eliphalet Nott," *Orations and Poetry, on Moral and Religious Subjects.* Albany: C. Van Benthuysen, 1858, p. 271.

S[eybolt], R[obert] F[rancis]. "Eliphalet Nott," *Dictionary of American Biography*, vol. XIII, New York: Charles Scribner's Sons, 1934.

Silliman, B[enjamin], Jr., and J. S. Whitney. *Report of the Examination of the Bristol Copper Mine in Bristol, Conn.* New Haven, Conn.: Ezekial Hayes, 1855.

Spencer, John C. *Argument in Defence of the Rev. Eliphalet Nott D.D., President of Union College, and in Answer to the Charges Made Against Him by Levinus Vanderheyden and James W. Beekman: Presented before the Committee of the Senate, Appointed to Investigate Certain Pecuniary Affairs of Union College.* Albany: C. Van Benthuysen, printer to the Legislature, 1853.

Union College. *Eliphalet Nott (President 1804–1866)* Schenectady: Union College [1954]. (Union Worthies number 9) Eliphalet Nott [by] Codman Hislop – the Future of the College President [by] Henry M. Wriston.

Van Santvoord, C[ornelius]. *Memoirs of Eliphalet Nott, D.D., LL.D. for sixty-two years President of Union College . . . : With contribution and revision by Professor Tayler Lewis of Union College.* New York: Sheldon & Company, [c. 1876].

Walworth, Ellen H. "Dr. Nott and His Stove," *Life Sketches of Father Walworth with Notes and Letters*, 2nd ed. Albany: 1907, p. 34ff.

Yates, Charles. *Reply to the Argument of John C. Spencer, Esq.: Presented Before the Committee of the Senate Appointed to Investigate the Affairs of Union College, in Refutation of Certain Charges Made Therein.* Albany: 1854.

ON UNION COLLEGE
Manuscripts

Adelphic Society. "Ledger," 1865–1905.

"Articles of Agreement," 1785. Union College Library.

Axen, Richard F. "History and Analysis of a Liberal Arts College Curriculum: Four Perspectives of Union College." Unpub. diss., University of California, 1952.

Dailey, W.N.P. "The Seals of Union College and Union University" [1936]. Union College Library.

Gardner, Harold Brooks, " 'Old Union' in the Forties," 1916. Union College Library.

Graham, Roy Eugene. "Joseph Jacques Ramée and the French Emigré Architects in America." M.A. thesis, University of Virginia, 1968.

Ingham, Albert C. "Private Journal." Microfilm copy from Rutgers University; Union College Library.

_____, In Waldron, Charles N., " 'Twas Here the Old Alumni Sat,' " Union Alumni Monthly, 29:116 April 1940.

Graham, Roy Eugene. "Joseph Jacques Ramée and the French Emigré Architects in America." M.A. thesis, University of Virginia, 1968.

Martin, Harold Edgar. "A Documentary History of Union College: 1779–1804." Union College Library.

Pearson, Jonathan. "Pearson Diary":
    vol. A. Nov. 10, 1828–Dec. 31, 1829;
    vol. B. July 5, 1830–Nov. 28, 1830;
    vol. C. Apr. 13, 1831–Jan. 17, 1832;
    vol. 1, April 27, 1832–July 17, 1834;
        Sept. 12, 1834–Jan. 5, 1835;
    vol. 1A. Journal of a tour from Schenectady to the White hills, Boston, New York, &c., July 18, 1834–Sept. 11, 1834;
    vol. 1B. Journal of a tour from Schenectady to Niagara Falls in August, 1833;
    vol. 2. Jan. 6, 1835–June 17, 1837, Sept. 1–6, 1837;
    vol. 3. Oct. 1, 1837–Feb. 10, 1838, August 22, 1838–Oct. 14, 1838, Jan. 3, 1840–May 29, 1840, Sept. 20, 1840–Aug. 10, 1841;
    vol. 4. Sept. 25, 1841–June 4, 1842, Sept. 9, 1842–Feb. 21, 1843, Dec. 25, 1844–Jan. 22, 1845, March 1845–Oct. 26, 1845, Dec. 4, 1845–Dec. 17, 1845, March 24, 1846–March 31, 1846, March 10, 1854–Dec. 28, 1854 [Brief notes on graduates of Union] ;
    vol. 4A. Dec. 29, 1854–July 8, 1855;
    vol. 5. July 9, 1855–May 12, 1856, Aug. 24, 1856–Aug. 5, 1857, Nov. 9, 1857–Dec. 30, 1857;
    vol. 6. Jan. 1, 1858–Aug. 3, 1858, Sept. 7, 1858–June 21, 1859;
    vol. 7. June 22, 1859–Sept. 24, 1860;
    vol. 8. Sept. 25, 1860–July 10, 1862, Jan. 1, 1863–June 19, 1864;
    vol. 9. Single entries for years 1866, 1868, 1869, 1871, March 22, 1875–June 5, 1875.

Sayre, M. F. "Early Engineering Education and Union College." [1941?] Union College Library.

Union College alumni, faculty, and trustees. Biographical material is scattered throughout the considerable number of Union College publications; see especially "Pearson Diary" (MS). There is a great deal of random biographical material filed chronologically and by categories at the Union College Alumni Office.

Published Materials

[Alexander, Robert C.] "Union College, 1795," in Sherwood, Sidney. *The University of the State of New York: History of Higher Education in the State of New York*. Washington, D.C.: Government Printing Office, 1900, p. 198–228.

Annual Reports of the Regents of the University of the State of New York. Albany: [various publishers]. [See for Union College annual reports during the Nott years].

Appel, Theodore. *Life and Work of John Williamson Nevin D.D., LL.D.* Philadelphia: Reformed Church Publication House, 1889, p. 35.

Bronner, Frederick L. "Union College and the West," *Union Alumni Monthly*, 21:11–16 (November 1931).

Catalogue of the Officers and Alumni of Union College, in the City of Schenectady, N.Y. from 1797 to 1884. Albany: C. Van Benthuysen & Sons, 1884.

Cavert, Samuel McCrea. "Union College and the Frontier Spirit," *Union College Bulletin*, v. 36, Commencement Number, June 1945.

The Celebration of the Fiftieth Anniversary of Dr. Nott's Presidency of Union College July 25, 1854. Schenectady: G. Y. Vandebogert, 1854.

Centennial Souvenir, Union College, 1795–1895. Albany: G. F. Williams, 1895.

Cowley, William H. "Two Men of Union," *Union Alumni Monthly*, 29:92–94 (March 1940).

The First Semi-Centennial Anniversary of Union College, Celebrated July 22, 1845. Albany: W. C. Little & Co.; Schenectady: I. Riggs, 1845.

Foot, Samuel A. *Autobiography: Collateral Reminiscences, Arguments in Important Causes, Speeches, Addresses, Lectures, and other Writings of Samuel A. Foot, LL.D., Counsellor at Law, and Late Judge of the Court of Appeals*, 2 v. New York: 1873.

Fox, Dixon Ryan. *Union College: An Unfinished History*. Schenectady: [1945].

Fox, Marion Osgood. "In a College Garden," (Union College) *Symposium*, 1:24–25 (Fall of 1962).

Hale, Edward Everett, Jr. "College Life in 1850." *Union Alumni Monthly*, 13:284–290 (June 1924).

———, "Union Men in the Field of Education." *Union College Maker of Men* (Series), v. 10, March 1921. [Supplement, *Union Alumni Monthly*].

Hislop, Codman. "The Ghost College That Came to Life." *American Heritage*, Spring 1952, 29-31.

———, "Jonathan Pearson's 'Thinking Books,' " *Union Alumni Monthly*, 25:85-95 (January 1936).

———, "What I Found in the Attic," *Union Alumni Monthly*, 21:99-106 (February 1932).

Hough, Franklin Benjamin. *Historical Sketch of Union College: [Now a Branch of Union University] Founded at Schenectady, N.Y., February 25, 1795*. Washington: Government Printing Office, 1876.

Laws of Union College. Albany: Charles R. and George Webster, 1802.

Larrabee, Harold A. "How Ramée Came to Schenectady," *Union Alumni Monthly*, 26:111-113 (February 1937).

———, *Phi Beta Kappa, Sesquicentennial History of the Alpha of New York: 1817-1967*. Schenectady: Union College.

Raymond, Andrew Van Vranken. *Union University: Its History, Influence, Characteristics and Equipment, with the Lives and Works of Its Founders, Benefactors, Officers, Regents, Faculty, and the Achievements of Its Alumni*. New York: Lewis Publishing Co., 1907.

Schermerhorn, Richard, Jr. "Union College and the Jackson Garden," *The American Architect and the Architectural Review*, 124: 541-544 (December 19, 1923).

Truax, James R. "Union College at the Close of Its First Century," *College and School* (Utica, N.Y.), 1:[165]-169 (June 1890).

Tunnard, Christopher. "Minerva's Union," *Architectural Review*. 101:57-62 (February 1947).

Union College. Catalogues, 1805–. Union College Library.

———, Commencement programs, 1814–.

———, Laws and regulations, 1796–.

———, Student publications: *The Censor*, 1833-1834; *The Crucible*, 1841 (conducted by the Deliberative Club); *The Floriad*, 1811 (Philomathean and Adelphic Societies publication); *The Frying Pan for Poor Sinners, Edited by Sir Christopher Porcupine*, 1839; *The Insinuator*, 1840; *The Leech*, July 1864; *The Parthenon and Academian's Magazine*, 1832-1899; *The Pastime*, Payne, John Howard, ed., 1807-1808; *The Scroll*, 1848-1851; *The Sophmore Independent*, v. 1, no. 1, November 4, 1854; *The Student's Album*, 1827; *Student Satires*, ca. 1833-1859 [binder's title]:

"Bona res," Oct. 24, 1855 (MS)

College Legends

Dunciad by Incog., Feb. 20, 1835

"The Fizzle," Oct. 24, 1855 (MS)

The Hornet, Mar. 13, 1838

Sophmore Mere-sham, July 1859
Truth by Invisible [ca. 1833]
The Vision [ca. 1838]
The Warning [ca. 1833]
Union College Chronicle, 1854 (published by the Sophmore Class); *Union College Magazine*, 1850-1875 (conducted by the Literary Societies); *The Union Offering and Freshman Review*, 1855; *Union Meerschaum*, July 1859; *The Union Ram*, fall term, 1865; *The Unionian*, 1860-1871 (title varies—*Union Resumé, The Union Annual*); *The Wizard*, 1858.

Union College: A Record of the Commemoration, June Twenty-First to Twenty-Seventh, 1895, of the One Hundredth Anniversary of the Founding of Union College, Including a Sketch of the History. New York: [DeVinne Press], 1897.

Union University. *Catalogue of the Officers and Alumni of Union College in the City of Schenectady, N.Y., from 1797-1884*. Albany: 1884.

Union Worthies Series. Schenectady: Union College, 1946-1968.

Waldron, Charles N. *The Union College I Remember, 1902-1946*. Boston: privately printed, 1954.

SELECTED GENERAL BIBLIOGRAPHY

Baker, George Edward, ed. *The Life of William H. Seward with Selections from His Works*. New York: Redfield, 1855.

Bancroft, Frederick. *The Life of William Henry Seward*. 2 vols. New York and London: Harper & Brothers, 1900.

Barnes, Thurlow Weed, and Harriet A. Weed, eds. *Life of Thurlow Weed. Including His Autobiography and a Memoir*: Vol. 1, *Autobiography of Thurlow Weed edited by His Daughter, Harriet A. Weed*; Vol. 2, *Memoir of Thurlow Weed by his Grandson, Thurlow Weed Barnes*. Boston and New York: Houghton, Mifflin and Company, 1883-1884.

Benedict, Henry Marvin. *The Genealogy of the Benedicts in America*. Albany: J. Munsell, 1870.

Bigelow, John. *Retrospections of an Active Life*. 5 vols. New York: The Baker & Taylor Co., 1909-1913.

Bliss, Neziah, in Armbruster, Eugene L. *Brooklyn's Eastern District*. Brooklyn: 1942, p. 38, 163, 199, 207, 224, 248, 249, 263.

_____, in Stiles, Henry R. *A History of the City of Brooklyn. Including the Old Town and Village of Brooklyn, the Town of Bushwick, and the Village and City of Williamsburgh*. 3 vols. Brooklyn: 1867-1870, vol. 2, p. 410-417.

Cajori, Florian. *The Chequered Career of Ferdinand Rudolph Hassler, First Superintendent of the United States Coast Survey: A Chapter in the*

History of Science in America. Boston: The Christopher Publishing House, n.d. [c. 1929].

Chiles, Rosa Pendleton. *John Howard Payne: American Poet, Actor, Playwright, Consul, and the Author of 'Home, Sweet Home.'* Reprinted from vols. 31 and 32 of the records of the Columbia Historical Society. Washington: n.d. [c. 1930].

Coons, William S. "The Tibbitts or Tibbetts Family: Descendants of George Tippett of Yonkers, N.Y.," *The New York Genealogical and Biographical Record: Devoted to the Interests of American Genealogy and Biography*, 51:346–359; 52:79–87 (October 1920 and January 1921).

Conrad, Earl. *The Governor and His Lady: The Story of William Henry Seward and His Wife Frances.* New York: G. P. Putnam's Sons, 1960.

Crane, Theodore R. "Francis Wayland and Brown University, 1796–1841." Unpublished dissertation, Harvard University, 1959.

———, *Francis Wayland: Political Economist as Educator.* Providence, R.I.: Brown University Press, 1962.

DeLancey, Edward Floyd. *Memoir of James William Beekman. Prepared at the request of the Saint Nicholas Society of the City of New York.* New York: The Saint Nicholas Society, 1877.

Dix, Morgan, comp. *Memoirs of John Adams Dix.* 2 vols. New York: Harper & Brothers, 1883.

Elton, Romeo. *The Literary Remains of the Reverend Jonathan Maxcy, D.D. . . . with a Memoir of his Life.* New York: A. V. Blake, 1844.

Garraty, John A. *Silas Wright.* New York: Columbia University Press, 1949.

Hale, Edward Everett, Jr. *William Seward.* Philadelphia: G. W. Jacobs & Co., 1910.

Hamilton, Allan McLane. *The Intimate Life of Alexander Hamilton, Based Chiefly upon Original Family Letters and Other Documents, Many of Which Have Never Been Published . . .* New York: Charles Scribner's Sons, 1910.

Hanson, Willis T., Jr. *The Early Life of John Howard Payne with Contemporary Letters Heretofore Unpublished.* Boston: Printed for Members of the Bibliophile Society [Cambridge, the University Press], 1913.

Hodges, George. *Henry Codman Potter Seventh Bishop of New York.* New York: The Macmillan Company, 1915.

Howe, M. A. DeWolfe. *Memoirs of the Life and Services of the Rt. Rev. Alonzo Potter, D.D., LL.D., Bishop of the Protestant Episcopal Church in the Diocese of Pennsylvania.* Philadelphia: 1871.

Lichterman, Martin. "John Adams Dix 1798–1879." New York: Columbia University, 1952.

Lothrop, Thornton Kirkland. *William Henry Seward*. Boston and New York: Houghton, Mifflin and Company, 1896.

McAllister, Ethel M. *Amos Eaton: Scientist and Educator, 1776-1842*. Philadelphia: University of Pennsylvania Press; London: H. Milford, Oxford University Press, 1941.

McIntyre, Archibald, in *History of Montgomery and Fulton Counties, N.Y.: with Illustrations Descriptive of Scenery . . . and Portraits of Old Pioneers and Prominent Residents*. New York: F. W. Beers & Co., 1878.

————, in Roberts, James A. *1797-1897: A Century in the Comptroller's Office, State of New York*. Albany: 1897. pp. 17-27; portrait facing p. 14.

Murray, James Ormsbee. *Francis Wayland*. Boston and New York: Houghton, Mifflin and Company, 1891.

Perry, Charles M. *Henry Philip Tappan: Philosopher and University President*. Ann Arbor: University of Michigan, 1933.

[Potter, Frank Hunter]. *The Alonzo Potter Family*. Privately printed. Concord, N.H.: The Rumford Press, 1923.

Roberts, James A. *1797-1897: A Century in the Comptroller's Office, State of New York*. Albany: 1897.

Roelker, Wm. G. "Francis Wayland, a Neglected Pioneer of Higher Education," in *Proceedings of the American Antiquarian Society, April 1943*. Worcester, Mass: 1944.

Sebring, Lewis Beck,. "Dirck Romeyn 1744-1804: Minister of the Word of God, Doctor of Divinity, Professor of Sacred Theology. A Biographical Account Comprising Excerpts from Family and Church Records, Printed Reference Works, and Other Historical Sources . . . ." Unpublished Ms., 1938. Union College Library.

Seward, Frederick W. *William H. Seward: An Autobiography*. 3 vols.: Vol. 1, *From 1801 to 1834 with a Memoir of his Life, and Selections from his Letters, 1831-1846* Vol. 2, *Seward at Washington, as Senator and Secretary of State, a Memoir of his Life, with Selections from his Letters, 1846-1861;*; Vol. 3, *Seward at Washington, as Senator and Secretary of State, a Memoir of his Life, with Selections from his Letters, 1861-1872*. New York: Derby and Miller, 1891.

Smith, Edward S. C. *Ferdinand Rudolph Hassler. Union Worthies, No. 13*. Schenectady: 1959.

Sprague, W. B. *Annals of the American Pulpit: or Commemorative Notices of Distinguished American Clergymen of Various Denominations from the Early Settlement of the Country to the Close of the Year Eighteen Hundred and Fifty-Five, with Historical Introduction*. 9 vols. New York: R. Carter and Brothers, 1857-1869.

Stillman, William James. *The Autobiography of a Journalist*. 2 vols. London: Grant Richards, 1901; Boston and New York: Houghton, Mifflin and Company, 1901.

Van Deusen, Glyndon Garlock. *Thurlow Weed, Wizard of the Lobby*. Boston: Little, Brown & Co., 1947.

_____, *William Henry Seward*. New York: Oxford University Press, 1967.

Warren, Austin. *The Elder Henry James*. New York: The Macmillan Company, 1934.

Watson, Winslow C., ed. *Men and Times of the Revolution: or Memoirs of Elkanah Watson, Including Journals of Travels in Europe and America, from 1777 to 1842, with His Correspondence with Public Men and Reminiscences and Incidents of the Revolution*. New-York: Dana and Company, 1856.

Wayland, Francis and Wayland, H. L. *A Memoir of the Life and Labors of Francis Wayland ... late President of Brown University, including Selections from his Personal Reminiscences and Correspondence. By his Sons Francis and H. L. Wayland*. 2 vols. New York: Sheldon and Company, 1867.

White, Philip. *The Beekmans of New York, in Politics and Commerce, 1647–1877, with an Introduction by Fenwick Beekman*. New York: New-York Historical Society, 1956.

Wikoff, Henry. *The Reminiscences of an Idler*. New York: Fords, Howard & Hulbert, 1880.

Yates, John Barentse, in Smith, John E., ed. *Our Country and Its People: A Descriptive and Biographical Record of Madison County, New York*. Boston: The Boston History Company, 1899.

_____, in Lanman, Charles. *Biographical Annals of the Civil Government of the United States During Its First Century, from Original and Official Sources*. Washington: J. Anglim, 1876, p. 480.

Index

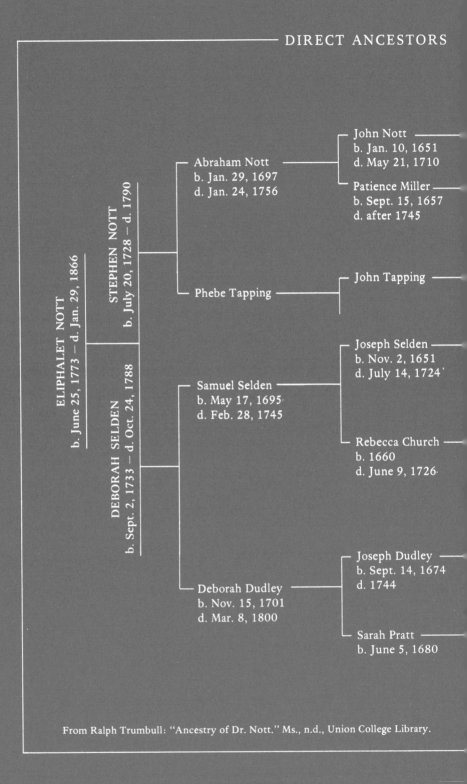

ELIPHALET NOTT
b. June 25, 1773 — d. Jan. 29, 1866

STEPHEN NOTT
b. July 20, 1728 — d. 1790

Abraham Nott
b. Jan. 29, 1697
d. Jan. 24, 1756

John Nott
b. Jan. 10, 1651
d. May 21, 1710

Patience Miller
b. Sept. 15, 1657
d. after 1745

Phebe Tapping

John Tapping

DEBORAH SELDEN
b. Sept. 2, 1733 — d. Oct. 24, 1788

Samuel Selden
b. May 17, 1695
d. Feb. 28, 1745

Joseph Selden
b. Nov. 2, 1651
d. July 14, 1724

Rebecca Church
b. 1660
d. June 9, 1726

Deborah Dudley
b. Nov. 15, 1701
d. Mar. 8, 1800

Joseph Dudley
b. Sept. 14, 1674
d. 1744

Sarah Pratt
b. June 5, 1680

From Ralph Trumbull: "Ancestry of Dr. Nott." Ms., n.d., Union College Library.